Lecture Notes in Computer Scien

T0238507

Commenced Publication in 1973
Founding and Former Series Editors:
Gerhard Goos, Juris Hartmanis, and Jan van Leeuwen

Advanced Research in Computing and Software Science

Subline of Lectures Notes in Computer Science

Antoine Miné   David Schmidt (Eds.)

Static Analysis

19th International Symposium, SAS 2012
Deauville, France, September 11-13, 2012
Proceedings

 Springer

Volume Editors

Antoine Miné
École Normale Supérieure
Département d'Informatique
45, rue d'Ulm
75005 Paris, France
E-mail: mine@di.ens.fr

David Schmidt
Kansas State University
Department of Computing and Information Sciences
234 Nichols Hall
Manhattan, KS 66506, USA
E-mail: das@ksu.edu

ISSN 0302-9743   e-ISSN 1611-3349
ISBN 978-3-642-33124-4   e-ISBN 978-3-642-33125-1
DOI 10.1007/978-3-642-33125-1
Springer Heidelberg Dordrecht London New York

Library of Congress Control Number: 2012945543

CR Subject Classification (1998): D.2.4-5, D.2.7, D.3.1-2, D.3.4, F.3.1-3, F.4.1

LNCS Sublibrary: SL 2 – Programming and Software Engineering

Typesetting: Camera-ready by author, data conversion by Scientific Publishing Services, Chennai, India

Printed on acid-free paper

Springer is part of Springer Science+Business Media (www.springer.com)

Preface

Static analysis is increasingly recognized as a fundamental tool for program verification, bug detection, compiler optimization, program understanding, and software maintenance. The series of Static Analysis Symposia has served as the primary venue for presentation of theoretical, practical, and application advances in the area.

This volume contains the proceedings of the 19th International Static Analysis Symposium, SAS 2012, which was held during September 11–13 in Deauville, France. Previous symposia were held in Venice, Perpignan, Los Angeles, Valencia, Kongens Lyngby, Seoul, London, Verona, San Diego, Madrid, Paris, Santa Barbara, Pisa, Aachen, Glasgow, and Namur.

As in the last two years, the 19th International Static Analysis Symposium was held together with three workshops. The 4th Workshop on Numerical and Symbolic Abstract Domains (NSAD 2012) and the Third Workshop on Static Analysis and Systems Biology (SASB 2012) were held in parallel on September 10. The Third Workshop on Tools for Automatic Program AnalysiS (TAPAS 2012) was held on September 14.

The program of the 19th International Static Analysis Symposium consisted in the presentation of 25 articles selected among 62 submissions from 23 countries. The contributions were selected by the Program Committee based on scientific quality, originality, and relevance to SAS, after a rigorous reviewing process involving at least three Program Committee members and external reviewers. In addition to the contributed papers, the program of the symposium featured four invited presentations by Gilles Barthe (IMDEA Software Institute, Spain), Dino Distefano (Queen Mary University of London and Monoidics, UK), Shriram Krishnamurthi (Brown University, USA), and Jens Palsberg (University of California, Los Angeles, USA). This volume includes an invited article by Jens Palsberg et al.

We would like to thank the external reviewers for their participation in the reviewing process. We would also like to thank the Département d'informatique de l'École normale supérieure and the Délegation régionale du CNRS Paris B for their administrative support. We thank the EasyChair team for the use of their software. We are grateful to our sponsors: CNRS, École normale supérieure, and INRIA.

September 2012

Antoine Miné
Dave Schmidt

Organization

Program Chairs

Antoine Miné   CNRS and École Normale Supérieure, France
David Schmidt   Kansas State University, USA

Program Committee

Elvira Albert	Complutense University of Madrid, Spain
Patrick Cousot	École Normale Supérieure, France and New York University, USA
Pietro Ferrara	ETH Zurich, Switzerland
Gilberto Filè	University of Padova, Italy
Chris Hankin	Imperial College London, UK
Suresh Jagannathan	Purdue University, USA
Matthieu Martel	Université de Perpignan Via Domitia, France
Matthew Might	University of Utah, USA
Anders Møller	Aarhus University, Denmark
David Monniaux	CNRS, Verimag, France
Markus Müller-Olm	Universität Münster, Germany
Andreas Podelski	University of Freiburg, Germany
G. Ramalingam	Microsoft Research, India
Sriram Sankaranarayanan	University of Colorado Boulder, USA
Francesca Scozzari	Università di Chieti-Pescara, Italy
Manu Sridharan	IBM Research, USA
Thomas Wies	New York University, USA
Eran Yahav	Technion, Israel
Kwangkeun Yi	Seoul National University, Korea

Steering Committee

Patrick Cousot	École Normale Supérieure, France and New York University, USA
Radhia Cousot	CNRS and École Normale Supérieure, France
Roberto Giacobazzi	University of Verona, Italy
Gilberto Filè	University of Padova, Italy
Manuel Hermenegildo	IMDEA Software Institute, Spain
David Schmidt	Kansas State University, USA

Additional Reviewers

Diego Esteban Alonso-Blas
Gianluca Amato
Sylvie Boldo
Olivier Bouissou
Hugues Cassé
Pavol Černý
Alexandre Chapoutot
Sungkeun Cho
Livio Colussi
Mauro Conti
Jesús Correas Fernández
Antonio Flores-Montoya
Goran Frehse
Sumit Gulwani
Arie Gurfinkel
Miguel Gómez-Zamalloa
Julien Henry
Kihong Heo
Jochen Hoenicke
Arnault Ioualalen
François Irigoin
Deokhwan Kim
Andy King
Tim King
Soonho Kong
Michael Kuperstein
Vincent Laviron
Oukseh Lee

Wonchan Lee
Woosuk Lee
Shuying Liang
Mark Marron
Isabella Mastroeni
Laurent Mauborgne
Yuri Meshman
Andrzej Murawski
Benedikt Nordhoff
Aditya Nori
Hakjoo Oh
Nimrod Partush
Simon Perdrix
Gustavo Petri
Ruzica Piskac
Corneliu Popeea
Noam Rinetzky
Sukyoung Ryu
Oliver Rüthing
Yassamine Seladji
Mihaela Sighireanu
Axel Simon
Fausto Spoto
Tullio Vardanega
Alexander Wenner
Enea Zaffanella
Damiano Zanardini

Sponsoring Institutions

École Normale Supérieure, CNRS, INRIA

Table of Contents

Computer-Aided Cryptographic Proofs

Gilles Barthe[1], Benjamin Grégoire[2], and Santiago Zanella Béguelin[3]

[1] IMDEA Software Institute
[2] INRIA Sophia Antipolis - Méditerranée
[3] Microsoft Research

Provable security [6] is at the heart of modern cryptography. It advocates a mathematical approach in which the security of new cryptographic constructions is defined rigorously, and provably reduced to one or several assumptions, such as the hardness of a computational problem, or the existence of an ideal functionality. A typical provable security statement is of the form: for all adversary $\mathcal{A}$ against the cryptographic construction $\mathcal{S}$, there exists an adversary $\mathcal{B}$ against a security assumption $\mathcal{H}$, such that if $\mathcal{A}$ has a high probability of breaking the scheme $\mathcal{S}$ in time t, then $\mathcal{B}$ has a high probability of breaking the assumption $\mathcal{H}$ in time t' (defined as a function of t).

EasyCrypt [1] is a framework for building and verifying machine-checked security proofs for cryptographic constructions in the computational model. Following the code-based approach [4], EasyCrypt uses probabilistic programs with adversarial computations to formulate unambiguously reductionist arguments. In EasyCrypt, cryptographic constructions are modelled as probabilistic programs, and their security is given by the probability of an event in a experiment, where an adversary interacts with the construction; similarly, security assumptions are stated in terms of the probability of an event in a probabilistic experiment. The key novelty of EasyCrypt (and its predecessor CertiCrypt [2]) is to provide programming languages tools to capture common reasoning patterns in cryptographic proofs. In particular, EasyCrypt provides support for a probabilistic relational Hoare Logic (pRHL) [2], whose judgments $\models c_1 \sim c_2 : \Psi \Rightarrow \Phi$ relate two probabilistic programs c_1 and c_2 (that typically involve adversarial code) relative to a pre-condition Ψ and a post-condition Φ, both defined as relations over program states. Informally, a judgment is valid iff for every initial memories that are related by the pre-condition, the sub-distributions of final memories are related by the lifting of the post-condition to distributions; the definition of the lifting operator $\mathcal{L}$ is adopted from probabilistic process algebra [7], and has close connections with the Kantorovich metric, and with flow networks [5]. As security properties are typically expressed in terms of probability of events rather than pRHL judgments, EasyCrypt implements mechanisms to derive from valid judgments probability claims, i.e. inequalities between expressions of the form $\Pr[c, m : S]$ that denote the probability of the event S in the sub-distribution $\llbracket c \rrbracket\, m$.

To automate reasoning in pRHL, EasyCrypt implements an automated procedure that given a logical judgment involving loop-free closed programs, computes

A. Miné and D. Schmidt (Eds.): SAS 2012, LNCS 7460, pp. 1–2, 2012.

a set of sufficient conditions for its validity, known as verification conditions. In the presence of loops or adversarial code, we require the user to provide the necessary annotations. The outstanding feature of this procedure, and the key to its effectiveness, is that verification conditions are expressed as first-order formulae, without any mention of probability, and thus can be discharged automatically using off-the-shelf SMT solvers and theorem provers.

To date, EasyCrypt (and its predecessor CertiCrypt) have been used to verify prominent examples of cryptographic constructions, including the OAEP padding scheme, the Cramer-Shoup encryption scheme, the Full Domain Hash signature scheme, the Merkle-Damgård hash function design, and zero-knowledge proofs. Moreover, CertiCrypt and EasyCrypt have been extended to reason about differentially private computations [3]. More recently, EasyCrypt has been used for the first time to prove the security of a novel cryptographic construction. Specifically, we have used EasyCrypt to prove the IND-CCA security of ZAEP, a redundancy-free public-key encryption scheme based on the Rabin function and RSA with exponent 3.

More information about the project can be found at:

`http://easycrypt.gforge.inria.fr`

References

1. Barthe, G., Grégoire, B., Heraud, S., Béguelin, S.Z.: Computer-Aided Security Proofs for the Working Cryptographer. In: Rogaway, P. (ed.) CRYPTO 2011. LNCS, vol. 6841, pp. 71–90. Springer, Heidelberg (2011)
2. Barthe, G., Grégoire, B., Béguelin, S.Z.: Formal certification of code-based cryptographic proofs. In: 36th ACM SIGPLAN-SIGACT Symposium on Principles of Programming Languages, POPL 2009, pp. 90–101. ACM, New York (2009)
3. Barthe, G., Köpf, B., Olmedo, F., Béguelin, S.Z.: Probabilistic reasoning for differential privacy. In: 39th ACM SIGPLAN-SIGACT Symposium on Principles of Programming Languages, POPL 2012, pp. 97–110. ACM, New York (2012)
4. Bellare, M., Rogaway, P.: The Security of Triple Encryption and a Framework for Code-Based Game-Playing Proofs. In: Vaudenay, S. (ed.) EUROCRYPT 2006. LNCS, vol. 4004, pp. 409–426. Springer, Heidelberg (2006)
5. Deng, Y., Du, W.: Logical, metric, and algorithmic characterisations of probabilistic bisimulation. Technical Report CMU-CS-11-110, Carnegie Mellon University (March 2011)
6. Goldwasser, S., Micali, S.: Probabilistic encryption. J. Comput. Syst. Sci. 28(2), 270–299 (1984)
7. Jonsson, B., Yi, W., Larsen, K.G.: Probabilistic extensions of process algebras. In: Bergstra, J.A., Ponse, A., Smolka, S.A. (eds.) Handbook of Process Algebra, pp. 685–710. Elsevier, Amsterdam (2001)

A Voyage to the Deep-Heap

Dino Distefano

Queen Mary University of London
and Monoidics Ltd.

This talk is the diary of a journey that brought the theoretical advances of Separation Logic all the way to a commercial static analyzer. It reports on some of the key insights which made this journey possible. It reviews the difficulties we have encountered along the way, the present status, and some of the challenges that remain open.

I have shared this journey with Cristiano Calcagno, Peter O'Hearn, and Hongseok Yang.

A. Miné and D. Schmidt (Eds.): SAS 2012, LNCS 7460, p. 3, 2012.

Semantics and Analyses
for JavaScript and the Web

Shriram Krishnamurthi

Brown University

The Web's lingua franca, JavaScript, is a large and complex language with an unconventional object model, a highly dynamic semantics, and many non-orthogonal features. We therefore defined λ_{JS}, a core language for JavaScript that presents just a small set of essential constructs. This core language was designed to be friendly to the needs of analysis and proof.

Of course, many have defined purported core calculi for large and complex languages. Somewhat unconventionally, we actually implemented a compiler from the source language to λ_{JS}. This compiler, composed with a small interpreter for λ_{JS}, results in a new implementation for JavaScript, which we can compare to those used in the real world. The heart of our effort on λ_{JS} is to make the results from the λ_{JS} implementation produce results as similar as possible to those of real implementations, yielding a semantics that matches what users actually use (and attackers actually attack).

We have used and are using λ_{JS} to build both tools and applications of these tools. These include:

- a sophisticated type system that captures the idioms of JavaScript
- the verification of the actual source of a Web sandbox

We have also created a Coq embedding of the semantics, and are building other tools such as a symbolic evaluator. In addition, many of our underlying theories apply broadly to many scripting languages, such as Python, Ruby, and Lua.

In addition to focusing on the JavaScript in a Web page, we must also address its execution context. Client-side JavaScript runs inside the browser, which has multiple consequences. For one, the JavaScript in a page is effectively inert: it only runs in response to events. Thus, to reflect a page's behavior, we have developed a (tested) semantics to capture the browser's complex event model. In addition, most browsers enable their users to install JavaScript modules to extend the browser's behavior. These extensions, written by third parties, may violate the browser's invariants, such as preserving privacy choices. We are therefore adapting our type system to enable reasoning about browser extensions.

All our models and tools are available from our project site:

www.jswebtools.org

Our tools are all Open Source, and we are happy to support others who want to use them. We welcome you to give them a try!

This work was done with a talented group of colleagues: Arjun Guha, Joe Gibbs Politz, Benjamin S. Lerner, Claudiu Saftoiu, Matthew J. Carroll, Hannah Quay-de la Vallee, Dan P. Kimmel, and Spiridon Eliopoulos. It has been partially supported by the US National Science Foundation and by Google.

A. Miné and D. Schmidt (Eds.): SAS 2012, LNCS 7460, p. 4, 2012.

Efficient May Happen in Parallel Analysis for Async-Finish Parallelism

Jonathan K. Lee, Jens Palsberg, Rupak Majumdar, and Hong Hong

UCLA Computer Science Department, University of California, Los Angeles, USA

Abstract. For concurrent and parallel languages, the may-happen-in-parallel (MHP) decision problem asks, given two actions in the program, if there is an execution in which they can execute in parallel. Closely related, the MHP computation problem asks, given a program, which pairs of statements may happen in parallel. MHP analysis is the basis for many program analysis problems, such as data race detection and determinism checking, and researchers have devised MHP analyses for a variety of programming models.

We present algorithms for static MHP analysis of a storeless abstraction of X10-like languages that have async-finish parallelism and procedures. For a program of size n, our first algorithm solves the MHP decision problem in $O(n)$ time, via a reduction to constrained dynamic pushdown networks (CDPNs). Our second algorithm solves the MHP computation problem in $O(n \cdot \max(n, k))$ time, where k is a statically determined upper bound on the number of pairs that may happen in parallel. The second algorithm first runs a type-based analysis that produces a set of candidate pairs, and then it runs the decision procedure on each of those pairs. For programs without recursion, the type-based analysis is exact and gives an output-sensitive algorithm for the MHP computation problem, while for recursive programs, the type-based analysis may produce spurious pairs that the decision procedure will then remove. Our experiments on a large suite of X10 benchmarks suggest that our approach scales well. Our experiments also show that while k is $O(n^2)$ in the worst case, k is often $O(n)$ in practice.

1 Introduction

For concurrent and parallel languages, the may-happen-in-parallel (MHP) decision problem asks, given two actions in the program, if there is an execution in which they can execute in parallel. Closely related, the MHP computation problem asks, given a program, which pairs of statements may happen in parallel. MHP analyses are useful as a basis for tools such as data race detectors [6,14] and determinism checkers.

In this paper we study MHP analysis of a storeless model of X10-like languages that have async-finish parallelism and procedures. In X10 [5], the *async* statement enables programs to create threads, while the *finish* statement provides a form of synchronization. Specifically, a finish statement *finish s* waits for termination of all *async* statement bodies started while executing *s*.

A. Miné and D. Schmidt (Eds.): SAS 2012, LNCS 7460, pp. 5–23, 2012.

Researchers have studied static MHP analysis for a variety of storeless programming models. Roughly, there are three categories of decidability results.

First, consider models with threads and synchronization mechanisms such as rendezvous. In case there are no procedures, Taylor proved in his seminal paper [21] that the MHP decision problem is NP-complete for a set of tasks that each contains only straight-line code, even when the set of possible rendezvous is known. The decision problem becomes undecidable if, in addition, procedure calls are allowed [18]. The decision problem is decidable if restricted synchronization techniques, such as nested locks, are used [9], but the complexity is exponential. The async-finish concurrency constructs of X10-like languages are different from threads with synchronization idioms such as rendezvous and locks, so the intractability results above do not immediately apply; indeed, we demonstrate a linear-time algorithm for the decision problem.

Second, consider models with syntactically specified synchronization, such as fork-join parallelism (e.g., Cilk). For fork-join parallelism, Seidl and Steffen [19] showed that the MHP decision problem is decidable in linear time. This result was extended by Lammich and Müller-Olm [10] in the presence of the *async* operator (called *spawn* in [10]) which can create new threads. Neither of these results immediately captures the *finish* construct of X10, in which an unbounded number of concurrently executing processes must synchronize. In the Seidl-Steffen paper, the fork-join construct ensures that there is at most a syntactically bounded number of processes executing and synchronizing in parallel. In the Lammich-Müller-Olm paper, spawned threads do not synchronize and synchronization is limited to an additional fork-join construct. Gawlitza et al. [8] made major progress and showed that MHP analysis is decidable for a model with nested locking and a join construct that has similarities with the *finish* construct in X10.

Finally, decidability results for MHP analysis have so far been mostly of theoretical interest. In particular, the decision procedures in [19,19,8] weren't applied to realistic benchmarks. Instead, most previous papers on practical MHP analysis present static analyses that give conservative, approximate answers to the MHP computation problem [7,13,15,16,12,3,1,11]. The relationship between the approximate analyses and the theoretically optimal algorithms is unclear; if the theoretically optimal algorithms are also practically efficient, then that would make research into approximate analyses moot.

We study MHP analysis of Featherweight X10 [11], which is a core calculus for async-finish parallelism and procedures, and which is essentially a subset of X10. We give a store-less abstract semantics of Featherweight X10 and define the MHP decision problem and the MHP computation problem in terms of this semantics. The resulting MHP problems are all about control flow.

The Challenge. For async-finish parallelism and procedures, is optimal MHP computation practical?

Our Results. For Featherweight X10, we present two new algorithms for the MHP decision and computation problems, and we show that they scale well in practice.

```
1   void  f () {
2     a1
3   }
4
5   void  main () {
6     finish {
7       async {
8         a2
9       };
10        a3
11      };
12      loop {
13        async {
14          f ()
15        }
16      }
17  }
```

```
1   void  g () {
2     g ()
3   }
4
5   void  main () {
6     loop {
7       async { a1 };
8       g ()
9     }
10  }
```

```
1   void  main () {
2     loop {
3       async {
4         chain0 ();
5       }
6     }
7   }
8
9   void  chain0 () {
10    a0;  chain1 ();
11  }
12  void  chain1 () {
13    a1;  chain2 ();
14  } ...
15  void  chainN () {
16    an;  chain0 ();
17  }
```

Fig. 1. Three Featherweight X10 programs

Our first algorithm solves the MHP decision problem in linear time, via a reduction from Featherweight X10 programs to constrained dynamic pushdown networks (CDPNs) [4]. We give a careful complexity analysis of a known decision procedure for CDPNs [4] for when it is applied to the CDPNs produced by our reduction.

Our second algorithm solves the MHP computation problem in $O(n{\cdot}\max(n,k))$ time, where k is a statically determined upper bound on the number of pairs that may happen in parallel. The second algorithm first runs a type-based analysis that produces a set of candidate pairs, and then it runs the decision procedure on each of those pairs. Following Lee and Palsberg [11], we recast the type analysis problem as a constraint solving problem that we can solve in $O(n \cdot \max(n,k))$ time. For programs without recursion, the type-based analysis is exact and gives an output-sensitive algorithm for the problem, while for recursive programs, the type-based analysis may produce spurious pairs that the decision procedure will then remove.

Our experiments on a large suite of X10 benchmarks suggest that our approach scales well. Our experiments also show that while k is $O(n^2)$ in the worst case, k is often $O(n)$ in practice. Thus, output-sensitivity is often crucial in getting algorithms to scale.

In summary, our results demonstrate two *tractable* MHP analyses for a *practical* parallel programming language.

In the following section we recall Featherweight X10 and give it an abstract semantics, and in Section 3 we define the MHP analysis problems. In Section 4 we present our type-based algorithm that produces a set of candidate pairs, in Section 5 we present our CDPN-based algorithm for the MHP decision problem, and in Section 6 we present our algorithm for solving the MHP computation

$$(Statement) \quad s ::= \quad s\;;s \mid loop\;s \mid async\;s \mid finish\;s \mid a^l \mid skip \mid f()$$
$$(Context) \quad C ::= \quad C\;;s \mid P\;;C \mid async\;C \mid finish\;C \mid \square$$
$$(ParStatement) \quad P ::= \quad P\;;P \mid async\;s$$
$$(Redex) \quad R ::= \quad skip\;;s \quad \mid \quad P\;;skip \quad \mid \quad loop\;s \quad \mid \quad async\;skip$$
$$\mid \quad finish\;skip \quad \mid \quad a^l \quad \mid \quad f()$$

$$\_[\_] : Context \times Statement \to Statement$$

$$(\square)[s'] = s' \qquad (C\;;s)[s'] = (C[s'])\;;s \qquad (P\;;C)[s'] = P\;;(C[s'])$$
$$(async\;C)[s'] = (async\;C[s']) \qquad (finish\;C)[s'] = (finish\;C[s'])$$

Fig. 2. Syntax of Featherweight X10

problem. Finally in Section 7 we present experimental results. We have omitted a large example and most of the proofs of correctness of our two algorithms; they are given in the appendices of the full version of the paper.

2 Featherweight X10

We now recall Featherweight X10 [11], and provide a store-less abstract semantics. In contrast to [11], we give a semantics based on evaluation contexts. Figure 1 shows three Featherweight X10 programs.

A program is a collection of procedures of the form

void $f()$ { s }

where f is a procedure name and s is the procedure body. We use body(f) to refer to the body of the procedure f. The procedure body is a statement generated by the grammar in Figure 2. We assume there is a procedure with the name *main*. The execution of a program begins by executing the body of *main*.

Syntax. Figure 2 gives the syntax of statements, contexts, parallel statements, and redexes, as well as a function for plugging a statement into a context. In the production for *Statement*, $s\;;s$ denotes statement sequence, $loop\;s$ executes s zero, one, or more times, $async\;s$ spawns off s in a separate thread, $finish\;s$ waits for termination of all $async$ statement bodies started while executing s, a^l is a primitive statement with label l, $skip$ is the empty statement, and $f()$ is a procedure call.

A context is a statement with a hole into which we can plug a statement. A parstatement is a statement in which multiple statements can execute in parallel. A redex is a statement that can execute at least one step of computation.

Featherweight X10 has no conditional statement; however, all the results in this paper can be extended easily to a conditional statement with nondeterministic branching.

The following theorem, proved by straightforward induction on s, characterizes statements in terms of contexts and redexes.

Theorem 1 (Statement Characterization). *For every statement s, either $s = skip$, or there exists a context C and a redex R such that $s = C[R]$.*

The characterization in Theorem 1 isn't necessarily unique. For example, if $s = (async\ a^5); (async\ skip)$, we can choose $C_1 = (async\ \Box); (async\ skip)$ and $R_1 = a^5$ and get $s = C_1[R_1]$, and we can choose $C_2 = (async\ a^5); \Box$ and $R_2 = async\ skip$ and get $s = C_2[R_2]$. The non-uniqueness reflects the nature of parallel computation: more than one statement can execute next, in some cases.

Abstract Semantics. We will define a small-step abstract store-less operational semantics. First we give some of the intuition behind the semantics by explaining how the semantics models the *finish* construct. Consider the statement:

$$(finish\ s_1); s_2 \tag{1}$$

Notice that the context $P\ ; C$ does not match (1) because $finish\ s_1$ is not a *ParStatement*. Thus, we cannot execute s_2. Rather, the only context that matches (1) is $C; s$. Thus, we will have to execute s_1 and if s_1 eventually becomes $skip$, then we will have rules that can bring us from $(finish\ skip); s_2$ to s_2.

We define a relation $\rightarrow\ \subseteq Redex \times Statement$:

$$skip\ ; s \rightarrow s \tag{2}$$
$$P\ ; skip \rightarrow P \tag{3}$$
$$loop\ s \rightarrow skip \tag{4}$$
$$loop\ s \rightarrow s\ ; loop\ s \tag{5}$$
$$async\ skip \rightarrow skip \tag{6}$$
$$finish\ skip \rightarrow skip \tag{7}$$
$$a^l \rightarrow skip \tag{8}$$
$$f()\ \rightarrow \mathsf{body}(f) \tag{9}$$

The program is fixed and implicit in the rules. Notice that for every redex R there exists s such that $R \rightarrow s$.

Intuitively, Rules (2)–Rule (3) say that $skip$ is left unit for all statements and a right unit for *ParStatement*'s. Rules (4)–Rule (5) say that a loop executes its body zero or more times. Rules (6)–(7) say that *async* and *finish* have outplayed their roles when their body is $skip$. Rule (8) models primitive statements; in our store-less semantics, we don't record any effort. Rule (9) replaces a call to a procedure with the body of that procedure.

Next we define a relation $\longmapsto\ \subseteq Statement \times Statement$:

$$C[R] \longmapsto C[s] \quad \Longleftrightarrow \quad R \rightarrow s$$

We write $\longmapsto^*$ for the reflexive transitive closure of $\longmapsto$. The context $C\ ; s$ ensures that we can execute the first statement in a sequence, as usual. The contexts

$P\;;C$ and $async\;C$ ensure that in a statement such as $(async\;s_1); (async\;s_2)$, we can execute either of s_1 or s_2 next. The context $finish\;C$ ensures that we can execute the body a finish statement.

3   The May-Happen-in-Parallel Problems

We now define the May Happen in Parallel decision and computation problems. We define:

$$CBE(s, l_1, l_2) = \exists C_1, C_2 : C_1 \neq C_2 \wedge s = C_1[a^{l_1}] = C_2[a^{l_2}]$$
$$CBE(s) = \{\ (l_1, l_2) \mid CBE(s, l_1, l_2)\ \}$$
$$MHP_{sem}(s) = \bigcup_{s' : s \longmapsto^* s'} CBE(s')$$

Intuitively, $CBE(s, l_1, l_2)$ holds if statements labeled l_1 and l_2 can both execute at s. We use the subscript sem in MHP_{sem} to emphasize that the definition is semantics-based.

For example, if $s = (async\;a^5); a^6$, we can choose $C_1 = (async\;\square); a^6$ and $R_1 = a^5$ and get $s = C_1[R_1]$, and we can choose $C_2 = (async\;a^5); \square$ and $R_2 = a^6$ and get $s = C_2[R_2]$. We conclude $CBE(s, 5, 6)$ and $(5, 6) \in CBE(s)$.

We define the MHP decision problem as follows.

MAY HAPPEN IN PARALLEL (DECISION PROBLEM)
Instance: (s, l_1, l_2) where s is a statement and l_1, l_2 are labels.
Problem: $(l_1, l_2) \in MHP_{sem}(s)$?

Equivalently, we can phrase the decision problem as: does there exist s' such that $s \longmapsto^* s'$ and $CBE(s', l_1, l_2)$?

We define the MHP computation problem as follows.

MAY HAPPEN IN PARALLEL (COMPUTATION PROBLEM)
Input: a statement s.
Output: $MHP_{sem}(s)$.

4   A Type System for Producing Candidate Pairs

We now present a type system that gives a conservative solution to the MHP computation problem.

Type Rules. We define

$$symcross\ :\ Set \times Set \to PairSet$$
$$symcross(S_1, S_2) = (S_1 \times S_2) \cup (S_2 \times S_1)$$

We use *symcross* to help produce a symmetric set of pairs of labels.

$$\frac{B \vdash s_1 : M_1, O_1, L_1 \qquad B \vdash s_2 : M_2, O_2, L_2}{B \vdash s_1 \ ; s_2 : M_1 \cup M_2 \cup symcross(O_1, L_2), O_1 \cup O_2, L_1 \cup L_2} \qquad (10)$$

$$\frac{B \vdash s : M, O, L}{B \vdash loop \ s : M \cup symcross(O, L), O, L} \qquad (11)$$

$$\frac{B \vdash s : M, O, L}{B \vdash async \ s : M, L, L} \qquad (12)$$

$$\frac{B \vdash s : M, O, L}{B \vdash finish \ s : M, \emptyset, L} \qquad (13)$$

$$B \vdash a^l : \emptyset, \emptyset, \{l\} \qquad (14)$$

$$B \vdash skip : \emptyset, \emptyset, \emptyset \qquad (15)$$

$$B \vdash f() : M, O, L \qquad (\text{if } B(f) = (M, O, L)) \qquad (16)$$

$$\frac{B \vdash s_i : M_i, O_i, L_i \qquad B(f_i) = (M_i, O_i, L_i) \qquad i \in 1..n}{\vdash \textbf{void } f_1()\{ \ s_1 \ \} \ \dots \ \textbf{void } f_n()\{ \ s_n \ \} : B} \qquad (17)$$

Fig. 3. Type rules

We will use judgments of the forms $B \vdash s : M, O, L$ and $\vdash p : B$. Here, s is a statement, p is a program, M is a set of label pairs, O and L are sets of labels, and B is a type environment that maps procedure names to triples of the form (M, O, L). The meaning of $B \vdash s : M, O, L$ is that in type environment B, (1) the statement s has MHP information M, (2) while s is executing statements with labels in L will be executed, and (3) when s terminates, statements with labels in O may still be executing. The meaning of $\vdash p : B$ is that the program p has procedures that can be described by B. Figure 3 shows the eight rules for deriving such judgments.

Notice that if a derivation of $\vdash p : B$ contains the judgment $B \vdash s : M, O, L$, then $O \subseteq L$.

Let us now explain the eight rules in Figure 3. Rule (10) says that we can combine information for s_1 and information for s_2 into information for $s_1; s_2$ mainly by set union and also by adding the term $symcross(O_1, L_2)$ to the set of pairs. The role of $symcross(O_1, L_2)$ is to capture that the statements (with labels in O_1) that may still be executing when s_1 terminates may happen in parallel with the statements (with labels in L_2) that will be executed by s_2. Rule (11) has the term $symcross(O_1, L_2)$ as part of the set of pairs because the loop body may happen in parallel with itself. Rule (12) says that the body of $async$ may still be executing when the $async$ statement itself terminates. Note here that the second piece of derived information is written as L rather than $O \cup L$ because, as noted above, $O \subseteq L$. Rule (13) says that no statements in the body of $finish$ will still be executing when the $finish$ statement terminates. Rule (14) states that just the statement a^l will execute. Rule (15) states no labeled statements will execute. Rule (16) states that B contains all the information we need about a procedure. Rule (17) says that if B correctly describes every procedure, then it correctly describes the entire program.

Example. As an example, let us show a type derivation for the first program in Figure 1. Let

$$B = [\ f \mapsto (\emptyset, \emptyset, \{1\}),\quad main \mapsto (\{(1,1), (2,3)\}, \{1\}, \{1,2,3\})\ ]$$

From Rule (17) we have that to show that the entire program has type B, we must derive the following two judgments:

$$B \vdash \mathsf{body}(f) : \emptyset, \emptyset, \{1\} \tag{18}$$

$$B \vdash \mathsf{body}(main) : \{(1,1), (2,3)\}, \{1\}, \{1,2,3\}) \tag{19}$$

Let us consider those judgments in turn.

We have that $\mathsf{body}(f) = a^1$ so Rule (14) gives us the judgment (18).

We have that $\mathsf{body}(main) = s_1 ; s_2$ where

$$s_1 = finish\ \{\ async\ \{\ a^2\ \};\ a^3\ \}$$
$$s_2 = loop\ \{\ async\ \{\ f()\ \}\ \}$$

From Rules (13), (10), (12), (14), we can produce this derivation:

$$\cfrac{\cfrac{B \vdash a^2 : \emptyset, \emptyset, \{2\}}{B \vdash async\ \{\ a^2\ \} : \emptyset, \{2\}, \{2\}} \qquad B \vdash a^3 : \emptyset, \emptyset, \{3\}}{\cfrac{B \vdash async\ \{\ a^2\ \};\ a^3 : \{(2,3)\}, \{2\}, \{2,3\}}{B \vdash s_1 : \{(2,3)\}, \emptyset, \{2,3\}}}$$

From Rules (11), (12), (16), we can produce this derivation:

$$\cfrac{\cfrac{B \vdash f() : \emptyset, \emptyset, \{1\}}{B \vdash async\ \{\ f()\ \} : \emptyset, \{1\}, \{1\}}}{B \vdash s_2 : \{(1,1)\}, \{1\}, \{1\}}$$

Finally, we can use Rule (10) to produce the judgment (19).

Properties. The following four theorems are standard and have straightforward proofs.

Theorem 2 (Existence of Typing). *For all B, there exists M, O, L such that $B \vdash s : M, O, L$.*

Theorem 3 (Unique Typing). *If $B \vdash s : M_1, O_1, L_1$ and $B \vdash s : M_2, O_2, L_2$, then $M_1 = M_2$ and $O_1 = O_2$ and $L_1 = L_2$.*

Theorem 4 (Subject Reduction). *For a program p, if $\vdash p : B$ and $B \vdash R : M, O, L$ and $R \to s'$, then there exists M', O', L' such that $B \vdash s' : M', O', L'$ and $M' \subseteq M$ and $O' \subseteq O$ and $L' \subseteq L$.*

Theorem 5 (Preservation). *For a program p, if $\vdash p : B$ and $B \vdash s : M, O, L$ and $s \longmapsto s'$, then there exists M', O', L' such that $B \vdash s' : M', O', L'$ and $M' \subseteq M$ and $O' \subseteq O$ and $L' \subseteq L$.*

Proof. From $s \longmapsto s'$ we have that there exist a context C and a redex R such that $s = C[R]$, and that there exists s'' such that $C[R] \longmapsto C[s'']$ and $R \to s''$. The proof proceeds by straightforward induction on C.   □

For a statement s and a type environment B, we have from Theorem 2 and Theorem 3 that there exist unique M, O, L such that $B \vdash s : M, O, L$, so we define

$$\mathsf{MHP}^B_{type}(s) = M$$

We use the subscript *type* to emphasize that the definition is type based.

The following two theorems say that the type system gives a conservative approximation to the MHP computation problem, and an exact solution for programs without recursion.

Theorem 6 (Overapproximation). *For a program p, a statement s in p, and a type environment B such that $\vdash p : B$, we have $\mathsf{MHP}_{sem}(s) \subseteq \mathsf{MHP}^B_{type}(s)$.*

We patterned Theorem 6 after [11, Theorem 3]. In the case where s is the body of the main procedure, Theorem 6 says that $\mathsf{MHP}^B_{type}(s)$ is an overapproximation of the MHP information for the entire program.

The next theorem shows that there is no loss of precision in the type-based approach for programs without recursion. See Appendix B of the full version for a proof.

Theorem 7 (Equivalence). *For a program without recursion, where the body of main is the statement s, we have that there exists B such that $\mathsf{MHP}_{sem}(s) = \mathsf{MHP}^B_{type}(s)$.*

Complexity. We can now state the complexity of the type-based approach.

Theorem 8. *For a program of size n, we can compute B and $\mathsf{MHP}^B_{type}(s)$ in $O(n \cdot \max(n, k))$ time, where $k = |\mathsf{MHP}^B_{type}(s)|$ is the size of the output produced by the type system.*

Proof. We first note that we can use the approach of Lee and Palsberg [11] to rephrase the problem of computing B and $\mathsf{MHP}^B_{type}(s)$ as the problem of finding the minimal solution to a collection of set constraints that are generated from the program text. For our type system, those set constraints are all of the forms:

$$l \in v \tag{20}$$

$$v \subseteq v' \tag{21}$$

$$symcross(v, v') \subseteq w \tag{22}$$

$$w \subseteq w' \tag{23}$$

Here v, v' range over sets of labels, while w, w' range over sets of pairs of labels. The maximal size of each set of labels is $O(n)$, the maximal size of each set of pairs of labels is k (by definition), and the number of constraints is $O(n)$. We proceed by first solving the constraints of the forms (20) and (21) by a straightforward propagation-based algorithm akin to the one that Palsberg and Schwartzbach used to solve a related kind of set constraints [17]; this takes $O(n^2)$ time. Then we solve the constraints of the forms (22) and (23) by the same algorithm but this time we propagate pairs of labels rather than single labels; this takes $O(n \cdot k)$ time. In total, we spent $O(n \cdot \max(n, k))$ time. □

Since $k = O(n^2)$ in the worst case, we get a cubic algorithm, but our experiments show that k is $O(n)$ in practice.

When we combine Theorem 7 and Theorem 8, we get that we can solve the MHP computation problem for programs without recursion in $O(n \cdot \max(n, k))$ time, while we get a conservative approximation for programs with recursion.

Programs with Recursion. Theorems 6 and 7 indicate that some uses of recursion cause the type system to produce an approximate result rather than an accurate result. Specifically, our type system may be conservative if recursive calls introduce non-termination. For example, see the second program in Figure 1. The program has a loop with the statement $async\{a^1\}$ in the body so one might think that a^1 may happen in parallel with itself. However, the loop body also calls the procedure g that is non-terminating. So, the program execution will never get around to executing $async\{a^1\}$ a second time. In summary, for the second program in Figure 1, the MHP set is empty.

Let us now take a look at how the type system analyzes the second program in Figure 1. Let

$$B = [\ g \mapsto (\emptyset, \emptyset, \emptyset),\ \ main \mapsto (\{(1,1)\}, \{1\}, \{1\})\ ]$$

From Rule (17) we have that to show that the entire program has type B, we must derive the following two judgments:

$$B \vdash \mathsf{body}(g) : \emptyset, \emptyset, \emptyset \tag{24}$$
$$B \vdash \mathsf{body}(main) : \{(1,1)\}, \{1\}, \{1\} \tag{25}$$

Let us consider those judgments in turn.

We have that $\mathsf{body}(g) = g()$ so Rule (16) gives us the judgment (24).

We have that $\mathsf{body}(main) = loop\ \{\ async\ \{\ a^1\ \};\ g()\ \}$ so from Rules (11), (12), (14), (16) we can produce this derivation that concludes with judgment (25):

$$\cfrac{\cfrac{\cfrac{B \vdash a^1 : \emptyset, \emptyset, \{1\}}{B \vdash async\ \{\ a^1\ \} : \emptyset, \{1\}, \{1\}} \qquad B \vdash g() : \emptyset, \emptyset, \emptyset}{B \vdash async\ \{\ a^1\ \};\ g() : \emptyset, \{1\}, \{1\}}}{B \vdash \mathsf{body}(main) : \{(1,1)\}, \{1\}, \{1\}}$$

In conclusion, the type system over-approximates non-termination and therefore concludes that a^1 may happen in parallel with itself.

5   An Algorithm for the MHP Decision Problem

We now give a linear-time algorithm for the MHP decision problem, even in the presence of recursion and potential non-termination. Our algorithm is based on constrained dynamic pushdown networks (CDPNs) [4], an infinite model of computation with nice decidability properties. Informally, CDPNs model collections of sequential pushdown processes running in parallel, where each process can "spawn" a new process or, under some conditions, observe the state of its children. We follow the presentation in [4].

Preliminaries. Let Σ be an alphabet, and let $\rho \subseteq \Sigma \times \Sigma$ be a binary relation on Σ. A set $S \subseteq \Sigma$ is ρ-*stable* if and only if for each $s \in S$ and for each $t \in \Sigma$, if $(s,t) \in \rho$ then t is also in S. A ρ-stable regular expression over Σ is defined inductively by the grammar:

$$e ::= S \mid e \cdot e \mid e^*$$

where S is a ρ-stable set. We derive a ρ-stable regular language from a ρ-stable regular expression in the obvious way and identify the expression with the language it denotes.

CDPNs. A *constrained dynamic pushdown network* (CDPN) [4] (A, P, Γ, Δ) consists of a finite set A of *actions*, a finite set P of *control locations*, a finite alphabet Γ of *stack symbols* (disjoint from P), and a finite set Δ of *transitions* of the following forms:

$$\phi : p\gamma \xrightarrow{a} p_1 w_1 \qquad \text{or} \qquad \phi : p\gamma \xrightarrow{a} p_1 w_1 \rhd p_2 w_2,$$

where $p, p_1, p_2 \in P$, $\gamma \in \Gamma$, $a \in A$, $w_1, w_2 \in \Gamma^*$, and ϕ is a ρ_Δ-stable regular expression over P with

$$\rho_\Delta = \{\, (p,p') \in P \times P \mid \exists \psi : p\gamma \xrightarrow{a} p'w \text{ in } \Delta, \text{ or } \exists \psi : p\gamma \xrightarrow{a} p'w \rhd p''w' \text{ in } \Delta \,\}$$

The ρ-stable property guarantees that whenever a control location p is matched by an expression ϕ, all its successors' control locations are also matched.

Semantics. CDPN *configurations* model the execution states of CDPN instances. Intuitively, a configuration of a CDPN is a tree with each node marked with the configuration of a pushdown process, and the children of a node are configurations of pushdown processes spawned by it, which are ordered by age (the more recently spawned child is to the right). The configuration of each pushdown process models a single thread execution state in a parallel program, which includes control location describing the thread state and stack symbols modeling the stack storage. Formally, given a set $X = \{x_1, \ldots, x_n\}$ of variables, define the set $\mathcal{T}[X]$ of M-terms over $X \cup P \cup \Gamma$ as the smallest set satisfying:

(a) $X \subseteq \mathcal{T}[X]$;
(b) If $t \in \mathcal{T}[X]$ and $\gamma \in \Gamma$, then $\gamma(t) \in \mathcal{T}[X]$;
(c) For each $n \geq 0$, if $t_1, \ldots, t_n \in \mathcal{T}[X]$ and $p \in P$, then $p(t_1, \ldots, t_n) \in \mathcal{T}[X]$.

Notice that n can be zero in case (c); we often write p for the term $p()$. A *ground M-term* is an M-term without free variables. The set of ground M-terms is denoted $\mathcal{T}$.

We now define the semantics of CDPNs as a transition system. An M-configuration is a ground M-term; we write Conf^M to denote the set of M-configurations. We define a context C as a M-term with one free variable, which moreover appears at most once in the term. If t is a ground M-term, then $C[t]$ is the ground M-term obtained by substituting the free variable with t.

The M-configuration $\gamma_m \ldots \gamma_1 p(t_1, \ldots, t_n)$, for $n, m \geq 0$ represents a process in control location p and $\gamma_m \ldots \gamma_1$ on the stack (with γ_1 on top), which has spawned n child processes. The ith child, along with all its descendants, is given by t_i. The child processes are ordered so that the rightmost child t_n is latest spawned. We call $\gamma_m \ldots \gamma_1 p$ the topmost process in the M-configuration.

The semantics of a CDPN is given as a binary transition relation $\rightarrow_M$ between M-configurations. Given an M-configuration t of one of the forms $\gamma_m \ldots \gamma_1 p(t_1, \ldots, t_n), n \geq 1$ or $\gamma_m \ldots \gamma_1 p$, we define $root(t)$ to be the control location p of the topmost process in t. We define $\rightarrow_M$ as the smallest relation such that the following hold:

(a) if $(\phi : p\gamma \xrightarrow{a} p_1 w_1) \in \Delta$ and $root(t_1) \ldots root(t_n) \in \phi$, then
$C[\gamma p(t_1, \ldots, t_n)] \rightarrow_M C[w_1^R p_1(t_1, \ldots, t_n)]$; and
(b) if $(\phi : p\gamma \xrightarrow{a} p_1 w_1 \rhd p_2 w_2) \in \Delta$ and $root(t_1) \ldots root(t_n) \in \phi$, then
$C[\gamma p(t_1, \ldots, t_n)] \rightarrow_M C[w_1^R p_1(t_1, \ldots, t_n, w_2^R p_2)]$.

Intuitively, transitions between M-configurations model parallel program execution. With a CDPN transition rule $\phi : p\gamma \xrightarrow{a} p_1 w_1$, a process in the M-configuration steps to its next state and updates its stack; with a CDPN transition rule $\phi : p\gamma \xrightarrow{a} p_1 w_1 \rhd p_2 w_2$, a process in the M-configuration spawns a new pushdown process as its newest child. The constraint ϕ in a transition rule provides a simple way to communicate between the parent process and its children. For example, given control location $\natural \in P$ standing for termination state, a parent process cannot step over a transition rule $\natural^* : p\gamma \xrightarrow{a} p_1 w_1$ until all its children have terminated.

Given the transition relation $\rightarrow_M$, we define the operators pre and pre^* on sets of M-configurations in the standard way.

Regular Sets of M-configurations. We define M-tree automata that accept a set of M-configurations. Formally, an M-tree automaton (Q, F, δ) consists in a finite set Q of states, a set $F \subseteq Q$ of final states, and a set δ of rules of the following two forms: (a) $\gamma(q) \rightarrow q'$, where $\gamma \in \Gamma$, and $q, q' \in Q$, and (b) $p(L) \rightarrow q$ where $p \in P$, $q \in Q$, and L is a regular language over Q. We define the relation $\rightarrow_\delta$ between terms over $P \cup \Gamma \cup Q$ as: $t \rightarrow_\delta t'$ if and only if there exists a context C, statements s, s', and a rule $r \in \delta$ such that $t = C[s]$, $t' = C[s']$, and (a) either $r = \gamma(q) \rightarrow q'$ and $s = \gamma(q)$ and $s' = q'$, or (b) $r = p(L) \rightarrow q$, $s = p(q_1, \ldots, q_n)$, $q_1 \ldots q_n \in L$, and $s' = q$. A term t is accepted by the M-tree automaton A^M denoted as $t \in L(A^M)$ if $t \rightarrow_\delta^* q$ for some $q \in F$, where $\rightarrow_\delta^*$ is the reflexive transitive closure of $\rightarrow_\delta$. The language of an M-tree automaton is the set of all M-terms accepted by it.

From X10 to CDPNs. We now give a translation from programs in our syntax to CDPNs. Our translation starts with a control-flow graph (CFG) representation of a program, in which each procedure f is represented as a labeled, directed graph $G_f = (V_f, E_f, entry_f, exit_f)$ where V_f is a set of control nodes, $E_f \subseteq V_f \times \text{ops} \times V_f$ is a set of labeled directed edges labeled by operations from ops (defined below), and $entry_f$ and $exit_f$ are nodes in V_f denoting the entry and exit nodes of a CFG. Each edge label is either a labeled action a^l, a call call(g) to a procedure g, an asynchronous call async(g) to a procedure g, or a finish finish(g) to a procedure g. A control flow graph representation can be computed from the program syntax using standard compiler techniques [2].

Additionally, we make the simplifying assumption that each label l is used at most once, and that if the primitive statement a^l is translated to the edge (u, a^l, v), then the node u has no other outgoing edges. Thus, the node u uniquely determines the label l which is about to be executed, and we can identify node u with l.

As usual, we assume $V_f \cap V_g = \emptyset$ for two distinct procedures f, g. Let

$$V = \cup\{ V_f \mid f \text{ is a procedure } \} \qquad E = \cup\{ E_f \mid f \text{ is a procedure } \}.$$

We now define a CDPN $M_{\mathcal{G}}$ from a CFG representation $\mathcal{G}$. The set of actions consists of all actions a in ops, together with a new "silent" action τ. The set of control locations $P = \{\#, \natural\}$. The set of stack symbols $\Gamma = V \cup \{\text{wait}[u, g, v] \mid (u, \text{finish}(g), v) \in E\} \cup \{\$\}$. Intuitively, we will use the stack to maintain the program stack, with the topmost symbol being the current program point. The control location $\#$ is the dummy location used to orchestrate program steps, and the control location $\natural$ is used to indicate the process execution has terminated. We shall implicitly assume that each stack has a bottom symbol $\$$.

Now for the transitions in Δ. For each $(u, a, v) \in E$, we have the rule P^* : $\# u \xrightarrow{a} \# v$. For each edge $(u, \text{call}(g), v)$, we have the rule P^* : $\# u \xrightarrow{\tau} \# entry_g v$. For each edge $(u, \text{async}(g), v)$, we have the rules P^* : $\# u \xrightarrow{\tau} \# v \triangleright \# entry_g$. To model returns from a procedure g, we add the rule P^* : $\# exit_g \xrightarrow{\tau} \#$. For each edge $(u, \text{finish}(g), v)$, we add the rule P^* : $\# u \xrightarrow{\tau} \# \text{wait}[u, g, v] \triangleright \# entry_g$.

Next, we give the rules performing the synchronization at the end of a finish statement. The first rule, $\natural^*$: $\# \$ \xrightarrow{\tau} \natural$, encodes that a process on its last stack symbol "$\$$" goes to the control state $\natural$ when all its children terminated. The second rule, $P^*\natural$: $\# \text{wait}[u, p, v] \xrightarrow{\tau} \# v$, encodes that the "top level" finish call finishes when the entire finish (spawned as its youngest child) finishes. These two rules ensure that a process makes progress beyond a finish(g) statement only when all processes spawned transitively from g terminate.

It is easy to see that for every CFG $\mathcal{G}$, the CDPN $M_{\mathcal{G}}$ preserves all the behaviors of $\mathcal{G}$. Moreover, $M_{\mathcal{G}}$ is *linear* in the size of $\mathcal{G}$.

Solving the MHP Decision Problem. We solve the MHP decision problem by performing a reachability test between the initial program M-configuration and a family of interesting M-configurations. In particular, for the MHP problem given two labels l and l', we are interested in the family of M-configurations $\mathsf{Conf}^M_{l,l'}$ in which there exists two processes, one about to execute l and the other about to execute l'. Formally, for edges $l \xrightarrow{a} v$, $l' \xrightarrow{a'} v'$ on $\mathcal{G}$ with labels l, l' and primitive statements a, a', we define M-configuration $c \in \mathsf{Conf}^M_{l,l'}$ if and only if there exists two processes in c of the form $\gamma l(p(t_1, \ldots, t_n))$ and $\gamma' l'(p(t'_1, \ldots, t'_m))$ in c where $\gamma, \gamma' \in \Gamma^*$, $t_1, \ldots, t_n$, $t'_1, \ldots, t'_m$ are ground M-terms. Both processes have program points l, l' on the top of the stacks, and thus, l and l' may happen in parallel.

We now give a M-tree automaton $A^M_{l,l'}$ that can recognize exactly the M-configurations in $\mathsf{Conf}^M_{l,l'}$. Given CDPN M with two labels l, l' (program points on $\mathcal{G}$), we define the M-tree automaton $A^M_{l,l'} = (Q, F, \delta)$ as follow. The state set is defined as

$$Q = Q_p \cup Q_r$$

where two symmetric subsets

$$Q_p = \{q_{\mathsf{p00}}, q_{\mathsf{p10}}, q_{\mathsf{p01}}, q_{\mathsf{p11}}\} \qquad Q_r = \{q_{\mathsf{r00}}, q_{\mathsf{r10}}, q_{\mathsf{r01}}, q_{\mathsf{r11}}\}$$

give all states for P-transitions and Γ-transitions. We define q_{pi} as the i-th state in Q_p, and q_{ri} as the i-th state in Q_r for $i = 1, 2, 3, 4$. The 4 states in both sets Q_p and Q_r with tags $00, 10, 01, 11$ on subscripts give the intuitive meanings that neither stack symbol l nor l' has been recognized yet, stack symbol l has been recognized (the first bit is set), stack symbol l' has been recognized (the second bit is set), both stack symbol l and stack symbol l' have been recognized (both bits are set). The terminal state set is defined as

$$F = \{q_{\mathsf{r11}}, q_{\mathsf{p11}}\}.$$

The transition rule set is defined as

$$\delta = \{p() \to q_{\mathsf{p00}} \ , \ l(q_{\mathsf{p01}}) \to q_{\mathsf{r11}} \ , \ l'(q_{\mathsf{p10}}) \to q_{\mathsf{r11}} \ , \ l(q_{\mathsf{p00}}) \to q_{\mathsf{r10}} \ ,$$
$$l'(q_{\mathsf{p00}}) \to q_{\mathsf{r01}} \ , \ p(Q^*, q_{10}, Q^*, q_{01}, Q^*) \to q_{\mathsf{p11}} \ ,$$
$$p(Q^*, q_{01}, Q^*, q_{10}, Q^*) \to q_{\mathsf{p11}} \ , \ \gamma(q_i) \to q_{ri} \ , \ p(Q^*, q_i, Q^*) \to q_{pi}\}.$$

In the transition rule set above, notice that q_i is the state in $\{q_{ri}, q_{pi}\}$, and similarly $q_{00}, q_{10}, q_{01}, q_{11}$ are states in $\{q_{\mathsf{r00}}, q_{\mathsf{p00}}\}$, $\{q_{\mathsf{r10}}, q_{\mathsf{p10}}\}$, $\{q_{\mathsf{r01}}, q_{\mathsf{p01}}\}$, $\{q_{\mathsf{r11}}, q_{\mathsf{p11}}\}$ respectively; $\gamma \in \Gamma$ is an arbitrary stack symbol; and $p \in P$ is an arbitrary control location. We will follow this convention in the rest of this paper.

It is easy to perform a bottom up scan on any M-configuration t with M-tree automaton $A^M_{l,l'}$. The M-tree automaton $A^M_{l,l'}$ recognizes t if and only if there are two processes in t running at program points l, l' in parallel. To be noted that the M-configuration t is not necessary a valid program configuration to be recognized by $A^M_{l,l'}$ as long as it belongs to $\mathsf{Conf}^M_{l,l'}$. A valid program configuration means the configuration is reachable from the initial program configuration by execution. The following theorem is proved in Appendix C of the full version.

Theorem 9. $\text{Conf}_{l,l'}^{M} = L(A_{l,l'}^{M})$.

Algorithm and Complexity. The key to our decision procedure is the following main result of [4].

Theorem 10. *[4] For every CDPN M, and for every M-tree automaton A, there is an effective procedure to construct an M-tree automaton A^* such that $L(A^*) = \text{pre}^*(L(A))$.*

The procedure in [4] applies backward saturation rules to the automaton A. Given a CFG $\mathcal{G}$, the MHP decision problem is solved by:

(a) Constructing CDPN $M_{\mathcal{G}}$ and M-tree automaton $A_{l,l'}^{M}$;
(b) Finding the pre^*-image of $L(A_{l,l'}^{M})$ using Theorem 10, and checking if the initial configuration $\#entry_{main}$ is in $\text{pre}^*(L(A_{l,l'}^{M}))$.

Step (a) can be performed in time linear in the size of the input $\mathcal{G}$. The M-tree automaton $A_{l,l'}^{M}$ is clearly constant and independent of the input program. A careful observation of the construction in [4] shows that (b) is also linear. Thus, we have the following theorem.

Theorem 11. *The MHP decision problem can be solved in linear time in the size of a program.*

Appendix A of the full version gives a detailed example of the CDPN-based approach applied to the first program in Figure 1.

6   Solving the MHP Computation Problem

We can compute all pairs of statements that may happen in parallel with this two-step algorithm:

1. Run the type-based analysis (Section 4) and produce a set of candidate pairs.
2. For each of the candidate pairs, run the CDPN-based decision procedure (Section 5), and remove those pairs that cannot happen in parallel.

Theorem 12. *For a program of size n, for which the type-based analysis produces k candidate pairs, the MHP computation problem can be solved in $O(n \cdot \max(n, k))$ time.*

Proof. Theorem 8 says that Step 1 runs in $O(n \cdot \max(n, k))$ time, and Theorem 11 implies that Step 2 runs in $O(n \cdot k)$ time because we apply an $O(n)$ algorithm k times. The total run time of the two-step algorithm is $O(n \cdot \max(n, k)) + O(n \cdot k) = O(n \cdot \max(n, k))$. ☐

7   Experimental Results

We now show experimental results that show (1) how to use our MHP analysis for race detection and (2) how much time is spent on the two parts of the algorithm in Section 6. We ran our experiments on a Apple iMac with Mac OS X and a 2.16 GHz Intel Core 2 Duo processor and 1 Gigabyte of memory.

Benchmarks	Static counts		Data-race detection			Analysis time (ms)		
	LOC	#async	MHP	MHP +Types	MHP+Types +Andersen	Step:1	Steps:1+2	All-pairs
stream	70	4	160	21	9	7	33	318
sor	185	7	31	8	3	16	21	169
series	290	3	3	3	3	11	13	237
sparsemm	366	4	55	4	2	14	52	2,201
crypt	562	2	366	100	100	54	164	2,289
moldyn	699	14	31882	880	588	43	14,992	57,308
linpack	781	8	67	33	33	14	60	5,618
mg	1,858	57	4884	431	421	69	9,970	114,239
mapreduce	53	3	3	2	2	3	16	78
plasma	4,623	151	8475	2084	760	503	36,491	5,001,310

Fig. 4. Data-race detection

Benchmarks. We use 10 benchmarks taken from the HPC challenge benchmarks (stream), the Java Grande benchmarks in X10 (sor, series, sparsemm, crypt, moldyn, linpack), the NAS benchmarks (mg), and two benchmarks written by ourselves (mapreduce, plasma). In Figure 4, columns 2+3 show the number of lines of code (LOC) and the number of asyncs. The number of asyncs includes the number of foreach and ateach loops, which are X10 constructs that let all the loop iterations run in parallel. We can think of foreach and ateach as plain loops where the body is wrapped in an async. Our own plasma simulation benchmark, called plasma, is the longest and by far the most complicated benchmark with 151 asyncs and 84 finishes. None of the benchmarks use recursion! In particular, none of the benchmarks use the problematic programming style illustrated in the second program in Figure 1.

Measurements. In Figure 4, columns 4–6 show results from doing race detection on our 10 benchmarks. The column MHP shows the number of pairs of primitive statements that read or write nonlocal variables that our analysis found may happen in parallel. Given that none of the benchmarks use recursion, we needed to use only Step 1 of the algorithm in Section 6.

The MHP analysis problem is all about control flow. We complement the control-flow analysis with two data flow analyses, one that uses types and one that uses pointer analysis. The column Type Check refines the MHP column by allowing only pairs of statements for which the accesses are to variables of the same type. The column Andersen Algo refines the Type Check column by allowing only pairs of statements for which Andersen's pointer analysis algorithm finds that the statements may access the same variable.

Note that we can give an alternative and slower algorithm for the MHP computation problem by running the CDPN-based decision procedure on all possible pairs. In Figure 4, column 7 shows the analysis time for the type-based Step 1 that is sufficient for our benchmarks, column 8 shows how long it would take to run Step 1+2 in case we were unable to determine that Step 2 was unnecessary,

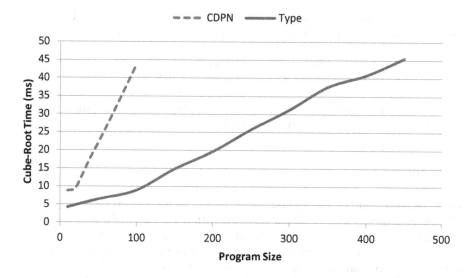

Fig. 5. The cubic root of the analysis time for the third program in Figure 1

and column 9 shows the analysis times for the CDPN-based decision procedure on all pairs. For all benchmarks, it much faster to run Step 1 only rather than Step 1+2, which, in turn, is much faster than to run the decision procedure on all pairs.

Assessment. The combination of the control-flow-oriented MHP analysis and the data-flow-oriented Type Check and Andersen's algorithm is powerful. The final column in Figure 4 contains numbers that are low enough that they are a good starting point for other analyses or testing techniques that depend on MHP information. One such approach is the Race Directed Random Testing of Sen [20] that needs MHP information as a starting point.

Scalability. Our X10 benchmarks form one extreme for the algorithm in Section 6: Step 2 isn't needed at all for those benchmarks. Let us now consider the other extreme where Step 1 provides no savings because the program is recursive and the size of the output is $O(n^2)$. Our question is then: how much time is spent on Step 1 and how much time is spent on Step 2? As our benchmarks, we will use the family of programs that are shown as the third program in Figure 1. For each N, we have one such program. The Nth program contains N procedures that call each other recursively in a closed chain. The main procedure executes a parallel loop that calls the 0'th procedure.

Our experiments show that the running times for the type-based Step 1 grow more slowly than the running times for the CDPN-based Step 2. The type-based Step 1 can handle $N = 450$ within 100 seconds, while for $N = 100$, the CDPN-based Step 2 takes a lot more than 100 seconds. Figure 5 shows the cubic-root of the analysis time for N up to 500. The near-linear curves in Figure 5 suggest that both steps use cubic time for the third program in Figure 1. Two linear regressions on the data in Figure 5 lead to these formulas for the running times:

Type-based Step 1: $time(n) = .00109 \times n^3 + \ldots$

CDPN-based Step 2: $time(n) = .06943 \times n^3 + \ldots$

The constant in front of n^3 is more than 63 times bigger for Step 2 than for Step 1 so in the worst case Step 2 dwarfs Step 1.

8   Conclusion

We have presented two algorithms for static may-happen-in-parallel analysis of X10 programs, including a linear-time algorithm for the MHP decision problem and a two-step algorithm for the MHP computation problem that runs in $O(n \cdot \max(n, k))$ time, where k is a statically determined upper bound on the number of pairs that may happen in parallel. Our results show that the may-happen-in-parallel analysis problem for languages with async-finish parallelism is computationally tractable, as opposed to the situation for concurrent languages with rendezvous or locks. Our results are applicable to various forms of parallelism and synchronization, including fork-join parallelism.

Acknowledgements. This material is based upon research performed in collaborative facilities renovated with funds from the National Science Foundation under Grant No. 0963183, an award funded under the American Recovery and Reinvestment Act of 2009 (ARRA).

References

1. Agarwal, S., Barik, R., Sarkar, V., Shyamasundar, R.K.: May-happen-in-parallel analysis of X10 programs. In: Yelick, K.A., Mellor-Crummey, J.M. (eds.) PPOPP, pp. 183–193. ACM (2007)
2. Aho, A.V., Sethi, R.I., Ullman, J.D.: Compilers: Principles, Techniques, and Tools, 2nd edn. Addison-Wesley, Reading (1986)
3. Barik, R.: Efficient Computation of May-Happen-in-Parallel Information for Concurrent Java Programs. In: Ayguadé, E., Baumgartner, G., Ramanujam, J., Sadayappan, P. (eds.) LCPC 2005. LNCS, vol. 4339, pp. 152–169. Springer, Heidelberg (2006)
4. Bouajjani, A., Müller-Olm, M., Touili, T.: Regular Symbolic Analysis of Dynamic Networks of Pushdown Systems. In: Abadi, M., de Alfaro, L. (eds.) CONCUR 2005. LNCS, vol. 3653, pp. 473–487. Springer, Heidelberg (2005)
5. Charles, P., Donawa, C., Ebcioglu, K., Grothoff, C., Kielstra, A., Sarkar, V., Von Praun, C.: X10: An object-oriented approach to non-uniform cluster computing. In: Proceedings of the 20th ACM SIGPLAN Conference on Object-oriented Programing, Systems, Languages, and Applications, pp. 519–538. ACM SIGPLAN (2005)

6. Choi, J.-D., Lee, K., Loginov, A., O'Callahan, R., Sarkar, V., Sridharan, M.: Efficient and precise datarace detection for multithreaded object-oriented programs. In: PLDI, pp. 258–269 (2002)
7. Duesterwald, E., Soffa, M.L.: Concurrency analysis in the presence of procedures using a data-flow framework. In: Symposium on Testing, Analysis, and Verification, pp. 36–48 (1991)
8. Gawlitza, T.M., Lammich, P., Müller-Olm, M., Seidl, H., Wenner, A.: Join-Lock-Sensitive Forward Reachability Analysis for Concurrent Programs with Dynamic Process Creation. In: Jhala, R., Schmidt, D. (eds.) VMCAI 2011. LNCS, vol. 6538, pp. 199–213. Springer, Heidelberg (2011)
9. Kahlon, V.: Boundedness vs. unboundedness of lock chains: Characterizing decidability of pairwise CFL-reachability for threads communicating via locks. In: LICS 2009, 24th Annual Symposium on Logic in Computer Science, pp. 27–36 (2009)
10. Lammich, P., Müller-Olm, M.: Precise Fixpoint-Based Analysis of Programs with Thread-Creation and Procedures. In: Caires, L., Vasconcelos, V.T. (eds.) CONCUR 2007. LNCS, vol. 4703, pp. 287–302. Springer, Heidelberg (2007)
11. Lee, J.K., Palsberg, J.: Featherweight X10: a core calculus for async-finish parallelism. In: Proceedings of PPOPP 2010, 15th ACM SIGPLAN Annual Symposium on Principles and Practice of Parallel Programming, Bangalore, India (January 2010)
12. Li, L., Verbrugge, C.: A Practical MHP Information Analysis for Concurrent Java Programs. In: Eigenmann, R., Li, Z., Midkiff, S.P. (eds.) LCPC 2004. LNCS, vol. 3602, pp. 194–208. Springer, Heidelberg (2005)
13. Masticola, S.P., Ryder, B.G.: Non-concurrency analysis. In: PPOPP, pp. 129–138 (1993)
14. Naik, M., Aiken, A.: Conditional must not aliasing for static race detection. In: Proceedings of POPL 2007, SIGPLAN–SIGACT Symposium on Principles of Programming Languages, pp. 327–338 (2007)
15. Naumovich, G., Avrunin, G.S.: A conservative data flow algorithm for detecting all pairs of statement that happen in parallel. In: SIGSOFT FSE, pp. 24–34 (1998)
16. Naumovich, G., Avrunin, G.S., Clarke, L.A.: An Efficient Algorithm for Computing MHP Information for Concurrent Java Programs. In: Wang, J., Lemoine, M. (eds.) ESEC 1999 and ESEC-FSE 1999. LNCS, vol. 1687, pp. 338–354. Springer, Heidelberg (1999)
17. Palsberg, J., Schwartzbach, M.I.: Object-Oriented Type Systems. John Wiley & Sons (1994)
18. Ramalingam, G.: Context-sensitive synchronization-sensitive analysis is undecidable. ACM Transactions on Programming Languages and Systems 22(2), 416–430 (2000)
19. Seidl, H., Steffen, B.: Constraint-Based Inter-Procedural Analysis of Parallel Programs. In: Smolka, G. (ed.) ESOP 2000. LNCS, vol. 1782, pp. 351–365. Springer, Heidelberg (2000)
20. Sen, K.: Race directed random testing of concurrent programs. In: Proceedings of PLDI 2008, ACM SIGPLAN Conference on Programming Language Design and Implementation, Tucson, Arizona, pp. 11–21 (June 2008)
21. Taylor, R.N.: Complexity of analyzing the synchronization structure of concurrent programs. Acta Inf. 19, 57–84 (1983)

Modular Static Analysis with Zonotopes

Eric Goubault, Sylvie Putot, and Franck Védrine

CEA Saclay Nano-INNOV, CEA LIST,
Laboratory for the Modelling and Analysis of Interacting Systems,
Point Courrier 174, 91191 Gif sur Yvette CEDEX
{Eric.Goubault,Sylvie.Putot,Franck.Vedrine}@cea.fr

Abstract. Being able to analyze programs function by function, or module by module is a key ingredient to scalable static analyses. The main difficulty for modular static analysis is to be able to do so while not losing too much precision. In this paper, we present a new summary-based approach that builds on previous work of the authors, a zonotopic functional abstraction, that is economical both in space and time complexity. This approach has been implemented, and experiments on numerical programs, reported here, show that this approach is very efficient, and that we still obtain precise analyses in realistic cases.

1 Introduction

In this paper, we use the particular properties that the zonotopic abstract domain [GP06, GGP09, GGP10] exhibits, to design a new modular static analysis of numeric properties. This domain has some advantages over the other sub-polyhedric abstract domains such as [Min01, SSM05, CH78], namely that its abstract transfer functions are of low complexity, while being more precise for instance for non-linear computations. This makes it a good candidate for scalable analyses of numeric properties. It has been the basis for the static analyzer FLUCTUAT, that extends this domain to deal with finite-precision arithmetic semantics (e.g. floating-point numbers) as in [GP11]. Experiments with FLUCTUAT [DGP+09] have proved the usefulness of this domain for analysing mid-sized programs (up to 50KLoCs typically, on standard laptop computers). As we are dealing with precise numerical invariants (ranges of variables or functional properties, numerical errors and their provenance), the standard global interpretation of programs, re-analysing every function at each call site, may still prove too costly for analysing large programs of over 100KLoCs to several MLoCs.

But this zonotopic domain exhibits other properties that make it a perfect candidate for being used in modular static analyses: as shown in [GP09], our domain is a *functional* abstraction, meaning that the transfer functions we define abstract input/output relationships. This paper builds on this property, to design a precise and fast modular static analysis for numerical programs.

The program of Figure 1 will be used to exemplify the basic constructs in our modular analysis. Let us quickly sketch on this example, the behavior of the zonotopic modular abstraction that will be detailed in the rest of the paper. Intuitively, affine sets abstract a program variable x by a form $\hat{x} = \sum_i c_i^x \varepsilon_i + \sum_j p_j^x \eta_j$,

A. Miné and D. Schmidt (Eds.): SAS 2012, LNCS 7460, pp. 24–40, 2012.

```
real mult(real a, real b)
{ return a*(b-2); }

compute(x ∈ [-1,1]);
```

```
real compute(real x)
{ real y1 = mult(x+1, x);
  real y2 = mult(x, 2*x);
  return y2-y1;
}
```

Fig. 1. Running example

where c_i^x and p_j^x are real coefficients that define the abstract value, ε_i are symbolic variables with values in $[-1, 1]$ that abstract uncertain inputs and parameters, and η_j are symbolic variables with values in $[-1, 1]$ that abstract uncertainty on the value of x due to the analysis (i.e. to non-affine operations). The symbolic variables ε_i and η_j are shared by program variables, which implicitly expresses correlation. An affine form $\hat{x}$ is thus a function of the inputs of the program: it is a linear form of the noise symbols ε_i, which are directly related to these inputs.

Here, function `compute` is called with $\hat{x} = \varepsilon_1$ (input in [-1,1]). We build a summary for function `mult` after its first call (`y1 = mult(x+1, x);`). Using the semantics on affine sets to abstract the body of the function, we get as summary the ordered pair of affine sets (I, O) such that $I = (\varepsilon_1 + 1, \varepsilon_1), O = (-1.5 - \varepsilon_1 + 0.5\eta_1)$, where I abstracts the calling context and O the output.

At the next call (`y1 = mult(x, 2*x);`), we try to see if the previous summary can be used, that is if the calling context is contained in the input I of the summary: it is not the case as $(\varepsilon_1, 2\varepsilon_1) \leq (\varepsilon_1 + 1, \varepsilon_1)$ does not hold (with the order on affine sets defined by Equation 3).

We merge the two calling contexts with the join operator of Definition 4, and analyze again the body of the function: this gives a new (larger) summary for function `mult`: $I = (0.5 + \varepsilon_1 + 0.5\eta_2, 1.5\varepsilon_1 + 0.5\eta_3), O = (-\frac{1}{4} - \frac{5}{4}\varepsilon_1 - \eta_2 + \frac{1}{4}\eta_3 + \frac{9}{4}\eta_4)$.

Then, this new summary can be instantiated to the two calls (or any other call with calling context contained in affine set $I = (0.5 + \varepsilon_1 + 0.5\eta_2, 1.5\varepsilon_1 + 0.5\eta_3)$). Without instantiation, the output value of the summary ranges in $[-5, 4.5]$, using concretization of Definition 3. But the summary is a function defined over input ε_1 of the program, and over the symbols η_2 and η_3 that allow expressing the inputs of function `mult`: we will thus get a tighter range for the output, as well as a function of input ε_1, by instantiating η_2 and η_3 and substituting them in the output of the summary. For instance, for the second call of function `mult`, with $(\varepsilon_1, 2\varepsilon_1)$, we identify ε_1 with $0.5 + \varepsilon_1 + 0.5\eta_2$ and $2\varepsilon_1$ with $1.5\varepsilon_1 + 0.5\eta_3$, and deduce $\eta_2 = -1$ and $\eta_3 = \varepsilon_1$, which yields for the output $\frac{3}{4} - \varepsilon_1 + \frac{9}{4}\eta_4 \in [-\frac{5}{2}, 4]$. Direct computation gives $1 - 2\varepsilon_1 + \eta_4 \in [-2, 4]$, which is just slightly tighter.

We illustrate this in Figure 2: we represent on the left picture, the calling contexts (a, b) for the two calls (I_1 is first call, I_2 is second call), and the zonotopic concretization of the calling context after merge, $I_1 \sqcup I_2$. On the right part of the figure, the parabola is the exact results of the second call, $ExM(I_2)$. The dashed zonotope is the result of the abstraction with the semantics of affine sets of the second call, $Mult(I_2)$. The zonotope in plain lines is the output of the summary, $Mult(I_1 \sqcup I_2)$. The zonotope in dotted lines is the summary instantiated to the second call.

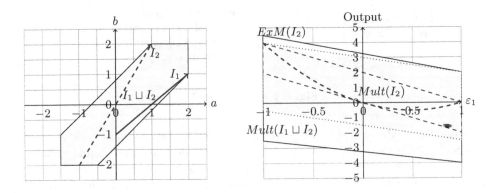

Fig. 2. Summary and instantiation (left is input, right output)

The performances of this modular analysis with our prototype implementation are demonstrated in Section 5.2.

Related Work and Contributions. Finding efficient ways to analyze inter procedural code is a long standing problem. A first class of methods consists in analyzing the whole control flow graph, re-analysing every procedure for each context. This may prove to be rather inefficient, as this may impose to analyze several times the same functions in very similar contexts. A second class considers separate analyses of procedures in a context-insensitive way. The same abstract return value is used for each call site. The advantage is that functions are only analyzed once, but the drawback is that the results that are used at each call site of a function may be a gross over-approximation of the correct result. This might lead to both imprecise and even time inefficient analyses, since imprecise abstractions might lead to lengthy imprecise least fixed point computations. Another approach is based on call strings abstractions [SP81]: the results of different calls to the same function are joined when the abstraction of the call stack (without considering environments, just the string of functions called) is the same. Among the classic abstractions of the call stack is the k-limiting abstraction, that considers equal all patterns of calls to functions that have their last k names of functions called, in order, equal. A way to improve on this is to use summary-based analyses. One creates an abstract value for each procedure, that summarizes its abstract transfer function, and which is instantiated for each call site. Most approaches use tabulation-based procedure summaries, see [SP81, CC77, RHS95, SRH96]. These tabulation-based approaches may be time and memory consuming while not always precise.

We develop here a context sensitive, summary-based approach, that corresponds to a symbolic relational separate analysis in the sense of [CC02], which is a relational function-abstraction in the sense of [JGR05]. The main originality of our work lies in the fact that we use a particular zonotopic domain [GP06, GP09], which abstracts functions (somewhat similarly, but in a much more efficient way, than the classic augmentation process with the polyhedric abstract domain [CC02]), and can thus be naturally instantiated. We will also briefly elaborate on improvements of our method, using a dynamic partitioning approach, as introduced in [Bou92]: one uses several summaries for a function, controlling their number by joining the closest (in a semantic sense) ones.

As already mentioned, the subject of modular analyses is huge, we mention here the closest work to ours. Some linear invariants are also found in a modular way in [MOS04]. Procedure summaries are inferred, but this time by using a backward analysis, in [GT07]. In the realm of pointer and shape analysis, which is orthogonal to our work, numerous techniques have been tried and implemented. See for instance [RC11, YYC08] for alias analysis, to mention but a few recent ones. Some complementary approaches can be found for instance in [Log07] for object-oriented features, and in [QR04] for dealing with concurrent programs.

Contents. We first state some of the basics of our zonotopic (or affine sets) functional abstract domain in Section 2. We describe in Section 3 how we create *summaries*, which associate to a given input context I, encoded as a zonotope, a zonotope O abstracting the input/output relationship, valid for all inputs that are included in I. We demonstrate how the input-output relationship abstracted in our zonotopic domain makes it very convenient to retrieve precise information on smaller contexts, through an instantiation process of the summary. We end up by presenting benchmarks in Section 5.

2   Functional Abstraction with Zonotopes

In this section, we quickly describe the abstract domain based on affine sets which is the basis for our modular analysis. Affine sets define an abstract domain for static analysis of numerical programs, based on affine arithmetic. The geometric concretization of an abstract value of affine sets is a zonotope, but the order we define on affine sets is stronger than the inclusion of the geometric concretization: it is equivalent to the inclusion of the zonotopes describing the abstract value and the inputs of the program. We thus get an input/output abstraction, which is naturally well suited for modular abstraction. The intersection, and thus the interpretation of tests, is a problematic operation: we partially by-pass this difficulty by enhancing our affine sets with constraints on the noise symbols [GGP10] used to define the affine sets. For a lighter presentation, the modular analysis will be presented here on affine sets without these constraints, but it can of course be used in the same manner with constrained affine sets.

2.1   Basics: Affine Sets and Zonotopes

Affine arithmetic is an extension of interval arithmetic on affine forms, first introduced in [CS93], that takes into account affine correlations between variables. An *affine form* is a formal sum over a set of *noise symbols* ε_i

$$\hat{x} \overset{\text{def}}{=} \alpha_0^x + \sum_{i=1}^{n} \alpha_i^x \varepsilon_i, \tag{1}$$

with $\alpha_i^x \in \mathbb{R}$ for all i. Each noise symbol ε_i stands for an independent component of the total uncertainty on the quantity $\hat{x}$, its value is unknown but bounded in [-1,1]; the corresponding coefficient α_i^x is a known real value, which gives the magnitude of that component. The same noise symbol can be shared by several quantities, indicating correlations among them.

The semantics of affine operations is straightforward, they are exact in affine arithmetic. Non-affine operations are linearized, and new noise symbols are introduced to handle the approximation term. In our analysis, we indicate these new noise symbols as η_j noise symbols, thus introducing two kinds of symbols in affine forms of Equation 1: the ε_i noise symbols model uncertainty in data or parameters, while the η_j noise symbols model uncertainty coming from the analysis. For instance, the multiplication of two affine forms, defined, for simplicity of presentation, on ε_i only, writes

$$\hat{x}\hat{y} = \alpha_0^x\alpha_0^y + \sum_{i=1}^{n}(\alpha_i^x\alpha_0^y + \alpha_i^y\alpha_0^x)\varepsilon_i + \left(\sum_{i=1}^{n}|\alpha_i^x\alpha_i^y| + \sum_{i<j}|\alpha_i^x\alpha_j^y + \alpha_j^x\alpha_i^y|\right)\eta_1.$$

More generally, non-affine operations are abstracted by an approximate affine form obtained for instance by a first-order Taylor expansion, plus an approximation term attached to a new noise symbol. Affine operations have linear complexity in the number of noise symbols, whereas non-affine operations can be defined with quadratic cost.

Example 1. Let us demonstrate the abstraction on the following program:
a = [-2,0]; b = [1,3]; x = a + b; y = -a; z = x * y;
The assignments of a and b create new noise symbols ε_1, ε_2: $\hat{a} = -1 + \varepsilon_1$, $\hat{b} = 2+\varepsilon_2$. Affine expressions are handled exactly, we get $\hat{x} = 1+\varepsilon_1+\varepsilon_2, \hat{y} = 1-\varepsilon_1$. The multiplication produces a new η_1 symbol, we get $\hat{z} = 0.5 + \varepsilon_2 + 1.5\eta_1$. The range of z given by $\hat{z}$ is $[-2, 3]$ while the exact range is $[-2, 2.25]$.

In what follows, we introduce matrix notations to handle tuples of affine forms. We note $\mathcal{M}(n, p)$ the space of matrices with n lines and p columns of real coefficients. A tuple of affine forms expressing the set of values taken by p variables over n noise symbols ε_i, $1 \leq i \leq n$, can be represented by a matrix $A \in \mathcal{M}(n + 1, p)$. Let ^tA denote the transpose of matrix A. We define the zonotopic concretization of such tuples by :

Definition 1. *Let a tuple of affine forms with p variables over n noise symbols, defined by a matrix $A \in \mathcal{M}(n + 1, p)$. Its concretization is the zonotope*

$$\gamma(A) = \left\{{}^tA\begin{pmatrix}1\\\varepsilon\end{pmatrix} \mid \varepsilon \in [-1, 1]^n\right\} \subseteq \mathbb{R}^p .$$

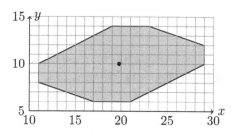

For instance, for $n = 4$ and $p = 2$, the gray zonotope is the concretization of the affine set $(\hat{x}, \hat{y})$, with $\hat{x} = 20 - 4\varepsilon_1 + 2\varepsilon_3 + 3\varepsilon_4$, $\hat{y} = 10 - 2\varepsilon_1 + \varepsilon_2 - \varepsilon_4$, and
$$
{}^tA = \begin{pmatrix} 20 & -4 & 0 & 2 & 3 \\ 10 & -2 & 1 & 0 & -1 \end{pmatrix}.
$$

Now, we saw in the Definition of non-linear arithmetic operations, that our affine forms are defined over two kind of noise symbols, the ε_i and η_j. We thus define affine sets as Minkowski sums of a *central* zonotope, $\gamma(C^X)$ and of a *perturbation* zonotope centered on 0, $\gamma(P^X)$. Central zonotopes depend on central noise symbols ε_i, that represent the uncertainty on input values to the program, with which we want to keep as many relations as possible. Perturbation zonotopes depend on perturbation symbols η_j which are created along the interpretation of the program and represent the uncertainty of values due to operations that are not interpreted exactly: for instance the control-flow abstraction while computing the join of two abstract values, or non-affine arithmetic operations.

Definition 2. *We define an affine set by the pair of matrices* $X = (C^X, P^X) \in \mathcal{M}(n+1, p) \times \mathcal{M}(m, p)$. *The affine form* $X_k = c_{0k}^X + \sum_{i=1}^{n} c_{ik}^X \varepsilon_i + \sum_{j=1}^{m} p_{jk}^X \eta_j$ *describes its kth variable.*

2.2   Geometric and Functional Orders

Definition 3. *Let* $X = (C^X, P^X)$ *be an affine set in* $\mathcal{M}(n+1, p) \times \mathcal{M}(m, p)$. *Its concretization in* $\mathcal{P}(\mathbb{R}^p)$ *is*

$$
\gamma(X) = \left\{ {}^tC^X \begin{pmatrix} 1 \\ \varepsilon \end{pmatrix} + {}^tP^X \eta \mid (\varepsilon, \eta) \in [-1, 1]^{n+m} \right\} .
$$

If we were only interested in abstractions of current values of variables, the partial order to consider would be the subset inclusion of their concretization, as formalized in Definition 3. But we are interested in abstracting input/output relations, this will be instrumental in our modular analysis.

Let $\mathcal{X}$ be a set of functions of the form $x : \mathbb{R}^q \to \mathbb{R}^p$. We write $x_1, \ldots, x_p$ its p components. Our goal is to abstract the input/output relationship of functions in $\mathcal{X}$ using an affine set X, i.e. to automatically determine an over-approximation X of the set of values that $e_1, \ldots, e_q, x_1, \ldots, x_p$ can take, conjointly, where $e_1, \ldots, e_q$ are slack variables representing the initial values of the q input variables of functions $x \in \mathcal{X}$: to one particular run of the program, corresponds exactly one fixed tuple of values $e_1, \ldots, e_q$. This fits in the *relational function-abstraction* of [JGR05]. Let $\gamma(\tilde{X})$ be such an augmented zonotope, $\tilde{X} \in \mathcal{M}(r, p+q)$, where the set of symbols is decomposed in $r = n + m$ symbols $\varepsilon_1, \ldots, \varepsilon_n$, the central noise symbols, and $\eta_1, \ldots, \eta_m$, the perturbation symbols, as introduced in Definition 2. From now on, we will consider the augmented affine set $\tilde{X}$:

$$\tilde{X} = \begin{pmatrix} E & C^X \\ 0 & P^X \end{pmatrix} \tag{2}$$

where $E \in \mathcal{M}(n+1, q)$ is the affine set describing the inputs to the functions in $\mathcal{X}$. The concretization γ_f of such augmented affine sets in terms of sets of functions from $\mathbb{R}^q$ to $\mathbb{R}^p$ is as follows:

$$\gamma_f(\tilde{X}) = \left\{ f : \mathbb{R}^q \to \mathbb{R}^p \ \middle|\ \begin{array}{l} \forall \varepsilon \in [-1,1]^n, \exists \eta \in [-1,1]^m, \\ f({}^tE\begin{pmatrix}1\\\varepsilon\end{pmatrix}) = {}^tC^X\begin{pmatrix}1\\\varepsilon\end{pmatrix} + {}^tP^X\eta \end{array} \right\}$$

The (partial) order relation on augmented affine sets $\tilde{X}, \tilde{Y}$, is given by: $\tilde{X} \leq_f \tilde{Y}$ if $\gamma_f(\tilde{X}) \subseteq \gamma_f(\tilde{Y})$, which in turn is equivalent to $\gamma(\tilde{X}) \subseteq \gamma(\tilde{Y})$, hence correctness of our functional abstraction is given naturally as for any concretization-based abstract interpretation [CC92]: $\tilde{X}$ is a correct abstraction of a set $\mathcal{X}$ of functions if $\mathcal{X} \subseteq \gamma_f(\tilde{X})$. Then, similarly for the interpretation of an abstraction F of a function $\mathcal{F}$ on augmented affine sets: $\forall \mathcal{X} \in \mathbb{R}^{n+p}, \mathcal{F}(\mathcal{X}) \subseteq \gamma(F(\tilde{X}))$.

Now, the order relation on augmented affine sets can be reformulated in terms of the current parameterization of abstract values for variables $x_1, \ldots, x_p$, without having to consider the extra n variables $e_1, \ldots, e_n$: let X and Y be two affine sets. We say that $X \leq Y$ iff for all $t \in \mathbb{R}^p$,

$$\|(C^Y - C^X)t\|_1 \leq \|P^Y t\|_1 - \|P^X t\|_1 . \tag{3}$$

This functional (pre-)order $\leq$ always implies $\leq_f$, and is equivalent in most interesting situations, for instance when matrix E of equation 2, without its first line, is invertible: this covers in particular the case when the inputs are given in intervals and have unknown dependency. We do not prove this property here as this is not central to the rest of the paper, some hints about it can be found in [GP09].

Example 2. Take $X : (X_1 = \varepsilon_1, X_2 = \varepsilon_2)$ and $Y : (Y_1 = \varepsilon_2, Y_2 = \varepsilon_1)$. We have $\gamma(X) = \gamma(Y) = [-1,1]^2$. But X and Y are incomparable for the functional ordering of Equation 3. Indeed, X and Y represent two very different functions from the inputs $(\varepsilon_1, \varepsilon_2)$ to the values of the variables (x_1, x_2).

2.3 Join Operation

In general, there exists no least upper bound for affine sets. We define a join operator over affine sets which gives a minimal upper bound in some cases, can always be computed efficiently, and presents some nice properties: for instance, the range of the joined value on each variable is equal to the union of the interval ranges on the variable. We refer the reader to [GP09] for details.

Let us first introduce some notations. For two real numbers α and β, let $\alpha \wedge \beta$ denote their minimum and $\alpha \vee \beta$ their maximum. We define

$$\mathrm{argmin}_{|.|}(\alpha, \beta) = \gamma \text{ such that } \gamma \in [\alpha \wedge \beta, \alpha \vee \beta] \text{ and } |\gamma| \text{ is minimal}$$

Let x and y be two intervals. We say that x and y are in generic positions if, whenever $x \subseteq y$, $\inf x = \inf y$ or $\sup x = \sup y$. And for an interval x, we note $mid(x)$ its center.

Definition 4. *Let two affine sets X and Y where (C^X, P^X) and (C^Y, P^Y) are in $\mathcal{M}(n+1, p) \times \mathcal{M}(m, p)$, we define $Z = X \sqcup Y$ such that for all $k, l \in [1, p]$, $i \in [1, n]$, $j \in [1, m]$:*
If $\gamma(X_k)$ and $\gamma(Y_k)$ are in generic position:

$$c_{0,k}^Z = mid\left(\gamma(X_k) \cup \gamma(Y_k)\right)$$

$$c_{i,k}^Z = argmin_{|.|}(c_{i,k}^X, c_{i,k}^Y), p_{j,k}^Z = argmin_{|.|}(p_{j,k}^X, p_{j,k}^Y)$$

$$p_{m+k,k}^Z = \sup(\gamma(X_k) \cup \gamma(Y_k)) - c_{0,k}^Z - \left(\sum_{i=1}^{n} \mid c_{i,k}^Z \mid + \sum_{j=1}^{m} \mid p_{j,k}^Z \mid \right)$$

Else: $c_{0,k}^Z = \dfrac{c_{0,k}^X + c_{0,k}^Y}{2}, c_{i,k}^Z = \dfrac{c_{i,k}^X + c_{i,k}^Y}{2}, p_{j,k}^Z = \dfrac{p_{j,k}^X + p_{j,k}^Y}{2}$

$$\boldsymbol{p}_{m+k,k}^Z = \frac{1}{2} \sum_{i=0}^{n} |c_{i,k}^Y - c_{i,k}^X| + \frac{1}{2} \sum_{j=1}^{m} |p_{j,k}^Y - p_{j,k}^X|$$

And in both cases: $p_{m+l,k}^Z = 0$ *for $l \neq k$*

Intuitively, by using the *argmin* operator, this join operator keeps the dependencies to the inputs that are common to both form joined.

We then have the following result (whose second item is proved in [GP09]):

Lemma 1. *$Z = X \sqcup Y$ is an upper bound of X and Y such that:*

- *for all $k \in [1, p]$, Z_k is a minimal upper bound of X_k and Y_k*
- *if X_k and Y_k are in generic positions, then $k \in [1, p]$, $\gamma(Z_k) = \gamma(X_k) \cup \gamma(Y_k)$ where $\cup$ is here the union in the lattice of intervals.*

Example 3. Take $X : (X_1 = 1 + \varepsilon_1, X_2 = \varepsilon_1)$ and $Y : (Y_1 = 2\varepsilon_1, Y_2 = \varepsilon_1)$. We have $\gamma(X_1) = [0, 2]$, $\gamma(Y_1) = [-2, 2]$, so that X_1 and Y_1 are in generic positions. Then $Z = X \cup Y : (Z_1 = \varepsilon_1 + \eta_1, Z_2 = \varepsilon_1)$ is a minimal upper bound of X, Y.

3   Affine Sets Summary and Specialization

We will now define function summaries as pairs (I, O) of input and output zonotopes, I and O being defined as introduced in Section 2. These zonotopes I and O are parametrized by the same central noise symbols $\varepsilon_1, \dots, \varepsilon_n$ representing the inputs of the program, and thus each represent a function of these inputs. But the pair also represents functions from $\gamma(I)$ to $\gamma(O)$, and we will introduce a new functional concretization $\gamma_f(I, O)$ that extends the γ_f of Section 2.

Pairs (I, O) abstract sets of functions from $\gamma(I)$ to $\gamma(O)$, deduced from I and O seen as sets of functions of the inputs of the program (the noise symbols ε_i), and of uncertainties introduced by the analysis (the noise symbols η_j). Indeed, as O represents some computation on entries I, O contains the perturbation symbols of I: say $\eta_1, \ldots, \eta_{m_1}$ for I, $\eta_{m_1+1}, \ldots, \eta_m$ for the symbols only appearing in O. More formally, the concretization of a pair (I, O) of input and output zonotopes, in terms of functions F from $\gamma(I)$ to $\gamma(O)$, is as follows:

$$\gamma_f(I, O) = \left\{ \begin{array}{l} F : \gamma(I) \to \gamma(O) \mid \forall \varepsilon_1, \ldots, \varepsilon_n, \eta_1, \ldots, \eta_{m_1} \\ \exists \eta_{m_1+1}, \ldots, \eta_m \text{ with } (\varepsilon, \eta) \in [-1, 1]^{n+m} \\ \text{and } F({}^t I^t(1, \varepsilon, \eta_1, \ldots, \eta_{m_1})) = {}^t O^t(1, \varepsilon, \eta) \end{array} \right\}$$

As outputs are defined over these same noise symbols, the summaries can be instantiated to a given calling context, by substituting some of these perturbation noise symbols by their expression for the particular calling context.

Consider a current calling context C, and a current function summary $S_f = (I, O)$ for f, the interpretation of the function call $f(C)$ in our inter-procedural analysis is given in Algorithm 1. Its different steps are detailed in the sections that follow.

Algorithm 1. Interpretation of function call $f(C)$, given calling context C, and function summary $S_f = (I, O)$

---

    if $!(C \leq I)$ // test if calling context C matches summary input I **then**
        $I \leftarrow I \sqcup C$ // join calling context and summary input (Definition 4)
        $S_f \leftarrow (I, [\![f]\!](I))$ // new summary creation (Section 3.2)
    end if
    return $[\![I == C]\!]O$ // summary instantiation (Section 3.3)

3.1   Program Syntax and Semantics

Programs *Prog* we are considering in what follows are sets of functions $f \in Prog$, acting on an environment made up of variables $\mathcal{V}_f$ local to function f, and global variables $\mathcal{G}$. We suppose that the $\mathcal{V}_f$, $f \in Prog$, and $\mathcal{G}$, form a partition of the set of program variables $\mathcal{V}$. There is a unique data type: the real numbers. Function definitions are as follows:

$$\begin{array}{l} funct = \text{function } f(v_1, \ldots, v_p) \ \{ \\ \qquad instr; \ \text{return } r \ \} \qquad v_1, \ldots, v_p \in \mathcal{V}_f, r \in \mathcal{V}_f \end{array}$$

Function calls $f(expr_1, \ldots, expr_p)$, where $expr_1$ to $expr_p$ are p expressions, have the call by value semantics: their evaluation correspond to computing the value of each expression $expr_1$ to $expr_p$ in that order, and assigning each local variable v_i with the corresponding value of $expr_i$ $(i = 1, \ldots, p)$ in the environment of the call. The body of the functions is standard, it is made of a classic set of instructions *instr* for imperative languages: assignment of expressions to variables, tests, loops. The *return* at the end of the definition of f just returns the value of one of the local variables, r, of f, to the caller. We consider global variables as part of the calling context and output of functions. A function f is thus defined from $\mathbb{R}^p$ to $\mathbb{R}^q$, for some $q \leq card(\mathcal{G}) + 1$.

We suppose given a set of control points attached to instructions of our language, including $(call^i_f)$ just before executing the ith call to f: $f(expr, \ldots, expr)$ in an expression, and $(return^i_f)$, right after the ith call to function f has returned the flow of execution to the calling expression.

The concrete collecting semantics is given in terms of concrete environments $e \in Env = \mathcal{V} \to \mathbb{R}$, and a semantics function, partitioned over the control points $d \in \mathcal{D}$, $[instr]_c : Env \to Env$, such that $[E]^d_c e$ ($E \in instr$, $e \in Env$) gives the change of concrete environment when interpreting instruction E in context e, at control point d. The concrete collecting semantics $[P]_c e$, partitioned over $d \in \mathcal{D}$ as $[P]^d_c e$, of a program P, is obtained as the least solution in $\wp(Env)$ (with subset ordering), over some set of initial environments $e \in \wp(Env)$, of the semantic equations given by $[E]^d_c$ lifted from Env to $\wp(Env)$, at each control point of P.

For the abstract collecting semantics, we use the abstract domain of affine sets $\mathcal{Z}$ for all instructions, except for calls to functions. In order to define a modular static analysis, we suppose now abstract environments in Env_a are made of bindings of variables to affine sets, as well as bindings of function names to summaries, i.e. pairs of affine sets: $Env_a = \mathcal{Z} \times (Prog \to \mathcal{Z} \times \mathcal{Z})$. We call $[instr]^d_a : Env_a \to Env_a$ the corresponding semantics functions (forward abstract transformers). The correctness of the abstract semantics with respect to the concrete one is formalized as follows. For all initial possible sets of environments $e \in \wp(Env)$, we form $e^\sharp = (e^\sharp_\mathcal{V}, \perp)$ where $e^\sharp_\mathcal{V}$ is any abstract environment in $\mathcal{Z}$, dealing only with program variables, such that $e \in \gamma(e^\sharp_\mathcal{V})$, and $\perp$ in the second component of $e^\sharp$ means that for all functions f of $Prog$, we start in an environment where we do not have any summary of f, then we must have, for all control points $d \in \mathcal{D}$:

$$[P]^d_c e \subseteq \gamma \left(\pi_1([P]^d_a e^\sharp) \right) \tag{4}$$

where $\pi_1 : Env_a \to \mathcal{Z}$ is the projection on the first component of environments.

3.2 Summary Creation

The operations involved, order $\leq$ and join, have already been described in Section 2. Let us just here consider Example 1. Function `compute` is called with $x \in [-1, 1]$, which can be abstracted by $x = \varepsilon_1$. The first call to function `mult` is then interpreted in Algorithm 1 as a new summary creation, since the current summary for `mult` is $\perp$. We thus interpret `mult` with arguments $a_1 = 1 + \varepsilon_1$ and $b_1 = \varepsilon_1$. Multiplication $a_1 \times (b_1 - 2)$ in the abstract domain of affine sets produces $a_1 \times (b_1 - 2) = -1.5 - \varepsilon_1 + 0.5\eta_1$, where η_1 is a new noise symbol with values in $[-1, 1]$. The abstract environment at the end of this first call to `mult` contains the entry, for `mult` $(I = (a_1 = 1 + \varepsilon_1, b_1 = \varepsilon_1), O = -1.5 - \varepsilon_1 + 0.5\eta_1)$.

3.3 Summary Instantiation

The instantiation of a summary for a given calling context resembles the meet operation on constrained affine sets [GGP10]: indeed, it consists in adding constraints on noise symbols that correspond to component-wise equality of affine forms. Still, it does not require the formalism of constrained affine sets as we do not abstract constraints, they are immediately used to substitute in the summary the noise symbols introduced by the join operation due to merging contexts, by the affine expression of the other noise symbols.

The instantiation operator is thus a function that takes a summary (I, O), an input affine set C such that $C \leq I$ and returns $Z = [\![I == C]\!]O$. We form the following matrix U, given $I = (C^I, P^I)$ and $C = (C^C, P^C)$ two affine sets with $(C^I, P^I), (C^C, P^C) \in \mathcal{M}(n+1, p) \times \mathcal{M}(m, p)$:

$$
U = \begin{pmatrix}
p^I_{m,1} - p^C_{m,1} \cdots p^I_{1,1} - p^C_{1,1} \; c^I_{n,1} - c^C_{n,1} \cdots c^C_{0,1} - c^C_{0,1} \\
\cdots \\
p^I_{m,p} - p^C_{m,p} \cdots p^I_{1,p} - p^C_{1,p} \; c^I_{n,p} - c^C_{n,p} \cdots c^C_{0,p} - c^C_{0,p}
\end{pmatrix}
$$

Performing Gauss elimination [Bee06], on U we obtain the row-echelon form for U: $U' = {}^t(U_1 | U_2)$ where $U_1 \in \mathcal{M}(n+m+1, r)$ and $U_2 \in \mathcal{M}(n+m+1, p-r)$ with $r = min(m, p)$ and U_1 and U_2 upper triangular. Matrix U_1 encodes the fact that we must have, when "interpreting" $I == C$, relations of the form $\eta_{k_1} = R_1(\eta_{k_1-1}, \ldots, \eta_1, \varepsilon_n, \ldots, \varepsilon_1)$, $\eta_{k_2} = R_2(\eta_{k_2-1}, \ldots, \eta_1, \varepsilon_n, \ldots, \varepsilon_1)$, $\ldots$, $\eta_{k_r} = R_r(\eta_{k_r-1}, \ldots, \eta_1, \varepsilon_n, \ldots, \varepsilon_1)$, with $k_1 > k_2 > \ldots k_r$.

The principle of the instantiation operator defined below is, first, to interpret the relation $U^t(\eta_m, \ldots, \eta_1, \varepsilon_n, \ldots, \varepsilon_1) = 0$ as constraints on the values taken by noise symbols, and to use the r relations $R_1, \ldots, R_{k_r}$ to eliminate the perturbation symbols that have been introduced the most recently in the summary output O of function f, $\eta_{k_1}, \ldots, \eta_{k_r}$:

Definition 5. *Let* $I = (C^I, P^I)$, $C = (C^C, P^C)$ *and* $O = (C^O, P^O)$ *be three affine sets with* $(C^I, P^I), (C^C, P^C) \in \mathcal{M}(n+1, p) \times \mathcal{M}(m, p)$ *and* $(C^O, P^O) \in \mathcal{M}(n+1, q) \times \mathcal{M}(m, q)$ *(by convention, m is the total number of perturbation noise symbols, some lines in P^I, P^C and P^O may contain only zeros). In $Z = [\![I == C]\!]O$, the (C^Z, P^Z) are defined by substituting in (C^O, P^O) the values of η_{k_1} to η_{k_r} given by $R_1(\eta_{k_1-1}, \ldots, \eta_1, \varepsilon_n, \ldots, \varepsilon_1)$ to $R_{k_r}(\eta_{k_r-1}, \ldots, \eta_1, \varepsilon_n, \ldots, \varepsilon_1)$ respectively, in terms of the η_j of lower indices, and of the ε_j.*

In practice, there is actually no need to first perform the Gauss elimination on U: constraints $I == C$ are of such a particular form that it is enough (and this is what is implemented and tested in this article) to substitute in (C^O, P^O), in order to obtain (C^Z, P^Z), only the relations in U that are already in row-echelon form.

Note that when a function contains only operations that are affine with respect to the calling context (no join operation), the instantiation of the summary to a particular context gives the same result as would do the direct abstraction of the function in that context. When non-affine operations are involved, such as in the running example, we will see that the instantiation also gives tight results.

Let us consider the second call to function `mult` in our running example, with $a_2 = \varepsilon_1$ and $b_2 = 2\varepsilon_1$. This calling context is not included in the previous one, so in Algorithm 1 we need first to merge the current summary input context I with the current call context, giving $(a_3, b_3) = (a_2, b_2) \sqcup (a_1, b_1) = (0.5 + \varepsilon_1 + 0.5\eta_2, 1.5\varepsilon_1 + 0.5\eta_3)$ (note that we are in the non-generic case of Definition 4). The zonotopic concretizations of the two calling contexts, and of the merged value giving the input context of the summary, are represented on the left picture of Figure 2 (and respectively named I_1, I_2 and $I_1 \sqcup I_2$).

The result of the multiplication for the merged context is then $a_3 \times (b_3 - 2) = -\frac{1}{4} - \frac{5}{4}\varepsilon_1 - \eta_2 + \frac{1}{4}\eta_3 + \frac{9}{4}\eta_4 \in [-5, \frac{9}{2}]$, so we create the new summary for `mult`: $(I = (a_3 = 0.5 + \varepsilon_1 + 0.5\eta_2, b_3 = 1.5\varepsilon_1 + 0.5\eta_3), O = -\frac{1}{4} - \frac{5}{4}\varepsilon_1 - \eta_2 + \frac{1}{4}\eta_3 + \frac{9}{4}\eta_4)$. This is the zonotope (parallelepiped, here), represented in plain lines on the right picture of Figure 2.

Let us now instantiate this summary for the second call (last part of Algorithm 1), when $a = \varepsilon_1 = 0.5 + \varepsilon_1 + 0.5\eta_2$ and $b = 2\varepsilon_1 = 1.5\varepsilon_1 + 0.5\eta_3$: we deduce by elimination $\eta_2 = -1$ and $\eta_3 = \varepsilon_1$. Instantiating the summary with these values of η_2 and η_3 yields $a_3 \times (b_3 - 2) = \frac{3}{4} - \varepsilon_1 + \frac{9}{4}\eta_4 \in [-\frac{5}{2}, 4]$. While direct computation $a_2 \times (b_2 - 2) = 1 - 2\varepsilon_1 + \eta_4 \in [-2, 4]$, which is just slightly tighter. The instantiated and directly computed zonotopes are also represented on the right picture of Figure 2, respectively in dotted and dashed lines.

3.4   Correctness and Complexity

The correctness of instantiation comes from the fact that, writing $F_{|\gamma(C)}$ for the restriction of a function $F : \gamma(I) \to \gamma(O) \in \gamma_f(I, O)$ (remember that $C \leq I$, hence $\gamma(C) \subseteq \gamma(I)$), first, $F(\gamma(C)) \subseteq \gamma(Z)$ and

$$\{F_{|\gamma(C)} : \gamma(C) \to \gamma(Z) | F \in \gamma_f(I, O)\} \subseteq \gamma_f(C, Z) \tag{5}$$

The last statement meaning that (C, Z) is a correct summary for restrictions of functions F summarized by the more general summary (I, O).

We can conclude from this that Algorithm 1 is correct in the sense of Equation 4. This is done by showing inductively on the semantics that, for any program P, and for any concrete environment e and abstract environment $e^\sharp$ such as in the premises of Equation 4,

$$\{F | \forall x \in [\![P]\!]_c^{(call_g^i)} e, F(x) = [\![g]\!]_c^{(return_g^i)} x\} \subseteq \gamma_f \left(\pi_2 \left([\![P]\!]_a^{(return_g^i)} e^\sharp \right) (g) \right) \tag{6}$$

$$[\![P]\!]_c^{(call_g^i)} e \subseteq \gamma \left(\pi_1 \left([\![P]\!]_a^{(call_g^i)} e^\sharp \right) \right) \tag{7}$$

In Equation 6, $\pi_2 : (Env_a = Z \times (Prog \to Z \times Z)) \to (Prog \to Z \times Z)$, extracts the part of the abstract semantics which accounts for the representation of summaries. The fact that Equation 6 is true comes from the fact that summary instantiations compute correct over-approximations of concrete functions on the calling contexts, see Equation 5. The fact that Equation 7 is true comes from the fact that in Algorithm 1 we join the calling context with the current summary context as soon as it is not included in it, so we safely over-approximate all calling contexts in the abstract fixed-point.

Without the inclusion test, the complexity of Algorithm 1 and of (the simpler version of) summary instantiation is $O(q \times nb\_noise)$, where q is the number of arguments of the called function and nb_noise is the number of noise symbols involved in the affine form of the calling context. The main contribution to the complexity comes from the (particularized) Gauss elimination in the substitution. The inclusion test is by default exponential in the number of noise symbols. However, simpler $O(q \times nb\_noise)$ versions can be used as a necessary condition for inclusion, and in many cases the full test can be avoided, see [GP09]. Also, the use of a modular abstraction as proposed here helps to keep the number of noise symbols quite low.

4   Summary Creation Strategies

In order to control the loss of accuracy due to summarizing, it is natural to use several (a bounded number n of) summaries instead of a unique one. We present here a method inspired from tabulation-based procedure summaries [SP81] and dynamic partitioning [Bou92].

We consider a function call $f(C)$, when k summaries (I_j, O_j), $j = 1, \ldots, k$ exist for function f. Either C is included in one of the inputs I_j, and the call reduces to instantiating O_j and thus returning $[\![I_j == C]\!]O_j$. Or else, we distinguish two cases. If the maximal number n of pairs (I_j, O_j) is not reached, we add a new summary $(C, [\![f]\!](C))$. And if it is reached, we take the closest calling context I_j to C (such that the cost $c(C, I_j)$ is minimal) and replace in the table of summaries, (I_j, O_j) by the new summary $(I_j \sqcup C, [\![f]\!](I_j \sqcup C))$.

For instance, the cost function c could be chosen as follows: let $(e_l)_{1 \le l \le p}$ be the canonical basis of $\mathbb{R}^p$,

$$c(X, Y) = \sum_{l=1}^{p} \left(\| (C^Y - C^X)e_l \|_1 - | \; \|P^Y e_l\|_1 - \|P^X e_l\|_1 \; | \right) \; .$$

By definition of the order relation 3, if $X \le Y$ or $Y \le X$ then $c(X, Y) \le 0$. This function, which defines a heuristic to create or not new summaries, expresses a cost function on the component-wise concretizations of the affine sets X and Y. And it can be computed more efficiently (in $O(p(n + m))$ operations, where p is the number of variables and $n + m$ the number of noise symbols) than if we used a stronger condition linked to the order on the concretizations of these affine sets.

5   Examples

We have implemented the zonotopic summarizing in a small analyzer of C programs. The part dedicated to zonotopes and summarizing represents about 7000 lines of C++ code. We present experiments showing the good behavior in time and accuracy of summaries, then some results on realistic examples. The examples are available on http://www.lix.polytechnique.fr/Labo/Sylvie.Putot/benchs.html.

5.1 Performance of the Modular Analysis

To evaluate the performance of the summarizing process, we slightly transform the running example of Figure 1, so that `mult` is called with different calling contexts (Figure 3 below). We analyze it with different numbers n of noise symbols for input x. Note that even though the interval abstraction for x is always $[-1, 1]$, the relational information between the arguments of `mult` evolves.

We now compare the summary-based modular analysis to the classic zonotopic iterations when n evolves (see Figure 3). We see the much better performance of the modular analysis when the instantiation succeeds: it is linear in the number n of noise symbols, whereas the non-modular one is quadratic, because of the multiplication. This is of course a toy example, where increasing the number of noise symbols brings no additional information. But in the analysis of large programs, which is the context where modularity makes the more sense, we will often encounter this kind of situation, with possibly many noise symbols if we want a fine abstraction of correlations and functional behavior (sensitivity to inputs and parameters). This complexity gain is thus crucial. Note that the results for the modular analysis are still very accurate: we obtain, for $y1$, $[-6.5, 2.5]$, to be compared to $[-3, 0]$ with the non-modular analysis, and for $y2$, $[-4, 4]$, to be compared to $[-2, 4]$.

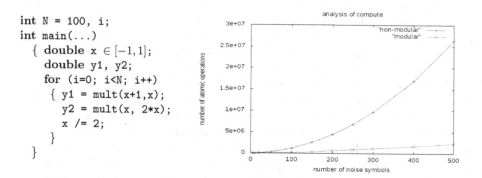

```
int N = 100, i;
int main(...)
  { double x ∈ [-1,1];
    double y1, y2;
    for (i=0; i<N; i++)
    { y1 = mult(x+1,x);
      y2 = mult(x, 2*x);
      x /= 2;
    }
}
```

Fig. 3. Number of operations in the analysis, function of the number of symbols

5.2 Application of Summarizing on Benchmarks

We consider the following set of simple benchmarks: *img_filter* is a simple filter that performs edge detection on a small image composed of 20 pixels. The algorithm uses iterative filtering that calls a blur filter followed by 6 calls to a Sobel filter. The application thus filters 40 different descriptions of the initial pixels.

sincos computes an approximation of the sin and the cos functions with different order 5 polynomials, depending on the range of the inputs. The application makes 64 different calls to the function computing the results. At the end of each call, we formally verify that $\sin^2 + \cos^2 - 1$ remains in small ranges.

order2_filter is a linear filter of order two: $S = a*E + b*E0 + c*E1 + d*S0 + e*S1$. The formal parameters of the function are a close to 0.7, b close to -1.3, c close to 1.1, d close to 1.4 and e close to -0.7; inputs E are independent, within $[-1, 1]$. Close to means that the value of these coefficients is only known to be in a range of width 2% of their value. The filter is called 8 times.

The results are shown in Table 1. Even on a rather small number of function calls, we have a significant time gain (at least 5 times as fast as the non-modular analysis) without losing too much precision (worst case being around 2).

Table 1. Comparison of modular and non-modular analyses

		img_filter	*sincos*	*filter*
	example			
Characteristics	#lines of C/#vars	194/135	208/135	96/19
Non-modular analysis	time (s)	11.8	3.84	49
	average interval	$[0.056, 0.067]$	$[-0.026, 0.026]$	$[-1.24, 2.99]$
Modular analysis	time(s)	1.7	0.79	10
	instantiations	18/20	63/65	6/8
	average interval	$[0.056, 0.067]$	$[-0.058, 0.058]$	$[-1.58, 3.33]$
Comparison	time gain	6.9	4.9	4.9
	precision loss	1	2.23	1.27

Our aim is of course to apply this modular analysis to real industrial control software for numerical validation. The applications we target are large reactive systems. Most of the source code for these applications is generated automatically from high-level synchronous data-flow specifications written in SCADE or SIMULINK. These languages allow programming the control software in a highly hierarchical way, with many calls to different levels of blocks. The structure of the C source generated in such a way is one main function that calls many numerical blocks, generally iterating on a large number of cycles.

We report here on a partially manual, partially automated simulation of our method to a real industrial test case, part of a control command software used in the aeronautics industry. This program is about 37500 lines of C, consisting of an infinite loop. The core of the loop first updates the inputs with the sensors' data and then calls a function composed of eight different blocks. We unroll this loop 6 times here, after which the ranges are stable. The program has about 20 input variables, more than 500 sensor variables, more than 10000 constant and local variables, and about 30 output variables. The automated part was done on an interactive version of FLUCTUAT [DGP+09], but we manually simulated the instantiation and call mechanisms. We did not use our standalone prototype here since the code contained features (in particular arrays), that are not treated in the prototype we specifically developed for this article.

A summary is built for the whole function in the loop, and it is reused or updated if necessary by the next iterations. The input summary has 70 variables, the output summary has 90. The analysis takes about 10 minutes for each cycle / function call on a standard Linux desktop. The summary applications is immediate (less than 1 second), and only one summary creation is needed here. For the 6 iterations, the analysis takes 60 minutes without summaries, and 10 minutes with summaries. The time gain may be less impressive than on the smaller examples, but it depends on the structure of the program, and this one is not especially modular. Also, if more loop iterations were needed (thus more function calls), the gain would of course have been higher. The final results are similar with and without summaries; only some partial results are less precise with summaries, but the loss of accuracy is always within 20%.

6   Conclusion and Future Work

We showed in this paper that zonotopic abstractions are particularly well suited as a basis for modular static analysis, by the fact that they form a natural parameterization of input-output relationships between program variables. The algorithm we presented and tested is both simple and efficient. Future work includes the proper testing and improvement of the dynamic partitioning extension to our algorithm (Section 4) and the combination of this numerical modular abstract interpretation together with modular alias analyses. One possibility is to use recent work on shape analysis [RC11], that eases such combinations.

Acknowledgement. This work was funded by CEA Carnot program and ANR projects ASOPT and DEFIS (grants ANR 2008 SEGI 023 02 and ANR 2011 INS 008 05).

References

[Bee06]   Beezer, R.: A First Course in Linear Algebra (2006),
            http://linear.ups.edu/online.html
[Bou92]   Bourdoncle, F.: Abstract interpretation by dynamic partitioning. J. Funct.
            Program. 2(4), 407–423 (1992)
[CC77]   Cousot, P., Cousot, R.: Static determination of dynamic properties of recursive procedures. In: Formal Description of Programming Concepts, pp.
            237–277. North-Holland (1977)
[CC92]   Cousot, P., Cousot, R.: Abstract interpretation frameworks. Journal of
            Logic and Computation 2(4), 511–547 (1992)
[CC02]   Cousot, P., Cousot, R.: Modular Static Program Analysis. In: Horspool,
            R.N. (ed.) CC 2002. LNCS, vol. 2304, pp. 159–179. Springer, Heidelberg
            (2002)
[CH78]   Cousot, P., Halbwachs, N.: Automatic discovery of linear restraints among
            variables of a program. In: POPL 1978, pp. 84–96. ACM (1978)
[CS93]   Comba, J.L.D., Stolfi, J.: Affine arithmetic and its applications to computer
            graphics. In: SIBGRAPI 1993 (1993)

[DGP+09] Delmas, D., Goubault, E., Putot, S., Souyris, J., Tekkal, K., Védrine, F.:
          Towards an Industrial Use of FLUCTUAT on Safety-Critical Avionics Soft-
          ware. In: Alpuente, M., Cook, B., Joubert, C. (eds.) FMICS 2009. LNCS,
          vol. 5825, pp. 53–69. Springer, Heidelberg (2009)

[GGP09]   Ghorbal, K., Goubault, E., Putot, S.: The Zonotope Abstract Domain Tay-
          lor1+. In: Bouajjani, A., Maler, O. (eds.) CAV 2009. LNCS, vol. 5643, pp.
          627–633. Springer, Heidelberg (2009)

[GGP10]   Ghorbal, K., Goubault, E., Putot, S.: A Logical Product Approach to Zono-
          tope Intersection. In: Touili, T., Cook, B., Jackson, P. (eds.) CAV 2010.
          LNCS, vol. 6174, pp. 212–226. Springer, Heidelberg (2010)

[GP06]   Goubault, É., Putot, S.: Static Analysis of Numerical Algorithms. In: Yi,
          K. (ed.) SAS 2006. LNCS, vol. 4134, pp. 18–34. Springer, Heidelberg (2006)

[GP09]   Goubault, E., Putot, S.: A zonotopic framework for functional abstractions.
          CoRR, abs/0910.1763 (2009)

[GP11]   Goubault, E., Putot, S.: Static Analysis of Finite Precision Computations.
          In: Jhala, R., Schmidt, D. (eds.) VMCAI 2011. LNCS, vol. 6538, pp. 232–
          247. Springer, Heidelberg (2011)

[GT07]   Gulwani, S., Tiwari, A.: Computing Procedure Summaries for Interproce-
          dural Analysis. In: De Nicola, R. (ed.) ESOP 2007. LNCS, vol. 4421, pp.
          253–267. Springer, Heidelberg (2007)

[JGR05]   Jeannet, B., Gopan, D., Reps, T.: A relational abstraction for functions. In:
          Int. Workshop on Numerical and Symbolic Abstract Domains (2005)

[Log07]   Logozzo, F.: Cibai: An Abstract Interpretation-Based Static Analyzer for
          Modular Analysis and Verification of Java Classes. In: Cook, B., Podelski,
          A. (eds.) VMCAI 2007. LNCS, vol. 4349, pp. 283–298. Springer, Heidelberg
          (2007)

[Min01]   Miné, A.: A New Numerical Abstract Domain Based on Difference-Bound
          Matrices. In: Danvy, O., Filinski, A. (eds.) PADO 2001. LNCS, vol. 2053,
          pp. 155–172. Springer, Heidelberg (2001)

[MOS04]   Müller-Olm, M., Seidl, H.: Precise interprocedural analysis through linear
          algebra. In: POPL 2004, pp. 330–341. ACM (2004)

[QR04]   Qadeer, S., Rajamani, S.K.: Summarizing procedures in concurrent pro-
          grams. In: POPL 2004, pp. 245–255. ACM Press (2004)

[RC11]   Rival, X., Chang, B.-Y.E.: Calling context abstraction with shapes. In:
          POPL, pp. 173–186. ACM Press (2011)

[RHS95]   Reps, T., Horwitz, S., Sagiv, M.: Precise interprocedural dataflow analysis
          via graph reachability. In: POPL 1995, pp. 49–61. ACM (1995)

[SP81]   Sharir, M., Pnueli, A.: Two approaches to interprocedural data-flow analy-
          sis. In: Program Flow Analysis: Theory and Applications (1981)

[SRH96]   Sagiv, S., Reps, T.W., Horwitz, S.: Precise interprocedural dataflow analysis
          with applications to constant propagation. TCS 167, 131–170 (1996)

[SSM05]   Sankaranarayanan, S., Sipma, H.B., Manna, Z.: Scalable Analysis of Linear
          Systems Using Mathematical Programming. In: Cousot, R. (ed.) VMCAI
          2005. LNCS, vol. 3385, pp. 25–41. Springer, Heidelberg (2005)

[YYC08]   Yorsh, G., Yahav, E., Chandra, S.: Generating precise and concise procedure
          summaries. In: POPL 2008, pp. 221–234. ACM (2008)

Polyhedral Analysis
Using Parametric Objectives

Jacob M. Howe[1] and Andy King[2]

[1] School of Informatics, City University London, EC1V 0HB, UK
[2] School of Computing, University of Kent, CT2 7NF, UK

Abstract. The abstract domain of polyhedra lies at the heart of many program analysis techniques. However, its operations can be expensive, precluding their application to polyhedra that involve many variables. This paper describes a new approach to computing polyhedral domain operations. The core of this approach is an algorithm to calculate variable elimination (projection) based on parametric linear programming. The algorithm enumerates only non-redundant inequalities of the projection space, hence permits anytime approximation of the output.

1 Introduction

Polyhedra [10] form the basis of a wide range of tools for static analysis and model checking. Their attraction is the expressivity of linear inequalities which capture not only the range of values that a variable can assume, but also dependencies between them. The drawback of polyhedra is the cost of the domain operations – this has motivated much recent work investigating the tradeoff of expressivity for efficiency. This paper introduces a new approach to polyhedral domain operations that sidesteps many of the problems associated with current approaches. At the heart of the work is a new approach to variable elimination (projection, or existential quantifier elimination).

Many polyhedral libraries are based on the double description method (DDM) [3,5,6,24,28,35]. DDM maintains two representations: the constraint representation in which the polyhedron is described as the solutions of a system of linear inequalities, and the frame representation in which the polyhedron is generated from a finite set of points, rays and lines. The method has proved popular since the constraint representation is convenient when computing the meet of two polyhedra (intersection) and the frame representation is convenient when computing join (the frame representation of the join of two polyhedra is merely the union of their frame representations). The maintenance of the two representations requires an algorithm to convert between the two, and this is the core of the method. The drawback of working with a double description is that maintenance algorithms are expensive. For example, to apply join to two polyhedra in constraint representation they both have to be converted to the frame representation, a potentially exponential operation [21]. The dominating cost of maintaining the double description can be avoided by working solely with constraints and reformulating join in terms of variable elimination [32]. Variable elimination can be performed with Fourier-Motzkin elimination [27], but the

A. Miné and D. Schmidt (Eds.): SAS 2012, LNCS 7460, pp. 41–57, 2012.

technique needs to be applied together with techniques for avoiding the generation of redundant inequalities [12,17,22] or methods for removing them after generation [23]. Even then, Fourier-Motzkin shares the problem with DDM that an intermediate result can be exponentially larger than the input, in addition to the problem of generation of redundant constraints that cannot always be removed until variable elimination is completed.

The algorithms deployed for manipulating unrestricted polyhedra [3,24,35] have barely changed since the inception of polyhedral analysis over 30 years ago [10]. This paper presents a radically different approach to the computation of projection and hence convex hull which can be reduced to projection [32]. The approach is based on the constraint representation, admits anytime approximation and invites parallelisation. The approach has two key steps. The first step describes the projection of the input constraint system as a bounded polyhedron (polytope) in a dual space. The vertices in this dual description of the projection correspond to non-redundant inequalities in the constraint representation of the projection. The second step is to enumerate these vertices. This is achieved by using parametric linear programming (PLP). The formulation of projection as PLP implementing vertex enumeration of a dual description of the projection space is not obvious, therefore this paper makes the following contributions:

- Lemma 3.2 of [19] builds on the projection lemma [36] to explain how projection can be reformulated as a vertex enumeration problem. Alas, this lemma is not correct to the level of generality that is required and the starting point of this paper is a reworking of this result.
- In a somewhat different way to [19] it is shown how PLP can be used to enumerate the vertices of a polytope. When this polytope is a description of the projection space, the output corresponds to irredundant inequalities of the constraint description of the projection.
- Together this gives an algorithm that projects arbitrary (possibly unbounded) polyhedra onto lower dimensions. (This fundamental algorithm may well find application outside static analysis, for example in control theory [19,29].)
- It is shown that this formulation enables inequalities in the projection space to be enumerated one-by-one, without requiring any post-processing to remove redundant inequalities. A consequence of this is that projection is naturally anytime – it can be stopped prematurely to yield a safe overapproximation of the projection. This compares favourably with DDM which is monolithic in the sense that the inequalities need to be completely converted to a frame, and then the projected frame is completely converted to the constraints representation before a single inequality in the projection space is found. The force of the anytime property is that if the projection is found to be excessively large, then the projection need only be computed up to that point and no further whilst still yielding a useful result.

Given the novelty of the contributions to theory (and the length of their exposition) a description of the implementation is postponed to a later paper; to the best of the authors' knowledge the implementions techniques are themselves novel and require space in their own right.

2   Background

2.1   Matrices and Vectors

Let $a = \langle a_1, \ldots, a_n \rangle \in \mathbb{R}^n$ denote a column vector which is an $n \times 1$ matrix. If $a = \langle a_1, \ldots, a_n \rangle$ then $a :: a = \langle a, a_1, \ldots, a_n \rangle$. The dot product of two column vectors $a, b \in \mathbb{R}^n$ is defined $a \cdot b = a^T b$ where A^T denotes transpose of a matrix A. For any matrix A, $(A)_j$ refers to the jth column of A and $(A)_J$ refers to the submatrix of columns indexed by J. Likewise $(A)^j$ refers to the jth row and $(A)^J$ refers to the submatrix of rows indexed by J. Similar notations are used for vectors, though bracketing is omitted when the column and row operator is clear. If $A = \{a_1, \ldots, a_n\} \subseteq \mathbb{R}$ and $a_1 < a_2 < \ldots < a_n$ then $(A)_i = (a)_i$ where $a = \langle a_1, \ldots, a_n \rangle$. The lexicographical ordering relation on vectors is defined by $\langle \rangle \preceq \langle \rangle$ and $(a :: a) \preceq (b :: b)$ iff $a \leq b$ or $(a = b$ and $a \preceq b)$. If $A = \{a_1, \ldots, a_m\} \subseteq \mathbb{R}^n$ then $\min(A) = a_i$ such that $a_i \preceq a_j$ for all $1 \leq j \leq m$. A vector (row) is lex-positive iff its first non-zero element is positive.

2.2   Basic and Non-basic Variables

The simplex algorithm [7,34] is formulated in terms of pivoting operations on bases. To introduce simplex consider maximising the cost function $c \cdot \lambda$, where $c = \langle 1, 1, -3, -3, -1, -1, 0 \rangle$, subject to the constraints $A\lambda = b$ where $\lambda \geq 0$ and

$$A = \begin{bmatrix} 1 & -1 & 1 & -1 & 2 & -2 & 0 \\ 2 & 2 & 2 & 2 & 8 & 8 & 2 \end{bmatrix} \qquad b = \begin{bmatrix} 0 \\ 1 \end{bmatrix}$$

Let $B = \{1, 6\}$ and $N = \{1, \ldots, 7\} \setminus B$ so that $\lambda_B = \langle \lambda_1, \lambda_6 \rangle$ and $\lambda_N = \langle \lambda_2, \ldots, \lambda_5, \lambda_7 \rangle$ and moreover

$$A_B = \begin{bmatrix} 1 & -2 \\ 2 & 8 \end{bmatrix} \qquad A_N = \begin{bmatrix} -1 & 1 & -1 & 2 & 0 \\ 2 & 2 & 2 & 8 & 2 \end{bmatrix}$$

Then $A\lambda = b$ can be expressed as $A_B\lambda_B + A_N\lambda_N = b$ hence $A_B\lambda_B = b - A_N\lambda_N$. Since the square matrix A_B is nonsingular this is equivalent to

$$\lambda_B = A_B^{-1} b - A_B^{-1} A_N \lambda_N \qquad (1)$$

This suggests putting $\lambda_N = 0$ to give

$$\lambda_B = A_B^{-1} b = \frac{1}{12} \begin{bmatrix} 8 & 2 \\ -2 & 1 \end{bmatrix} \begin{bmatrix} 0 \\ 1 \end{bmatrix} = \frac{1}{12} \begin{bmatrix} 2 \\ 1 \end{bmatrix}$$

Since $\lambda_B \geq 0$ the point $\lambda = \langle \frac{1}{6}, 0, 0, 0, 0, \frac{1}{12}, 0 \rangle$ satisfies both the equality constraints $A\lambda = b$ and inequalities $\lambda \geq 0$, five of which are saturated by λ. Geometrically, λ is a vertex of the polyhedron $\{\lambda \geq 0 \mid A\lambda = b\}$ and for this point $c \cdot \lambda = \frac{1}{12}$. In fact a vertex is defined by any B for which A_B is invertible (though a vertex may be defined by different B). In this classical set up, B is called the basis, N the co-basis and λ_B and λ_N are, respectively, the basic and non-basic variables. Moreover, the objective function $c \cdot \lambda$ too can be considered to be a function of the non-basic variables λ_N. To see this, observe

$$c \cdot \lambda = c_B \cdot \lambda_B + c_N \cdot \lambda_N = c_B \cdot A_B^{-1} b + (c_N^T - c_B^T A_B^{-1} A_N) \cdot \lambda_N \qquad (2)$$

The equalities of (1) and the objective given in (2) constitute the dictionary.

2.3   Pivoting

In the (revised) simplex method [11], a path is found between adjacent bases that terminates with a basis that maximises the objective. Adjacent bases differ by one index and pivoting is used to transition from one basis to another. In each pivoting step, the basis B is updated with $B' = (B \setminus \{i\}) \cup \{j\}$ where $i \in B$ is the index of a basic variable that leaves B and $j \in N$ is the index for a non-basic variable that enters B. The index $j \in N$ is chosen so that the corresponding element of $c_N^T - c_B^T A_B^{-1} A_N$ is positive. This is achieved by solving $y^T A_B = c_B^T$ since then $y^T = c_B^T A_B^{-1}$ hence $c_N^T - c_B^T A_B^{-1} A_N = c_N^T - y^T A_N$. To illustrate for $B = \{1, 6\}$, so that $c_B = \langle 1, -1 \rangle$ and $c_N = \langle 1, -3, -3, -1, 0 \rangle$. Then

$$y^T = c_B^T A_B^{-1} = \frac{1}{12} [1 \; {-1}] \begin{bmatrix} 8 & 2 \\ -2 & 1 \end{bmatrix} = \frac{1}{12} [10 \; 1]$$

$$c_N^T - y^T A_N = [1 \; {-3} \; {-3} \; {-1} \; 0] - \frac{1}{12} [10 \; 1] \begin{bmatrix} -1 & 1 & -1 & 2 & 0 \\ 2 & 2 & 2 & 8 & 2 \end{bmatrix}$$

$$= \frac{1}{6} [2 \; {-24} \; {-22} \; {-20} \; {-1}]$$

The entering variable can only be λ_2. To find a leaving variable for $i = 2$, let

$$d = A_B^{-1} (A)_2 = \frac{1}{12} \begin{bmatrix} 8 & 2 \\ -2 & 1 \end{bmatrix} \begin{bmatrix} -1 \\ 2 \end{bmatrix} = \frac{1}{12} \begin{bmatrix} -4 \\ 4 \end{bmatrix}$$

Then the largest $t \geq 0$ is found such that $\lambda_B - td \geq 0$. This occurs when $t = \frac{1}{4}$ and then $\lambda_B - td = \langle \frac{1}{4}, 0 \rangle$. The second element of this vector is 0 hence the second variable of B, namely λ_6, leaves the basis. This gives the new basis $B = \{1, 2\}$ for which $\lambda_B = \langle \frac{1}{4}, \frac{1}{4} \rangle$ and $c \cdot \lambda = \frac{1}{2}$ which has increased as desired. Repeating the process with $B = \{1, 2\}$ gives $c_B = \langle 1, 1 \rangle$, $c_N = \langle -3, -3, -1, -1, 0 \rangle$ and

$$y^T = \frac{1}{12} [6 \; 3] \qquad c_N^T - y^T A_N = \frac{1}{2} [-8 \; {-6} \; {-8} \; {-4} \; {-1}]$$

Hence there is no variable to enter B and $c \cdot \lambda$ is maximal. Although revised simplex is usually introduced with this pivoting rule, alternative rules may be attractive in certain situations.

2.4   Avoiding Cycling with Lexicographic Pivoting

Cycling, hence non-termination, can be resolved [2] by lexicographic pivot selection [7]. This pivoting rule is defined for a subset of the bases which are called lex-positive; each vertex, including degenerate ones, has a unique lex-positive basis. The graph of lex-positive bases is a subgraph of the basis graph yet still covers all the vertices. In the rest of this paper the dictionary is embedded into $A\lambda = b$ by extending it to the system $C(\mu :: \lambda) = (0 :: b)$ where

$$C = \begin{bmatrix} 1 & -c \\ \hline 0 & A \end{bmatrix}$$

The rows and columns of C (and only this matrix) are indexed from 0 to preserve the correspondance with $A\lambda = b$. To illustrate, if $B = \{0, 1, 6\}$ then

$$C = \begin{bmatrix} 1 & -1 & -1 & 3 & 3 & 1 & 1 & 0 \\ \hline 0 & 1 & -1 & 1 & -1 & 2 & -2 & 0 \\ 0 & 2 & 2 & 2 & 2 & 8 & 8 & 2 \end{bmatrix} \qquad C_B = \begin{bmatrix} 1 & -1 & 1 \\ 0 & 1 & -2 \\ 0 & 2 & 8 \end{bmatrix}$$

A basis B is said to be lex-positive if each row $(L)^j$ is lex-positive where $j > 0$ and $L = [C_B^{-1}(0 :: b) \mid C_B^{-1}]$. For example, B is lex-positive since

$$C_B^{-1} = \frac{1}{12} \begin{bmatrix} 12 & 10 & 1 \\ 0 & 8 & 2 \\ 0 & -2 & 1 \end{bmatrix} \qquad L = \frac{1}{12} \begin{bmatrix} 1 & 12 & 10 & 1 \\ 2 & 0 & 8 & 2 \\ 1 & 0 & -2 & 1 \end{bmatrix}$$

Lexicographic pivoting pivots whilst preserving the lex-positive basis property. In each pivoting step, row zero $r = (C_B^{-1}C)^0$ is inspected to find an index $j \in N$ such that $(r)_j < 0$. For

$$C_B^{-1}C = \frac{1}{12} \begin{bmatrix} 12 & 0 & -20 & 48 & 28 & 40 & 0 & 2 \\ 0 & 12 & -4 & 12 & -4 & 32 & 0 & 4 \\ 0 & 0 & 4 & 0 & 4 & 4 & 12 & 2 \end{bmatrix}$$

this would give $j = 2$. Then $i = \mathsf{lexminratio}(B, j) > 0$ is computed which prescribes which $i \in B$ should be replaced with j. The $\mathsf{lexminratio}$ operation is defined

$$\mathsf{lexminratio}(B, j) = \begin{cases} 0 & \text{if } S = \emptyset \\ (B)_{k+1} & \text{else if } (L)^k/(d)_k = \min(S) \end{cases}$$

where $d = C_B^{-1}(C)_j$ and $S = \{(L)^k/(d)_k \mid 0 < k \wedge 0 < (d)_k\}$. Crucially if B is lex-positive then so is $B' = (B \setminus \{i\}) \cup \{j\}$. Continuing with $j = 2$, $d = \langle -20, -4, 4 \rangle$, $S = \{\frac{1}{48}[1, 0, -2, 1]\}$ and $i = (B)_2 = 6$. Hence $B' = \{0, 1, 2\}$. Observe that B' is lex-positive since

$$[C_{B'}^{-1}(0 :: b) \mid C_{B'}^{-1}] = \frac{1}{4} \begin{bmatrix} 2 & 4 & 0 & 2 \\ 1 & 0 & 2 & 1 \\ 1 & 0 & -2 & 1 \end{bmatrix}$$

Then

$$C_{B'}^{-1}C = \frac{1}{4} \begin{bmatrix} 4 & 0 & 0 & 16 & 16 & 20 & 20 & 4 \\ 0 & 4 & 0 & 4 & 0 & 12 & 4 & 2 \\ 0 & 0 & 4 & 0 & 4 & 4 & 12 & 2 \end{bmatrix}$$

and since all elements of row $(C_{B'}^{-1}C)^0$ are positive, no new variable can enter B' and $c \cdot \lambda$ is maximal.

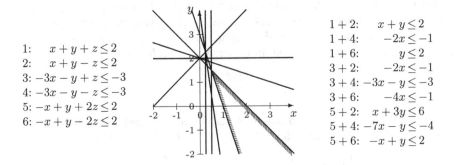

1:     $x + y + z \leq 2$
2:     $x + y - z \leq 2$
3: $-3x - y + z \leq -3$
4: $-3x - y - z \leq -3$
5: $-x + y + 2z \leq 2$
6: $-x + y - 2z \leq 2$

$1 + 2$: $x + y \leq 2$
$1 + 4$: $-2x \leq -1$
$1 + 6$: $y \leq 2$
$3 + 2$: $-2x \leq -1$
$3 + 4$: $-3x - y \leq -3$
$3 + 6$: $-4x \leq -1$
$5 + 2$: $x + 3y \leq 6$
$5 + 4$: $-7x - y \leq -4$
$5 + 6$: $-x + y \leq 2$

Fig. 1. (a) Inequalities (b) Projection (graphically) (c) Projection (Fourier-Motzkin)

3   Worked Example

This section centres on a worked example that illustrates the steps involved in setting up and applying the projection algorithm. The more formal aspects of the algorithm are detailed in the next section. The example involves eliminating the variable z from the following system of inequalities given in Fig 1(a). The system of inequalities is sufficiently simple for Fourier-Motzkin elimination to be applied. The projection is obtained by combining all the inequalities with a positive coefficient for z with those that have a negative coefficient for z. The resulting inequalities are given in Fig 1(c), where the left hand column indicates how the inequalities of Fig 1(a) are combined.

The system contains many redundant inequalities as is illustrated in the diagram given in Fig 1(b) – it can be seen that the projection is a cone that can be described by just two inequalities, namely $-3x - y \leq -3$ and $x + y \leq 2$. The challenge is to derive these constraints without generating the redundant inequalities, a problem that is magnified when eliminating many variables.

3.1   Overview

The algorithm presented in this section proceeds in three separate steps, each of which is detailed in its own section. Sect. 3.2 shows how to formulate the projection problem in a dual fashion so that any inequality entailed by the projection corresponds to points in a cone. Sect. 3.3 shows how to compute a slice through the cone yielding a polytope (a bounded polyhedra). The vertices of the polytope then represent the non-redundant inequalities in the projection. Sect. 3.5 explains how to use PLP to enumerate the vertices of this polytope. By enumerating each vertex exactly once, the inequalities are generated with no repetition and no redundancy other than the enumeration of the trivial constraint $0 \leq 1$.

3.2   Describing the Output Inequalities as a Cone

To represent the inequalities in the projection as a cone, a formulation of [19] is adapted in which a set of points of the form $\langle \alpha_1, \alpha_2, \beta \rangle$ is used to represent inequalities $\alpha_1 x + \alpha_2 y \leq \beta$ that are entailed by the system given in Fig 1(a). The inequalities are augmented with the trivial constraint $0 \leq 1$. These points are defined as solutions to the systems (3) and (4) below:

$$
\begin{bmatrix} \alpha_1 \\ \alpha_2 \\ \beta \end{bmatrix} = E^T \lambda \qquad
E^T = \begin{bmatrix} 1 & 1 & -3 & -3 & -1 & -1 & 0 \\ 1 & 1 & -1 & -1 & 1 & 1 & 0 \\ 2 & 2 & -3 & -3 & 2 & 2 & 1 \end{bmatrix} \tag{3}
$$

where $\lambda = \langle \lambda_1, \ldots, \lambda_7 \rangle \geq 0$ and

$$
D = \begin{bmatrix} 1 & -1 & 1 & -1 & 2 & -2 & 0 \end{bmatrix} \qquad D\lambda = [0] \tag{4}
$$

The matrix E^T represents the x, y coefficients and constants of the input inequalities. The λ variables are interpreted as weightings that prescribe positive linear combinations of the input inequalities that yield an entailed inequality. The equation given in (4) stipulates that the sum of the z coefficients is zero, in other words z is eliminated.

Let $\Lambda = \{\lambda \in \mathbb{R}^7 \mid D\lambda = 0 \wedge \lambda \geq 0\}$ and $E^T \Lambda = \{E^T \lambda \mid \lambda \in \Lambda\}$. Observe that if $\langle \alpha_1, \alpha_2, \beta \rangle \in E^T \Lambda$, that is, the point $\langle \alpha_1, \alpha_2, \beta \rangle$ satisfies (3) and (4), then $\mu \langle \alpha_1, \alpha_2, \beta \rangle \in E^T \Lambda$ for any $\mu \geq 0$ hence $E^T \Lambda$ constitutes a cone. Importantly the final column of E^T permits the constant β of an inequality to be relaxed: if $\alpha_1 x + \alpha_2 y \leq \beta$ is entailed and $\beta \leq \beta'$, then $\alpha_1 x + \alpha_2 y \leq \beta'$ is also entailed.

3.3   Slicing the Cone with a Plane to Obtain a Polytope

In order to construct a polytope in the $\langle \alpha_1, \alpha_2, \beta \rangle$ space, a plane slicing through the cone $E^T \Lambda$ is required. To find such a plane, consider the inequalities that are entailed by the initial system given in Fig 1(a), again represented dually as a set of points, denoted G. Any inequality $\alpha_1 x + \alpha_2 y + \alpha_3 z \leq \beta$ entailed by the inequalities of Fig 1(a) is represented by a point $\langle \alpha_1, \alpha_2, \alpha_3, \beta \rangle \in G$ where $G = \{R\mu \mid \mu \geq 0\}$ and

$$
R = \begin{bmatrix} 1 & 1 & -3 & -3 & -1 & -1 & 0 \\ 1 & 1 & -1 & -1 & 1 & 1 & 0 \\ 1 & -1 & 1 & -1 & 2 & -2 & 0 \\ 2 & 2 & -3 & -3 & 2 & 2 & 1 \end{bmatrix}
$$

Each column of R gives the coefficients α_i and the constant β of an inequality of Fig 1(a), again augmented with the additional inequality $0 \leq 1$. G is a cone incident to the origin where the columns of R are extremal rays of G (rays that cannot be obtained as positive linear combinations of others).

A plane that slices $E^T \Lambda$ can be derived from one that slices G. Let $a\alpha_1 + b\alpha_2 + c\alpha_3 + d\beta = 0$ be a plane that supports the cone G at the origin, hence all the rays of G are strictly above this plane. By setting $\mu = \langle 1, \ldots, 1 \rangle$ in G, the ray $\{\mu \langle 1, 1, 1, 2 \rangle \mid \mu \geq 0\}$ gives the point $\langle 1, 1, 1, 2 \rangle$, similarly $\{\mu \langle 1, 1, -1, 2 \rangle \mid \mu \geq 0\}$ gives $\langle 1, 1, -1, 2 \rangle$, etc. Values for a, b, c, d can be found by setting up a linear program which asserts that each of these 7 points are strictly above the plane by at least some quantity ϵ:

Maximise ϵ subject to

$$\epsilon \leq a+b+c+2d \qquad -1 \leq a \leq 1$$
$$\epsilon \leq a+b-c+2d \qquad -1 \leq b \leq 1$$
$$\epsilon \leq -3a-b+c-3d \qquad -1 \leq c \leq 1$$
$$\epsilon \leq -3a-b-c-3d \qquad -1 \leq d \leq 1$$
$$\epsilon \leq -a+b+2c+2d \qquad 0 \leq \epsilon$$
$$\epsilon \leq -a+b-2c+2d \qquad \epsilon \leq d$$

The bounds $-1 \leq a,b,c,d \leq 1$ are included for normalisation since the plane $a\alpha_1 + b\alpha_2 + c\alpha_3 + d\beta = 0$ can also be described by $\mu a\alpha_1 + \mu b\alpha_2 + \mu c\alpha_3 + \mu d\beta = 0$ where $\mu \geq 0$ is any positive multiplier. Solving the linear program gives $a = -1$, $b = \frac{1}{3}$, $c = 0$, $d = \frac{2}{3}$ and $\epsilon = \frac{2}{3}$. The value of ϵ is discarded and the equation of the plane that supports G is $-3\alpha_1 + \alpha_2 + 0\alpha_3 + 2\beta = 0$.

Next observe that $E^T \Lambda = \{\langle \alpha_1, \alpha_2, \beta \rangle \mid \langle \alpha_1, \alpha_2, 0, \beta \rangle \in G\}$. As a consequence, a supporting plane for $E^T \Lambda$ can be found merely by removing the α_3 component (note that $c = 0$ is an oddity of this particular example). This gives $-3\alpha_1 + \alpha_2 + 2\beta = 0$ which indeed supports $E^T \Lambda$. Finally the constant for the plane is adjusted so that it slices through $E^T \Lambda$. Any positive value may be chosen, here the plane is set to have constant 1, that is, $-3\alpha_1 + \alpha_2 + 2\beta = 1$. Since $\langle \alpha_1, \alpha_2, \beta \rangle = E^T \boldsymbol{\lambda}$ the equation of the plane induces a further constraint on $\boldsymbol{\lambda}$:

$$1 = -3\alpha_1 + \alpha_2 + 2\beta = -3 \begin{bmatrix} 1 & 1 & -3 & -3 & -1 & -1 & 0 \end{bmatrix} \boldsymbol{\lambda} +$$
$$\begin{bmatrix} 1 & 1 & -1 & -1 & 1 & 1 & 0 \end{bmatrix} \boldsymbol{\lambda} +$$
$$2 \begin{bmatrix} 2 & 2 & -3 & -3 & 2 & 2 & 1 \end{bmatrix} \boldsymbol{\lambda} = \begin{bmatrix} 2 & 2 & 2 & 2 & 8 & 8 & 2 \end{bmatrix} \boldsymbol{\lambda}$$

Augmenting equation (4) the system $A\boldsymbol{\lambda} = \boldsymbol{c}$ is obtained where:

$$A = \begin{bmatrix} 1 & -1 & 1 & -1 & 2 & -2 & 0 \\ 2 & 2 & 2 & 2 & 8 & 8 & 2 \end{bmatrix} \qquad \boldsymbol{c} = \begin{bmatrix} 0 \\ 1 \end{bmatrix} \tag{5}$$

Under this construction, the set $\Lambda' = \{\boldsymbol{\lambda} \in \mathbb{R}^7 \mid A\boldsymbol{\lambda} = \boldsymbol{c} \wedge \boldsymbol{\lambda} \geq 0\}$ is not a cone; it is a polytope. $E^T \Lambda'$ is a polytope as a consequence.

3.4 The Vertices of the Polytope as Irredundant Inequalities

For each non-redundant inequality $\alpha_1 x + \alpha_2 y \leq \beta$ in the projection there exists a unique vertex $\langle \alpha_1, \alpha_2, \beta \rangle \in E^T \Lambda'$. Moreover, if $\langle \alpha_1, \alpha_2, \beta \rangle$ is a vertex of $E^T \Lambda'$ there exists a vertex $\boldsymbol{\lambda}$ of Λ' such that $\langle \alpha_1, \alpha_2, \beta \rangle = E^T \boldsymbol{\lambda}$. However, the converse does not hold. If $\boldsymbol{\lambda}$ is a vertex of Λ' then $E^T \boldsymbol{\lambda}$ is not necessarily a vertex of $E^T \Lambda'$. To illustrate, the following table gives the vertices $\boldsymbol{\lambda}$ of Λ' for the system given in (5) and $\langle \alpha_1, \alpha_2, \beta \rangle = E^T \boldsymbol{\lambda}$:

λ_1	λ_2	λ_3	λ_4	λ_5	λ_6	λ_7	α_1	α_2	β
$\frac{1}{4}$	$\frac{1}{4}$	0	0	0	0	0	$\frac{1}{2}$	$\frac{1}{2}$	1
$\frac{1}{4}$	0	0	$\frac{1}{4}$	0	0	0	$-\frac{1}{2}$	0	$-\frac{1}{4}$
$\frac{1}{6}$	0	0	0	0	$\frac{1}{12}$	0	$\frac{1}{12}$	$\frac{1}{4}$	$\frac{1}{2}$
0	$\frac{1}{4}$	$\frac{1}{4}$	0	0	0	0	$-\frac{1}{2}$	0	$-\frac{1}{4}$
0	0	$\frac{1}{4}$	$\frac{1}{4}$	0	0	0	$-\frac{3}{2}$	$-\frac{1}{2}$	$-\frac{3}{2}$

λ_1	λ_2	λ_3	λ_4	λ_5	λ_6	λ_7	α_1	α_2	β
0	0	$\frac{1}{6}$	0	0	$\frac{1}{12}$	0	$-\frac{7}{12}$	$-\frac{1}{12}$	$-\frac{1}{3}$
0	$\frac{1}{6}$	0	0	$\frac{1}{12}$	0	0	$\frac{1}{12}$	$\frac{1}{4}$	$\frac{1}{2}$
0	0	0	$\frac{1}{6}$	$\frac{1}{12}$	0	0	$-\frac{7}{12}$	$-\frac{1}{12}$	$-\frac{1}{3}$
0	0	0	0	$\frac{1}{16}$	$\frac{1}{16}$	0	$-\frac{1}{8}$	$\frac{1}{8}$	$\frac{1}{4}$
0	0	0	0	0	0	$\frac{1}{2}$	0	0	$\frac{1}{2}$

First observe that $E^T \langle 0, 0, \frac{1}{6}, 0, 0, \frac{1}{12}, 0 \rangle = \langle -\frac{7}{12}, -\frac{1}{12}, -\frac{1}{3} \rangle = E^T \langle 0, 0, 0, \frac{1}{6}, \frac{1}{12}, 0, 0 \rangle$ and second that $-\frac{7}{12}x - \frac{1}{12}y \le -\frac{1}{3}$ is a redundant inequality. In fact, only rows 1 and 5 give non-redundant inequalities; row 10 gives the trivial inequality $0 \le 1$ and the remaining rows give inequalities that are redundant. (Note that this table is only given for the purposes of exposition and is not actually calculated as part of the projection algorithm.)

3.5 Enumerating Inequalities Using PLP

To enumerate the vertices of the polytope defined in section 3.3, hence the irredundant inequalities of the projection space, PLP is used. As the parameters vary the basis representing the optimum changes – a subset of these bases correspond to the vertices. Consider an objective function parameterised by variables δ_1 and δ_2:

$$\delta_1 \alpha_1 + \delta_2 \alpha_2 = \delta_1 (E^T)^1 \cdot \lambda + \delta_2 (E^T)^2 \cdot \lambda = c \cdot \lambda$$

where $c = \langle \delta_1 + \delta_2, \delta_1 + \delta_2, -3\delta_1 - \delta_2, -3\delta_1 - \delta_2, -\delta_1 + \delta_2, -\delta_1 + \delta_2, 0 \rangle$. The range of values taken by δ_1 and δ_2 can be constrained to $-1 \le \delta_1, \delta_2 \le 1$ without changing the set of possible objectives. This leads to tableau:

$$C = \begin{bmatrix} 1 & -c & 0 \\ \hline 0 & A & b \end{bmatrix} = \begin{bmatrix} 1 & (-\delta_1 - \delta_2) & (-\delta_1 - \delta_2) & (3\delta_1 + \delta_2) & (3\delta_1 + \delta_2) & (\delta_1 - \delta_2) & (\delta_1 - \delta_2) & 0 & 0 \\ \hline 0 & 1 & -1 & 1 & -1 & 2 & -2 & 0 & 0 \\ 0 & 2 & 2 & 2 & 2 & 8 & 8 & 2 & 1 \end{bmatrix}$$

An initial basis (hence vertex) is found by fixing δ_1 and δ_2 and optimising. Here, $\delta_1 = \delta_2 = 1$, hence $\alpha_1 + \alpha_2$ is maximised, to give $B = \{0, 1, 2\}$. The pivots involved in this optimisation lead to:

$$C_B = \begin{bmatrix} 1 & (-\delta_1 - \delta_2) & (-\delta_1 - \delta_2) \\ 0 & 1 & -1 \\ 0 & 2 & 2 \end{bmatrix} \qquad C_B^{-1} = \frac{1}{4} \begin{bmatrix} 4 & 0 & (2\delta_1 + 2\delta_2) \\ 0 & 2 & 1 \\ 0 & -2 & 1 \end{bmatrix}$$

$$T_1 = C_B^{-1} C = \begin{bmatrix} 1 & 0 & 0 & (4\delta_1 + 2\delta_2) & (4\delta_1 + 2\delta_2) & (5\delta_1 + 3\delta_2) & (5\delta_1 + 3\delta_2) & (\delta_1 + \delta_2) & (2\delta_1 + 2\delta_2) \\ 0 & 1 & 0 & 1 & 0 & 3 & 1 & \frac{1}{2} & \frac{1}{4} \\ 0 & 0 & 1 & 0 & 1 & 1 & 3 & \frac{1}{2} & \frac{1}{4} \end{bmatrix}$$

Observe that with $\delta_1 = \delta_2 = 1$ this tableau represents an optimum since (in row T_1^0) the objective entry for each non-basic column is positive. However, decreasing the δ_1 parameter to $-\frac{1}{2}$ leads to the objective entries for columns 3 and 4 to be 0. Hence with the new parameters there are potential alternative bases that correspond to points optimal with respect to the objective (optimal bases). These possibilities are explored, that is, columns 3 and 4 are considered as candidates to enter the basis with objective $-\frac{1}{2}\alpha_1 + \alpha_2$. Note that this treatment of pivoting is slightly non-standard – when optimising with respect to an objective a column is considered as a candidate to enter the basis when its objective entry is strictly negative; here, it is optimal bases that are of interest and the condition is that objective entries that are zero. In the example column 3 is selected as the candidate to enter the basis, lexminratio$(B, 3) = 1$ so that column 1 leaves, with the result that B is now $\{0, 2, 3\}$. Pivoting gives:

$$T_2 = \begin{bmatrix} 1 & (-4\delta_1 - 2\delta_2) & 0\ 0 & (4\delta_1 + 2\delta_2) & (-7\delta_1 - 3\delta_2) & (\delta_1 + \delta_2) & -\delta_1 & -\frac{\delta_1}{2} \\ 0 & & 1\ 0\ 1 & 0 & 3 & 1 & \frac{1}{2} & \frac{1}{4} \\ 0 & & 0\ 1\ 0 & 1 & 1 & 3 & \frac{1}{2} & \frac{1}{4} \end{bmatrix}$$

Observe that with $\delta_1 = -\frac{1}{2}$ and $\delta_2 = 1$ this still represents an optimum. However, this tableau does not represent a vertex of the projection space. At a vertex, the parameters should have sufficient freedom that a perturbation in one parameter can be balanced by perturbations in the other parameters such that the perturbed objective is still optimal. In T_2, columns 1 and 4 can only be non-negative with the current parameter values – any perturbation cannot be balanced, leaving the objective non-optimal. Now column 4 enters the basis and column 2 leaves. The basis is now $\{0, 3, 4\}$ and pivoting gives:

$$T_3 = \begin{bmatrix} 1 & (-4\delta_1 - 2\delta_2) & (-4\delta_1 - 2\delta_2) & 0\ 0 & (-11\delta_1 - 5\delta_2) & (-11\delta_1 - 5\delta_2) & (-3\delta_1 - \delta_2) & (-\frac{3\delta_1}{2} - \frac{\delta_2}{2}) \\ 0 & 1 & 0\ 1\ 0 & 3 & 1 & \frac{1}{2} & \frac{1}{4} \\ 0 & 0 & 1\ 0\ 1 & 1 & 3 & \frac{1}{2} & \frac{1}{4} \end{bmatrix}$$

Observe that T_3 is a vertex – the columns with value zero (columns 1 and 2) can remain with non-negative entries when the values of δ_1 or δ_2 are perturbed. Next observe that no further pivots are available with $-1 \le \delta_1 < -\frac{1}{2}$. Again, with $\delta_1 = -\frac{1}{2}$ fixed, there are no pivots available for any value $-1 \le \delta_2 \le 1$.

Returning to the original basis and tableau, and this time allowing the δ_2 parameter to vary, it can be observed that an alternative basis may be optimal when $\delta_2 = -1$, see column 7. When 7 enters the basis, 2 is chosen to leave the basis, giving basis $\{0, 1, 7\}$. Pivoting gives:

$$T_4 = \begin{bmatrix} 1\ 0 & (-2\delta_1 - 2\delta_2) & (4\delta_1 + 2\delta_2) & 2\delta_1 & (3\delta_1 + \delta_2) & (-\delta_1 - 3\delta_2) & 0\ 0 \\ 0\ 1 & -1 & 1\ -1 & 2 & -2\ 0\ 0 \\ 0\ 0 & 2 & 0\ \ 2 & 2 & 6\ 1\frac{1}{2} \end{bmatrix}$$

Again this represents a vertex. A further sequence of pivots is explored, with the basis becoming $\{0, 4, 7\}$ when $\delta_1 = \frac{1}{2}$ and $\delta_2 = -1$, then $\{0, 3, 4\}$ when $\delta_1 = \frac{1}{3}$, $\delta_2 = -1$. This leads again to the tableau T_3. No further vertices are generated, that is, the output is the three basis $\{0, 1, 2\}$, $\{0, 3, 4\}$, $\{0, 1, 7\}$ corresponding to the tableaux T_1, T_3 and T_4. The constant columns for these tableaux are:

$$\begin{bmatrix} -\frac{1}{2} \\ \frac{1}{4} \\ \frac{1}{4} \end{bmatrix} \quad \begin{bmatrix} -2 \\ \frac{1}{4} \\ \frac{1}{4} \end{bmatrix} \quad \begin{bmatrix} 0 \\ \frac{1}{4} \\ 0 \end{bmatrix}$$

The basis and the weighting of the basis elements indicates how inequalities from the input are combined in order to give a non-redundant output inequality. In the $\{0, 1, 2\}$ basis the 1 and 2 inequalities are weighted equally giving $x + y \le 2$, in the $\{0, 3, 4\}$ basis the 3 and 4 inequalities are weighted equally giving $-3x - y \le -3$ and in the $\{0, 7, 2\}$ basis the 2 inequality is not weighted, giving the $0 \le 1$ trivial constraint. That is, the output is, up to the trivial constraint, the non-redundant inequalities of the projection space.

4   Anytime Projection Using Vertex Enumeration

This section explains how an anytime projection algorithm can be obtained through vertex enumeration, where each vertex is in one-to-one correspondence with an irredundant inequality in the projection (with the exception of a single vacuous inequality that is a by-product of the construction). To concisely formulate the projection problem consider the system $C\boldsymbol{x} + D\boldsymbol{y} \leq \boldsymbol{b}$ where C and D are matrices of coefficients of dimension $m \times d$ and $m \times d'$, $\boldsymbol{x}$ and $\boldsymbol{y}$ are d-ary and d'-ary vectors of (distinct) variables, and $\boldsymbol{b}$ is an m-ary vector of constants. The construction starts with the well-known projection lemma [36]. The lemma states that points in the projection satisfy linear combinations of the input inequalities:

Lemma 1. If $P = \{\boldsymbol{x} :: \boldsymbol{y} \in \mathbb{R}^{d+d'} \mid C\boldsymbol{x} + D\boldsymbol{y} \leq \boldsymbol{b}\}$ is a polyhedron, and $\Lambda = \{\boldsymbol{\lambda} \in \mathbb{R}^m \mid D^T\boldsymbol{\lambda} = 0 \wedge \boldsymbol{\lambda} \geq 0\}$, then the projection of P onto $\boldsymbol{x}$ is given by

$$\pi_{\boldsymbol{x}}(P) = \{\boldsymbol{x} \in \mathbb{R}^d \mid \forall \boldsymbol{\lambda} \in \Lambda \,.\, \boldsymbol{\lambda}^T C\boldsymbol{x} \leq \boldsymbol{\lambda}^T \boldsymbol{b}\}$$

The next step in the construction is, on the face of it, rather odd. $C\boldsymbol{x} + D\boldsymbol{y} \leq \boldsymbol{b}$ is augmented with the vacuous inequality $0 \leq 1$. Thus let C' be the $m + 1 \times d$ matrix where $C'_{m+1} = \boldsymbol{0}$, D' be the $m + 1 \times d$ matrix where $D'_{m+1} = \boldsymbol{0}$, and $\boldsymbol{b}' = \boldsymbol{b} :: 1$ and :: denotes concatenation. To match against the previous section, define $E = [C' \mid \boldsymbol{b}']$. The main result can now be stated:

Theorem 1. Suppose

$$P = \left\{\boldsymbol{x} :: \boldsymbol{y} \in \mathbb{R}^{d+d'} \mid C\boldsymbol{x} + D\boldsymbol{y} \leq \boldsymbol{b}\right\} \quad \Lambda' = \left\{\boldsymbol{\lambda}' \in \mathbb{R}^{m+1} \mid D'^T\boldsymbol{\lambda}' = 0 \wedge \boldsymbol{\lambda}' \geq 0\right\}$$

$$S = \left\{\boldsymbol{\alpha} :: \beta \in \mathbb{R}^{d+1} \mid \exists \boldsymbol{\lambda}' \in \Lambda' \wedge \boldsymbol{\alpha} = C'^T\boldsymbol{\lambda}' \wedge \beta = \boldsymbol{b}'^T\boldsymbol{\lambda}'\right\}$$

and the plane $S' = \{(\boldsymbol{\alpha} :: \beta) \in \mathbb{R}^{d+1} \mid \boldsymbol{\alpha}^T\boldsymbol{c} + \beta = 1\}$ slices the cone S where $\boldsymbol{c} \in \mathbb{R}^d$. Then the following representation of $\pi_{\boldsymbol{x}}(P)$ is irredundant

$$\pi_{\boldsymbol{x}}(P) = \{\boldsymbol{x} \in \mathbb{R}^d \mid \boldsymbol{\alpha}^T\boldsymbol{x} \leq \beta \wedge \boldsymbol{\alpha} :: \beta \in vertex(S \cap S') \wedge \boldsymbol{\alpha} :: \beta \neq \boldsymbol{0} :: 1\}$$

where $vertex(S \cap S')$ denotes the vertices of $S \cap S'$.

Proof.

- Let $\boldsymbol{\alpha} :: \beta \in S$ and $\boldsymbol{x} \in \pi_{\boldsymbol{x}}(P)$. Thus there exists $\boldsymbol{\lambda}' = \langle \lambda_1, \ldots, \lambda_{m+1} \rangle \in \Lambda'$ such that $\boldsymbol{\alpha} = C'^T\boldsymbol{\lambda}'$ and $\beta = \boldsymbol{b}'^T\boldsymbol{\lambda}'$. Let $\boldsymbol{\lambda} = \langle \lambda_1, \ldots, \lambda_m \rangle$. Since $D^T\boldsymbol{\lambda} = 0$ by lemma 1 it follows $\boldsymbol{\lambda}^T C\boldsymbol{x} \leq \boldsymbol{\lambda}^T \boldsymbol{b}$. But $\boldsymbol{\alpha} = C^T\boldsymbol{\lambda}$ hence $\boldsymbol{\alpha}^T = \boldsymbol{\lambda}^T C$ and $\beta = \boldsymbol{\lambda}^T\boldsymbol{b} + \lambda_{m+1}$ where $\lambda_{m+1} \geq 0$. Thus $\boldsymbol{\alpha}^T\boldsymbol{x} = \boldsymbol{\lambda}^T C\boldsymbol{x} \leq \boldsymbol{\lambda}^T\boldsymbol{b} \leq \beta$.
- Let $\boldsymbol{\alpha} :: \beta \in vertex(S \cap S')$ such that $\boldsymbol{\alpha} :: \beta \neq \boldsymbol{0} :: 1$. Suppose $\boldsymbol{\alpha} :: \beta = \mu_0 + \sum_{i=1}^{\ell} \mu_i(\boldsymbol{\alpha}_i :: \beta_i)$ for some $\boldsymbol{\alpha}_1 :: \beta_1, \ldots, \boldsymbol{\alpha}_\ell :: \beta_\ell \in S$ and $\mu_0 \geq 0, \mu_1 \geq 0, \ldots, \mu_\ell \geq 0$. Observe $\boldsymbol{0} :: 1 \in S \cap S'$ and put $\boldsymbol{\alpha}_0 :: \beta_0 = \boldsymbol{0} :: 1$. Thus $\boldsymbol{\alpha} :: \beta = \sum_{i=0}^{\ell} \mu_i(\boldsymbol{\alpha}_i :: \beta_i)$. But $1 = (\boldsymbol{\alpha} :: \beta)^T(\boldsymbol{c} :: 1) = \sum_{i=0}^{\ell} \mu_i(\boldsymbol{\alpha}_i :: \beta_i)^T(\boldsymbol{c} :: 1) = \sum_{i=0}^{\ell} \mu_i$ hence $1 = \sum_{i=0}^{\ell} \mu_i$. Since $\boldsymbol{\alpha} :: \beta \neq \boldsymbol{0} :: 1$ there exists $1 \leq i \leq \ell$ such that $\boldsymbol{\alpha} :: \beta = \boldsymbol{\alpha}_i :: \beta_i$ thus $\boldsymbol{\alpha}^T\boldsymbol{x} \leq \beta$ is irredundant.   □

Note that the plane $\alpha^T c + \beta = 1$ used to define S' does not compromise generality. Indeed if it where $\alpha^T c + \beta.c_{n+1} = 1$ for some $c_{n+1} \in \mathbb{R}$ then it would follow that $c_{n+1} > 0$ since S' cuts the ray $\mathbf{0} :: 1$. Yet the translated plane $\alpha^T c + \beta.c_{n+1} = c_{n+1}$ also cuts the rays, hence the assumption $\alpha^T c + \beta = 1$. The force of the theorem is that it shows how inequalities in the projection can be found independently, one-by-one, except for the removal of the vacuous inequality. The sequel explains how vertex enumeration can be realised with PLP.

5 Vertex Enumeration Using PLP

The algorithm to enumerate the vertices of the projection space using PLP is presented across Algorithms 1, 2 and 3, that are described separately below.

5.1 Vertex Enumeration

Algorithm 1 takes as its argument the tableau of form C as described in section 3.5. The vector δ represents the parameters of the objective. Each parameter δ_i assumes a value in range $[-1, 1]$ though initially $\delta = 1$.

The algorithm uses a worklist WL of tableau/parameter pairs to drive the vertex enumeration. The output OP is a set of tableaux representing the vertices. The first step on line 3 of Algorithm 1 finds the tableau with the initial value of δ optimised. The main loop removes a pair from the worklist, then for every parameter δ_i finds a tableau corresponding to an adjacent vertex and a corresponding value for that parameter such that the vertex is optimal.

These values are returned from the calls to nextVertex on lines 11 and 15, with first call searching for further vertices with the current parameters and the second call invoked when line 11 does not give a new tableau. Note that in some cases only δ_i changes its value and that *null* returns are possible for the tableau, indicating that pivoting is not possible. If no new tableau is found then δ_i is updated to -1 and this is added to the worklist (line 18). Otherwise, both the worklist and the output are updated.

5.2 Next Parameter

Algorithm 2 returns for parameter δ_i the highest value less than its current value that induces a pivot. Again note that since it is optimal bases that are of interest, pivots occur when objective entries become zero, rather than when they are negative. Line 2 of the algorithm finds the set Δ' of values (less than δ_i) that the parameter can take in order that a non-basis objective entry can take value 0. Here $T_j^0(\delta)$ evaluates the objective entry in column j with parameters δ. If Δ' is non-empty the largest value less than the current value is returned (line 3). Otherwise the return is -1.

Algorithm 1. Vertex enumeration with PLP

```
 1: function enumVertices(T_in)
 2:   WL = [], OP = [], δ = 1
 3:   T = maximise(T_in, δ)
 4:   WL.add(T, δ), OP.add(T)
 5:   while WL ≠ [] do
 6:     (T, δ) = WL.remove()
 7:     for i = 1 to |δ| do
 8:       if δ_i ≠ -1 then
 9:         T' = null
10:         if ∃j ∈ (T.cobasis).T_j^0(δ) = 0 then
11:           (T', δ') = nextVertex(T, δ, i)
12:         end if
13:         if T' = null then
14:           δ'' = nextDelta(T, δ, i)
15:           (T', δ') = nextVertex(T, δ'', i)
16:         end if
17:         if T' = null then
18:           WL.add(T, δ')
19:         else
20:           WL.add(T', δ'), OP.add(T')
21:         end if
22:       end if
23:     end for
24:   end while
25:   return OP
```

5.3   Next Vertex

Algorithm 3 defines a recursive function that returns a tableau/parameter pair representing a vertex. That a tableau represents a vertex can be tested by solving a linear program describing that at a vertex the parameters should have sufficient freedom that a perturbation in one parameter can be balanced by perturbations in the others so that a pivot is not induced. Recall the example in section 3.5.

The algorithm performs a lexicographic pivot step with a candidate entering column at line 4. If the pivot leads to a basis that has already been generated, the resulting tableau is *null* and the loop moves on to the next j column. This avoids the cycling phenomena in which a vertex is visited repeatedly. Otherwise, if the new tableau/parameter pair does not represent a vertex, then the function calls itself, continuing its search for a vertex. The algorithm returns $(null, δ)$ if there are no pivots available.

The combined effect of the three algorithms is to systematically explore the tableaux corresponding to optima with respect to the parameter space. By returning those tableaux corresponding to vertices the inequalities of the projection space can be found. In summary, projection is reduced to repeated pivoting.

Proposition 1. *Algorithm 1 is complete, that is, if $\alpha :: \beta \in vertex(S \cap S')$, $\alpha :: \beta$ is in its output.*

Algorithm 2. Finding the next δ value

1: **function** nextDelta(T, δ, i)
2: $\quad \Delta' = \{\delta_i' \mid \exists j \in (T.\text{cobasis}).T_j^0(\delta[i \mapsto \delta_i']) = 0 \ \wedge \ \delta_i' < \delta_i\}$
3: $\quad \delta_i^* = \max(\Delta' \cup \{-1\})$
4: **return** $\delta[i \mapsto \delta_i^*]$

Algorithm 3. Finding the next vertex

1: **function** nextVertex(T, δ, i)
2: **for** $j = 1$ *to* $|\delta|$ **do**
3: $\quad$ **if** $j \in T.\text{cobasis} \ \wedge \ T_j^0(\delta) = 0$ **then**
4: $\qquad T' = T.\text{pivot}(j)$
5: $\qquad$ **if** $T' \neq null$ **then**
6: $\qquad\quad$ **if** $T'.\text{isVertex}(\delta)$ **then**
7: $\qquad\qquad$ **return** (T', δ)
8: $\qquad\quad$ **else**
9: $\qquad\qquad$ **return** nextVertex(T', δ, i)
10: $\qquad\quad$ **end if**
11: $\qquad$ **end if**
12: $\quad$ **end if**
13: **end for**
14: **return** $(null, \delta)$

Proof. (Outline) The algorithm is complete if it gives a series of pivots from the initial tableau to a tableau representing any vertex of the output space. Consider some vertex v, then there exists objective δ_v such that a tableau for v is optimal with respect to δ_v. Now consider the initial tableau which is optimal with respect to 1. With objective δ_v there must be a series of pivots from the initial tableau to that for vertex v. The parameter values δ always suggest an entering column for pivoting. To see this consider a tableau representing vertex v' that is optimal with respect to δ: for some i a decrease in δ_i will suggest a pivot to a tableau that gives a higher value for δ_v than that for v', hence this pivot must also be selectable when optimising δ_v from v'. Therefore v is output by Algorithm 1. $\square$

6   Related Work

This paper can be considered to be a response to the agenda promoted by the weakly relational domains [14,16,25,26,33] which seek to curtail the expressiveness of the linear inequalities up front so as to recover tractability. These domains are classically formulated in terms of a closure operation which computes the planar shadows [1] of a higher-dimensional polyhedron defined over $x_1, \ldots, x_n$; one shadow for each x_i, x_j pair. Operations such as join are straightforward once the shadows are known. This hints at the centrality of projection in the design of a numeric domain, an idea that is taken to the limit in this paper. Other ingenious ways of realising weakly relational domains include representing inequalities with unary coefficients as binary decision diagrams [8], using an array of size n to compactly represent a system of two variable equality constraints over n variables [13], and employing k-dimensional simplices as descriptions since they can be represented as $k + 1$ linearly independent frame elements [31].

An interesting class of weakly relational domain are the template domains [30] in which the inequalities conform to patterns given prior to analysis, say, $ax_2 + bx_3 + cx_6 \leq d$. During analysis values for coefficients a, b and c (on the left) and constants d (on the right) are inferred using linear programming. This domain has recently been relaxed [9] so that the right-hand side can be generalised to any parametric two-variable linear expression. The advance in this work is that the domain operations can then be performed in an output sensitive way: the computational effort is governed not only by the size of the input but the output too, rather than that of any intermediate representation. Fractional linear programming [4] is used to simulate the Jarvis march [18] and thereby project a higher dimensional polyhedron onto a plane in an output sensitive fashion.

Further afield, finite-horizon optimal problems can be formulated as PLP [19]. PLPs allow the control action to be pre-computed off-line for every possible value of the parameter μ, simplifying an on-line implementation. In a study of how to solve PLPs, the link between PLP and projection has been explored [19], a connection that is hinted at in the seminal work on PLP [15]. Yet the foundation result of [19], lemma 3.2, overlooks the need to relax constants and only addresses the problem of the uniqueness of the representation of a vertex by making a general position assumption. This assumption is unrealistic in program analysis where polyhedra can be degenerate, hence the use of lexicographical pivoting in this work. As a separate work, there has been interest in realising PLP using reverse search [2,20] though again making a general position assumption.

7 Conclusions

This paper has revisited the abstract domain of polyhedra, presenting a new algorithm to calculate projection. Apart from one trivial inequality that can be recognised syntactically the projection does not enumerate redundant inequalities, hence does not incur expensive post-processing. Moreover, if there are an excessively large number of inequalities in the projection then, since projection is computed incrementally, one inequality at a time, the calculation can be aborted prematurely yielding an over-approximation of the result without compromising soundness. The new algorithm is based on pivoting which is known to have fast implementations and even appears to be amenable to parallelisation. Since convex hull can be calculated using meet and projection [32] the presented algorithm can form the core of a polyhedra analysis.

Acknowledgements. This work was funded by a Royal Society Industrial Fellowship number IF081178, the EPSRC VIP grant, and a Royal Society International Grant number JP101405. London Mathematical Society Scheme 7 enabled the authors to visit Freie Universität Berlin and they are indebted to Günter Rote for alerting them to the connection between projection and PLP. The authors also thank Darko Dimitrov, Axel Simon and Sriram Sankaranarayanan for interesting discussions.

References

1. Amenta, N., Ziegler, G.: Shadows and Slices of Polytopes. In: Symposium on Computational Geometry, pp. 10–19. ACM Press (1996)
2. Avis, D.: lrs: A Revised Implementation of the Reverse Search Vertex Enumeration Algorithm. In: Kalai, G., Ziegler, G.M. (eds.) Polytopes – Combinatorics and Computation, pp. 177–198. Brikhäuser, Basel (2000)
3. Bagnara, R., Hill, P.M., Zaffanella, E.: The Parma Polyhedra Library: Toward a Complete Set of Numerical Abstractions for the Analysis and Verification of Hardware and Software Systems. Science of Computer Programming 72(1-2), 3–21 (2008)
4. Boyd, S., Vandenberghe, S.: Convex Optimization. Cambridge University Press (2004)
5. Burger, E.: Über Homogene Lineare Ungleichungssysteme. Zeitschrift für Angewandte Mathematik und Mechanik 36, 135–139 (1956)
6. Chernikova, N.V.: Algorithm for Discovering the Set of All the Solutions of a Linear Programming Problem. Computational Mathematics and Mathematical Physics 8(6), 1387–1395 (1968)
7. Chvátal, V.: Linear Programming. W.H. Freeman and Company (1983)
8. Clarisó, R., Cortadella, J.: The Octahedron Abstract Domain. Science of Computer Programming 64(1), 115–139 (2007)
9. Colón, M.A., Sankaranarayanan, S.: Generalizing the Template Polyhedral Domain. In: Barthe, G. (ed.) ESOP 2011. LNCS, vol. 6602, pp. 176–195. Springer, Heidelberg (2011)
10. Cousot, P., Halbwachs, N.: Automatic Discovery of Linear Restraints among Variables of a Program. In: Principles of Programming Languages, pp. 84–97. ACM Press (1978)
11. Dantzig, G.B., Orchard-Hays, W.: The Product Form for the Inverse in the Simplex Method. Mathematical Tables and other Aids to Computation 8(46), 64–67 (1954)
12. Duffin, R.J.: On Fourier's Analysis of Linear Inequality Systems. Mathematical Programming Studies 1, 71–95 (1974)
13. Flexeder, A., Müller-Olm, M., Petter, M., Seidl, H.: Fast Interprocedural Linear Two-Variable Equalities. ACM Transactions on Programming Languages and Systems 33(6) (2011)
14. Fulara, J., Durnoga, K., Jakubczyk, K., Shubert, A.: Relational Abstract Domain of Weighted Hexagons. Electronic Notes in Theoretical Computer Science 267(1), 59–72 (2010)
15. Gass, S., Saaty, T.: The Computational Algorithm for the Parametric Objective Function. Naval Research Logistics Quarterly 2(1-2), 39–45 (1955)
16. Howe, J.M., King, A.: Logahedra: A New Weakly Relational Domain. In: Liu, Z., Ravn, A.P. (eds.) ATVA 2009. LNCS, vol. 5799, pp. 306–320. Springer, Heidelberg (2009)
17. Imbert, J.-L.: Fourier's Elimination: Which to Choose?. In: First Workshop on Principles and Practice of Constraint Programming, pp. 117–129 (1993)
18. Jarvis, R.A.: On the identification of the convex hull of a finite set of points in the plane. Information Processing Letters 2(1), 18–21 (1973)
19. Jones, C.N., Kerrigan, E.C., Maciejowski, J.M.: On Polyhedral Projection and Parametric Programming. Journal of Optimization Theory and Applications 138(2), 207–220 (2008)

20. Jones, C.N., Maciejowski, J.M.: Reverse Search for Parametric Linear Programming. In: IEEE Conference on Decision and Control, pp. 1504–1509 (2006)
21. Khachiyan, L., Boros, E., Borys, K., Elbassioni, K., Gurvich, V.: Generating All Vertices of a Polyhedron is Hard. Discrete and Computational Geometry 39, 174–190 (2008)
22. Kohler, D.A.: Projections of Convex Polyhedral Sets. Technical Report 67-29, Operations Research Centre, University of California, Berkeley (1967)
23. Lassez, J.-L., Huynh, T., McAloon, K.: Simplification and Elimination of Redundant Linear Arithmetic Constraints. In: Benhamou, F., Colmerauer, A. (eds.) Constraint Logic Programming, pp. 73–87. MIT Press (1993)
24. Le Verge, H.: A Note on Chernikova's algorithm. Technical Report 1662, Institut de Recherche en Informatique, Campus Universitaire de Beaulieu, France (1992)
25. Miné, A.: A New Numerical Abstract Domain Based on Difference-Bound Matrices. In: Danvy, O., Filinski, A. (eds.) PADO 2001. LNCS, vol. 2053, pp. 155–172. Springer, Heidelberg (2001)
26. Miné, A.: The Octagon Abstract Domain. Higher-Order and Symbolic Computation 19(1), 31–100 (2006)
27. Motzkin, T.S.: Beiträge zur Theorie der Linearen Ungleichungen. PhD thesis, Universität Zurich (1936)
28. Motzkin, T.S., Raiffa, H., Thompson, G.L., Thrall, R.M.: The Double Description Method. In: Annals of Mathematics Studies, vol. 2, pp. 51–73. Princeton University Press (1953)
29. Ponce, J., Sullivan, S., Sudsang, A., Boissonnat, J.-D., Merlet, J.-P.: On Computing Four-Finger Equilibrium and Force-Closure Grasps of Polyhedral Objects. International Journal of Robotics Research 16(2), 11–35 (1997)
30. Sankaranarayanan, S., Colón, M.A., Sipma, H., Manna, Z.: Efficient Strongly Relational Polyhedral Analysis. In: Emerson, E.A., Namjoshi, K.S. (eds.) VMCAI 2006. LNCS, vol. 3855, pp. 111–125. Springer, Heidelberg (2005)
31. Seidl, H., Flexeder, A., Petter, M.: Interprocedurally Analysing Linear Inequality Relations. In: De Nicola, R. (ed.) ESOP 2007. LNCS, vol. 4421, pp. 284–299. Springer, Heidelberg (2007)
32. Simon, A., King, A.: Exploiting Sparsity in Polyhedral Analysis. In: Hankin, C., Siveroni, I. (eds.) SAS 2005. LNCS, vol. 3672, pp. 336–351. Springer, Heidelberg (2005)
33. Simon, A., King, A., Howe, J.M.: Two Variables per Linear Inequality as an Abstract Domain. In: Leuschel, M. (ed.) LOPSTR 2002. LNCS, vol. 2664, pp. 71–89. Springer, Heidelberg (2003)
34. Todd, M.J.: The Many Facets of Linear Programming. Mathematical Programming 91(3), 417–436 (2002)
35. Wilde, D.K.: A Library for Doing Polyhedral Operations. Technical Report 785, Institut de Recherche en Informatique, Campus Universitaire de Beaulieu, France (1993)
36. Ziegler, G.M.: Lectures on Polytopes. Springer (2007)

Inference of Polynomial Invariants for Imperative Programs: A Farewell to Gröbner Bases*

David Cachera[1], Thomas Jensen[2], Arnaud Jobin[3], and Florent Kirchner[4],**

[1] ENS Cachan Bretagne, IRISA, Rennes, France
[2] Inria Rennes - Bretagne Atlantique, France
[3] Université Rennes 1, IRISA, Rennes, France
[4] CEA, LIST, Gif-sur-Yvette, France
{david.cachera,thomas.jensen,arnaud.jobin}@irisa.fr,
florent.kirchner@cea.fr

Abstract. We propose a static analysis for computing polynomial invariants for imperative programs. The analysis is derived from an abstract interpretation of a backwards semantics, and computes preconditions for equalities like $g = 0$ to hold at the end of execution. A distinguishing feature of the technique is that it computes polynomial loop invariants without resorting to Gröbner base computations. The analysis uses remainder computations over parameterized polynomials in order to handle conditionals and loops efficiently. The algorithm can analyse and find a large majority of loop invariants reported previously in the literature, and executes significantly faster than implementations using Gröbner bases.

1 Introduction

The problem of automatically inferring non-linear (polynomial) invariants of programs is a challenge in program verification. This stands in contrast to the case for linear invariants where the initial work by Karr [8] and Cousot and Halbwachs [5] has led to efficient implementations based on variants of the polyhedral domain. As an example of a polynomial invariant, consider the algorithm

```
1.      y₁ := 0; y₂ := 0; y₃ := x₁;
2.      while y₃ ≠ 0 do
3.          if x₂ = y₂ + 1 then
4.              y₁ := y₁ + 1;    y₂ := 0;    y₃ := y₃ − 1;
5.          else
6.              y₂ := y₂ + 1;    y₃ := y₃ − 1;
7.
```

Fig. 1. A division algorithm with polynomial invariant

---

* This work was partly supported by the ANR Decert and the *Région Bretagne* CertLogs projects.
** Work performed while at Inria Rennes - Bretagne Atlantique.

A. Miné and D. Schmidt (Eds.): SAS 2012, LNCS 7460, pp. 58–74, 2012.

in Figure 1 which computes the Euclidean division of x_1 by x_2 [10]. The invariant we want to compute for this example is non-linear, *viz.*, $y_1 * x_2 + y_2 + y_3 = x_1$. For more examples, see [16].

A central observation in existing work on generating polynomial invariants is that n-ary relations of the form $\{x \in \mathbb{R}^m | p_1(x) = \ldots = p_j(x) = 0\}$, *i.e.*, relations that can be described as the zeroes of a set of polynomials, correspond to a lattice of polynomials ideals. Such ideals are finitely generated which means that fixpoint iterations are guaranteed to terminate (more details in Section 2). The lattice of ideals have been used in several ways. Sankaranarayanan et al. [19] proposed a constraint-based strategy for generating non-linear invariants, derived from their previous work on linear invariants [3]. Müller-Olm and Seidl [11,12] define an abstract interpretation method that can generate polynomial invariants for a restrictive class of guarded-loop programs where tests in conditionals are polynomial disequalities. Their analysis is a backward propagation based method: they start from a polynomial p and compute the weakest preconditions of the relation $p = 0$. More precisely, in order to prove that a polynomial relation $p = 0$ is valid at the end of a program, they show that the set of zeroes of a polynomial p can be exactly abstracted by a polynomial ideal. The restrictions imposed on the language are sufficiently strong to ensure that their method can be proven complete. Rodríguez-Carbonell and Kapur [18,17] define the analysis as an abstract interpretation problem over a domain of ideals of variety, and use iteration-based techniques to compute polynomial invariants.

All these approaches rely on Gröbner base computations [6], either when checking the inclusion of one polynomial ideal within another when analysing loops [12], when analysing variable assignments [19] or when computing the intersection of ideals in [18,17]. Computing Gröbner bases however slows down considerably the overall analysis. It is made even slower when the techniques for generation of polynomial invariants employ parameterized polynomials [12,19] of the form $a_0 + a_1.x_1 + a_2.x_2 + a_3.x_1x_2 + a_4.x_1{}^2 + a_5.x_2{}^2$ (also called polynomial templates) and infer the coefficients of the polynomial in a second phase. This means that the computation has to calculate Gröbner bases for parameterized polynomials.

In this paper, we propose an abstract interpretation based method [4] for inferring polynomial invariants that entirely avoids computing Gröbner bases. The method is precise and efficient, and is obtained without restricting the expressiveness of the polynomial programming language. Our analysis consists in a backward propagation mechanism that extends Müller-Olm and Seidl's work [12] to a *general polynomial structured programming language* that includes **if** and **while** constructs where branching conditions are both polynomial equalities and disequalities. As in this previous approach, our analysis uses a form of weakest precondition calculus for showing that a polynomial relation $g = 0$ holds at the end of a program. We show that the backward approach, which was already observed to be well adapted to polynomial disequality guards [12] can be extended to **if** constructs with equality guards by using parameterized polynomial division.

The main contribution of the paper is a constraint-based algorithm for inferring polynomial invariants. Such constraint-based techniques (rather than iteration) when dealing with loops means that it becomes feasible to analyse conditionals precisely, using parameterized polynomial division. This leads to a backwards static analysis, expressed as a constraint generation algorithm that at the same time computes polynomial ideals and a set of constraints, which together characterize the program invariants. A salient feature of this analysis, which distinguishes it from previous analyses, is that it does not require the use of Gröbner base computations. We have implemented this algorithm in Maple and our benchmarks show that our analyzer can successfully infer invariants on a sizeable set of examples, while performing two orders of magnitude faster than other existing implementations.

The rest of the paper is organized as follows. Section 2 contains mathematical background material: multivariate polynomial algebra, division and remainder operators and the lattice structure of ideals. Section 3 defines the syntax and semantics of *polynomial programs*. In Section 4, we present the abstract semantics of polynomial programs over the lattice of ideals. Section 5 presents our method for fast inferring polynomial loop invariants without fixpoint iteration nor Gröbner base computation. We report on benchmarks for our implementation in Section 6 and discuss related work in Section 7.

2   Preliminaries

We consider polynomials in $\mathbb{R}[x_1, \ldots, x_m]$ where m represents the number of variables of the program[1]. In the rest of the paper, we will distinguish between x, element of $\mathbb{R}^m$, x_i element of $\mathbb{R}$, and x_i variable of the program.

A set of polynomial equalities $\{p_1 = 0, \ldots, p_s = 0\}$ enjoys the property of being stable under a few select arithmetic operations: this corresponds to the algebraic structure of an ideal, as recalled by the following definition.

Definition 1 (Polynomial ideal). *A set $I \subseteq \mathbb{R}[x_1, \ldots, x_m]$ is a polynomial ideal if it contains 0, is stable under addition (if $p_1, p_2 \in I$ then $p_1 + p_2 \in I$) and stable under external multiplication (if $q \in \mathbb{R}[x_1, \ldots, x_m]$ and $p \in I$ then $q \cdot p \in I$). We write $\mathcal{I}$ for the set of polynomial ideals of $\mathbb{R}[x_1, \ldots, x_m]$, and $<S>$ for the polynomial ideal generated by a set S of polynomials. By definition, $<S>$ is the smallest ideal containing all polynomials of S.*

The set $\mathcal{I}$ can be given a partial order structure by using the *reverse subset inclusion* between ideals. The least upper bound (lub) of a set of polynomial ideals is then the intersection of its elements, while the greatest lower bound (glb) is the ideal generated by the union of the elements[2].

---

[1] A careful reader will see that our analysis can be set in any $\mathbb{F}[x_1, \ldots, x_m]$ where $\mathbb{F}$ is a noetherian ring, *i.e.* a ring satisfiying the ascending chain condition on its ideal set.

[2] The union set of two ideals is not an ideal in general.

Definition 2 (Lattice structure of $\mathcal{I}$). *Given I and J two polynomial ideals, we define $I \sqcup^\sharp J = I \cap J$, $I \sqcap^\sharp J = <I \cup J>$ and $\sqsubseteq^\sharp = \supseteq$. Operators $\sqcup^\sharp$ and $\sqcap^\sharp$ are extended in a standard fashion to range over sets of polynomial ideals. Equipped with these operators, $\mathcal{I}$ is a complete lattice, where the least element is $\perp^\sharp = <1>$ and the greatest element is $\top^\sharp = <0>$.*

A crucial property of polynomial ideals is that they are finitely generated.

Theorem 1 (Hilbert). *Every polynomial ideal $I \in \mathcal{I}$ is finitely generated, i.e., $I = <S>$ for a finite subset S of I.*

Theorem 1 above also exhibits the tight link that exists between polynomial equality sets and an ideal structure. We have already seen that such a set can naturally be represented as an ideal. Conversely, any polynomial ideal can be represented by a finite set of polynomials, that can be seen as a polynomial equality set. A direct consequence of this theorem is that operations on ideals can be defined thanks to finite sets of generators representing these ideals. For instance, given the two ideals $I = <q_1, \ldots, q_r>$ and $J = <h_1, \ldots, h_s>$, their abstract glb is defined by $I \sqcap^\sharp J = <q_1, \ldots, q_r, h_1, \ldots, h_s>$. The reader should remember this finite representation for the rest of the paper.

The notion of *division* on multivariate polynomial rings will play an important role when defining the analysis. Contrary to the univariate case, the polynomial ring $\mathbb{R}[x_1, \ldots, x_m]$ is not equipped with a Euclidean division, nevertheless it is common to define a division according to a monomial ordering [6]. In our case, we define a general division operator as follows.

Definition 3 (Division operator, remainder). *A division operator $\boldsymbol{div}$ is a function mapping a pair of polynomials $(g, p) \in \mathbb{R}[x_1, \ldots, x_m]^2$ to a pair $(q, r) \in \mathbb{R}[x_1, \ldots, x_m]^2$ such that $g = pq + r$. Polynomial r is called the remainder of g by p according to $\boldsymbol{div}$, and is noted $Rem(g, p, \boldsymbol{div})$ or only $Rem(g, p)$ if the division operator doesn't need to be explicitly given.*
We extend this definition to any polynomial ideal $I = <g_1, \ldots, g_s>$ by defining $Rem(I, p) = <Rem(g_1, p), \ldots, Rem(g_s, p)>$.

Our concrete semantics will operate over the domain $(\mathcal{P}(\mathbb{R}^m), \subseteq, \bigcup, \bigcap)$ of subsets, whereas our abstract semantics will deal with polynomial ideals. The link between these two domains is given by the following Galois connection:

$$\alpha : \mathcal{P}(\mathbb{R}^m) \to \mathcal{I}$$
$$X \mapsto \{p \in \mathbb{R}[x_1, \ldots, x_m] \mid \forall x \in X, \ p(x) = 0\}$$
$$\gamma : \mathcal{I} \to \mathcal{P}(\mathbb{R}^m)$$
$$I \mapsto \{x \in \mathbb{R}^m \mid \forall p \in I, \ p(x) = 0\}$$

such that $\forall X \in \mathcal{P}(\mathbb{R}^m), \forall I \in \mathcal{I} : X \subseteq \gamma(I) \Leftrightarrow \alpha(X) \sqsubseteq^\sharp I$.

3 Syntax and Semantics of Polynomial Programs

Our analysis produces invariants of *polynomial programs*, *i.e.*, programs where assignments are polynomial and conditional tests are polynomial (dis)equalities.

Definition 4 (Syntax of polynomial programs). *Let* $\mathbb{V} = \{x_1, \ldots, x_m\}$ *a set of program variables. We denote by p an element of $\mathbb{R}[x_1, \ldots, x_m]$ and by var an element of $\mathbb{V}$.*

$\mathbb{T} \ni test ::= p = 0 \mid p \neq 0$

$\mathbb{P} \ni c \quad ::= var := p \mid c ; c \mid \textbf{if } test \textbf{ then } c \textbf{ else } c \mid \textbf{while } test \textbf{ do } c \mid \textbf{skip}$

We define the semantics of polynomial programs as a backwards collecting semantics (a weakest liberal precondition calculus [7]) over sets of states. This collecting semantics can be proved equivalent to a classical operational semantics [2].

Definition 5 (Backward collecting semantics (BCS))
Let $\bowtie$ stand for $=$ or $\neq$, and $[\![p \bowtie 0]\!] = \{x \in \mathbb{R}^m \mid p(x) \bowtie 0\}$.

$B^\nu[\![c]\!] : \mathcal{P}(\mathbb{R}^m) \to \mathcal{P}(\mathbb{R}^m)$

$B^\nu[\![x_j := p]\!] \, S = \{x \in \mathbb{R}^m \mid x[p(x)]_j \in S\}$
  where $x[p(x)]_j$ is the element $(x_1, \ldots, x_{j-1}, p(x), x_{j+1}, \ldots, x_m)$

$B^\nu[\![\textbf{skip}]\!] \, S = S$

$B^\nu[\![c_1; c_2]\!] \, S = B^\nu[\![c_1]\!] \, (B^\nu[\![c_2]\!] \, S)$

$B^\nu[\![\textbf{if } p \bowtie 0 \textbf{ then } c_1 \textbf{ else } c_2]\!] \, S = (B^\nu[\![c_1]\!] \, S \cap [\![p \bowtie 0]\!]) \bigcup (B^\nu[\![c_2]\!] \, S \cap [\![p \not\bowtie 0]\!])$

$B^\nu[\![\textbf{while } p \bowtie 0 \textbf{ do } c]\!] \, S = \nu F_{c,p,S}$
  where $F_{c,p,S} = \lambda X.([\![p \not\bowtie 0]\!] \cap S) \bigcup ([\![p \bowtie 0]\!] \cap B^\nu[\![c]\!] \, X)$

The polynomial analysis only deals with partial correctness, hence the weakest liberal precondition calculus is expressed using a *greatest* fixpoint definition in this semantics.

We can now give the formal definition of a *polynomial invariant*. Intuitively, a polynomial g is said to be invariant for a program if all final states of execution for this program are zeroes of g. As our semantics operates backwards, this is equivalent to saying that, starting from a state zeroing g, the collecting semantics reaches the whole set of potential initial states.

Definition 6 (Polynomial invariant). *A polynomial $g \in \mathbb{R}[x_1, \ldots, x_m]$ is said to be* invariant *at the end of a program c if $B^\nu[\![c]\!] \, (\gamma(<g>)) = \mathbb{R}^m$.*

Note that, for a program where any initial state leads to an infinite execution, every polynomial will be invariant, *i.e.*, the analysis provides no information for such programs.

4 Verifying and Generating Polynomial Invariants

The concrete semantics is not computable because of the presence of fixpoint computations in the infinite lattice $\mathcal{P}(\mathbb{R}^m)$ that does not satisfy the ascending chain condition. A classical idea to overcome this problem is to approximate the concrete semantics by using *polynomial ideals* [12,17,19]. This provides a method for both verifying and generating polynomial invariants.

$\llbracket c \rrbracket^{\sharp} : \mathcal{I} \to \mathcal{I}$

$\llbracket x_j := p \rrbracket^{\sharp} I = <\{q[x_j \mapsto p], q \in I\}>$
  where $q[x_j \mapsto p]$ is the polynomial $q(x_1, \ldots, x_{j-1}, p(x_1, \ldots, x_m), x_{j+1}, \ldots, x_m)$

$\llbracket skip \rrbracket^{\sharp} I = I$

$\llbracket s_1; s_2 \rrbracket^{\sharp} I = \llbracket s_1 \rrbracket^{\sharp}(\llbracket s_2 \rrbracket^{\sharp} I)$

$\llbracket if \ p \neq 0 \ then \ c_1 \ else \ c_2 \rrbracket^{\sharp} I = p \cdot (\llbracket c_1 \rrbracket^{\sharp} I) \sqcap^{\sharp} Rem(\llbracket c_2 \rrbracket^{\sharp} I, p)$

$\llbracket if \ p = 0 \ then \ c_1 \ else \ c_2 \rrbracket^{\sharp} I = p \cdot (\llbracket c_2 \rrbracket^{\sharp} I) \sqcap^{\sharp} Rem(\llbracket c_1 \rrbracket^{\sharp} I, p)$

$\llbracket while \ p \neq 0 \ do \ c \rrbracket^{\sharp} I = \nu(F_{c,p,I}^{\sharp})$
  where $F_{c,p,I}^{\sharp} = \lambda J. \ p \cdot (\llbracket c \rrbracket^{\sharp} J) \sqcap^{\sharp} Rem(I, p)$

$\llbracket while \ p = 0 \ do \ c \rrbracket^{\sharp} I = \nu(\overline{F}_{c,p,I}^{\sharp})$
  where $\overline{F}_{c,p,I}^{\sharp} = \lambda J. \ p \cdot I \sqcap^{\sharp} Rem(\llbracket c \rrbracket^{\sharp} J, p)$

Fig. 2. Abstract semantics for polynomial programs

The abstract interpretation of polynomial programs using ideals as interpretation domain is given on Figure 2. This semantics is derived from Müller-Olm and Seidl's work [12,13] (see Section 7 for a discussion on similarities and differences). A few remarks on this abstract semantics are in order. As it acts backwards, assignments only consist in a substitution. Also note that the semantics of the **if** and **while** constructs use the Rem-operator introduced in Definition 3. Indeed, consider an **if** statement guarded by a (dis)equality p: if we want to prove that relation $g = 0$ holds and we know that relation $p = 0$ holds, it suffices to compute $Rem(g, p) = g - pq$ for a given polynomial q, and prove that the relation $Rem(g, p) = 0$ holds. This property does not depend on the choice of q; in particular, this choice does not impact the correctness of our approach. We will show in the next section how parameterized quotients can be used to infer relevant invariants.

The semantics for **while** is defined by a greatest fixpoint definition, which follows the definition of the concrete semantics. The abstract transfer function for **while** can computed with a Kleene fixpoint iteration starting from $\top^{\sharp} = <0>$, the top element of the lattice $\mathcal{I}$.

For any given program c, the abstract semantics satisfies the following correctness property, expressed using the Galois connection defined in Section 2. It states that abstract computations under-approximate concrete behaviour.

$$\gamma(\llbracket c \rrbracket^{\sharp} <g>) \ \subseteq \ B^{\nu} \llbracket c \rrbracket \ \gamma(<g>) \tag{1}$$

A detailed proof of this property can be found in [2].

Thus, to verify that a given polynomial g is invariant it suffices to compute the abstract semantics $\llbracket c \rrbracket^{\sharp}$ on $<g>$ and verify that the initial state computed by the semantics is equal to the null ideal $<0>$. As $\gamma(<0>) = \mathbb{R}^m$, this ensures that g holds at the end of the execution of c, independently of the starting state.

In practice, the algorithms for computing polynomial invariants [19,12] operate on candidate polynomials of bounded degree and with unknown coefficients, expressed as parameters. For example, $a_0 + a_1.x_1 + a_2.x_2 + a_3.x_1 x_2 + a_4.x_1^2 + a_5.x_2^2$ is the most generic parameterized polynomial of $\mathbb{R}[x_1, x_2]$ of degree 2 for the set

$\{a_1, \ldots, a_5\}$ of coefficients. The algorithm for computing polynomial invariants of maximum degree d for a program c then starts from g, the most generic parameterized polynomial of degree d and computes the abstract semantics $[\![c]\!]^\sharp <g>$, using iteration over parameterized polynomials whenever loops are involved. The result is a set of parameterized polynomials whose coefficients are linear combinations of the initial a_is. Finding the parameters for which $[\![c]\!]^\sharp <g> = <0>$ then amounts to solving a linear system of equations where these coefficients are equal to zero.

The upshot of Hilbert's Theorem is that the fixpoint iteration induced by the semantics of the **while** construct terminates in finitely many steps. As this results in an increasing sequence, the stopping criterion consists in checking if the polynomials at step $n + 1$ belong to the ideal generated at step n. This ideal membership problem is decidable via Gröbner base computations [6]. As these are particularly costly for parameterized polynomials, we propose in the next section an analysis technique that will not iterate the semantics and hence avoid these computations.

5   Fast Inference of Loop Invariants

The basic idea for computing loop invariants fast is to avoid fixpoint iterations by using constraint-based techniques. A central observation for this approach to work is the fact that we can restrict attention to a particular set of invariant candidates: a polynomial g is a loop invariant if, starting from a state verifying the relation $g = 0$, the execution of the body of the loop leads to a state that satisfies this relation $g = 0$. In this section we will show how to reduce the inference of polynomial invariants to a search for such loop invariants. We first formalize this notion in Section 5.1, then show in Section 5.2 how it translates into a notion of constraints between ideals, resulting in our `Fastind` analysis. We then explain in Section 5.3 how to solve these constraints, before developing a detailed example in Section 5.4.

5.1   Loop Invariants

The informal definition of a loop invariant can be formalized using the backward concrete semantics.

Definition 7 (Loop invariant). *Let* $w \equiv$ ***while*** b ***do*** c *be a polynomial loop program and* $g \in \mathbb{R}[x_1, \ldots, x_m]$. *Then,* g *is a* loop invariant *for* w *if and only if* $\gamma(<g>) \subseteq B^\nu[\![c]\!] \; \gamma(<g>)$.

The first step of our method consists in finding a counterpart of the notion of loop invariant in the context of the abstract semantics. The following theorem gives a sufficient condition for a polynomial to be a loop invariant.

Definition 8 (Abstract loop invariant). *Assuming the notations of Definition 7, a polynomial* g *is an* abstract loop invariant *for program* w *if* $[\![c]\!]^\sharp <g> = <g>$.

Theorem 2. *If g is an abstract loop invariant for* w, *then g is a loop invariant for* w.

Proof. Correctness relation (1) states that $\gamma(\llbracket c \rrbracket^\sharp <g>) \subseteq B^\nu \llbracket c \rrbracket \gamma(<g>)$. Hypothesis $\llbracket c \rrbracket^\sharp <g> = <g>$ and Definition 7 allow to conclude the proof.

The benchmarks in Section 6 will show that the abstract loop invariant property is not a real restriction, but rather allows to infer a large number of invariants.

Theorem 2 and consequently Theorem 3 below have a direct consequence on fixpoint computations: by restricting our search to abstract loop invariants, iterations are not needed any more to compute abstract **while** statements guarded by a polynomial disequality. If we look closely at the semantics of a program $c \equiv$ **if** $p \neq 0$ **then** c_1 **else** *skip*, we have $\llbracket c \rrbracket^\sharp I = p \cdot (\llbracket c_1 \rrbracket^\sharp I) \, \bigsqcap^\sharp \, \mathrm{Rem}(I, p) = p \cdot (\llbracket c_1 \rrbracket^\sharp I) \, \bigsqcap^\sharp (I - p \cdot q)$ for a given polynomial quotient q. We thus remark that, without any *a priori* hypothesis on c_1, a correct choice for a quotient is given by $q = 0$, which defines $\mathrm{Rem}(g, p) = g$ for any g in I. Even if not the optimal one in some cases, this choice coincides with Müller-Olm and Seidl's abstract function and gives good results in practice. As the abstract transfer function for **while** is derived from $c \equiv$ **if** $p \neq 0$ **then** c_1 **else** *skip*, the abstract definition of a **while** statement guarded by a polynomial disequality is given by the trivial division operator that leaves its argument unchanged. As a direct consequence, the ideal that is taken as postcondition of this **while** statement is left unchanged when computing its semantics, as expressed by the following theorem.

Theorem 3. *Let $I \in \mathcal{I}$ and* w $\equiv$ **while** $p \neq 0$ **do** c *be a polynomial program. Suppose that* $\llbracket c \rrbracket^\sharp I = I$. *Then* $\llbracket w \rrbracket^\sharp I = I$.

Proof. With a null quotient for the Rem operator, the definition of $F^\sharp_{c,p,I}$ simplifies into $\lambda J.p \cdot (\llbracket c \rrbracket^\sharp J) \, \bigsqcap^\sharp \, I$. By hypothesis, $\llbracket c \rrbracket^\sharp I = I$, so $p \cdot (\llbracket c \rrbracket^\sharp I) = p \cdot I \subseteq I$, which proves that stabilization is reached immediately and concludes the proof.

The proof shows that, even if the semantics of the guard is taken into account in the product $p \cdot (\llbracket c \rrbracket^\sharp I)$, this effect is masked in the resulting ideal. Hence, the semantics of the **while** construct with polynomial disequality guard is expressed by the constraint $\llbracket c \rrbracket^\sharp I = I$, as will be made explicit in the new abstract semantics we propose in Section 5.2.

Note that Theorem 3 does not remain valid in the case of loops with equality guards. As loop guards of the form $p = 0$ are not frequent and taking them into account would increase the cost of the analysis significantly, we propose to ignore the information that could be obtained from such loop guards. This results in an approximation of the abstract semantics and brings us back to the quick single iteration case. As a summary, guards of **if** and **while** constructs will be handled as follows.

- Disequality guards in loops do not give rise to remainder computations. The iterative semantics of this kind of loops is replaced by the efficient computation of loop invariants.

- Loops with equality guards are handled by ignoring their guards. Thanks to this approximation, the iterative semantics of this kind of loops is also replaced by the efficient computation of loop invariants as in the previous case.
- Positive or negative guards for **if** constructs, which do not require iteration but still deserve precise abstract semantics are handled by introducing parameterized quotients, as explained below.

5.2 Inferring Loop Invariants by Fastind Analysis

As stated in Section 4 and as it is commonly done [19,12], our abstract semantics will operate on parameterized polynomials in order to infer, and not only verify, polynomial invariants.

Definition 9 (Linear a_i-parameterized polynomial). *Let $A = \{a_i \mid i \in \mathbb{N}\}$ be a set of parameters and $L_A = \{\sum_{j=1}^{n} \lambda_j \cdot a_{i_j} \mid n \in \mathbb{N} \text{ and } (i_1, \ldots i_n) \in \mathbb{N}^n \text{ and } (\lambda_1, \ldots, \lambda_n) \in \mathbb{R}^n\}$ be the set of finite linear combinations of the a_is over $\mathbb{R}$. The set of* linear a_i-parameterized (a_i-lpp) *polynomials is $L_A[x_1, \ldots, x_m]$. For example, $a_0 + a_1.x_1 + a_2.x_2 + a_3.x_1x_2 + a_4.x_1^2 + a_5.x_2^2$ is the most generic linear a_i-parameterized polynomial of $L_{\{a_0, \ldots, a_5\}}[x_1, x_2]$ of degree 2. An ideal is said to be a* linear a_i-parameterized *ideal if it is generated by linear a_i-parameterized polynomials[3]. The set of linear parameterized ideals is denoted by $\mathcal{I}_{par}$.*

The **Fastind** analysis consists in integrating the abstract loop invariant condition of Definition 8 into the polynomial inference process. This condition, which will be asserted for each loop of a program, is written as an equality between two polynomial ideals, under the form $[\![c]\!]^\sharp I = I$ where c stands for the body of a loop. We begin by defining the domain of constraints on polynomial ideals.

Definition 10 (Domain of ideal constraints). *An equality constraint between ideals is a finite set of pairs of linear parameterized ideals. Intuitively, this represents a conjunction of equalities of the form $I_0 \equiv I_1$ where I_0 and I_1 stand for a_i-lpp ideals. Formally, we define the domain $\mathcal{C}$ of equality constraints between ideals: $\mathcal{C} = \mathcal{P}_f(\mathcal{I}_{par} \times \mathcal{I}_{par})$. A solution to these constraints is a set of instantiations of the parameters by real values such that the ideal equalities are satisfied.*

The abstract semantics of **Fastind** analysis depicted on Figure 3 is derived from the abstract semantics $[\![.]\!]^\sharp$ by instrumentating it with the polynomial constraints resulting from the loop invariant property.

Note that abstract computations of **if** statements imply division operations of linear parameterized polynomials by polynomial guards. These operations, as explained in the following definition, require the introduction of new parameters.

Definition 11 (Parameterized division operator). *Let $p \in \mathbb{R}[x_1, \ldots, x_m]$ and $g \in L_A[x_1, \ldots, x_m]$ of respective degrees d and $d_1 \leq d$. Let $(b_i)_{i \in \mathbb{N}}$ be a set*

---

[3] Remark that a member of a linear parameterized ideal is a not a linear parameterized polynomial in general.

$$[\![c]\!]^{\sharp c} : \mathcal{I}_{par} \times \mathcal{C} \to \mathcal{I}_{par} \times \mathcal{C}$$

$$[\![\mathbf{x_j} := p]\!]^{\sharp c}(I, C) = (<\{q[\mathbf{x_j} \mapsto p], q \in I\}>, C)$$

$$[\![\mathbf{skip}]\!]^{\sharp c}(I, C) = (I, C)$$

$$[\![s_1; s_2]\!]^{\sharp c}(I, C) = ([\![s_1]\!]^{\sharp c}([\![s_2]\!]^{\sharp c}(I, C))$$

$$[\![\mathbf{if}\ p \neq 0\ \mathbf{then}\ c_1\ \mathbf{else}\ c_2]\!]^{\sharp c}(I, C) = (p \cdot I_1 \sqcap^{\sharp} \mathbf{Rem}_{par}(I_2, p), C_1 \cup C_2)$$

$$[\![\mathbf{if}\ p = 0\ \mathbf{then}\ c_1\ \mathbf{else}\ c_2]\!]^{\sharp c}(I, C) = (p \cdot I_2 \sqcap^{\sharp} \mathbf{Rem}_{par}(I_1, p), C_1 \cup C_2)$$

$$where\ [\![c_1]\!]^{\sharp c}(I, C) = (I_1, C_1)$$

$$and\ [\![c_2]\!]^{\sharp c}(I, C) = (I_2, C_2)$$

$$[\![\mathbf{while}\ p \neq 0\ \mathbf{do}\ c]\!]^{\sharp c}(I, C) = (I, C' \cup C_w)$$

$$[\![\mathbf{while}\ p = 0\ \mathbf{do}\ c]\!]^{\sharp c}(I, C) = (I, C' \cup C_w)$$

$$where\ [\![c_1]\!]^{\sharp c}(I, C) = (I', C')$$

$$and\ \qquad C_w = \{I \equiv I'\}$$

Fig. 3. Abstracting polynomial programs assuming loop invariant property

of fresh parameters. We will note $\mathbf{Rem}_{par}(g, p)$ the a_i, b_i-lpp polynomial defined by $\mathbf{Rem}_{par}(g, p) = g - q \cdot p$ where q is the most generic b_i-lpp of degree $d - d_1$. Considering a linear parameterized ideal $I = <g_1, \ldots, g_s> \in \mathcal{I}_{par}$, we will note $\mathbf{Rem}_{par}(I, p) = <\mathbf{Rem}_{par}(g_1, p), \ldots, \mathbf{Rem}_{par}(g_s, p)>$.

The use of this parameterized division operator will be illustrated in the example of Section 5.4.

This abstract semantics gives raise to Algorithm 1 that computes polynomial loop invariants. The correctness of this algorithm is asserted by Theorem 4 below.

---

input : $c \in \mathbb{P}$, $d \in \mathbb{N}$ and $a = \{a_i \mid i \in \mathbb{N}\}$ parameters
output: a set of polynomials $\mathcal{G}$

1 **begin**
2    $g :=$ the most generic a_i-polynomial of degree d;
3   computing abstract semantics $(I, C) = [\![c]\!]^{\sharp c} <g>$;
4   generating $\mathscr{C}_{g,c}$, the constraint $C \cup (I \equiv <0>)$;
5   computing $\mathscr{S}_{g,c}$, set of solutions of $\mathscr{C}_{g,c}$;
6    $\mathcal{G} :=$ set of polynomials obtained by a_i-instanciating g by elements of $\mathscr{S}_{g,c}$;
7 **end**

Algorithm 1. Inference of polynomial invariants assuming loop invariant property

Theorem 4. *Let* $c \in \mathbb{P}$ *and* $d \in \mathbb{N}$. *Polynomials computed by Algorithm 1 are polynomial invariants at the end of the program* c, *whose degree are less or equal to* d.

Proof. This theorem is a direct consequence of correctness relation (1) stated in Section 4 and of loop invariant property (Definition 8).

Let $c \in \mathbb{P}$, $d \in \mathbb{N}$ and $a = \{a_i \mid i \in \mathbb{N}\}$ a set of parameters. Let g be the most generic a_i-*lpp* polynomial of degree d and I and C such that $[\![c]\!]^{\sharp c} {<}g{>} = (I, C)$. The important point of this proof is that the abstract semantics $[\![.]\!]^{\sharp}$ and $[\![.]\!]^{\sharp c}$ coincide on all non-loop statements. Moreover, Theorem 3 states that the loop invariant hypothesis makes these two abstract semantics coincide on loop statements too. Thus, under loop invariant hypothesis, we can prove by induction on polynomial programs that $[\![c]\!]^{\sharp} {<}g{>} = I$. The correctness relation (1) then gives $\gamma(I) \subseteq B^{\nu}[\![c]\!] \, \gamma(g)$. Line 3 of Algorithm 1 enforces the constraint $I \equiv {<}0{>}$. Assuming this constraint on the coefficients of g, we have $B^{\nu}[\![c]\!] \, \gamma(g) = \mathbb{R}^{m}$, which proves that polynomials computed by Algorithm 1 are polynomial invariants at the end of the program c.

5.3 Handling and Solving Constraints

The `Fastind` analysis is based on an abstract domain mixing ideals and equality constraints between ideals, that allows eliminating iteration in the computation of the abstract semantics. The complexity of the whole analysis thus depends on the efficiency in constraint solving. However, checking equality of two a_i-*lpp* ideals I_0 and I_1 is not easy in general. Basically, one has to prove that each polynomial of I_0 belongs to I_1 and vice-versa. Such a complete proof could be achieved by Gröbner base computations, which are nonetheless very costly for parameterized polynomials. The goal is to avoid Gröbner base computations altogether in order to keep tractability, so we propose to assert ideal equality by imposing stronger predicates between *polynomials*, following a suggestion of Sankaranarayanan *et al.* [19]. We detail the different possible choices for polynomial equality predicates. The problem of ensuring equality $I_0 \equiv I_1$ depends on the nature of I_0 and I_1. We first consider the case where I_0 and I_1 are principal ideals, which means that $I_0 = {<}g{>}$ and $I_1 = {<}h{>}$ for some a_i-*lpp* polynomials g and h.

Ensuring ${<}g{>} \equiv {<}h{>}$. Equality between principal ideals can be strengthened by asserting *simple equality* between their base polynomials. Clearly,

$$g = h \quad \Rightarrow \quad {<}g{>} = {<}h{>} \tag{2}$$

Such an equality is then achieved by solving a linear system in the a_i parameters.

A weaker condition consists in asserting *constant scale equality*: equality between the polynomials g and h up to a multiplication by a constant also leads to the equality of the generated ideals

$$\exists \lambda, g = \lambda h \quad \Rightarrow \quad {<}g{>} = {<}h{>} \tag{3}$$

Imposing this equality comes to assuming the equality between coefficients of g and λh. This results into particular quadratic systems composed of equations of the form $l_0 + \lambda_1 l_1 + \cdots + \lambda_n l_n = 0$ where l_i denotes a linear combination of the a_i parameters. The way of solving these *parametric linear constraint systems* has already been studied in the literature [19] and is not developed here. The `Fastind` analysis first tries to use *simple equality* property. If this property does not succeed to produce a polynomial invariant, we switch to *constant scale equality*.

Ensuring $<g> \equiv [\![c]\!]^{\sharp}<g>$. Due to the possible presence of **if**-statements, $[\![c]\!]^{\sharp}<g>$ may not be a principal ideal but in the form $<h_1, \ldots, h_n>$ for $n > 1$. This kind of ideal equalities is managed by imposing simple equality or constant scale equality between g and each polynomial h_i.

Note that, in the case where $[\![c]\!]^{\sharp}<g>$ is of the form $<h_1, q \cdot h_2>$, we may alternatively chose a slightly different condition by asserting $<g> \equiv <h_1>$ and $<g> \equiv <h_2>$. This choice is correct because $<g, q \cdot g> = <g>$ and will be made when $deg(g) = deg(h_2)$.

Ensuring $<g_1, \ldots, g_s> \equiv [\![c]\!]^{\sharp}<g_1> \sqcap^{\sharp} \ldots \sqcap^{\sharp} [\![c]\!]^{\sharp}<g_s>$. This case is treated as the previous one by imposing simple equality or constant scale equality between $<g_i>$ and $[\![c]\!]^{\sharp}<g_i>$.

Note that, except for **dijkstra** and **wensley** programs, all the invariants presented in Section 6 have been inferred using the equality property (2).

5.4   Illustrating the Fastind Analysis on mannadiv Example

In this section, we develop the different steps of the **Fastind** analysis on the program **mannadiv** given in Figure 1 in the introduction of this paper. This program, that yields an invariant of degree 2, has been chosen in order to illustrate the different techniques that come into play for computing loop invariants. More precisely:

- it demonstrates the use of the loop invariant property,
- the presence of a conditional statement whose guard cannot be ignored in order to infer a non-trivial invariant illustrates the use of Rem_{par}-operations,
- it shows constraints generation and solving.

We will denote by (I_i, C_i) the element of $\mathcal{I}_{par} \times \mathcal{C}$ computed at line i. As the **Fastind** analysis acts backward, we start from the pair (I_7, C_7) where I_7 is the ideal generated by the most generic quadratic a_i-*lpp* polynomial g ($I_7 = <g>$) and $C_7 = \emptyset$. In other words, the abstract semantics of **mannadiv** program is given by

$$(I_1, C_1) = [\![\text{mannadiv}]\!]^{\sharp c}(I_7, C_7)$$
$$= [\![y_1 := 0; y_2 := 0; y_3 := x_1; \textbf{while } y_3 \neq 0 \textbf{ do } c_{\textbf{if}}]\!]^{\sharp c}(I_7, C_7)$$
$$= [\![y_1 := 0; y_2 := 0; y_3 := x_1]\!]^{\sharp c}([\![\textbf{while } y_3 \neq 0 \textbf{ do } c_{\textbf{if}}]\!]^{\sharp c}(I_7, C_7))$$

where $c_{\textbf{if}}$ denotes the **if**-statement of the program and $p_{\textbf{if}}$ its guard ($p_{\textbf{if}} = x_2 - y_2 - 1$). According to the abstract semantics presented in Figure 3, we have

$$[\![\textbf{while } y_3 \neq 0 \textbf{ do } c_{\textbf{if}}]\!]^{\sharp c}(I_7, C_7) = (I_7, C_3 \cup C_w)$$

where $C_w = (I_3 \equiv I_7)$ is the constraint set resulting from imposing the loop invariant property and $[\![c]\!]^{\sharp c} = (I_3, C_3)$. As $c_{\textbf{if}}$ is an **if**-statement, it does not modify the set of constraints and we have $C_3 = C_7 = \emptyset$. It remains to express I_3 as the weakest precondition of $c_{\mathbf{if}}$ w.r.t. I_7. For the **then**-branch, we have

$$[\![\mathbf{y_1} := \mathbf{y_1} + 1; \mathbf{y_2} := 0; \mathbf{y_3} := \mathbf{y_3} - 1]\!]^{\sharp c}(I_7, C_w) = (I_4, C_w)$$

where $I_4 = \ <g_4>\ $ and $g_4 = g[^{y_3-1}/_{y_3}; {}^0/_{y_2}; {}^{y_1+1}/_{y_1}]$. In the same way, the abstract semantics of the **else**-branch is given by

$$[\![\mathbf{y_2} := \mathbf{y_2} + 1; \mathbf{y_3} := \mathbf{y_3} - 1]\!]^{\sharp c}(I_7, C_w) = (I_6, C_w)$$

where $I_6 = \ <g_6>\ $ and $g_6 = g[^{y_3-1}/_{y_3}; {}^{y_2+1}/_{y_2}]$. Finally, ideal I_3 is given by $I_3 = p_{\mathbf{if}} \cdot I_6 \ \sqcap^{\sharp} \ \mathrm{Rem}_{par}(I_4, p_{\mathbf{if}})$. According to Definition 11, the computation of $\mathrm{Rem}_{par}(I_4, p_{\mathbf{if}})$ requires the introduction of q, the most generic b_i-*lpp* of degree $deg(g_4) - deg(p_{\mathbf{if}}) = 1$, and yields

$$\mathrm{Rem}_{par}(g_4, p) = g_4 - q \cdot p = g_4 - (b_0 + b_1\, x_1 + b_2\, x_2 + b_3\, y_1 + b_4\, y_2 + b_5\, y_3) \cdot (x_2 - y_2 - 1).$$

Note that the resulting polynomial is in $\{a_i, b_i\}$-*lpp* form, which is essential for the linearity of the constraints generated further. Finally, we get

$$[\![\mathtt{mannadiv}]\!]^{\sharp c}(I_7, C_7) = [\![\mathbf{y_1} := 0; \mathbf{y_2} := 0; \mathbf{y_3} := \mathbf{x_1}]\!]^{\sharp c}(I_7, C_w) = (I_1, C_w)$$

where $I_1 = \ <g_1>\ $ and $g_1 = g[^{x_1}/_{y_3}; {}^0/_{y_2}; {}^0/_{y_1}]$.

The last step of the algorithm consists in solving the constraints in $C_w \cup C_0$ where C_0 is the constraint set obtained by initial nullness, namely $C_0 = (I_1 \equiv \ <0>)$, and C_w corresponds to the ideal equality $<g> \equiv <p_{\mathbf{if}} \cdot g_6, \mathrm{Rem}_{par}(g_4, p_{\mathbf{if}})>$. This equality will be ensured by the special case of *simple equality*, which means that this constraint is satisfied by enforcing both $\mathrm{Rem}_{par}(g_4, p_{\mathbf{if}}) = g$ and $g_6 = g$. By definition, initial nullness is equivalent to $g_1 = 0$. We note C_4, C_6 and C_0 the respective linear systems induced by these polynomial equalities.

C_0	C_6	C_4	
$a_6 + a_{10} + a_{20} = 0$	$a_{20} = a_{18}$	$a_{10} = a_8$	$a_{18} + a_{13} = 0$
$a_1 + a_5 = 0$	$a_{19} = 2\,a_{18}$	$a_{20} = a_{15}$	$a_9 = a_{16} = a_{19} = 0$
$a_7 + a_{14} = 0$	$a_{17} = a_{16}$	$b_4 + a_{13} = 0$	$b_1 = b_2 = b_3 = b_5 = 0$
$a_0 = a_2 = a_{11} = 0$	$a_4 = a_5$	$b_0 = a_{12} - a_{14}$	
	$a_{10} = a_9$	$a_5 = a_3 - a_{14} + a_{12}$	
	$a_7 + a_{14}$	$a_4 = a_{12} - a_{13} - a_{14}$	
	$a_{14} = a_{13}$	$a_{17} = 2\,a_{15}$	

These resolve into $a_{12} = a_5 = a_4 = b_0 = -a_1$, all other parameters equating to 0. Finally, the direct instantiation of the a_i-*lpp* polynomial g returns the single program invariant: $x_1 = y_1\, x_2 + y_2 + y_3$.

6   Benchmarks

Column **Fastind** of Table 1 presents the results of the **Maple** implementation of the **Fastind** analysis, run on Rodríguez-Carbonell and Kapur's benchmarks [18] and **mannadiv** example. Even if our method is incomplete due to our way to solve constraints, our analysis was able to find all the invariants inferred by Rodríguez-Carbonell and Kapur's first approach [18] and a large majority of invariants of Rodríguez-Carbonell and Kapur's second technique [17]. Our tests were run on a 2.8 GHz Intel Core 2 Duo with 4 GB of DDR3 RAM. The other columns of the table are the results of the implementations of literature approaches [12,18,17]. Execution times (in seconds) are given by the authors [14,18,17]. More precisely,

MOS column gives the results of Petter implementation [14,15] of Müller-Olm and Seidl approach. It uses the algebra system `Singular` (2.0.5) to deal with polynomial operations, and was run on an Intel architecture with an AMD Athlon XP 3000+ and 1Gb of memory. **RCK** columns present the results of the implementation of the two Rodríguez-Carbonell and Kapur's approaches [18,17]. First column gives the time taken by the `Maple` implementation of their *simple loop* approach [18]. Second column gives the time taken by the `Macaulay2` implementation of their *general* approach [17]. These two implementations were run on a 3.4 GHz Pentium 4 with 2 Gb of memory.

Table 1. Performance results for the Maple implementation

Name	d	Var	MOS	RCK simple loop [18]	RCK general [17]	Fastind
dijkstra	2	5	−	1.5	1.31	0.043
divbin	2	5	−	2.1	0.99	0.005
freire1	2	3	−	0.7	0.38	0.006
freire2	2	4	−	0.7	0.85	0.007
cohencu	2	4	−	0.7	0.94	0.009
fermat	2	5	−	0.8	0.92	0.006
wensley	2	5	−	1.1	0.99	0.037
euclidex	2	8	−	1.4	1.95	0.008
lcm	2	6	3.5	1.0	1.22	0.006
prod4	3	6	−	2.1	4.63	0.013
knuth	3	9	−	55.4	2.61	0.084
mannadiv	2	5	−	−	1.12	0.005
petter1	2	2	0.776	1.0	0.5	0.003
petter2	3	2	1.47	1.1	0.8	0.003
petter3	4	2	2.71	1.3	4.2	0.004
petter4	5	2	10.3	1.3	> 300	0.004
petter5	6	2	787.2	1.4	> 300	0.006
petter30	31	2	−	−	−	1.423

In this table d is the degree of the invariants; **Var** is the number of variables in the initial polynomial. All times are in seconds, and the dash symbol (−) is used when no result is available. Examples and their provenance can be found at [16], and in [18].

Results displayed on column **Fastind** proves the efficiency of the analysis. Even if Müller-Olm *et al.* [13] propose in their implementation to optimize Gröbner base computations by using modules, the iterative process and the cost of module inclusion checking still show a high computational cost, as shown by the Petter5 example. Last line of the table presents the result of the **Fastind** analysis on the program **petter30** that computes the integer 30 power sum ($\sum_{i=0}^{N} i^{30}$) and yields an invariant of degree 31. This shows that our method can effectively infer invariants of high degree. A thorough analysis of these results can be found in the technical report [2]. Our `Maple` sheets are available from www.irisa.fr/celtique/ext/polyinv.

7 Related Work

Our approach to computing polynomial invariants is developed from a combination of two techniques developed in literature [12,19]. From Müller-Olm and

Seidl's analysis [12], we have taken the idea to compute pre-conditions for equalities like $g = 0$ to hold at he end of execution. From Sankaranarayanan *et al.*'s work [19], we have pursued the idea of searching for loop invariants by a constraint based approach.

More precisely, the abstract semantics presented in Figure 2 extends the initial work of Müller-Olm and Seidl [12] to a structured language with both polynomial equality and disequality guards. This extension relies on our computation of quotients and remainders for parameterized polynomials. In the special case of a program $c \equiv$ **if** $p \neq 0$ **then** c_1 **else** *skip*, chosing $q = 0$ as a quotient coincides with Müller-Olm and Seidl's abstract function. Note that the same authors mentionned the possibility of using non-null quotients for handling polynomial equality guards [13], but without pursuing this idea. Indeed, the analysis of Müller-Olm and Seidl is based on fixpoint iterations using Gröbner bases and iterating Rem_{par}-operations in loops would give rise to an excessively expensive analysis. The constraint-based technique that we propose in the abstract semantics given on Figure 3 eliminates the need for iteration. We are thus able to compute with parameterized quotients in our analysis.

In terms of computational complexity, we propose a practical alternative to iteration-based methods by focussing on a particular form of loop invariants, as suggested by Sankaranarayanan *et al.* [19]. More precisely, condition (2) which provides the most efficient invariant computation corresponds to their notion of *constant value consecution*, and condition (3), which is the loop invariant hypothesis of Definition 8, corresponds to their notion of *constant-scale consecution*. Sankaranarayanan *et al.* are concerned with computing a *forwards* analysis whereas our analysis works backwards. In a forwards analysis, abstract assignments are handled by fresh variable introduction and elimination which requires computing ideal intersections using Gröbner bases. In a backwards analysis, assignments are abstracted by a simple substitution, which avoids Gröbner bases.

Rodríguez-Carbonell and Kapur [17] propose a method adapted to both kinds of guards, but at the price of a high degree of computational complexity. First, their abstract domain is the set of ideal varieties, *i.e.*, ideals such that $\alpha \circ \gamma(I) = I$ (called the IV property). The transfer function for disequality guards comes down to computing ideal quotients in this abstract domain. The IV property is costly to maintain, since it relies on the computation of radical ideals, which again involves Gröbner bases. By default, their implementation skips these computations and ignores disequality guards, inducing over-approximations. As above, their forwards analysis uses Gröbner bases for handling assignment. Abstract equality tests, which are easier to handle in this kind of approach, still need IV computations due to the nature of the abstract domain: these are often skipped in practice. Because their transfer function can be non-terminating, they have to introduce a widening operator that removes all polynomials above a given degree.

Finally, taking the alternative approach of restricting expressiveness, Rodríguez-Carbonell and Kapur [18] propose an analysis restricted to assignments involving only *solvable mappings*, which essentially amounts to having invertible abstract assignments. This leads to a complete analysis for which the number of iterations is bounded; nevertheless it systematically demands iterative fixpoint computations. The process of computing all polynomial invariants for a restricted class of programs was extended by Kovács in [9] which provides, again through iterative fixpoint computation, a complete invariant generation method for a specific loop pattern with nested conditionals.

8   Conclusion

We have presented a method for inferring polynomial invariants based on a backwards abstract interpretation of imperative programs. The inference technique is constraint-based rather than iteration-based, relies on parameterized polynomial division for improved precision when analyzing conditionals, and reduces the analysis problem to constraint solving on ideals of polynomials. The central result of the paper is that combining constraint-based techniques with backwards analysis has as consequence that the analysis can be implemented without the use of Gröbner base computations. Benchmarks show that the resulting analyzer achieves both good precision, even if not complete, and fast execution, compared to existing implementations using Gröbner bases.

This contribution constitutes a foundation for extensions to an analysis tool that covers a full-fledged language. Our technique should have good scalability properties as the limiting factor is the number of variables and not the degree of the polynomials nor the size of the code. We have began its integration into the Sawja static analysis framework for Java (`sawja.inria.fr`) with promising results.

We have undertaken the mechanized formalization of all the material of this paper with the Coq proof assistant, following Besson *et al.*'s approach [1] to linear invariant generation. In addition to the gain in confidence, this lays the groundwork for a certifying analysis toolchain, *i.e.*, the combination of an analyzer that generates certificates in predefined format, and a formally verified checker that validates them.

References

1. Besson, F., Jensen, T., Pichardie, D., Turpin, T.: Certified Result Checking for Polyhedral Analysis of Bytecode Programs. In: Wirsing, M., Hofmann, M., Rauschmayer, A. (eds.) TGC 2010, LNCS, vol. 6084, pp. 253–267. Springer, Heidelberg (2010)

2. Cachera, D., Jensen, T., Jobin, A., Kirchner, F.: Fast inference of polynomial invariants for imperative programs. Research Report RR-7627, INRIA (2011)

3. Colón, M., Sankaranarayanan, S., Sipma, H.: Linear Invariant Generation Using Non-linear Constraint Solving. In: Hunt Jr., W.A., Somenzi, F. (eds.) CAV 2003. LNCS, vol. 2725, pp. 420–432. Springer, Heidelberg (2003)

4. Cousot, P., Cousot, R.: Abstract interpretation: A unified lattice model for static analysis of programs by construction or approximation of fixpoints. In: POPL, pp. 238–252. ACM Press (1977)

5. Cousot, P., Halbwachs, N.: Automatic discovery of linear restraints among variables of a program. In: POPL, pp. 84–96. ACM Press (1978)
6. Cox, D., Little, J., O'Shea, D.: Ideals, varieties, and algorithms, 3rd edn. Undergraduate Texts in Mathematics. Springer (2007)
7. Dijkstra, E.: A Discipline of Programming. Prentice-Hall (1976)
8. Karr, M.: Affine relationships among variables of a program. Acta Informatica 6, 133–151 (1976)
9. Kovács, L.: A Complete Invariant Generation Approach for P-solvable Loops. In: Pnueli, A., Virbitskaite, I., Voronkov, A. (eds.) PSI 2009. LNCS, vol. 5947, pp. 242–256. Springer, Heidelberg (2010)
10. Manna, Z.: Mathematical Theory of Computation. McGraw-Hill (1974)
11. Müller-Olm, M., Seidl, H.: Polynomial Constants Are Decidable. In: Hermenegildo, M.V., Puebla, G. (eds.) SAS 2002. LNCS, vol. 2477, pp. 4–19. Springer, Heidelberg (2002)
12. Müller-Olm, M., Seidl, H.: Computing polynomial program invariants. Information Processing Letters 91(5), 233–244 (2004)
13. Müller-Olm, M., Petter, M., Seidl, H.: Interprocedurally Analyzing Polynomial Identities. In: Durand, B., Thomas, W. (eds.) STACS 2006. LNCS, vol. 3884, pp. 50–67. Springer, Heidelberg (2006)
14. Petter, M.: Berechnung von polynomiellen Invarianten. Master's thesis, Technische Universität München (2004)
15. Petter, M., Seidl, H.: Inferring polynomial program invariants with Polyinvar. Short paper, NSAD (2005)
16. Rodríguez-Carbonell, E.: Some programs that need polynomial invariants in order to be verified,
http://www.lsi.upc.edu/~erodri/webpage/polynomial_invariants/list.html
17. Rodríguez-Carbonell, E., Kapur, D.: Automatic generation of polynomial invariants of bounded degree using abstract interpretation. Science of Computer Programming 64(1), 54–75 (2007)
18. Rodríguez-Carbonell, E., Kapur, D.: Generating all polynomial invariants in simple loops. Journal of Symbolic Computation 42(4), 443–476 (2007)
19. Sankaranarayanan, S., Sipma, H., Manna, Z.: Non-linear loop invariant generation using Gröbner bases. In: POPL, pp. 318–329. ACM Press (2004)

A New Abstract Domain for the Representation of Mathematically Equivalent Expressions*

Arnault Ioualalen[1,2,3] and Matthieu Martel[1,2,3]

[1] Univ. Perpignan Via Domitia, Digits,
Architectures et Logiciels Informatiques, F-66860, Perpignan, France
[2] Univ. Montpellier II,
Laboratoire d'Informatique Robotique et de Microélectronique de Montpellier,
UMR 5506, F-34095, Montpellier, France
[3] CNRS,
Laboratoire d'Informatique Robotique et de Microélectronique de Montpellier,
UMR 5506, F-34095, Montpellier, France
{arnault.ioualalen,matthieu.martel}@univ-perp.fr

Abstract. Exact computations being in general not tractable for computers, they are approximated by floating-point computations. This is the source of many errors in numerical programs. Because the floating-point arithmetic is not intuitive, these errors are very difficult to detect and to correct by hand and we consider the problem of automatically synthesizing accurate formulas. We consider that a program would return an exact result if the computations were carried out using real numbers. In practice, roundoff errors arise during the execution and these errors are closely related to the way formulas are written. Our approach is based on abstract interpretation. We introduce Abstract Program Equivalence Graphs (APEGs) to represent in polynomial size an exponential number of mathematically equivalent expressions. The concretization of an APEG yields expressions of very different shapes and accuracies. Then, we extract optimized expressions from APEGs by searching the most accurate concrete expressions among the set of represented expressions.

1 Introduction

In computers, exact computations are approximated by the floating-point arithmetic which relies on a finite representation of the numbers [1,12,15]. Although this approximation is often accurate enough, in some cases, it may lead to irrelevant or too inaccurate results. In programs, these roundoff errors are very difficult to understand and to rectify by hand. At least this task is strongly time consuming and, sometimes, it is almost impossible. Recently, validation techniques based on abstract interpretation [2] have been developed to assert the numerical accuracy of floating-point computations and to help the programmer to correct their codes [11,10]. For example, Fluctuat is a static analyzer that

---

* This work was partly supported by the SARDANES project from the french Aeronautic and Space National Foundation.

A. Miné and D. Schmidt (Eds.): SAS 2012, LNCS 7460, pp. 75–93, 2012.

computes the inaccuracies of floating-point computations in C codes and helps to understand their origin [5,6]. This tool has been successfully used in many industrial projects, in aeronautics and other industries [4]. However, this method does not indicate how to correct programs in order to produce smaller errors. It is up to the programmers to write a new version of their program until they reach a version with the desired accuracy. As floating-point arithmetic is not intuitive and as there are many ways to write a program this process can be long and tedious.

Our work concerns the automatic optimization, at compile-time, of the accuracy of arithmetic expressions. To synthesize an accurate expression, we proceed in two phases. In the first phase, we build a large but yet polynomial under-approximation of all its mathematically equivalent expressions. In the second phase, we explore our abstract representation to find, still in polynomial-time, the expression with the best accuracy. More precisely, we select an expression which minimizes the roundoff errors in the worst case, i.e. for the worst inputs taken in the ranges specified by the user. This article mainly focuses on the first phase, the second phase not being described in details because of space limitations. Briefly speaking, this second phase uses an analysis *à la* Fluctuat to guide a local exploration of the abstract structure in order to extract an accurate expression. In this article, we present a new method to generate a large set of arithmetic expressions all mathematically equivalent. This kind of semantics-based transformation [3] has been introduced in [10,11] and the current work strongly improves the existing transformations as it allows the generation of alternative expressions of very different shapes.

Technically, we define a intermediate representation called Abstract Program Expression Graph (APEG), presented in Section 2 and defined in Section 3, which is inspired from the Equivalence Program Expression Graphs (EPEG) introduced in [17]. Our APEGs are built thanks to a set of polynomial algorithms presented in Section 4. We have proven the correctness of our approach in Section 5, by introducing a Galois connection between sets of equivalent expressions and APEGs and we introduce an abstract semantics to under-approximate by APEGs the set of transformation traces of an arithmetic expression. We present in Section 6 an overview of how we extract an accurate expression from an APEG. Finally, Section 7 describes experimental results obtained with the Sardana tool which implements these techniques.

2   Overview

In this section, we give an overview of the methodology used to construct APEGs. APEGs are designed to represent, in polynomial size, many expressions that are *equal* to the original one we intend to optimize. Mathematical equality is defined with respect to a certain set $\triangleright$ of transformation rules of expressions, for example associativity and distributivity. Our goal is to build a tractable abstraction of the set of equal expressions and then to explore this abstract set to find an expression which minimizes the roundoff errors arising during its evaluation.

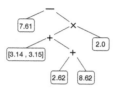

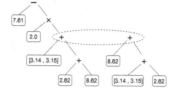

Fig. 1. Syntactic tree of expression e **Fig. 2.** APEG built on e by associativity

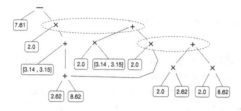

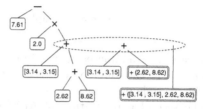

Fig. 3. Example of product propagation   **Fig. 4.** APEG with abstraction boxes

First of all, an APEG is built upon the syntactic tree of an arithmetic expression. We assume that, for each input variable, an interval describing its range is provided by the user. An APEG then contains the usual arithmetic operators (like $+$, $\times$ or $-$), variables and constants in the interval domain. An example of syntactic tree is given in Figure 1 (intervals are written between brackets). An APEG has two main features: First, it is a compact data structure, of polynomial size, which is able to cope with the issue of a combinatorial explosion thanks to the concept of classes of *equivalent nodes*. Next, it contains *abstraction boxes* which represent an exponential number of expressions.

The first feature of APEGs is the notion of equivalent nodes. Equivalent nodes are obtained by attaching to each node of the tree a set of additional nodes (written inside dashed ellipses in the figures). An APEG is always built by adding new nodes in these sets of equivalent nodes, or by adding a new node with its own set of equivalent nodes. An important point is that nodes are never discarded. For example, if $\triangleright$ contains only the associativity of addition, we construct the APEG of Figure 2 over the expression $e = 7.61 - 2.0 \times ([3.14; 3.15] + (2.62 + 8.62))$. Remark that the APEG of Figure 2 represents the expressions $7.61 - 2.0 \times ([3.14; 3.15] + (2.62 + 8.62))$ and $7.61 - 2.0 \times (([3.14; 3.15] + 2.62) + 8.62)$ without duplicating the common parts of both expressions.

In order to produce various shapes of expressions, we use several algorithms to expand the APEG while keeping its size polynomial. First, by propagating the products in the APEG of Figure 2, we obtain the APEG of Figure 3. Next, we propagate the subtraction in products and sums. This transformation underlines the interest of APEGs: A naive approach would introduce a combinatorial explosion, since the propagation of a negation into each product can be done in two ways ($-(a \times b) = (-a) \times b = a \times (-b)$). Instead, as APEGs do not

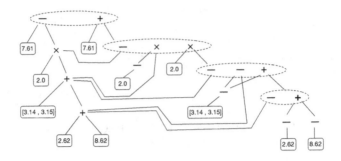

Fig. 5. Example of subtraction propagation

duplicate the common parts, we simply add to each multiplication a new branch connected to the lower part of the structure (see Figure 5). Thus we represent all the possible propagations of the subtraction without growing exponentially.

The second main feature of APEGs is the notion of abstraction box. We add abstraction boxes into APEGs in the sub-trees where the same operator is uniformly applied. Abstraction boxes are represented in our figures by rectangles with a double outline. Intuitively, an abstraction box is an abstraction of all the parsings that we can obtain with the sub-expressions contained in the box and a specific operator. For example, the box $\boxed{+, (a, b, c)}$ stands for any parsing of the sum of a, b and c. Abstraction boxes allow to represent exactly $(2n - 1)!!$ [13, §6.3] equivalent expressions. An example of the abstraction boxes we add to the APEG of Figure 2 is given in Figure 4.

Our approach consists of combining all these transformations, in order to generate the largest (yet polynomial) APEG. The key idea is that we only add to APEGs expressions which are equivalent to the original one. The correctness relies on a Galois connection between a collecting semantics containing traces of transformation and evaluation of expressions and APEGs. This Galois connection is constructed as an under-approximation of the set of equivalent expressions in order to cover only equivalent expressions. Hence, we do not cover all the equivalent expressions but we represent an exponential number of them.

3   Formal Definition of APEGs

APEGs are inspired from the EPEG intermediate representation introduced in [17]. Initially, EPEGs were defined for the phase ordering problem, to represent multiple equivalent versions of an imperative program. They are built upon a C program by application of a set of rewriting rules until saturation. These rules correspond for example to constant propagations or loop unfoldings. This process is arbitrary stopped at a certain depth to avoid infinite processing. Our APEGs are not built from a set of rewriting rules applied until saturation. Instead, we use a set of deterministic and polynomial algorithms described in Section 4.

An APEG is built from an initial expression e with respect to a certain set of binary relations $\rhd = \{\rhd_i, 1 \leq i \leq n\}$, representing the mathematically equivalent transformations we allow to perform on e. Usually we define $\rhd$ as a subset of rules of the real field containing associativity, commutativity, distributivity and factorization. Formally, if an expression e_1 can be transformed into the expression e_2 using a relation of $\rhd$, then e_1 and e_2 are mathematically equivalent. We generalize this property with the $\rhd$-equal relation.

Definition 1. $\rhd$-equal : *Let e_1 and e_2 be two arithmetic expressions, e_1 is $\rhd$-equal to e_2 if $(e_1, e_2) \in \rhd^*$ where $\rhd^*$ is the transitive reflexive closure of the set of $\rhd_i$ relations.*

APEGs are syntactic trees whose nodes are sets of $\rhd$-equal expressions, and which contain abstraction boxes representing efficiently large sets of $\rhd$-equal expressions. Abstraction boxes are defined by a binary symmetric operator $*$ (like $+$ or $\times$) and a set of operands L. Note that L may contain constants, variables, expressions or other abstraction boxes (abstraction boxes may be nested). The abstraction box $B = \boxed{*, L}$ represents the set of expressions made of the $*$ operator applied to the operands of L. For example, $\boxed{+, (x_1, x_2, x_3, x_4)}$ abstracts all the parsings of $\sum_{i=1}^{i=4} x_i$ and, for a nested box, $\boxed{+, (x_1, x_2, \boxed{+, (y_1, y_2, y_3)})}$ abstracts all the parsings of $\cup_{x_3 \in Y}\{\sum_{i=1}^{i=3} x_i\}$ where Y denotes all the parsings of $\sum_{i=1}^{i=3} y_i$.

Abstraction boxes are essential for our abstraction as they allow to represent efficiently an exponential number of $\rhd$-equal expressions.

From a formal point of view, the set $\Pi_\rhd$ of APEGs is defined inductively as the smallest set such that:

(i) $a \in \Pi_\rhd$ where a is a leaf (a constant or an identifier or an interval $[x, y]$ abstracting all the values a such that $x \leq a \leq x$),

(ii) $*(lop, rop) \in \Pi_\rhd$ where $*$ is a binary operator, lop and rop are APEGs representing the left and right operands of $*$,

(iii) $\boxed{*, (p_1, \ldots, p_n)} \in \Pi_\rhd$ is an abstraction box defined by the operator $*$ and the APEGs $p_1, \ldots, p_n$ as operands,

(iv) $\langle p_1, \ldots, p_n \rangle \in \Pi_\rhd$ is a class of $\rhd$-equal expressions, where $p_1, \ldots, p_n$ are APEGS. Note that $p_1, \ldots, p_n$ cannot be classes of $\rhd$-equal expressions themselves, i.e. $p_1, \ldots, p_n$ must be induced by the cases (i) to (iii) of the definition.

Case (iv) of the definition forbids nested equivalence classes since any equivalence class of the form $\langle p_1, \ldots, p_n, \langle p'_1, \ldots, p'_m \rangle \rangle$ could always be rewritten in $\langle p_1, \ldots, p_n, p'_1, \ldots, p'_m \rangle$. Examples of APEGs are given in figures 2 to 4. Equivalence classes are represented by dashed ellipses in the pictures.

4   APEG Construction

In this section, we introduce the transformations which add to APEGs new ▷-equal expressions and abstraction boxes. Each transformation is intended to only add new nodes into the APEGs without discarding any other node. First of all, recall from Section 3 that abstraction boxes are defined by a symmetric operator and a set of expressions. In order to produce the largest abstraction boxes, we have to introduce *homogeneous* parts inside APEGs.

Definition 2. Full homogeneity *Let $*$ be a symmetric binary operator and π an APEG. We say that π is fully homogeneous if it contains only variables or constants and the operator $*$.*
Partial homogeneity *We say that an APEG is partially homogeneous if it contains a fully homogeneous sub-expression $e_1 * \ldots * e_n$ where $\forall i, 1 \leq i \leq n, e_i$ is any sub-expression.*

For example, the expression $e = a + (b + c)$ is a fully homogeneous expression, while $e' = ((a \times b) + (c + d)) \times e$ is partially homogeneous since, for $e_1 = a \times b$ the sub-expression $e_1 + (c + d)$ of e' is fully homogeneous.

We introduce two kinds of transformations. First, we perform the homogenization of the APEG by adding new nodes which introduce new homogeneous sub-expressions. Next we apply the expansion functions which insert abstraction boxes in the homogenized APEGs. Both transformations are designed to be executed in sequence, in polynomial-time. The homogenization transformations insert into an APEG as many ▷-equal expressions as possible.

4.1   Homogenization Transformations

Transformation of Multiplication: Multiplication may yield two ▷-equal expressions: Either by applying the distributivity over the addition or subtraction, or by applying a further factorization to one or both of its operands (whenever it is possible). For example, the expression $e = a \times (b + c) + a \times d$ can be distributed either in $e_1 = (a \times b + a \times c) + a \times d$ or factorized into the expression $e_2 = a \times ((b + c) + d)$. In both cases e_1 and e_2 contain an homogeneous part for the $+$ operator. This transformation is illustrated in the upper part of Figure 6.

Transformation of Minus: The minus operator introduces three kinds of transformations depending on which expression it is applied to. If the minus operator is applied to an addition then it transforms the addition into a subtraction plus an unary minus operator. For example, $-(a + b)$ is transformed into $(-a) - b$. If the minus operator is applied to a multiplication then it generates two ▷-equal expressions, depending on the operands. For example, $-(a \times b)$ generates the ▷-equal expressions $(-a) \times b$ and $a \times (-b)$. If the minus operator is applied on another minus operator they anneal each other. This transformation is illustrated in the lower part of Figure 6. Note that, as shown in the graphical representation of the transformation given in Figure 6, in both cases

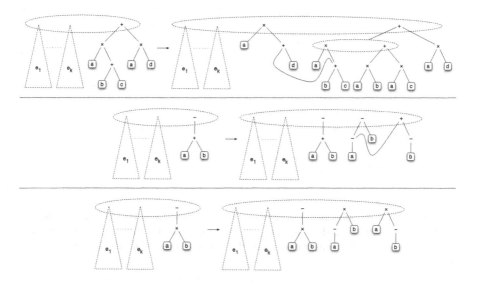

Fig. 6. Graphical representation of the homogenization transformations. ▷-equal expressions $e_1 \ldots e_k$ are represented by dashed trees. The top transformation corresponds to the transformation over multiplication and the next two schemes illustrate the transformation over minus, for an addition and a product respectively.

(transformation of multiplication and minus), we add as few nodes as possible to the pre-existing APEG. Each transformation only adds a polynomial number of node.

4.2   Expansion Functions

The expansion functions insert abstraction boxes with as many operands as possible. Currently, we have defined three expansion functions. From an algorithmic point of view, each expansion function is applied through all the nodes of the APEG, recursively. As the size of an APEG is polynomial in the number of its leaves, the expansion functions can be performed in polynomial-time.

Horizontal Expansion: The horizontal expansion introduces abstraction boxes which are built on some fully or partially homogeneous some sub-trees of an homogeneous part. If we split an homogeneous part in two, both parts are also homogeneous. Then we can either build an abstraction box containing the leaves of the left part of the homogeneous tree, or the leaves of the right part. For example let us consider the expression described in the top of Figure 7 where we perform and addition between the left sub-tree grouping the leaves $l_1, \ldots, l_k$ and the right sub-tree grouping the leaves $l'_1, \ldots, l'_{k'}$. We can either create a box $B_1 = (\boxed{+, (l_1, \ldots, l_k)})$ or a box $B_2 = (\boxed{+, (l'_1, \ldots, l'_{k'})})$. In one case we

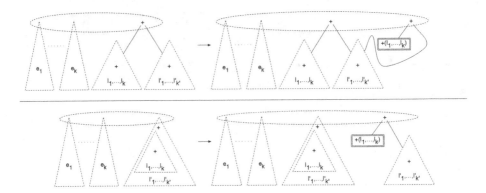

Fig. 7. Graphical representation of the expansion transformations. The dotted triangles with $l_1, \ldots, l_k$ written inside represent homogeneous parts. From top to bottom, the figure represents the horizontal and vertical expansion transformations.

collapse all the parsings of $\sum_{i=1}^{k} l_i$ and keep a certain parsing of $\sum_{j=1}^{k'} l'_j$ (in an englobing expression). In the other case we keep a certain parsing of $\sum_{i=1}^{k} l_i$ plus any parsing of $\sum_{j=1}^{k'} l'_j$. This transformation is illustrated in Figure 7. We introduce only $O(2n)$ boxes, among the exponential number of possible combinations.

Vertical Expansion: The vertical expansion introduces abstraction boxes in an homogeneous structure by splitting it into two parts. Here, the splitting is performed by considering in one hand the leaves contained in a sub-expression and in the other hand the leaves contained in the englobing expression. Let us consider an homogeneous structure defined by a set $P = \{p_1, \ldots, p_n\}$ of operands and the binary operator $*$. Each occurrence of $*$ defines a sub-expression with a set $\{p'_1, \ldots, p'_k\} \subseteq P$ of leaves. The vertical expansion introduces for each occurrence of $*$, an abstraction box defined by $*$ and the set $P \setminus \{p'_1, \ldots, p'_k\}$ of leaves. Also the vertical expansion introduces for each leaf an abstraction box containing all the others. This transformation is illustrated in Figure 7. It introduces $O(2n)$ boxes into an homogeneous part of size n.

Box Expansion: The box expansion is designed to add new abstraction boxes over the existing ones. As we allow abstraction boxes to be recursive, then for any abstraction box $B' = (\boxed{*', P'})$ which is contained in $B = (\boxed{*, P})$, if $* = *'$ then we can merge P and P' into a new abstraction box $B'' = (\boxed{*, P \cup P'})$. It is obvious that $\triangleright$-equal expressions represented by B'' strictly includes the $\triangleright$-equal expressions represented by B.

5   Correctness

5.1   Collecting Semantics

For the sake of clarity, we define a collecting semantics enabling only the transformation of expressions and we omit to include the reduction rules corresponding to the usual evaluation of expressions. Let $(\!|e|\!)_\triangleright$ be the set of partial traces for the transformation of e into $\triangleright$-equal expressions. To define this collecting semantics, we need to introduce some transformation rules of arithmetic expressions into other equivalent expressions. We define $\mathcal{R} = \cup_{i=1}^{n} \triangleright_i$ with $\forall i$, $1 \leq i \leq n$, $\triangleright_i \subseteq Expr \times Expr$. We do not require the $\triangleright_i$ relations to be transitive since $\triangleright$ may be applied many times along a trace. For example, we can set $\triangleright_1 = \{((a+b)+c, \, a+(b+c)) \in Expr^2 : a,b,c \in Expr\}$, $\triangleright_2 = \{((a+b) \times c, \, a \times c + b \times c) \in Expr^2 : a,b,c \in Expr\}$ and $\triangleright_3$ and $\triangleright_4$ the symmetric relations of $\triangleright_1$ and $\triangleright_2$. We define the transformation relation $\triangleright$ by means of the rules below, where $*$ stands for $+$, $-$ or $\times$:

$$\frac{e \triangleright_i e', \; \triangleright_i \in \mathcal{R}}{e \triangleright e'} \qquad \frac{e_1 \triangleright e_1'}{e_1 * e_2 \triangleright e_1' * e_2} \qquad \frac{e_2 \triangleright e_2'}{e_1 * e_2 \triangleright e_1 * e_2'} \qquad (1)$$

Next we define $(\!|e|\!)_\triangleright$ as the set $\triangleright^*$ of $\triangleright$-chains, i.e. the set of all the sequences $e \triangleright e_1 \triangleright \ldots \triangleright e_n$ such that $\forall i$, $1 \leq i < n$, $e_i \in Expr$ and $e_i \triangleright e_{i+1}$ and $e \triangleright e_1$.

Obviously, the collecting semantics $(\!|e|\!)_\triangleright$ is often intractable on a computer. For example the number of $\triangleright$-equal expressions is exponential if $\triangleright$ contains the usual laws of the real field (associativity, distributivity, etc.) Our abstraction of the collecting semantics by APEGs is an *under-approximation*. We compute our APEG abstract value by iterating a function $\Phi : \Pi_\triangleright \to \Pi_\triangleright$ until a fixed point is reached: $[\![e]\!]^\sharp = Fix \, \Phi(\bot)$. The function Φ corresponds to the transformations introduced in Section 4. The correctness stems from the fact that we require that a) Φ is extensive, ie. $\forall t^\sharp \in \Pi_\triangleright$, $t^\sharp \sqsubseteq \Phi(t^\sharp)$, b) Φ is Scott-continuous (ie. $x \sqsubseteq y \Rightarrow \Phi(x) \sqsubseteq \Phi(y)$ and for any increasing chain X, $\sqcup_{x \in X}\Phi(x) = \Phi(\sqcup X)$) and c) for any set of abstract traces $t^\sharp$, $\gamma(t^\sharp) \subseteq (\!|e|\!)_\triangleright \Rightarrow \gamma(\Phi(t^\sharp)) \subseteq (\!|e|\!)_\triangleright$. These conditions holds for the transformations of Section 4 which only add $\triangleright$-equal elements in APEGs and never discard existing elements. By condition a), the chain C made of the iterates $\bot$, $\Phi(\bot)$, $\Phi^{(2)}(\bot)$, ... is increasing. Then C has an upper bound since $\Pi_\triangleright$ is a CPO (see Section 5.3). The function Φ being continuous, $\sqcup_{c \in C}\Phi(c) = \Phi(\sqcup C)$ and, finally, by condition c) $\gamma([\![e]\!]^\sharp) = \gamma(Fix \, \Phi(\bot)) = \gamma(\sqcup_{c \in C}\Phi(c)) = \gamma(\Phi(\sqcup C)) \sqsubseteq (\!|e|\!)_\triangleright$.

Intuitively, computing an under-approximation of the collecting semantics ensures that we do not introduce into the APEG some expressions that would not be mathematically equivalent to e using the relations in $\triangleright$. This is needed to ensure the correctness of the transformed expression. Using our conditions, any abstract trace of the resulting APEG is mathematically correct wrt. the transformation rules of $\triangleright$ and can be chosen to generate a new expression.

5.2 Abstraction and Concretization Functions

For an initial expression e, the set $(\!|e|\!)_{\triangleright}$ contains transformations of the expression e into $\triangleright$-equal expressions as defined in Equation (1). The elements of $(\!|e|\!)_{\triangleright}$ are of the form $e \triangleright e' \triangleright \ldots \triangleright e^n$, where $e, e', \ldots, e^n$ are $\triangleright$-equal and we may aggregate them into a global APEG since this structure has been introduced to represent multiple $\triangleright$-equal expressions. So we define the abstraction function α, as the function that aggregates each expression contained in the traces in a single APEG. In order to define the concretization function γ we introduce the following functions:

- the function $\mathcal{C}(p, \pi)$ which returns the set of sub-APEGs of π which are in the same equivalence class than p, In other words, $\mathcal{C}(p, \pi) = \{p_1, \ldots p_n\}$ if there exists an equivalence class $\langle p_1, \ldots p_n \rangle$ in π such as $p \in \langle p_1, \ldots p_n \rangle$,
- the composition $\circ_*$ of two traces by some operator $*$. Intuitively, given evaluation traces t_1 and t_2 for two expressions e_1 and e_2, we aim at building the evaluation trace of $e_1 * e_2$. Following the rules of Equation (1), $\circ_*(t_1, t_2)$ is the trace in which, at each step, one of the sub-expressions e_1 or e_2 of $e_1 * e_2$ is transformed as they were transformed in t_1 or t_2.

The concretization γ of an APEG $\pi \in \Pi_{\triangleright}$ is defined by induction by:

(i) if $\pi = a$ where a is a leaf (i.e. a constant or a variable) then $\gamma(\pi) = \{a\}$,

(ii) if $\pi = *(lop, rop)$ where $*$ is a binary operator, and lop and rop are the operands of $*$, if the traces of $\gamma(\mathcal{C}(lop, \pi))$ are of the form $t = t_0 \triangleright \ldots \triangleright t_n$, and the traces of $\gamma(\mathcal{C}(rop, \pi))$ are of the form $s = s_0 \triangleright \ldots \triangleright s_m$, then we have

$$\gamma(*(lop, rop)) = \bigcup_{\substack{t \in \gamma(\mathcal{C}(lop, \pi)), |t| = n \\ s \in \gamma(\mathcal{C}(rop, \pi)), |s| = m}} t_0 * s_0 \triangleright t_1 * s_1 \triangleright \ldots \triangleright t_{n+m} * s_{n+m}$$

(2)

where at each step either $t_i \triangleright t_{i+1}$ and $s_i = s_{i+1}$, or $t_i = t_{i+1}$ and $s_i \triangleright s_{i+1}$, and where $|t|$ is the length of the trace t.

(iii) if $\pi = \langle p_1, \ldots, p_n \rangle$, let us take p_i and p_j, two distinct nodes in π. Let $t \in \gamma(p_i)$ and $t' \in \gamma(p_j)$ such as $t = t_0 \triangleright \ldots \triangleright t_n$ and $t' = t'_0 \triangleright \ldots \triangleright t'_m$. We defined $\mathcal{J}_{ij}$ the set of all pairs (k, l) with $0 \leq k \leq n$ and $0 \leq l \leq m$ such as $t_k \triangleright t'_l$ is a valid transformation. Then we defined $\gamma(\pi)$ as all the $\triangleright$-compatible junction of pieces of traces of $\gamma(pi)$ and $\gamma(p_j)$ for all p_i and p_j. Formally

$$\gamma(\pi) = \bigcup_{\substack{p_i, p_j \in \pi \\ (k, l) \in \mathcal{J}_{ij}}} t_0 \triangleright \ldots \triangleright t_k \triangleright t'_l \triangleright \ldots \triangleright t_m$$

(3)

This definition works for one function point between two traces, but it could be generalized to multiple junction points.

(iv) if $\pi = \boxed{*, (p_1, \ldots, p_2)}$ then, by definition of an abstraction box, $\gamma(\pi) = \bigcup_{p \in P} \gamma(p)$, where P is the set of all the parsing of $p_1, \ldots, p_n$ using the binary operator $*(lop, rop)$ whose concretization is defined in Point *(ii)*.

5.3 The Abstract Domain of APEGs

In this section, we show that the set of APEGs is a complete partial order. Then we show the existence of a Galois connection between sets of traces and APEGs.

First, we define $\sqsubseteq_\square$, the partial order on the set of abstraction boxes. Let $B_1 = \boxed{*, (p_1, \ldots, p_n)}$ and let $B_2 = \boxed{*', (p'_1, \ldots, p'_m)}$, we say that $B_2 \sqsubseteq_\square B_1$ if and only if the following conditions are fulfilled:

(i) $* = *'$,

(ii) $\forall p'_i \in \{p'_1, \ldots, p'_m\}$, if p'_i is not an abstraction box, $\exists p_j \in \{p_1, \ldots, p_n\}$ such that $p_j = p'_i$,

(iii) $\forall p'_i \in \{p'_1, \ldots, p'_m\}$, if p'_i is an abstract box $B_3 = \boxed{*'', (p''_1, \ldots, p''_k)}$ we have:

   (a) if $*'' = *$ then $\forall p''_j \in \{p''_1, \ldots, p''_k\}$ if p''_j is not an abstraction box then $p''_j \in \{p_1, \ldots, p_n\}$, else if p''_j is an abstract box then $\exists p_i \in \{p_1, \ldots, p_n\}$ such that p_i is an abstract box and $p''_j \sqsubseteq_\square p_i$,

   (b) if $*'' \neq *$ then $\exists p_j \in \{p_1, \ldots, p_n\}$ such that p_j is an abstraction box and $p'_i \sqsubseteq_\square p_j$.

In order to define the join $\sqcup_\square$ of two boxes $B_1 = \boxed{*, (p_1, \ldots, p_n)}$ and $B_2 = \boxed{*', (p'_1, \ldots, p'_m)}$, we introduce $B_3 = \boxed{*, (p_1, \ldots, p_n, p'_1, \ldots, p'_m)}$. By definition, $B_1 \sqcup_\square B_2 = B_3$ if $* = *'$, otherwise, if $* \neq *'$ then $B_1 \sqcup_\square B_2 = \top$. Next we extend the operators $\sqsubseteq_\square$ and $\sqcup_\square$ to whole APEGs. We obtain new operators $\sqsubseteq$ and $\sqcup$ defined as follows. For $\sqsubseteq$, given two APEGs $\pi_1, \pi_2 \in \Pi_\rhd$ we have $\pi_1 \sqsubseteq \pi_2$ if and only if one of the following conditions hold:

(i) $\pi_1 = a$, $\pi_2 = a'$ and $a = a'$, where a is a constant or an identifier,

(ii) if π_1 and π_2 fulfill all of the following conditions: $\pi_1 = *(lop, rop)$, $\pi_2 = *'(lop', rop')$, $* = *'$, $lop \sqsubseteq lop'$ and $rop \sqsubseteq rop'$,

(iii) if $\pi_1 = \langle p_1, \ldots, p_n \rangle$, $\pi_2 = \langle p'_1, \ldots, p'_m \rangle$ and $\forall i, 1 \leq i \leq n, \exists j, 1 \leq j \leq m$ such that $p_i \sqsubseteq p'_j$,

(iv) if π_1 is a fully homogeneous APEG defined by $*$ and the nodes $\{p_1, \ldots, p_n\}$, and π_2 contains an abstraction box B' such that $\boxed{*, (p_i, \ldots, p_n)} \sqsubseteq_\square B'$,

(v) if $\pi_1 = \langle p_1, \ldots, p_n \rangle$, $\pi_2 = *(lop, rop)$, $lop \in \langle p^l_1, \ldots, p^l_{k_l} \rangle$, $rop \in \langle p^r_1, \ldots, p^r_{k_r} \rangle$ and $\forall p_i \in \pi_1, \exists p^l_j \in \mathcal{C}(lop, \pi)$ and $\exists p^r_k \in \mathcal{C}(rop, \pi)$ such that $p_i \sqsubseteq *(p^l_j, p^r_k)$.

In order to define $\pi_1 \sqcup \pi_2$, with $\pi_1, \pi_2 \in \Pi_\rhd$, we observe first that π_1 and π_2 only contain $\rhd$-equal expressions. The join of two APEGs π_1 and π_2 is defined as the union of the corresponding trees. Boxes are joined using $\sqcup_\square$ and the join of two nodes of the syntactic tree p_1 and p_2 yields the equivalence class $\langle p_1, p_2 \rangle$. Finally we define $\bot$ as the empty APEG, and $\top$ as the APEG built with all the possible expression transformations of $\rhd$.

We have the following Galois connection between the collecting semantics and the APEGs where $\wp(X)$ denotes the powerset of X:

$$\langle \wp((|e|)_{\triangleright}), \subseteq \rangle \xleftrightarrow[\alpha]{\gamma} \langle \Pi_{\triangleright}, \sqsubseteq \rangle \tag{4}$$

6 Profitability Analysis

In this section we give an overview of how our profitability analysis works. First, we recall how the roundoff errors are computed, and next we briefly describe the search algorithm employed to explore APEGs.

We use a non-standard arithmetic where error terms are attached to the floating-point numbers [1,9,11]. They indicate a range for the roundoff error due to the rounding of the exact value in the current rounding mode. The exact error term being possibly not representable in finite precision, we compute an over-approximation and return an interval with bounds made of multiple precision floating-point numbers. Indeed, the error interval may be computed in an arbitrarily large precision since it aims at binding a real number and, in practice, we use the GMP multi-precision library [18]. Note that the errors can be either positive or negative. This depends on the direction of the rounding operation which can create either an upper or a lower approximation.

Error terms are propagated among computations. The error on the result of some operation $x * y$ is the propagation of the errors on x and y through the operator $*$ plus the new error due to the rounding of the result of the operation itself. Let x and y be to values represented in our arithmetic by the pairs (f_x, e_x) and (f_y, e_y) where f_x and f_y are the floating-point or fixed-point numbers approximating x and y and e_x and e_y the error terms on both operands. Let $\circ(v)$ be the rounding of the value v in the current rounding mode and let $\varepsilon(v)$ be the roundoff error, i.e. the error arising when rounding v into $\circ(v)$. We have by definition $\varepsilon(v) = v - \circ(v)$ and, in practice, when v is an interval, we approximate $\circ(v)$ by $[-\frac{1}{2}ulp(m), \frac{1}{2}ulp(m)]$ in floating-point arithmetic, or by $[0, ulp(m)]$ in fixed-point arithmetic, where m is the maximal bound of v, in absolute value, and ulp is the function which computes the unit in the last place of m [14]. The elementary operations are defined in equations (5) to (7).

$$x + y = \left(\circ (f_x + f_y), e_x + e_y + \varepsilon(f_x + f_y) \right) \tag{5}$$

$$x - y = \left(\circ (f_x - f_y), e_x - e_y + \varepsilon(f_x - f_y) \right) \tag{6}$$

$$x \times y = \left(\circ (f_x \times f_y), f_y \times e_x + f_x \times e_y + e_x \times e_y + \varepsilon(f_x \times f_y) \right) \tag{7}$$

For an addition, the errors on the operands are added to the error due to the roundoff of the result. For a subtraction, the errors on the operands are subtracted. The semantics of the multiplication comes from the development of $(f_x + e_x) \times (f_y + e_y)$. For other operators, like division and square root, we use power series developments to compute the propagation of errors [9].

We use the former semantics to evaluate which expression in an APEG yields the smallest error. The main difficulty is that it is possible to extract an exponential number of expressions from an APEG. For example, let us consider an operator $*(p_1, p_2)$ where p_1 and p_2 are equivalence classes $p_1 = \langle p'_1, \ldots p'_n \rangle$ and $p_2 = \langle p''_1, \ldots p''_m \rangle$. Then we have to consider all the expressions $*(p'_i, p''_j)$ for $1 \leq i \leq n$ and $1 \leq j \leq m$. In general, the sub-APEGs contained in p_1 and p_2 may be operations whose operands are again equivalence classes. To cope with this combinatorial explosion, we use a limited depth search strategy. We select the way an expression is evaluated by considering only the best way to evaluate its sub-expressions. This corresponds to a local choice. In our example, synthesizing an expression for $*(p_1, p_2)$ consists of searching the expression $p'_i * p''_j$ whose error is minimal with respect to any $p'_i \in p_1$ and any $p''_j \in p_2$.

For a box $B = \boxed{*, (p_1, \ldots, p_n)}$ we use an heuristic which synthesizes an accurate expression (yet not always optimal). This heuristic is defined as a greedy algorithm which searches at each step the pair p_i and p_j such that the error term carried out by the expression $p_i * p_j$ is minimal. Then p_i and p_j are removed from the box and a new term p_{ij} is added whose accuracy is equal to the error term of $p_i * p_j$ defined by Equations (5) to (7). This process is repeated until there is only one node left in the box. This last node corresponds to the root of the expression synthesized for the abstraction box. Remark that other algorithms could be used including algorithms performing additional computations to compensate the errors [19,16].

7   Experimental Results

In this section, we present experimental results obtained using our tool, Sardana. We present statistical results on randomly generated expressions. Then we show exhaustive tests on summations and polynomial functions.

7.1   Statistical Results

In this section, we present statistical results concerning the reduction of the roundoff errors on randomly generated expressions. First, we consider summations whose operands belong to intervals. Summations are fundamental in our domain since they correspond to the core of many numerical algorithms (scalar products, matrix products, means, integrators, etc). Despite their apparent simplicity, summations may introduce many accuracy errors and many algorithms have been proposed (this is still an active research field e.g. [19]). Hence, a main challenge for our analysis is to improve the accuracy of sums.

We use 4 configurations taken from [8] and which illustrate several pitfalls of the summation algorithms in floating-point arithmetic. We call *large value* a floating-point interval around 10^{16}, *medium value* an interval around 1, and *small value* an interval around 10^{-16}. We consider the following configurations:

Table 1. Statistical improvement of accuracy for summation and polynomials

expression form	interval width	10 terms expression		20 terms expression	
		large	small	large	small
100%+	Configuration 1	35.3%	33.4%	16.2%	16.5%
	Configuration 2	35.2%	34.3%	15.8%	34.3%
	Configuration 3	54.2%	59%	46.5%	51.9%
	Configuration 4	46.2%	52.9%	41.4%	46.3%
45%+, 10%×, 45%−	Configuration 1	12.9%	14.5%	13.1%	15%
	Configuration 2	11.8%	12.9%	11.8%	12%
	Configuration 3	15.1%	14.9%	13.9%	14.5%
	Configuration 4	10.0%	11.3%	11%	11.4%
50%+, 25%×, 25%−	Configuration 1	15%	16.4%	15.2%	16.4%
	Configuration 2	12.9%	13.6%	12.2%	13.1%
	Configuration 3	18.4%	17.7%	16.4%	16.9%
	Configuration 4	12.7%	13.5%	12.2%	12.3%

1) Only positive sign, 20% of large values among small values. Accurate sums should first add the smallest terms,

3) Only positive sign, 20% of large values among small and medium values. Accurate sums should add terms in increasing order,

3) Both signs, 20% of large values that cancel, among small values. Accurate sums should add terms in decreasing order of absolute values,

4) Both signs, 20% small values and same number of large and medium values. Accurate sums should add terms in decreasing order of absolute values.

For all these configurations, we present in the first row of Table 1 the average improvement on the error bound, i.e. the percentage of reduction of the error bound. We test each configuration on two expression sizes: With 10 or 20 terms, and with two widths of intervals: Small width (interval width about 10^{-12} times the values) or large width (interval width about 10% of the values). Each result is an average of the error reduction on 10^3 randomly generated expressions. Each source expression has been analyzed in the IEEE-754 binary 64 format by our tool in matter of milliseconds on a laptop computer. We can see that our tool is able to reduce the roundoff error on the result by 30% to 50% for a 10 terms, and between 16% and 45% for 20 terms. This means that our tool synthesize new expressions whose evaluation yields smaller roundoff errors than the original ones in the worst case, for any concrete configuration taken into the intervals for which the transformation has been performed.

Table 1 presents also the average improvement for more complex expressions. We used the same configurations as before but on two new sets of randomly generated expressions: The former with 45% of sums, 10% of products and 45% of subtractions, and the latter with 50% of additions, 25% of products and 25% subtractions. We obtained an accuracy improvement by 10% to 18% in average. We believe that the accuracy improvement is less significant because the data are not specifically ill-conditioned for these kind of expressions.

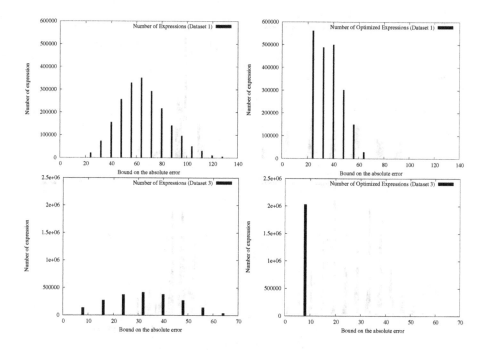

Fig. 8. First line: Results for the sum of 9 terms, Configuration 1. Second line: Results with Configuration 2. Left and right part illustrate the initial and optimized accuracy.

7.2   Benchmarks

Transformation of Summations. First we present some exhaustive tests concerning the summations. Our goal is to determine the performance of our tool for all the possible initial parsings of a sum. Let us remark that a sum of n terms has $(2n-1)!!$ evaluation schemes [13, §6.3] which can all have various accuracies. For example, a 9 term sum yields 2 millions evaluation schemes, and a 10 term sum yields almost 40 millions schemes. We performed our benchmarks on all the initial parsings of sums going from 5 to 9 terms. For each parsing we have tested the same four configurations and the two interval widths of value described in Section 7.1. We present the results obtained using the IEEE-754 binary 64 format to perform 9 terms summations with large interval width (other interval widths yield similar observations and this configuration presents the most significant results of our benchmarks).

Our results are depict by histograms organized as follows: The x-axis indicates the roundoff error on the result of the evaluation of one summation (i.e. for a specific parsing) using the configuration mentioned in the caption and the y-axis indicates how many parsings among all the initial parsings have introduced the corresponding roundoff error (note that many parsings yield the same error, for instance about $3,5 \cdot 10^6$ yield an absolute error of magnitude 64 in the first histogram of figure 1). We have first performed an analysis to determine the

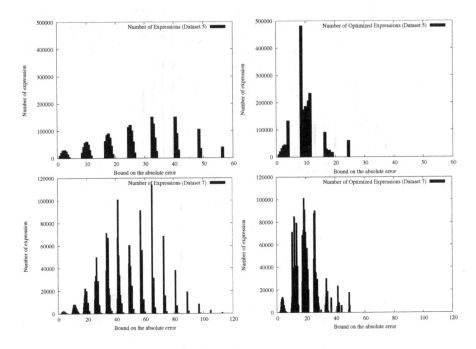

Fig. 9. Sum of 9 terms for configurations 3 and 4 (first and second line resp.)

maximal error bound on each source sum. This corresponds to the leftmost histograms of Figures 1 and 9. Then we have applied our tool to each source sum with the same data in order to obtain the error bounds on the optimized sums. The right-hand side of Figure 1 gives the number of sums corresponding to each accuracy after program transformation. Intuitively, the more the bars are shifted to the left, the better it is. In all the figures presented in this section, both the leftmost and rightmost histograms of each line have the same scale.

First, let us remark that, initially, the distribution of the errors is similar for each configuration (leftmost histograms of figures 1 and 9). The distribution looks like gaussian: There are few optimal parsings (leftmost bar) and few parsings returning the worst accuracy (rightmost bar). Remark that on configurations 1, 3 and 4 our tool is able to shift the gaussian-like distribution of the bars to the left, which corresponds to an average gain of 50% of accuracy.

For each sum in Configuration 2 our tool is able to produce a parsing of optimal accuracy. This result is due to how we generate code when we reify an abstraction box: We perform a greedy association of terms and, in the case of positive values, it corresponds to sorting them by increasing order of magnitude which is the optimal solution in this case.

Transformation of Polynomials. We focus now on the transformation of monovariate polynomials. Polynomials are pervasives in numerical codes yet it is less famous that numerical errors arise during their evaluation close to a root

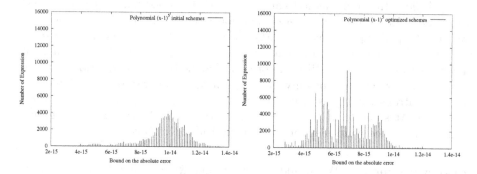

Fig. 10. Leftmost histogram illustrates the initial accuracy of the polynomials $P^5(x)$, the rightmost histogram yields the accuracy of the optimized one

(and even more close to a multiple root [7]). We have tested exhaustively all the polynomials defined by $P^n(x) = \sum_{k=0}^{n}(-1)^k \times \binom{n}{k} \times x^k$ which correspond to the developed form of the function $(x-1)^n$. In our source expressions, x^n is written as the product $\prod_{i=1}^{n} x$. We let n range from 2 to 5. The variable x is set to an interval around 1 ± 10^{-12} in the IEEE-754 binary 64 format. To grasp the combinatorial explosion in the number of ways to evaluate the polynomial, note that for $n = 5$ there are 2.3 million distinct schemes, and for $n = 6$ there are 1.3 billion schemes [13, §6.2.2]. Left part of Figure 10 shows the error distribution of the initial schemes of $P^5(x)$ and the right part shows the error distribution of the optimized schemes. We can see that initially most of the schemes induces a rounding error which is between $8.0 \cdot 10^{-15}$ and $1.2 \cdot 10^{-14}$. Our tool produces optimized schemes of $P^5(x)$ with an error bound between $4.0 \cdot 10^{-15}$ and $9.0 \cdot 10^{-15}$, which represents a 25% to 50% improvement of the numerical accuracy.

8   Conclusion

In this article, we have introduced a new technique to represent a large set of mathematically equal arithmetic expressions. Our goal is to improve the numerical accuracy of an expression in floating-point arithmetic. We have define an abstract intermediate representation called APEG which represents very large set of arithmetic expressions that are equal to an original one. We construct APEGs by using only deterministic and polynomial functions, which allow us to represent an exponential number of equal expressions of very various shapes. The correctness is based on a Galois connection between the collecting semantics of transformations of arithmetic expressions and our abstract domain of APEG. Our experimental results show that, statistically, the roundoff error on summations may be reduced by 40% to 50% and by 20% for polynomials. We intend to present in more details the approach we use to explore APEGs and select expressions, as well as the implementation of our tool.

We believe that our method can be improved and extended in many ways. First, we want to introduce more expansion functions in order to increase the variety of equal expressions in APEGs. We already think about defining some expansion functions to achieve partial regroupings of identical terms in a sum. Then we want to extend APEGs in order to handle the transformation of whole pieces of programs and not only isolated arithmetic expressions. We intend to handle control structure as well as recursive definitions of variables or iteration structure. At short term, we aim at transforming small standalone programs such as embedded controllers or small numerical algorithms.

Acknowledgments. We would like to thank Radhia and Patrick Cousot, Damien Massé and all the members of the Abstraction team for inspiring discussions about various aspects of this work.

References

1. ANSI/IEEE. IEEE Standard for Binary Floating-point Arithmetic, std 754-2008 edition (2008)
2. Cousot, P., Cousot, R.: Abstract interpretation: A unified lattice model for static analysis of programs by construction of approximations of fixed points. In: POPL, pp. 238–252. ACM (1977)
3. Cousot, P., Cousot, R.: Systematic design of program transformation frameworks by abstract interpretation. In: POPL, pp. 178–190. ACM (2002)
4. Delmas, D., Goubault, E., Putot, S., Souyris, J., Tekkal, K., Védrine, F.: Towards an Industrial Use of FLUCTUAT on Safety-Critical Avionics Software. In: Alpuente, M., Cook, B., Joubert, C. (eds.) FMICS 2009. LNCS, vol. 5825, pp. 53–69. Springer, Heidelberg (2009)
5. Putot, S., Goubault, É., Martel, M.: Static Analysis-Based Validation of Floating-Point Computations. In: Alt, R., Frommer, A., Kearfott, R.B., Luther, W. (eds.) Numerical Software with Result Verification. LNCS, vol. 2991, pp. 306–313. Springer, Heidelberg (2004)
6. Goubault, E., Putot, S.: Static Analysis of Finite Precision Computations. In: Jhala, R., Schmidt, D. (eds.) VMCAI 2011. LNCS, vol. 6538, pp. 232–247. Springer, Heidelberg (2011)
7. Higham, N.J.: Accuracy and Stability of Numerical Algorithms, 2nd edn. Society for Industrial and Applied Mathematics, Philadelphia (2002)
8. Langlois, P., Martel, M., Thévenoux, L.: Accuracy Versus Time: A Case Study with Summation Algorithms. In: PASCO, pp. 121–130. ACM (2010)
9. Martel, M.: Semantics of roundoff error propagation in finite precision calculations. Journal of Higher Order and Symbolic Computation 19, 7–30 (2006)
10. Martel, M.: Semantics-Based Transformation of Arithmetic Expressions. In: Riis Nielson, H., Filé, G. (eds.) SAS 2007. LNCS, vol. 4634, pp. 298–314. Springer, Heidelberg (2007)
11. Martel, M.: Enhancing the implementation of mathematical formulas for fixed-point and floating-point arithmetics. Journal of Formal Methods in System Design 35, 265–278 (2009)
12. Monniaux, D.: The pitfalls of verifying floating-point computations. ACM Transactions of Programming Language Systems (TOPLAS) 30(3), 12 (2008)

13. Mouilleron, C.: Efficient computation with structured matrices and arithmetic expressions. PhD thesis, Université de Lyon–ENS de Lyon (November 2011)
14. Muller, J.-M.: On the definition of ulp(x). Technical Report 5504, INRIA (2005)
15. Muller, J.-M., Brisebarre, N., de Dinechin, F., Jeannerod, C.-P., Lefèvre, V., Melquiond, G., Revol, N., Stehlé, D., Torres, S.: Handbook of Floating-Point Arithmetic. Birkhäuser, Boston (2010)
16. Ogita, T., Rump, S.M., Oishi, S.: Accurate sum and dot product. SIAM Journal on Scientific Computing (SISC) 26(6), 1955–1988 (2005)
17. Tate, R., Stepp, M., Tatlock, Z., Lerner, S.: Equality saturation: A new approach to optimization. In: POPL, pp. 264–276. ACM (2009)
18. Torbjorn Granlund and the GMP development team. The GNU Multiple Precision Arithmetic Library, 5.0.2 edn. (2011), http://gmplib.org
19. Zhu, Y.-K., Hayes, W.B.: Algorithm 908: Online exact summation of floating-point streams. Transactions on Mathematical Software 37(3), 1–13 (2010)

An Abstract Domain
to Infer Types over Zones in Spreadsheets⋆

Tie Cheng[1,2,3] and Xavier Rival[1,2]

[1] École Normale Supérieure, Paris, France
[2] INRIA Paris–Rocquencourt, France
[3] École Polytechnique, Palaiseau, France
{tie.cheng,xavier.rival}@ens.fr

Abstract. Spreadsheet languages are very commonly used, by large user bases, yet they are error prone. However, many semantic issues and errors could be avoided by enforcing a stricter type discipline. As declaring and specifying type information would represent a prohibitive amount of work for users, we propose an abstract interpretation based static analysis for spreadsheet programs that infers type constraints over zones of spreadsheets, viewed as two-dimensional arrays. Our abstract domain consists in a cardinal power from a numerical abstraction describing zones in a spreadsheet to an abstraction of cell values, including type properties. We formalize this abstract domain and its operators (transfer functions, join, widening and reduction) as well as a static analysis for a simplified spreadsheet language. Last, we propose a representation for abstract values and present an implementation of our analysis.

1 Introduction

Spreadsheet softwares such as Excel or OpenOffice are very widely used, and include not only an interface to visualize and manipulate two-dimensional arrays of cells but also a programming language which permits complex calculations. For instance, Excel includes Visual Basic for Applications (VBA) and OpenOffice includes a Basic like language.

These programming languages are used in many industrial and financial areas for important applications such as statistics, organization and management. Reports of spreadsheet related errors appear in the global media at a fairly consistent rate. It is not surprising that, as an example, a consulting firm, Coopers and Lybrand in England, found that 90% of all spreadsheets with more than 150 rows that it audited contained errors [1]. Spreadsheet errors result in various problems such as additional audit costs, money loss, false information to public, wrong decision making, etc. As the risks they incur are not considered acceptable, the defects in such applications have attracted increasing attention from communities such as Excel advanced users and IT professionals.

⋆ The research leading to these results has received funding from the European Research Council under the European Union's seventh framework programme (FP7/2007-2013), grant agreement 278673, Project MemCAD.

A. Miné and D. Schmidt (Eds.): SAS 2012, LNCS 7460, pp. 94–110, 2012.

Various techniques were considered in order to tackle spreadsheet risks. One class of existing work enhances the functional aspect of spreadsheets, viewed as a first-order functional environment [2,3,4,5]. Another body of work attempts to improving quality of spreadsheets using model-driven engineering spreadsheet development environments [6,7,8,9]. Last, ad hoc methods [10,11,12] were proposed to detect specific kinds of problems, using most of the time algorithms with no mathematical foundation, that neither sound nor complete. One major drawback of the existing work is that currently they only consider spreadsheet interface, but not consider applications attached to the spreadsheets, which are written e.g., in VBA.

In this paper, we address the lack of static types in current spreadsheet applications. For instance, it is impossible to declare abstract types (e.g. integer, boolean, etc.) for a cell in Microsoft Excel; a value of any type may be assigned to any cell at any time. This feature of spreadsheet applications may provide users with a high level of flexibility but it becomes a serious source of errors which would be avoided in well typed languages.

Therefore, we verify the absence of some class of type errors to improve the safety of spreadsheet programs, that existing research in enhancing spreadsheet languages or focusing on spreadsheet interface hardly deals with. Our approach is based on a static analysis by abstract interpretation, which guarantees the soundness of our approach and makes it possible to existing abstract domains and tools.

More precisely, our analysis aims at inferring type information about zones in spreadsheets, taking into account an initial condition on the spreadsheet, and all possible sequences of operations of the associated programs. We make the following contributions:

- we introduce an abstract domain to express type properties of array zones, based on a cardinal power of zone abstractions and type abstractions (Sect. 4);
- we propose a set of transfer functions and join and widening operators for the analysis of spreadsheet programs (Sect. 5);
- we validate our approach using a prototype implementation (Sect. 6) with the analysis of simple spreadsheet programs.

2   Overview

We show a simple program 1 in a restricted spreadsheet language that we consider in the paper. Although its syntax is not exactly the same as that of VBA or Basic in OpenOffice, its task of selecting data sharing certain properties is realistic and common in practice. The rectangle zone $[1, 100] \times [1, 1]$ of the sheet has already been initialized to integer values. The main procedure goes through column 1, for each cell, we compare its value to 9 and assign the boolean result to the cell in the same line in column 2. If the integer value is less than 9, it is copied to the first empty cell in column 3. Our analyzer infers invariants about types of different parts of the sheet, and it also detects different sorts of type conflicts hidden in the code, which may result in strange behaviors in VBA for instance. The index error in line 16, operand error in line 17, condition error in line 18 and assignment error in line 21 will be more explained further.

1 **program**		12	$j := j + 1$
2 **var**		13	**end fi**
3 i, j : int;		14	$i := i + 1$
4 **name**		15	**od**;
5 $([1, 100], [1, 1])$: int;		16	$i :=$ **Sheet**$(\text{true}, 1)$;
6 **begin**		17	$i := 1 +$ **Sheet**$(11, 2)$;
7 $i := 1; j := 1$;		18	**if Sheet**$(j, 3)$ **then**
8 **while** $i < 51$ **do**		19	$j := 1$ **else**
9 **Sheet**$(i, 2) :=$ **Sheet**$(i, 1) < 9$;		20	$j := 2$ **fi**
10 **if Sheet**$(i, 2)$ **then begin**		21	**Sheet**$(i - 1, 1) :=$ true
11 **Sheet**$(j, 3) :=$ **Sheet**$(i, 1)$;		22	**end.**

Fig. 1. An example program

The concrete states refer to the concrete value of variables and the run-time contents of the sheet cells. Figure 2 represents a concrete state of loop between line 8 and line 9. Precisely, the cells $[1, 7] \times [2, 2]$ store boolean values, the cells $[1, 4] \times [3, 3]$ store integer values. $[1, 100] \times [1, 1]$ is reserved by the declaration **name** at lines 4 and 5 of the program, which means only integer values should be stored in that area.

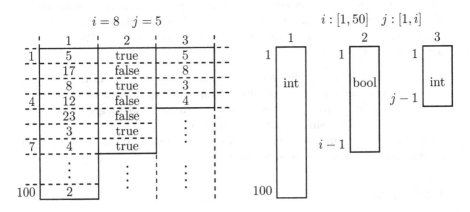

Fig. 2. A concrete state   **Fig. 3.** An abstract state

In order to verify that no illegal operation will be performed in the spreadsheet program due to type issue, and that type properties in the reserved zone are not violated, the analysis should relate type information to spreadsheet cells. Attaching a type predicate to each cell would not be effective, and it would not be even doable for spreadsheet regions of non fixed size. Moreover, users naturally view a spreadsheet as a set of zones where they store homogeneous sorts of data. Therefore, we consider an abstraction, where type information are attached to spreadsheet zones. Precisely, an abstract state will consist in a pair made of an abstraction of integer variables, and an abstraction of type properties of sheet cells (e.g.. Figure 3 is an intuitive image of the abstract state corresponding to the concrete state of Figure 2). The abstraction of integer variables relies on inequality constraints over variables and constants. The abstraction of type properties of sheet cells consists in a form of cardinal power [13] from the abstraction of sheet zones to type properties, where zones are characterized by set of constraints tying cell coordinates to program variables. Although analyzing the simple program, chosen to facilitate the illustration, needs only column abstraction, the abstraction of a large variety of zones is necessary in practice and can be achieved by our domain (e.g. rectangular abstraction is performed to analyze programs in Sect. 6).

3 Spreadsheet Programs

In this paper, we focus on a restricted spreadsheet language, where instructions are assignments, "if" and "while" statements, with data-types ranging in $\mathbb{T} = \{\text{int}, \text{bool}, \ldots\}$. We assume program variables all have type int, whereas spreadsheet cells may store values of any type. Compared to a classical imperative language, our language has two specific features. First, the keyword "**Sheet**" denotes a cell in the spreadsheet. For instance, expression "**Sheet**(br, bc)" evaluates into the value stored in cell (br, bc); "**Sheet**$(br, bc) := e$" affects the value of e to the cell (br, bc). In the paper, we restrict to cell indexes (br and bc) which are either an integer constant c or an integer variable plus an integer constant $x + c$. Other variables are assumed to be declared at the beginning of the program. Second, spreadsheet areas can be reserved to a type by the keyword "**name**". For instance, "**name** $([1, 100], [1, 1]) : \text{int}$" in Program 1 means that only integer values should be stored in that area (storing a value of another type would be considered a semantic error).

In the following, we let $\mathbb{V}$ (resp., $\mathbb{V}_i$) denote the set of values (resp., integer values). We let $\mathbb{X}$ denote the set of program variables, augmented with two special variables $\overline{x}, \overline{y}$ which we will use to express relations over cell indexes. Moreover, $\mathbb{N}^2$ represents the set of cells. We use an operational semantics, which collects all program executions. An execution is a sequence of states (or trace), where a state is a pair made of a control state l and a memory state $\rho = (\rho_v, \rho_s)$, where $\rho_v : \mathbb{X} \to \mathbb{V}_i$ and $\rho_s : \mathbb{N}^2 \to \mathbb{V}$ are respectively functions mapping integer variables and sheet cells into values. We let $\to$ denote the transition relation from one state to another (modelling one step of computation) and Ω represent the error state (no transition from Ω is possible). For a detailed presentation of the syntax and concrete semantics of our restricted spreadsheet language, see [14].

4 Abstract Domain

In this section, we formalize the abstract domain used in our analysis as a cardinal power. First, we consider in Sect. 4.1 the abstraction of a set of spreadsheets using one type and constraints of one zone. Then, we show the case of a set of zones in Sect. 4.2. Last, we specialize our abstraction using Difference-Bound Matrices (DBMs) as a base abstraction in Sect. 4.3.

4.1   Abstraction of a Typed Zone

We assume a numerical abstract domain $\mathbb{D}_i^\sharp$ is fixed for the abstraction of numerical variables, with a concretization function $\gamma_i : \mathbb{D}_i^\sharp \to \mathcal{P}(\mathbb{X} \to \mathbb{V}_i)$.

Abstraction of a Typed Zone. An abstract value in the typed zone abstract domain $\mathbb{D}_{z,1}^\sharp$ consists in a pair $(\mathcal{Z}, t)$ where $\mathcal{Z} \in \mathbb{D}_i^\sharp$ describes a set of numerical constraints (binding $\overline{x}, \overline{y}$ to other variables and constants in the store) and t is a data-type. The meaning of such an abstract value is that all cells the coordinates $(\overline{x}, \overline{y})$ of which satisfy constraints $\mathcal{Z}$ store a value of type t. More formally, this yields the concretization relation below:

$$\gamma_{z,1}(\mathcal{Z}, t) \stackrel{\triangle}{=} \{(\rho_v, \rho_s) \mid \forall x, y \in \mathbb{N}^2, \rho_v \in \gamma_i(\mathcal{Z}|_{\overline{x}=x, \overline{y}=y}) \Rightarrow \rho_s(x,y) : t\}$$

The concrete state shown in Figure 2 can be approximated by the following typed zone abstract elements:

- $(\mathcal{Z}_0, t_0)$ where $\mathcal{Z}_0 = 1 \leq \overline{x} \wedge \overline{x} \leq 100 \wedge \overline{y} = 1$ and $t_0 = \text{int}$
- $(\mathcal{Z}_1, t_1)$ where $\mathcal{Z}_1 = 1 \leq \overline{x} \wedge \overline{x} \leq i - 1 \wedge \overline{y} = 2$ and $t_1 = \text{bool}$
- $(\mathcal{Z}_2, t_2)$ where $\mathcal{Z}_2 = 1 \leq \overline{x} \wedge \overline{x} \leq j - 1 \wedge \overline{y} = 3$ and $t_2 = \text{int}$

This construction is an abstraction of the cardinal power [13]. Indeed the cardinal power abstract domain would collect all monotone function from an abstraction of zones into a type domain. We perform here an additional step of abstraction, where functions from zones to types are approximated with only one pair leaving the other zones unconstrained.

Product Abstraction. In practice, we always consider an abstraction over the variables together with an abstraction of the spreadsheet contents, using a product domain $\mathbb{D}_{\times,1}^\sharp = \mathbb{D}_i^\sharp \times \mathbb{D}_{z,1}^\sharp$. An abstract value consists in a pair $(\mathcal{V}, \{(\mathcal{Z}, t)\})$ where $\mathcal{V} \in \mathbb{D}_i^\sharp$ describes constraints over variables and $(\mathcal{Z}, t) \in \mathbb{D}_{z,1}^\sharp$ describes constraints over one zone and its type. Therefore, the combined domain concretization boils down to

$$\gamma_{\times,1}(\mathcal{V}, \{(\mathcal{Z}, t)\}) \stackrel{\triangle}{=} \{(\rho_v, \rho_s) \mid \rho_v \in \gamma_i(\mathcal{V}) \wedge (\rho_v, \rho_s) \in \gamma_{z,1}(\mathcal{Z}, t)\}$$

As an example, the concrete state shown in Figure 2 can be approximated by abstract state $(\mathcal{V}, \{(\mathcal{Z}, t)\}))$ where $\mathcal{V} = 1 \leq i \wedge i \leq 50 \wedge 1 \leq j \wedge j \leq i$, $\mathcal{Z} = 1 \leq \overline{x} \wedge \overline{x} \leq 100 \wedge \overline{y} = 1$ and $t = \text{int}$. We will consider the case of a combined abstraction with several typed zones in Sect. 4.2, after studying some properties of the product abstraction.

Properties. The definition of $\gamma_{z,1}$ and $\gamma_\times$ allows to prove the properties below:

1. Propagating constraints over variables into the zone abstraction preserves concretization: $\gamma_\times(\mathcal{V}, \{(\mathcal{Z}, t)\}) = \gamma_\times(\mathcal{V}, \{(\mathcal{Z} \sqcap \mathcal{V}, t)\})$, where $\sqcap$ simply joins two sets of constraints.

2. Replacing the abstraction of variables (resp. zones) with an equivalent abstraction preserves concretization: if $\gamma_i(\mathcal{V}) = \gamma_i(\mathcal{V}') \wedge \gamma_i(\mathcal{Z}) = \gamma_i(\mathcal{Z}')$ then $\gamma_\times(\mathcal{V}, \{(\mathcal{Z}, t)\}) = \gamma_\times(\mathcal{V}', \{(\mathcal{Z}', t)\})$

3. Replacing the abstraction of variables with a weaker abstraction results in a weaker abstract state: if $\gamma_i(\mathcal{V}) \subseteq \gamma_i(\mathcal{V}')$ then $\gamma_\times(\mathcal{V}, \{(\mathcal{Z}, t)\}) \subseteq \gamma_\times(\mathcal{V}', \{(\mathcal{Z}, t)\})$

4. Replacing the zone abstraction with a weaker abstraction results in a stronger abstract state: if $\gamma_i(\mathcal{Z}) \subseteq \gamma_i(\mathcal{Z}')$ then $\gamma_\times(\mathcal{V}, \{(\mathcal{Z}, t)\}) \supseteq \gamma_\times(\mathcal{V}, \{(\mathcal{Z}', t)\})$

4.2 Abstraction of a Set of Typed Zones

In practice, we need to bind several distinct zones in the spreadsheet to type information. For instance, three zones are needed to faithfully abstract the concrete state of Figure 2. Therefore, we define $\mathbb{D}_Z^\sharp$ as the set of finite sets of elements of $\mathbb{D}_{z,1}^\sharp$, with concretization $\gamma_\mathbf{Z}$ defined by:

$$\gamma_\mathbf{Z}(\{(\mathcal{Z}_0, t_0), \ldots, (\mathcal{Z}_n, t_n)\}) \triangleq \bigcap_{0 \leq k \leq n} \gamma_{z,1}(\mathcal{Z}_k, t_k)$$

The definition of the product domain given in Sect. 4.1 extends in a straightforward manner, and the properties mentioned in Sect. 4.1 still hold:

$$\gamma_\times(\mathcal{V}, \{(\mathcal{Z}_0, t_0), \ldots, (\mathcal{Z}_n, t_n)\})$$
$$\triangleq \{(\rho_v, \rho_s) \mid \rho_v \in \gamma_i(\mathcal{V}) \wedge (\rho_v, \rho_s) \in \gamma_\mathbf{Z}(\{(\mathcal{Z}_0, t_0), \ldots, (\mathcal{Z}_n, t_n)\})\}$$

Then, the concrete state of Figure 2 can be described by the abstract state $(\mathcal{V}, \{(\mathcal{Z}_0, t_0), (\mathcal{Z}_1, t_1), (\mathcal{Z}_2, t_2)\})$ with the notations used in Sect. 4.1. This abstract state actually corresponds to Figure 3.

4.3 An Instantiation with Difference-Bound Matrices

When abstracting array properties, bounds of the form c or $x + c$ are often expressive enough to capture large classes of invariants. Similarly, we found that such bounds are usually adequate to describe spreadsheet zones. This suggests using an abstraction based on Difference-Bound Matrices (DBM) (a weaker form of octagons [15], where constraints are either of the form $c \leq x$, $x \leq c$ or $x - y \leq c$) in order to describe zones. We actually do not need full expressiveness of DBMs in order to describe zones, as we will be interested only in relations that relate an index variable ($\bar{x}$ or $\bar{y}$) to a constant or an expression of the form $x + c$. Therefore, in the following, we set the following abstraction:

- program variables abstractions ($\mathcal{V}$) are described by DBMs;
- zones abstractions ($\mathcal{Z}$) are described by a weaker form of DBMs, where no relation among pairs of variables $u, v \notin \{\bar{x}, \bar{y}\}$ is represented.

A large variety of zones can be expressed using this abstraction, including in particular rectangular ($c_0 \leq \bar{x} \leq c_1, c_2 \leq \bar{y} \leq c_3$), triangular ($c_0 \leq \bar{x} \leq \bar{y}, c_0 \leq \bar{y} \leq c_3$), and trapezoidal ($c_0 \leq \bar{x} \leq \bar{y} + c_1, c_2 \leq \bar{y} \leq c_3$) zones. As shown in Sect. 4.1, this set of constraints allows us to describe all zones relevant in the example program of Fig. 1.

In this step, the classical representation of DBMs using matrices of difference appears unnecessarily heavy for zone constraints $\mathcal{Z}_p$, as no relation needs to be stored for pairs of program variables in $\mathcal{Z}_p$. This leads us to a hollow representation of the $\mathcal{Z}_p$ DBMs, where the submatrix corresponding to the integer variables is removed. We call this representation "Matrix Minus Matrix" (or MMM).

For instance, letting $\mathbf{d}$ (resp., $\mathbf{m}$) denote a DBM (resp., MMM) in the following, all concrete states at the beginning of line 9 in Program 1 can be over-approximated by the abstract value $(\mathbf{d}, \{(\mathbf{m}_0, \text{int}), (\mathbf{m}_1, \text{bool}), (\mathbf{m}_2, \text{int})\})$ (depicted in Figure 3), where

$\mathbf{d} =$

	i	j	0
i	0	0	-1
j	$+\infty$	0	-1
0	50	$+\infty$	0

$\mathbf{m}_0 =$

	$\overline{x}$	$\overline{y}$	i	j	0
$\overline{x}$	0	$+\infty$	$+\infty$	$+\infty$	-1
$\overline{y}$	$+\infty$	0	$+\infty$	$+\infty$	-1
i	$+\infty$	$+\infty$			
j	$+\infty$	$+\infty$			
0	100	1			

$\mathbf{m}_1 =$

	$\overline{x}$	$\overline{y}$	i	j	0
$\overline{x}$	0	$+\infty$	$+\infty$	$+\infty$	-1
$\overline{y}$	$+\infty$	0	$+\infty$	$+\infty$	-2
i	-1	$+\infty$			
j	$+\infty$	$+\infty$			
0	$+\infty$	2			

$\mathbf{m}_2 =$

$\dots$

5   Domain Operations

In this section, we describe the operations of the domain based on DBM and MMM structures, including transfer functions, reduction, union and widening.

5.1   Transfer Functions

Transfer functions have two purposes:

- compute a sound post-condition for a program statement, that is accounting for all concrete states reachable after executing the statement from a given pre-state;
- report alarms for operations that could not be proved exempt of type error.

The alarm reporting reduces to the checking that all operations are applied to data of valid type. For instance, if a program statement contains expression $i + \mathbf{Sheet}(k, l)$, and the analysis current abstract state at that point is of the form $(\mathbf{d}, \{(\mathbf{m}_0, t_0), \dots, (\mathbf{m}_n, t_n)\})$, then it should check that for all $\rho_v \in \gamma_i(\mathbf{d})$ there exists j such that $0 \leq j \leq n$ and $(\overline{x} = k|_{\rho_v}, \overline{y} = l|_{\rho_v}) \in \mathbf{m}_j|_{\rho_v}$, which guarantees that cell $\mathbf{Sheet}(k, l)$ has integer type. In the following, we discuss the computation of post-conditions only.

Assignment Transfer Function. Assignment instructions are either of the form $x := e$ where x is a program variable and e is an expression or of the form $\mathbf{Sheet}(e_0, e_1) := e$ where e_0, e_1 and e are expressions. In the first case, the standard assignment transfer function of DBMs shown in [15] leads to define a sound result for transfer function $\mathbf{assign}^\sharp$ in the combined domain (when the right hand side e reads a spreadsheet cell, we conservatively assume this read operation may return any possible value, as our abstraction does not carry a precise information about the values stored in the spreadsheet besides type).

In the second case, the typed zones abstractions need to be updated. Let us assume we are computing an abstract post-condition for abstract state $X^\sharp = (\mathbf{d}, \{(\mathbf{m}_0, t_0), \ldots, (\mathbf{m}_n, t_n)\})$. Then:

- when the cell modified in the assignment can be proved to belong to zone $\mathbf{m}_k$ the type of the right hand side is t_k, then typed zone abstractions do not need be modified, and $X^\sharp$ is a valid abstract post-condition;
- otherwise zones need be updated, by removing zone information that may not be preserved in the assignment operation and adding a new zone reduced to the cell that has been modified.

Let us illustrate by an example with an abstract value $X^\sharp = (\mathbf{d}, \{(\mathbf{m}, t)\}) = (\{i : [3,5]\}, \{(\{\overline{x} : [1,i], \overline{y} : [1,3]\}, \text{int})\})$. For $\mathbf{Sheet}(i-1, 2) := 5$, the assignment transfer function infers that $\gamma_i(\overline{x} = i - 1 \wedge \overline{y} = 2) \subseteq \gamma_i(\mathbf{m})$ under $\mathbf{d} = \{i : [3,5]\}$, and the type of the expression on the right of the assignment is same as the one of the zone, so $X^\sharp$ remains the same. However, for $\mathbf{Sheet}(i-1, 2) := \text{true}$, the type of the expression of the assignment value is different, if $\mathbf{Sheet}(i-1, 2)$ is within a zone reserved to int, an assignment error Ω_{assign} will be raised, otherwise the abstract zone needs to be split as shown below.

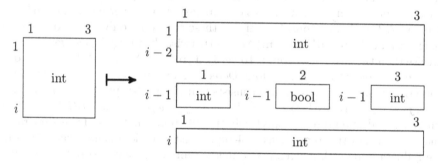

Many zone splitting strategies could be used, e.g. either vertically first or horizontally first. All strategies would yield a sound result. Reduction (Sect. 5.2) tends to remove unnecessary partitions, so that the choice of the splitting strategy is not so crucial.

Condition Test Transfer Function. Condition tests are analyzed with a $\mathbf{guard}^\sharp$ abstract function, which inputs an abstract state $X^\sharp$ and a condition c and computes an over-approximation of the concrete states in $\gamma_{\times}(X^\sharp)$ such that c evaluates to true. When c involves only program variables, we simply let $\mathbf{guard}^\sharp$ call the condition test function of DBMs [15]. When c involves spreadsheet cells, we let it return $X^\sharp$ (which is always a sound result) as our abstraction ignores spreadsheet values.

5.2 Reduction

As we can see in Sect. 5.1, assignments may generate additional abstract zones, resulting in increasingly large sets of zones. For instance, constraints $(\{\overline{x} : [1, i-1], \overline{y} = 2\}, \text{bool}), \{(\{\overline{x} = i, \overline{y} = 2\}, \text{bool})\}$ could be described by just one constraint. Performing this simplification is the purpose of a (partial) reduction operator, by merging zones when this can be done with no loss in precision.

In the following we let $\mathbf{d}^*$ denote the *closure* of $\mathbf{d}$, the *closure* $\mathbf{m}^*$ *associated with* $\mathbf{d}^*$ is obtained by computing $\mathbf{m}^*$ from the information in both $\mathbf{m}$ and $\mathbf{d}^*$. We write $\vee$ for the point-wise least upper bound over DBMs (resp., MMMs), thus $(\mathbf{d} \vee \mathbf{d}')_{ij} = \max(\mathbf{d}_{ij}, \mathbf{d}'_{ij})$ (resp., $(\mathbf{m} \vee \mathbf{m}')_{ij} = \max(\mathbf{m}_{ij}, \mathbf{m}'_{ij})$). We allow the intersection $\wedge$ over an MMM and a DBM if their sizes and the variables they describe are consistent, the result is a DBM. We define the intersection of a $(h \times l - h' \times l')$ MMM $\mathbf{m}$ and a $h' \times l'$ DBM $\mathbf{d}$ by:

$$\begin{cases} \mathbf{d}'_{i+h-h',j+l-l'} \stackrel{\triangle}{=} \mathbf{d}_{ij} & \text{if } (i,j) \in [1 \times h'] \times [1 \times l'] \\ \mathbf{d}'_{ij} \stackrel{\triangle}{=} \mathbf{m}_{ij} & \text{otherwise} \end{cases}$$

We assume an abstract value $(\mathbf{d}, \{(\mathbf{m}_0, t_0), \ldots, (\mathbf{m}_n, t_n)\})$ is given. Let us first look at a pair of its zones $(\mathbf{m}_i, t_i)$ and $(\mathbf{m}_j, t_j)$. Obviously we don't consider merging the two zones if $t_i \neq t_j$. In the other case, we first carry out the normalization, and obtain the closures $\mathbf{d}^*$, $\mathbf{m}_i^*$ and $\mathbf{m}_j^*$ associated with $\mathbf{d}^*$. Then we let $\mathbf{m}^\vee$ be the result of $\mathbf{m}_i^* \vee \mathbf{m}_j^*$, which ensures that $\mathbf{m}^\vee \wedge \mathbf{d}^*$ is an upper bound for $(\mathbf{m}_i^* \wedge \mathbf{d}^*)$ and $(\mathbf{m}_j^* \wedge \mathbf{d}^*)$. But we consider merging these two zones only when $(\mathbf{m}^\vee \wedge \mathbf{d}^*)$ is an exact join of $(\mathbf{m}_i^* \wedge \mathbf{d}^*)$ and $(\mathbf{m}_j^* \wedge \mathbf{d}^*)$, otherwise the merged zone would be less precise than the two initial zones. To verify if $(\mathbf{m}^\vee \wedge \mathbf{d}^*) = (\mathbf{m}_i^* \wedge \mathbf{d}^*) \vee (\mathbf{m}_j^* \wedge \mathbf{d}^*)$, we use the algorithm "Exact Join Detection for Integer Bounded Difference Shapes" introduced in [16], which consists in finding a 4-tuple (i, j, l, k) such that $w_1(i,j) < w_2(i,j) \wedge w_2(k,l) < w_1(k,l) \wedge w_1(i,j) + w_2(k,l) + 2 \leq w(i,l) + w(k,j)$, where w_k and w represent respectively the difference matrices of the 2 operands and the result of the join. If such a 4-tuple exists, the join is not exact. Overall, the reduction algorithm attempts to merge pairs of zone constraints with equal type. Then, the merging rule of two abstract typed zones writes down:

$$\{(\mathbf{m}_i, t_i), (\mathbf{m}_j, t_j)\} \xrightarrow{\substack{t_i = t_j \text{ and} \\ (\mathbf{m}^\vee \wedge \mathbf{d}^*) \text{ is an exact join of } (\mathbf{m}_i^* \wedge \mathbf{d}^*) \text{ and } (\mathbf{m}_j^* \wedge \mathbf{d}^*)}} \{(\mathbf{m}^\vee, t_i)\}$$

where $\mathbf{m}^\vee \stackrel{\triangle}{=} \mathbf{m}_i \vee \mathbf{m}_j$. In the above example, the following reduction can be performed:

$$(\{i : [1, +\infty]\}, \{(\{\overline{x} : [1, i-1], \overline{y} = 2\}, \text{bool}); \{(\{x = i, y = 2\}, \text{bool})\})$$
$$\longrightarrow (\{i : [1, +\infty]\}, \{(\{\overline{x} : [1, i], \overline{y} = 2\}, \text{bool})\})$$

Now given the whole abstract value $(\mathbf{d}, \{(\mathbf{m}_0, t_0), \ldots, (\mathbf{m}_n, t_n)\})$ which may contain several typed zones, we compute the normalization of all the zones at once. Then reduction picks one zone $\mathcal{Z}_i$, and goes through the other zones, looks for a zone that can be merged with $\mathcal{Z}_i$. A join needs to be calculated, and if the join is exact, the reduction merges both zones into one new zone and proceeds with the other zones. The complexity of a normalization (Floyd-Warshall algorithm) is $O(l^3)$, where l is the length of the side of $\mathbf{m}_k$ (number of program and index variables). The most costly part of the algorithm, the exact join detection, has a worst-case complexity bound in $O(l^3 + r_1 r_2)$, where r_k is the number of edges in difference matrix w_r, but the detection may finish quickly when the join is not exact, which occurs often in practice. Overall the worst-case complexity of the reduction is $O(n^2 \times l^3)$. The algorithm is sound:

Theorem 1 (Soundness). $r^\sharp$ *is an abstract reduction,*

$$\gamma_\times (X^\sharp) \subseteq \gamma_\times (r^\sharp(X^\sharp))$$

5.3   Upper Bound Operator

We now propose an algorithm to compute upper bounds for typed zone constraints, which will also serve as a basis for a widening operator (Sect. 5.4).

We assume two abstract values $X_0^\sharp, X_1^\sharp \in \mathbb{D}_\times^\sharp$ are given, and we assume $X_k^\sharp = (\mathbf{d}_k, \{(\mathbf{m}_k, t)\})$ (the cases where types do not match or where there are several zones will be discussed afterward). Property 3 and Property 4 (Sect. 4.1) provide a straightforward way to compute a common over-approximation for $X_0^\sharp$ and $X_1^\sharp$: indeed, if we let $\mathbf{d} = \mathbf{d}_0 \vee \mathbf{d}_1$ and $\mathbf{m} = \mathbf{m}_0 \wedge \mathbf{m}_1$, we clearly have $\gamma_\times (X_i^\sharp) \subseteq \gamma_\times (\mathbf{d}, \{\mathbf{m}, t\})$, thus $X^\sharp = (\mathbf{d}, \{\mathbf{m}, t\})$ provides a sound upper bound.

Unfortunately, this straightforward technique is not very precise. Indeed, let us consider the case of $X_0^\sharp = (\{i : [2,2]\}, \{(\{\overline{x} : [i+6, i+6], \overline{y} = 1\}, \mathrm{int})\})$ and $X_1^\sharp = (\{i : [3,3]\}, \{(\{\overline{x} : [i+5, i+6], \overline{y} = 1\}, \mathrm{int})\})$ (these abstract elements would naturally arise in the first two iterations over a loop that fills a zone with integer values). Then, we obtain $\mathbf{d} = \{i : [2,3]\}$ and $\mathbf{m} = \{\overline{x} : [i+6, i+6], \overline{y} = 1\}$. While the variable abstraction is satisfactory, the zone is not precise: both $X_0^\sharp$ and $X_1^\sharp$ express the existence of a zone of values of type int with bounds $8 \le \overline{x} \le i+6 \wedge \overline{y} = 1$. When $i = 3$, that zone contains two cells, whereas the zone described by $\{\overline{x} : [i+6, i+6], \overline{y} = 1\}$ only remembers that $\mathbf{Sheet}(9, 1)$ has type int, but forgets about $\mathbf{Sheet}(8, 1)$.

In order to avoid such imprecision, the abstract join algorithm should perform some rewriting steps on both inputs before it actually computes the lower bound on zones. In the case of our example, $X_0^\sharp$ is equivalent (in the sense of $\gamma_\times$) to $(\{i : [2,2]\}, \{(\{\overline{x} : [8, i+6], \overline{y} = 1\}, \mathrm{int})\})$ and $X_1^\sharp$ is equivalent to $(\{i : [3,3]\}, \{(\{\overline{x} : [8, i+6], \overline{y} = 1\}, \mathrm{int})\})$. Applying the lower bounds on zone constraints will then produce the desired result. These transformations do not modify the concretization, as shown by Property 2.

For a better illustration, we summarize the general algorithm in Figure 4 and show a step-by-step execution of the algorithm, on the case of the above example in Figure 5. For the sake of simplicity, we omit the constraint $\overline{y} = 1$ as it is appears in both operands and can be handled trivially. So the general algorithm consists of five steps:

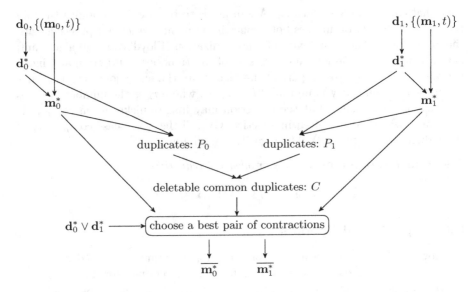

Fig. 4. $(\mathbf{d}_0, \{(\mathbf{m}_0, t)\}) \sqcup^{\sharp} (\mathbf{d}_1, \{(\mathbf{m}_1, t)\}) \triangleq (\mathbf{d}_0^* \vee \mathbf{d}_1^*, \{(\overline{\mathbf{m}_0^*} \wedge \overline{\mathbf{m}_1^*}, t)\})$

– *Normalize.* Given two abstract values $(\mathbf{d}_k, \{(\mathbf{m}_k, t)\})$, we first carry out the normalization, and obtain the closures $\mathbf{d}_k^*$ and $\mathbf{m}_k^*$ associated with $\mathbf{d}_k^*$.

– *Calculate Duplicates.* A difference matrix can be seen as a representation of a directed graph $\mathcal{G} = (\mathcal{V}, \mathcal{A}, w)$ with weighted edges. From its (shortest-path) closure, there are some edges which can be *restored* by other edges. E.g., in $\mathbf{m}_0^* \wedge \mathbf{d}_0^*$, $w(\overline{x}, i) = -6$ is *deletable*, because it can be restored by the sum of $w(\overline{x}, 0) = -8$ and $w(0, i) = 2$. We say $w(\overline{x}, i)$ is a *duplicate* of $w(\overline{x}, 0)$ and $w(0, i)$, and we let $(\overline{x}, i) \leftrightarrow 0$ denote this duplication. A *contraction* $\overline{\mathbf{m}^*}$ of an MMM $\mathbf{m}^*$ *associated with* $\mathbf{d}^*$, refers to an MMM deleting some duplicates, and $\mathbf{m}^*$ can still be restored from $\overline{\mathbf{m}^*} \wedge \mathbf{d}^*$. E.g., $\mathbf{m}_0^* \wedge \mathbf{d}_0^*$ without $w(\overline{x}, i)$ is actually one contraction of $\mathbf{m}_0^* \wedge \mathbf{d}_0^*$. So this step aims at finding the set of all the possible duplicates P_k in $\mathbf{m}_k^* \wedge \mathbf{d}_k^*$.

– *Find Deletable Common Duplicates.* Considering now the 2 operands together, we can find the set of the common duplicates of the 2 operands: $P_0 \cap P_1$. Then some subsets of this set, which are actually some common duplicates, can be deleted from both operands to compute two contractions. This step searches for the set of this kind of subsets that C denotes.

– *Choose a Best Pair of Contractions.* Taking the 2 operands of our example, C contains both $\{(\overline{x}, i), (0, \overline{x})\}$ and $\{(i, \overline{x}), (\overline{x}, 0)\}$. Although the concretization of a contraction is always the same as the one of the original matrix, if we forecast the next step – the intersection of both contractions, the choice of the set of duplicates to delete, resulting in the contractions, makes actually a real difference: Both contractions formed by deleting $\{(\overline{x}, i), (0, \overline{x})\}$ gives a larger intersection than the ones formed by deleting $\{(i, \overline{x}), (\overline{x}, 0)\}$. So based on C, $\mathbf{m}_k^*$

Initial operands:

$$
\begin{array}{cc}
\begin{array}{c|cc}
 & i & 0 \\
\hline
i & 0 & -2 \\
0 & 2 & 0
\end{array}
&
\left(
\begin{array}{c|cccc}
 & \overline{x} & \overline{y} & i & 0 \\
\hline
\overline{x} & 0 & & & -6 \\
\overline{y} & & 0 & & \\
i & 6 & & & \\
0 & & & &
\end{array}
\right), \text{int}
\end{array}
\qquad
\begin{array}{cc}
\begin{array}{c|cc}
 & i & 0 \\
\hline
i & 0 & -3 \\
0 & 3 & 0
\end{array}
&
\left(
\begin{array}{c|cccc}
 & \overline{x} & \overline{y} & i & 0 \\
\hline
\overline{x} & 0 & & & -5 \\
\overline{y} & & 0 & & \\
i & 6 & & & \\
0 & & & &
\end{array}
\right), \text{int}
\end{array}
$$

After normalization:

$$
\begin{array}{cc}
\begin{array}{c|cc}
 & i & 0 \\
\hline
i & 0 & -2 \\
0 & 2 & 0
\end{array}
&
\left(
\begin{array}{c|cccc}
 & \overline{x} & \overline{y} & i & 0 \\
\hline
\overline{x} & 0 & & & -6 & -8 \\
\overline{y} & & 0 & & \\
i & 6 & & 0 & -2 \\
0 & 8 & & 2 & 0
\end{array}
\right), \text{int}
\end{array}
\qquad
\begin{array}{cc}
\begin{array}{c|cc}
 & i & 0 \\
\hline
i & 0 & -3 \\
0 & 3 & 0
\end{array}
&
\left(
\begin{array}{c|cccc}
 & \overline{x} & \overline{y} & i & 0 \\
\hline
\overline{x} & 0 & & & -5 & -8 \\
\overline{y} & & 0 & & \\
i & 6 & & 0 & -3 \\
0 & 9 & & 3 & 0
\end{array}
\right), \text{int}
\end{array}
$$

2 sets of duplicates:

$$P_0 = \{(\overline{x}, i) \leftarrow 0, (\overline{x}, 0) \leftarrow i,$$
$$(i, \overline{x}) \leftarrow 0, (0, \overline{x}) \leftarrow i, \ldots\}$$

$$P_1 = \{(\overline{x}, i) \leftarrow 0, (\overline{x}, 0) \leftarrow i,$$
$$(i, \overline{x}) \leftarrow 0, (0, \overline{x}) \leftarrow i, \ldots\}$$

Sets of deletable common duplicates:

$$C = \{\{(\overline{x}, i), (0, \overline{x})\}, \{(\overline{x}, i), (i, \overline{x})\}, \{(\overline{x}, 0), (0, \overline{x})\}, \{(i, \overline{x}), (\overline{x}, 0)\}, \ldots\}$$

Choose a best pair of contractions:

$$
\begin{array}{cc}
\begin{array}{c|cc}
 & i & 0 \\
\hline
i & 0 & -2 \\
0 & 2 & 0
\end{array}
&
\left(
\begin{array}{c|cccc}
 & \overline{x} & \overline{y} & i & 0 \\
\hline
\overline{x} & 0 & & & -8 \\
\overline{y} & & 0 & & \\
i & 6 & & 0 & -2 \\
0 & & & 2 & 0
\end{array}
\right), \text{int}
\end{array}
\qquad
\begin{array}{cc}
\begin{array}{c|cc}
 & i & 0 \\
\hline
i & 0 & -3 \\
0 & 3 & 0
\end{array}
&
\left(
\begin{array}{c|cccc}
 & \overline{x} & \overline{y} & i & 0 \\
\hline
\overline{x} & 0 & & & -8 \\
\overline{y} & & 0 & & \\
i & 6 & & 0 & -3 \\
0 & & & 3 & 0
\end{array}
\right), \text{int}
\end{array}
$$

Final join:

$$
\begin{array}{cc}
\begin{array}{c|cc}
 & i & 0 \\
\hline
i & 0 & -2 \\
0 & 3 & 0
\end{array}
&
\left(
\begin{array}{c|cccc}
 & \overline{x} & \overline{y} & i & 0 \\
\hline
\overline{x} & 0 & & & -8 \\
\overline{y} & & 0 & & \\
i & 6 & & & \\
0 & & & &
\end{array}
\right), \text{int}
\end{array}
$$

Fig. 5. Computation of a join

and $d_0^* \vee d_1^*$, this step finds a set of duplicates to delete, thus computes a pair of contractions m_k^* for the next step.

– *Join of DBMs and Intersection of MMMs.* The final step joins the two transformed operands by joining their DBMs and intersecting their MMMs.
As all steps either preserve concretization or return an over-approximation of the arguments (under-approximating zones), this algorithm is sound:

Theorem 2 (Soundness). *With the above notations:*

$$\gamma_\times(X_0^\sharp) \cup \gamma_\times(X_1^\sharp) \subseteq \gamma_\times(X^\sharp)$$

Computation of a New Zone. So far, we focused on the case where both operands of $\sqcup^\sharp$ consist of exactly one zone. In practice, most cases fall out of this scope. We consider here the case where the left argument contains no zone and

After normalization:

$$\begin{array}{c|cc} & i & 0 \\ \hline i & 0 & -1 \\ 0 & 1 & 0 \end{array} \quad (\perp_{\mathbf{zone}}, \mathrm{int})$$

$$\left(\begin{array}{c|cc} & i & 0 \\ \hline i & 0 & -2 \\ 0 & 2 & 0 \end{array}\left|\begin{array}{c|cccc} & \overline{x} & \overline{y} & i & 0 \\ \hline \overline{x} & 0 & & 1 & -1 \\ \overline{y} & & 0 & & \\ i & -1 & & 0 & -2 \\ 0 & 1 & & 2 & 0 \end{array}\right.\right), \mathrm{int}$$

Sets of duplicates:

$P_0 = $ not applicable

$$P_1 = \{(\overline{x}, i) \hookleftarrow 0, (\overline{x}, 0) \hookleftarrow i,$$
$$(i, \overline{x}) \hookleftarrow 0, (0, \overline{x}) \hookleftarrow i, \ldots\}$$

Sets of deletable duplicates:

$D_0 = $ not applicable

$$D_1$$
$$= \{\{(\overline{x}, i), (0, \overline{x})\}, \{(\overline{x}, i), (i, \overline{x})\},$$
$$\{(\overline{x}, 0), (0, \overline{x})\}, \{(i, \overline{x}), (\overline{x}, 0)\}, \ldots\}$$

Choose a best contraction:

$$\left(\begin{array}{c|cc} & i & 0 \\ \hline i & 0 & -1 \\ 0 & 1 & 0 \end{array}\left|\begin{array}{c|cccc} & \overline{x} & \overline{y} & i & 0 \\ \hline \overline{x} & 0 & & & -1 \\ \overline{y} & & 0 & & \\ i & -1 & & 0 & -1 \\ 0 & & & 1 & 0 \end{array}\right.\right), \mathrm{int}$$

$$\left(\begin{array}{c|cc} & i & 0 \\ \hline i & 0 & -2 \\ 0 & 2 & 0 \end{array}\left|\begin{array}{c|cccc} & \overline{x} & \overline{y} & i & 0 \\ \hline \overline{x} & 0 & & & -1 \\ \overline{y} & & 0 & & \\ i & -1 & & 0 & -2 \\ 0 & & & 2 & 0 \end{array}\right.\right), \mathrm{int}$$

Final join:

$$\left(\begin{array}{c|cc} & i & 0 \\ \hline i & 0 & -1 \\ 0 & 2 & 0 \end{array}\left|\begin{array}{c|cccc} & \overline{x} & \overline{y} & i & 0 \\ \hline \overline{x} & 0 & & & -1 \\ \overline{y} & & 0 & & \\ i & -1 & & & \\ 0 & & & & \end{array}\right.\right), \mathrm{int}$$

Fig. 6. Creation of a new typed zone in join

the right operand contains one zone, and we will treat the general case in the next paragraph. This case is typically encountered when computing an abstract join after the first iteration of a loop that initializes a spreadsheet zone. For instance, such a program would give us abstract states $X_0^\sharp = (\{i = 1\}, \emptyset)$ at iteration 0 and $X_1^\sharp = (\{i = 2\}, \{((\overline{x} = 1, \overline{y} = 1\}, \mathrm{int})\})$ at iteration 1. Then $X_0^\sharp$ is actually equivalent to abstract state $(\{i = 1\}, \{(\perp_{\mathbf{zone}}, \mathrm{int})\})$ where $\perp_{\mathbf{zone}}$ denotes the MMM with empty concretization, hence the empty zone. We remark that the constraints of the zone can in both cases be rewritten into $\{1 \le \overline{x} \le i - 1, \overline{y} = 1\}$: indeed, when $i = 1$, this is equivalent to the empty MMM. Thus, $(\{i : [1, 2]\}, \{((\overline{x} : [1, i - 1], \overline{y} = 2\}, \mathrm{int})\})$ is an over-approximation for both operands, hence a valid result for $\sqcup^\sharp$.

We assume that operands are of the form $X_0^\sharp = (\mathbf{d}_0, \{(\perp_{\mathbf{zone}}, t)\})$ and $X_1^\sharp = (\mathbf{d}_1, \{(\mathbf{m}_1, t)\})$. Then, we follow the algorithm given in the case of two abstract states with exactly one zone up to the step normalization. Then for the following two steps about duplicates, as the zone of the left operand is $\perp_{\mathbf{zone}}$, we calculate only the part of the right operand. Then for the step of choosing a contraction, we search for a set of deletable duplicates in D_1 to delete, thus computes a contraction $\overline{\mathbf{m}_1^*}$ of $\mathbf{m}_1^*$ associated with $\mathbf{d}_1^*$ (therefore $\gamma_i(\overline{\mathbf{m}_1^*} \wedge \mathbf{d}_1^*) = \gamma_i(\mathbf{m}_1^* \wedge \mathbf{d}_1^*)$), such that

$\overline{\mathbf{m}_1^*} \wedge \mathbf{d}_0 = \emptyset$. If such a $\overline{\mathbf{m}_1^*}$ can be found, $\sqcup^\sharp$ keeps it for MMMs of both operands, and computes a join for the DBMs of both operands. Otherwise, the right hand zone is discarded. Fig. 6 shows this algorithm on the above example.

Case of an Arbitrary Number of Zones. We now consider the case of two $\mathbb{D}_\times^\sharp$ elements $X_k^\sharp = (\mathbf{d}_k, \{(\mathbf{m}_{k,0}, t_{k,0}), \ldots, (\mathbf{m}_{k,n}, t_{k,n})\}), k \in \{0, 1\}$. In that case, abstract join operator $\sqcup^\sharp$ should identify pairs of zones that can be over-approximated with minimal loss of precision, and zones in the right hand side argument that can be joined with an empty zone with no loss of precision. Precisely, the steps of the normalization and the calculation of duplicates can be first done on every zone of both operands at once. Then for one zone $(\mathbf{m}_{0,i}, t_{0,i})$ of $X_0^\sharp$, the algorithm goes through the zones of $X_1^\sharp$, proceed the step of deletable common duplicates and see if an optimal pair of contractions can be found. If so, the algorithm considers the pair of zones is identified; otherwise, it continues to examine the rest of the zones in $X_1^\sharp$. In the end if a pair of zones is identified, it adds their join to the result set, and remove them from both operands; otherwise, it adds the join of $(\mathbf{m}_{0,i}, t_{0,i})$ and $(\perp_{\mathbf{zone}}, t_{0,i})$ to the result set, and remove the zone from $X_0^\sharp$. The whole algorithm proceeds this way for each zone in $X_0^\sharp$. The most costly step of a join of 2 zones is to compute the sets of deletable common duplicates C: larger the sets of duplicates and their intersection are, more computation it requires. The complexity of the step to choose a best pair of contractions is proportional to the size of C and the one of each element. Finally the number of zones in each operand and the size of $\mathbf{m}_k$ also determines the complexity of the entire operation.

5.4   Widening Operator

Abstract join operator $\sqcup^\sharp$ shown in Sect. 5.3 returns an upper bound of its argument, but does not enforce termination of abstract iterates. However, we can extend $\sqcup^\sharp$ into a widening operator as follows:

- we let $\nabla^\sharp$ use a widening operator $\nabla_{\mathbf{d}}^\sharp$ over DBMs instead of $\vee$;
- after a fixed number of iterations $N_{\nabla^\sharp}$, the steps of the computation of $\overline{\mathbf{m}_k^*}$ and their intersection are replaced by a lower bound computation:

$$\overline{\mathbf{m}_0^*} \wedge \overline{\mathbf{m}_1^*} = \begin{cases} \mathbf{m}_0^* & \text{if } \forall i, j, (\mathbf{m}_0^*)_{ij} \leq (\mathbf{m}_1^*)_{ij}, \\ \perp_{\mathbf{zone}} & \text{otherwise} \end{cases}$$

(in practice, empty zones are pruned out of $\mathbb{D}_{\mathbf{Z}}^\sharp$ elements).

This provides a sound and terminating widening operator $\nabla^\sharp$ over $\mathbb{D}_\times^\sharp$.

5.5   Analysis

Transfer functions shown in Sect. 5.1 and the reduction, join and widening operators of Sect. 5.2-5.4 allow us to define a standard abstract interpretation based static analysis for the restricted spreadsheet language of Sect. 3. Our analysis implements a classic iteration engine over the program control flow graphs, and performs widening at loop heads. We use a delayed widening iteration strategy, where the regular join operator $\sqcup^\sharp$ is used in the first iterations over each loop, and $\nabla^\sharp$ is used for the following iterations. The reduction operator of Sect. 5.2 is used after the computation of transfer functions which modify the structure of zones. It is not applied to the widening output, as this might break termination. Our analysis is sound in the sense of the correctness theorem below:

Theorem 3 (Correctness)
If (l, ρ) is reachable for $\rightarrow$, then $\rho \in \gamma_\times(X_l^\sharp)$ where $X_l^\sharp$ is the invariant at l.
If (l, ρ) is reachable for $\rightarrow$, and $(l, \rho) \rightarrow \Omega$, then an alarm is reported at l.

6   Prototype and Results

The analysis was implemented in OCaml and represents around 3000 lines of code, including a front-end for our restricted spreadsheet language. We have applied our analysis to a number of small programs and examined type properties of the arrays that they manipulate. We ran the analysis on programs consisting of a single loop as well as programs with nested loops. In the table, we show the size in pre-processed lines of code and the analysis time without any spurious type warning on a 2.80 GHz Intel Core Duo with 4GB RAM. The analyzer raises various type errors (e.g., Ω_{assign}) if they exist in the programs.

Benchmark	Loop Level	Code Size (loc)	Run Time (sec)
initialization of a row	1	13	0.042
creation of 2 columns (program 1)	1	31	0.258
copy of a matrix	2	20	0.071
insertion sort of a column	2	29	0.135
multiplication of 2 matrices	3	35	0.096

7   Conclusion and Future Work

Our proposal enables static analysis of spreadsheet programs and verifies that an important class of type errors will not occur. It is based on a combination of numeric abstraction to describe spreadsheet zones and a type abstraction over cell contents.

The upper bound operators of our abstract domain accommodates an under-approximation operation of a sub-domain. [17] presents generic procedures that work for any base domain to compute under-approximations. In comparison with their approach, our domain is adapted specifically for the application, thus closer to a precise and efficient analysis for spreadsheet programs.

Substituting other lattices to the type lattice used in this paper will allow us to carry out other analyses. E.g. in practice we may relax the exact type charac-terization and permit approximate types (e.g. "int or bool") to more compactly capture zones which maybe otherwise need to be split to a large number of smaller zones. Existing work has considered other type properties, such as units and dimensions properties [18,19] (e.g., distinguishing hours, minutes, seconds, etc.), albeit only at the interface level, whereas we are considering the spreadsheet programs. Our work could be extended to deal with notions of units in a very straightforward manner by only substituting lattices. Information to build that lattice could be determined from header and labels in the spreadsheets.

Another important extension of our work would be to deal with a full spreadsheet language instead of the restricted language considered in this paper, so as to analyze industrial applications.

Our work also opens some more theoretical abstract domain design issues. In particular, it would be interesting to explore other instantiations of the abstract domain, with other kinds of numerical constraints over zones. For instance, we may consider octagons [20] (also allowing constraints of the form $\bar{x} + i \geq c$ where i is a program variable), or simple disequalities [21]. This would require a more general representation of zone constraints, and operators to cope with this more general representation. Last, it would also be interesting to extend array content analysis such as [22,23] to our two dimensional zones, so as to discover relations between program variable data and more complex properties of contents of spreadsheet zones.

Acknowledgments. We would like to thank Antoine Miné, Enea Zaffanella and members of the EuSpRIG (European Spreadsheet Risks Interest Group) for helpful discussions. We are grateful to the referees for their encouraging and useful comments on the early version of the article.

References

1. Panko, R.R.: What we know about spreadsheet errors. Journal of End User Computing 10, 15–21 (1998)
2. Jones, S.P., Blackwell, A., Burnett, M.: A user-centred approach to functions in excel. In: ICFP 2003: Proceedings of the Eighth ACM SIGPLAN International Conference on Functional Programming, pp. 165–176. ACM (2003)
3. Sestoft, P.: Implementing function spreadsheets. In: WEUSE 2008: Proceedings of the 4th International Workshop on End-user Software Engineering, pp. 91–94. ACM, New York (2008)
4. Cheng, T.: Excel Functional Programming. In: Explore Another Dimension of Spreadsheet Programming (2010)
5. Wakeling, D.: Spreadsheet functional programming. J. Funct. Program. 17(1), 131–143 (2007)
6. Erwig, M., Abraham, R., Kollmansberger, S., Cooperstein, I.: Gencel: a program generator for correct spreadsheets. J. Funct. Program. 16, 293–325 (2006)
7. Abraham, R., Erwig, M.: Inferring templates from spreadsheets. In: Proceedings of the 28th International Conference on Software Engineering, ICSE 2006, pp. 182–191. ACM Press, New York (2006)
8. Silva, A.: Strong Types for Relational Data Stored in Databases or Spreadsheets. PhD thesis, University of Minho (2006)

9. Cunha, J., Saraiva, J., Visser, J.: From spreadsheets to relational databases and back. In: PEPM 2009: Proceedings of the 2009 ACM SIGPLAN Workshop on Partial Evaluation and Program Manipulation, pp. 179–188. ACM (2009)
10. Rajalingham, K., Chadwick, D.R., Knight, B.: Classification of spreadsheet errors. In: EuSpRIG 2000 Symposium: Spreadsheet Risks, Audit and Development Methods (2001)
11. Bradley, L., McDaid, K.: Using bayesian statistical methods to determine the level of error in large spreadsheets. In: ICSE Companion, pp. 351–354 (2009)
12. Bishop, B., McDaid, K.: Spreadsheet debugging behaviour of expert and novice end-users. In: Proceedings of the 4th International Workshop on End-user Software Engineering, WEUSE 2008, pp. 56–60. ACM, New York (2008)
13. Cousot, P., Cousot, R.: Systematic design of program analysis frameworks. In: Conference Record of the Sixth Annual ACM SIGPLAN-SIGACT Symposium on Principles of Programming Languages, San Antonio, Texas, pp. 269–282. ACM Press, New York (1979)
14. Cheng, T.: Verification of spreadsheet programs by abstract interpretation. Master's thesis, École Polytechnique (2011)
15. Miné, A.: A New Numerical Abstract Domain Based on Difference-Bound Matrices. In: Danvy, O., Filinski, A. (eds.) PADO II. LNCS, vol. 2053, pp. 155–172. Springer, Heidelberg (2001)
16. Bagnara, R., Hill, P.M., Zaffanella, E.: Exact join detection for convex polyhedra and other numerical abstractions. Computational Geometry: Theory and Applications 43(5), 453–473 (2010)
17. Gulwani, S., McCloskey, B., Tiwari, A.: Lifting abstract interpreters to quantified logical domains. In: Proceedings of the 35th Annual ACM SIGPLAN-SIGACT Symposium on Principles of Programming Languages, POPL 2008, pp. 235–246. ACM, New York (2008)
18. Chambers, C., Erwig, M.: Automatic detection of dimension errors in spreadsheets. Journal of Visual Languages and Computing 20(4), 269–283 (2009)
19. Antoniu, T., Steckler, P.A., Krishnamurthi, S., Neuwirth, E., Felleisen, M.: Validating the unit correctness of spreadsheet programs. In: ICSE 2004: Proceedings of the 26th International Conference on Software Engineering, pp. 439–448. IEEE Computer Society, Washington, DC (2004)
20. Miné, A.: The octagon abstract domain. Higher-Order and Symbolic Computation 19(1), 31–100 (2006)
21. Péron, M., Halbwachs, N.: An Abstract Domain Extending Difference-Bound Matrices with Disequality Constraints. In: Cook, B., Podelski, A. (eds.) VMCAI 2007. LNCS, vol. 4349, pp. 268–282. Springer, Heidelberg (2007)
22. Halbwachs, N., Péron, M.: Discovering properties about arrays in simple programs. In: PLDI 2008: 2008 ACM SIGPLAN Conference on Programming Language Design and Implementation, pp. 339–348. ACM (June 2008)
23. Cousot, P., Cousot, R., Logozzo, F.: A parametric segmentation functor for fully automatic and scalable array content analysis. In: Conference Record of the 38th Annual ACM SIGPLAN-SIGACT Symposium on Principles of Programming Languages, pp. 105–118. ACM Press, New York (2011)

Bilateral Algorithms for Symbolic Abstraction[*]

Aditya Thakur[1], Matt Elder[1], and Thomas Reps[1,2,**]

[1] University of Wisconsin, Madison, WI, USA
[2] GrammaTech, Inc., Ithaca, NY, USA

Abstract. Given a concrete domain $\mathcal{C}$, a concrete operation $\tau : \mathcal{C} \to \mathcal{C}$, and an abstract domain $\mathcal{A}$, a fundamental problem in abstract interpretation is to find the *best abstract transformer* $\tau^\# : \mathcal{A} \to \mathcal{A}$ that over-approximates τ. This problem, as well as several other operations needed by an abstract interpreter, can be reduced to the problem of *symbolic abstraction*: the symbolic abstraction of a formula φ in logic $\mathcal{L}$, denoted by $\widehat{\alpha}(\varphi)$, is the best value in $\mathcal{A}$ that over-approximates the meaning of φ. When the concrete semantics of τ is defined in $\mathcal{L}$ using a formula φ_τ that specifies the relation between input and output states, the best abstract transformer $\tau^\#$ can be computed as $\widehat{\alpha}(\varphi_\tau)$.

In this paper, we present a new framework for performing symbolic abstraction, discuss its properties, and present several instantiations for various logics and abstract domains. The key innovation is to use a *bilateral* successive-approximation algorithm, which maintains both an over-approximation and an under-approximation of the desired answer.

1 Introduction

For several years, we have been investigating connections between abstract interpretation and logic—in particular, how to harness decision procedures to obtain algorithms for several fundamental primitives used in abstract interpretation. Automation ensures correctness and precision of these primitives [3, §1.1], and drastically reduces the time taken to implement the primitives [19, §2.5] This paper presents new results on this topic.

Like several previous papers [25,15,11,34], this paper concentrates on the problem of developing an algorithm for *symbolic abstraction*: the symbolic abstraction of a formula φ in logic $\mathcal{L}$, denoted by $\widehat{\alpha}(\varphi)$, is the best value in a given abstract domain $\mathcal{A}$ that over-approximates the meaning of φ [25]. To be more precise, given a formula $\varphi \in \mathcal{L}$, let $[\![\varphi]\!]$ denote the meaning of φ—i.e., the set of concrete states that satisfy φ. Then $\widehat{\alpha}(\varphi)$ is the unique value $a \in \mathcal{A}$ such that (i)

[*] Supported, in part, by NSF under grants CCF-{0810053, 0904371}, by ONR under grants N00014-{09-1-0510, 10-M-0251, 11-C-0447}, by ARL under grant W911NF-09-1-0413, by AFRL under grants FA9550-09-1-0279 and FA8650-10-C-7088; and by DARPA under cooperative agreement HR0011-12-2-0012. Any opinions, findings, and conclusions or recommendations expressed in this publication are those of the authors, and do not necessarily reflect the views of the sponsoring agencies.

[**] T. Reps has an ownership interest in GrammaTech, Inc., which has licensed elements of the technology discussed in this publication.

A. Miné and D. Schmidt (Eds.): SAS 2012, LNCS 7460, pp. 111–128, 2012.
© Springer-Verlag Berlin Heidelberg 2012

$[\![\varphi]\!] \subseteq \gamma(a)$, and (ii) for all $a' \in \mathcal{A}$ for which $[\![\varphi]\!] \subseteq \gamma(a')$, $a \sqsubseteq a'$. In this paper, we present a new framework for performing symbolic abstraction, discuss its properties, and present several instantiations for various logics and abstract domains.

Several key operations needed by an abstract interpreter can be reduced to symbolic abstraction. For instance, one use of symbolic abstraction is to bridge the gap between concrete semantics and an abstract domain. Cousot and Cousot [5] gave a *specification* of the most-precise abstract interpretation of a concrete operation τ that is possible in a given abstract domain:

> Given a Galois connection $\mathcal{C} \xrightarrow[\alpha]{\gamma} \mathcal{A}$, the *best abstract transformer*, $\tau^{\#} : \mathcal{A} \to \mathcal{A}$, is the most precise abstract operator possible that over-approximates τ. $\tau^{\#}$ can be expressed as follows: $\tau^{\#} = \alpha \circ \tau \circ \gamma$.

The latter equation defines the limit of precision obtainable using abstraction $\mathcal{A}$. However, the definition is non-constructive; it does not provide an *algorithm*, either for applying $\tau^{\#}$ or for finding a representation of the function $\tau^{\#}$. In particular, in many cases, the explicit application of γ to an abstract value would yield an intermediate result—a set of concrete states—that is either infinite or too large to fit in computer memory.

In contrast, it is often convenient to use a logic $\mathcal{L}$ to state the concrete semantics of transformer τ as a formula $\varphi_{\tau} \in \mathcal{L}$ that specifies the relation between input and output states. Then, using an *algorithm for symbolic abstraction*, a representation of $\tau^{\#}$ can be computed as $\widehat{\alpha}(\varphi_{\tau})$.

To see how symbolic abstraction can yield better results than conventional approaches to the creation of abstract transformers, consider an example from machine-code analysis: the x86 instruction "add bh,al" adds al, the low-order byte of 32-bit register eax, to bh, the second-to-lowest byte of 32-bit register ebx. The semantics of this instruction can be expressed in quantifier-free bit-vector (QFBV) logic as

$$\varphi_I \overset{\text{def}}{=} \mathsf{ebx}' = \left(\begin{array}{l} (\mathsf{ebx} \ \& \ \mathsf{0xFFFF00FF}) \\ | \ ((\mathsf{ebx} + 256 * (\mathsf{eax} \ \& \ \mathsf{0xFF})) \ \& \ \mathsf{0xFF00}) \end{array} \right) \wedge \mathsf{eax}' = \mathsf{eax}, \quad (1)$$

where "&" and "|" denote bitwise-and and bitwise-or. Eqn. (1) shows that the semantics of the instruction involves non-linear bit-masking operations.

Now suppose that abstract domain $\mathcal{A}$ is the domain of affine relations over integers mod 2^{32} [11]. For this domain, $\widehat{\alpha}(\varphi_I)$ is $(2^{16}\mathsf{ebx}' = 2^{16}\mathsf{ebx} + 2^{24}\mathsf{eax})$ $\wedge(\mathsf{eax}' = \mathsf{eax})$, which captures the relationship between the low-order two bytes of ebx and the low-order byte of eax. It is the best over-approximation to Eqn. (1) that can be expressed as an affine relation. In contrast, a more conventional approach to creating an abstract transformer for φ_I is to use operator-by-operator reinterpretation of Eqn. (1). The resulting abstract transformer would be $(\mathsf{eax}' = \mathsf{eax})$, which loses all information about ebx. Such loss in precision is exacerbated when considering larger loop-free blocks of instructions.

Motivation. Reps, Sagiv, and Yorsh (RSY) [25] presented a framework for computing $\widehat{\alpha}$ that applies to any logic and abstract domain that satisfies certain conditions. King and Søndergaard [15] gave a specific $\widehat{\alpha}$ algorithm for an abstract domain of Boolean affine relations. Elder et al. [11] extended their algorithm to affine relations in arithmetic modulo 2^w—i.e., for some bit-width w of bounded integers. (When the generalized algorithm is applied to φ_I from Eqn. (1), it finds the $\widehat{\alpha}(\varphi_I)$ formula indicated above.) Because the generalized algorithm is similar to the Boolean one, we refer to it as KS. We use RSY[AR] to denote the RSY framework instantiated for the abstract domain of affine relations modulo 2^w.

The RSY[AR] and KS algorithms resemble one another in that they both find $\widehat{\alpha}(\varphi)$ via successive approximation from "below". However, *the two algorithms are not the same.* As discussed in §2, although both the RSY[AR] and KS algorithms issue queries to a decision procedure, compared to the RSY[AR] algorithm, the KS algorithm issues *comparatively inexpensive* decision-procedure queries. Moreover, the differences in the two algorithms cause an order-of-magnitude difference in performance: in our experiments, *KS is approximately ten times faster* than RSY[AR].

These issues motivated us to (i) investigate the fundamental principles underlying the difference between the RSY[AR] and KS algorithms, and (ii) seek a *framework* into which the KS algorithm could be placed, so that its advantages could be transferred to other domains. A third motivating issue was that neither the RSY framework nor the KS algorithm are resilient to timeouts. Because the algorithms maintain only under-approximations of the desired answer, if the successive-approximation process takes too much time and needs to be stopped, they must return $\top$ to be sound. We desired an algorithm that could return a nontrivial (non-$\top$) value in case of a timeout.

The outcome of our work is a new *framework* for symbolic abstraction that

- is applicable to any abstract domain that satisfies certain conditions (similar to the RSY algorithm)
- uses a successive-approximation algorithm that is *parsimonious* in its use of the decision procedure (similar to the KS algorithm)
- is *bilateral*; that is, it maintains both an under-approximation and a (non-trivial) over-approximation of the desired answer, and hence is resilient to timeouts: the procedure can return the over-approximation if it is stopped at any point (unlike the RSY and KS algorithms).

The key concept used in generalizing the KS algorithm is an operation that we call AbstractConsequence (Defn. 1, §3). We show that many abstract domains have an AbstractConsequence operation that enables the kind of inexpensive decision-procedure queries that we see in the KS algorithm (Thm. 2, §3).

Our experiments show that the bilateral algorithm for the AR domain improves precision at up to 15% of a program's control points (i.e., the beginning of a basic block that ends with a branch), and on average is more precise for 3.1% of the control points (computed as the arithmetic mean).

Algorithm 1. $\widehat{\alpha}_{\text{RSY}}^{\uparrow}\langle \mathcal{L}, \mathcal{A}\rangle(\varphi)$	**Algorithm 2.** $\widehat{\alpha}_{\text{KS}}^{\uparrow}(\varphi)$
1 $lower \leftarrow \bot$	1 $lower \leftarrow \bot$
2	2 $i \leftarrow 1$
3 **while** true **do**	3 **while** $i \leq \text{rows}(lower)$ **do**
4	4 $p \leftarrow \text{Row}(lower, -i)$ // $p \sqsupseteq lower$
5 $S \leftarrow \text{Model}(\varphi \wedge \neg\widehat{\gamma}(lower))$	5 $S \leftarrow \text{Model}(\varphi \wedge \neg\widehat{\gamma}(p))$
6 **if** S is TimeOut **then**	6 **if** S is TimeOut **then**
7 **return** $\top$	7 **return** $\top$
8 **else if** S is None **then**	8 **else if** S is None **then**
9 **break** // $\varphi \Rightarrow \widehat{\gamma}(lower)$	9 $i \leftarrow i + 1$ // $\varphi \Rightarrow \widehat{\gamma}(p)$
10 **else** // $S \not\models \widehat{\gamma}(lower)$	10 **else** // $S \not\models \widehat{\gamma}(p)$
11 $lower \leftarrow lower \sqcup \beta(S)$	11 $lower \leftarrow lower \sqcup \beta(S)$
12 $ans \leftarrow lower$	12 $ans \leftarrow lower$
13 **return** ans	13 **return** ans

Contributions. The contributions of the paper can be summarized as follows:

- We show how the KS algorithm can be modified into a *bilateral algorithm* that maintains sound under- and over-approximations of the answer (§2).
- We present a framework for symbolic abstraction based on a bilateral algorithm for computing $\widehat{\alpha}$ (§3).
- We give several instantiations of the framework (§3 and §4).
- We compare the performance of various algorithms (§2 and §5).

§6 discusses related work. A longer version is available as a technical report [32].

2   Towards a Bilateral Algorithm

Alg. 1 shows the general RSY algorithm ($\widehat{\alpha}_{\text{RSY}}^{\uparrow}\langle \mathcal{L}, \mathcal{A}\rangle$) [25], which is parameterized on logic $\mathcal{L}$ and abstract domain $\mathcal{A}$. Alg. 2 shows the KS algorithm ($\widehat{\alpha}_{\text{KS}}^{\uparrow}$) [15,11], which is specific to the QFBV logic and the affine-relations (AR) domain. The following notation is used in the algorithms:

- The operation of *symbolic concretization* (line 5 of Algs. 1 and 2), denoted by $\widehat{\gamma}$, maps an abstract value $a \in \mathcal{A}$ to a formula $\widehat{\gamma}(a) \in \mathcal{L}$ such that a and $\widehat{\gamma}(a)$ represent the same set of concrete states (i.e., $\gamma(a) = [\![\widehat{\gamma}(a)]\!]$).
- Given a formula $\psi \in \mathcal{L}$, $\text{Model}(\psi)$ returns (i) a satisfying model S if a decision procedure was able to determine that ψ is satisfiable in a given time limit, (ii) None if a decision procedure was able to determine that ψ is unsatisfiable in a given time limit, and (iii) TimeOut otherwise.
- The *representation function* β (line 11 of Algs. 1 and 2) maps a singleton concrete state $S \in \mathcal{C}$ to the least value in $\mathcal{A}$ that over-approximates $\{S\}$.

An abstract value in the AR domain is a conjunction of affine equalities, which can be represented in a normal form as a matrix in which each row expresses a non-redundant affine equality [11]. (Rows are 0-indexed.) Given a matrix m,

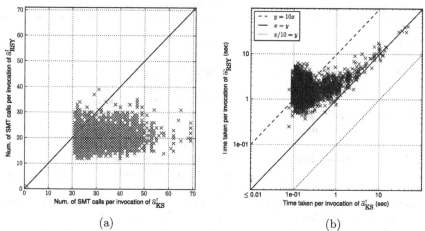

(a)   (b)

Fig. 1. (a) Scatter plot showing of the number of decision-procedure queries during each pair of invocations of $\widehat{\alpha}_{RSY}^{\uparrow}$ and $\widehat{\alpha}_{KS}^{\uparrow}$, when neither invocation had a decision-procedure timeout. (b) Log-log scatter plot showing the times taken by each pair of invocations of $\widehat{\alpha}_{RSY}^{\uparrow}$ and $\widehat{\alpha}_{KS}^{\uparrow}$, when neither invocation had a decision-procedure timeout.

$\mathtt{rows}(m)$ returns the number of rows of m (line 3 in Alg. 2), and $\mathtt{Row}(m, -i)$, for $1 \leq i \leq \mathtt{rows}(m)$, returns row $(\mathtt{rows}(m) - i)$ of m (line 4 in Alg. 2).

Both algorithms have a similar overall structure. Both are successive approximation algorithms: they compute a sequence of successively "larger" approximations to the set of states described by φ. Both maintain an under-approximation of the final answer in the variable *lower*, which is initialized to $\bot$ on line 1. Both call a decision procedure (line 5), and having found a model S that satisfies the query, the under-approximation is updated by performing a join (line 11).

The differences between Algs. 1 and 2 are highlighted in gray. The key difference is the nature of the decision-procedure query on line 5. $\widehat{\alpha}_{RSY}^{\uparrow}$ uses *all* of *lower* to construct the query, while $\widehat{\alpha}_{KS}^{\uparrow}$ uses only a single row from *lower* (line 4)—i.e., just a *single affine equality*, which has two consequences. First, $\widehat{\alpha}_{KS}^{\uparrow}$ should issue a larger number of queries, compared with $\widehat{\alpha}_{RSY}^{\uparrow}$. Suppose that the value of *lower* has converged to the final answer via a sequence of joins performed by the algorithm. To discover that convergence has occurred, $\widehat{\alpha}_{RSY}^{\uparrow}$ has to issue just a single decision-procedure query, whereas $\widehat{\alpha}_{KS}^{\uparrow}$ has to confirm it by issuing $\mathtt{rows}(lower) - i$ number of queries, proceeding row-by-row. Second, each individual query issued by $\widehat{\alpha}_{KS}^{\uparrow}$ is simpler than the ones issued by $\widehat{\alpha}_{RSY}^{\uparrow}$. Thus, *a priori*, it is not clear which algorithm will perform better in practice.

We compared the time for $\widehat{\alpha}_{RSY}^{\uparrow}$ (instantiated for QFBV and the AR domain) and $\widehat{\alpha}_{KS}^{\uparrow}$ to compute basic-block transformers for a set of x86 executables. There was no overall timeout imposed on the invocation of the procedures, but each invocation of the decision procedure (line 5 in Algs. 1 and 2) had a timeout of 3 seconds. (Details of the experimental setup are described in §5.) Fig. 1(a) shows a scatter-plot of the *number of decision-procedure calls* in each invocation of $\widehat{\alpha}_{RSY}^{\uparrow}$

Algorithm 3. $\widehat{\alpha}_{KS}^{\uparrow}(\varphi)$	**Algorithm 4.** $\widetilde{\alpha}_{KS+}^{\updownarrow}(\varphi)$
1	1 *upper* $\leftarrow \top$
2 *lower* $\leftarrow \bot$	2 *lower* $\leftarrow \bot$
3 $i \leftarrow 1$	3 $i \leftarrow 1$
4 **while** $i \leq \mathbf{rows}(lower)$ **do**	4 **while** $i \leq \mathbf{rows}(lower)$ **do**
5 $p \leftarrow \mathbf{Row}(lower, -i)$	5 $p \leftarrow \mathbf{Row}(lower, -i)$
// $p \sqsupseteq lower$	// $p \sqsupseteq lower$, $p \not\sqsupseteq upper$
6 $S \leftarrow \mathbf{Model}(\varphi \wedge \neg\widehat{\gamma}(p))$	6 $S \leftarrow \mathbf{Model}(\varphi \wedge \neg\widehat{\gamma}(p))$
7 **if** S is TimeOut **then**	7 **if** S is TimeOut **then**
8 **return** $\top$	8 **return** *upper*
9 **else if** S is None **then**	9 **else if** S is None **then**
// $\varphi \Rightarrow \widehat{\gamma}(p)$	10 *upper* $\leftarrow upper \sqcap p$ // $\varphi \Rightarrow \widehat{\gamma}(p)$
10 $i \leftarrow i + 1$	$i \leftarrow i + 1$
11 **else** // $S \not\models \widehat{\gamma}(p)$	11 **else** // $S \not\models \widehat{\gamma}(p)$
12 *lower* $\leftarrow lower \sqcup \beta(S)$	12 *lower* $\leftarrow lower \sqcup \beta(S)$
13 *ans* $\leftarrow lower$	13 *ans* $\leftarrow lower$
14 **return** *ans*	14 **return** *ans*

versus the corresponding invocation of $\widehat{\alpha}_{KS}^{\uparrow}$, when neither of the procedures had a decision-procedure timeout. $\widehat{\alpha}_{RSY}^{\uparrow}$ issues fewer decision-procedure queries: on average (computed as an arithmetic mean), $\widehat{\alpha}_{KS}^{\uparrow}$ invokes 42% more calls to the decision procedure. Fig. 1(b) shows a log-log scatter-plot of the *total time* taken by each invocation of $\widehat{\alpha}_{RSY}^{\uparrow}$ versus the time taken by $\widehat{\alpha}_{KS}^{\uparrow}$. $\widehat{\alpha}_{KS}^{\uparrow}$ is much faster than $\widehat{\alpha}_{RSY}^{\uparrow}$: overall, computed as the geometric mean of the speedups on each of the x86 executables, $\widehat{\alpha}_{KS}^{\uparrow}$ is about ten times faster than $\widehat{\alpha}_{RSY}^{\uparrow}$.

The order-of-magnitude speedup can be attributed to the fact that each of the $\widehat{\alpha}_{KS}^{\uparrow}$ decision-procedure queries is less expensive than the ones issued by $\widehat{\alpha}_{RSY}^{\uparrow}$. At line 4 in $\widehat{\alpha}_{KS}^{\uparrow}$, p is a single constraint; consequently, the decision-procedure query contains the *single* conjunct $\neg\widehat{\gamma}(p)$ (line 5). In contrast, at line 5 in $\widehat{\alpha}_{RSY}^{\uparrow}$, *lower* is a *conjunction* of constraints, and consequently the decision-procedure query contains $\neg\widehat{\gamma}(lower)$, which is a *disjunction* of constraints.

Neither $\widehat{\alpha}_{RSY}^{\uparrow}$ nor $\widehat{\alpha}_{KS}^{\uparrow}$ is resilient to timeouts. A decision-procedure query—or the cumulative time for $\widehat{\alpha}^{\uparrow}$—might take too long, in which case the only safe answer that can be returned is $\top$ (line 6 in Algs. 1 and 2). To remedy this situation, we show how $\widehat{\alpha}_{KS}^{\uparrow}$ can be modified to maintain a non-trivial over-approximation of the desired answer. Alg. 4 is such a *bilateral* algorithm that maintains both an under-approximation and over-approximation of $\widehat{\alpha}(\varphi)$. The original $\widehat{\alpha}_{KS}^{\uparrow}$ is shown in Alg. 3 for comparison; the differences in the algorithms are highlighted in gray. (Note that line numbers are different in Algs. 2 and 3.)

The $\widetilde{\alpha}_{KS+}^{\updownarrow}$ algorithm (Alg. 4) initializes the over-approximation (*upper*) to $\top$ on line 1. At any stage in the algorithm $\varphi \Rightarrow \widehat{\gamma}(upper)$. On line 10, it is sound to update *upper* by performing a meet with p because $\varphi \Rightarrow \widehat{\gamma}(p)$. Progress is guaranteed because $p \not\sqsupseteq upper$. In case of a decision-procedure timeout (line 7),

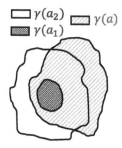

Fig. 2. Abstract Consequence: For all $a_1, a_2 \in \mathcal{A}$ where $\gamma(a_1) \subsetneq \gamma(a_2)$, if $a =$ AbstractConsequence(a_1, a_2), then $\gamma(a_1) \subseteq \gamma(a)$ and $\gamma(a) \not\supseteq \gamma(a_2)$

Algorithm 5. $\widetilde{\alpha}^{\updownarrow}\langle \mathcal{L}, \mathcal{A}\rangle(\varphi)$

---

1 $upper \leftarrow \top$
2 $lower \leftarrow \bot$
3 **while** $lower \neq upper \wedge$ ResourcesLeft **do**
   // $lower \subsetneq upper$
4    $p \leftarrow$ AbstractConsequence$(lower, upper)$
     // $p \sqsupseteq lower, p \not\sqsupseteq upper$
5    $S \leftarrow$ Model$(\varphi \wedge \neg\widehat{\gamma}(p))$
6   **if** S is TimeOut **then**
7   **return** $upper$
8   **else if** S is None **then**   // $\varphi \Rightarrow \widehat{\gamma}(p)$
9      $upper \leftarrow upper \sqcap p$
10   **else**   // $S \not\models \widehat{\gamma}(p)$
11     $lower \leftarrow lower \sqcup \beta(S)$
12 $ans \leftarrow upper$
13 **return** ans

Alg. 4 returns $upper$ as the answer (line 8). We use " $\sim$ " to emphasize the fact that $\widetilde{\alpha}^{\updownarrow}_{\mathrm{KS+}}(\varphi)$ can return an over-approximation of $\widehat{\alpha}(\varphi)$ in case of a timeout. However, if the loop exits without a timeout, then $\widetilde{\alpha}^{\updownarrow}_{\mathrm{KS+}}(\varphi)$ returns $\widehat{\alpha}(\varphi)$.

3   A Parametric Bilateral Algorithm

Like the original KS algorithm, $\widetilde{\alpha}^{\updownarrow}_{\mathrm{KS+}}$ applies only to the AR domain. The results presented in §2 provide motivation to generalize $\widetilde{\alpha}^{\updownarrow}_{\mathrm{KS+}}$ so that we can take advantage of its benefits with domains other than AR. In this section, we present the bilateral framework we developed. Proofs for all theorems are found in [32].

We first introduce the *abstract-consequence* operation, which is the key operation in our generalized algorithm:

Definition 1. *An operation* AbstractConsequence$(\cdot, \cdot)$ *is an **acceptable abstract-consequence operation** iff for all $a_1, a_2 \in \mathcal{A}$ such that $a_1 \subsetneq a_2$, $a =$ AbstractConsequence(a_1, a_2) implies $a_1 \sqsubseteq a$ and $a \not\sqsupseteq a_2$.*   □

Fig. 2 illustrates Defn. 1 graphically, using the concretizations of a_1, a_2, and a.

Alg. 5 presents the parametric bilateral algorithm $\widetilde{\alpha}^{\updownarrow}\langle \mathcal{L}, \mathcal{A}\rangle(\varphi)$, which performs symbolic abstraction of $\varphi \in \mathcal{L}$ for abstract domain $\mathcal{A}$. The differences between Alg. 5 and Alg. 4 are highlighted in gray.

The assumptions placed on the logic and the abstract domain are as follows:

1. There is a Galois connection $\mathcal{C} \xrightleftharpoons[\alpha]{\gamma} \mathcal{A}$ between $\mathcal{A}$ and concrete domain $\mathcal{C}$.
2. Given $a_1, a_2 \in \mathcal{A}$, there are algorithms to evaluate $a_1 \sqcup a_2$ and $a_1 \sqcap a_2$, and to check $a_1 = a_2$.
3. There is a symbolic-concretization operation $\widehat{\gamma}$ that maps an abstract value $a \in \mathcal{A}$ to a formula $\widehat{\gamma}(a)$ in $\mathcal{L}$.

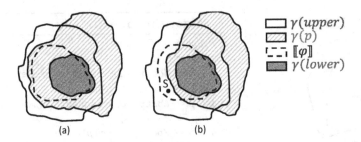

(a)   (b)

Fig. 3. The two cases arising in Alg. 5: $\varphi \wedge \neg\widehat{\gamma}(p)$ is either (a) unsatisfiable, or (b) satisfiable with $S \models \varphi$ and $S \not\models \widehat{\gamma}(p)$. (Note that although $lower \sqsubseteq \widehat{\alpha}(\varphi) \sqsubseteq upper$ and $[[\varphi]] \subseteq \gamma(upper)$ are invariants of Alg. 5, $\gamma(lower) \subseteq [[\varphi]]$ does not necessarily hold, as depicted above.)

4. There is a decision procedure for the logic $\mathcal{L}$ that is also capable of returning a model satisfying a formula in $\mathcal{L}$.
5. The logic $\mathcal{L}$ is closed under conjunction and negation.
6. There is an acceptable abstract-consequence operation for $\mathcal{A}$ (Defn. 1).

The abstract value p returned by `AbstractConsequence` (line 4 of Alg. 5) is used to generate the decision-procedure query (line 5); Fig. 3 illustrates the two cases arising based on whether $\varphi \wedge \neg\widehat{\gamma}(p)$ is satisfiable or unsatisfiable. The overall resources, such as time, used by Alg. 5 can be controlled via the ResourcesLeft flag (line 3).

Theorem 1. [**Correctness of Alg. 5**] *Suppose that $\mathcal{L}$ and $\mathcal{A}$ satisfy requirements 1–6, and $\varphi \in \mathcal{L}$. Let $a \in \mathcal{A}$ be the value returned by $\widetilde{\alpha}^{\updownarrow}\langle\mathcal{L}, \mathcal{A}\rangle(\varphi)$. Then*
1. *a over-approximates $\widehat{\alpha}(\varphi)$; i.e., $\widehat{\alpha}(\varphi) \sqsubseteq a$.*
2. *If $\mathcal{A}$ has neither infinite ascending nor infinite descending chains and $\widetilde{\alpha}^{\updownarrow}\langle\mathcal{L}, \mathcal{A}\rangle(\varphi)$ returns with no timeout, then $a = \widehat{\alpha}(\varphi)$.* □

Defn. 1 allows `AbstractConsequence`(a_1, a_2) to return any $a \in \mathcal{A}$ as long as a satisfies $a_1 \sqsubseteq a$ and $a \not\sqsupseteq a_2$. Thus, for a given abstract domain $\mathcal{A}$ there could be multiple implementations of the `AbstractConsequence` operation. In particular, `AbstractConsequence`(a_1, a_2) can return a_1, because $a_1 \sqsubseteq a_1$ and $a_1 \not\sqsupseteq a_2$. If this particular implementation of `AbstractConsequence` is used, then Alg. 5 reduces to the RSY algorithm (Alg. 1). However, as illustrated in §2, the decision-procedure queries issued by the RSY algorithm can be very expensive.

Conjunctive Domains. We now define a class of *conjunctive domains*, for which `AbstractConsequence` can be implemented by the method presented as Alg. 6. The benefit of Alg. 6 is that it causes Alg. 5 to issue the kind of inexpensive queries that we see in $\widehat{\alpha}^{\uparrow}_{\text{KS}}$. Let $\varPhi$ be a given set of formulas expressed in $\mathcal{L}$. A *conjunctive domain* over $\varPhi$ is an abstract domain $\mathcal{A}$ such that:

Algorithm 6. AbstractConsequence(a_1, a_2) for conjunctive domains

---

1 **if** $a_1 = \perp$ **then return** $\perp$
2 Let $\Psi \subseteq \Phi$ be the set of formulas such that $\widehat{\gamma}(a_1) = \bigwedge \Psi$
3 **foreach** $\psi \in \Psi$ **do**
4      $a \leftarrow \mu\widehat{\alpha}(\psi)$
5   **if** $a \not\sqsupseteq a_2$ **then return** a

- For any $a \in \mathcal{A}$, there exists a finite subset $\Psi \subseteq \Phi$ such that $\widehat{\gamma}(a) = \bigwedge \Psi$.
- For any finite $\Psi \subseteq \Phi$, there exists an $a \in \mathcal{A}$ such that $\gamma(a) = [\![\bigwedge \Psi]\!]$.
- There is an algorithm $\mu\widehat{\alpha}(\varphi)$ ("micro-$\widehat{\alpha}$") that, for each singleton formula $\varphi \in \Phi$, returns $a_\varphi \in \mathcal{A}$ such that $\widehat{\alpha}(\varphi) = a_\varphi$.
- There is an algorithm that, for all $a_1, a_2 \in \mathcal{A}$, checks $a_1 \sqsubseteq a_2$.

Many common domains are conjunctive domains. For example, using v, v_i for program variables and c, c_i for constants:

Domain	Φ
Interval domain	inequalities of the form $c_1 \leq v$ and $v \leq c_2$
Octagon domain [20]	inequalities of the form $\pm v_1 \pm v_2 \leq c$
Polyhedral domain [7]	linear inequalities over reals or rationals
KS domain [15,11]	linear equalities over integers mod 2^w

Theorem 2. *When $\mathcal{A}$ is a conjunctive domain over Φ, Alg. 6 is an acceptable abstract-consequence operation.*   □

Discussion. We can weaken part 2 of Thm. 1 to allow $\mathcal{A}$ to have infinite descending chains by modifying Alg. 5 slightly. The modified algorithm has to ensure that it does not get trapped updating *upper* along an infinite descending chain, and that it exits when *lower* has converged to $\widehat{\alpha}(\varphi)$. We can accomplish these goals by forcing the algorithm to perform the basic RSY iteration step at least once every N iterations, for some fixed N. A version of Alg. 5 that implements this strategy is presented in [32].

As presented, Alg. 5 exits and returns the value of *upper* the first time the decision procedure times out. We can improve the precision of Alg. 5 by not exiting after the first timeout, and instead trying other abstract consequences. The algorithm will exit and return *upper* only if it cannot find an abstract consequence for which the decision-procedure terminates within the time bound. For conjunctive domains, Alg. 5 can be modified to enumerate all conjuncts of *lower* that are abstract consequences; to implement this strategy, lines 4–7 of Alg. 5 are replaced with

---

```
progress ← false                                    // Initialize progress
foreach p such that p = AbstractConsequence(lower, upper) do
    S ← Model(φ ∧ ¬γ̂(p))
    if S is not TimeOut then
        progress ← true                             // Can make progress
        break
if ¬progress then return upper                       // Could not make progress
```

Henceforth, when we refer to $\widetilde{\alpha}^{\ddagger}$, we mean Alg. 5 with the above two changes.

Relationship of `AbstractConsequence` to Interpolation. To avoid the potential for confusion, we now discuss how the notion of abstract consequence differs from the well-known concept of *interpolation* [8]:

> A logic $\mathcal{L}$ *supports interpolation* if for all $\varphi_1, \varphi_2 \in \mathcal{L}$ such that $\varphi_1 \Rightarrow \varphi_2$, there exists a formula I such that (i) $\varphi_1 \Rightarrow I$, (ii) $I \Rightarrow \varphi_2$, and (iii) I uses only symbols in the shared vocabulary of φ_1 and φ_2.

Although condition (i) is part of Defn. 1, the restrictions imposed by conditions (ii) and (iii) are not part of Defn. 1. From an operational standpoint, condition (iii) in the definition of interpolation serves as a heuristic that generally allows interpolants to be expressed as small formulas. In the context of $\widetilde{\alpha}^{\ddagger}$, we are interested in obtaining small formulas to use in the decision-procedure query (line 5 of Alg. 5). Thus, given $a_1, a_2 \in \mathcal{A}$, it might appear plausible to use an interpolant I of $\widehat{\gamma}(a_1)$ and $\widehat{\gamma}(a_2)$ in $\widetilde{\alpha}^{\ddagger}$ instead of the abstract consequence of a_1 and a_2. However, there are a few problems with such an approach:

- There is no guarantee that I will indeed be simple; for instance, if the vocabulary of $\widehat{\gamma}(a_1)$ is a subset of the vocabulary of $\widehat{\gamma}(a_2)$, then I could be $\widehat{\gamma}(a_1)$ itself, in which case Alg. 5 performs the more expensive RSY iteration step.
- Converting the formula I into an abstract value $p \in \mathcal{A}$ for use in line 9 of Alg. 5 itself requires performing $\widehat{\alpha}$ on I.

As discussed above, many domains are conjunctive domains, and for conjunctive domains is it always possible to find a *single conjunct* that is an abstract consequence (see Thm. 2). Moreover, such a conjunct is not necessarily an interpolant.

4   Instantiations

4.1   Herbrand-Equalities Domain

Herbrand equalities are used in analyses for partial redundancy elimination, loop-invariant code motion [30], and strength reduction [31]. In these analyses, arithmetic operations (e.g., $+$ and $*$) are treated as term constructors. Two program variables are known to hold equal values if the analyzer determines that the variables hold equal terms. Herbrand equalities can also be used to analyze programs whose types are user-defined algebraic data-types.

Basic Definitions. Let $\mathcal{F}$ be a set of function symbols. The function $arity \colon \mathcal{F} \rightarrow \mathbb{N}$ yields the number of parameters of each function symbol. *Terms* over $\mathcal{F}$ are defined in the usual way; each function symbol f always requires $arity(f)$ parameters. Let $\mathcal{T}(\mathcal{F}, X)$ denote the set of finite terms generated by $\mathcal{F}$ and variable set X. The *Herbrand universe* of $\mathcal{F}$ is $\mathcal{T}(\mathcal{F}, \emptyset)$, the set of *ground terms* over $\mathcal{F}$.

A *Herbrand state* is a mapping from program variables $\mathcal{V}$ to ground terms (i.e., a function in $\mathcal{V} \rightarrow \mathcal{T}(\mathcal{F}, \emptyset)$). The concrete domain consists of all sets of Herbrand states: $\mathcal{C} \stackrel{\text{def}}{=} \mathcal{P}(\mathcal{V} \rightarrow \mathcal{T}(\mathcal{F}, \emptyset))$. We can apply a Herbrand state σ to a term $t \in \mathcal{T}(\mathcal{F}, \mathcal{V})$ as follows:

$$\sigma[t] \stackrel{\text{def}}{=} \begin{cases} \sigma(t) & \text{if } t \in \mathcal{V} \\ f(\sigma[t_1], \ldots, \sigma[t_k]) & \text{if } t = f(t_1, \ldots, t_k) \end{cases}$$

The Herbrand-Equalities Domain. Sets of Herbrand states can be abstracted in several ways. One way is to use conjunctions of equations among terms (whence the name "Herbrand-equalities domain"). Such systems of equations can be represented using Equivalence DAGs [30]. A different, but equivalent, approach is to use a representation based on *idempotent substitutions*: $\mathcal{A} = (\mathcal{V} \to \mathcal{T}(\mathcal{F}, \mathcal{V}))_\perp$. Idempotence means that for each $\sigma \neq \perp$ and $v \in \mathcal{V}$, $\sigma[\sigma(v)] = \sigma(v)$. The meaning of an idempotent substitution $\sigma \in \mathcal{A}$ is given by its concretization, $\gamma \colon \mathcal{A} \to \mathcal{C}$, where $\gamma(\perp) = \emptyset$, and otherwise

$$\gamma(\sigma) = \{\rho \colon \mathcal{V} \to \mathcal{T}(\mathcal{F}, \emptyset) \mid \forall v \in \mathcal{V} \colon \rho(v) = \rho[\sigma(v)]\}. \tag{2}$$

We now show that the Herbrand-equalities domain satisfies the requirements of the bilateral framework. We will assume that the logical language $\mathcal{L}$ has all the function symbols and constant symbols from $\mathcal{F}$, equality, and a constant symbol for each element from $\mathcal{V}$. (In a minor abuse of notation, the set of such constant symbols will also be denoted by $\mathcal{V}$.) The logic's universe is the Herbrand universe of $\mathcal{F}$ (i.e., $\mathcal{T}(\mathcal{F}, \emptyset)$). An interpretation maps the constants in $\mathcal{V}$ to terms in $\mathcal{T}(\mathcal{F}, \emptyset)$. To be able to express $\widehat{\gamma}(p)$ and $\neg\widehat{\gamma}(p)$ (see item 5 below), we assume that $\mathcal{L}$ contains at least the following productions:

$$\begin{aligned} F &::= F \wedge F \mid \neg F \mid v = T \text{ for } v \in \mathcal{V} \mid \text{ false} \\ T &::= v \in \mathcal{V} \mid f(T_1, \ldots, T_k) \text{ when } arity(f) = k \end{aligned} \tag{3}$$

1. There is a Galois connection $\mathcal{C} \xrightleftharpoons[\alpha]{\gamma} \mathcal{A}$:
   - The ordering on $\mathcal{C}$ is the subset relation on sets of Herbrand states.
   - $\gamma(\sigma)$ is given in Eqn. (2).
   - $\alpha(S) = \bigsqcap\{a \mid \gamma(a) \supseteq S\}$.
   - For $a, b \in \mathcal{A}$, $a \sqsubseteq b$ iff $\gamma(a) \subseteq \gamma(b)$.
2. Meet is most-general unification of substitutions, computed by standard unification techniques [18, Thm. 3.1].
3. Join is most-specific generalization, computed by "dual unification" or "anti-unification" [23,26], [18, Thm. 5.8].
4. Equality checking is described by Lassez et al. [18, Prop. 4.10].
5. $\widehat{\gamma}\colon \widehat{\gamma}(\perp) = \text{false}$; otherwise, $\widehat{\gamma}(\sigma)$ is $\bigwedge_{v \in \mathcal{V}} v = \sigma(v)$.
6. One can obtain a decision procedure for $\mathcal{L}$ formulas using the built-in datatype mechanism of, e.g., Z3 [9] or Yices [10], and obtain the necessary decision procedure using an existing SMT solver.
7. $\mathcal{L}$ is closed under conjunction and negation.
8. `AbstractConsequence`: The domain is a conjunctive domain, as can be seen from the definition of $\widehat{\gamma}$.

Thm. 1 ensures that Alg. 5 returns $\widehat{\alpha}(\varphi)$ when abstract domain $\mathcal{A}$ has neither infinite ascending nor infinite descending chains. The Herbrand-equalities domain has no infinite ascending chains [18, Lem. 3.15]. The domain described here also has no infinite descending chains, essentially because every right-hand term in every Herbrand state has no variables but those in $\mathcal{V}$. (Worked examples of $\widetilde{\alpha}^{\updownarrow}$ (Alg. 5) for the Herbrand-equalities domain are given in [32].)

4.2 Polyhedral Domain

An element of the polyhedral domain [7] is a convex polyhedron, bounded by hyperplanes. It may be unbounded in some directions. The symbolic concretization of a polyhedron is a conjunction of linear inequalities. The polyhedral domain is a conjunctive domain:

– Each polyhedron can be expressed as some conjunction of linear inequalities ("half-spaces") from the set $\mathcal{F} = \left\{ \sum_{v \in \mathcal{V}} c_v v \geq c \,\middle|\, c, c_v \text{ are constants} \right\}$.
– Every finite conjunction of facts from $\mathcal{F}$ can be represented as a polyhedron.
– $\mu\widehat{\alpha}$: Each formula in $\mathcal{F}$ corresponds to a simple, one-constraint polyhedron.
– There is an algorithm for comparing two polyhedra [7].

In addition, there are algorithms for join, meet, and checking equality.

The logic QF_LRA (quantifier-free linear real arithmetic) supported by SMT solvers provides a decision procedure for the fragment of logic that is required to express negation, conjunction, and $\widehat{\gamma}$ of a polyhedron. Consequently, the polyhedral domain satisfies the bilateral framework, and therefore supports the $\widetilde{\alpha}^{\updownarrow}$ algorithm. The polyhedral domain has both infinite ascending chains and infinite descending chains, and hence Alg. 5 is only guaranteed to compute an over-approximation of $\widehat{\alpha}(\varphi)$.

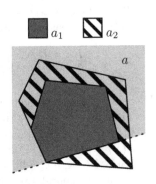

Fig. 4. Abs. conseq. for polyhedra. $a = \texttt{AbstractConsequence}(a_1, a_2)$.

Because the polyhedral domain is a conjunctive domain, if $a_1 \subsetneqq a_2$, then some single constraint a of a_1 satisfies $a \not\sqsupseteq a_2$. For instance, for the polyhedra a_1 and a_2 in Fig. 4, the region a above the dotted line is an acceptable abstract consequence.

5 Experiments

In this section, we compare two algorithms for performing symbolic abstraction for the affine-relations (AR) domain [15,11]:

– the $\widehat{\alpha}^{\uparrow}_{\text{KS}}$ procedure of Alg. 2 [11].
– the $\widetilde{\alpha}^{\updownarrow}\langle\text{AR}\rangle$ procedure that is the instantiation of Alg. 5 for the affine-relations (AR) domain and QFBV logic.

| Prog. | Measures of size | | | | Performance (x86) | | | Better |
| name | instrs | procs | BBs | brs | $\widehat{\alpha}_{KS}^{\uparrow}$ | | $\widetilde{\alpha}^{\updownarrow}\langle AR\rangle$ | $\widetilde{\alpha}^{\updownarrow}\langle AR\rangle$ |
					WPDS	t/o	WPDS	precision
finger	532	18	298	48	104.0	4	138.9	**6.3%**
subst	1093	16	609	74	196.7	4	214.6	0%
label	1167	16	573	103	146.1	2	171.6	0%
chkdsk	1468	18	787	119	377.2	16	417.9	0%
convert	1927	38	1013	161	287.1	10	310.5	0%
route	1982	40	931	243	618.4	14	589.9	**2.5%**
logoff	2470	46	1145	306	611.2	16	644.6	**15.0%**
setup	4751	67	1862	589	1499	60	1576	**1.0%**

Fig. 5. WPDS experiments. The columns show the number of instructions (instrs); the number of procedures (procs); the number of basic blocks (BBs); the number of branch instructions (brs); the times, in seconds, for $\widehat{\alpha}_{KS}^{\uparrow}$ and $\widetilde{\alpha}^{\updownarrow}\langle AR\rangle$ WPDS construction; the number of invocations of $\widehat{\alpha}_{KS}^{\uparrow}$ that had a decision procedure timeout (t/o); and the degree of improvement gained by using $\widetilde{\alpha}^{\updownarrow}\langle AR\rangle$-generated ARA weights rather than $\widehat{\alpha}_{KS}^{\uparrow}$ weights (measured as the percentage of control points whose inferred one-vocabulary affine relation was strictly more precise under $\widetilde{\alpha}^{\updownarrow}\langle AR\rangle$-based analysis).

Although the bilateral algorithm $\widetilde{\alpha}^{\updownarrow}\langle AR\rangle$ benefits from being resilient to time-outs, it maintains *both* an over-approximation and an under-approximation. Thus, the experiments were designed to understand the trade-off between performance and precision. In particular, the experiments were designed to answer the following questions:

1. How does the speed of $\widetilde{\alpha}^{\updownarrow}\langle AR\rangle$ compare with that of $\widehat{\alpha}_{KS}^{\uparrow}$?
2. How does the precision of $\widetilde{\alpha}^{\updownarrow}\langle AR\rangle$ compare with that of $\widehat{\alpha}_{KS}^{\uparrow}$?

To address these questions, we performed affine-relations analysis (ARA) on x86 machine code, computing affine relations over the x86 registers. Our experiments were run on a single core of a quad-core 3.0 GHz Xeon computer running 64-bit Windows XP (SP2), configured so that a user process has 4GB of memory. We analyzed a corpus of Windows utilities using the WALi [14] system for weighted pushdown systems (WPDSs). For the $\widehat{\alpha}_{KS}^{\uparrow}$-based ($\widetilde{\alpha}^{\updownarrow}\langle AR\rangle$-based) analysis we used a weight domain of $\widehat{\alpha}^{\uparrow}$-generated ($\widetilde{\alpha}^{\updownarrow}\langle AR\rangle$-generated) ARA transformers. The weight on each WPDS rule encodes the ARA transformer for a basic block B of the program, including a jump or branch to a successor block. A formula φ_B is created that captures the concrete semantics of B, and then the ARA weight for B is obtained by performing $\widehat{\alpha}(\varphi_B)$. We used EWPDS merge functions [17] to preserve caller-save and callee-save registers across call sites. The post* query used the FWPDS algorithm [16].

Fig. 5 lists several size parameters of the examples (number of instructions, procedures, basic blocks, and branches).[1] Prior research [11] shows that the calls to $\widehat{\alpha}$ during WPDS construction dominate the total time for ARA. Although the overall time taken by $\widehat{\alpha}$ is not limited by a timeout, we use a 3-second timeout for each invocation of the decision procedure (as in Elder et al. [11]). Column 7 of Fig. 5 lists the number invocations of $\widehat{\alpha}^{\uparrow}_{\text{KS}}$ that had a decision-procedure timeout, and hence returned $\top$. (Note that, in general, $\widehat{\alpha}^{\uparrow}_{\text{KS}}$ implements an over-approximating $\widetilde{\alpha}$ operation.)

Columns 6 and 8 of Fig. 5 list the time taken, in seconds, for $\widehat{\alpha}^{\uparrow}_{\text{KS}}$ and $\widetilde{\alpha}^{\downarrow}\langle\text{AR}\rangle$ WPDS construction. We observe that on average $\widetilde{\alpha}^{\downarrow}\langle\text{AR}\rangle$ is about 10% slower than $\widehat{\alpha}^{\uparrow}_{\text{KS}}$ (computed as the geometric mean), which answers question 1.

To answer question 2 we compared the precision of the WPDS analysis when using $\widehat{\alpha}^{\uparrow}_{\text{KS}}$ with the precision obtained using $\widetilde{\alpha}^{\downarrow}\langle\text{AR}\rangle$. In particular, we compare the affine-relation invariants computed by the $\widehat{\alpha}^{\uparrow}_{\text{KS}}$-based and $\widetilde{\alpha}^{\downarrow}\langle\text{AR}\rangle$-based analyses for each *control point*—i.e., the beginning of a basic block that ends with a branch. The last column of Fig. 5 shows the percentage of control points for which the $\widetilde{\alpha}^{\downarrow}\langle\text{AR}\rangle$-based analysis computed a strictly more precise affine relation. We see that the $\widetilde{\alpha}^{\downarrow}\langle\text{AR}\rangle$-based analysis improves precision at up to 15% of control points, and, on average, the $\widetilde{\alpha}^{\downarrow}\langle\text{AR}\rangle$-based analysis is more precise for 3.1% of the control points (computed as the arithmetic mean), which answers question 2.

6   Related Work

6.1   Related Work on Symbolic Abstraction

Previous work on symbolic abstraction falls into three categories:

1. algorithms for specific domains [24,3,2,15,11]
2. algorithms for parameterized abstract domains [12,35,28,22]
3. abstract-domain frameworks [25,34].

What distinguishes category 3 from category 2 is that each of the results cited in category 2 applies to a specific *family* of abstract domains, defined by a *parameterized Galois connection* (e.g., with an abstraction function equipped with a readily identifiable parameter for controlling the abstraction). In contrast, the results in category 3 are defined by an *interface*; for any abstract domain that satisfies the requirements of the interface, one has a method for symbolic abstraction. The approach presented in this paper falls into category 3.

Algorithms for Specific Domains. Regehr and Reid [24] present a method that constructs abstract transformers for machine instructions, for interval and

---

1 Due to the high cost of the ARA-based WPDS construction, all analyses excluded the code for libraries. Because register `eax` holds the return value from a call, library functions were modeled approximately (albeit unsoundly, in general) by "`havoc(eax)`".

bitwise abstract domains. Their method does not call a SAT solver, but instead uses the physical processor (or a simulator of a processor) as a black box.

Brauer and King [3] developed a method that works from below to derive abstract transformers for the interval domain. Their method is based on an approach due to Monniaux [22] (see below), but they changed two aspects:

1. They express the concrete semantics with a Boolean formula (via "bit-blasting"), which allows a formula equivalent to $\forall x.\varphi$ to be obtained from φ (in CNF) by removing the x and $\neg x$ literals from all of the clauses of φ.
2. Whereas Monniaux's method performs abstraction and then quantifier elimination, Brauer and King's method performs quantifier elimination on the concrete specification, and then performs abstraction.

Barrett and King [2] describe a method for generating range and set abstractions for bit-vectors that are constrained by Boolean formulas. For range analysis, the algorithm separately computes the minimum and maximum value of the range for an n-bit bit-vector using $2n$ calls to a SAT solver, with each SAT query determining a single bit of the output. The result is the best over-approximation of the value that an integer variable can take on (i.e., $\widehat{\alpha}$).

Algorithms for Parameterized Abstract Domains. Graf and Saïdi [12] showed that decision procedures can be used to generate best abstract transformers for predicate-abstraction domains. Other work has investigated more efficient methods to generate approximate transformers that are not best transformers, but approach the precision of best transformers [1,4].

Yorsh et al. [35] developed a method that works from above to perform $\widetilde{\alpha}(\varphi)$ for the kind of abstract domains used in shape analysis (i.e., "canonical abstraction" of logical structures [27]).

Template Constraint Matrices (TCMs) are a parametrized family of linear-inequality domains for expressing invariants in linear real arithmetic. Sankaranarayanan et al. [28] gave a parametrized meet, join, and set of abstract transformers for all TCM domains. Monniaux [22] gave an algorithm that finds the best transformer in a TCM domain across a straight-line block (assuming that concrete operations consist of piecewise linear functions), and good transformers across more complicated control flow. However, the algorithm uses quantifier elimination, and no polynomial-time elimination algorithm is known for piecewise-linear systems.

Abstract-Domain Frameworks. Thakur and Reps [34] recently discovered a new framework for performing symbolic abstraction from "above": $\widetilde{\alpha}^{\downarrow}$. The $\widetilde{\alpha}^{\downarrow}$ framework builds upon the insight that Stålmarck's algorithm for propositional validity checking [29] can be explained using abstract-interpretation terminology [33]. The $\widetilde{\alpha}^{\downarrow}$ framework adapts the same algorithmic components of this generalization to perform symbolic abstraction. Because $\widetilde{\alpha}^{\downarrow}$ maintains an over-approximation of $\widehat{\alpha}$, it is resilient to timeouts.

The $\widetilde{\alpha}^{\downarrow}$ framework is based on much different principles from the RSY and bilateral frameworks. The latter frameworks use an *inductive-learning approach* to learn from examples, while the $\widetilde{\alpha}^{\downarrow}$ framework uses a *deductive approach* by using inference rules to deduce the answer. Thus, they represent two different classes of frameworks, with different requirements for the abstract domain.

6.2   Other Related Work

Cover Algorithms. Gulwani and Musuvathi [13] defined what they termed the "cover problem", which addresses *approximate existential quantifier elimination*: Given a formula φ in logic $\mathcal{L}$, and a set of variables V, find the strongest quantifier-free formula $\overline{\varphi}$ in $\mathcal{L}$ such that $[\![\exists V : \varphi]\!] \subseteq [\![\overline{\varphi}]\!]$. They presented cover algorithms for the theories of uninterpreted functions and linear arithmetic, and showed that covers exist in some theories that do not support quantifier elimination.

The notion of a cover has similarities to the notion of symbolic abstraction, but the two notions are distinct. Our technical report [32] discusses the differences in detail, describing symbolic abstraction as over-approximating a formula φ using an impoverished logic fragment (e.g., approximating an arbitrary QFBV formula, such as Eqn. (1), using conjunctions of modular-arithmetic affine equalities) while a cover algorithm only removes variables V from the vocabulary of φ. The two approaches yield different over-approximations of φ, and the over-approximation obtained by a cover algorithm does not, in general, yield suitable abstract values and abstract transformers.

Logical Abstract Domains. Cousot et al. [6] define a method of abstract interpretation based on using particular sets of logical formulas as abstract-domain elements (so-called *logical abstract domains*). They face the problems of (i) performing abstraction from unrestricted formulas to the elements of a logical abstract domain [6, §7.1], and (ii) creating abstract transformers that transform input elements of a logical abstract domain to output elements of the domain [6, §7.2]. Their problems are particular cases of $\widehat{\alpha}(\varphi)$. They present heuristic methods for creating over-approximations of $\widehat{\alpha}(\varphi)$.

Connections to Machine-Learning Algorithms. In [25], a connection was made between symbolic abstraction (in abstract interpretation) and the problem of *concept learning* (in machine learning). In machine-learning terms, an abstract domain $\mathcal{A}$ is a *hypothesis space*; each domain element corresponds to a *concept*. Given a formula φ, the symbolic-abstraction problem is to find the most specific concept that explains the meaning of φ.

$\widehat{\alpha}_{\text{RSY}}^{\uparrow}$ (Alg. 1) is related to the Find-S algorithm [21, §2.4] for concept learning. Both algorithms start with the most-specific hypothesis (i.e., $\bot$) and work bottom-up to find the most-specific hypothesis that is consistent with positive examples of the concept. Both algorithms generalize their current hypothesis each time they process a (positive) training example that is not explained by the current hypothesis. A major difference is that Find-S receives a sequence of positive and negative examples of the concept (e.g., from nature). It discards negative examples, and its generalization steps are based solely on the positive examples. In contrast, $\widehat{\alpha}^{\uparrow}_{RSY}$ repeatedly calls a decision procedure to generate the next positive example; $\widehat{\alpha}^{\uparrow}_{RSY}$ never sees a negative example.

A similar connection exists between $\widetilde{\alpha}^{\updownarrow}$ (Alg. 5) and a different concept-learning algorithm, called the Candidate-Elimination algorithm [21, §2.5]. Both algorithms maintain two approximations of the concept, one that is an over-approximation and one that is an under-approximation.

References

1. Ball, T., Podelski, A., Rajamani, S.K.: Boolean and Cartesian Abstraction for Model Checking C Programs. In: Margaria, T., Yi, W. (eds.) TACAS 2001. LNCS, vol. 2031, pp. 268–283. Springer, Heidelberg (2001)
2. Barrett, E., King, A.: Range and set abstraction using SAT. ENTCS 267(1) (2010)
3. Brauer, J., King, A.: Automatic Abstraction for Intervals Using Boolean Formulae. In: Cousot, R., Martel, M. (eds.) SAS 2010. LNCS, vol. 6337, pp. 167–183. Springer, Heidelberg (2010)
4. Clarke, E., Kroening, D., Sharygina, N., Yorav, K.: Predicate abstraction of ANSI-C programs using SAT. FMSD 25(2-3) (2004)
5. Cousot, P., Cousot, R.: Systematic design of program analysis frameworks. In: POPL, pp. 269–282 (1979)
6. Cousot, P., Cousot, R., Mauborgne, L.: Logical abstract domains and interpretations. In: The Future of Software Engineering (2011)
7. Cousot, P., Halbwachs, N.: Automatic discovery of linear constraints among variables of a program. In: POPL (1978)
8. Craig, W.: Three uses of the Herbrand-Gentzen theorem in relating model theory and proof theory. J. Sym. Logic 22(3) (September 1957)
9. de Moura, L., Bjørner, N.: Z3: An Efficient SMT Solver. In: Ramakrishnan, C.R., Rehof, J. (eds.) TACAS 2008. LNCS, vol. 4963, pp. 337–340. Springer, Heidelberg (2008)
10. Dutertre, B., de Moura, L.: Yices: An SMT solver (2006), yices.csl.sri.com/
11. Elder, M., Lim, J., Sharma, T., Andersen, T., Reps, T.: Abstract Domains of Affine Relations. In: Yahav, E. (ed.) SAS 2011. LNCS, vol. 6887, pp. 198–215. Springer, Heidelberg (2011)
12. Graf, S., Saïdi, H.: Construction of Abstract State Graphs with PVS. In: Grumberg, O. (ed.) CAV 1997. LNCS, vol. 1254, pp. 72–83. Springer, Heidelberg (1997)
13. Gulwani, S., Musuvathi, M.: Cover Algorithms and Their Combination. In: Drossopoulou, S. (ed.) ESOP 2008. LNCS, vol. 4960, pp. 193–207. Springer, Heidelberg (2008)
14. Kidd, N., Lal, A., Reps, T.: WALi: The Weighted Automaton Library (2007), http://www.cs.wisc.edu/wpis/wpds/download.php
15. King, A., Søndergaard, H.: Automatic Abstraction for Congruences. In: Barthe, G., Hermenegildo, M. (eds.) VMCAI 2010. LNCS, vol. 5944, pp. 197–213. Springer, Heidelberg (2010)
16. Lal, A., Reps, T.: Improving Pushdown System Model Checking. In: Ball, T., Jones, R.B. (eds.) CAV 2006. LNCS, vol. 4144, pp. 343–357. Springer, Heidelberg (2006)

17. Lal, A., Reps, T., Balakrishnan, G.: Extended Weighted Pushdown Systems. In: Etessami, K., Rajamani, S.K. (eds.) CAV 2005. LNCS, vol. 3576, pp. 434–448. Springer, Heidelberg (2005)

18. Lassez, J.-L., Maher, M.J., Marriott, K.: Unification Revisited. In: Boscarol, M., Carlucci Aiello, L., Levi, G. (eds.) Foundations of Logic and Functional Programming. LNCS, vol. 306, pp. 67–113. Springer, Heidelberg (1988)

19. Lim, J., Reps, T.: A System for Generating Static Analyzers for Machine Instructions. In: Hendren, L. (ed.) CC 2008. LNCS, vol. 4959, pp. 36–52. Springer, Heidelberg (2008)

20. Miné, A.: The octagon abstract domain. In: WCRE, pp. 310–322 (2001)

21. Mitchell, T.: Machine Learning. WCB/McGraw-Hill, Boston (1997)

22. Monniaux, D.: Automatic modular abstractions for template numerical constraints. Logical Methods in Comp. Sci. 6(3) (2010)

23. Plotkin, G.: A note on inductive generalization. In: Machine Intelligence, vol. 5, pp. 153–165. Edinburgh Univ. Press (1970)

24. Regehr, J., Reid, A.: HOIST: A system for automatically deriving static analyzers for embedded systems. In: ASPLOS (2004)

25. Reps, T., Sagiv, M., Yorsh, G.: Symbolic Implementation of the Best Transformer. In: Steffen, B., Levi, G. (eds.) VMCAI 2004. LNCS, vol. 2937, pp. 252–266. Springer, Heidelberg (2004)

26. Reynolds, J.: Transformational systems and the algebraic structure of atomic formulas. Machine Intelligence 5(1), 135–151 (1970)

27. Sagiv, M., Reps, T., Wilhelm, R.: Parametric shape analysis via 3-valued logic. TOPLAS 24(3), 217–298 (2002)

28. Sankaranarayanan, S., Sipma, H.B., Manna, Z.: Scalable Analysis of Linear Systems Using Mathematical Programming. In: Cousot, R. (ed.) VMCAI 2005. LNCS, vol. 3385, pp. 25–41. Springer, Heidelberg (2005)

29. Sheeran, M., Stålmarck, G.: A tutorial on Stålmarck's proof procedure for propositional logic. FMSD 16(1), 23–58 (2000)

30. Steffen, B., Knoop, J., Rüthing, O.: The value flow graph: A program representation for optimal program transformations. In: ESOP (1990)

31. Steffen, B., Knoop, J., Rüthing, O.: Efficient Code Motion and an Adaption to Strength Reduction. In: Abramsky, S., Maibaum, T.S.E. (eds.) TAPSOFT 1991, CCPSD 1991, and ADC-Talks 1991. LNCS, vol. 494, pp. 394–415. Springer, Heidelberg (1991)

32. Thakur, A., Elder, M., Reps, T.: Bilateral algorithms for symbolic abstraction. TR 1713, CS Dept., Univ. of Wisconsin, Madison, WI (March 2012), http://www.cs.wisc.edu/wpis/papers/tr1713.pdf

33. Thakur, A., Reps, T.: A Generalization of Stålmarck's Method. In: SAS (2012)

34. Thakur, A., Reps, T.: A Method for Symbolic Computation of Abstract Operations. In: Madhusudan, P., Seshia, S.A. (eds.) CAV 2012. LNCS, vol. 7358, pp. 174–192. Springer, Heidelberg (2012)

35. Yorsh, G., Reps, T., Sagiv, M.: Symbolically Computing Most-Precise Abstract Operations for Shape Analysis. In: Jensen, K., Podelski, A. (eds.) TACAS 2004. LNCS, vol. 2988, pp. 530–545. Springer, Heidelberg (2004)

Making Abstract Interpretation Incomplete: Modeling the Potency of Obfuscation

Roberto Giacobazzi and Isabella Mastroeni

Dipartimento di Informatica, Università di Verona, Verona, Italy
{roberto.giacobazzi,isabella.mastroeni}@univr.it

Abstract. Recent studies on code protection showed that incompleteness, in the abstract interpretation framework, has a key role in understanding program obfuscation. In particular, it is well known that completeness corresponds to exactness of a given analysis for a fixed program semantics, hence incompleteness implies the imprecision of an analysis with respect to the program semantics. In code protection, if the analysis corresponds to attacker capability of understanding a program semantics, then to study incompleteness means to study how to make an attacker harmless. We recently showed that this is possible by transforming the program semantics towards incompleteness, which corresponds to a code obfuscation. In this paper, we show that incompleteness can be induced also by transforming abstract domains. In this way we can associate with each obfuscated program (semantics) the most imprecise, harmless, analysis. We show that, for both the forms of completeness, backward and forward, we can uniquely simplify domains towards incompleteness, while in general it is not possible to uniquely refine domains. Finally, we show some examples of known code protection techniques that can be characterized in the new framework of abstract interpretation incompleteness.

1 Introduction

Abstract interpretation [7] is not only a theory for the approximation of the semantics of dynamic systems, but also a way of *understanding* information and computation. In particular, the notion of completeness/incompleteness in abstract interpretation provides a deep insight into the meaning of precise/imprecise analyses of programs. Abstract interpretation-based static analysis consists in fixing a level of abstraction for observing/analyzing the program behaviour in order to determine whether programs satisfy given properties in a sound way. For instance, if we analyse the sign property of variables, we compute the values of program variables looking only at their sign. Suppose to analyze $x := a + b$, then if $a \geq 0$ and $b \geq 0$ we surely know that $x \geq 0$, but if $b < 0$ then we cannot say anything about the sign of x. This situation depends on the incompleteness of the sign analysis with respect to the integer addition. In other words, the sign analysis is, in this case, *imprecise*, meaning that the abstract observer loses information about the program behaviour that it is unable to rebuild. Consider $x := a * b$, in this case we can check that, whichever is the sign of a and b we are always able to precisely characterize the sign of x (the rule sign of product). In this case we say that the analysis is precise, *complete*, since it captures exactly the property of x. This means that the concrete information the analysis ignores, by abstracting the program semantics, is useless for the computation of the program property.

A. Miné and D. Schmidt (Eds.): SAS 2012, LNCS 7460, pp. 129–145, 2012.

Why This Framework Can Be Useful in Code Protection? Code protection, and in particular code obfuscation, relies upon making security inseparable from code: *a program, or parts of it, are transformed in order to make them hard to understand or analyze* [4]. In programming languages, this means that the transformed code has to preserve the same desired behaviour, as the original program, yet making untrusted users analyses unable to reveal certain program (secret) properties. Hence, the connection between incompleteness and successful code obfuscation is clear, since the main objective of code obfuscation is that of making attacker program analysis useless, namely imprecise, and incompleteness models precisely the degree of imprecision of a given analysis [15]. Recently, this strong connection has been exploited for designing incompleteness-driven obfuscation techniques [23]. The idea is to combine two different frameworks: the obfuscators are designed as *program interpreters*, guaranteeing by construction the preservation of the semantics, and *incompleteness* is used to determine what kind of transformation we have to design in order to make a given analysis (the attacker model) imprecise. For instance, if we prove that by adding opaque predicates (predicates that are always true or false) [2] we make the control-flow graph analysis incomplete, then we know that we have to add precisely opaque predicates for making it obscure for an attacker able to analyze exactly the control-flow graph structure.

Our Idea: Incompleteness Transformers for "Measuring" Potency. Measuring the potency of obfuscating transformations is a key challenge in code protection. The classical notion of code obfuscation [3,5] defines an obfuscator as a *potent* transformation that preserves observable behaviour of programs. In this setting a transformation is potent when the obfuscated program is more complex (*to analyze*) than the original one. In other words, if there exists at least one analysis that is made harder, or even impossible to perform, namely imprecise. Again, the connection between (in)completeness and potency is quite straightforward, namely if, given the obfuscated program, we can find an incomplete analysis, then we can say that the obfuscation technique is potent.

The idea we propose in this paper is to extend the (in)completeness transformers framework in order to provide a formal model of the potency of obfuscation and a systematic method for characterizing it. The idea is to start from the systematic method existing for making an abstract domain *Obs* complete [20] and to invert/adjoin this construction. Hence, instead of constructing the most abstract *complete* refinement of *Obs*, i.e., $\mathcal{R}(Obs)$, we characterize the most abstract *incomplete* simplification $\mathcal{UR}(Obs)$ that (in order not to go too far) shares the same complete refinement with *Obs*. In this way we characterize the potency of an obfuscation technique by providing a "range" of potency: we guarantee that all the analyses between $\mathcal{R}(Obs)$ (excluded) and $\mathcal{UR}(Obs)$ (included) are imprecise, and therefore harmless, for the obfuscated program. In this case, the minimality of $\mathcal{UR}(Obs)$ systematically characterize a canonical imprecise analysis for which the obfuscation is potent. In contrast with completeness, where the problem of transforming domains for making them complete/precise has been widely studied [17,20], the problem of making domains incomplete by abstract domain transformations is still unexplored. We solve this problem for generic abstract domains in the Galois connection based abstract interpretation theory and show that the potency of well known obfuscation techniques such as opaque predicates [5], data-type obfuscation [11] and slicing obfuscation [24], can analyzed in this framework.

2 Abstract Domains Individually and Collectively

Standard abstract domain definition is formalised in [7] and [8] in terms of Galois connections. It is well known that this is a restriction for abstract interpretation because relevant abstractions do not form Galois connections and Galois connections are not expressive enough for modelling dynamic fix-point approximation [9]. Formally, if $\langle C, \leq, \top, \bot, \vee, \wedge \rangle$ is a complete lattice, monotone functions $\alpha : C \xrightarrow{m} A$ and $\gamma : A \xrightarrow{m} C$ form an *adjunction* or a *Galois connection* if for any $x \in C$ and $y \in A$: $\alpha(x) \leq_A y \Leftrightarrow x \leq_C \gamma(y)$. α [resp. γ] is the *left- [right-]adjoint* to γ [α] and it is additive [co-additive], i.e. it preserves *lub*'s [*glb*] of all subsets of the domain (emptyset included). The right adjoint of a function α is $\alpha^+ \stackrel{\text{def}}{=} \lambda x. \bigvee \{ y \mid \alpha(y) \leq x \}$. Conversely the left adjoint of γ is $\gamma^- \stackrel{\text{def}}{=} \lambda x. \bigwedge \{ y \mid x \leq \gamma(y) \}$ [8]. Abstract domains can be also equivalently formalized as closure operators on the concrete domain. An *upper [lower] closure operator* $\rho : C \longrightarrow C$ on a poset C is monotone, idempotent, and extensive: $\forall x \in C. \ x \leq_C \rho(x)$ [reductive: $\forall x \in C. \ x \geq_C \rho(x)$]. Closures are uniquely determined by their fix-points $\rho(C)$. The set of all upper [lower] closure operators on C is denoted by $uco(C)$ [$lco(C)$]. The *lattice of abstract domains* of C, is therefore isomorphic to $uco(C)$, (cf. [7, Section 7] and [8, Section 8]). Recall that if C is a complete lattice, then $\langle uco(C), \sqsubseteq, \sqcup, \sqcap, \lambda x. \top, id \rangle$ is a complete lattice [27], where $id \stackrel{\text{def}}{=} \lambda x.x$ and for every $\rho, \eta \in uco(C)$, $\rho \sqsubseteq \eta$ iff $\forall y \in C. \ \rho(y) \leq \eta(y)$ iff $\eta(C) \subseteq \rho(C)$. A_1 is more precise than A_2 (i.e., A_2 is an abstraction of A_1) iff $A_1 \sqsubseteq A_2$ in $uco(C)$. An element $x \in C$ is *meet-irreducible* if $x \neq \top$ and $x = a \wedge b$ implies $x \in \{a, b\}$. The set of meet-irreducible elements in C is denoted $\text{Mirr}(C)$. The downward closure of $S \subseteq C$ is defined as $\downarrow S \stackrel{\text{def}}{=} \{x \in C \mid \exists y \in S. \ x \leq_C y\}$, and for $x \in C$, $\downarrow x$ is a shorthand for $\downarrow \{x\}$. Given $X \subseteq C$, the least abstract domain containing X is the least closure including X as fix-points, which is the *Moore-closure* $\mathcal{M}(X) \stackrel{\text{def}}{=} \{\bigwedge S \mid S \subseteq X\}$.

Precision of an abstract interpretation typically relies upon the structure of the abstract domain [20]. Depending on where we compare the concrete and the abstract computations we obtain two different notions of completeness. If we compare the results in the abstract domain, we obtain what is called *backward completeness* ($\mathscr{B}$), while, if we compare the results in the concrete domain we obtain the so called *forward completeness* ($\mathscr{F}$) [8,17,20]. Formally, if $f : C \xrightarrow{m} C$ and $\rho \in uco(C)$, then ρ is $\mathscr{B}$-complete if $\rho \circ f \circ \rho = \rho \circ f$, while it is $\mathscr{F}$-complete if $\rho \circ f \circ \rho = f \circ \rho$. The problem of making abstract domains $\mathscr{B}$-complete has been solved in [20] and later generalised to $\mathscr{F}$-completeness in [17]. In a more general setting let $f : C_1 \longrightarrow C_2$ and $\rho \in uco(C_2)$ and $\eta \in uco(C_1)$. $\langle \rho, \eta \rangle$ is a pair of $\mathscr{B}[\mathscr{F}]$-complete abstractions for f if $\rho \circ f = \rho \circ f \circ \eta$ [$f \circ \eta = \rho \circ f \circ \eta$]. A pair of domain transformers has been associated with any completeness problem [12,18], which are respectively a *domain refinement* and *simplification*. In [20] and [17], a constructive characterization of the most abstract refinement, called *complete shell*, and of the most concrete simplification, called *complete core*, of any domain, making it $\mathscr{F}$ or $\mathscr{B}$-complete, for a given continuous function f, is given as a solution of simple domain equations based on the following basic operators:

$$R_f^{\mathscr{F}} \stackrel{\text{def}}{=} \lambda X. \mathcal{M}(f(X)) \quad \Big| \quad R_f^{\mathscr{B}} \stackrel{\text{def}}{=} \lambda X. \mathcal{M}(\bigcup_{y \in X} \max(f^{-1}(\downarrow y)))$$
$$C_f^{\mathscr{F}} \stackrel{\text{def}}{=} \lambda X. \{ y \in L \mid f(y) \subseteq X \} \quad \Big| \quad C_f^{\mathscr{B}} \stackrel{\text{def}}{=} \lambda X. \{ y \in L \mid \max(f^{-1}(\downarrow y)) \subseteq X \}$$

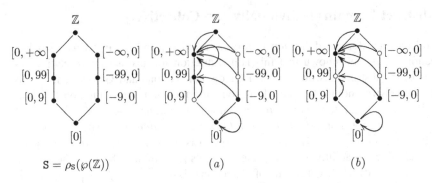

Fig. 1. The abstract domain S and two abstractions

Let $\ell \in \{\mathscr{F}, \mathscr{B}\}$. In [20] the authors proved that the most concrete $\beta \sqsupseteq \rho$ such that $\langle \beta, \eta \rangle$ is ℓ-complete and the most abstract $\beta \sqsubseteq \eta$ such that $\langle \rho, \beta \rangle$ is ℓ-complete are respectively the ℓ-complete core and ℓ-complete shell, which are: $\mathcal{C}^{\mathscr{B}}_{f,\eta}(\rho) \stackrel{\text{def}}{=} \rho \sqcup C^{\mathscr{B}}_f(\eta)$ $[\mathcal{C}^{\mathscr{F}}_{f,\rho}(\eta) \stackrel{\text{def}}{=} \eta \sqcup C^{\mathscr{F}}_f(\rho)]$ and $\mathcal{R}^{\mathscr{B}}_{f,\rho}(\eta) \stackrel{\text{def}}{=} \eta \sqcap R^{\mathscr{B}}_f(\rho)$ $[\mathcal{R}^{\mathscr{F}}_{f,\eta}(\rho) \stackrel{\text{def}}{=} \rho \sqcap R^{\mathscr{F}}_f(\eta)]$.

When $\eta = \rho$, then the fix-point iteration on abstract domains of the above function $\mathcal{R}^{\ell}_f(\rho) = \text{gfp}(\lambda X. \rho \sqcap R^{\ell}_f(X))$ is called the *absolute ℓ-complete shell*. By construction if f is additive then $\mathcal{R}^{\mathscr{B}}_f = \mathcal{R}^{\mathscr{F}}_{f+}$ (analogously $\mathcal{C}^{\mathscr{B}}_f = \mathcal{C}^{\mathscr{F}}_{f+}$) [17]. This means that when we have to solve a problem of $\mathscr{B}$-completeness for an additive function then we can equivalently solve the corresponding $\mathscr{F}$-completeness problem for its right adjoint.

Example 1. Assume S be the domain in Fig. 1, which is an abstraction of $\langle \wp(\mathbb{Z}), \subseteq \rangle$ for the analysis of integer variables and $sq : \wp(\mathbb{Z}) \to \wp(\mathbb{Z})$ be the square operation defined as follows: $sq(X) = \{ x^2 \mid x \in X \}$ for $X \in \wp(\mathbb{Z})$. Let $\rho_S \in uco(\wp(\mathbb{Z}))$ be the closure operator associated with S. The best correct approximation of sq in S is $sq^S : S \to S$ such that $sq^S(X) = \rho_S(sq(X))$, with $X \in S$ (the arrows in Fig. 1 (a)). It is easy to see that the abstraction $\rho_a = \{\mathbb{Z}, [0, +\infty], [0, 99], [-9, 0], [0]\}$ (black dots in Fig. 1 (a)) is not $\mathscr{B}$-complete on the concrete domain S for sq^S (for instance $\rho_a(sq^S(\rho_a([0,9]))) = [0, +\infty]$ but $\rho_a(sq^S([0,9])) = [0,99]$). The complete shell adds the maximal of inverse images of sq^S, namely it adds $[0,9]$. Note that, the shell does not add $[-99, 0]$ and $[-\infty, 0]$ since $\max \{ X \mid sq^S(X) \subseteq [0, +\infty] \} = \top$, hence all the other elements X such that $sq^S(X) = [0, +\infty]$ are not added. The complete core erases $[0, 99]$ hence it is $\{\mathbb{Z}, [0, +\infty], [-9, 0], [0]\}$.

On the other hand, $\rho_b = \{\mathbb{Z}, [0, +\infty], [0, 9], [-9, 0], [0]\}$ (black dots in Fig. 1 (b)) is not $\mathscr{F}$-complete on the concrete domain S for sq^S (for instance $\rho_b(sq^S(\rho_b([-9, 0]))) = [0, +\infty]$ but $sq^S(\rho_b([-9, 0])) = [0, 99]$). The complete shell adds the direct images of ρ_b fix points, i.e., $[0, 99]$, while the core erases the incomplete elements obtaining the domain $\{\mathbb{Z}, [0, +\infty], [0]\}$.

2.1   Adjoining Closure Operators

In the following we will make an extensive use of adjunction, in particular of closure operators. Janowitz [22] characterized the structure of *residuated* (adjoint) closure operators. The following result strengthen the characterization provided in [22] by showing the order-theoretic structure of residuated closures.

Proposition 2. *[16] Let $\tau \in lco(C)$ and $\eta \in uco(C)$. If $\langle \tau, \tau^+ \rangle$ and $\langle \eta^-, \eta \rangle$ are pairs of adjoint functions then we have $\tau^+ = \lambda X. \bigvee \{Y | \tau(Y) = \tau(X)\}$ and $\eta^- = \lambda X. \bigwedge \{Y | \eta(X) = \eta(Y)\}$.*

In particular this result leads to the observation that the existence of adjunction is related to the notion of *closure uniformity*. Uniform closures have been introduced in [19] for specifying the notion of *abstract domain compression*, namely the operation for reducing abstract domains to their minimal structure with respect to some given abstraction refinement $\eta \in lco(uco(C))$. An upper closure η is *meet-uniform* [19] if $\eta(\bigwedge \{Y | \eta(X) = \eta(Y)\}) = \eta(X)$. Join-uniformity is dually defined for lower closures. Well-known non-co-additive upper closures are meet-uniform, such as the downward closure $\downarrow$ of a subset of a partially ordered set [19].

It is known that any $\rho \in uco(C)$ is join-uniform and the set of meet-uniform upper closures $uco^*(C)$ is a Moore-family of $uco(C)$. Dually, the same holds for lower closure operators, namely $\tau \in lco(C)$ is meet-uniform and the set of join-uniform lower closures $lco^*(C)$ is a Moore-family of $lco(C)$. As observed in [19] when only uniformity holds, the adjoint function may fail monotonicity. In [19] the authors proved that the adjoint function is monotone on a lifted order induced by τ, $\leq_\tau \subseteq C \times C$, defined as: $x \leq_\tau y \Leftrightarrow (\tau(x) \leq \tau(y)) \wedge (\tau(x) = \tau(y) \Rightarrow x \leq y)$. $\leq_\tau$ is such that $\leq \Rightarrow \leq_\tau$. The following result is immediate by [22] and Prop. 2.

Proposition 3. *[16] Let $\tau \in lco(C)$ [$\eta \in uco(C)$]. $\langle \tau, \tau^+ \rangle$ [$\langle \eta^-, \eta \rangle$] is a pair of adjoint closures on the lifted order iff τ is join-uniform [η is meet-uniform].*

Example 4. Consider the *Sign* domain in Fig. 2, let us consider $uco(Sign)$:

$$
\begin{array}{llll}
D_1 = \{\top\} & D_2 = \{\top, 0+\} & D_3 = \{\top, 0\} & D_4 = \{\top, \bot\} \\
D_5 = \{\top, 0-\} & D_6 = \{\top, 0+, \bot\} & D_7 = \{\top, 0+, 0\} & D_8 = \{\top, 0, \bot\} \\
D_9 = \{\top, 0-, 0\} & D_{10} = \{\top, 0-, \bot\} & D_{11} = \{\top, 0+, 0, \bot\} & D_{12} = \{\top, 0+, 0-, 0\} \\
D_{13} = \{\top, 0-, 0, \bot\} & D_{14} = D
\end{array}
$$

Consider the domain transformer $\tau_a = \lambda X. X \sqcap D_7$. The lco domain with respect to the lifted order $\sqsubseteq_\tau$ is depicted in Fig 2 (a), where the circled domains are the fix points. Fig 2 (b) provides another example of lifted order where $\tau_b = \lambda X. X \sqcap D_3$. It is worth noting that both the domain transformers are join-uniform, implying additivity on the lifted $lco(Sign)$, namely admitting the right adjoints.

3   Potency by Incompleteness

In this paper we aim to use incompleteness domain transformers for modeling the potency of obfuscation. Before formally introducing the transformers we aim to describe what we mean by modeling potency by incompleteness, in particular with respect to related works, and then we show, by means of an example, how the transformers should modify abstract domains for inducing incompleteness and how this is used for measuring potency in code obfuscation.

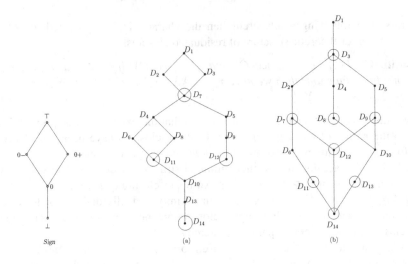

Fig. 2. Lifted $lco(Sign)$

3.1   Modeling Potency of Code Obfuscation

In this paper, we start from the model of potency introduced in [15] and used in [23]. First of all, consider a program P and let $\llbracket P \rrbracket$ denotes its semantics, computed as fixpoint of the operator f_P, namely $\llbracket P \rrbracket = \{\ lfp_s\ f_P \mid s \in \Sigma\ \}$. Let Σ be the set of states of P and $\rho, \eta \in uco(\Sigma)$. Finally, let $\mathfrak{O}$ a program obfuscation transformer. Then, consider the following conditions that have to hold when dealing with code obfuscation:

(1) $\llbracket P \rrbracket = \llbracket \mathfrak{O}(P) \rrbracket$, by definition of code obfuscation [2]

(2) $\rho(\llbracket P \rrbracket) = \llbracket P \rrbracket^{(\rho,\eta)} \stackrel{\text{def}}{=} \{\ lfp_s\rho \circ f_P \circ \eta \mid s \in \Sigma\ \}$
       i.e., suppose (ρ, η) $\mathscr{B}$-complete for $\llbracket P \rrbracket$, implying the need of obfuscation when (ρ, η) is the property to protect in P.

Hence, the property (ρ, η) is obfuscated if $\llbracket P \rrbracket^{(\rho,\eta)} \sqsubset \llbracket \mathfrak{O}(P) \rrbracket^{(\rho,\eta)}$, which holds iff $\rho(\llbracket \mathfrak{O}(P) \rrbracket) \sqsubset \llbracket \mathfrak{O}(P) \rrbracket^{(\rho,\eta)}$ (see [15]). In other words, a property is obfuscated iff it is incomplete for the obfuscated program.

In [15] and in [23] the objective is to provide an incompleteness-driven *construction* of a potent obfuscator, while here we aim to use this incompleteness-based characterization for "measuring" potency. In fact, we aim to define formal domain transformers inducing incompleteness that allow to systematically characterize a range of analyses that are made incomplete, and therefore imprecise, by the performed code obfuscation. In particular, if *Obs* can be precisely analyzed by the attacker, the incomplete compression $\mathcal{UR}(Obs)$ (that will be defined in the next section) systematically characterizes the most abstract domain such that any abstract analysis between *Obs* (excluded) and $\mathcal{UR}(Obs)$ (included) is obfuscated.

This not the first attempt to model potency by means of abstract interpretation. In [10], the basic idea is to define potency in terms of the most concrete *output* observation left unchanged by the obfuscation, i.e., $\delta_{\mathfrak{O}}$ such that $\delta_{\mathfrak{O}}(\llbracket P \rrbracket) = \delta_{\mathfrak{O}}(\llbracket \mathfrak{O}(P) \rrbracket)$.

The set of all the obfuscated properties, making the obfuscator potent, is determined by all the analyses $\{\ Obs\ |\ Obs$ not more abstract than $\delta_{\mathcal{O}}\ \}$. This characterization does not use (in)completeness since it is based on the observation of the computed output of programs, and not on the iterative computation of program semantics.

3.2   Example: Control-Flow Obfuscation

Let us consider the obfuscation technique based on the use of opaque predicate [5], and let us recall the incompleteness characterization already provided in [23].

Opacity is an obfuscation technique based on the idea of confusing the control structure of a program by inserting predicates that are always true (or false) independently of the memory [5]. In [23] we show that opacity is making incomplete an abstract interpreter, we characterize the construction of the control-flow graph (the attack) as an abstract interpretation and we prove that a program contains opaque predicates if and only if this abstract interpretation is incomplete. Let us consider the graph semantics $[\![P]\!]_{\mathbb{G}}$ modeling the semantics of a program, keeping trace also of its control-flow graph [23].

Example 5. Consider the following program and the generated graph when $x = 1$:

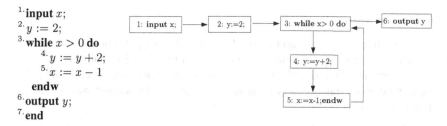

```
1. input x;
2. y := 2;
3. while x > 0 do
4.    y := y + 2;
5.    x := x − 1
   endw
6. output y;
7. end
```

States in Σ are defined as $\langle\sigma, \langle l, l'\rangle, \mathsf{G}_l\rangle$, where σ is a memory, namely the actual values of variables, $l \in \mathbb{N}$ is the executed statement of P, $l' \in \mathbb{N}$ is next statement to execute, and G_l is the computed control-flow graph. The transition relation is $g_{\mathsf{P}}(\langle\sigma, \langle l, l'\rangle, \mathsf{G}\rangle) = \langle\sigma', \langle l', \mathtt{Next_P}(l')\rangle, \mathsf{G}'\rangle$, where the nodes are $Nodes(\mathsf{G}') = Nodes(\mathsf{G}) \cup \{l, l'\}$ and the edges are $Arcs(\mathsf{G}') = Arcs(\mathsf{G}) \cup \{\langle l, l'\rangle\}$ (for details on the computation of σ and on definition of $\mathtt{Next_P}$ see [23]). Hence, we build the executed control-flow graph as the fix-point iteration of this transition function, starting from any state s: $[\![P]\!]_{\mathbb{G}} = \{\ lfp_s\ \mathcal{C} \circ g_{\mathsf{P}} \mid s \in \Sigma\ \}$, where $\mathcal{C}$ ignores the memory (unnecessary when looking at the control structure of programs) and merges the collected histories of computations.

At this point, for *measuring* precision of the obfuscation technique adding opaque predicates, we consider the completeness equation $lfp_s\ \mathcal{C} \circ g_{\mathsf{P}} = lfp_s \mathcal{C} \circ g_{\mathsf{P}} \circ id$ (for $s \in \Sigma$) where P contains at least one opaque predicate, and we look for the input abstraction $\mathcal{B}$ (abstracting the graph component of states augmenting the set of edges) such that $lfp_s \mathcal{C} \circ g_{\mathsf{P}} \neq lfp_s \mathcal{C} \circ g_{\mathsf{P}} \circ \mathcal{B}$. Intuitively, in $lfp_s \mathcal{C} \circ g_{\mathsf{P}}$, due to the $\mathcal{C}$ abstraction, we evaluate the opaque predicates on the set of all the possible memories, and since these predicates are opaque, only one branch is always followed. In other words, the resulting graph contains nodes corresponding to control structures with only one outgoing edge. Hence, for inducing incompleteness the input abstraction $\mathcal{B}$ has to abstract states in order to force any control structure node to follow always both the possible branches. $\mathcal{B}$ can be obtained from the identity abstraction by erasing all the states that lead to follow only one branch, namely all the states corresponding to the evaluation of an opaque predicate. In other words, $\mathcal{B}$ has to ignore the evaluation of *any* control statement guard, considering always both the branches of computation.

This abstraction, informally described here as an incompleteness driven simplification of the identity domain, corresponds precisely to the abstraction statically characterizing the control-flow semantics in [23]. Namely, the control-flow graph of an imperative program is the fix-point abstraction of the concrete semantics: $[\![P]\!]_{\text{CFG}} = lfp_{s}(g_{\text{P}}^{\text{CFG}})$ where $g_{\text{P}}^{\text{CFG}} \stackrel{\text{def}}{=} \mathcal{C} \circ g_{\text{P}} \circ \mathcal{B}$. Note that, in [23] opacity is characterized by the absence of completeness, showing that $\mathcal{C}([\![P]\!]_{\text{G}}) =_{\text{G}} [\![P]\!]_{\text{CFG}}$ *iff* P *doesn't contain opaque predicates*.

4 Making Abstract Domains Incomplete

In this section, we formalize the construction of the most abstract domain having a fixed complete refinement, i.e., the *incomplete domain compressor*. The idea is to consider the complete shell in [20], and to show that it admits right adjoint and that this right adjoint is exactly the incomplete compressor.

4.1 Simplifying Abstractions

First of all, we observe that a complete shell always admits right adjoint. Indeed, by Prop. 3 we know that the right adjoint of an lco exists iff the lco is join-uniform. At this point, since complete shells have the form of *pattern completion*, we observe that pattern completion domain transformers are always join-uniform (this result was observed for the first time in [19]).

Lemma 6. *Let C a complete lattice and $\eta \in \text{uco}(C)$ then the pattern completion function $f_\eta \stackrel{\text{def}}{=} \lambda\delta.\delta \sqcap \eta$ is join-uniform.*

Note that, the domain transformers defined in Ex. 4 are exactly of this form, and indeed, the fact that they admit right adjoint on the lifted orders depends precisely on the fact that these transformers are join-uniform by Lemma 6.

Forward Incomplete Compressor

Consider $\mathscr{F}$ completeness, i.e., $\rho \circ f \circ \eta = f \circ \eta$ with $\rho, \eta \in \text{uco}(C)$, C complete lattice, and $f : C \longrightarrow C$, denoting also its additive lift to $\wp(C)$. The completeness shell is $\mathcal{R}_{f,\eta}^{\mathscr{F}}$ which refines the output domain by adding all the f-images of elements of η to ρ. Hence, by Lemma 6 we have the following result.

Proposition 7. $\mathcal{R}_{f,\eta}^{\mathscr{F}} = \lambda\rho. \rho \sqcap \mathcal{M}(f(\eta))^{1}$ *is join-uniform on* $\text{uco}(C)$.

Being $\mathcal{R} \stackrel{\text{def}}{=} \mathcal{R}_{f,\eta}^{\mathscr{F}}$ join-uniform, its right adjoint exists (Prop. 3) and by Prop. 2 it is

$$\mathcal{R}^{+} = \lambda\rho. \bigsqcup \{ \delta \mid \mathcal{R}(\delta) = \mathcal{R}(\rho) \} = \lambda\rho. \bigsqcup \{ \delta \mid \delta \sqcap \mathcal{M}(f(\eta)) = \rho \sqcap \mathcal{M}(f(\eta)) \}$$

---

[1] $f(\eta)$ stands for $f(\eta(C))$.

By join-uniformity we know that $\mathcal{R} \circ \mathcal{R}^+(\rho) = \mathcal{R}(\rho)$, namely $\mathcal{R}^+(\rho)$ is the most abstract domain such that $\mathcal{R}^+(\rho) \sqcap \mathcal{M}(f(\eta)) = \rho \sqcap \mathcal{M}(f(\eta))$, which by definition is exactly the pseudo-complement $(\rho \sqcap \mathcal{M}(f(\eta))) \ominus \mathcal{M}(f(\eta))^2$. By [13] we know that if C is meet-generated by $Mirr(C)$ then $uco(C)$ is pseudo-complemented and for any $A \in uco(C)$, $C \ominus A = \mathcal{M}(Mirr(C) \smallsetminus A)$. Hence we define

$$\mathcal{UR}^{\mathcal{F}}_{f,\eta} \stackrel{\text{def}}{=} \lambda\rho.\, \mathcal{M}(Mirr(\rho \sqcap \mathcal{M}(f(\eta))) \smallsetminus \mathcal{M}(f(\eta)))$$

This transformation first erases all the elements that we should avoid, and then by the Moore-family completion adds only those necessary for obtaining a Moore-family, i.e., an abstract domain. We call this transformation *incomplete compressor*.

Proposition 8. $\mathcal{UR}^{\mathcal{F}}_{f,\eta} = (\mathcal{R}^{\mathcal{F}}_{f,\eta})^+$

Example 9. Consider the operation $sq(X) = \{ x^2 \mid x \in X \}$ for $X \in \wp(\mathbb{Z})$, this time on the lattice of integer intervals $Int \stackrel{\text{def}}{=} \{ [a,b] \mid a,b \in \mathbb{Z} \} \cup \{ [-\infty, b] \mid b \in \mathbb{Z} \} \cup \{ [a, +\infty] \mid a \in \mathbb{Z} \}$ [6,7]. In this case the best correct approximation of sq in Int is $sq^\sharp : Int \to Int$ such that $sq^\sharp(X) = Int(sq(X))$, with $X \in Int$. Note that, by definition of $sq^\sharp$, we trivially have $Int \circ sq^\sharp \circ Int = sq^\sharp \circ Int$, i.e., $\mathcal{F}$-completeness. For instance $sq^\sharp([3,4]) = [9, 16] \in Int$. Let us transform the output Int domain in order to induce incompleteness, namely let us derive the forward incomplete compression of Int. Note that $Mirr(Int) = \{ [-\infty, b] \mid b \in \mathbb{Z} \} \cup \{ [a, +\infty] \mid a \in \mathbb{Z} \}$ [20] and that $\mathcal{M}(sq^\sharp(Int)) = \{ [a^2, b^2] \mid a,b \in \mathbb{Z} \} \cup \{ [-\infty, b^2] \mid b \in \mathbb{Z} \} \cup \{ [a^2, +\infty] \mid a \in \mathbb{Z} \} \sqsupseteq Int$. Hence we have that $Int' \stackrel{\text{def}}{=} \mathcal{UR}^{\mathcal{F}}_{sq^\sharp, Int}(Int) = \mathcal{M}(Mirr(Int) \smallsetminus \mathcal{M}(sq^\sharp(Int)))$ namely

$$
\begin{aligned}
Int' &= \mathcal{M}(\{ [-\infty, b] \mid b \in \mathbb{Z}, \nexists c \in \mathbb{Z}.\, b = c^2 \} \cup \{ [a, +\infty] \mid a \in \mathbb{Z}, \nexists c \in \mathbb{Z}.\, a = c^2 \}) \\
&= \{ [a, b] \mid a, b \in \mathbb{Z}, \nexists c, d \in \mathbb{Z}.\, a = c^2 \wedge b = d^2 \} \cup \\
&\quad\ \{ [-\infty, b] \mid b \in \mathbb{Z}, \nexists c \in \mathbb{Z}.\, b = c^2 \} \cup \{ [a, +\infty] \mid a \in \mathbb{Z}, \nexists c \in \mathbb{Z}.\, a = c^2 \}
\end{aligned}
$$

So, for instance, we have that $sq^\sharp([3,4]) = [9, 16] \notin Int'$, meaning incompleteness.

Note that this transformation does not always generate an incomplete domain. The following result provides the formal conditions that have to hold in order to induce incompleteness, namely in order to guarantee the existence of incomplete compression. The domains that does not satisfy these conditions are complete and are complete shells of only themselves, namely we cannot find a unique most concrete simplification which is incomplete.

Theorem 10. *Let* $\eta, \rho \in uco(C)$ *and* $f : C \longrightarrow C$. $\mathcal{UR}^{\mathcal{F}}_{f,\eta}(\rho)$ *(here denoted* $\mathcal{UR}$*) is such that* $\mathcal{UR}(\rho) \circ f \circ \eta \neq f \circ \eta$ *iff one of the following conditions hold:*

1. $\rho \circ f \circ \eta \neq f \circ \eta$, *i.e.,* ρ *was incomplete before simplification;*
2. $\mathcal{M}(f(\eta)) \cap Mirr(\rho) \neq \varnothing$;

In the following examples we show the meaning of these conditions.

---

[2] If C is a meet-semilattice with bottom, then the pseudo-complement of $x \in C$, when it exists, is the unique element $x^* \in C$ such that $x \wedge x^* = \bot$ and such that $\forall y \in C.\, (x \wedge y = \bot) \Rightarrow (y \leq x^*)$ [1].

Example 11. Consider the *Sign* domain in Fig. 2. Consider a complete shell such that $\mathcal{M}(f(\eta)) = D_7$, then the completeness transformer is $\mathcal{R} = \lambda X.X \sqcap D_7$. The resulting lco on the corresponding lifted order is in Fig 2(a), where the circled domains are the complete ones, i.e., $\{D_7, D_{11}, D_{12}, D_{14}\}$. All of them contain the meet-irreducible elements of D_7 (condition (2) of Th. 10 is satisfied) and therefore we can find the incomplete compression of any domain, e.g., $\mathcal{UR}(D_{12}) = D_5$.

Th. 10 says that some conditions have to hold in order to have a *unique* incomplete simplification, this does not mean that we cannot find anyway an incomplete simplification, even if it is not unique. Consider the following example.

Example 12. Consider again the domain in Fig 2 and suppose the shell now is $\mathcal{R} = \lambda X.X \sqcap D_3$. The lifted lco is depicted in Fig. 1(b). In this case the complete domains are $\{D_3, D_7, D_8, D_9, D_{11}, D_{12}, D_{13}, D_{14}\}$. We can observe that not all of them have meet-irreducibles in common with D_3. In particular, D_{12} and D_{14} are shell only of themselves. In this case we could only choose one of the closest complete domains that contains meet-irreducible elements of D_3, e.g., for D_{14} we can choose between D_{11} or D_{13}, and then we can transform one of the chosen domains for finding one of the closest incomplete domains, i.e., D_6 or D_{10}.

Absolute Incomplete Compressor. We can exploit the previous transformation relative to a starting input abstraction ρ, in order to characterize the abstract domain which is incomplete for a given function, both in input and in output. This is possible without fix-point iteration since, the domain transformer reaches the fix-point in one iteration.

Theorem 13. *Let $f : C \longrightarrow C$ be a monotone function, $\rho \in uco(C)$.*
Let $\mathcal{UR}(\rho) \stackrel{def}{=} \mathcal{UR}^{\mathcal{F}}_{f,\rho}(\rho) \in uco(C)$ be an incomplete compression of ρ such that we have $\mathcal{UR}(\rho) \neq \top$. Then $\mathcal{UR}(\rho) \circ f \circ \mathcal{UR}(\rho) \neq f \circ \mathcal{UR}(\rho)$.

Note that, if $\mathcal{UR}(\rho) = \top$ we cannot find the absolute incomplete compressor since $\top \circ f \circ \top = \top \circ f$ always holds.

Example 14. Consider the situation described in Ex. 9, and compute $\mathcal{UR}^{\mathcal{F}}_{sq^\sharp,Int}(Int')$.
Recall the following facts

$$Mirr(Int') = \{ [-\infty, b] \mid b \in \mathbb{Z}, \nexists c \in \mathbb{Z}. b = c^2 \} \cup \{ [a, +\infty] \mid a \in \mathbb{Z}, \nexists c \in \mathbb{Z}. a = c^2 \}$$

$$\mathcal{M}(sq^\sharp(Int')) = \{ [a^2, b^2] \mid a, b \in \mathbb{Z}, \nexists c, d \in \mathbb{Z}. a = c^2 \wedge b = d^2 \} \cup$$
$$\{ [-\infty, b^2] \mid b \in \mathbb{Z}, \nexists c \in \mathbb{Z}. b = c^2 \} \cup \{ [a^2, +\infty] \mid a \in \mathbb{Z}, \nexists c \in \mathbb{Z}. a = c^2 \}$$

Now we show that Th. 13 holds. Note that, $Mirr(Int') \cap \mathcal{M}(sq^\sharp(Int')) = \varnothing$, for instance, $[a, +\infty] \in Mirr(Int')$ then $\nexists c \in \mathbb{Z}. a = c^2$, which means that $[a, +\infty] \notin \mathcal{M}(sq^\sharp(Int'))$, since by construction the elements of this form are of the kind $[c^2, +\infty]$ (with the additional, but useless, condition that c is not the square of any integer), and viceversa.

Moreover, $Mirr(Int') \subseteq Mirr(Int' \sqcap \mathcal{M}(sq^\sharp(Int')))$, since by construction if $x \in Mirr(Int')$ then we also have $x \in Mirr(Int)$, on the other hand $\mathcal{M}(sq^\sharp(Int')) \subseteq Int$, therefore x remain meet-irreducible also in the reduced product. Therefore,

$$Mirr(Int') = Mirr(Int') \smallsetminus \mathcal{M}(sq^\sharp(Int')) \subseteq Mirr(Int' \sqcap \mathcal{M}(sq^\sharp(Int'))) \smallsetminus \mathcal{M}(sq^\sharp(Int'))$$

namely $Int' \sqsupseteq \mathcal{UR}^{\mathcal{F}}_{sq^\sharp,Int}(Int')$, and since by construction we have the other inclusion, we showed the equality, i.e., $\mathcal{UR}^{\mathcal{F}}_{sq^\sharp,Int}(Int') = Int'$.

Example 15. Consider the ρ_b domain in Fig. 1(b).
Then $Mirr(\rho_b) = \{[0, +\infty], [-9, 0], [0, 9]\}$ and $\mathcal{M}(sq^{s}(\rho_b)) = \{\mathbb{Z}, [0, +\infty], [0, 99], [0]\}$.

$$S' \stackrel{def}{=} \mathcal{U}\mathcal{R}^{\mathcal{F}}_{sq^{s}, \rho_b}(\rho_b) = \mathcal{M}(Mirr(\rho_b \sqcap \mathcal{M}(sq^{s}(\rho_b))) \setminus \mathcal{M}(sq^{s}(\rho_b)))$$
$$= \mathcal{M}(Mirr(\rho_b) \setminus \mathcal{M}(sq^{s}(\rho_b))) = \mathcal{M}(\{[0, +\infty], [-9, 0], [0, 9]\}) = \{\mathbb{Z}, [-9, 0], [0, 9], [0]\}$$

Finally, we can easily check that $S' \circ sq^{s} \circ S' \neq sq^{s} \circ S'$.

Backward Incompleteness Compressor

In this section we show that all the results holding for $\mathcal{F}$ completeness can be instantiated also to $\mathcal{B}$ completeness. First of all, by Lemma 6 we have that

Proposition 16. $\mathcal{R}^{\mathcal{B}}_{f, \rho}$ *is join-uniform on the domain of upper closure operators.*

This result tells us that also the $\mathcal{B}$ shell admits right adjoint, and as before, its adjoint can be characterized as a pseudo-complement in the following way.

Proposition 17. *Let* $R_f \stackrel{def}{=} \lambda\delta. \mathcal{M}(\bigcup_{y \in \delta} \max(f^{-1}(\downarrow y))) \in uco(C)$, *then we have that* $\mathcal{U}\mathcal{R}^{\mathcal{B}}_{f, \rho} \stackrel{def}{=} \lambda\eta. \mathcal{M}(Mirr(\eta \sqcap R_f(\rho)) \setminus R_f(\rho)) = (\mathcal{R}^{\mathcal{B}}_{f, \rho})^{+}.$

Finally, also for $\mathcal{B}$ completeness we can prove that the $\mathcal{B}$ incomplete compressor exists iff some conditions hold, as stated in the following theorem.

Theorem 18. *Let* $\eta, \rho \in uco(C)$ *and* $f : C \longrightarrow C$. $\mathcal{U}\mathcal{R}^{\mathcal{B}}_{f, \rho}(\eta)$ *(here denoted simply* $\mathcal{U}\mathcal{R}$*) is such that* $\rho \circ f \circ \mathcal{U}\mathcal{R}(\eta) \neq \rho \circ f$ *iff one of the following conditions hold:*

1. $\rho \circ f \circ \eta \neq \rho \circ f$, *i.e.,* η *was incomplete before simplification;*
2. $R_f(\rho) \cap Mirr(\eta) \neq \emptyset$;

Finally, we can characterize also the absolute $\mathcal{B}$ incomplete compressor.

Theorem 19. *Let* $f : C \longrightarrow C$ *be a monotone function,* $\eta \in uco(C)$.
Let $\mathcal{U}\mathcal{R}(\eta) \stackrel{def}{=} (\mathcal{R}^{\mathcal{B}}_{f, \eta})^{+}(\eta) \in uco(C)$ *be an incomplete compressor such that we have* $\mathcal{U}\mathcal{R}(\eta) \neq \top$. *Then* $\mathcal{U}\mathcal{R}(\eta) \circ f \circ \mathcal{U}\mathcal{R}(\eta) \neq \mathcal{U}\mathcal{R}(\eta) \circ f$.

Example 20. Let us consider data obfuscation, and in particular the incompleteness characterization provided in [23]. This obfuscation technique is based on the encoding of data [11]. In this case obfuscation is achieved by data-refinement, namely by exploiting the complexity of different data-structures or values in such a way that actual computations can be viewed as abstractions of the refined (obfuscated) ones. The idea consists in choosing a pair of statements c^{α} and c^{γ} such that $c^{\gamma}; c^{\alpha} \equiv \mathbf{skip}$. This means that both c^{α} and c^{γ} are statements of the form: $c^{\alpha} \equiv x := G(x)$ and $c^{\gamma} \equiv x := F(x)$, for some function F and G. A program transformation $\mathfrak{O}(P) \stackrel{def}{=} c^{\gamma}; \tau_x(P); c^{\alpha}$ is data-type obfuscation for data-type x if $\mathfrak{O}(P) \equiv P$, where τ_x adjusts the data-type computation for x on the refined type (see [11]). It is known that data-type obfuscation can be modeled as adjoint functions (Galois connections), where c^{γ} represents the program concretizing , viz. refining, the datum x and c^{α} represents the program abstracting the refined datum x back to the original data-type. As proved in [15], this is precisely modeled as a pair of adjoint functions: $\alpha : \mathbb{V} \longrightarrow \mathbb{V}^{\Re}$ and $\gamma : \mathbb{V}^{\Re} \longrightarrow \mathbb{V}$ relating the standard data-type $\mathbb{V}$ for x with its refined version $\mathbb{V}^{\Re}$. For instance, consider $P = x := x + 2$;,

$c^\alpha \equiv x := x/2$ and $c^\gamma \equiv x := 2x$, then we have $\tau_x(\mathrm{P}) = x := 2(x/2 + 2)$, namely $x := x + 4$, therefore: $\mathfrak{O}(\mathrm{P}) \equiv x := 2x; x := x + 4; x := x/2$. Consider, for instance the program: $\mathrm{P} = x := 1; s := 0;$ **while** $x < 15$ **do** $s := s + x; x := x + 1;$ **endw.** Then $\tau_x(\mathrm{P}) = x := 2; s := 0;$ **while** $x < 30$ **do** $s := s + x/2; x := x + 2;$ **endw.** α, γ, $\mathbb{V}$, and $\mathbb{V}^{\mathfrak{R}}$ are the most obvious ones. In [23], given $\rho \in uco(\mathbb{V})$, we showed that for any pair of adjoint functions (α, γ) such that $\gamma\alpha \sqsubseteq \rho$ and program refinement τ_x (for some variable x in P) mapping programs into incomplete structures for ρ: $\rho([\![\mathrm{P}_{[\mathfrak{O}(\mathbb{Q})]}]\!]) \sqsubseteq \rho[\![\mathrm{P}_{[\mathfrak{O}(\mathbb{Q})]}]\!]\rho$.

Hence, let op_{p} be a syntactic operation in a programming language. Then $\mathcal{UR}^{\mathscr{B}}(\rho)$ is the absolute incomplete compression of ρ, unable to precisely analyze the semantics of op_{p}. Namely, it is such that $\mathcal{UR}^{\mathscr{B}}(\rho) \circ [\![op_{\mathrm{p}}]\!] \circ \mathcal{UR}^{\mathscr{B}}(\rho) \neq \mathcal{UR}^{\mathscr{B}}(\rho) \circ [\![op_{\mathrm{p}}]\!]$.

Consider, for instance $op_{\mathrm{p}} \stackrel{def}{=} sq^{\mathrm{S}}$ and ρ_a defined in Ex. 1 and consider the abstraction $\rho' \stackrel{def}{=} \mathcal{R}^{\mathscr{B}}(\rho_a) = \{\mathbb{Z}, [0, +\infty], [0, 99], [0, 9], [-9, 0], [0]\}$. ρ' is complete for op_{p} by construction, hence for characterizing the potency of the obfuscation technique consisting in using the operator op_{p} in a program. Hence, we can compute $\mathcal{UR}^{\mathscr{B}}(\rho') = \mathcal{UR}^{\mathscr{B}}(\rho_a) = \mathcal{M}(Mirr(\rho' \sqcap R_{sq^{\mathrm{S}}}(\rho')) \smallsetminus R_{sq^{\mathrm{S}}}(\rho')) = \mathcal{M}(Mirr(\rho') \smallsetminus R_{sq^{\mathrm{S}}}(\rho'))$. Noting that $R_{sq^{\mathrm{S}}}(\rho')) = \{\mathbb{Z}, [0, 9], [-9, 0], [0]\}$, the resulting incomplete compression is $\mathcal{UR}^{\mathscr{B}}(\rho') = \{\mathbb{Z}, [0, +\infty], [0, 99]\}$. In this way we provide a model of the potency of the obfuscation technique since we know that all the analyses between ρ' (excluded) and $\mathcal{UR}^{\mathscr{B}}(\rho')$ (included) are made imprecise by the performed code transformation.

4.2   Refining Abstractions: Incomplete Expanders

If we consider the other direction, when we want to transform the input abstraction, it is well known (see [20]) that, for inducing $\mathscr{F}$ [$\mathscr{B}$] completeness we can simplify the domain by erasing all the η-elements whose f [inverse] image goes out of ρ. In this case we are considering the completeness core $\mathcal{C}^{\mathscr{F}}_{\rho, f}$ [$\mathcal{C}^{\mathscr{B}}_{\eta, f}$]. If we aim to induce incompleteness we should add all the elements such that the f [inverse] image is out of ρ, i.e., $\{x \mid f(x) \notin \rho\}$ [$\{y \mid \max\{x \mid f(x) \leq y\} \not\sqsubseteq \eta\}$]. We wonder if this transformation always exists.

Unfortunately, the following result implies, by Prop. 3, that we cannot find the most concrete abstraction that refines ρ and which is incomplete.

Theorem 21. *The operator $\mathcal{C}^{\mathscr{F}}_{\rho, f}$ [$\mathcal{C}^{\mathscr{B}}_{\eta, f}$] is not meet-uniform.*

5   The Potency of Data Dependency Obfuscation

In this section we describe program slicing [21,28] as an abstraction of a program semantics constructing the program dependency graph (*PDG* for short). In particular we show that slicing obfuscation [24], against attackers performing slicing analyses, is potent when there are syntactic dependencies between variables that do not correspond to semantic dependencies. We will call these dependencies *fake dependencies*. For instance, in the assignment $y = x + 1$ there is a semantic dependency of y on x, while in $y = x + 5 - x$ there is a fake dependency between y and x since the value of y does not depend on x. We show that slicing can be modeled as an abstraction of program semantics and it is precisely the most abstract incomplete compression of the concrete semantics that is obfuscated by fake dependencies.

5.1 Program Slicing

Let us provide a brief overview on program slicing [28] and on the way slices are computed in [21].

Definition 22 ((Semantic) Program slicing). *For a variable v and a statement (program point) s (final use of v), the slice S of program P with respect to the slicing criterion $\langle s, v \rangle$ is any executable program such that S can be obtained by deleting zero or more statements from P and if P halts on input I then the value of v at the statement s, each time s is reached in P, is the same in P and in S. If P fails to terminate then s may be reached more times in S than in P, but P and S execute the same value for v each time s is executed by P.*

The standard approach for characterizing slices is based on *PDG* [21]. A *program dependence graph* [14] $\mathcal{P}_P$ for a program P is a directed graph with vertexes denoting program components and edges denoting *dependencies* between components. The vertexes of $\mathcal{P}_P$, $Nodes(\mathcal{P}_P)$, represent the assignment statements and control predicates that occur in P. In addition $Nodes(\mathcal{P}_P)$ includes a distinguished vertex called *Entry* denoting the starting vertex. An edge represents either a *control dependence* or a *flow dependence*. Control dependence edges $u \longrightarrow_c v$ are such that (1) u is the *Entry* vertex and v represents a component of P that is not nested within any control predicate; or (2) u represents a control predicate and v represents a component of P immediately nested within the control predicate represented by u. Flow dependence edges $u \longrightarrow_f v$ are such that (1) u is a vertex that defines variable x (an assignment), (2) v is a vertex that uses x, and (3) Control can reach v after u via an execution path along which there is no intervening definition of x. Finally, on these graphs, a slice for a criterion $\langle s, v \rangle$ is the sub-graph containing all the vertexes that can reach s via flow/control edges. It is worth noting that these slices are characterized by means of syntax-based dependencies, therefore in general they are not the smallest program fragments satisfying Def. 22 [25].

Example 23. Consider the following programs [26], Note that P_2 is a slice of P_1.

$$P_1 \begin{bmatrix} ^{1.}x := 0 \, ; \\ ^{2.}i := 1 \, ; \ ^{3.}\textbf{while } i > 0 \textbf{ do } i := i + 1 \, ; \\ ^{4.}y := x \, ; \end{bmatrix} \qquad P_2 \begin{bmatrix} ^{1.}x := 0 \, ; \\ \\ ^{4.}y := x \, ; \end{bmatrix}$$

On the right we find a representation of the program dependence graph of P_1. In this representation we have only control and flow dependence edges, without distinction. In this graph we can note that slice P_2 (with criterion the value of y) can be computed by following backwards the edges starting from node $y := x$, the final definition of y.

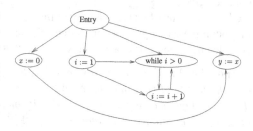

5.2 Semantic *PDG* as Abstraction of Program Semantics

We define now the abstractions characterizing the program semantics that can be abstracted in the program slicing. In particular, we first define a semantics, similar to graph semantics [23] (briefly described in Sect. 3.2) which, instead of computing the control flow graph, computes the semantic *PDG*, namely the *PDG* including only semantic/real dependencies among variables.

The program semantics is a transition system with states in Σ of the form $\langle \sigma, \langle l, l' \rangle, \mathcal{P}_l \rangle$, where σ is the memory, namely the actual values of program variables, $\langle l, l' \rangle \in \mathbb{N} \times \mathbb{N}$ is a pair of program states, l is the executed statement and l' is next statement to execute, finally $\mathcal{P}_l$ is the computed *PDG*. Let us concentrate on the structure and on the iterative construction of $\mathcal{P}$. A *PDG* $\mathcal{P}_l$ is defined as a triple $\langle Nodes_l, Arcs_l, D_l \rangle$, where $Nodes_l \subset \mathbb{N}$ and $Arcs_l \subset \mathbb{N} \times \mathbb{N}$ describe respectively the nodes and the edges of the *PDG* graph. In particular, we have two kinds of edges, the *control* dependence edges $Control_l$ and the *flow* dependence edges $Flow_l$, hence $Arcs_l = Control_l \cup Flow_l$. Finally, D_l is an auxiliary information, necessary for constructing flow dependencies. In fact $D_l : Var \longrightarrow \mathbb{N}$ associates with each variable the last statement where the variable has been defined. For instance, in Ex. 23, $D_4(x) = 1$ while $D_4(y) = 4$.

For each program point $l' \in \mathbb{N}$ we can also define the following auxiliary maps:

$\mathtt{Stm_P} : \mathbb{N} \longrightarrow \mathbb{P}$ s.t. $\mathtt{Stm_P}(l)$ is the statement in program line l
$\mathtt{Dep} : \mathbb{N} \longrightarrow Var$ s.t. $\mathtt{Dep}(l)$ is the set of variables the statement in l depends on
$\mathtt{Use} : \mathbb{N} \longrightarrow Var$ s.t. $\mathtt{Use}(l)$ is the set of variables used in l

In general, $\mathtt{Dep}(l) \subseteq \mathtt{Use}(l)$, if there are not fake dependencies we have the equality.

The transition function is $p_P(\langle \sigma, \langle l_1, l_2 \rangle, \mathcal{P}_{l_1} \rangle) = \langle \sigma', \langle l_2, \mathtt{Next_P}(l_2) \rangle, \mathcal{P}_{l_2} \rangle$ where σ' is the memory modified by executing statement in l_1 and $\mathtt{Next_P}$ computes the following statement to execute (see [23] for details) and $\mathcal{P}_{l_2}$ is computed as follows:

$$D_{l_2} = D_{l_1}[D_x = l_2] \text{ if } \mathtt{Stm}(l_2) = x := e \text{ (it is } D_{l_1} \text{ otherwise)}$$
$$Nodes_{l_2} = Nodes_{l_1} \cup \{l_2\}$$
$$Control_{l_2} = Control_{l_1} \cup \{ \langle l_2, l \rangle \mid \mathtt{Stm}(l_2) \in \{\textbf{if}, \textbf{while}\} \text{ and } \mathtt{Stm}(l) \text{ is nested in } l_1 \}$$
$$Flow_{l_2} = Flow_{l_1} \cup \{ \langle D_{l_1}(x), l_2 \rangle \mid x \in \mathtt{Dep}(l_2) \}$$

We compute the *PDG* semantics as $[\![P]\!]_{PDG} \overset{\text{def}}{=} \{ lfp_s \, id \circ p_P \mid s \in \Sigma \}$. The precision measure of an input abstraction α of this semantics is provided by the $\mathcal{B}$ completeness equation $[\![P]\!]_{PDG} = [\![P]\!]_{PDG}^{\alpha}$, where $[\![P]\!]_{PDG}^{\alpha} \overset{\text{def}}{=} \{ lfp_s \, id \circ p_P \circ \alpha \mid s \in \Sigma \}$, where the considered abstractions of states α augment the set of *PDG* (flow) edges. Hence, we can use the incomplete compressor for characterizing a simplification of the identity inducing completeness, and it is exactly the syntactic *PDG*-based computation of slices [21].

Proposition 24. *Consider a program* P *with fake dependencies. The input abstraction* S *computing the* PDG_P *in terms of* $Flow_{l_2} = Flow_{l_1} \cup \{ \langle D_{l_1}(x), l_2 \rangle \mid x \in \mathtt{Use}(l_2) \}$ *is the* $\mathcal{B}$ *incomplete compressor of the identity map on states unable to precisely compute program slices, namely such that* $[\![P]\!]_{PDG} \neq [\![P]\!]_{PDG}^{S}$.

In order to understand this transformation observe that it consists in erasing the (maximal) inverse images of the semantics $[\![P]\!]_{PDG}$ of a program containing fake dependencies. This means that $[\![P]\!]_{PDG}$ generates flow branches where not all the *used* variables are connected to the defined one, for instance in $y := x + z - x$ we have an edge from z to y but not from x to y which is a fake dependence. Hence in order to force incompleteness

$[\![P]\!]^{\mathcal{S}}_{PDG}$ has to generate *PDG*s where, for each variable definition, all the used variables are taken into account in the flow edges construction. In this way we guarantee, due to the presence of fake dependencies, that the resulting *PDG*s are different. This construction suggests also the following result, which perfectly fits in the approach to program obfuscation proposed in [23], where programs are obfuscated by specializing interpreters distorted with respect to a fixed syntactic feature that has to be added into the program in order to make imprecise a given analysis.

Proposition 25. $[\![P]\!]_{PDG} = [\![P]\!]^{\mathcal{S}}_{PDG}$ *iff* P *does not contain fake dependencies.*

6 Conclusion

The paper provides two main contributions. The first consists in extending (an in some sense completing) the framework of abstract domain transformers for completeness and incompleteness in abstract interpretation. This is achieved by formalizing the abstract domain simplifications making abstract domains incomplete, i.e., incompleteness compressors. The second contribution consists in modeling the potency of code obfuscation by associating attackers (i.e., abstract interpretations [15]) with their incomplete compressor. In particular, we showed that the potency of well known obfuscation techniques such as opaque predicates and data-type obfuscation can be modeled in our incompleteness framework. Moreover, we formally showed that if the attacker is able to perform program slicing, then we obtain a *potent* obfuscation technique by adding fake dependencies among variables. The minimality of our result implies the minimality of fake dependencies for protecting programs against slicing. We believe that most code obfuscation strategies can be modeled in this way or, equivalently, that we can characterize the obfuscation techniques potent with respect to most of attackers that can be specified as approximate interpreters.

As far as the formal framework is concerned, we already know how to make abstract domains complete [17,20], and how to transform semantics in order to induce both completeness and incompleteness [16]. In particular, the incompleteness transformers, both of domains (developed in this paper) and of semantics [16], have been obtained by adjoining the corresponding completeness transformers. It would be interesting to study the formal relation between domain and semantics transformers. We believe that this would provide an important contribution in the obfuscation field due to the strong relation between obfuscation and incompleteness. Indeed, it is clear that to transform semantics for inducing incompleteness corresponds to obfuscate programs [15], while, as we underlined, transforming domains for inducing incompleteness characterize the harmless attackers. Hence, understanding the relation between incomplete domains and semantics transformers allows to formally study the relation between the power of attackers and the obfuscation transformations devoted to protect code.

References

1. Birkhoff, G.: Lattice Theory, 3rd edn. AMS Colloquium Publication, AMS (1967)
2. Collberg, C., Nagra, J.: Surreptitious Software: Obfuscation, Watermarking, and Tamper-proofing for Software Protection. Addison-Wesley Professional (2009)

3. Collberg, C., Thomborson, C.: Breaking abstrcations and unstructural data structures. In: Proc. of the 1994 IEEE Internat. Conf. on Computer Languages, ICCL 1998, pp. 28–37 (1998)
4. Collberg, C., Thomborson, C.: Watermarking, tamper-proofing, and obduscation-tools for software protection. IEEE Trans. Software Eng., 735–746 (2002)
5. Collberg, C., Thomborson, C.D., Low, D.: Manufactoring cheap, resilient, and stealthy opaque constructs. In: Proc. of Conf. Record of the 25th ACM Symp. on Principles of Programming Languages, POPL 1998, pp. 184–196. ACM Press (1998)
6. Cousot, P., Cousot, R.: Static determination of dynamic properties of programs. In: Proceedings of the 2nd International Symposium on Programming, pp. 106–130. Dunod, Paris (1976)
7. Cousot, P., Cousot, R.: Abstract interpretation: A unified lattice model for static analysis of programs by construction or approximation of fixpoints. In: Conference Record of the 4th ACM Symposium on Principles of Programming Languages, POPL 1977, pp. 238–252. ACM Press (1977)
8. Cousot, P., Cousot, R.: Systematic design of program analysis frameworks. In: Conference Record of the 6th ACM Symposium on Principles of Programming Languages, POPL 1979, pp. 269–282. ACM Press (1979)
9. Cousot, P., Cousot, R.: Comparing the Galois Connection and Widening/Narrowing Approaches to Abstract Interpretation (Invited Paper). In: Bruynooghe, M., Wirsing, M. (eds.) PLILP 1992. LNCS, vol. 631, pp. 269–295. Springer, Heidelberg (1992)
10. Dalla Preda, M., Giacobazzi, R.: Semantic-Based Code Obfuscation by Abstract Interpretation. In: Caires, L., Italiano, G.F., Monteiro, L., Palamidessi, C., Yung, M. (eds.) ICALP 2005. LNCS, vol. 3580, pp. 1325–1336. Springer, Heidelberg (2005)
11. Drape, S., Thomborson, C., Majumdar, A.: Specifying Imperative Data Obfuscations. In: Garay, J.A., Lenstra, A.K., Mambo, M., Peralta, R. (eds.) ISC 2007. LNCS, vol. 4779, pp. 299–314. Springer, Heidelberg (2007)
12. Filé, G., Giacobazzi, R., Ranzato, F.: A unifying view of abstract domain design. ACM Comput. Surv. 28(2), 333–336 (1996)
13. Filé, G., Ranzato, F.: Complementation of abstract domains made easy. In: Maher, M. (ed.) Proceedings of the 1996 Joint International Conference and Symposium on Logic Programming, JICSLP 1996, pp. 348–362. The MIT Press (1996)
14. Gallagher, K.B., Lyle, J.R.: Using program slicing in software maintenance. IEEE Trans. on Software Engineering 17(8), 751–761 (1991)
15. Giacobazzi, R.: Hiding information in completeness holes - new perspectives in code obfuscation and watermarking. In: Proc. of the 6th IEEE International Conferences on Software Engineering and Formal Methods (SEFM 2008), pp. 7–20. IEEE Press (2008)
16. Giacobazzi, R., Mastroeni, I.: Transforming Abstract Interpretations by Abstract Interpretation. In: Alpuente, M., Vidal, G. (eds.) SAS 2008. LNCS, vol. 5079, pp. 1–17. Springer, Heidelberg (2008)
17. Giacobazzi, R., Quintarelli, E.: Incompleteness, Counterexamples, and Refinements in Abstract Model-Checking. In: Cousot, P. (ed.) SAS 2001. LNCS, vol. 2126, pp. 356–373. Springer, Heidelberg (2001)
18. Giacobazzi, R., Ranzato, F.: Refining and Compressing Abstract Domains. In: Degano, P., Gorrieri, R., Marchetti-Spaccamela, A. (eds.) ICALP 1997. LNCS, vol. 1256, pp. 771–781. Springer, Heidelberg (1997)
19. Giacobazzi, R., Ranzato, F.: Uniform closures: order-theoretically reconstructing logic program semantics and abstract domain refinements. Inform. and Comput. 145(2), 153–190 (1998)
20. Giacobazzi, R., Ranzato, F., Scozzari, F.: Making abstract interpretation complete. Journal of the ACM 47(2), 361–416 (2000)

21. Horwitz, S., Reps, T.W., Binkley, D.: Interprocedural slicing using dependence graphs. ACM Trans. Program. Lang. Syst. 12(1), 26–60 (1990)
22. Janowitz, M.F.: Residuated closure operators. Portug. Math. 26(2), 221–252 (1967)
23. Jones, N.D., Giacobazzi, R., Mastroeni, I.: Obfuscation by partial evaluation of distorted interpreters. In: Kiselyov, O., Thompson, S. (eds.) Proc. of the ACM SIGPLAN Symp. on Partial Evaluation and Semantics-Based Program Manipulation (PEPM 2012), pp. 63–72. ACM Press (2012)
24. Majumdar, A., Drape, S.J., Thomborson, C.D.: Slicing obfuscations: design, correctness, and evaluation. In: DRM 2007: Proceedings of the 2007 ACM Workshop on Digital Rights Management, pp. 70–81. ACM (2007)
25. Mastroeni, I., Zanardini, D.: Data dependencies and program slicing: From syntax to abstract semantics. In: Proc. of the ACM SIGPLAN Symp. on Partial Evaluation and Semantics-Based Program Manipulation (PEPM 2008), pp. 125–134. ACM Press (2008)
26. Reps, T., Turnidge, T.: Program Specialization via Program Slicing. In: Danvy, O., Gltick, R., Thiemann, P. (eds.) Partial Evaluation. LNCS, vol. 1110, pp. 409–429. Springer, Heidelberg (1996)
27. Ward, M.: The Closure Operators of a Lattice. Annals of Mathematics 43(2), 191–196 (1942)
28. Weiser, M.: Program slicing. In: ICSE 1981: Proceedings of the 5th International Conference on Software Engineering, pp. 439–449. IEEE Press (1981)

Invariant Generation
for Parametrized Systems Using Self-reflection

Alejandro Sanchez[1], Sriram Sankaranarayanan[2],
César Sánchez[1,3], and Bor-Yuh Evan Chang[2,*]

[1] IMDEA Software Institute, Madrid, Spain
{firstname.lastname@imdea.org}
[2] University of Colorado, Boulder, CO, USA
{firstname.lastname@colorado.edu}
[3] Institute for Applied Physics, CSIC, Spain

Abstract. We examine the problem of inferring invariants for parametrized systems. Parametrized systems are concurrent systems consisting of an *a priori* unbounded number of process instances running the same program. Such systems are commonly encountered in many situations including device drivers, distributed systems, and robotic swarms. In this paper we describe a technique that enables leveraging off-the-shelf invariant generators designed for sequential programs to infer invariants of parametrized systems. The central challenge in invariant inference for parametrized systems is that naïvely exploding the transition system with all interleavings is not just impractical but impossible. In our approach, the key enabler is the notion of a *reflective abstraction* that we prove has an important correspondence with inductive invariants. This correspondence naturally gives rise to an iterative invariant generation procedure that alternates between computing candidate invariants and creating reflective abstractions.

1 Introduction

We study the problem of automatically inferring invariants for parametrized systems. Parametrized systems are multi-threaded programs that may be executed by a finite but unbounded number of thread instances executing in parallel. The individual thread instances belonging to the same process type execute the same set of program instructions involving local variables that are unique to each thread instance, as well as the global shared variables. Parametrized programs are useful in many settings including device drivers, distributed algorithms, concurrent data structures, robotic swarms, and biological systems. The thread instances in a parametrized program communicate through shared memory and synchronization mechanisms including locks, synchronous rendezvous, and broadcast communication.

In this paper, we define an abstract-interpretation–based framework for inferring indexed invariants of parametrized programs. A k-indexed invariant of a parametrized

---

* This work was supported in part by the US National Science Foundation (NSF) under grants CNS-0953941 and CCF-1055066; the EU project FET IST-231620 *HATS*, MICINN project TIN-2008-05624 *DOVES*, CAM project S2009TIC-1465 *PROMETIDOS*, and by the COST Action IC0901 *Rich ModelToolkit-An Infrastructure for Reliable Computer Systems*.

A. Miné and D. Schmidt (Eds.): SAS 2012, LNCS 7460, pp. 146–163, 2012.

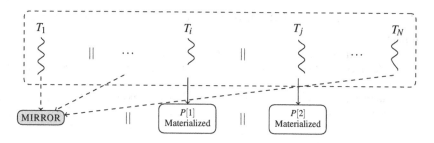

Fig. 1. A reflective abstraction to infer 2-indexed invariants of a parametrized system. We abstract the system as two materialized processes and the mirror process.

system is an invariant over the local variables of an arbitrary k distinct thread instances and the global shared variables. The main idea is to build what we call a *reflective abstraction* of the parametrized program that consists of a fixed number of *materialized* processes composed with a *mirror* abstraction that summarizes the effect of the remaining thread instances on the global variables. In Fig. 1, we hint at this construction for deriving 2-indexed invariants (and discussed further in Sect. 2).

We show how invariants computed at various program locations of the materialized processes can be transferred in a suitable way into guards of the mirror process. In this way, the abstraction of other interfering threads via the mirror process varies during the course of the analysis — much like how materialization in shape analysis enables the heap abstraction to vary for better precision. Our approach can be viewed as an abstract interpretation over the cartesian product of the abstract domain of state assertions over program variables and the reflective abstractions of the environment. This allows us to cast existing methods for invariant generation for parametrized systems [4,30] as different iteration schemes for computing fixed points. Finally, we define new iteration schemes and compare their effectiveness empirically. In summary, we arrive at a characterization of invariants of the parametrized program as fixed points of a monotone functional that (a) computes a (post-) fixed point on the reflective abstraction and (b) transfers the fixed point to the guards of the mirror processes.

Overall, this paper contains the following contributions. We present the notion of a *reflective abstraction*, which gives a means to summarize the effects of other threads dynamically during the analysis (Sect. 3). We then formally prove a correspondence between reflective abstractions and inductive invariants, which leads naturally to an iterative invariant generation procedure that allows leveraging off-the-shelf invariant generators for sequential programs (Sect. 4.1). We discuss how the reflective abstraction framework encompasses interference abstractions (Sect. 4.2), as well as practical considerations for an implementation (Sect. 4.3). Finally, we present some initial experience on evaluating applications of our reflective abstraction framework (Sect. 5). In particular, we study three variants of reflective abstraction and one variant of interference abstraction and how they compare with respect to the invariants they obtain. We find that surprisingly, widening appears to have a less predictable effect for parametrized systems than for sequential systems.

```
     global data: int array(len) where len > 0, next: int where next = 0;
     thread P {
       local c: int where c = 0, end: int where end = 0;
0      atomic if (next + 10 <= len) { c := next; next := end := next + 10; }
1      while (c < end) {
2         assert(0 <= c && c < len); data[c]:= ... process data[c] ...;
3         c := c + 1;
4      }
     }
```

Fig. 2. WORKSTEAL: A parametrized array processing program. Each thread processes a "chunk" with 10 elements.

2   Overview: Self-reflection

In this section, we illustrate the basic idea behind reflective abstractions of parametrized systems, and we give a sense of how such a construction enables inference of k-indexed invariants. Consider the program WORKSTEAL in Fig. 2. Parametrized programs consist of a fixed but unbounded number of thread instances $T_1, \ldots, T_N$ where $N \geq 1$. In the rest of this paper, we use $[N]$ to denote the set of indices $\{1, \ldots, N\}$. Each thread runs the set of statements in P. In this program, there is a global array data of size len and a global variable next that holds the current unprocessed index. Each instance T_i has thread local variables $c[i]$ and $end[i]$ for $i \in [N]$, that is, local variables are replicated for and indexed by each thread instance. The local variable $c[i]$ holds a current index of the data element being processed by the thread instance T_i. The variable $end[i]$ holds the limiting index for thread T_i.

Our goal is to prove properties about the behavior of parametrized systems that must hold regardless of the number of running thread instances N. The simplest properties involve only global variables, such as ψ_0: (next mod $10 = 0$). Other properties may also involve local variables, as well as globals. In case local variables are involved, we differentiate instances of local variables by indexing them. A 1-indexed property refers to a local variable from a single thread instance. In our example, we wish to prove the 1-indexed property corresponding to the assertion at location 2:

$$\psi_1: (\forall i)\ 0 \leq c[i] < \text{len} \qquad \text{(i.e., access of array data is in bounds).} \qquad (1)$$

An example of a 2-indexed property is where we wish to establish race-freedom for *distinct* thread instances i_1, i_2 whenever one of the instances resides at location 2:

$$\psi_2: (\forall i_1, i_2)\ c[i_1] \neq c[i_2] \qquad \text{(i.e., access of array data is race free).} \qquad (2)$$

We will use $i, i_1, i_2, \ldots$ to refer to process instances ranging within the set of thread indices $[N]$. We will assume implicitly that different symbols i_j, i_k involved in a given assertion ψ are used to refer to different process instances (e.g., there is an implicit pre-condition that $i_1 \neq i_2$ in ψ_2).

In this paper, we adapt existing invariant synthesis techniques to parametrized programs. Our technique allows us to generate invariants such as ψ_0, ψ_1, and ψ_2 for the

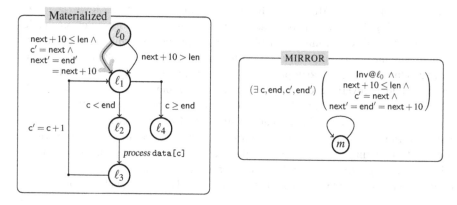

Fig. 3. Transition system models for a materialized thread and the MIRROR process. The guard $\mathsf{Inv@}\ell_0$ for the MIRROR transition comes from the invariant computed at location ℓ_0 in a materialized thread.

parametrized program in Fig. 2. Our approach, inspired by the idea of materialization in shape analysis [33], is based on identifying a fixed number of *materialized processes* and summarizing the remaining processes into a single, separate process that we will call the MIRROR. We show this idea pictorially in Fig. 1 where a parametrized system with N thread instances is modeled by three threads: 2 materialized thread instances $P[1], P[2]$ and the mirror process that summarizes the effects of the $N - 2$ remaining thread instances on the shared global variables. The number of materialized processes is fixed *a priori* based on the desired form of the invariants. For example, we need to materialize at least 2 threads to infer 2-indexed invariants. The novel aspect of our *reflective* approach is that the MIRROR process is *not* fixed *a priori* but rather is derived as part of the fixed point analysis.

Fig. 3 shows the basic setup for invariant synthesis for the WORKSTEAL program. The composition of the materialized thread(s) and the MIRROR yields a regular sequential transition system that can be analyzed using a standard abstract interpretation engine. The MIRROR process simulates the effect that the remaining (non-materialized) threads in the system have on the shared variables next and len. In particular, the MIRROR process has no local variables. The running example has a single transition from location ℓ_0 to ℓ_1 that affects the shared variable next (highlighted), and variable len is never updated anywhere. This transition is copied as a self-loop around a single location in the MIRROR process, and the local variable updates are quantified away. However, to maintain precision, it is preferable to restrict the scope of this transition only to those states of the program that are actually reachable at location ℓ_0. We will over-approximate these states by an assertion $\mathsf{Inv@}\ell_0$. The main question is then to precisely determine what $\mathsf{Inv@}\ell_0$ is. A simple solution is to assume $\mathsf{Inv@}\ell_0$: *true* to yield a valid over-approximation of all states that are reachable whenever some process resides at location ℓ_0, but *true* is very often a coarse over-approximation. Our key observation is that $\mathsf{Inv@}\ell_0$ and correspondingly the construction of the MIRROR process need not be fixed *a priori*. Instead, we build a more precise abstraction by incrementally constructing MIRROR as follows. The first iteration sets $\mathsf{Inv}@\ell_0 : false$, in effect, disabling the mirror. This iteration approximates only those states reachable by the materialized threads running in isolation. Subsequently, we run an abstract interpreter and compute invariants of the composition of the current MIRROR process and the materialized threads. The MIRROR process for the next iteration is updated with $\mathsf{Inv}@\ell_0$ set to the candidate invariants computed at location ℓ_0 in the materialized threads with the local variables projected out. This *candidate invariant reflection* allows the MIRROR to run from a larger portion of the reachable state space. Convergence is achieved whenever the invariants obtained at some iteration are subsumed by those at the previous iteration. At this point, the effect of the mirror and the materialized processes in the invariants and the guards is stable. Upon convergence, we obtain k-indexed invariants that relate the local variables of the k materialized threads to the global variables.

3   Reflective Abstractions and Inductive Invariants

In this section, we define the notion of a *reflective abstraction* of a parametrized system. We first present the basic model of parametrized systems. The main result of this section (Theorem 1) proves the soundness of reflective abstractions.

A parametrized system consists of a large, *a priori* unbounded set of processes that (a) run the same sequence of instructions and (b) interact with each other through some synchronization primitives. The model presented here is based on concurrent systems communicating through shared memory. For convenience, we use the fair transition system model [27]. To simplify the presentation further, all program variables are assumed to be of integer type.

A *parametrized transition system* Π is described by $\langle G, X, Trs, \ell_0, \Theta \rangle$ consisting of a set of shared (global) variables $g \in G$, a set of local variables $x \in X$, a finite set of locations $\ell \in Loc$, a finite set of transitions $\tau \in Trs$, an initial location ℓ_0, and an initial condition Θ that denotes the set of possible initial values of the global and local variables. A transition $\tau : \langle \ell_{src}, \ell_{tgt}, \rho \rangle$ consists of a pre-location ℓ_{src}, a post-location ℓ_{tgt} and a transition relation ρ that relates the values of the variables (global and local) before the transition with the values after it. We use primed variables (e.g., $g' \in G'$ and $x' \in X'$) to refer to the values of the corresponding variables in the post-location.

Example 1 (Parametrized Transition System). Consider the WORKSTEAL program from Fig. 2. Its corresponding parametrized transition system Π consists of globals $G = \{\mathsf{len}, \mathsf{next}\}$, locals $X = \{\mathsf{c}, \mathsf{end}\}$, and locations $Loc = \{\ell_0, \ell_1, \ell_2, \ell_3, \ell_4\}$ with the initial location being ℓ_0. Ignoring the MIRROR process, Fig. 3 depicts the transition relations Trs of the parametrized transition system (solid edges). Not modeling the array data means the transition relation ρ between ℓ_2 and ℓ_3 is a no-op, that is, $\rho = \mathsf{preserve}(G \cup X)$. We define $\mathsf{preserve}(Z) \stackrel{\mathsf{def}}{=} \wedge_{z \in Z} z' = z$ for any set of variables Z, that is, the transition relation where all variables in Z are preserved.

The semantics of a parametrized system is given with respect to a positive number N of *thread instances*. The overall *state* of a parametrized system with N thread instances is described by valuations of the shared (global) variables, the *local variable instances*, and the *location instances* of each thread. That is, a local variable instance $x[i]$ is the instance of local variable $x \in X$ for thread instance $i \in [N]$. The set $X[i]$ refers to the local variable instances of thread instance i.

A state $\sigma : \langle L, V \rangle$ is characterized by a map $L : [N] \rightharpoonup_{\mathrm{fin}} Loc$ that associates a location $L(i)$ for each thread instance i and a valuation map V that maps each shared (global) variable and each local variable instance to its integer value. We write $V(G)$ to denote the valuations to all global variables and $V(X[i])$ to denote the valuations of locals of thread i. We write $V \models \varphi$ for a valuation V satisfying a formula φ. Where helpful for clarity in presentation, we write $\varphi[G, X]$ to indicate the variables over which the formula φ is defined. A *run* of a parametrized system instantiated with N thread instances is a finite or infinite sequence of states such that (1) the initial state satisfies the initial condition, and (2) a step between two successive states is obtained by executing one transition in one thread instance. More detailed definitions of parametrized systems and their runs are given in our companion TR [34].

Definition 1 (1-Indexed Invariant). *A pair $\langle \ell, \varphi \rangle$ consisting of a location ℓ and assertion $\varphi[G, X]$ is a 1-index invariant of a parametrized program Π iff for every reachable state $\sigma : (L, V)$ with $N > 0$ thread instances, and for every $i \in [N]$*

$$\text{if } L(i) = \ell \text{ then } (V(G), V(X[i])) \models \varphi .$$

In other words, the valuations of the local variables $X[i]$ and global variables G for any thread instance i reaching the location ℓ satisfies φ.

The notion of 1-indexed invariants generalizes to k-indexed invariants involving the global variables and the local variables of some $k > 0$ threads. This generalization is given explicitly in our companion TR [34].

Example 2 (k-Indexed Invariants). Property ψ_1 (see (1) on page 148) is an example of a 1-indexed invariant for the parametrized system in Example 1 (i.e., $\langle \ell_2, 0 \leq c < \mathsf{len} \rangle$). Property ψ_2 (see (2) in page 148) corresponds to many 2-indexed invariants at different pairs of locations. Each invariant is of the form $\langle \ell_2, \_, c[1] \neq c[2] \rangle$ or $\langle \_, \ell_2, c[1] \neq c[2] \rangle$ where $\_$ refers to any location. These invariants say that one of the thread instances resides at location ℓ_2 (and the other anywhere else) with the respective instances of the local variable c holding different values.

Reflective Abstractions. In essence, a reflective abstraction is an over-approximation of a parametrized transition system by a sequential one. What makes an abstraction *reflective* is that the over-approximation is computed *under an assertion map*.

We skip the formal definition of sequential transition systems, noting that these correspond to single thread instances of parametrized transition systems. To denote specifically a sequentially transition system, we use the meta-variable Σ. Let $\Gamma[X]$ be some fixed first-order language of assertions, such as the theory of integer arithmetic, involving free variables X. We overload $\models$ to denote the semantic entailment relation between these formulae. An *assertion map* $\eta : Loc \rightharpoonup_{\mathrm{fin}} \Gamma[X]$ maps each location to an assertion in $\Gamma[X]$. An assertion map η is *inductive* whenever (1) the assertion at the initial location subsumes the initial condition (i.e., initiation) and (2) the assertion map respects the (strongest) post-condition transformer (i.e., consecution): for any transition

τ between ℓ_{src} and ℓ_{tgt}, the post-condition transformer for τ applied to $\eta(\ell_{src})$ entails $\eta(\ell_{tgt})$. Standard definitions for the post-condition transformer and inductive assertion maps are given in our TR [34]. Inductive invariants are fundamental to the process of verifying safety properties of programs. In order to prove an assertion φ over all reachable states at a location ℓ, we seek an inductive assertion map η over the entire program such that $\eta(\ell) \models \varphi$. The map η is termed an *inductive strengthening* of φ.

We now formally define the notion of a *reflective abstraction*, which abstracts a parametrized system by a system with a $k > 0$ materialized processes, and a MIRROR process that models the "interference" of the remaining threads on the shared variables G. Our key result is that *an invariant of a reflective abstraction is that of a parametrized system*. To simplify the presentation, the rest of this section will describe reflective abstractions with a single materialized thread (i.e., $k = 1$). Our definitions readily extend to the case when $k > 1$.

Let η be an assertion map over the locations of a parametrized system Π. Our goal is to define a sequential system $\mathrm{REFLECT}_\Pi(\eta)$. Such a system will contain transitions to model one specific thread instance, termed the *materialized thread*, and the MIRROR process, which models the influence of the other threads on the shared variables.

Definition 2 (Reflective Abstraction). *The* reflective abstraction *of a parametrized system* Π: $\langle G, X, Loc, Trs, \ell_0, \Theta \rangle$ *with respect to an assertion map* η *is a sequential transition system, written* $\mathrm{REFLECT}_\Pi(\eta)$, *over variables* $G \cup X$, *with locations given by Loc and transitions given by* $Trs \cup \{ \mathrm{MIRROR}(\tau, \eta, \ell) \mid \tau \in Trs \text{ and } \ell \in Loc \}$.
The original transitions Trs model the materialized thread, while the MIRROR *transitions model the visible effects of the remaining threads.*

For transition τ: $\langle \ell_{src}, \ell_{tgt}, \rho \rangle$ *and some location* $\ell \in Loc$, *the corresponding* MIRROR *transition* $\mathrm{MIRROR}(\tau, \eta, \ell)$ *is defined as follows:*

$$\Big\langle \ell, \ \ell, \ \mathrm{preserve}(X) \wedge (\exists Y, Y') \left(\underline{\eta(\ell_{src})[G, Y]} \wedge \rho[G, Y, G', Y'] \right) \Big\rangle.$$

Finally, the initial location of the reflective abstraction is ℓ_0 *and the initial condition* Θ *(i.e., comes directly from the parametrized system).*

Note that each MIRROR transition is a self-loop at location ℓ of the materialized thread, or equivalently, MIRROR can be seen as a process with a single location and self-looping transitions that is composed with the materialized thread. Note that each MIRROR transition preserves the local variables of the materialized thread. Also, observe that the (underlined) guard of the MIRROR transition includes the invariant $\eta(\ell_{src})$ of the interfering thread at the pre-location, which can be seen as reflecting the invariant of the materialized thread at ℓ_{src} on to the interfering thread. Finally, the local variables are projected away from the transition relation using existential quantification to model the effect of the materialized transition on the shared variables.

Example 3 (Reflective Abstraction). The following table shows a part of an assertion map η for the program in Fig. 2, along with the corresponding mirror transitions computed from it, that is, of $\mathrm{REFLECT}_\Pi(\eta)$. We write $\rho(\tau)$ for the transition relation of transition τ (in the original parametrized system Π) and $\rho(m)$ for the transition relation of a MIRROR transition in the reflective abstraction. Note that the assertion map η is not necessarily inductive.

Name	Invariant/Relation
$\eta(\ell_0)$	$\text{next} = 0 \,\wedge\, c = 0 \,\wedge\, \text{end} = 10$
$\rho(\tau_0 \colon \langle \ell_0, \ell_1, \rho_0 \rangle)$	$\text{next} + 10 \le \text{len} \,\wedge\, c' = \text{next} \,\wedge\, \text{next}' = \text{end}' = \text{next} + 10$ $\wedge\,\text{preserve}(\{\text{len}\})$
$\rho(m_0 \colon \text{MIRROR}(\tau_0, \eta, \_))$	$\text{next} = 0 \,\wedge\, 10 \le \text{len} \,\wedge\, \text{next}' = 10 \,\wedge\, \text{preserve}(\{\text{len}, c, \text{end}\})$
$\rho(\tau_0' \colon \langle \ell_0, \ell_1, \rho_0' \rangle)$	$\text{next} + 10 > \text{len} \,\wedge\, \text{preserve}(\{\text{next}, \text{len}, c, \text{end}\})$
$\rho(m_0' \colon \text{MIRROR}(\tau_0', \eta, \_))$	$10 > \text{len} \,\wedge\, \text{preserve}(\{\text{next}, \text{len}, c, \text{end}\})$
$\eta(\ell_3)$	$\text{next} \ge 0 \,\wedge\, c \ge 0 \,\wedge\, c < \text{end}$
$\rho(\tau_3 \colon \langle \ell_3, \ell_1, \rho_3 \rangle)$	$c' = c + 1 \,\wedge\, \text{preserve}(\{\text{next}, \text{len}, \text{end}\})$
$\rho(m_3 \colon \text{MIRROR}(\tau_3, \eta, \_))$	$\text{next} \ge 0 \,\wedge\, \text{preserve}(\{\text{next}, \text{len}, c, \text{end}\})$
$\eta(\ell_4)$	$\text{next} \ge 0 \,\wedge\, c \ge 10$

The transition relation of the MIRROR transition m_0 is derived from the original transition τ_0 by computing: $\text{preserve}(\{c, \text{end}\}) \wedge ((\exists\, c, \text{end}, c', \text{end}')\,\eta(\ell_0) \wedge \rho_0)$. Eliminating the existential quantifier from

$$
\text{preserve}(\{c, \text{end}\}) \,\wedge \\
(\exists\, c, \text{end}, c', \text{end}') \left[\begin{array}{c} \text{next} = 0 \,\wedge\, c = 0 \,\wedge\, \text{end} = 10 \,\wedge \\ \text{next} + 10 \le \text{len} \,\wedge\, c' = \text{next} \,\wedge\, \text{next}' = \text{end}' = \text{next} + 10 \,\wedge \\ \text{preserve}(\{\text{len}\}) \end{array} \right]
$$

yields the MIRROR transition relation of m_0 shown above. We note that other MIRROR transitions preserve the global variables next and len (e.g., m_0' or m_3). Thus, these transitions may be omitted from the MIRROR process while preserving all behaviors. Mirror transition m_0 is the one illustrated in Fig. 3.

We now present the main result involving reflective abstractions: if η is an inductive invariant of the reflective abstraction $\text{REFLECT}_\Pi(\eta)$ for a parametrized program Π, then for every location ℓ, the assertion $\eta(\ell)$ is a 1-indexed invariant (Cf. Definition 1).

Theorem 1 (Reflection Soundness). *Let η be an assertion map such that η is inductive for the system $\text{REFLECT}_\Pi(\eta)$. It follows that for each location ℓ of Π, $\eta(\ell)$ is a 1-index invariant.*

The proof proceeds by induction on the runs of the parametrized system Π. The full proof is provided in our companion TR [34]. To summarize, if one discovers a map η that is inductive for the system $\text{REFLECT}_\Pi(\eta)$, then we may conclude that $\eta(\ell)$ is a 1-index invariant for location ℓ in Π. In spite of its circularity, this characterization naturally suggests that the process of constructing a suitable η can be cast as a fixed point and solved using abstract interpretation.

   To generalize reflective abstraction to $k > 1$ materialized threads, we first construct a transition system that is the product of k-copies of the parametrized program Π. This transition system uses k-copies of the locals and a single instance of the globals from Π. Then, given an assertion map η, we add MIRROR transitions to construct the reflective abstraction following Definition 2 on this product system. Each transition τ is projected onto the (global) shared variables guarded by the assertion given by η in the transition's pre-location. An inductive assertion derived on the reflective abstraction of the product system is a k-indexed invariant for the original parametrized system.

4   Reflective Abstract Interpretation

In this section, we present an iterative procedure to generate invariants of a parametrized system by applying abstract interpretation on reflective abstractions. We explain a *lazy* and an *eager* approach to reflective abstract interpretation and contrast reflective abstraction with *interference abstraction*, a commonly-used approach when analyzing multi-thread programs (e.g., [30]).

First, we briefly recall the theory of abstract interpretation [13,14,5] for finding inductive assertion maps as the fixed point of a monotone operator over an *abstract domain*. Abstract interpretation is based on the observation that invariants of a program are over-approximations of the *concrete collecting semantics* η^*, an assertion map that associates each location ℓ with a first-order assertion $\eta^*(\ell)$ characterizing all reachable states at the location ℓ. Formally, we write $\eta^* = \text{lfp } \mathscr{F}_\Sigma(false)$. Here, $\mathscr{F}_\Sigma(\eta)$ is a "single-step" semantics—a monotone operator over the lattice of assertion maps that collects all the states reachable in at most one step of the system Σ, and *false* maps every location to *false*. For this presentation, we will rewrite slightly that familiar equation, making the transition system Σ an explicit argument of $\mathscr{F}$ (rather than fixed):

$$\eta^* = \text{lfp } \mathscr{F}(false, \Sigma). \tag{3}$$

We can also define a *structural pre-order* on sequential transition systems. We say Σ structurally refines Σ', written $\Sigma \preceq \Sigma'$, as simply saying that Σ and Σ' have the same structure—in terms of their variables, locations, and transitions—and where the initial conditions and the corresponding transition relations are ordered by $\models$. It is clear that if $\Sigma \preceq \Sigma'$, then the behaviors of Σ' over-approximate the behaviors of Σ. A more detailed definition is given in our companion TR [34]. Now, we can see that the concrete collecting semantics functional $\mathscr{F}(\eta, \Sigma)$ is monotone over both arguments: (a) over concrete assertion maps ordered by $\models$ location-wise and (b) over sequential transition systems using the structural pre-order.

The abstract interpretation framework allows one to approximate the *collecting semantics* of programs in an abstract domain $\mathscr{A}$: $\langle A, \sqsubseteq, \bot, \top, \sqcup, \sqcap \rangle$ defined by a lattice. The abstract lattice is related to the concrete lattice of first-order assertions $\Gamma[X]$ through a *Galois connection* described by an abstraction function $\alpha : \Gamma[X] \to A$ that maps assertions in the concrete domain to abstract objects and $\gamma : A \to \Gamma[X]$ that interprets abstract objects as concrete assertions representing sets of states. In the abstract interpretation framework, we lift the operator $\mathscr{F}$ defined over the concrete domain to the corresponding monotone operator $\widehat{\mathscr{F}}$ over the abstract domain $\mathscr{A}$. Analogously, we write $\widehat{\eta} : Loc \to_{\text{fin}} A$ for an abstract assertion map. A fixed point computation in (3) is then expressed in terms of the abstract domain $\mathscr{A}$ as follows: $\widehat{\eta}^* = \text{lfp } \widehat{\mathscr{F}}(\bot, \Sigma)$. Here, $\bot$ is the abstract assertion map that maps every location to the bottom element of the abstract domain $\bot$. If $\mathscr{A}$ is an abstract domain, then it follows that $\gamma \circ \widehat{\eta}^*$ yields an inductive assertion map over the concrete domain.

If the domain $\mathscr{A}$ is finite or has the *ascending chain condition*, the least-fixed point lfp operator may be computed iteratively. On the other hand, many domains of interest fail to satisfy these conditions. Herein, abstract interpretation provides us a framework using the *widening* operator that can be repeatedly applied to guarantee convergence to a *post-fixed point* that over-approximates the least-fixed point. Concretizing this post-fixed point leads to a valid (but weaker) inductive assertion map.

4.1 Abstract Interpretation Using Reflection

The overall idea behind our invariant generation technique is to alternate between constructing a (sequential) reflective abstraction of the given parametrized system Π and applying abstract interpretation for sequential systems on the reflective abstraction. We distinguish two abstract interpretation schemes: *lazy* and *eager*.

Lazy Reflective Abstract Interpretation. Lazy reflective abstract interpretation for a parametrized system Π proceeds as follows: First, begin with an initial abstract candidate invariant map $\widehat{\eta}_0$ that maps each location to the least abstract element $\bot$. Then, iterate the following steps until convergence: (a) compute the reflective abstraction Σ_j Using $\widehat{\eta}_j$; (b) on the reflective abstraction Σ_j, apply an abstract interpreter for sequential systems to obtain the next candidate invariant map $\widehat{\eta}_{j+1}$; (c) terminate the iteration whenever $\widehat{\eta}_{j+1}(\ell) \sqsubseteq \widehat{\eta}_j(\ell)$ for all $\ell \in Loc$. We now proceed formally to derive the lazy abstract interpretation scheme above. Let $\widehat{\mathcal{G}}_{\text{LAZY},\Pi}$ be the following operator defined over the abstract lattice:

$$\widehat{\mathcal{G}}_{\text{LAZY},\Pi}(\widehat{\eta}) \stackrel{\text{def}}{=} \text{lfp } \widehat{\mathcal{F}}(\bot, \text{REFLECT}_\Pi(\gamma \circ \widehat{\eta})). \tag{4}$$

Given a map $\widehat{\eta}$ associating locations with abstract objects, the operator $\widehat{\mathcal{G}}_{\text{LAZY},\Pi}$ is implemented by (a) concretizing $\widehat{\eta}$ to compute $\text{REFLECT}_\Pi(\gamma \circ \widehat{\eta})$, the reflective abstraction; and (b) applying the least fixed point of $\widehat{\mathcal{F}}$ over the reflection. We note that the monotonicity of $\widehat{\mathcal{G}}_{\text{LAZY}}$ holds where lfp is computable. In particular, we note that $\text{REFLECT}_\Pi(\eta)$ is a monotone operator. The overall scheme for inferring invariants of the original system Π consists of computing the following:

$$\widehat{\eta}^* = \text{lfp } \widehat{\mathcal{G}}_{\text{LAZY},\Pi}(\bot) \qquad \text{and let map } \eta_{\text{inv}} \stackrel{\text{def}}{=} \gamma \circ \widehat{\eta}^*. \tag{5}$$

Soundness follows from the soundness of abstract interpretation and reflection soundness (Theorem 1). In practice, we implement the operator $\widehat{\mathcal{G}}_{\text{LAZY}}$ by constructing a reflective abstraction and calling an abstract interpreter as a black-box. Note that if the abstract interpreter uses widening to enforce convergence, $\widehat{\mathcal{G}}_{\text{LAZY}}$ is not necessarily monotone since the post-fixed point computation cannot be guaranteed to be monotone. We revisit these considerations in Sect. 4.3.

Eager Reflective Abstract Interpretation. In contrast with the lazy scheme, it is possible to construct an eager scheme that weaves the computation of a least-fixed point and the reflective abstractions in a single iteration. This scheme can be thought of as abstract interpretation on the Cartesian product of the abstract domain $\mathcal{A}$ and the space of reflective abstractions $\text{REFLECT}_\Pi(\gamma \circ \widehat{\eta})$ for $\widehat{\eta} \in (Loc \rightharpoonup_{\text{fin}} A)$ ordered by the structural pre-order relation $\preceq$.

The eager scheme consists of using an eager operator and an eager reflective abstract interpretation as a least-fixed point computation with that operation starting at $\bot$:

$$\widehat{\mathcal{G}}_{\text{EAGER},\Pi}(\widehat{\eta}) \stackrel{\text{def}}{=} \widehat{\mathcal{F}}(\widehat{\eta}, \text{REFLECT}_\Pi(\gamma \circ \widehat{\eta})) \qquad \text{and} \qquad \widehat{\eta}^* = \text{lfp } \widehat{\mathcal{G}}_{\text{EAGER},\Pi}(\bot). \tag{6}$$

In other words, we apply a single step of the abstract operator $\widehat{\mathcal{F}}$ starting from the map $\widehat{\eta}$ over the reflective abstraction from $\gamma \circ \widehat{\eta}$.

4.2   Interference Abstraction versus Reflective Abstraction

We compare and contrast the eager and lazy reflective abstraction approaches with the commonly used interference abstraction. The goal of interference abstraction (see for example [30]) is to capture the effect of interfering transitions flow-insensitively much like a reflective abstraction. The *interference semantics* can be expressed concisely in the formalism developed in this section by the following operator:

$$\widehat{\eta}^* = \mathsf{lfp}\ \widehat{\mathscr{F}}(\bot, \Sigma_\top) \quad \text{where } \Sigma_\top \stackrel{\text{def}}{=} \text{REFLECT}_\Pi(\textit{true}). \tag{7}$$

Here $\top$ represents the abstract assertion map that associates each location with $\top \in A$. In particular, the mirror process is fixed to say that any transition in Π (i.e., of an interfering thread) can fire at any point.

As a concrete example, consider the parametrized system with a global variable g and a local variable x shown on the right. At location 0, a thread waits until the value of the global g is positive and then saves that value into its local variable x while setting g to 0. It then increments that value saved locally and writes it back to the global g signaling completion of its processing. Our first goal is to establish that g $\geq$ 0 everywhere.

```
global g: int where g >= 0;
thread P {
    local x: int where x = 0;
0   atomic { await(g > 0);
        x := g; g := 0; }
1   x := x + 1;
2   atomic { g := x; }
3 }
```

Consider the transition from location ℓ_2 to ℓ_3. Following the framework described in this paper, the ideal transition relation for the corresponding MIRROR transition is $((\exists\ \mathsf{x})\ \eta^*(\ell_2) \wedge \mathsf{g}' = \mathsf{x})$. The interference semantics over-approximates $\eta^*(\ell_2)$ with *true*, so this interference transition is simply a non-deterministic update to g, which causes a failure to derive g $\geq$ 0 anywhere. In contrast, the reflective abstraction approach described in this paper over-approximates η^* incrementally starting from $\bot$ in the abstract domain. Doing so enables inferring invariants on x that can then be used to derive g $\geq$ 0—in particular, using that x $>$ 0 for any thread instance at location ℓ_2. However, the reflective abstraction approach is not complete either. For instance, reflective abstractions cannot be used to establish the invariant g $=$ 0 when all threads are at location ℓ_1 or ℓ_2 without the use of additional auxiliary variables.

4.3   Theory versus Practice: The Effect of Widening

Thus far in this section, we have defined all iterations via least-fixed points of monotone operators, implicitly assuming abstract domains for which the least-fixed point is computable. However, in practice, abstract interpretation is used with abstract domains that do not enjoy this property. In particular, we want to be able to use abstract domains that rely on widening to enforce convergence to a post-fixed point that over-approximates the least-fixed point.

Applying abstract interpretation with widening instead of lfp in the previous definitions of this section raises a number of issues in an implementation. First, the lazy reflective operator $\widehat{\mathscr{G}}_{\text{LAZY}}$ defined in (4) on page 155 is not necessarily monotonic. To remedy this in our implementation we enforce monotonicity by applying an "outer join" that joins the assertion maps from the previous iteration with the one from the current iteration. To enforce convergence of this iteration, we must apply an "outer widening" should the abstract domain warrant it.

Another consequence is that the relative precision of the reflective abstract interpretation schemes are unclear. Perhaps counter-intuitively, the interference abstraction approach described in Sect. 4.2 is not necessarily less precise than the reflective abstract interpretation with $\mathscr{G}_{\text{EAGER}}$ as defined in (6). To see this possibility, let $\widehat{\eta}^*_{\text{EAGER}}$ be the fixed point abstract assertion map computed by iterating $\mathscr{G}_{\text{EAGER}}$. While the final reflective abstraction $\Sigma_{\text{EAGER}} : \text{REFLECT}_\Pi(\gamma \circ \widehat{\eta}^*_{\text{EAGER}})$ using $\mathscr{G}_{\text{EAGER}}$ is trivially no less precise than the interference abstraction $\Sigma_{\text{INTERFERE}} : \text{REFLECT}_\Pi(true)$, the abstract interpretation with widening is not guaranteed to be monotonic. Instead, this observation suggests another scheme, which we call eager+. The eager+ scheme runs $\mathscr{G}_{\text{EAGER}}$ to completion to get Σ_{EAGER} and then applies standard abstract interpretation over this sequential transition system. In other words, the eager+ scheme is defined as follows:

$$\widehat{\eta}^*_{\text{EAGER}} = \text{lfp } \mathscr{G}_{\text{EAGER},\Pi}(\bot) \qquad \widehat{\eta}^*_{\text{EAGER}+} = \text{lfp } \widehat{\mathscr{F}}(\bot, \text{REFLECT}_\Pi(\gamma \circ \widehat{\eta}^*_{\text{EAGER}})). \quad (8)$$

5 Empirical Evaluation: Studying Iteration Schemes

We present here an empirical evaluation of implementations of the eager, eager+, lazy, and interference schemes. The main questions that we seek to answer are: (a) how effective are each of these schemes at generating invariants of interest, and (b) how do the invariants generated by each scheme compare with each other in terms of precision? We also look at performance of the analyses secondarily.

Methodology. We consider a set of five benchmarks, including a simple barrier algorithm [29], a centralized barrier [29], the work stealing algorithm presented in Fig. 2, a generalized version of dinning philosophers with a bounded number of resources, and a parametrized system model of autonomous swarming robots inside a $m \times n$ grid [12]. They range in size from 2–75 locations, 6–24 variables, and 4–49 transitions. For each problem, we specify a set of target invariants, with the intention to check whether the automatically generated invariants imply a given program's safety specification. The number of target invariants ranges from 4–16. Our study focuses on examining the technique space rather than the benchmark space, so we do not discuss the details of the benchmarks. Those details are available in our companion TR [34].

We have implemented the reflective and interference abstraction schemes in the LEAP theorem proving framework for verifying functional correctness properties of parametrized programs, currently being developed at the IMDEA Software Institute. The approaches proposed here extend LEAP by generating invariant assertions automatically. After compiling a parametrized program written in an imperative language into a transition system, we generate inductive assertions using the lazy, eager, and eager+ reflective abstraction schemes and the interference abstraction scheme. Our framework directly uses the abstract domains implemented in the Apron library [23]. Narrowing is used for the eager, eager+, and interference schemes but not the lazy scheme.

Results. Table 1 presents a comparison of timings and precision across the lazy, eager, eager+, and interference schemes. The running time in seconds is given for each method

Table 1. Timing and precision results for Lazy, Eager, Eager+ and Interference abstract interpretations. Legend: **ID:** benchmark identifier, **Dom:** abstract domains, **I:** intervals, **O:** octagons, **P:** polyhedra, **Prps:** total number of properties to be proven, **Time:** seconds, **Prp:** number of properties proved, **TO:** timed out (≥ 1.5 hours), **Wid:** number of widening iterations (*) for the lazy scheme we report external widening applications.

ID	Dom	Prps	Lazy			Eager			Eager+			Interf.		
			Time	Wid*	Prp	Time	Wid	Prp	Time	Wid	Prp	Time	Wid	Prp
Tbar	I	4	0.1	2	0	0.1	5	0	0.1	5	0	0.1	4	0
	P		0.2	4	4	0.1	5	4	0.1	5	4	0.1	4	4
	O		0.8	3	3	0.1	5	3	0.1	5	3	0.1	4	3
Wsteal	I	5	0.3	6	2	0.1	5	1	0.1	5	1	0.1	4	0
	P		2.4	6	1	0.1	7	1	0.2	7	3	0.1	7	5
	O		8.2	6	4	7.5	6	4	0.2	6	4	6.2	5	4
Cbar	I	9	0.9	3	4	0.1	7	0	0.1	8	0	0.1	7	0
	P		TO		0	1.7	11	4	2.7	12	5	1.1	10	6
	O		TO		0	7.5	9	6	11.3	9	6	6.2	8	4
Phil	I	14	1.9	4	2	0.1	8	2	0.1	8	2	0.1	7	0
	P		11.8	6	14	1.1	11	8	1.8	11	8	6.3	13	14
	O		TO		0	25	12	4	40	12	4	20	12	4
Rb(2,2)	I	16	31.3	8	4	0.4	10	4	0.4	11	4	0.2	10	0
	P		TO		0	9.3	22	3	15	23	3	5.8	15	4
	O		TO		0	142	25	3	225	26	3	105	18	3
Rb(2,3)	I	18	133	8	6	0.7	10	6	0.9	11	6	0.5	10	0
	P		TO		0	23	22	5	36.8	23	5	16	15	5
	O		TO		0	404	25	5	629	26	5	320	18	5
Rb(3,3)	I	23	1141	8	9	1.6	10	9	2.1	11	9	0.9	10	0
	P		TO		0	68.2	22	8	111.5	23	8	52	15	8
	O		TO		0	1414	25	8	2139	26	8	1168	18	8
Rb(4,4)	I	29	TO		0	6.7	11	16	9.4	11	16	3.2	11	0
	P		TO		0	49	23	15	396	23	15	303	15	15
	O		TO		0	TO		0	TO		0	TO		0

under the Time columns. While interference abstractions are the fastest, as expected, it is perhaps surprising to note that the lazy scheme was markedly slower than the remaining techniques considered. In fact, it times out on many instances. Likewise, we note that eager and eager+ were only slower by a factor of 1.1–1.5 on most benchmarks when compared to interference abstraction. Also surprisingly, the time for using polyhedra is generally faster than octagons. According to the Apron authors, the execution time of polyhedra can vary widely between good and bad cases, while the worst case and best case execution time of octagons is the same, which may explain this observation.

The properties proved by each method are given under the Prp columns. Again, surprisingly, the interference semantics fares noticeably better than the other schemes for the polyhedral domain but noticeably worse on the interval domain. Also, the interval domain itself seems to fare surprisingly better than the polyhedral domain in terms of properties proved. In many cases, however, the properties proved by these domains were non-overlapping. Perhaps the simplest explanation for this result is that the properties themselves mostly concern proving bounds on variables. It is not surprising that the interval domain can establish this. Yet another factor is the use of polyhedral widening. Since a widening needs to be carried out at every location in the program, the loss of precision in the polyhedral domain can be considerable.

In Table 2, we compare each pair of methods in terms of the relative strengths of the invariants inferred. Some surprising patterns are revealed. For one, lazy (L), eager (E), and eager+ (E+) prove stronger invariants for the interval domain when compared to the interference (In) scheme. On the other hand, the trend is reversed for the polyhedral domain. In many cases, the invariants are either incomparable or invariants of one technique are stronger at some location and weaker at others. Conjoining the invariants in these cases can produce stronger invariants overall.

Table 2. Comparing the strength of the inference. For a comparison $A{:}B$, $+$ means A's invariants are stronger than B in at least one location and not weaker elsewhere (conversely for $-$), $=$ means the same everywhere, and $\neq$ means incomparable somewhere.

ID	Dom	L:E	L:E+	L:In	E:In	E+:In	E:E+
Tbar	I	—	—	+	+	+	=
	P	=	=	+	+	+	=
	O	=	=	+	+	+	=
Wsteal	I	+	+	+	+	+	=
	P	+	≠	≠	≠	≠	—
	O	=	=	+	+	+	=
Cbar	I	≠	≠	+	+	+	=
	P	TO	TO	TO	≠	≠	—
	O	TO	TO	TO	+	+	=
Phil	I	+	+	+	+	+	=
	P	+	+	+	—	—	=
	O	TO	TO	TO	+	+	=
Rb(2,2)	I	+	+	+	+	+	=
	P	TO	TO	TO	≠	≠	—
	O	TO	TO	TO	≠	+	—
Rb(2,3)	I	+	+	+	+	+	=
	P	TO	TO	TO	≠	≠	—
	O	TO	TO	TO	≠	+	—
Rb(3,3)	I	+	+	+	+	+	=
	P	TO	TO	TO	≠	≠	—
	O	TO	TO	TO	≠	+	—
Rb(4,4)	I	TO	TO	TO	+	+	=
	P	TO	TO	TO	≠	≠	—
	O	TO	TO	TO	TO	TO	TO

Interpretation of Results. In theory, all the methods presented can be viewed as post-fixed point computations in the product domain representing sets of states and reflective abstractions. Our intuition with abstract interpretation suggests that the interference scheme, which applies a single iteration on the sequential system generated from the $\top$ reflection, should fare worse than the eager scheme which computes a least fixed point using Kleene iteration. The comparison results are quite surprising, however. We conclude that widening and the associated non-monotonicity play a significant role for parametrized systems. This effect is much more so than for sequential systems, wherein, our past experience suggests that non-monotonicity of widening plays a more limited role. A future direction of research might focus on minimizing the use of widenings or avoiding them altogether using constraint-based techniques [11] or recent advances based on policy and strategy iterations [19,20].

6 Related Work

The problem of verifying parametrized systems has received a lot of attention in recent years. This problem is, in general, undecidable [3]. However, numerous decidable subclasses have been identified [7,15,21,16,25,8,1,2,6]. Our approach here is an instance of the general framework of thread-modular reasoning [18,22,26,9], wherein one reasons about a thread in isolation given some assumptions about its environment (i.e., the other concurrently executing threads). Notably, the approach considered here builds up the assumptions incrementally via self-reflection.

One of the main issues in verifying parametrized programs is the interaction between a given thread and its environment, consisting of the remaining threads. Abstracting this interaction finitely has been considered by many, recently by Berdine et al. [4] and Farzan et al. [17]. In particular, the approach of Berdine et al. is very closely related. Similarities include the notion of transferring invariants from a materialized thread to the abstraction of the remaining threads. However, Berdine et al. do not explicitly specify an iteration scheme, that is, how the inferred candidate invariants are transferred to the environment abstraction. Furthermore, the effects of widening, including the potential non-monotonicity in many domains, are not studied. As observed in this paper, such considerations have a significant impact on the generated invariants. Another recent contribution is that of Farzan et al. that explores the interleaving of control and data-flow analyses to better model the thread interference in parametrized programs. In our framework, their setup roughly corresponds to the lazy scheme. However, Farzan et al. do not incrementally consider the transference of data properties, and instead they focus on ruling out infeasible interferences due to control.

The idea of abstracting away the effects of interacting threads by projecting away the local variables is quite standard. The recent work of Miné et al. [30] analyzes multi-threaded embedded systems using this abstraction. Likewise, Kahlon et al. present a framework for the abstract interpretation of multi-threaded programs with finitely-many threads. Therein, a *melding operator* is used to model the effect of an interfering thread on the abstract state of the current thread [24].

Our approach presented here does not explicitly handle synchronization constructs such as locks and pairwise rendezvous. These constructs can be handled using the framework of *transaction delineation* presented by Kahlon et al. [24]. Here, a single-threaded sequential analysis pass is first carried out to identify sections of the program which can be executed "atomically" while safely ignoring the interferences by the remaining threads. Exploring the use of the delineated transactions to construct the reflective abstraction in the framework of this paper is a promising future direction that will enable us to analyze larger and more complex software systems.

Another class of approaches relies on finite model properties wherein invariants of finite instantiations generalize to the parametrized system as a whole. One such approach is that of *invisible invariants* pioneered by Pnueli et al. [32,35]. This approach finds inductive invariants by fixing the number of processes and computing invariants of the instantiated system. These invariants are heuristically generalized to the parametrized system, which are then checked to be inductive. In [28], invisible invariants are generalized in the abstract interpretation framework as fixed points. In specific instances, a finite model property is used to justify the completeness of this technique. A related method is that of *splitting invariants* [31,10] that ease the automation of invariant generation but also assumes finite state processes and the existence of a cut-off [15].

7   Conclusion

We have described the *reflective abstraction* approach for inferring k-indexed invariants of parametrized systems. This approach was inspired partly by the notions of materialization-summarization from shape analysis. The central idea was that inferences made on materialized threads can be transferred or *reflected* on to the summarized threads (i.e., the MIRROR process). This perspective not only suggests a new technique but describes a space of possible invariant inference techniques, including previously-defined interference abstractions. As such, we studied three variants of reflective abstraction that we defined and the interference abstraction to better understand their relative strength in inferring invariants. To our surprise, our study revealed what appears to be a significant amount of unpredictability in invariant inference strength as the result of widening. The effect of widening seems to be larger for reflective abstract interpretation of parametrized systems than for standard abstract interpretation of sequential systems. We hypothesize that the presence of loops at each program location (from the composition with the MIRROR process) is the primary culprit behind this observation, suggesting a direction for future inquiry. Another future direction is to examine how additional structure can be imposed on the summarized threads.

References

1. Abdulla, P.A., Bouajjani, A., Jonsson, B., Nilsson, M.: Handling Global Conditions in Parameterized System Verification. In: Halbwachs, N., Peled, D.A. (eds.) CAV 1999. LNCS, vol. 1633, pp. 134–145. Springer, Heidelberg (1999)
2. Abdulla, P.A., Delzanno, G., Rezine, A.: Parameterized Verification of Infinite-State Processes with Global Conditions. In: Damm, W., Hermanns, H. (eds.) CAV 2007. LNCS, vol. 4590, pp. 145–157. Springer, Heidelberg (2007)
3. Apt, K.R., Kozen, D.C.: Limits for automatic verification of finite-state concurrent systems. Info. Proc. Letters 22(6), 307–309 (1986)
4. Berdine, J., Lev-Ami, T., Manevich, R., Ramalingam, G., Sagiv, M.: Thread Quantification for Concurrent Shape Analysis. In: Gupta, A., Malik, S. (eds.) CAV 2008. LNCS, vol. 5123, pp. 399–413. Springer, Heidelberg (2008)
5. Blanchet, B., Cousot, P., Cousot, R., Feret, J., Mauborgne, L., Miné, A., Monniaux, D., Rival, X.: Design and Implementation of a Special-Purpose Static Program Analyzer for Safety-Critical Real-Time Embedded Software. In: Mogensen, T.Æ., Schmidt, D.A., Hal Sudborough, I. (eds.) The Essence of Computation. LNCS, vol. 2566, pp. 85–108. Springer, Heidelberg (2002)
6. Bozzano, M., Delzanno, G.: Beyond Parameterized Verification. In: Katoen, J.-P., Stevens, P. (eds.) TACAS 2002. LNCS, vol. 2280, pp. 221–235. Springer, Heidelberg (2002)
7. Clarke, E.M., Grumberg, O., Browne, M.C.: Reasoning about networks with many identical finite-state processes. In: PODC 1986, pp. 240–248. ACM (1986)
8. Clarke, E.M., Grumberg, O., Jha, S.: Veryfying Parameterized Networks using Abstraction and Regular Languages. In: Lee, I., Smolka, S.A. (eds.) CONCUR 1995. LNCS, vol. 962, pp. 395–407. Springer, Heidelberg (1995)
9. Clarke, E., Talupur, M., Veith, H.: Proving Ptolemy Right: The Environment Abstraction Framework for Model Checking Concurrent Systems. In: Ramakrishnan, C.R., Rehof, J. (eds.) TACAS 2008. LNCS, vol. 4963, pp. 33–47. Springer, Heidelberg (2008)
10. Cohen, A., Namjoshi, K.S.: Local proofs for global safety properties. FMSD 34(2), 104–125 (2009)
11. Colón, M.A., Sankaranarayanan, S., Sipma, H.B.: Linear Invariant Generation Using Nonlinear Constraint Solving. In: Hunt Jr., W.A., Somenzi, F. (eds.) CAV 2003. LNCS, vol. 2725, pp. 420–432. Springer, Heidelberg (2003)
12. Correll, N., Martinoli, A.: Collective inspection of regular structures using a swarm of miniature robots. In: ISER. Springer Tracts in Advanced Robotics, vol. 21, pp. 375–386. Springer (2004)

13. Cousot, P., Cousot, R.: Abstract Interpretation: A unified lattice model for static analysis of programs by construction or approximation of fixpoints. In: POPL 1977, pp. 238–252. ACM (1977)

14. Cousot, P., Cousot, R.: Comparing the Galois Connection and Widening/Narrowing Approaches to Abstract Interpretation (Invited Paper). In: Bruynooghe, M., Wirsing, M. (eds.) PLILP 1992. LNCS, vol. 631, pp. 269–295. Springer, Heidelberg (1992)

15. Allen Emerson, E., Kahlon, V.: Reducing Model Checking of the Many to the Few. In: McAllester, D. (ed.) CADE 2000. LNCS (LNAI), vol. 1831, pp. 236–254. Springer, Heidelberg (2000)

16. Emerson, E.A., Namjoshi, K.S.: Automatic Verification of Parameterized Synchronous Systems. In: Alur, R., Henzinger, T.A. (eds.) CAV 1996. LNCS, vol. 1102, pp. 87–98. Springer, Heidelberg (1996)

17. Farzan, A., Kincaid, Z.: Verification of parameterized concurrent programs by modular reasoning about data and control. In: POPL 2012, pp. 297–308. ACM (2012)

18. Flanagan, C., Qadeer, S.: Thread-Modular Model Checking. In: Ball, T., Rajamani, S.K. (eds.) SPIN 2003. LNCS, vol. 2648, pp. 213–224. Springer, Heidelberg (2003)

19. Gaubert, S., Goubault, É., Taly, A., Zennou, S.: Static Analysis by Policy Iteration on Relational Domains. In: De Nicola, R. (ed.) ESOP 2007. LNCS, vol. 4421, pp. 237–252. Springer, Heidelberg (2007)

20. Gawlitza, T., Seidl, H.: Precise Fixpoint Computation Through Strategy Iteration. In: De Nicola, R. (ed.) ESOP 2007. LNCS, vol. 4421, pp. 300–315. Springer, Heidelberg (2007)

21. German, S.M., Sistla, A.P.: Reasoning about systems with many processes. J. of the ACM 39(3), 675–735 (1992)

22. Henzinger, T.A., Jhala, R., Majumdar, R., Qadeer, S.: Thread-Modular Abstraction Refinement. In: Hunt Jr., W.A., Somenzi, F. (eds.) CAV 2003. LNCS, vol. 2725, pp. 262–274. Springer, Heidelberg (2003)

23. Jeannet, B., Miné, A.: APRON: A Library of Numerical Abstract Domains for Static Analysis. In: Bouajjani, A., Maler, O. (eds.) CAV 2009. LNCS, vol. 5643, pp. 661–667. Springer, Heidelberg (2009)

24. Kahlon, V., Sankaranarayanan, S., Gupta, A.: Semantic Reduction of Thread Interleavings in Concurrent Programs. In: Kowalewski, S., Philippou, A. (eds.) TACAS 2009. LNCS, vol. 5505, pp. 124–138. Springer, Heidelberg (2009)

25. Lesens, D., Halbwachs, N., Raymond, P.: Automatic verification of parameterized linear networks of processes. In: POPL 1997, pp. 346–357. ACM (1997)

26. Malkis, A., Podelski, A., Rybalchenko, A.: Precise Thread-Modular Verification. In: Riis Nielson, H., Filé, G. (eds.) SAS 2007. LNCS, vol. 4634, pp. 218–232. Springer, Heidelberg (2007)

27. Manna, Z., Pnueli, A.: Temporal Verification of Reactive Systems: Safety. Springer (1995)

28. McMillan, K.L., Zuck, L.D.: Invisible Invariants and Abstract Interpretation. In: Yahav, E. (ed.) SAS 2011. LNCS (LNAI), vol. 6887, pp. 249–262. Springer, Heidelberg (2011)

29. Mellor-Crummey, J.M., Scott, M.L.: Barriers for the sequent symmetry, ftp://ftp.cs.rochester.edu/pub/packages/scalable_synch/locks_and_barriers/Symmetry.tar.Z

30. Miné, A.: Static Analysis of Run-Time Errors in Embedded Critical Parallel C Programs. In: Barthe, G. (ed.) ESOP 2011. LNCS, vol. 6602, pp. 398–418. Springer, Heidelberg (2011)

31. Namjoshi, K.S.: Symmetry and Completeness in the Analysis of Parameterized Systems. In: Cook, B., Podelski, A. (eds.) VMCAI 2007. LNCS, vol. 4349, pp. 299–313. Springer, Heidelberg (2007)

32. Pnueli, A., Ruah, S., Zuck, L.D.: Automatic Deductive Verification with Invisible Invariants. In: Margaria, T., Yi, W. (eds.) TACAS 2001. LNCS, vol. 2031, pp. 82–97. Springer, Heidelberg (2001)
33. Sagiv, M., Reps, T., Wilhelm, R.: Solving shape-analysis problems in languages with destructive updating. ACM Trans. Program. Lang. Syst. 20(1), 1–50 (1998)
34. Sanchez, A., Sankaranarayanan, S., Sánchez, C., Chang, B.Y.E.: Invariant generation for parametrized systems using self-reflection (extended version). Tech. Rep. CU-CS-1094-12, University of Colorado Boulder (2012)
35. Zuck, L.D., Pnueli, A.: Model checking and abstraction to the aid of parameterized systems (a survey). Computer Languages, Systems & Structures 30, 139–169 (2004)

Automatic Fence Insertion
in Integer Programs via Predicate Abstraction*

Parosh Aziz Abdulla[1], Mohamed Faouzi Atig[1],
Yu-Fang Chen[2], Carl Leonardsson[1], and Ahmed Rezine[3]

[1] Uppsala University, Sweden
[2] Academia Sinica, Taiwan
[3] Linköping University, Sweden

Abstract. We propose an automatic fence insertion and verification framework for concurrent programs running under relaxed memory. Unlike previous approaches to this problem, which allow only variables of finite domain, we target programs with (unbounded) integer variables. The problem is difficult because it has two different sources of infiniteness: unbounded store buffers and unbounded integer variables. Our framework consists of three main components: (1) a finite abstraction technique for the store buffers, (2) a finite abstraction technique for the integer variables, and (3) a counterexample guided abstraction refinement loop of the model obtained from the combination of the two abstraction techniques. We have implemented a prototype based on the framework and run it successfully on all standard benchmarks together with several challenging examples that are beyond the applicability of existing methods.

1 Introduction

Modern concurrent process architectures allow *relaxed* memory, in which certain memory operations may overtake each other. The use of weak memory models makes reasoning about the behaviors of concurrent programs much more difficult and error-prone compared to the classical *sequential consistency* (SC) memory model. In fact, several algorithms that are designed for the synchronization of concurrent processes, such as mutual exclusion and producer-consumer protocols, are not correct when run on weak memories [3]. One way to eliminate the non-desired behaviors resulting from the use of weak memory models is to insert memory *fence* instructions in the program code. A fence instruction forbids certain reordering between instructions issued by the same process. For example, a fence may forbid an operation issued after the fence instruction to overtake an operation issued before it. Recently, several research efforts [9,8,14,6,15,13,18,5,4,10,11,2] have targeted developing automatic verification and fence insertion algorithms of concurrent programs under relaxed memory. However, all these approaches target finite state programs. For the problem of analyzing algorithms/programs with mathematical integer variables (i.e., variables of an infinite data domain), these approaches can only approximate them by, e.g., restricting the upper and lower bounds of variables. The main challenge of the problem is that it contains

---

* This research was in part funded by the Swedish Research Council within the UPMARC Linnaeus centre of Excellence.

A. Miné and D. Schmidt (Eds.): SAS 2012, LNCS 7460, pp. 164–180, 2012.

two different dimensions of infiniteness. First, under relaxed memory, memory operations may be temporarily stored in a buffer before they become effective and the size of the buffer is *unbounded*. Second, the variables are ranging over an *infinite* data domain.

In this paper, we propose a framework (Fig. 1) that can automatically verify a concurrent system S (will be defined in Sec. 2) with integer variables under relaxed memory and insert fences as necessary to make it correct. The framework consists of three main components. The first component (Sec. 4) is responsible for finding a finite abstraction of the unbounded store buffers. In the paper, we choose to instantiate it with a technique introduced in [15]. Each store buffer in the system keeps only the first k operations and makes a finite over-approximation of the rest. For convenience, we call this technique *k-abstraction* in this paper. The second component (Sec. 5) (1) finds a finite abstraction of the data and then (2) combines it with the first abstraction to form a finite *combined abstraction* for both the buffer and data. For the data abstraction, in this paper we choose to instantiate it with *predicate abstraction*; a finite set of predicates over integer variables in the system is applied to partition the infinite data domain into finitely many parts. The combined abstraction gives us a finite state abstraction of the concurrent system S. A standard reachability algorithm (Sec. 6) is then performed on the finite abstraction. For the case that a counterexample is returned, the third component analyzes it (Sec. 7) and depending on the result of the analysis it may refine the concurrent system by adding fences, refine the abstract model by increasing k or adding more predicates, or report that ce is an unpreventable counterexample trace, i.e., a bad behavior exists even in the SC model and cannot be removed by adding fences.

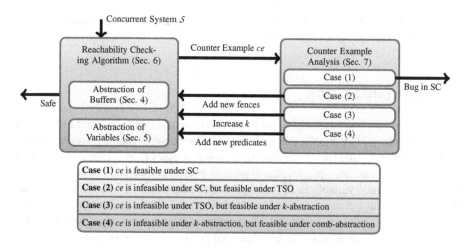

Fig. 1. Our fence insertion/verification framework

Because of the space limit and in order to simplify presentation, we demonstrate our technique under the total store order (TSO) memory model. However, our technique can be generalized to other memory models such as the partial store order (PSO) memory model. In this paper, we use the usual formal model of TSO, developed in, e.g., [20,22], and assume that it gives a faithful description of the actual hardware on which we run our programs. Conceptually, the TSO model adds a FIFO buffer between each process and the main memory (Fig. 2). The buffer is used to store the write operations performed by the process. Thus, a process executing a write operation inserts it into its store buffer and immediately continues executing subsequent operations. Memory updates are then performed by non-deterministically choosing a process and executing the oldest write operation in its buffer. A read operation by a process p on a variable x can overtake some write operations stored in its own buffer if all these operations concern variables that are different from x. Thus, if the buffer contains some write operations to x, then the read value must correspond to the value of the most recent write operation to x. Otherwise, the value is fetched from the memory. A fence means that the buffer of the process must be flushed before the program can continue beyond the fence. Notice that the store buffers of the processes are unbounded since there is *a priori* no limit on the number of write operations that can be issued by a process before a memory update occurs.

To our knowledge, our approach is the first automatic verification and fence insertion method for concurrent *integer* programs under relaxed memory. We implemented a prototype and run it successfully on all standard benchmarks together with challenging examples that are beyond the applicability of existing methods. For instance, we can verify Lamport's Bakery algorithm without assuming an upper bound on ticket numbers.

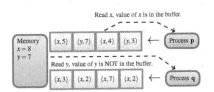

Fig. 2. TSO memory model

2   Concurrent Systems

Our goal is to verify safety properties of *concurrent systems* under relaxed memory. A *concurrent system* (P, A, X_S, X_L) consists of a set of processes P running in parallel with shared variables X_S and local variables X_L. These processes P are modeled by a set of finite automata $A = \{A_p \mid p \in P\}$. Each process p in P corresponds to an automaton A_p in A. Each local variable in X_L belongs to one process in P, i.e., we assume that two processes will not use the same local variable in X_L. The automaton A_p is a triple $(Q_p, q_p^{init}, \delta_p)$, where Q_p is a finite set of *program locations* (sometimes "locations" for short), q_p^{init} is the initial program location, and δ_p is a finite set of transitions. Each transition is a triple (l, op, l'), where l, l' are locations and op is an operation in one of the following forms: (1) read operation $read(x, v)$, (2) write operation $write(x, v)$, (3) fence operation $fence$, (4) atomic read write operation $arw(x, v, w)$, (5) assignment operation $v := e$, and (6) guard operation $e_1 \circ e_2$, for $\circ \in \{>, =, <\}$. In the above, x is a shared variable in X_S, v, w are local variables in X_L, and e, e_1, e_2 are quantifier-free Presburger formulae over X_L. We write $l \xrightarrow{op}_p l'$ to denote that $(l, op, l') \in \delta_p$. We assume that $Q_p \cap Q_q = \emptyset$ for all $p, q \in P$ such that $p \neq q$ and use Q to denote the set of all locations in the concurrent program, i.e., $Q = \bigcup_{p \in P} Q_p$. In the next section, we formally define the semantics of concurrent systems under TSO and the verification problem we are interested in.

3   The TSO Transition System

We define the semantics of concurrent systems under TSO in this section. We begin with the definition of some terms and notations that will be used in this paper. In the rest of the paper, we fix a concurrent system $S = (P, A, X_S, X_L)$.

3.1   Definitions and Notations

We write $\mathcal{N}$ for the set of natural numbers (the set of positive integers) and $\mathcal{Z}$ for the set of integers. Given a set S, we use $|S|$ to denote the cardinality of S. For each process $p \in P$ and an integer value $i \in \mathcal{N}$, we use the variable $b_{p,i}$ to denote the i-th operation of the store buffer of p. We assume that the smaller the value i is, the closer it is to the memory, i.e., the longer it stayed in the buffer. We use X_B to denote the set $\{b_{p,i} \mid p \in P \wedge i \in \mathcal{N}\}$ and call it the set of *buffer variables*. For a partial function f, we use the notation $f(x) = \bot$ to denote that f is undefined on x.

After these basic definitions, we will start to explain the semantics of concurrent systems under TSO. This is done by first defining system configurations and then the transition relation between these configurations w.r.t different operations.

3.2   Configurations

A *configuration* is a snapshot of a concurrent system, which captures values of shared and local variables, the current location of each process, and the content of the store buffers. Formally, we define a *configuration* as a tuple (M, L, pc, B_x, B_v), where $M : X_S \to \mathcal{Z}$ maps a shared variable to its value, $L : X_L \to \mathcal{Z}$ maps a local variable to its value, the function $pc : P \to Q$ maps a process p to its current location in Q_p, $B_x : X_B \to X_S$ maps a buffer variable to its corresponding shared variable, and $B_v : X_B \to \mathcal{Z}$ maps a buffer variable to its value. For example, if the i-th operation in the buffer of process p is $(x, 3)$ (update the value of x to 3), then $B_x(b_{p,i}) = x$ and $B_v(b_{p,i}) = 3$. Notice that here the functions B_x and B_v are partial. A configuration (M, L, pc, B_x, B_v) is said to be *initial* if $pc(p) = q_p^{init}$ for all $p \in P$, $M(x) = 0$, $L(v) = 0$, $B_x(b) = \bot$, $B_v(b) = \bot$ for all $x \in X_S$, $v \in X_L$ and $b \in X_B$[1].

3.3   Transition Relation

The transition relation between configurations is defined as follows. Assume that in the concurrent system S, we have $l \xrightarrow{op}_p l'$. There exists a transition from the configuration (M, L, pc, B) to a next configuration (M', L', pc', B') if the following hold: (1) $pc(p) = l$, $pc'(p) = l'$, $\forall q \in P.q \neq p \to pc(q) = pc'(q)$ and (2) at least one of the transition rules in Fig.3 is satisfied. Below we explain the rules in Fig.3.

---

[1] Notice that for simplicity we assume the initial values of all shared and local variables are 0. This can be generalized by defining a new symbol $\top$ representing arbitrary integer values and assigning the initial values of all shared and local variables to $\top$.

$$\frac{Contain(x)}{L'(v)=LastWrite(x)} \text{ READ-B} \quad \frac{\neg Contain(x)}{L'(v)=M(x)} \text{ READ-M} \quad \frac{|B_p|=i}{B'_x(b_{p,i+1})=x \quad B'_v(b_{p,i+1})=L(v)} \text{ WRITE}$$

$$\frac{Empty}{} \text{ FENCE} \quad \frac{Empty \quad M(x)=L(v)}{M'(x)=L(w)} \text{ ARW} \quad \frac{}{L'(v)=e[L]} \text{ ASSIGN} \quad \frac{e_1[L] \circ e_2[L]}{} \text{ GUARD}$$

$$\frac{|B_p|=i \quad B_x(b_{p,1})=x_1 \quad \ldots \quad B_x(b_{p,i})=x_i \quad B_v(b_{p,1})=v_1 \quad \ldots \quad B_v(b_{p,i})=v_i}{M'(x_1)=v_1 \quad B'_x(b_{p,1})=x_2 \quad \ldots \quad B'_x(b_{p,i-1})=x_i \quad B'_v(b_{p,1})=v_2 \quad \ldots \quad B'_v(b_{p,i-1})=v_i \quad B'_x(b_{p,i})=B'_v(b_{p,i})=\bot} \text{ UPDATE}$$

Fig. 3. Transition Rules of a Transition System under TSO. The conditions above the horizontal line are the "pre-condition" that decide whether this transition can be triggered and those below the line are the "post-condition" that decide what the next configuration should be. For a more clear presentation, in the post-condition of the rules defined in this paper (including those in the other sections), we focus only on the component that has been changed. For the components that has not been changed, we assume implicitly that the primed version (the component in the next configuration) is equal to the non-primed version (the same component in the current configuration). For example, for all shared variables $x \in X_S$, if $M'(x)$ has not been assigned a value in the rule, we assume implicitly $M'(x) = M(x)$.

READ-B Rule: When $op=read(x, v)$, if the buffer of p contains write operations to x, we read the value of the last write operation to x in p's buffer. We use $Contain(x)$ as a shorthand for $(\exists i \in \mathcal{N}.B_x(b_{p,i}) = x)$, or, informally, there exists some write operations to x in the buffer. We use $LastWrite(x)$ to denote the most recent value written to x in the buffer of p. Formally, $LastWrite(x) = X_v(b_{p,i})$, where $i = Max(\{j \in \mathcal{N} \mid B_x(b_{p,j}) = x\})$.

READ-M Rule: When $op=read(x, v)$, if the buffer of p does not contain write operations to x, we read the value of x from the memory.

WRITE Rule: When $op=write(x, v)$, we put the operation (x, v) to the end of the buffer. We use $|B_p|$ to denote the length of the buffer of p. Notice that this number equals the index of the most recent operation in p's buffer. Formally, $|B_p| = Max(\{j \in \mathcal{N} \mid B_x(b_{p,j}) \neq \bot\} \cup \{0\})$.

FENCE Rule: When $op=fence$, the transition can be executed only when the buffer of p is empty. Here we use the predicate $Empty$ as a shorthand for $B_x(b_{p,1}) = \bot$.

ARW Rule: When $op=arw(x,v,w)$, the transition can be executed only when the buffer of p is empty and the value of x in the memory equals the value of v in p. When it is executed, the value of x in the memory is immediately changed to the value of w in p.

UPDATE Rule: The write operations in the buffer can be at any time nondeterministically delivered to the memory. This is handled by implicitly adding self-loop transitions $l \xrightarrow{update} l$ from all the locations in Q. Notice that the transition $l \xrightarrow{update} l$ is internal, i.e., it never appears explicitly in the definition of the concurrent system. In this rule, the oldest operation in p's buffer (the one with index 1) will be used to update the memory while all the other operations in the buffer are shifted one step closer to the memory, i.e., their indices are reduced by 1.

ASSIGN Rule: When $op = (v := e)$, where e is a Presburger expression over X_L, we update the value of v to the *evaluation* of e under the assignment L (denoted as $e[L]$).

GUARD Rule: When $op = (e_1 \circ e_2)$, where e_1 and e_2 are Presburger expressions over X_L, the transition can be executed only when $(e_1[L] \circ e_2[L])$ holds, i.e., the evaluations of e_1 and e_2 under L is in the binary relation $\circ$. Here we let $\circ \in \{>, =, <\}$.

3.4 The Reachability Problem

The problem of verifying safety properties can be reduced to reachability problems. We use c^{init} to denote the initial configuration (defined in Section 3.2) and assume that a partial function $Bad : P \to Q$ is given. We use C^{Bad} to denote the set of bad configurations $\{(M, L, pc, B_x, B_v) \mid \forall p \in P.Bad(p) = \perp \lor pc(p) = Bad(p)\}$. Intuitively, taking a mutex problem of processes p_1, p_2, and p_3 as an example. If we want to describe the property that p_1 and p_2 cannot enter their critical sections at the same time, we define $Bad(p_1) = l_{cs1} \land Bad(p_2) = l_{cs2} \land Bad(p_3) = \perp$, where l_{cs1} and l_{cs2} are the locations of the critical sections. The reachability problem of a concurrent system under TSO asks if there exists some configuration in C^{Bad} reachable from the initial configuration c^{init} following the transition rules described in Fig. 3. We say that the concurrent system is "correct" iff all configurations in C^{Bad} are not reachable from c^{init}. Notice that we can extend this approach to allow finitely many bad functions $Bad_1 : P \to Q, \ldots, Bad_m : P \to Q$. In this case, the set of bad configurations becomes $\{(M, L, pc, B_x, B_v) \mid \bigvee_{1 \le i \le m} \forall p \in P.Bad_i(p) = \perp \lor pc(p) = Bad_i(p)\}$.

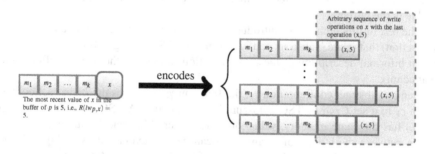

Fig. 4. A k-abstract buffer and the TSO buffer it encodes

4   k-Abstraction

Notice that the store buffers under TSO may grow infinitely large. Therefore, a naive algorithm that would explores all reachable configurations would not work. One way to deal with the problem is to find a proper finite abstraction of the buffer. In this section, we introduce a finite abstraction technique of the buffer and the corresponding abstract transition system [15]. We call this technique k-abstraction (for a given integer k). The basic idea is that, for a buffer with more than k write operations, we keep only the oldest k operations and assume that any operation can appear in the buffer after these k operations. To be more specific, for the operations with index larger than k, we only use (1) a set to record the variable part of those write operations together with (2) a function to record the most recent value of each shared variable in the buffer and abstract away other information. In Fig. 4, we illustrate the relation between a k-*abstract buffer* and the set of TSO buffers it encodes.

4.1   Definitions and Notations

In the sequel, we refer to the transition system induced from the concurrent system under TSO as "TSO system" and the system after k-abstraction as "k-abstract system". As a consequence, we call a configuration, a buffer, and a transition in the TSO system a "TSO configuration", a "TSO buffer", and a "TSO transition", respectively. We call a configuration, a buffer, and a transition in a k-abstract system a "k-abstract configuration", a "k-abstract buffer", and a "k-abstract transition", respectively. In a similar manner, to the case of buffer variables, for a process $p \in P$ and a shared variable $x \in X_S$, we use the variable $lw_{p,x}$ to refer to the value of the last write operation to x in the buffer of p. Let $X_{LW} = \{lw_{p,x} \mid p \in P \wedge x \in X_S\}$.

4.2 k-Abstract Configurations

Formally, a k-abstract configuration is a tuple $(M, L, pc, B_x, B_v, S, R)$, where M, L, pc, B_x, and B_v are defined in the same way as in a TSO configuration, $S : P \to 2^{X_S}$ records, for each process in P, the set of variables in the TSO buffer with index larger than k, and $R : X_{LW} \to \mathcal{Z}$ is a partial function that records the most recent value of each shared variable in the buffer.

In the rest of this section, we introduce the two functions γ_k (concretization) and α_k (abstraction) that relate k-abstract configurations and TSO configurations. Here we only give an informal description of these two functions and leave the formal definition to the appendix.

Given a k-abstract configuration c_k, the function $\gamma_k(c_k)$ maps the k-abstract configuration c_k to a set C_{TSO} of TSO configurations it encodes. A TSO configuration c_{TSO} in C_{TSO} has the same memory, valuation to local variables, and locations as c_s. The relation between the buffers of c_k and c_{TSO} can be best explained using Fig.4. If the buffer of c_k is the k-abstract buffer on the left of Fig.4, then the buffer of c_{TSO} is one of the TSO buffers on the right. Similarly, given a TSO configuration c_{TSO}, the function $\alpha_k(c_{TSO})$ maps it to a k-abstract configuration c_k with the same memory, valuation to local variables, and locations. The relation between their buffers can again be explained using Fig.4. The buffer of c_{TSO} corresponds to one of the buffers on the right of Fig. 4. After k-abstraction, we should obtain the k-abstract buffer on the left of Fig.4.

4.3 k-Abstract Transition Relation

Assume that we have $l \xrightarrow{op}_p l'$ in the concurrent system $\mathcal{S}$. There exists a k-abstract transition from a k-abstract configuration $(M, L, pc, B_x, B_v, S, R)$ to the other k-abstract configuration $(M', L', pc', B'_x, B'_v, S', R')$ if the following holds (1) $pc(p) = l$, $pc'(p) = l'$, $\forall q \in P.q \neq p \rightarrow pc(q) = pc'(q)$ and (2) one of the k-abstract transition rules (Fig.5) holds.

$$\frac{|B_p| = k \vee S(p) \neq \emptyset}{R'(lw_{p,x}) = L(v) \quad S'(p) = S(p) \cup \{x\}} \; \textbf{WRITE-G} \qquad \frac{|B_p| = i < k \quad S(p) = \emptyset}{B'_x(b_{p,i+1}) = x \quad B'_v(b_{p,i+1}) = R'(lw_{p,x}) = L(v)} \; \textbf{WRITE-L}$$

$$\frac{|B_p| = i \neq 0 \quad B_x(b_{p,1}) = x_1 \ldots B_x(b_{p,i}) = x_i \quad B_v(b_{p,1}) = v_1 \ldots B_v(b_{p,i}) = v_i}{M'(x_1) = v_1 \quad B'_x(b_{p,1}) = x_2 \ldots B'_x(b_{p,i-1}) = x_i \quad B'_v(b_{p,1}) = v_2 \ldots B'_v(b_{p,i-1}) = v_i \quad B'_x(b_{p,i}) = B'_v(b_{p,i}) = \perp} \; \textbf{UPDATE-NE}$$

$$\frac{x \in S(p) \quad |B_p| = 0}{M'(x) = M'(x)} \; \textbf{UPDATE-AM} \qquad \frac{x \in S(p) \quad |B_p| = 0}{M'(x) = R(lw_{p,x}) \quad S'(p) = S(p) \setminus \{x\}} \; \textbf{UPDATE-AS}$$

Fig. 5. k-Abstract Transition Rules. We list only rules that are different from the rules in Fig.3.

READ-B, READ-M, FENCE, ARW, ASSIGN, GUARD Rules: For $op = read(x,v)$, the rule of k-abstract transitions is almost the same as the one of TSO transitions. The only exception is that the definition of the predicate $Contain(x)$ should be changed to $(x \in S) \vee (\exists i \in \mathcal{N}.B_x(b_{p,i}) = x)$ and $LastWrite(x) = R(lw_{p,x})$. The case of $op = fence$ or $op = arw(x,v,w)$ can be handled in a similar way. We only need to change the definition of $Empty$ to $(B_x(b_{p,1}) = \perp \wedge S(p) = \emptyset)$. The case of local operations $op = (v := e)$ and $op = (e_1 \circ e_2)$ can be handled by exactly the same rule as in a TSO transition.

WRITE Rules: When $op = write(x,v)$, we need to consider the cases where the size of the abstract buffer is less than k (**WRITE-L**) and equal to or greater than k (**WRITE-G**). When the size is smaller than k, it behaves the same as in the TSO system. For the case that the size is equals to or greater than k, we (1) modify the record of the last write operation of x and (2) add x to the set $S(p)$.

UPDATE Rules: When $op = update$, different cases have to be considered. When the k-bounded buffer is not empty, i.e., $B(b_{p,1}) \neq \perp$ (**UPDATE-NE**), the oldest operation in the buffer (the one with index 1) is sent to the memory and all the other operations in the buffer are shifted one step closer to the memory. For the case that the k-bounded buffer is empty, i.e., $B(b_{p,1}) = \perp$, but the k-abstract buffer is already an over-approximation, i.e, $S(p) \neq \emptyset$, there are two possible sub-cases. One is when the corresponding TSO buffer has more than one operation on x (**UPDATE-AM**) and one is when the TSO buffer has only one operation on x left (**UPDATE-AS**). For the former case, the update operation may change the memory value of any variables in $S(p)$ to any value in $\mathbb{Z}$. Hence we do not need any constraint on $M'(x)$ and put a tautology $M'(x) = M'(x)$ to show that the value of x in the memory has been changed. For the latter case, since only one write operation to x is left in the buffer, the most recent and the oldest write operation to x in the buffer coincide. Therefore, the update operation changes the memory value of the variable x in $S(p)$ to $R(lw_{p,x})$.

5   Combined Abstraction

The elements in a k-abstract state $(M, L, pc, B_x, B_v, S, R)$ can be categorized into two parts. The *data components* include M, L, B_v, R, which are assignments to variables ranging over Z, and the rest belongs to the *control components*. Since the numbers of shared variables $|X_S|$, processes $|P|$, locations of each process $|Q|$, and the lengths of the k-bounded buffers are finite, there exists only a finite number of different control components. However, this is not the case for data components. Since the data domain Z is an infinite set, there exists an infinite number of different data components. It follows that the number of possible configurations can be infinite. In this case, the reachability problem becomes non-trivial. One possible solution is to also apply abstraction techniques on data in order to get a finite abstraction of reachable configurations. Then the reachability problem can be solved by simple depth first or breadth first search algorithms. In this section, we will demonstrate how to use *predicate abstraction* to form a finite abstraction of the data components and how k-abstraction and predicate abstraction are combined.

5.1   Definitions and Notations

We have $X = X_S \cup X_L \cup X_B \cup X_{LW}$, the set of all integer variables in the k-abstract system (recall that X_S, X_L, X_B, X_{LW}, is the set of shared, local, buffer, and last-write variables, respectively). Given a formula e, we define the substitution operation $e[x/x']$ as the formula obtained by replacing all free occurrences of x in e with x'. Given a set of variables $X = \{x_1, \ldots, x_n\}$, we use X' to denote the primed version of X, i.e., $X' = \{x' \mid x \in X\}$. If X and X' are two disjoint sets, we write $e[x/x']_{x \in X}$ as a shorthand for $e[x_1/x'_1][x_2/x'_2] \ldots [x_n/x'_n]$, i.e., replacing all free occurrences of elements $x \in X$ appearing in e with their new variants x'. In the paper, we refer to a transition system on the combined abstraction domain as a "comb-abstract system". As a consequence, we call a configuration, a buffer, and a transition in a comb-abstract system a "comb-abstract configuration", a "comb-abstract buffer", and a "comb-abstract transition", respectively.

5.2   The Idea

The idea of *predicate abstraction* is to use predicates over variables in X to partition the data components of k-abstract configurations into finitely many parts. Each partition may encode an infinite number of different data components. An example can be found in Fig.6. In the figure on the left, we abstract the data components by a predicate $f = (x > y \wedge b_{p,4} = t \wedge lw_{p,y} = t)$ while we store the control component exactly. We call the result a *comb-abstract configuration*. In the example, the comb-abstract configuration encodes k-abstract configurations with the same control components and with data components satisfying the constraint defined in the predicate f. Taking the k-abstract configuration $(M, L, pc, B_x, B_v, S, R)$ [1] on the top-right of Fig 6 as an example, it has the same control components as the comb-abstract configuration on the left. By substituting x and y in f with $M(x)$ and $M(y)$, t with $L(t)$, $b_{p,4}$ with $B_v(b_{p,4})$, $lw_{p,y}$ with $R(lw_{p,y})$, we obtain the formula $8 > 7 \wedge 4 = 4 \wedge 4 = 4$, which evaluates to *true*. Hence it is a k-abstract configuration encoded by the comb-abstract configuration.

---

[1] Recall that $S : P \to 2^{X_S}$ records, for each process in P, the set of variables in the TSO buffer with index larger than k, and $R : X_{LW} \to Z$ is a partial function that records the most recent value of each shared variable in the buffer.

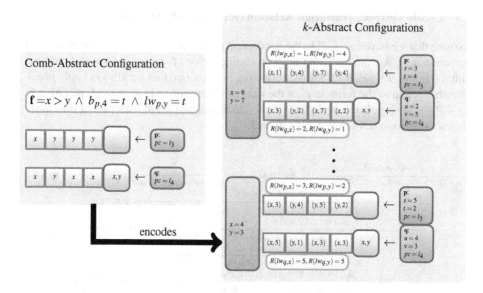

Fig. 6. A comb-abstract configuration and the k-abstract configurations it encodes. Here $X_S = \{x,y\}$ and $X_L = \{s,t,u,v\}$. All the configurations in the figure have the same control components pc, B_x, and S, where $pc(p) = l_3 \wedge pc(q) = l_4$, $B_x(b_{p,1}) = B_x(b_{q,1}) = B_x(b_{q,3}) = B_x(b_{q,4}) = x \wedge B_x(b_{p,2}) = B_x(b_{p,3}) = B_x(b_{p,4}) = B_x(b_{q,2}) = y$, and $S(p) = \emptyset \wedge S(q) = \{x,y\}$.

5.3 Comb-Abstract Configurations

Formally, a comb-abstract configuration is a tuple (f, pc, B_x, S), where f is a formula over X that encodes data components, and the control components pc, B_x, S are defined in a similar manner as in a k-abstract configuration. Given a k-abstract configuration $c_k = (M, L, pc, B_x, B_v, S, R)$ and a formula f over X, we define the *evaluation* of f in c_k, denoted as $f[c_k]$, as the value obtained by substituting all free occurrences of $x \in X_S$ in f with $M(x)$, $v \in X_L$ in f with $L(v)$, $b \in X_B$ in f with $B_v(b)$, and $lw \in X_{LW}$ in f with $R(lw)$. Given a comb-abstract configuration $c_c = (f, pc, B_x, S)$, we define the concretization function $\gamma_c(c_c) = \{c_k = (M, L, pc, B_x, B_v, S, R) \mid f[c_k]\}$. Given a set of comb-abstract configurations C_b, we define $\gamma_c(C_b) = \bigcup_{c_b \in C_b} \gamma_c(c_b)$. Given a set of k-abstract configurations C_k, we use $\alpha_c(C_k)$ to denote the set of comb-abstract configurations that encodes exactly C_k, i.e., $C_k = \gamma_c(\alpha_c(C_k))$.

5.4 Predicate Abstraction

Let f be a formula over X and $\mathcal{P}$ a set of predicates over X. Each predicate in $\mathcal{P}$ partitions the valuation of variables in X into two parts. For each predicate $\pi \in \mathcal{P}$ such that $f \to \pi$ is valid, or equivalently, $f \wedge \neg\pi$ is unsatisfiable, π characterizes a superset of data components of those characterized by f. The predicate abstraction function $\alpha_{pa}(f, \mathcal{P})$ returns a conjunction of all predicates $\pi \in \mathcal{P}$ such that $f \to \pi$ is valid.

5.5 Comb-Abstract Transition Relation (w.r.t a Set of Predicates $\mathcal{P}$)

Assume that we have $l \xrightarrow{op}_p l'$ in the concurrent system $\mathcal{S}$. There exists a comb-abstract transition w.r.t. $\mathcal{P}$ from the comb-abstract configuration (f, pc, B_x, S) to a next configuration $(\alpha_{pa}(f', \mathcal{P}), pc', B_x', S')$ if the following hold (notice that we always apply predicate abstraction to the formula f' of the next configuration): (1) $pc(p) = l$, $pc'(p) = l'$, $\forall q \in P.q \neq p \rightarrow pc(q) = pc'(q)$, (2) f' is satisfiable, and (3) at least one of the comb-abstract transition rules in Fig.7 is satisfied.

$$\frac{\neg Contain(x)}{f' = (\exists X.f \wedge v' = x \wedge Equ(X \setminus \{v\}))[x'/x]_{x' \in X'}} \text{ READ-M} \qquad \frac{Contain(x)}{f' = (\exists X.f \wedge v' = lw_{p,x} \wedge Equ(X \setminus \{v\}))[x'/x]_{x' \in X'}} \text{ READ-B}$$

$$\frac{|B_p| = k \vee S(p) \neq \emptyset}{f' = (\exists X.f \wedge lw_{p,x}' = v \wedge Equ(X \setminus \{lw_{p,x}\}))[x'/x]_{x' \in X'} \quad S'(p) = S(p) \cup \{x\}} \text{ WRITE-G}$$

$$\frac{|B_p| = i < k \quad S(p) = \emptyset}{f' = (\exists X.f \wedge b_{p,i}' = lw_{p,x}' = v \wedge Equ(X \setminus \{b_{p,i}, lw_{p,x}\}))[x'/x]_{x' \in X'} \quad B_x'(b_{p,i}) = x} \text{ WRITE-L} \quad \frac{Empty}{} \text{ FENCE}$$

$$\frac{Empty}{f' = (\exists X.f \wedge x = v \wedge x' = w \wedge Equ(X \setminus \{x\}))[x'/x]_{x' \in X'}} \text{ ARW}$$

$$\frac{|B_p| = i \neq 0 \quad B_x(b_{p,1}) = x_1 \dots B_x(b_{p,i}) = x_i}{B_x'(b_{p,1}) = x_2 \dots B_x'(b_{p,i-1}) = x_i \quad B_x'(b_{p,i}) = \perp} \text{ UPDATE-NE}$$

$$\frac{B_x'(b_{p,1}) = x_2 \dots B_x'(b_{p,i-1}) = x_i \quad B_x'(b_{p,i}) = \perp}{f' = (\exists X.f \wedge x_1' = b_{p,1} \wedge \bigwedge_{1 \leq k \leq i-1} b_{p,k}' = b_{p,k+1} \wedge Equ(X \setminus \{x_1, b_{p,1}, \dots, b_{p,i-1}\}))[x'/x]_{x' \in X'}}$$

$$\frac{x \in S(p) \quad |B_p| = 0}{f' = (\exists X.f \wedge Equ(X \setminus \{x\}))[x'/x]_{x' \in X'}} \text{ UPDATE-AM}$$

$$\frac{x \in S(p) \quad |B_p| = 0}{f' = (\exists X.f \wedge x' = lw_{p,x} \wedge Equ(X \setminus \{x\}))[x'/x]_{x' \in X'} \quad S'(p) = S(p) \setminus \{x\}} \text{ UPDATE-AS}$$

$$\frac{}{f' = (\exists X.f \wedge v' = e \wedge Equ(X \setminus \{v\}))[x'/x]_{x' \in X'}} \text{ ASSIGN} \quad \frac{f \wedge (e_1 \circ e_2)\}}{} \text{ GUARD}$$

Fig. 7. Comb-Abstract Transition Rules. We use the predicate $Equ(V)$ to denote $\bigwedge_{v \in V} v' = v$, i.e., no change made to variables in V in this transition. We assume all bounded variables are renamed to fresh variables that are not in $X \cup X'$ so the substitution will not assign the names of bounded variables to some free variable.

6 The Reachability Checking Algorithm

Alg.1 solves they reachability problem of a comb-abstract system derived from a given concurrent system. The inputs of the algorithm include a value k, a set of predicates $\mathcal{P}$, a concurrent system $\mathcal{S} = (P, A, X_S, X_L)$, and a partial function $Bad : P \rightarrow Q$. We first generate the initial comb-abstract configuration $c^{init} = (true, pc, B_x, S)$, where $\forall p \in P.(pc(p) = q_p^{init} \wedge S(p) = \emptyset) \wedge \forall b \in X_B.B_x(b) = \perp$.

For the reachability algorithm, we maintain two sets, $Next$ and $Visited$ (Line 2). $Next$ contains pairs of a comb-abstract configuration c and a path that leads to c. $Visited$ contains comb-abstract configurations that have been visited. Notice that $Visited$ stores comb-abstract configurations in an efficient way; if both the comb-abstract configurations (f_1, pc, B_x, S) and (f_2, pc, B_x, S) should be put into $Visited$, we put $(f_1 \vee f_2, pc, B_x, S)$ instead. When $Next$ is not empty (Line 3), a pair $((pd, pc, B_x, S), ce)$ is removed from $Next$ and the algorithm tests if (pd, pc, B_x, S) encodes some bad TSO configurations (Line 5). For the case that it does, the algorithm stops and returns ce as a counterexample. Otherwise (pd, pc, B_x, S) is merged into $Visited$ (Line 6). Then the

Algorithm 1. Reachability Algorithm

Input : $S = (P, A, X_S, X_L)$, an integer k, a set of predicates $\mathcal{P}$, a partial function $Bad : P \to Q$
Output: Either the program is safe or a counterexample ce

1 $c^{init} = (true, pc, B_x, S)$, where $\forall p \in P.(pc(p) = q_p^{init} \wedge S(p) = \emptyset) \wedge \forall b \in X_B.B_x(b) = \bot$;
2 $Next := \{(c^{init}, \varepsilon)\}$, $Visited := \emptyset$;
3 **while** $Next \neq \emptyset$ **do**
4   Pick and remove $((pd, pc, B_x, S), ce)$ from $Next$;
5   **if** $\forall p \in P.Bad(p) \neq \bot \to pc(p) = Bad(p)$ **then return** ce is a counterexample;
6   **if** $\exists (f, pc, B_x, S) \in Visited$ **then** replace it with $(f \vee pd, pc, B_x, S)$ **else** add (pd, pc, B_x, S) to $Visited$;
7   **foreach** $l \xrightarrow{op}_p l'$ such that $pc(p) = l$ **do**
8   **foreach** comb-abstract transition rule r **do**
9   compute the next configuration (pd', pc', B_x', S') of (pd, pc, B_x, S) w.r.t $l \xrightarrow{op}_p l'$, r, and $\mathcal{P}$;
10   **if** $\neg(\exists (f, pc', B_x', S') \in Visited$ s.t. $pd' \to f)$ **then**
11   add $((pd', pc', B_x', S'), ce \cdot (l \xrightarrow{op}_p l', r))$ to $Next$;
12 **return** The program is safe;

---

reachability algorithm explores the next configurations of (pd, pc, B_x, S) w.r.t the transitions in S and the comb-abstract transition rules (Lines 7-11). Once $Next$ becomes empty, the algorithm reports that the program is safe. Notice that in the counterexample ce, we record not only the sequence of transitions of S but also the sequence of transition rules that have been applied. We need this in order to remove non-determinism in the comb-abstract system and thus simplify the counterexample analysis. To be more specific, assume that $l \xrightarrow{op}_p l'$ and a comb-abstract configuration c is given, it is possible that there exists more than one transition rules that can be applied and thus the same transition $l \xrightarrow{op}_p l'$ may lead to two different comb-abstract configurations. For example, assume that $op = update$ and the length of the TSO buffer is larger than k. It could happen that both of the rules **UPDATE-AM** and **UPDATE-AS** can be applied. Then the current comb-abstract configuration c may have two different next comb-abstract configurations w.r.t the same transition $l \xrightarrow{op}_p l'$.

7 Counter Example Guided Abstraction Refinement

The counterexample detected by the reachability checking algorithm is a sequence of pairs in the form of (δ, r), where δ is a transition in S and r is a comb-abstract transition rule. Let $ce = (l_1 \xrightarrow{op_1}_{p_1} l_1', r_1)(l_2 \xrightarrow{op_2}_{p_2} l_2', r_2) \ldots (l_n \xrightarrow{op_n}_{p_n} l_n', r_n)$ be the counterexample returned from the reachability module. We next analyze ce and decide how to respond to it. Four possible responses are described in Fig.1.

Case (1): We will not formally define the transition system induced from the concurrent system under sequential consistency (SC) model for lack of space. Informally, under the SC model, all operations will be immediately sent to the memory without buffering. We simulate ce under SC and if ce is feasible under SC, ce is not a bug caused by the relaxation of the memory model. In this case, it cannot be fixed by just adding fences. The algorithm reports that ce is a bug of the concurrent system under the SC model.

Case (2): We can check if the counterexample ce is feasible under TSO by simulating it on the TSO system following the rules defined in Fig. 3. For the case that ce is

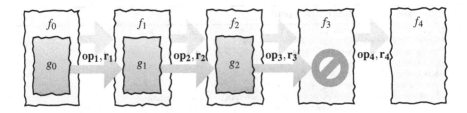

Fig. 8. Data components produced by *ce*

infeasible under SC, but feasible under TSO, we can find a set of fences that can help to remove the spurious counterexample *ce* by the following steps. First we add fences immediately after all write operations in *ce*. We then repeatedly remove these newly added fences while keeping it infeasible under the TSO system. We do this until we reach a point where removing any fences would make *ce* feasible under TSO. In such case, the subsequently remaining such fences are those that need to be added. A more efficient algorithm of extracting fences from error traces can be found in [2].

Case (3): When *ce* is infeasible under TSO, but feasible under k-abstraction, we keep increasing the value of k until we reach a value i such that *ce* is feasible under $(i\text{-}1)$-abstraction, but infeasible under i-abstraction. In such case, we know that we need to increase the value of k to i in order to remove this spurious counterexample. Such a value i always exists, because the length of the sequence *ce* is finite, which means that it contains a finite number of write operations, say n operations, and thus the size of the buffer will not exceed n. When we set k to n, then in fact the behavior of *ce* will be the same under TSO and under k-abstraction. It follows that it is infeasible under k-abstraction when k equals n.

Case (4): When *ce* is infeasible under k-abstraction, but is feasible in the comb-abstract system, it must be the case that predicate abstraction made a too coarse over-approximation of the data components and has to be refined. An example can be found in Fig. 8, where g_0 (respectively, f_0) characterizes the data components of the initial k-abstract configuration (respectively, comb-abstract configuration) and g_i (respectively, f_i) characterizes the data components of the k-abstract configuration (respectively, comb-abstract configuration) after i steps of *ce* are executed. The rule r_3 has a precondition on data components such that g_2 cannot meet this condition, but f_2 can (note that this can happen only when r_3 is a **GUARD** rule or an **ARW** rule). This situation arises because the predicate abstraction in the first 2 steps of *ce* made a too coarse over-approximation. That is, some data components encoded in $f_2 \wedge \neg g_2$ that satisfy the pre-condition of transition rule r_3 are produced from the predication abstraction. In order to fix the problem, we have to find some proper predicates to refine f_0, f_1, and f_2 so the *ce* cannot be executed further after 2 steps in the comb-abstract system. Hence we have to generate some more predicates to refine the comb-abstract system. This can be done using the classical predicate extraction technique based on *Craig interpolation* [7].

8   Discussion

How to Generalize the Proposed Technique?   The proposed technique can be generalized to memory models such as the partial store order memory model or the power memory model. Such models use infinite buffers and one can define finite abstractions by applying the k-abstraction technique [15]. Predicate abstraction and counterexample analysis can be done in the same way as we described in this paper. The Presburger expressions used in this paper can also be extended to any theory for which satisfiability and interpolation are efficiently computable. Notice that although the formula f' in the comb-abstract transtion rules has existential quantifiers, we do not need to assume that quantifier elimination is efficiently computable for the given theory. This is because in predicate abstraction, for a given predicate π, instead of checking whether $f' \rightarrow \pi$ is valid, we check if $f' \wedge \neg \pi$ is unsatisfiable. For satisfiability checking, we can ignore the outermost existential quantifiers in f'.

Further Optimizations.   Assume that two local variables v, u of process p and a predicate $v < u$ describing their relation are given. When the size of the buffer of p is k and p executes the operation $write(x, v)$, the value of the buffer variable $b_{p,k+1}$ will be assigned to the value of v. Then the relation $v < u$ should propagate to the buffer variable and hence we should also have $b_{p,k+1} < u$. However, in order to generate this predicate, it requires another counterexample guided abstraction refinement iteration. It would require even more loop iterations for the relation $v < u$ to propagate to the variable x and generate the relation $x < u$. Notice that for such situations, the "shapes" of the predicates remain the same while propagating in the buffer. Based on this observation, we propose an idea called "predicate template". In this example, instead of only keeping $v < u$ in the set $\mathcal{P}$ of predicates, we keep a predicate template $\square < \square$. The formulae returned by the predicate abstraction function $\alpha_{pa}(f, \mathcal{P})$ are then allowed to contain predicates $x_0 < x_1$ for any $x_0, x_1 \in X$ s.t. $f \rightarrow x_0 < x_1$ is valid. We call predicates in this form *parameterized predicates*.

Modules in the Framework   Our framework is in fact flexible. The k-abstraction can be replaced with any abstraction technique that abstracts the buffers to finite sequences. E.g., instead of keeping the oldest k operations in the buffer, one can also choose to keep the newest k operations and abstract away others. For the integer variable, instead of applying predicate abstraction techniques, we also have other choices. In fact, a k-abstract system essentially can be encoded as a sequential program with integer variables running under the SC model. Then one can choose to verify it using model checkers for sequential programs such as BLAST or CBMC.

9   Experimental Results

We have implemented the method described in this paper in C++ geared with parameterized predicates. Instead of keeping the oldest k operations in the buffer, we choose to keep the newest k

Table 1. Experimental results

	LOC	Time	Fences/proc	# Predicates
1. Burns [19]	9	0.02 s	1	1
2. Simple Dekker [23]	10	0.04 s	1	1
3. Full Dekker [12]	22	0.06 s	1	1
4. Dijkstra [19]	22	0.35 s	1	4
5. Lamport Bakery [16]	20	154 s	2	17
6. Lamport Fast [17]	32	2 s	2	4
7. Peterson [21]	12	2 s	1	6
8. Linux Ticket Lock[2]	16	2 s	0	2

operations and abstract away older operations. In the counter-example guided refinement loop, for Case 2 (fence placement) we use the more efficient algorithm described in [2].

We applied it to several classical examples. Among these examples, the Lamport Bakery and Linux Ticket Lock involves integer variables whose values can grow unboundedly. To our knowledge, these examples cannot be handled by any existing algorithm. The experiments were run on a 2.27 GHz laptop with 4 GB of memory. The MathSat4 [1] solver is used as the procedure for deciding satisfiability and computing interpolants. All of the examples involve two processes. The results are given in Table 1. For each protocol we give the total number of instructions in the program, the total time to infer fence positions, the number of necessary fences per process, and the greatest number of parameterized predicates used in any refinement step.

References

1. MATHSat4, http://mathsat4.disi.unitn.it/
2. Abdulla, P.A., Atig, M.F., Chen, Y.-F., Leonardsson, C., Rezine, A.: Counter-Example Guided Fence Insertion under TSO. In: Flanagan, C., König, B. (eds.) TACAS 2012. LNCS, vol. 7214, pp. 204–219. Springer, Heidelberg (2012)
3. Adve, S., Gharachorloo, K.: Shared memory consistency models: a tutorial. Computer 29(12) (1996)
4. Alglave, J., Maranget, L.: Stability in Weak Memory Models. In: Gopalakrishnan, G., Qadeer, S. (eds.) CAV 2011. LNCS, vol. 6806, pp. 50–66. Springer, Heidelberg (2011)
5. Atig, M.F., Bouajjani, A., Burckhardt, S., Musuvathi, M.: On the verification problem for weak memory models. In: POPL (2010)
6. Atig, M.F., Bouajjani, A., Parlato, G.: Getting Rid of Store-Buffers in TSO Analysis. In: Gopalakrishnan, G., Qadeer, S. (eds.) CAV 2011. LNCS, vol. 6806, pp. 99–115. Springer, Heidelberg (2011)
7. Beyer, D., Henzinger, T.A., Jhala, R., Majumdar, R.: The software model checker blast: Applications to software engineering. In: STTT (2007)
8. Burckhardt, S., Alur, R., Martin, M.: CheckFence: Checking consistency of concurrent data types on relaxed memory models. In: PLDI (2007)
9. Burckhardt, S., Alur, R., Martin, M.M.K.: Bounded Model Checking of Concurrent Data Types on Relaxed Memory Models: A Case Study. In: Ball, T., Jones, R.B. (eds.) CAV 2006. LNCS, vol. 4144, pp. 489–502. Springer, Heidelberg (2006)
10. Burckhardt, S., Musuvathi, M.: Effective Program Verification for Relaxed Memory Models. In: Gupta, A., Malik, S. (eds.) CAV 2008. LNCS, vol. 5123, pp. 107–120. Springer, Heidelberg (2008)
11. Burnim, J., Sen, K., Stergiou, C.: Sound and Complete Monitoring of Sequential Consistency for Relaxed Memory Models. In: Abdulla, P.A., Leino, K.R.M. (eds.) TACAS 2011. LNCS, vol. 6605, Springer, Heidelberg (2011)
12. Dijkstra, E.W.: Cooperating sequential processes. Springer-Verlag New York, Inc., New York (2002)

---

[2] The "Linux Ticket Lock" protocol was taken from the Linux kernel. Its correctness on x86 was the topic of a lively debate among the developers on the Linux Kernel Mailing List in 1999. (See the mail thread starting with https://lkml.org/lkml/1999/11/20/76.)

13. Huynh, T.Q., Roychoudhury, A.: A Memory Model Sensitive Checker for C#. In: Misra, J., Nipkow, T., Karakostas, G. (eds.) FM 2006. LNCS, vol. 4085, pp. 476–491. Springer, Heidelberg (2006)
14. Kuperstein, M., Vechev, M., Yahav, E.: Automatic inference of memory fences. In: FMCAD (2011)
15. Kuperstein, M., Vechev, M., Yahav, E.: Partial-coherence abstractions for relaxed memory models. In: PLDI (2011)
16. Lamport, L.: A new solution of Dijkstra's concurrent programming problem. CACM 17 (August 1974)
17. Lamport, L.: A fast mutual exclusion algorithm (1986)
18. Linden, A., Wolper, P.: A Verification-Based Approach to Memory Fence Insertion in Relaxed Memory Systems. In: Groce, A., Musuvathi, M. (eds.) SPIN 2011. LNCS, vol. 6823, pp. 144–160. Springer, Heidelberg (2011)
19. Lynch, N., Patt-Shamir, B.: Distributed Algorithms, Lecture Notes for 6.852 FALL 1992. Technical report, MIT, Cambridge, MA, USA (1993)
20. Owens, S., Sarkar, S., Sewell, P.: A Better x86 Memory Model: x86-TSO. In: Berghofer, S., Nipkow, T., Urban, C., Wenzel, M. (eds.) TPHOLs 2009. LNCS, vol. 5674, pp. 391–407. Springer, Heidelberg (2009)
21. Peterson, G.L.: Myths About the Mutual Exclusion Problem. IPL 12(3) (1981)
22. Sewell, P., Sarkar, S., Owens, S., Nardelli, F.Z., Myreen, M.O.: x86-tso: A rigorous and usable programmer's model for x86 multiprocessors. CACM 53 (2010)
23. Weaver, D., Germond, T. (eds.): The SPARC Architecture Manual Version 9. PTR Prentice Hall (1994)

A   Abstraction and Concretization Functions for k-Abstraction

Given a k-abstract configuration $c_k = (M, L, pc, B_x, B_v, S, R)$. Let $|B_p| = Max(\{i \in \mathcal{N} \mid B_x(b_{p,i}) \neq \bot\} \cup \{0\})$ denote the length of the buffer of process p, as encoded by B_x and B_v. We define $LastWrite_p(x, B'_x, B'_v) = B'_v(b_{p,i})$, where $i = Max(\{j \in \mathcal{N} \mid B'_x(b_{p,j}) = x\})$ and the last write constraint $LW(p, c_k, B'_x, B'_v) = \forall x \in S(p).LastWrite_p(x, B'_x, B'_v) = R(lw_{p,x})$. Let the buffer constraint $BC(p, m, c_k, B'_x, B'_v)$ equal the following

$$\forall 0 < i \leq |B_p|.(B'_x(b_{p,i}) = B_x(b_{p,i}) \wedge B'_v(b_{p,i}) = B_v(b_{p,i}))$$
$$\wedge$$
$$S(p) \neq \emptyset \rightarrow \left(\begin{array}{c} \forall x \in S(p).\exists |B_p| < i < m.B'_x(b_{p,i}) = x \\ \wedge \\ \forall |B_p| < i < m.(B'_x(b_{p,i}) \in S(p) \wedge B'_v(b_{p,i}) \neq \bot) \\ \wedge \\ \forall m \leq i.(B'_x(b_{p,i}) = B'_v(b_{p,i}) = \bot) \end{array} \right)$$
$$\wedge$$
$$S(p) = \emptyset \rightarrow (\forall |B_p| < i.(B'_x(b_{p,i}) = B'_v(b_{p,i}) = \bot))$$

We use $\gamma_k(c_k)$ to denote the set of TSO configurations encoded in c_k, which equals the set $\{(M, L, pc, B'_x, B'_v) \mid \forall p \in P.((\exists m \in \mathcal{N}.BC(p, m, c_k, B'_x, B'_v)) \wedge LW(p, c_k, B'_x, B'_v))\}$

On the other hand, given a TSO configuration $c_{TSO} = (M, L, pc, B_x, B_v)$, we define $\alpha_k(c_{TSO}) = (M, L, pc, B'_x, B'_v, S, R)$, where (1) $\forall 0 < i \leq k, p \in P.(B'_x(b_{p,i}) = B_x(b_{p,i}) \wedge B'_v(b_{p,i}) = B_v(b_{p,i}))$, (2) $\forall k < i, p \in P.((B_x(b_{p,i}) \neq \bot \rightarrow B_x(b_{p,i}) \in S(p)) \wedge (B'_x(b_{p,i}) = B'_v(b_{p,i}) = \bot))$, and (3) $\forall p \in P, x \in X_S.R(lw_{p,x}) = LastWrite_p(x, B_x, B_v)$.

Control Flow Analysis for the Join Calculus

Peter Calvert and Alan Mycroft

Computer Laboratory, University of Cambridge
William Gates Building, JJ Thomson Avenue,
Cambridge CB3 0FD, UK
firstname.lastname@cl.cam.ac.uk

Abstract. Since first being described, the Join Calculus has been incorporated into a variety of languages as an alternative concurrency primitive. While there has been some work on efficient library implementation of the calculus, there has been little on statically analysing and transforming it. This work explores adapting conventional analysis techniques to the Join Calculus. In particular, we present three variations of *control flow analysis* for a flattened version, and consider two important optimisations: *inlining* and *queue bounding*.

Keywords: program analysis, concurrency, optimisation.

1 Introduction

Over recent years, the elegant primitives of the Join Calculus [5] have been popular as language extensions—both functional [3,12] and imperative [1,18]—and libraries [15], as researchers have looked for paradigms that allow developers to express parallelism naturally, without introducing the intermittent bugs often associated with concurrency. However, consideration of efficient execution has mostly been focussed on the implementation of the primitives [17] rather than on employing any static analysis or transformations. This paper tries to redress the balance by building on the limited work that has been done [7].

Our main contribution is a variation of *control flow analysis* (Section 6) that we use to describe two optimisations. Consider the following example:

```
def ^memcell(i,k)    = val(i); k(get, set)
  | get(m)   & val(x) = val(x); m(x)
  | set(x,m) & val(y) = val(x); m()
```

Each *signal*[1] (i.e. memcell, get, val and set) has an associated unordered *message queue*. The *transition rules* in a *definition* then dictate what can occur after messages matching their left-hand-side *join pattern* are present on these queues. In this case, emitting a message to memcell (i.e. making a call) creates a new memory cell (since memcell is marked as a constructor with ^), returning a getter and setter via the continuation k. Note that the names get and set are not exported, and that continuations in the Join Calculus are just signal values.

---

[1] Signals are also called *channels* and *names* in other work.

A. Miné and D. Schmidt (Eds.): SAS 2012, LNCS 7460, pp. 181–197, 2012.
© Springer-Verlag Berlin Heidelberg 2012

It is clear that `val` never escapes from this definition, and also that it will always have exactly one message available. Therefore, we can optimise this to:

```
def ^memcell(i,k) = (loc := i); k(get, set)
  | get(m)       = m(!loc)
  | set(x,m)     = (loc := x); m()
```

where `loc` now refers to an (instance-local) ML-style memory location corresponding to the single `val` message. By analysing message queue lengths in order to reduce the number of *signals* in the left-hand-side patterns of transition rules, this optimisation (Section 7.1) removes both the overhead of manipulating the message queue and also of checking whether messages are available at `val` when trying to fire a transition.

While the first optimisation enables the removal of signals, the second removes rules by adapting *inlining* to the Join Calculus. Consider the following example for expressions P and Q, having free variables x and y respectively:

```
def ^p(x,k)             = k(P)
def ^q(y,k)             = k(Q)
def ^f(x,y,k)           = ^p(x,m); ^q(y,n); s(k)
  | m(a) & n(b) & s(k) = k(a * b)
```

The behaviour of a call `^f(x,y,k)` is to invoke k on P * Q. If there is insufficient parallelism to fire `^p` and `^q` concurrently, we prefer to inline these, and the final multiplication `a * b`, to eliminate the overheads associated with passing messages and firing transitions—resulting in the optimised code of:

```
def ^f(x,y,k) = k(P * Q)
```

We briefly introduce relevant background in Section 2, before setting out our contributions as follows:

- The language that we use throughout the paper is introduced in Section 3, along with its concrete semantics in terms of a simple abstract machine.
- Section 4 presents a direct translation of existing zeroth-order techniques.
- This is refined to be *instance-local* in Section 5 (0-LCFA).
- A more accurate k-LCFA analysis is given in Section 6. This forms the basis of all our transformations.
- Section 7 defines *queue bounding* to lower signal queues to raw memory operations and formulates *inlining* for the Join Calculus

We discuss our work in Section 8, offering examples where the analysis could be further improved, and also talk about opportunities for further work.

2   Background and Notation

Previously, only Le Fessant and Maranget's work with JoCaml [7] has discussed performing analysis on the Join Calculus. In their implementation, a signal can be in one of three states $\{0, 1, \mathbb{N}\}$ depending on the length of its message queue. Whereas 0 and 1 can be implemented efficiently with a single memory location, $\mathbb{N}$ requires an actual queue for the signal. They therefore describe how to use semantic analysis to eliminate the possibility of $\mathbb{N}$ where possible, but do not describe the semantic analysis itself, stating that they only have a *"rudimentary name usage analyzer"* that suffices for certain cases. This corresponds to the queue bounding transformation we describe later using our control-flow analysis.

In the literature, there are two main styles of control-flow analysis—the constraint-based approach developed by Faxén [4] and popularised in [11]; and the abstract interpretation method by Shivers [16] and more recently revisited by Might [9]. In constraint methods, we first describe the *flow* of data through the program using constraints, and then solve for these. Abstract interpretation techniques tend to merge the two steps, simply constructing the solution as it walks through the program.[2] Although it has been successfully used for concurrent versions of the λ-calculus [10], in the presence of non-deterministic join-pattern matching, ensuring that a direct abstraction of the operational semantics considers all cases is rather more difficult. Constraints, on the other hand, seem a natural choice, since they can describe all possible executions at once. As far as possible, we adopt the notation used by Faxén's *polyvariant analysis* [4], combined with the convention that 'hats' introduce abstract domains.

Throughout this paper, we make use of both multisets and sequences. The notation $\mathbf{m}(X)$ is used to denote *multisets* over the set X, and $+$ the addition of multisets. We abuse this slightly by writing $M + x$ instead of $M + \{x\}$. The set of all possible sequences over X is written X^*, and those bounded by length k as $X^{\leq k}$. Fixed-length sequences are referred to as tuples and written $\vec{v}$ (with elements v_i), while we use σ (or $\hat{\sigma}$) for variable-length stacks. Concatenation is denoted by $\cdot$ and ϵ gives the empty sequence.

3   The Flattened Join Calculus

Our source language syntax is given in Figure 1. Here x ranges over variables (local to a rule), *op* over arithmetic operators and f over *signal names*. Signal names play a similar role to function names in functional or object-oriented languages, except the Join Calculus allows *join patterns* (multiple signal names each with formal parameters) on the left-hand side of *transition rules*. Signals have definition-local scope and instances of them are first-class values. By contrast *constructor signal names* marked by $\hat{\ }f$ are exported from definitions, but do not give first-class values. However, when no ambiguity results we allow f to range over both constructor and non-constructor signal names. We write Constructor for the set of constructor signals in a given program; Rule represents its set of rules and CRule the subset of constructor rules. We require names to be globally unique and constructor and non-constructor names to be disjoint.

---

[2] Note that the *store* that is added for abstract interpretation provides a level of indirection that is similar in spirit to that provided by constraints.

$$
\begin{aligned}
e &::= x \mid f \mid op(e_1, \ldots e_n) & \text{(expressions)} \\
s &::= \mathbf{var}\, x = e & \text{(local variables)} \\
&\mid s; s' \mid \mathbf{if}\, e\, \mathbf{then}\, s\, \mathbf{else}\, s' & \text{(control flow)} \\
&\mid e_0(e_1, \ldots, e_n) \mid \,\widehat{}\,f(e_1, \ldots, e_n) \mid \mathbf{finish} & \text{(join calculus)} \\
r &::= f_1(x_1^1, \ldots, x_{k_1}^1)\, \&\, \ldots\, \&\, f_n(x_1^n, \ldots, x_{k_n}^n) = s & \text{(transition rules)} \\
&\mid \,\widehat{}\,f(x_1, \ldots, x_n) = s & \text{(constructor rules)} \\
d &::= \mathbf{def}\, r_1 \mid \cdots \mid r_n & \text{(definitions)} \\
p &::= d_1 \ldots d_n & \text{(program)}
\end{aligned}
$$

Fig. 1. Abstract Syntax of the Flattened Join Calculus

The main difference between our language and previous presentations of the calculus is to forbid nested join definitions. This both enables a clearer presentation of the CFA, and offers other benefits [2], without any loss of expressive power. Nested definitions can still be encoded through a process similar to *lambda-lifting*, or Java's encoding of inner classes.

Invoking a constructor creates an *instance* of the definition which consists of a *signal instance* (conceptually a message queue) for each of the definition's signal names. When sufficient messages are available on these queues, one of the transitions can be fired. Messages are placed on the queues by *emission* calls. Signal values are first-class values and resemble closures in the λ-calculus—semantically being (signal name, instance identifier) pairs. A constructor would normally pass out some of its definition's signal instances as these are not otherwise exported. Note that if we restrict rules to have a single signal in the left-hand-side pattern, we get a traditional functional language and definition instances play no interesting role.

Rather than the Chemical Abstract Machine [5] or rewriting [12] style of semantics previously used for the Join Calculus, we describe its operation in terms of a JVM-like stack-based abstract machine—the JCAM of Figure 2. Programs in the above syntax can easily be translated to this machine code by a post-order walk of the abstract syntax tree. This style uses an environment Γ which is typically the focus of abstraction in CFA techniques, and corresponds more closely to actual implementations of the calculus (although these would typically use per-signal-instance queues instead of the single large multiset Γ). The operand stack also allows the parameters of a transition rule to be implicitly concatenated, rather than needing complex indexing (as appears for *transition rules* in Figure 1). Indeed, this enables us to omit formal parameters when referring to JCAM transition rules (as for the *fire* rule in Figure 2). Our semantics runs the right-hand-side of a rule to completion (FINISH) before firing another rule, resulting in transition-level interleaving, although this gives the same observable behaviour as more fine-grained interleavings.

Instructions: $\mathtt{LOAD.SIGNAL{<}f{>}^l}$, $\mathtt{CONSTRUCT{<}f{>}^l}$, $\mathtt{EMIT}^l$, $\mathtt{FINISH}^l$, ...

where l is a unique label and $\mathrm{next}(l)$ gives the successor instruction.

Domains:

$$(f,t),(f,\theta) \in \mathrm{SignalValue} = \mathrm{Signal} \times \mathrm{Time}$$

$$\Gamma, \Delta \in \mathrm{Environment} = \mathbf{m}(\mathrm{SignalValue} \times \mathrm{Value}^*) \qquad \text{(available messages)}$$

$$t \in \mathrm{Time} = \mathbb{N}_0$$

$$\Sigma = (l,\theta,\sigma) \in \mathrm{State} = \mathrm{Label} \times \mathrm{Time} \times \mathrm{Value}^* \qquad \text{(PC, context, stack)}$$

$$v \in \mathrm{Value} = \mathrm{SignalValue} \cup \mathrm{Primitive}$$

Operational Semantics: $\Gamma, t, \Sigma \to \Gamma', t', \Sigma'$

$$\Gamma + \Delta,\ t,\ (\mathtt{FINISH}^l, \_, \_) \to \Gamma,\ t,\ (l_0, \theta, \vec{v_1} \cdot \ldots \cdot \vec{v_n}) \qquad \text{(fire)}$$

$$\text{where } \Delta = \{((f_i,\theta), \vec{v_i}) \mid 1 \le i \le n\}$$

$$\text{and } f_1\ \&\ \ldots\ \&\ f_n = \{l_0, l_1, \ldots\} \text{ is a rule.}$$

$$\Gamma,\ t,\ (\mathtt{EMIT}^l, \theta, s \cdot \vec{v} \cdot \sigma) \to \Gamma + (s, \vec{v}),\ t,\ (\mathrm{next}(l), \theta, \sigma) \qquad \text{(emit)}$$

$$\Gamma,\ t,\ (\mathtt{CONSTRUCT{<}f{>}}^l, \theta, \vec{v} \cdot \sigma) \to \Gamma + ((f,t), \vec{v}),\ t+1,\ (\mathrm{next}(l), \theta, \sigma) \qquad \text{(construct)}$$

$$\Gamma,\ t,\ (\mathtt{LOAD.SIGNAL{<}f{>}}^l, \theta, \sigma) \to \Gamma,\ t,\ (\mathrm{next}(l), \theta, (f, \theta) \cdot \sigma) \qquad \text{(load)}$$

Fig. 2. Key Operations of the Join Calculus Abstract Machine (JCAM)

The firing rule of the semantics defines the characteristic Join Calculus behaviour in a similar way to how Petri-net semantics are normally described. It requires that the current environment Γ contains messages Δ that match the join pattern of a rule. These messages must also all be associated with the same instance θ, which, in this semantics, constructors obtain by reading and incrementing the JCAM *time* t. The JCAM start state is as follows:

$$\{((\hat{}\mathtt{main}, 0), \vec{v})\}, 1, (\mathtt{FINISH}^l, 0, \epsilon)$$

We require that the program provides a *main* constructor typed in accordance with the input $\vec{v}$. This input must only contain primitive values, or signal values (e.g. giving access to system calls) that cannot conflict with any program definition instances—past, present or future. This can be achieved by drawing their instance identifiers from a disjoint set—e.g. the negative integers.

This work is part of a wider project that uses the JCAM as an architecture-neutral intermediate representation for concurrent and parallel languages.[3] The full JCAM also supports many JVM-style [8] control-flow and data structure instructions, excluding method-calls which are replaced by join-calculus primitives. However, our use as an architecture-neutral intermediate format for potentially distributed systems results in various JCAM design decisions: (i) we retain the continuation-passing style of the calculus as sugarings can be done

---

[3] Turon and Russo's work [17] supports this by showing that Join Calculus implementations of some primitives (e.g. barriers) can outperform the classic implementation.

at source-level; (*ii*) global mutable state is encoded by recursive rules (equivalent to cyclic Petri-nets) as in our `memcell` example; and (*iii*) local mutable state via structures or arrays is permitted but these must respect a memory-isolation property by only allowing writes when a transition firing holds the sole reference. A compiler for the JCAM may possibly use additional target-architecture shared-global-memory operations, for example to represent the optimised `memcell`. These are not discussed here—instead our queue-bounding analysis merely determines when such operations can be inserted by a code generator.

4   Translating Classical Techniques: 0-CFA

We start by offering a zeroth-order analysis for the JCAM. This provides an introduction to our notation in the context of a well-known technique. In many ways, the resultant technique is similar to the CFA used by Reppy and Xiao [14] for Concurrent ML, although we do not make use of type-sensitivity.

For this straightforward abstraction, we discard the instance identifier from each signal value. This effectively conflates all instances, as is done for the different environments that a closure might receive in a λ-calculus 0-CFA. As normal, values on the operand stack in the concrete semantics are abstracted to sets of 0-CFA values, although we slip between this and the isomorphic function-form that we can refine later. We are only interested in signal values, so all primitives are abstracted to `PRIM`.

$$\hat{s} \in \widehat{\text{SignalValue}} = \text{Signal}$$

$$\hat{v} \in \widehat{\text{Value}} = \wp(\widehat{\text{SignalValue}} \cup \{\texttt{PRIM}\})$$

$$\cong (\widehat{\text{SignalValue}} \cup \{\texttt{PRIM}\}) \rightarrow \{\bot, \top\}$$

We use c to range over $\widehat{\text{SignalValue}} \cup \{\texttt{PRIM}\}$, while f only ranges over signal values. $\widehat{\text{Value}}$ inherits the order $\bot \sqsubseteq \top$, which in the set view corresponds to $\subseteq$. However, rather than using these values directly, we use *flow variables* as is typical in a constraint-based approach, along with a constraint set S over these. The operand stack that represents intermediate values is abstracted to a list of flow variables $\hat{\sigma}$. A constant mapping $\hat{\varGamma} : \text{Signal} \rightarrow \text{FlowVar}^*$ associates a tuple of flow variables with each signal (i.e. one per argument to the signal). These represent all possible values that might be sent in messages to the signal. We build constraints using the rules in Figure 3. The *emission constraint* $\vec{\alpha} \mapsto \beta$ generated for `EMIT` and `CONSTRUCT` instructions can be read as saying that any tuple of values represented by the flow variables $\vec{\alpha}$ could be used to send a message to any of the signal values in β. Note that whilst $\Longrightarrow$ is formally logical implication in these rules, it also depicts an abstract execution step. We use $\exists \alpha$ to allocate a new flow variable. However, since there may be cycles in the control-flow graph of rule bodies, in general an implementation will need to reuse such α's to ensure termination. Typically, 0-CFA allocates one per program

Constraint Syntax:

$$S \subseteq \text{Constraint} ::= \alpha_1 \succeq \alpha_2 \mid \alpha \succeq \{c\} \mid \vec{\alpha} \mapsto \beta \quad \text{where } c \in \widehat{\text{SignalValue}} \cup \{\text{PRIM}\}$$

Constraint Generation Rules: (with judgement form $S, \hat{\Gamma} \vdash l, \hat{\sigma}$)

$$S, \hat{\Gamma} \vdash \text{EMIT}^l, \alpha \cdot \vec{\beta} \cdot \hat{\sigma} \implies (S, \hat{\Gamma} \vdash \text{next}(l), \hat{\sigma}) \wedge \{\vec{\beta} \mapsto \alpha\} \subseteq S$$

$$S, \hat{\Gamma} \vdash \text{CONSTRUCT<}f\text{>}^l, \vec{\beta} \cdot \hat{\sigma} \implies \exists \alpha.(S, \hat{\Gamma} \vdash \text{next}(l), \hat{\sigma}) \wedge \{\vec{\beta} \mapsto \alpha, \alpha \succeq \{f\}\} \subseteq S$$

$$S, \hat{\Gamma} \vdash \text{LOAD.SIGNAL<}f\text{>}^l, \hat{\sigma} \implies \exists \alpha.(S, \hat{\Gamma} \vdash \text{next}(l), \alpha \cdot \hat{\sigma}) \wedge \{\alpha \succeq \{f\}\} \subseteq S$$

$$S, \hat{\Gamma} \vdash \text{FINISH}^l, \hat{\sigma} \qquad \text{always holds}$$

Model of Constraints: ($\Phi, \hat{\Gamma} \models S$ iff $\Phi, \hat{\Gamma} \models s$ for all $s \in S$)

$$\Phi, \hat{\Gamma} \models \alpha_1 \succeq \alpha_2 \iff \Phi(\alpha_1) \sqsupseteq \Phi(\alpha_2)$$

$$\Phi, \hat{\Gamma} \models \alpha \succeq \{c\} \iff c \in \Phi(\alpha)$$

$$\Phi, \hat{\Gamma} \models \vec{\alpha} \mapsto \beta \iff \forall f \in \Phi(\beta). \forall j. \Phi(\hat{\Gamma}(f)_j) \sqsupseteq \Phi(\alpha_j)$$

Closure of Constraint Sets: $S^+ \supseteq S$

$$\{\alpha_1 \succeq \alpha_2, \alpha_2 \succeq \{c\}\} \subseteq S^+ \implies \{\alpha_1 \succeq \{c\}\} \subseteq S^+$$

$$\{\vec{\alpha} \mapsto \beta, \beta \succeq \{f\}\} \subseteq S^+ \implies \forall i.\{\hat{\Gamma}(f)_i \succeq \alpha_i\} \subseteq S^+$$

Fig. 3. Definition of 0-CFA

point—i.e. α is treated as α_l at program point l. The constraint set S is then defined as the least set that satisfies, for each rule $f_1 \& \ldots \& f_n = \{l_0, \ldots\}$:

$$S, \hat{\Gamma} \vdash l_0, \hat{\Gamma}(f_1) \cdot \ldots \cdot \hat{\Gamma}(f_n)$$

Solutions to the analysis are of the form $\Phi : \text{FlowVar} \to \widehat{\text{Value}}$. Figure 3 also defines what it means for such a Φ to be a valid model of the constraints, and gives a dynamic transitive closure algorithm for computing S^+. Given S^+, we can read off the (least) solution as:

$$\Phi(\alpha) = \{c \mid (\alpha \succeq \{c\}) \in S^+\}$$

5 Dealing with Message Interaction: 0-LCFA

Whilst 0-CFA is useful for functional languages, it is often insufficient for the Join Calculus as it cannot differentiate between different signal instances. In particular, the firing semantics only allows two messages to interact when they belong to the same instance. There is no need for such discrimination in functional languages (i.e. predicting whether two closures share the *same* environment, rather than two environments that bind the same values to variables).

To do so, we must abstract the times allocated by CONSTRUCT. In past techniques, it is typical to use a call-site history of depth k, in place of the unbounded

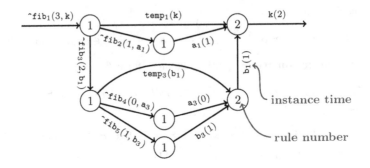

```
1. def ^fib(x, k) = if x < 2 then k(x)
                              else temp(k); ^fib(x-2,a); ^fib(x-1,b)
2.    | temp(k) & a(x) & b(y) = k(x + y)
```

Fig. 4. Call DAG for `^fib(3,k)`

Constraint Syntax:

$$S \subseteq \text{Constraint} ::= \alpha_1 \succeq \alpha_2 \mid \alpha \succeq \{c\} \mid \vec{\alpha} \mapsto \beta \quad \text{where } c \in \widehat{\text{SignalValue}} \cup \boxed{\{*\}}$$

Constraint Generation Rules: (with judgement form $S, \hat{\Gamma} \vdash l, \hat{\sigma}$)

$$S, \hat{\Gamma} \vdash \text{EMIT}^l, \alpha \cdot \vec{\beta} \cdot \hat{\sigma} \implies (S, \hat{\Gamma} \vdash \text{next}(l), \hat{\sigma}) \wedge \{\vec{\beta} \mapsto \alpha\} \subseteq S$$

$$S, \hat{\Gamma} \vdash \text{CONSTRUCT} \text{<} f \text{>}^l, \vec{\beta} \cdot \hat{\sigma} \implies \exists \alpha. (S, \hat{\Gamma} \vdash \text{next}(l), \hat{\sigma}) \wedge \{\vec{\beta} \mapsto \alpha, \alpha \succeq \boxed{\{*\}}\} \subseteq S$$

$$S, \hat{\Gamma} \vdash \text{LOAD.SIGNAL} \text{<} f \text{>}^l, \hat{\sigma} \implies \exists \alpha. (S, \hat{\Gamma} \vdash \text{next}(l), \alpha \cdot \hat{\sigma}) \wedge \{\alpha \succeq \{f\}\} \subseteq S$$

$$S, \hat{\Gamma} \vdash \text{FINISH}^l, \hat{\sigma} \qquad \text{always holds}$$

Model of Constraints: ($\Phi, \hat{\Gamma} \models S$ iff $\Phi, \hat{\Gamma} \models s$ for all $s \in S$)

$$\Phi, \hat{\Gamma} \models \alpha_1 \succeq \alpha_2 \iff \Phi(\alpha_1) \sqsupseteq \Phi(\alpha_2)$$

$$\Phi, \hat{\Gamma} \models \alpha \succeq \{c\} \iff c \in \Phi(\alpha)$$

$$\Phi, \hat{\Gamma} \models \vec{\alpha} \mapsto \beta \iff \left(\forall f \in \Phi(\beta). \forall j. \Phi(\hat{\Gamma}(f)_j) \sqsupseteq \Phi(\alpha_j) \right)$$

$$\wedge \boxed{\left(* \in \Phi(\beta) \implies \forall f \in \bigcup_i \Phi(\alpha_i). \forall j. \Phi(\hat{\Gamma}(f)_j) \sqsupseteq \{*\} \right)}$$

Closure of Constraint Sets: $S^+ \supseteq S$

$$\{\alpha_1 \succeq \alpha_2, \alpha_2 \succeq \{c\}\} \subseteq S^+ \implies \{\alpha_1 \succeq \{c\}\} \subseteq S^+$$

$$\{\vec{\alpha} \mapsto \beta, \beta \succeq \{f\}\} \subseteq S^+ \implies \forall i. \{\hat{\Gamma}(f)_i \succeq \alpha_i\} \subseteq S^+$$

$$\boxed{\{\alpha_i \succeq \{f\}, \vec{\alpha} \mapsto \beta, \beta \succeq \{*\}\} \subseteq S^+} \implies \boxed{\forall i. \{\hat{\Gamma}(f)_i \succeq \{*\}\} \subseteq S^+}$$

Fig. 5. Definition of 0-LCFA (changes highlighted)

concrete call string to give instance identifiers.[4] However, in the Join Calculus, call strings are replaced by more complex traces. These can be described by a *pomset* [13], or more intuitively a DAG where each node represents a rule firing (e.g. Figure 4). Forming an abstract version of these *call DAGs* is further complicated by the non-deterministic choice of messages that is made when a transition fires.

In Section 6, we show how to abstract these for the purposes of accuracy. However, that technique is not suitable for comparing abstract instances (i.e. it cannot imply either equality or inequality of concrete instances). Instead, we use a naïve refinement that uses two *abstract times*: definitely 'this' instance (i.e. *local*); and possibly another instance. We call the resultant analysis *zeroth-order local CFA* (0-LCFA).

We therefore abstract signal values as follows: a *local* signal value is abstracted as its signal name,[5] ranged over by f as before (discarding the time component); other signal values (either from other definitions or another instance of this definition) are abstracted to a *wildcard* $*$. This wildcard also represents local signals that have escaped the instance and might then be passed back in.[6] However, it does not represent local signals that do not escape.[7] We are not interested in primitive values, so for simplicity represent these by $*$ too—this conveniently captures the fact that other definition instances are able to fabricate any primitive value they wish. Our abstract value set therefore changes to:

$$\hat{v} \in \widehat{\text{Value}} = \wp(\widehat{\text{SignalValue}} \cup \{*\})$$

$$\cong (\widehat{\text{SignalValue}} \cup \{*\}) \rightarrow \{\bot, \top\}$$

The updated analysis (Figure 5) requires a new constraint generation rule for CONSTRUCT as well as changes to the model and closure algorithm for emission constraints. These simply ensure that whenever a local signal value may escape to another instance, its $\hat{\Gamma}$ flow variables are updated to include $*$ for each of its arguments. The initial conditions of the analysis must also include the following constraints, which specify that constructors may receive any external value:

$$\forall f \in \text{Constructor}.\{\hat{\Gamma}(f)_i \succeq \{*\} \mid 1 \leq i \leq \text{arity}(f)\} \subseteq S$$

Unlike 0-CFA, this new analysis can be used for both queue bounding and inlining (Section 7).

---

[4] Call strings can also improve accuracy (k-CFA). However, this and identifying instances are two distinct problems, and for the Join Calculus we solve them separately.

[5] The abstract value f in 0-LCFA corresponds to a single concrete value (f, this) whereas it previously gave (f, θ) for all θ in 0-CFA.

[6] The wildcard treatment is not dissimilar to the concept of a 'most general attacker' in security, or approaches used for address-taken variables.

[7] Clearly determining whether a signal escapes is undecidable, but simply requiring that the solution to the analysis is self-consistent results in a safe approximation.

6 Abstracting Call DAGs: k-LCFA

The limitations of our approach so far are the same as those of other zeroth-order and monovariant approaches for the λ-calculus. This is illustrated by two small examples ('handshake' and 'handshake-with-swap' respectively):

```
A:   a(x,m) & b(y,n) = m(x); n(y)
B:   a(x,m) & b(y,n) = m(y); n(x)
```

Consider the calls a(i,p), a(j,q), b(k,r) and b(l,s). The table below indicates the results of 0-LCFA, compared to the optimum—i.e. what could actually occur on a real execution:

	Example A		Example B	
	0-LCFA	Optimum	0-LCFA	Optimum
p	$\{i,j\}$	$\{i\}$	$\{k,l\}$	$\{k,l\}$
q	$\{i,j\}$	$\{j\}$	$\{k,l\}$	$\{k,l\}$
r	$\{k,l\}$	$\{k\}$	$\{i,j\}$	$\{i,j\}$
s	$\{k,l\}$	$\{l\}$	$\{i,j\}$	$\{i,j\}$

The case where the optimum solution is not attained is A. However, in some non-trivial situations the simple approach does as well as possible. As expected, the inaccuracy is due to arguments passed from different call-sites being conflated. It is this issue that we now address, while still allowing for the non-deterministic combination of call-sites (as exemplified by case B above).

In zeroth-order approaches, the problem is our simple approximation of a single flow variable per signal argument, as given by $\hat{\Gamma}$. More accurate k-CFA approaches for the λ-calculus refine this 'global' variable into a set of variables, indexed by the last k call-sites. However, as already discussed, the Join Calculus gives call DAGs rather than call strings. Furthermore, they include non-deterministic choices wherever different messages could have been combined.

Our approach is to continue to calculate zeroth-order results for the flow variables in $\hat{\Gamma}$, and then use these as *background* information while following each possible (*foreground*) path in the DAG (up to depth k). We arrange that the union of the analyses for each path gives a suitable result for the whole DAG. The trick is to ensure that the inaccurate background information is overridden by the more accurate constraints generated by the *foreground path*. In order to do this, we further refine the abstract value domain to tag each value:

$$\hat{v} \in \widehat{\text{Value}} = (\widehat{\text{SignalValue}} \cup \{*\}) \to \{\bot, \mathcal{B}, \mathcal{F}\}$$

The ordering $\bot \sqsubseteq \mathcal{B} \sqsubseteq \mathcal{F}$ ensures the $\mathcal{F}$ tag takes priority. For convenience, we continue to use set-style notation, with the tag given by annotations—e.g.

$$\{\mathcal{F}(c)\} \equiv \lambda x. \begin{cases} \mathcal{F} & \text{if } x = c \\ \bot & \text{otherwise} \end{cases}$$

Note $\{\mathcal{B}(c)\} \sqsubseteq \{\mathcal{F}(c)\}$ and, less obviously, that x ranges over both a and b in:

$$\forall \mathcal{B}(x) \in \{\mathcal{F}(a), \mathcal{B}(b)\}. \dots$$

Figure 6 presents the new analysis. Values always start off as being tagged $\mathcal{F}$, and it is only the emission constraint that later lowers them to $\mathcal{B}$. The only other change to the constraint generation rules is that we now maintain a *foreground call-string* context $h \in \text{Label}^{\leq k}$ that is used to implement $\exists \alpha$—for example, $\alpha = \alpha_{l,h}$. This context is also included on emission constraints.

Examining the model of the emission constraints, we first note that it only has any effect for destination values tagged with $\mathcal{F}$. This prevents the background $\mathcal{B}$ values causing inaccuracy. In the first and last lines, it states similar requirements to our 0-LCFA. The $\hat{\Gamma}$ flow variables are predominantly made up of $\mathcal{B}$ values, since these are used to give values to signal arguments not in the current foreground path. The exception is when a signal f escapes the instance, then $\mathcal{F}(*)$ is added to each $\hat{\Gamma}(f)_j$ since the $*$ values are not attributable to any particular call-site, so will not be considered on a foreground path. For this reason, we still require that the following holds for each rule $f_1 \& \ldots \& f_n = \{l_0, \ldots\}$, even though this typically generates very few constraints directly:

$$S, \hat{\Gamma} \vdash_\epsilon l_0, \hat{\Gamma}(f_1) \cdot \ldots \cdot \hat{\Gamma}(f_n)$$

As before, we pass $*$ (actually $\mathcal{F}(*)$) to the entry points of each definition:

$$\forall f \in \text{Constructor}. \ \{\hat{\Gamma}(f)_i \succeq \{\mathcal{F}(*)\} \mid 1 \leq i \leq \text{arity}(f)\} \subseteq S$$

The second line of the emission constraint's model is new, and performs the analysis along the foreground path. The $\exists \vec{\gamma}$ in both the model and closure algorithm is responsible for choosing new flow variables, and it is here that the choice of k affects an implementation, as it reuses flow variables for emissions with common h.

The dynamic transitive closure algorithm also changes to accommodate the alterations. In particular, it may introduce a new form of constraint that corresponds to raising tags from $\mathcal{B}$ to $\mathcal{F}$, and lowering them the other way.

Both our 0-LCFA and this k-LCFA essentially perform a form of *escape-analysis*. However, if we look at the results of our k-LCFA for the `memcell` example, we find that all three signals (`get`, `set` and `val`) receive $*$ (i.e. external values) for each of their arguments. Whilst this is correct, we would like to distinguish between `get` (or `set`), which could be called any number of times from outside the definition, and `val`, which is only called internally, despite receiving foreign values via `set`. We achieve this by also constructing an escape set $E \supseteq \text{Constructor}$, which is the minimal set satisfying:

$$(\vec{\alpha} \mapsto_h \beta) \in S \wedge \mathcal{F}(*) \in \Phi(\beta) \implies \forall \mathcal{B}(f) \in \bigcup_i \Phi(\alpha_i). \ f \in E$$

This is computed by initialising E to Constructor and closing under:

$$\{\alpha_i \succeq \{\mathcal{B}(f)\}, \ \vec{\alpha} \mapsto_h \beta, \ \beta \succeq \{\mathcal{F}(*)\}\} \subseteq S^+ \implies f \in E$$
$$\{\alpha_i \succeq \{\mathcal{F}(f)\}, \ \vec{\alpha} \mapsto_h \beta, \ \beta \succeq \{\mathcal{F}(*)\}\} \subseteq S^+ \implies f \in E$$

Constraint Syntax:

$$S \subseteq \text{Constraint} ::= \alpha_1 \succeq \mathcal{F}(\alpha_2) \mid \alpha_1 \succeq \mathcal{B}(\alpha_2) \mid \alpha \succeq \{\mathcal{F}(c)\} \mid \alpha \succeq \{\mathcal{B}(c)\} \mid \vec{\alpha} \mapsto_h \beta$$

Constraint Generation Rules: (with judgement form $S, \hat{\Gamma} \vdash_h l, \hat{\sigma}$)

$$S, \hat{\Gamma} \vdash_h \text{EMIT}^l, \alpha \cdot \vec{\beta} \cdot \hat{\sigma} \implies (S, \hat{\Gamma} \vdash_h \text{next}(l), \hat{\sigma}) \wedge \{\vec{\beta} \mapsto_{\text{first}_k(l \cdot h)} \alpha\} \subseteq S$$

$$S, \hat{\Gamma} \vdash_h \text{CONSTRUCT} \texttt{<} f \texttt{>}^l, \vec{\beta} \cdot \hat{\sigma} \implies \exists \alpha.(S, \hat{\Gamma} \vdash_h \text{next}(l), \hat{\sigma})$$
$$\wedge \{\vec{\beta} \mapsto_{\text{first}_k(l \cdot h)} \alpha, \alpha \succeq \{\mathcal{F}(*)\}\} \subseteq S$$

$$S, \hat{\Gamma} \vdash_h \text{LOAD.SIGNAL} \texttt{<} f \texttt{>}^l, \hat{\sigma} \implies \exists \alpha.(S, \hat{\Gamma} \vdash_h \text{next}(l), \alpha \cdot \hat{\sigma}) \wedge \{\alpha \succeq \{\mathcal{F}(f)\}\} \subseteq S$$

$$S, \hat{\Gamma} \vdash_h \text{FINISH}^l, \hat{\sigma} \qquad \text{always holds}$$

Notation:

$$\text{mkF}(X) = \{\mathcal{F}(x) \mid \mathcal{B}(x) \in X\} \qquad \text{and} \qquad \text{mkB}(X) = \{\mathcal{B}(x) \mid \mathcal{B}(x) \in X\}$$

Model of Constraints: $(\Phi, \hat{\Gamma} \models_h S$ iff $\Phi, \hat{\Gamma} \models_h s$ for all $s \in S)$

$$\Phi, \hat{\Gamma} \models \alpha_1 \succeq \mathcal{F}(\alpha_2) \iff \Phi(\alpha_1) \sqsupseteq \text{mkF}(\Phi(\alpha_2))$$

$$\Phi, \hat{\Gamma} \models \alpha_1 \succeq \mathcal{B}(\alpha_2) \iff \Phi(\alpha_1) \sqsupseteq \text{mkB}(\Phi(\alpha_2))$$

$$\Phi, \hat{\Gamma} \models \alpha \succeq \{\mathcal{F}(c)\} \iff \mathcal{F}(c) \in \Phi(\alpha)$$

$$\Phi, \hat{\Gamma} \models \alpha \succeq \{\mathcal{B}(c)\} \iff \mathcal{B}(c) \in \Phi(\alpha)$$

$$\Phi, \hat{\Gamma} \models \vec{\alpha} \mapsto_h \beta \iff$$
$$\forall \mathcal{F}(f_\bullet) \in \Phi(\beta).\left(\forall j.\Phi(\hat{\Gamma}(f_\bullet)_j) \sqsupseteq \text{mkB}(\Phi(\alpha_j))\right)$$
$$\wedge \forall (f_1 \& ... \& f_\bullet \& ... \& f_n = \{l_0, ...\}) \in \text{Rule}. \exists S, \vec{\gamma}. (\Phi, \hat{\Gamma} \models S)$$
$$\wedge (S, \hat{\Gamma} \vdash_h l_0, \hat{\Gamma}(f_1) \cdot ... \cdot \vec{\gamma} \cdot ... \cdot \hat{\Gamma}(f_n)) \wedge \forall j. \Phi(\gamma_j) \sqsupseteq \text{mkF}(\Phi(\alpha_j)))$$
$$\wedge \left(\mathcal{F}(*) \in \Phi(\beta) \implies \forall \mathcal{B}(f) \in \bigcup_i \Phi(\alpha_i).\forall j.\Phi(\hat{\Gamma}(f)_j) \sqsupseteq \{\mathcal{F}(*)\}\right)$$

Closure of Constraint Sets: $S^+ \supseteq S$

$$\{\alpha_1 \succeq \mathcal{F}(\alpha_2), \alpha_2 \succeq \{\mathcal{F}(c)\}\} \subseteq S^+ \implies \{\alpha_1 \succeq \{\mathcal{F}(c)\}\} \subseteq S^+$$

$$\{\alpha_1 \succeq \mathcal{F}(\alpha_2), \alpha_2 \succeq \{\mathcal{B}(c)\}\} \subseteq S^+ \implies \{\alpha_1 \succeq \{\mathcal{F}(c)\}\} \subseteq S^+$$

$$\{\alpha_1 \succeq \mathcal{B}(\alpha_2), \alpha_2 \succeq \{\mathcal{F}(c)\}\} \subseteq S^+ \implies \{\alpha_1 \succeq \{\mathcal{B}(c)\}\} \subseteq S^+$$

$$\{\alpha_1 \succeq \mathcal{B}(\alpha_2), \alpha_2 \succeq \{\mathcal{B}(c)\}\} \subseteq S^+ \implies \{\alpha_1 \succeq \{\mathcal{B}(c)\}\} \subseteq S^+$$

$$\{\vec{\alpha} \mapsto_h \beta, \beta \succeq \{\mathcal{F}(f)\}\} \subseteq S^+ \implies \forall i. \{\hat{\Gamma}(f)_i \succeq \mathcal{B}(\alpha_i)\} \subseteq S^+$$

$$\{\vec{\alpha} \mapsto_h \beta, \beta \succeq \{\mathcal{F}(f_\bullet)\}\} \subseteq S^+ \implies$$
$$\exists \vec{\gamma}.\forall i.\{\gamma_i \succeq \mathcal{F}(\alpha_i)\} \subseteq S^+$$
$$\wedge S^+, \hat{\Gamma} \vdash_h l_0, \hat{\Gamma}(f_1) \cdot ... \cdot \vec{\gamma} \cdot ... \cdot \hat{\Gamma}(f_n)$$
$$\text{for each rule of the form } f_1 \& ... \& f_\bullet \& ... \& f_n = \{l_0, ...\}$$

$$\{\alpha_i \succeq \{\mathcal{B}(f)\}, \vec{\alpha} \mapsto_h \beta, \beta \succeq \{\mathcal{F}(*)\}\} \subseteq S^+ \implies \forall i. \{\hat{\Gamma}(f)_i \succeq \{\mathcal{F}(*)\}\} \subseteq S^+$$

$$\{\alpha_i \succeq \{\mathcal{F}(f)\}, \vec{\alpha} \mapsto_h \beta, \beta \succeq \{\mathcal{F}(*)\}\} \subseteq S^+ \implies \forall i. \{\hat{\Gamma}(f)_i \succeq \{\mathcal{F}(*)\}\} \subseteq S^+$$

Fig. 6. Definition of k-LCFA (main changes highlighted)

Initialisation:

$$\lfloor f \rfloor = \min_{c \in \text{CRule}} \{ \lfloor c^\bullet(f) \rfloor \}$$

$$\lceil f \rceil = \begin{cases} \infty & \text{if } f \in (E \setminus \text{Constructor}) \\ \max_{c \in \text{CRule}} \{ \lceil c^\bullet(f) \rceil \} & \text{otherwise} \end{cases}$$

Computation: $\forall r \in (\text{Rule} \setminus \text{CRule})$

$$^\bullet r(f) > \lfloor r^\bullet(f) \rfloor \implies \lfloor f \rfloor = 0$$

$$^\bullet r(f) < \lceil r^\bullet(f) \rceil \implies \lceil f \rceil = \infty$$

Fig. 7. Algorithm for Computing Queue Bound of f

The escape set E is useful for both queue bounding and proving our k-LCFA technique to be sound with respect to the concrete semantics. The proof is available from the first author's homepage.

Returning to the examples presented earlier, this novel approach overcomes the inaccuracy of conflating call-sites while still allowing for the firing semantics. For the functional subset of the Join Calculus, our approach collapses to conventional k-CFA for a CPS lambda-lifted λ-calculus. In particular, $*$ represents only primitives when there is just a single instance, and if all rules are functional then we never make use of $\hat{\Gamma}$ and always deal with $\mathcal{F}$ values.

7   Applications

7.1   Queue Bounding

Our motivating example for queue bounding was the memory cell encoding. We hoped that the val signal could be replaced by a memory location and removed from patterns. To do this, we need to bound the possible queue lengths for each signal f. The result of this is a pair $(\lfloor f \rfloor, \lceil f \rceil) \in (\mathbb{N}_0 \times \mathbb{N}_0^\infty)$ giving the minimum and maximum queue size. We use helper functions inspired by Petri-net notation:

$$^\bullet\_ \in \text{Rule} \to (\text{Signal} \to \mathbb{N}_0) \qquad\qquad \text{(input count)}$$

$$\_^\bullet \in \text{Rule} \to (\text{Signal} \to (\mathbb{N}_0 \times \mathbb{N}_0^\infty)) \qquad \text{(output range)}$$

The first is defined by the number of occurrences of a signal in the left-hand-side pattern of a rule. The second requires analysis of the transition rule body's control-flow graph. There is insufficient space to give it here, but this amounts to a relatively straightforward use of the LCFA results and range arithmetic, incorporating dominator analysis to detect loops and prevent counting to ∞.

The queue bounds of a signal f can then be approximated by the simple algorithm in Figure 7. A more accurate solution would consider the interaction between signals in a similar manner to *boundness* checking, or *invariants* for Petri-nets, but we leave this for future work. Our approach accurately (with respect to $\_^\bullet$) finds signals with a constant queue length, so can still replace signals with memory locations in many situations.

The optimisation itself is straightforward: wherever $\lfloor f \rfloor = \lceil f \rceil$, we remove f, replacing it with $\lfloor f \rfloor$ memory locations. We also remove f from the left-hand-side of every rule that previously matched on it—and modify its body to use the memory locations and behave atomically (e.g. by using *transactional memory*).

7.2 Inlining

Our second optimisation—inlining—is very similar to its classical counterpart. Wherever our LCFA resolves the destination of an EMIT to a single signal, we can inline transitions to reduce firing overheads. As before, a heuristic or code annotations would determine when to do this, since inlining in the Join Calculus may reduce the available parallelism. However, the Join Calculus does present a few complications. Firstly, signals and join patterns are in a many-to-many relation, so we may need to resolve multiple EMITs before being able to inline, and might have to decide between multiple transitions (i.e. resolve non-determinism). Secondly, LCFA only considers message interaction within a single instance, so cannot support whole-program inlining. We now address these issues.

Transition Inlining. The inlinings that are possible become clearest by constructing a Petri-net version of the LCFA results for the definition. In this net, places correspond to signals, and the pre-places of a transition are given by its join pattern. The post-places are given by EMIT instructions with a resolved destination, which are statically known to be executed a fixed number of times. Valid inlinings then correspond to valid transition mergings in this Petri-net—these can be represented as pomset paths [13].

The pomset paths restrict the ordering of the original transition bodies within the merged transition. Any EMIT or FINISH instructions, which become internal due to inlining, should be removed, and local variables used to thread values between the original transition bodies. One complication occurs in the case that the new transition matches on a signal that it might also emit. In this case, the new transition may deadlock—for example, inlining just the signal b() in:

```
a()        = b(); c()
b() & c() = ...
```

gives:

```
a() & c() = c(); ...
```

Assuming c() does not appear elsewhere, then the former allows a() to fire but not the latter, potentially causing deadlock. One solution is to retain the original transitions along with the inlined version and make the scheduler responsible for picking the faster inlined option where possible.

Instance Inlining. The technique above can only perform inlining within a definition. To allow a more global effect, we now describe how whole 'child' instances can be inlined within a 'parent'. This clearly preserves semantics— just as two Petri-nets placed next to each other do not interact. However, since inlining is a static optimisation, we must know statically that a given CONSTRUCT instruction is called exactly once. Hence, we only inline definitions instantiated within a constructor, and outside a loop.

To do this, we copy non-constructor transitions into the parent definition, α-renaming to preserve globally unique signal names, and replace the CONSTRUCT instruction with the body of the child's constructor transition rule. Any FINISHes are replaced by branches to the successor of the original CONSTRUCT. For example, in the following code:

```
def ^main()           = ^mutex(s)
  | s(p,v)            = ...

def ^mutex(k)         = free(); k(lock,unlock)
  | lock(k) & free() = k()
  | unlock(k)        = k(); free()
```

inlining ^mutex gives:

```
def ^main()           = free(); s(lock, unlock)
  | s(p,v)            = ...
  | lock(k) & free() = k()
  | unlock(k)        = k(); free()
```

One issue with this approach, is that it does enlarge the possible state space of the parent definition, which grows exponentially with the number of signals. Ideally, the total state space would remain constant, with part of it simply being transferred from the child definition instance to the parent. An implementation can achieve this by considering *disjoint sets* of signals. We start by treating all signals as disjoint, then consider each rule in turn. Whenever two signals appear in a join pattern together, their respective sets must be unioned. The state spaces of the disjoint sets can then be considered separately leading to the result we hoped for (since the inlined signals will clearly be disjoint from all others).

8   Discussion and Further Work

It is worth considering a few cases where our k-LCFA produces inaccurate results (for any k). Firstly, it is unaware of any ordering of calls that might be enforced by the program. Consider the example (compare is assumed to be a system call which prints "Yes" or "No" depending on whether its arguments are equal):

```
def ^main()     = i(a); a()
  | a() & i(x) = i(b); b(); compare(a, x)
  | b() & i(x) =           compare(b, x)
```

Clearly the printed message should always be "Yes". However, our analysis cannot tell that specific calls to i are forced to join with each of the signals, and therefore concludes that either a or b could be passed as the second argument to compare on each occasion—a refinement of our approach might address this.

The second source of imprecision is more expected (and reminiscent of how tuples are analysed in an independent-attribute approach [6]). Consider:

```
a(k) & b(m,x) = k(m,x)
c(m,x)        = m(x)
```

with calls of a(c), b(p,q) and b(r,s). The call to c is considered while a is on the foreground path. It therefore receives the argument sets {p,r} and {q,s} for b, and cannot determine whether p receives argument q or s. A relational method would address this, but at some cost in algorithmic complexity.

9   Conclusion

This paper has developed a novel and accurate k-LCFA approach (Section 6) for the Join Calculus, along with a simpler 0-LCFA (Section 5). In addition, we have given two optimisations (Section 7) that make use of this information to remove some of the overheads associated with the calculus.

Our approach was targeted at a flattened Join Calculus Abstract Machine (Section 3) that we hope might be suitable as a universal IR for parallel architectures. This work should enable implementations to reduce the number of firings that occur. However, it is still unclear how effective inlining heuristics and scheduling can be in making intelligent use of resources as set out in [2].

Acknowledgements. We thank the Schiff Foundation, University of Cambridge, for funding this research through a PhD studentship. We are also grateful to the anonymous reviewers for their useful feedback on our submission.

References

1. Benton, N., Cardelli, L., Fournet, C.: Modern Concurrency Abstractions for C#. TOPLAS 26(5), 769–804 (2004)
2. Calvert, P., Mycroft, A.: Mapping the Join Calculus to Heterogeneous Hardware. In: 5th International Workshop on Programming Language Approaches to Concurrency and Communication-cEntric Software, PLACES, pp. 45–51 (2012)
3. Conchon, S., Le Fessant, F.: JoCaml: Mobile Agents for Objective-Caml. In: 1st International Symposium on Agent Systems and Applications, and 3rd International Symposium on Mobile Agents, ASAMA, pp. 22–29. IEEE (1999)
4. Faxén, K.-F.: Polyvariance, Polymorphism and Flow Analysis. In: Dam, M. (ed.) LOMAPS-WS 1996. LNCS, vol. 1192, pp. 260–278. Springer, Heidelberg (1997)
5. Fournet, C., Gonthier, G.: The Reflexive CHAM and the Join-Calculus. In: 23rd ACM SIGPLAN-SIGACT Symposium on Principles of Programming Languages, POPL, pp. 372–385. ACM (1996)

6. Jones, N.D., Muchnick, S.: Complexity of Flow Analysis, Inductive Assertion Synthesis and a Language due to Dijkstra. In: 21st Annual Symposium on Foundations of Computer Science, FOCS, pp. 185–190. IEEE (1980)
7. Le Fessant, F., Maranget, L.: Compiling Join-Patterns. In: 3rd International Workshop on High-Level Concurrent Languages, HLCL. Electronic Notes in Theoretical Computer Science, vol. 16(3), pp. 205–224 (1998)
8. Lindholm, T., Yellin, F., Bracha, G., Buckley, A.: The Java Virtual Machine Specification. Oracle (2011)
9. Might, M.: Abstract Interpreters for Free. In: Cousot, R., Martel, M. (eds.) SAS 2010. LNCS, vol. 6337, pp. 407–421. Springer, Heidelberg (2010)
10. Might, M., Van Horn, D.: A Family of Abstract Interpretations for Static Analysis of Concurrent Higher-Order Programs. In: Yahav, E. (ed.) SAS 2011. LNCS, vol. 6887, pp. 180–197. Springer, Heidelberg (2011)
11. Nielson, F., Nielson, H.R., Hankin, C.: Principles of Program Analysis. Springer (1999)
12. Odersky, M.: Functional Nets. In: Smolka, G. (ed.) ESOP/ETAPS 2000. LNCS, vol. 1782, pp. 1–25. Springer, Heidelberg (2000)
13. Pratt, V.: Modeling Concurrency with Partial Orders. International Journal of Parallel Programming 15(1), 33–71 (1986)
14. Reppy, J., Xiao, Y.: Specialization of CML Message-Passing Primitives. In: 34th Annual ACM SIGPLAN-SIGACT Symposium on Principles of Programming Languages, POPL, pp. 315–326. ACM (2007)
15. Russo, C.: The Joins Concurrency Library. In: Hanus, M. (ed.) PADL 2007. LNCS, vol. 4354, pp. 260–274. Springer, Heidelberg (2007)
16. Shivers, O.G.: Control-Flow Analysis of Higher-Order Languages. PhD thesis, Carnegie Mellon University (1991)
17. Turon, A., Russo, C.: Scalable Join Patterns. In: International Conference on Object-Oriented Programming Systems, Languages and Applications, OOPSLA, pp. 575–594. ACM (2011)
18. Von Itzstein, G.S.: Introduction of High Level Concurrency Semantics in Object Oriented Languages. PhD thesis, University of South Australia (2005)

When the Decreasing Sequence Fails[*]

Nicolas Halbwachs and Julien Henry

Vérimag[**], Grenoble University, France

Abstract. The classical method for program analysis by abstract interpretation consists in computing a increasing sequence with widening, which converges towards a correct solution, then computing a decreasing sequence of correct solutions without widening. It is generally admitted that, when the decreasing sequence reaches a fixpoint, it cannot be improved further. As a consequence, all efforts for improving the precision of an analysis have been devoted to improving the limit of the increasing sequence. In this paper, we propose a method to improve a fixpoint after its computation. The method consists in projecting the solution onto well-chosen components and to start again increasing and decreasing sequences from the result of the projection.

1 Introduction

Program analysis by abstract interpretation [CC77] consists in computing an upper approximation of the least fixpoint of an abstract semantic function in a suitable abstract lattice of properties. When the abstract lattice is of infinite depth, the standard approach [CC76, CC77] consists in computing an *increasing sequence* whose convergence is forced using a *widening operator*; then, from the obtained limit of the increasing sequence, one can improve the solution by computing a *decreasing sequence*, by iterating the function without widening. The decreasing sequence may either stop at a fixpoint of the semantic function, or be infinite, but since all its terms are correct solutions, one can stop the computation after a fixed number of terms, or limit its length using a *narrowing operator*.

Of course, the precision of the result depends both on the ability of the widening operator to "guess" a precise limit of the increasing sequence, and on the information gathered during the decreasing sequence. Intuitively, the increasing sequence extrapolates the behaviour of the program from the first steps of its execution, while the decreasing sequence gathers information about the end of the execution of the program, its loops, or more generally, the way the strongly connected components of its control flow graph are left.

While significant efforts have been devoted to improving the precision of the limit of the increasing sequence (see §1.2 for a quick survey), little attention

---

[*] This work has been partially supported by the ASOPT project of the "Agence Nationale de la Recherche" of the French Ministry of Research.

[**] Verimag is a joint laboratory of Université Joseph Fourier, CNRS and Grenoble-INP.

A. Miné and D. Schmidt (Eds.): SAS 2012, LNCS 7460, pp. 198–213, 2012.

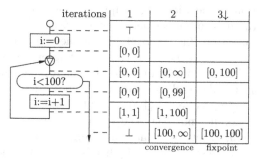

iterations	1	2	3↓
	⊤		
	[0, 0]		
	[0, 0]	[0, ∞]	[0, 100]
	[0, 0]	[0, 99]	
	[1, 1]	[1, 100]	
	⊥	[100, ∞]	[100, 100]
		convergence	fixpoint

(a) A classical example where the decreasing sequence reaches the least fixpoint

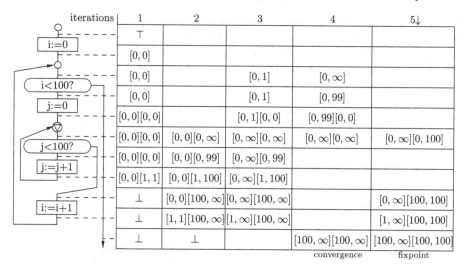

iterations	1	2	3	4	5↓
	⊤				
	[0, 0]				
	[0, 0]		[0, 1]	[0, ∞]	
	[0, 0]		[0, 1]	[0, 99]	
	[0, 0][0, 0]		[0, 1][0, 0]	[0, 99][0, 0]	
	[0, 0][0, 0]	[0, 0][0, ∞]	[0, ∞][0, ∞]	[0, ∞][0, ∞]	[0, ∞][0, 100]
	[0, 0][0, 0]	[0, 0][0, 99]	[0, ∞][0, 99]		
	[0, 0][1, 1]	[0, 0][1, 100]	[0, ∞][1, 100]		
	⊥	[0, 0][100, ∞]	[0, ∞][100, ∞]		[0, ∞][100, 100]
	⊥	[1, 1][100, ∞]	[1, ∞][100, ∞]		[1, ∞][100, 100]
	⊥	⊥		[100, ∞][100, ∞]	[100, ∞][100, 100]
				convergence	fixpoint

(b) A nested loop prevents the decreasing sequence to get precise results

Fig. 1. Example 1 – nested loops

has been paid to the decreasing sequence. It is generally admitted that, when the decreasing sequence reaches a fixpoint, it cannot be improved. However, it appears that such a fixpoint can be far from the least fixpoint, so improving it may have a significant influence. More specifically, we shall see in §1.1 that slight modifications in a program may have a surprising influence on the amount of information gathered during the decreasing sequence.

1.1 Motivating Examples

Let's illustrate the problem with two very simple examples:

Example 1. is a classical example of what can be obtained by interval analysis [CC76]. Fig. 1.a shows the control-flow graph (CFG) of a very simple loop incrementing a variable i from 0 to 100. The increasing sequence consists of 2 iterations; at iteration 2, the widening is applied, and the sequence converges. Iteration 3 shows the descending sequence, which reaches a fixpoint in 1 step. The results are the best possible: i ∈ [100, 100] at the end of the loop. Now, the CFG shown in Fig.1.b is obtained from the preceding one by nesting a second loop on another variable j within the first one. The increasing sequence converges after 4 steps. Again, the descending sequence reaches a fixpoint in 1 step, but now, the result for i is imprecise: i ∈ [100, ∞] at the end. The reason is that the nested loop neither modifies nor tests the variable i; so, as soon as its interval has been widened to [0, ∞], it will remain unchanged in the inside loop. Notice that it is also the case if we select both loop heads as widening nodes (see Note 1 in §2 on the selection of widening nodes).

Example 2: Our second example illustrates a situation which occurs commonly in reactive programs, cyclically sampling their environment. A first program (Fig. 2.a) is just an infinite loop with a counter modulo 60. It is properly analysed after 2 steps of increasing sequence and one descending step.

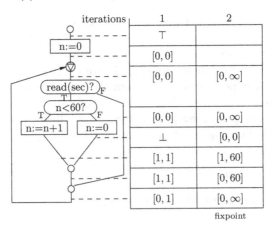

(a) An infinite loop with a counter modulo 60

(b) A loop counting the occurrences of "seconds"

Fig. 2. Example 2 – intermittent counting

Now, assume that we don't want to count all loop iterations, but only when some external event (e.g., a "second") is detected. This is done by the program of Fig. 2.b. As before, the increasing sequence converges after 2 steps, but now, the limit is a fixpoint, so there is no decreasing sequence, and the upper bound of the counter is missed. This second example can be simply explained as follows: let $(L, \sqsubseteq, \sqcup, \sqcap, \top, \bot)$ be the abstract lattice, and F be an abstract semantic function from L to L. Let $G = Id \sqcup F$ (i.e., $\lambda X.X \sqcup F(X)$). Then, it is easy to see that G has the same least fixpoint as F, but G is *extensive* (i.e., $\forall X \in L, X \sqsubseteq G(X)$). As a consequence, any postfixpoint of F is a fixpoint of G. So, while the limit of the increasing sequence with F may be a strict postfixpoint of F — which can be improved by a decreasing sequence —, this limit will be a fixpoint of G, meaning that there is no decreasing sequence with G. This is exactly what happens with our example, where the dummy branch in the loop of Fig. 2.b adds an identity term to the semantic function at the widening node.

1.2 Related Works

Beside researches proposing new abstract domains, many existing works aim at fighting the imprecision of analysis, considered to be essentially due to the widening operation. Apart from proposals of systematic design of widening and narrowing operators [CZ11], one can distinguish at least three big tracks: (1) designing smart widening operators, generally dedicated to some specific domains; (2) avoiding or minimising the use of widening, by focusing either on some classes of programs or on some classes of abstract domains; (3) applying widening and narrowing using smart strategies.

Smart Widening. Several proposals concern smart widening operators, especially for the polyhedra domain [CH78, BHRZ03]. Widening *up to* or *with thresholds* [Hal93, HPR97, BCC+03, LCJG11] consists in choosing — generally from the conditions appearing in the program — some tentative limits to the widening. Widening *with landmarks* follows the same idea, but the selection of limits is made dynamically. Widening *with care set* [WYGI07] makes use of a proof objective. Some of these proposals can properly deal with some of our examples, mainly because they can reach a precise solution at the end of the increasing sequence. However, they are not independent of the considered abstract domain. Our method will work for any abstract domain, and is compatible with any widening operation.

Avoiding Widening. Other authors try to avoid the use of widening. *Acceleration techniques* [BGP97, WB98, CJ98, BFLP03, GH06] are dedicated to some classes of programs or loops, the effect of which can be exactly computed. Other approaches can be applied only with some kinds of domains — namely "weakly relational domains" [Min04] or "templates" [SSM04, SSM05] — in which *policy iteration* [SW04, CGG+05, GS07] allows least fixpoints to be precisely computed. These methods generally solve our problem, but they are restricted either to some class of programs or to some abstract domains.

Widening Strategies. An obvious way of improving the precision of the widening is to *delay* its application [Hal93, BCC+03], i.e., applying it only after a fixed number of exact steps or intermittently, or applying it after some *loop unrolling* [Gou01, PGM03]. Some strategies adapt the application of the widening according to the discovery of *new feasible paths* [Hal93, HPR97, BCC+03] in the program. In particular, [GR06, GR07] proposes a very clever strategy, called *lookahead widening*, where a succession of increasing-decreasing sequences are computed for more and more feasible paths of the program. *Stratified analysis* [ML11] is a succession of analyses concerning more and more variables, according to their dependencies. None of these strategies provides a general solution to our problem.

Anyway, while some of these methods can work on some of our examples, none of them specifically address the problem of improving the result of the decreasing sequence. We don't pretend our method is better than these works, but that it is different and complementary.

1.3   Contribution and Summary

In this paper, we propose a method starting from the result of the decreasing sequence, and trying to improve it as follows: the solution will be projected on some of its components, whose propagation is likely to provide a more precise solution, according to some criteria. New increasing and decreasing sequences will be started from the result of the projection, providing a new solution which can be intersected with the previous one. The method is independent from the abstract domain. We'll show that it properly solves our running examples, and that in some cases, it can gather non trivial information about the end of program execution.

The paper is organised as follows: Section 2 introduce the necessary definitions and notations; our method is presented in Section 3 and illustrated on an example in Section 4; Section 5 proposes some ways for improving the performances and Section 6 gives some experimental results.

2   Definitions and Notations

Abstract Lattice. As said before, we assume that the analysis makes use of an abstract complete lattice $(L, \sqsubseteq, \sqcup, \sqcap, \top, \bot)$. We assume this lattice to be of infinite depth. The lattice operations are supposed to be available, together with a widening operator ∇, and the interpretation of each program statement s as a function (predicate transformer) $f_s : L \mapsto L$.

Control-Flow Graph. A control-flow graph (CFG) is a graph (N, E), where
- the finite set $N = \{\nu_1, ..., \nu_k\}$ is made of 3 types of nodes: the start nodes, the junction nodes, and the statement nodes. With each statement node ν_i is associated a function $f_i : L \mapsto L$.

– $E \subseteq N \times N$ is the set of edges. Start nodes have no incoming edge, statement nodes have one incoming edge, junction nodes have several incoming edges.

Remark: for simplicity, each node has a single output. This means that the classical "test nodes" (used in Figures 1 and 2) are split into pairs of statement nodes, whose associated function returns an abstraction of the intersection of its argument with the condition of the test ("then" part) or its negation ("else" part). As an example, Fig. 3 shows the CFG of our example 1.b.

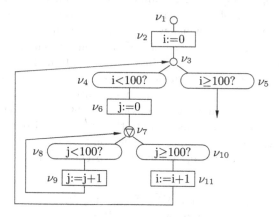

Fig. 3. CFG of the example 1.b

Semantic Equations. The analysis will associate with each node ν_i of the CFG an abstract value $X_i \in L$, these abstract values being defined by a system of recursive equations:

$$\forall i = 1..k, \ X_i = \begin{cases} \top & \text{if } \nu_i \text{ is a start node} \\ f_i(X_j) & \text{if } \nu_i \text{ is a statement node and } (\nu_j, \nu_i) \in E \\ \bigsqcup_{(\nu_j, \nu_i) \in E} X_j & \text{if } \nu_i \text{ is a junction node} \end{cases}$$

We'll often write this system of equations as a vectorial fixpoint equation: $X = F(X)$ in the lattice L^k.

Increasing Sequence. Since the lattice L is of infinite depth, the Kleene sequence $X_0 = \bot^k, X_{\ell+1} = F(X_\ell)$ may be infinite. The classical approach consists in computing the increasing sequence $Y_0 = \bot^k, Y_{\ell+1} = Y_\ell \nabla F(Y_\ell)$; from the properties of the widening operator, this sequence is guaranteed to converge after a finite number of steps towards a limit Y^∇, which is a postfixpoint of F, i.e., $F(Y^\nabla) \sqsubseteq Y^\nabla$. Of course, the increasing sequence is computed in a chaotic way (cf. Figures 1 and 2), by propagating changes along the paths of the CFG, and since the widening operation loses information, it is only applied on a selected set W of *widening nodes* intersecting each loop of the CFG.

Note 1 (On the Selection of Widening Nodes). The set W of widening nodes must be as small as possible, to minimise the number of applications of the widening operator. Since finding a minimal cutting set W is an NP-complete problem, the heuristic classically applied is the method of *strongly connected subcomponents* (SCSC) proposed by Bourdoncle [Bou93]: the method recursively uses Tarjan's algorithm [Tar72] to find the strongly connected components (SCC) of a directed graph, together with an entry node to each SCC. Entry nodes are the target of back edges, so *they are all junction nodes*. Bourdoncle's method consists in adding all SCC entry nodes to W, then removing them from the graph and recursively apply Tarjan's algorithm to the rest of each SCC. The result is a hierarchy of SCSC, each of which being cut by a junction node in W. An obvious improvement of this method (which we did not find published anywhere) consists in considering again the hierarchy of SCSC bottom-up, checking whether each SCSC is disconnected by the cut-points of its children. For instance, on the CFG of Fig. 3, a first application of Tarjan's algorithm finds one non-trivial SCC, $c_1 = \{\nu_3, \nu_4, \nu_6, \nu_7, \nu_8, \nu_9, \nu_{10}, \nu_{11}\}$, with entry node ν_3. Removing node ν_3 and applying again the algorithm provides the SCSC $c_2 = \{\nu_7, \nu_8, \nu_9\}$, with entry node ν_7, whose removal disconnects the graph. So, Bourdoncle's method provides $W = \{\nu_3, \nu_7\}$. Now, since the cut-point ν_7 of the leaf SCSC c_2 also disconnects the father SCSC c_1, it's enough to choose $W = \{\nu_7\}$, as done in Fig. 3.

Decreasing Sequence. The limit Y^∇ of the increasing sequence is a post-fixpoint of F. If it is a strict post-fixpoint ($F(Y^\nabla) \sqsubset Y^\nabla$), it can be improved by computing a decreasing sequence $Z_0 = Y^\nabla, Z_{\ell+1} = F(Z_\ell)$. This sequence can be infinite, or reach a fixpoint of F. In practice, it generally reaches a fixpoint after very few steps. Anyway, since all of its terms are post-fixpoints of F, hence correct approximations of the least fixpoint, one can stop it after a fixed number of steps, or force its convergence using a *narrowing operator*. In the following, we'll note Z^Δ the last term of the descending sequence, and we'll generally assume that Z^Δ is a fixpoint; however, the results still hold if Z^Δ is a strict post-fixpoint.

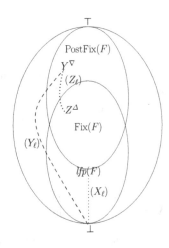

The above figure classically illustrates the sequences in the abstract lattice: $(X\ell)$ is the (generally infinite) Kleene's sequence, (Y_ℓ) is the (finite) increasing sequence, leading to the post-fixpoint Y^∇, and (Z_ℓ) is the decreasing sequence of post-fixpoints providing a solution Z^Δ.

3   Improving a (Post-)Fixpoint Solution

3.1   An Intuition of the Solution

Let's look again at example 1.b (see Fig. 3). At the widening node ν_7, during the decreasing sequence, we have $Z_7 = Z_6 \sqcup Z_9$. At the end of the decreasing sequence, we find $Z_7^{\Delta} = (i \in [0, \infty], j \in [0, 100])$, while $Z_6^{\Delta} = (i \in [0, 99], j \in [0, 0])$ and $Z_9^{\Delta} = (i \in [0, \infty], j \in [1, 100])$. Obviously, $i \in [0, 99]$, found in Z_6^{Δ}, is a correct invariant, which is lost in Z_7^{Δ} because of the least upper bound with $i \in [0, \infty]$ imprecisely found in Z_9^{Δ}. Our idea is to start again a propagation of Z_6^{Δ} after resetting Z_9^{Δ} to $\bot$.

3.2   Generalised Sequences

Restarting an iteration from an arbitrary point requires some changes in the definition of the iteration sequences. We must ensure that a widened sequence starting form an arbitrary point (not necessarily a pre-fixpoint) is increasing; moreover, widening operators are generally designed under the assumption that their first operand is smaller than the second one. We introduce the following notations: Let F be a monotone function from L to L. Let $X \in L$. Then,

- we note $F^{\nabla}(X)$ the limit of the sequence $Y_0 = X$, $Y_{\ell+1} = Y_\ell \nabla (X \sqcup F(Y_\ell))$;
- we note $F^{\nabla\Delta}(X)$ the last term Z^{Δ} of a descending sequence (Z_ℓ) starting at $Z_0 = F^{\nabla}(X)$

Remarks:

- The second operand $X \sqcup F(Y_\ell)$ of the widening is always greater than the first one, and the increasing sequence (Y_ℓ) is indeed increasing. Obviously, $F^{\nabla}(X)$ is the classical approximation of the least fixpoint of the function $\lambda X.(X \sqcup F(Y))$, i.e., of the least fixpoint of F greater than X.
- Notice also that, with $X = \bot$, these definitions of sequences and limits match the classical ones recalled in §2.
- For any X, $F^{\nabla\Delta}(X)$ is a correct approximation of the least fixpoint of F, i.e., $\forall X \in L$, $F^{\nabla\Delta}(X) \sqsupseteq lfp(F)$.
- Neither F^{∇} nor $F^{\nabla\Delta}$ is increasing. As a consequence, there can be some X such that $F^{\nabla\Delta}(X) \sqsubset F^{\nabla\Delta}(\bot)$, i.e., such that the limit obtained from X is more precise than the one computed by the classical iteration.

We address the problem of analysing an SCC of the graph, since the analysis of a complex graph considers each SCC in turn. We consider first the case of an SCC with only one widening node, before addressing the general case.

3.3   Case of a Single Widening Node

We need some additional definitions:

Path Transformers. Let ν_i, ν_j be two nodes. Let $\mathcal{P}_{i,j}$ denote the set of nodes belonging to an elementary path in the CFG going from ν_i to ν_j. Intuitively the *path transformer* from ν_i to ν_j is the function $F_{i,j} : L \mapsto L$, which, from an abstract value X associated with ν_i, provides the abstract value $F_{i,j}(X)$ corresponding to the propagation of X along the elementary paths from ν_i to ν_j. We have:

$$F_{i,j}(X) = \begin{cases} \bot & \text{if } \mathcal{P}_{i,j} = \emptyset \\ X & \text{if } \nu_i = \nu_j \\ f_j(F_{i,k}(X)) & \text{if } \nu_j \text{ is a statement node and } (\nu_k, \nu_j) \in E \\ \displaystyle\bigsqcup_{\substack{(\nu_k, \nu_j) \in E \\ \nu_k \in \mathcal{P}_{i,j}}} F_{i,k}(X) & \text{if } \nu_j \text{ is a junction node} \end{cases}$$

Now, let us consider an SCC with only one widening node, ν_i. ν_i is a junction node (from the way widening nodes are selected). The abstract value at ν_i depends on those at the preceding nodes in the SCC, and on abstract values propagated from outside (start nodes and preceding SCCs), which we note Y_i^0 since it is the first value $\neq \bot$ at node ν_i during the increasing sequence. Let $\nu_{j_1}, \ldots, \nu_{j_m}$ be the source nodes of incoming back edges to ν_i. The semantic equations considered during the descending sequence can be subsumed as:

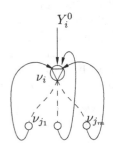

$$Z_i = Y_i^0 \sqcup Z_{j_1} \sqcup \ldots \sqcup Z_{j_m} \quad, \quad Z_{j_\ell} = F_{i,j_\ell}(Z_i), \ell = 1..m$$

At the end of the sequence, we have $Z_i^\Delta \sqsupseteq Y_i^0 \sqcup Z_{j_1}^\Delta \sqcup \ldots \sqcup Z_{j_m}^\Delta$ (an equality if Z^Δ is a fixpoint).

Projection According to Improving Components. The idea is to select a set S of nodes, such that the propagation of terms $\{Z_{j_\ell}^\Delta \mid \nu_{j_\ell} \in S\}$ is likely to improve the solution. More precisely, we define $Z^\Delta \Downarrow S$ by

$$(Z^\Delta \Downarrow S)_k = \begin{cases} Z_k^\Delta & \text{if } \nu_k \in S \\ \bot & \text{otherwise} \end{cases}$$

The choice of S should make $F^{\nabla\Delta}(Z^\Delta \Downarrow S)$ more precise or incomparable with Z^Δ, so that $Z^\Delta \sqcap F^{\nabla\Delta}(Z^\Delta \Downarrow S)$ is an improved result.

For instance, and following the intuition of §3.1, in our example 1.b (Fig. 3), we should choose $S = \{\nu_6\}$ and restart increasing and decreasing sequences from $Z^\Delta \Downarrow S$, i.e., a vector U such that

$$U_k = (\text{if } k = 6 \text{ then } ([0, 99], [0, 0]) \\ \text{else if } k = 1 \text{ then } \top \text{ else } \bot)$$

With this choice, $F^{\nabla\Delta}(U)$ is the best possible result (the least fixpoint of F), shown by the opposite vector.

	i	j
ν_3	[0,100]	
ν_7	[0,99]	[0,100]
ν_9	[0,99]	[1,100]
ν_{11}	[1,100]	[100,100]
ν_5	[100,100]	

The opposite figure shows the new sequences: the classical solution Z^Δ is projected on $U = Z^\Delta \Downarrow S$ (generally not a pre-fixpoint), from which a new increasing sequence (U_ℓ) and a new decreasing sequence (V_ℓ) provide a new limit V^Δ. The improved solution is the greatest lower bound $Z^\Delta \sqcap V^\Delta$.

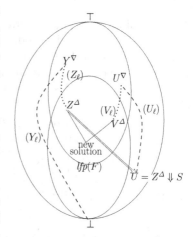

Choice of Improving Components. A component $Z^\Delta_{j_\ell}$ is likely to improve the solution if it is strictly smaller than Z^Δ_i. It may happen for two reasons:

- either some "initial states" in Y^0_i have been left on the paths from ν_i to $\nu_{j\ell}$; this case is not interesting since Y^0_i clearly consists of states which won't be shown to be unreachable. They will belong to any solution.
- or, during its propagation along these paths, Z^Δ_i has been "truncated" by some condition; this is the interesting case which can add some information.

As a consequence, ν_{j_ℓ} will be selected in S if

$$Y^0_i \sqcup Z^\Delta_{j_\ell} \sqsubset Z^\Delta_i \quad \text{(Criterion 1)}$$

Moreover, it is useless to propagate again Y^0_i, which already provided the existing result Z^Δ. So, ν_{j_ℓ} will be selected in S only if

$$Z^\Delta_{j_\ell} \not\sqsubseteq Y^0_i \quad \text{(Criterion 2)}$$

Now, let's consider our example 2.b. At convergence, no predecessor of the widening node satisfy our criteria. However, the widening node is preceded by a succession of two junction nodes, the first one being associated with an obviously interesting invariant: $n \in [0, 60]$. A simple change in the CFG taking into account the associativity of junction, would bring this node in the predecessors of the widening node. So, it can be useful to look for "improving nodes" further upstream the widening node. We change our selection process as follows:

A node ν_j will be selected in S if

- it precedes a junction node (possibly ν_i) (C0)
- $Y^0_i \sqcup F_{j,i}(Z^\Delta_j) \sqsubset Z^\Delta_i$ (C1)
- $F_{j,i}(Z^\Delta_j) \not\sqsubseteq Y^0_i$ (C2)

The criterion (C0) above comes from the fact that, during the descending sequence, only junction nodes lose information. The other two criteria generalise our preceding Criteria 1 and 2, by allowing the candidate node ν_j not to be an immediate predecessor of ν_i. Note that, in our example 2.b, the selected node ν_j is such that $F_{j,i} = Id$. However, our criteria allow also some statement nodes to be on the path from ν_j to ν_i.

3.4   General Case

The case of an SCC with several widening nodes is very similar. Only the definition of $\mathcal{P}_{i,j}$ needs to be modified: it denotes the set of nodes belonging to an elementary path in the CFG going from i to j *without going through a widening node*: only the extremities ν_i and/or ν_j can belong to W. Our criteria for selecting the improving nodes are essentially unchanged: a node ν_j will be selected in S if

- it precedes a junction node (C0)
- there exists a widening node ν_i such that
  - $Y_i^0 \sqcup F_{j,i}(Z_j^\Delta) \sqsubset Z_i^\Delta$ (C1)
  - $F_{j,i}(Z_j^\Delta) \not\sqsubseteq Y_i^0$ (C2)

and the definition of $Z^\Delta \Downarrow S$ is unchanged.

4   A More Illustrative Example

Our two running examples are properly analysed with the proposed method. They would be also solved with a smart choice of "thresholds" [Hal93, BCC$^+$03, LCJG11] for limiting the widening during the increasing sequence. Let us consider now another example to show that our method can discover constraints that don't appear as conditions in the program. The example is a rather ad-hoc modification of Example 1.b by variable change.

```
i := 0;
while i < 4 do {
    j := 0;
    while j < 4 do { i := i + 1; j := j + 1; }
    i := i - j + 1;
}
```

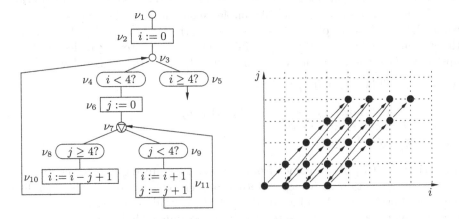

Fig. 4. Example 3

Fig. 4 shows the corresponding CFG together with the set of variable states traversed by the execution at ν_7. Fig. 5 shows the abstract values at widening node ν_7, during a polyhedra analysis:

- at the end of the classical increasing sequence, we get $(0 \leq j \leq i)$;
- the decreasing sequence reaches a fixpoint Z^Δ in one step, giving $(0 \leq j \leq i, j \leq 4)$;
- at node ν_6, we have $Z_6^\Delta = (0 \leq i \leq 3, j = 0)$, which satisfies all our criteria; we start again from $Z^\Delta \Downarrow \{\nu_6\}$;
- after a new increasing sequence, we get $(0 \leq j \leq i \leq j + 3)$;
- the decreasing sequence converges in one step, giving the best possible polyhedral invariant $(0 \leq j \leq i \leq j + 3, j \leq 4)$.

Notice that the constraint $i \leq j + 3$ doesn't appear in the program, so it could not be chosen as a "threshold" for widening.

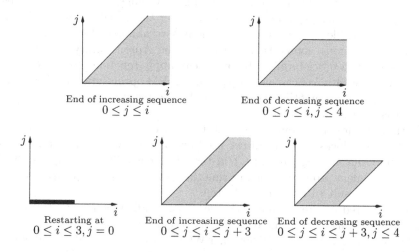

Fig. 5. Analysis of Example 3

5 Some Improvements

Of course, our method involves the computation of new iteration sequences, which may look expensive. We propose here two simple improvements to limit the cost of this computation.

The first one is obvious: since the result, in general, is the greatest lower bound of the classical solution Z^Δ and the new limit V^Δ, one can intersect with Z^Δ each term of the new increasing sequence. In our Example 3, this would force the convergence of the new increasing sequence directly on the fixpoint $(0 \leq j \leq i \leq j + 3, j \leq 4)$, without need of a decreasing sequence.

The second improvement is a compromise: it saves computation, but may lose precision (although we did not find any example where it happens). The selected components $\{Z_j^\Delta \mid \nu_j \in S\}$ are intended to lead to improvements of other components, but in general, they are not supposed to be improved by the new iteration. With this idea in mind, we can limit the computation of the new iteration to the part of the CFG which doesn't influence only the components in S. More precisely, a component at node ν_k must be computed again only if there is a path from ν_k to a widening node which doesn't intersect S. In our Example 3, this would limit the new iteration to the subgraph $\{\nu_7, \nu_9, \nu_{11}\}$, since any path from $\{\nu_8, \nu_{10}, \nu_3, \nu_4\}$ to the widening node ν_7 goes through the selected node ν_6.

6   Experimental Results

Our technique has been implemented inside our prototype static analyser, called Pagai, which computes numerical invariants in programs expressed in the LLVM internal representation [LA04]. In this representation, a function is a graph of basic blocks. The analyser takes as input such an LLVM file (that can be obtained from a C, C++, Fortran program by llvm-gcc or clang), and outputs for each basic block a numerical inductive invariant over the variables that are live at the head of this block. We can choose among several abstract domains : convex polyhedra, octagons, intervals, etc. through the Apron library [JM09]. Since Pagai is an intra-procedural analyser, we can apply function inlining to obtain more precise results. We can also apply some LLVM optimisation passes, such as loop unrolling, or promoting memory variables to registers (mem2reg), in order to increase precision.

In the current state of our implementation, we only choose as improving components basic-blocks that are direct predecessors of a widening point, i.e., we don't apply our criteria C0 and C1 in their full generality. We apply only the first improvement proposed in §5: during the new increasing sequence, we intersect our new result with Z^Δ at each step.

We compared our technique with the classical abstract interpretation with standard widening/narrowing, on a variety of benchmarks.

The benchmark from the Mälardalen WCET research group[1] contains interesting programs such as sorts, matrix transformations, fft, etc. These programs have been instrumented with a variable that counts the number of instructions being executed. These 98 functions have been analysed, using the polyhedra abstract domain. For 69 functions, the results of the new method are the same as the classical one, with a negligible time overhead (1.008 factor). For the other 29 functions, the new methods gives better results at 35% of widening points, with a 1.76 overhead factor. So, on this benchmark, not only the results are better for a significant subset of functions, but the new method costs almost nothing when it doesn't improve the results.

However, these encouraging experimental conclusions should not be overestimated: on a benchmark made of various highly used GNU functions (e.g., a2ps, gawk, gnuchess, gnugo, grep, gzip, lapack, make, sed and tar), the results are improved only at 4.14% of the widening points, with an overhead factor of 1.56 even on non improved functions.

---

[1] `www.mrtc.mdh.se/projects/wcet/benchmarks.html`

7   Conclusion

A claim of the present paper is that the information about the end of executions can be as rich, complex and useful than the one derived from their beginning. To permit a better gathering of this information, we presented a method to improve the solution obtained by classical analysis: this solution is projected on some of its components, and the result of the projection is used to start a new pair of increasing and decreasing sequences.

The method is independent of the abstract lattice, it is compatible with any smart widening operator and any iteration strategy.

Acknowledgement. We are indebted to Laure Gonnord and David Monniaux for having put our attention on the problem — and specially on Examples 1 and 2 — and for helpful discussions.

References

[BCC+03]   Blanchet, B., Cousot, P., Cousot, R., Feret, J., Mauborgne, L., Miné, A., Monniaux, D., Rival, X.: A static analyzer for large safety-critical software. In: ACM SIGPLAN SIGSOFT Conference on Programming Language Design and Implementation, PLDI 2003, San Diego (Ca.), pp. 196–207 (June 2003)

[BFLP03]   Bardin, S., Finkel, A., Leroux, J., Petrucci, L.: FAST: Fast Acceleration of Symbolic Transition Systems. In: Hunt Jr., W.A., Somenzi, F. (eds.) CAV 2003. LNCS, vol. 2725, pp. 118–121. Springer, Heidelberg (2003)

[BGP97]   Bultan, T., Gerber, R., Pugh, W.: Symbolic Model Checking of Infinite State Systems using Presburger Arithmetic. In: Grumberg, O. (ed.) CAV 1997. LNCS, vol. 1254, pp. 400–411. Springer, Heidelberg (1997)

[BHRZ03]   Bagnara, R., Hill, P.M., Ricci, E., Zaffanella, E.: Precise Widening Operators for Convex Polyhedra. In: Cousot, R. (ed.) SAS 2003. LNCS, vol. 2694, pp. 337–354. Springer, Heidelberg (2003)

[Bou93]   Bourdoncle, F.: Efficient Chaotic Iterations Strategies with Widening. In: Pottosin, I.V., Bjorner, D., Broy, M. (eds.) FMP&TA 1993. LNCS, vol. 735, pp. 128–141. Springer, Heidelberg (1993)

[CC76]   Cousot, P., Cousot, R.: Static determination of dynamic properties of programs. In: 2nd Int. Symp. on Programming. Dunod, Paris (1976)

[CC77]   Cousot, P., Cousot, R.: Abstract interpretation: a unified lattice model for static analysis of programs by construction or approximation of fixpoints. In: 4th ACM Symposium on Principles of Programming Languages, POPL 1977, Los Angeles (January 1977)

[CGG+05]   Costan, A., Gaubert, S., Goubault, É., Martel, M., Putot, S.: A Policy Iteration Algorithm for Computing Fixed Points in Static Analysis of Programs. In: Etessami, K., Rajamani, S.K. (eds.) CAV 2005. LNCS, vol. 3576, pp. 462–475. Springer, Heidelberg (2005)

[CH78]   Cousot, P., Halbwachs, N.: Automatic discovery of linear restraints among variables of a program. In: 5th ACM Symposium on Principles of Programming Languages, POPL 1978, Tucson, Arizona (January 1978)

[CJ98]   Comon, H., Jurski, Y.: Multiple Counters Automata, Safety Analysis and
            Presburger Arithmetic. In: Vardi, M.Y. (ed.) CAV 1998. LNCS, vol. 1427,
            pp. 268–279. Springer, Heidelberg (1998)

[CZ11]   Cortesi, A., Zanioli, M.: Widening and narrowing operators for abstract
            interpretation. Computer Languages, Systems & Structures 37(1), 24–42
            (2011)

[GH06]   Gonnord, L., Halbwachs, N.: Combining Widening and Acceleration in
            Linear Relation Analysis. In: Yi, K. (ed.) SAS 2006. LNCS, vol. 4134,
            pp. 144–160. Springer, Heidelberg (2006)

[Gou01]   Goubault, É.: Static Analyses of the Precision of Floating-Point Oper-
            ations. In: Cousot, P. (ed.) SAS 2001. LNCS, vol. 2126, pp. 234–259.
            Springer, Heidelberg (2001)

[GR06]   Gopan, D., Reps, T.: Lookahead Widening. In: Ball, T., Jones, R.B. (eds.)
            CAV 2006. LNCS, vol. 4144, pp. 452–466. Springer, Heidelberg (2006)

[GR07]   Gopan, D., Reps, T.: Guided Static Analysis. In: Riis Nielson, H., Filé,
            G. (eds.) SAS 2007. LNCS, vol. 4634, pp. 349–365. Springer, Heidelberg
            (2007)

[GS07]   Gawlitza, T., Seidl, H.: Precise Fixpoint Computation Through Strategy
            Iteration. In: De Nicola, R. (ed.) ESOP 2007. LNCS, vol. 4421, pp. 300–
            315. Springer, Heidelberg (2007)

[Hal93]   Halbwachs, N.: Delay Analysis in Synchronous Programs. In: Courcou-
            betis, C. (ed.) CAV 1993. LNCS, vol. 697, pp. 333–346. Springer, Heidel-
            berg (1993)

[HPR97]   Halbwachs, N., Proy, Y.E., Roumanoff, P.: Verification of real-time sys-
            tems using linear relation analysis. Formal Methods in System De-
            sign 11(2), 157–185 (1997)

[JM09]   Jeannet, B., Miné, A.: APRON: A Library of Numerical Abstract Domains
            for Static Analysis. In: Bouajjani, A., Maler, O. (eds.) CAV 2009. LNCS,
            vol. 5643, pp. 661–667. Springer, Heidelberg (2009)

[LA04]   Lattner, C., Adve, V.: LLVM: a compilation framework fopr lifelong pro-
            gram analysis & transformation. In: CGO 2004, pp. 75–86. IEEE Com-
            puter Society, Washington, DC (2004)

[LCJG11]   Lakhdar-Chaouch, L., Jeannet, B., Girault, A.: Widening with Thresh-
            olds for Programs with Complex Control Graphs. In: Bultan, T., Hsiung,
            P.-A. (eds.) ATVA 2011. LNCS, vol. 6996, pp. 492–502. Springer, Heidel-
            berg (2011)

[Min04]   Miné, A.: Weakly relational numerical abstract domains. PhD thesis,
            Ecole Polytechnique (2004)

[ML11]   Monniaux, D., Le Guen, J.: Stratified static analysis based on variable
            dependencies. In: Third International Workshop on Numerical and Sym-
            bolic Abstract Domains, Venice (September 2011)

[PGM03]   Putot, S., Goubault, É., Martel, M.: Static Analysis-Based Validation of
            Floating-Point Computations. In: Alt, R., Frommer, A., Kearfott, R.B.,
            Luther, W. (eds.) Numerical Software with Result Verification. LNCS,
            vol. 2991, pp. 306–313. Springer, Heidelberg (2004)

[SSM04]   Sankaranarayanan, S., Sipma, H.B., Manna, Z.: Constraint-Based Linear-
            Relations Analysis. In: Giacobazzi, R. (ed.) SAS 2004. LNCS, vol. 3148,
            pp. 53–68. Springer, Heidelberg (2004)

[SSM05]   Sankaranarayanan, S., Sipma, H.B., Manna, Z.: Scalable Analysis of Lin-
            ear Systems Using Mathematical Programming. In: Cousot, R. (ed.) VM-
            CAI 2005. LNCS, vol. 3385, pp. 25–41. Springer, Heidelberg (2005)

[SW04]   Su, Z., Wagner, D.: A Class of Polynomially Solvable Range Constraints for Interval Analysis without Widenings and Narrowings. In: Jensen, K., Podelski, A. (eds.) TACAS 2004. LNCS, vol. 2988, pp. 280–295. Springer, Heidelberg (2004)

[Tar72]   Tarjan, R.E.: Depth-first search and linear graph algorithms. SIAM Journal on Computing 1, 146–160 (1972)

[WB98]   Wolper, P., Boigelot, B.: Verifying Systems with Infinite but Regular State Spaces. In: Vardi, M.Y. (ed.) CAV 1998. LNCS, vol. 1427, pp. 88–97. Springer, Heidelberg (1998)

[WYGI07]   Wang, C., Yang, Z., Gupta, A., Ivančić, F.: Using Counterexamples for Improving the Precision of Reachability Computation with Polyhedra. In: Damm, W., Hermanns, H. (eds.) CAV 2007. LNCS, vol. 4590, pp. 352–365. Springer, Heidelberg (2007)

Loop Leaping with Closures

Sebastian Biallas[1], Jörg Brauer[1,2], Andy King[3,4], and Stefan Kowalewski[1]

[1] Embedded Software Laboratory, RWTH Aachen University, Germany
[2] Verified Systems International GmbH, Bremen, Germany
[3] Portcullis Computer Security, Pinner, UK
[4] School of Computing, University of Kent, UK

Abstract. Loop leaping is the colloquial name given to a form of program analysis in which summaries are derived for nested loops starting from the innermost loop and proceeding in a bottom-up fashion considering one more loop at a time. Loop leaping contrasts with classical approaches to finding loop invariants that are iterative; loop leaping is compositional requiring each stratum in the nest of loops to be considered exactly once. The approach is attractive in predicate abstraction where disjunctive domains are increasingly used that present long ascending chains. This paper proposes a simple and an efficient approach for loop leaping for these domains based on viewing loops as closure operators.

1   Introduction

Abstract interpretation [9] provides a compelling theory for modelling a program with descriptions of concrete data values. Not only does it show how domains can be defined, refined and related to their concrete counterparts, but it provides a methodology for constructing transformers that simulate the behaviour of the primitive operations that arise in a program. Best transformers can, at least in principle, always be automatically constructed for domains of finite height [30] which, notably, includes the abstract domain of conjunctions of predicates [4] that has proved so popular in verification [14]. Techniques for deriving transformers for whole blocks of code have recently emerged due, in part, to the development of robust decision procedures [6,21,25] and efficient quantifier elimination techniques [7,24,27]. The step beyond blocks is the automatic synthesis of transformers for loops.

Calculational techniques for deriving transformers for loops are colloquially referred to loop leaping [2] or loop frogging [22,23]. These evocative terms capture the central idea of jumping over the computational obstacle presented by repeatedly reaching, iterating and stabilising on each loop in a nest of loops. Instead, the whole loop nest is summarised in a straight-line block, ideally with the summary computed in a compositional fashion, starting with the innermost and ending with the outermost loop. The case for loop summarisation becomes more convincing for domains with long chains such as those admitted by Boolean formulae over large numbers of predicates [28]. Boolean formulae can be widened, even in ways that are sensitive to the underlying Boolean function rather than

A. Miné and D. Schmidt (Eds.): SAS 2012, LNCS 7460, pp. 214–230, 2012.

merely its representation [20], yet it is our contention that the rich structure of formulae aids rather than impedes loop analysis when loop leaping is applied.

Ideally one would derive a best transformer that summarises the execution of a loop, or loop nest, to the limits of what is expressible in the abstract domain. A best transformer is exactly that: a mapping from the set of input descriptions to the set of output descriptions where the output description given by the transformer is the most precise characterisation of the set of all the output states that are reachable from all the input states described by the input description. This immediately presents a problem for Boolean formulae: the number of input descriptions. Even for the sub-class of monotonic Boolean formulae, the simplest domain that can express both conjunctive and disjunctive properties, the number of formulae grows rapidly with the number of predicates: 2, 3, 6, 20, 168, 7581, 7828354, 2414682040998, 56130437228687557907788 [37]. It is therefore not surprising that previous work has sought to curtail the representation, for instance, by bounding the number of disjuncts [28]. Without exploiting common structure in and between the input and output formulae, the only realistic prospective is to design a transformer whose representation is suitably compact and whose summary is sufficiently precise: the former can be ensured through design but the latter can only be tested empirically.

The contribution of this paper is simple. It is to show how loop transformers can be computed from maps of the form $\uparrow\!f : \Sigma \to \wp(\wp(\Sigma))$ where $\Sigma = \{\sigma_1, \ldots, \sigma_n\}$ is the finite set of predicates under consideration. If $\sigma_i \in \Sigma$ then $\Delta_i = \uparrow\!f(\sigma_i)$ is interpreted as a monotonic formula in DNF. For example $\{\{\sigma_1, \sigma_2\}, \{\sigma_1, \sigma_3\}\}$ represents the formula $\theta = (\sigma_1 \wedge \sigma_2) \vee (\sigma_1 \wedge \sigma_3) = \sigma_1 \wedge (\sigma_2 \vee \sigma_3)$. Crucially the map $\uparrow\!f$ is defined by just n formulae $\Delta_1 = \uparrow\!f(\sigma_1), \ldots, \Delta_n = \uparrow\!f(\sigma_n)$. The map $\uparrow\!f$ does not constitute a loop transformer itself since it only specifies how to map an input formula, which is one of the predicates, to an output formula. Yet $\uparrow\!f$ is designed so that logical combinators can be applied to $\Delta_1, \ldots, \Delta_n$ to compute an output formula for an arbitrary input formula. To illustrate, if the input formula is θ then the output formula is $\Delta_1 \wedge (\Delta_2 \vee \Delta_3)$, where here the distinction between a monotonic Boolean function and its representation is blurred. The construction rests on $\uparrow\!f : \Sigma \to \wp(\wp(\Sigma))$, or rather its extension $\uparrow\!f : \wp(\wp(\Sigma)) \to \wp(\wp(\Sigma))$, being a closure operator, that is, a map which is monotonic, idempotent and extensive (extensivity means that the operator relaxes a formula whenever it is applied). The centrality of these three concepts explains the title of the paper and the (mysterious) $\uparrow$ symbol that indicates closure. These three properties square with the way a loop transformer maps an input formula to an output formula which describes the final state of a loop. This fit leads to a loop summarisation method that is both simple and effective.

Expositionally this paper is laid out as follows: First, Sect. 2 explains the key ingredients of our method for both, unnested and nested loops, by means of an example, followed by a formalisation and correctness arguments in Sect. 3. Then, Sect. 4 presents experimental evidence which compares the precision of our techniques to related ones based on predicate abstraction. Finally the paper concludes with a survey of related work in Sect. 5 and a discussion in Sect. 6.

(1) assume $i = 0$;	if $i < n$ then	(1) if $i < n$ then
(2) assume $n > 0$;	$\quad b := \text{nondet}();$	(2) $\quad b' := \text{nondet}();$
(3) while $i < n$ do	$\quad$ if $b \neq 0$ then	(3) $\quad$ if $b' \neq 0$ then
(4) $\quad b := \text{nondet}();$	$\quad\quad i := i + 1;$	(4) $\quad\quad i' := i + 1;$
(5) $\quad$ if $b \neq 0$ then	$\quad$ else	(5) $\quad$ else
(6) $\quad\quad i := i + 1;$	$\quad\quad$ skip;	(6) $\quad\quad i' := i;$
(7) $\quad$ else	$\quad$ endif	(7) $\quad$ endif
(8) $\quad\quad$ skip;	else	(8) else
(9) $\quad$ endif	$\quad$ skip	(9) $\quad i' := i;$
(10) endwhile	endif	(10) endif
		(11) $n' := n$

Fig. 1. Single loop example: (a) code; (b) loop block; (c) loop block in a SSA-form

2   Worked Examples

The ethos of our method is to summarise a loop with a closure operator on the domain of monotonic Boolean formulae, D, where the predicates are drawn from a given finite set of predicates, Σ, that is defined up-front. Monotonic Boolean formulae are a class of propositional functions which take the following syntactic form: if $\sigma \in \Sigma$ then $\sigma \in D$ and if $f_1, f_2 \in D$ then it follows $f_1 \wedge f_2 \in D$ and $f_1 \vee f_2 \in D$ [31]. The domain D is ordered by entailment $\models$ and with appropriate factoring (the details of which are postponed to the sequel) a finite lattice $\langle D, \models, \vee, \wedge \rangle$ can be obtained.

To illustrate how a loop can be summarised using closures over D consider the program that is listed to the leftmost column of Figure 1. Observe that the loop transforms the state that the program has when the loop is first encountered into the state that is obtained by repeated applications of the loop body. A loop summary expresses this transformation. Since state is described in terms of monotonic formulae, the summary is itself a mapping from an input formula to an output formula. The input formula describes the initial state at the head of the loop: the state of the program when the loop is first encountered. The output formula describes all the states that are reachable at the head of the loop, by repeatedly applying the loop body, from any of the initial states. Since the number of monotonic formulae grows rapidly with $|\Sigma|$ [37], the challenge is to find a way to summarise a loop that is both descriptive and yet can be represented compactly and derived straightforwardly.

Observe that the while loop is equivalent to repeated applications of the block of statements in the middle column that will collectively be referred to as S. Suppose too that the set of predicates is defined as $\Sigma = \Sigma_0 \cup \Sigma_1 \cup \Sigma_2$ where:

$$\Sigma_0 = \{ (n < 0), (n = 0), (n > 0)\}$$
$$\Sigma_1 = \{ (i < 0), (i = 0), (i > 0)\}$$
$$\Sigma_2 = \{ (i < n), (i = n), (i > n)\}$$

Although Σ is entirely natural given the predicates in the program, observe that S does not mutate n, hence S does not alter the truth or falsity of the predicates of Σ_0. We shall thus restrict our attention to summaries over the predicates $\Sigma_1 \cup \Sigma_2$; extending the summaries to Σ increases the number of cases that need to be considered without offering the reader fresh insight.

2.1   Closing the Loop over Σ

Using SMT-based reachability analysis [8,14], a function f is computed which maps input formulae, which coincide with each of the predicates $\sigma \in \Sigma_1 \cup \Sigma_2$, to their corresponding output formulae. To derive the output formulae, S is put into a form of single static assignment [10], which gives the block listed in the rightmost column, denoted S'. The three paths through S' correspond to three systems of constraints that are:

$$c_1 = (i < n) \wedge (b' \neq 0) \wedge (i' = i + 1) \wedge (n' = n)$$
$$c_2 = (i < n) \wedge \neg(b' \neq 0) \wedge (i' = i) \wedge (n' = n)$$
$$c_3 = \neg(i < n) \wedge (i' = i) \wedge (n' = n)$$

To illustrate, consider computing the abstract transformer $\alpha_{\Sigma_1' \cup \Sigma_2'}((i = 0) \wedge c_1)$ of $(i = 0) \in \Sigma_1$ subject to path c_1, where the abstraction map α is outlined below and Σ_1' and Σ_2' denote sets of predicates, analogous to Σ_1 and Σ_2 respectively, but defined over primed output variables. Passing $(i = 0) \wedge c_1$ to an SMT solver gives a model $\mathbf{m}_1$, e.g.:

$$\mathbf{m}_1 = \left\{ (i = 0) \wedge (n = 2) \wedge (i' = 1) \wedge (n' = 2) \right\}$$

Since we can check that a concrete model $\mathbf{m}$ satisfies a given predicate $\sigma \in \Sigma$, that is, $\mathbf{m} \in \gamma_\Sigma(\sigma)$, then $\alpha_\Sigma(\mathbf{m})$ can be computed thus:

$$\alpha_\Sigma(\mathbf{m}) = \bigwedge \{\sigma \in \Sigma \mid \mathbf{m} \in \gamma_\Sigma(\sigma)\}$$

Note that α is parametric in the set Σ. By abstracting $\mathbf{m}_1$, we obtain $\alpha_{\Sigma'}(\mathbf{m}_1) = (i' > 0) \wedge (i' < n')$. In a second iteration, we add $\neg\alpha_{\Sigma'}(\mathbf{m}_1)$ to the SMT instance as a blocking clause. Then, passing $(i = 0) \wedge c_1 \wedge \neg\alpha_{\Sigma'}(\mathbf{m}_1)$ to a solver yields a different model $\mathbf{m}_2$, in which all concrete values described by $\alpha_{\Sigma'}(\mathbf{m}_1)$ are blocked. Suppose $\mathbf{m}_2$ is defined as:

$$\mathbf{m}_2 = \left\{ (i = 0) \wedge (n = 1) \wedge (i' = 1) \wedge (n' = 1) \right\}$$

This model induces an output $\alpha_{\Sigma'}(\mathbf{m}_2) = (i' > 0) \wedge (i' = n')$. Then, the formula $(i = 0) \wedge c_1 \wedge \neg\alpha_{\Sigma'}(\mathbf{m}_1) \wedge \neg\alpha_{\Sigma'}(\mathbf{m}_2)$ becomes unsatisfiable, and thus $(i = 0) \wedge c_1 \models \alpha_{\Sigma'}(\mathbf{m}_1) \vee \alpha_{\Sigma'}(\mathbf{m}_2)$, which entails $f(i = 0 \wedge c_1) = (i' > 0) \wedge ((i < n') \vee (i' = n'))$. Applying this strategy to $(i = 0) \wedge c_2$ and $(i = 0) \wedge c_3$ gives:

$$f((i = 0) \wedge c_1) = (i' > 0) \wedge ((i' = n') \vee (i' < n'))$$
$$f((i = 0) \wedge c_2) = (i' = 0) \wedge (i' < n')$$
$$f((i = 0) \wedge c_3) = (i' = 0) \wedge ((i' = n') \vee (i' > n'))$$

Combining these three results we derive a formula which describes the effect of executing S under input that satisfies the predicate $\sigma = (i = 0)$. In what follows simplifications have been applied to make the presentation more accessible:

$$f(i = 0) = \bigvee_{j=1}^{3} f((i = 0) \wedge c_j)$$
$$= f((i = 0) \wedge c_1) \vee f((i = 0) \wedge c_2) \vee f((i = 0) \wedge c_3)$$
$$= (i' = 0) \vee ((i' > 0) \wedge ((i' < n') \vee (i' = n')))$$

Likewise, for the remaining predicates in Σ, we compute:

$$f(i < 0) = (i' < 0) \vee ((i' = 0) \wedge ((i' < n') \vee (i' = n')))$$
$$f(i > 0) = (i' > 0)$$
$$f(i < n) = (i' < n') \vee (i' = n')$$
$$f(i = n) = (i' = n')$$
$$f(i > n) = (i' > n')$$

The map f characterises one iteration of the block S. To describe many iterations, f is relaxed to a closure, that is, an operator over D which is idempotent, monotonic and extensive. Idempotent so as to capture the effect to repeatedly applying S until the output formula does not change; monotonic since if the input formula is relaxed then so is the output formula; and extensive so as to express that the output formula is weaker than in the input formula. The last point deserves amplification: the input formula characterises the state that holds when the loop is first encountered whereas the output summarises that states that hold when the loop head is first and then subsequently encountered, hence the former entails the latter.

With renaming applied to eliminate the auxiliary predicates of $\Sigma_1' \cup \Sigma_2'$, the closure of $f(i = 0)$, denoted $\uparrow\!f(i = 0)$, is computed so as to satisfy:

$$\uparrow\!f(i = 0) = \uparrow\!f(i = 0) \vee (\uparrow\!f(i > 0) \wedge \uparrow\!f(i < n)) \vee (\uparrow\!f(i > 0) \wedge \uparrow\!f(i = n))$$

Likewise, the closures for all predicates in Σ are required such that:

$$\uparrow\!f(i < 0) = \uparrow\!f(i < 0) \vee (\uparrow\!f(i = 0) \wedge \uparrow\!f(i < n)) \vee (\uparrow\!f(i = 0) \wedge \uparrow\!f(i = n))$$
$$\uparrow\!f(i > 0) = \uparrow\!f(i > 0)$$
$$\uparrow\!f(i < n) = \uparrow\!f(i < n) \vee \uparrow\!f(i = n)$$
$$\uparrow\!f(i = n) = \uparrow\!f(i = n)$$
$$\uparrow\!f(i > n) = \uparrow\!f(i > n)$$

This recursive equation system can be solved iteratively until it stabilises, a property that is guaranteed due to monotonicity and finiteness of the domain. In fact it is straightforward to see that $\uparrow\!f(i > 0) = (i > 0)$, $\uparrow\!f(i = n) = (i = n)$, and $\uparrow\!f(i > n) = (i > n)$. Using substitution, we then obtain $\uparrow\!f(i < n) = (i < n) \vee (i = n)$. Likewise, for $(i = 0)$, we compute:

$$\uparrow\!f(i = 0) = (i = 0) \vee ((i > 0) \wedge (i < n)) \vee ((i > 0) \wedge (i = n))$$

Also by simplification we obtain:

$$\uparrow\!f(i < 0) = (i < 0) \vee ((i > 0) \wedge ((i < n) \vee (i = n))) \vee (\uparrow\!f(i = 0) \wedge (i = n))$$
$$= (i < 0) \vee (i < n) \vee (i = n)$$

which completes the derivation of the closure.

2.2 Applying Closures

Thus far, we have computed a function $\mathord{\uparrow} f$ that maps each predicate $\sigma \in \Sigma$ to a formula that represents the states reachable at the head of the loop from σ. Yet $\mathord{\uparrow} f$ can be interpreted as more than a loop transformer over just Σ since if $\sigma_1, \sigma_2 \in \Sigma$ it follows that:

$$\mathord{\uparrow} f(\sigma_1 \wedge \sigma_2) \models \mathord{\uparrow} f(\sigma_1) \wedge \mathord{\uparrow} f(\sigma_2)$$

This holds because the closure operator is monotonic. Moreover, due to the rich structure of our domain, we also have:

$$\mathord{\uparrow} f(\sigma_1 \vee \sigma_2) = \mathord{\uparrow} f(\sigma_1) \vee \mathord{\uparrow} f(\sigma_2)$$

This follows from the way $\sigma_1 \vee \sigma_2$ is formally interpreted as set union and the operator $\mathord{\uparrow} f$ is defined so as to distribute over union. The force of this is that $\mathord{\uparrow} f$ can be lifted to an arbitrary formula over Σ, thereby prescribing a loop transformer that is sufficiently general to handle any conceivable input formula. As an example, suppose that the loop is first reached with state described by the input formula $(i = 0) \wedge (i < n)$. Then

$$
\begin{aligned}
\mathord{\uparrow} f(&(i = 0) \wedge (i < n)) \\
&\sqsubseteq \mathord{\uparrow} f(i = 0) \wedge \mathord{\uparrow} f(i < n) \\
&= ((i = 0) \vee ((i > 0) \wedge (i < n)) \vee ((i > 0) \wedge (i = n))) \wedge ((i < n) \vee (i = n)) \\
&= ((i = 0) \vee (i > 0)) \wedge ((i < n) \vee (i = n))
\end{aligned}
$$

which, with some simplifications applied, describes all the states that are reachable at the head of the loop. The complete loop transformer then amounts to intersecting this formula with the negation of the loop-condition, that is, $(i = n) \vee (i > n)$, which gives the formula $((i = 0) \vee (i > 0)) \wedge (i = n)$ which characterises the states that hold on exit from the loop as desired. The importance of this final step cannot be overlooked.

2.3 Leaping Nested Loops

The strength of the construction is that it can be used to compositionally summarise nested loops. Given an inner loop S_I, we first compute a loop transformer $\mathord{\uparrow} f_I$, which is then incorporated into the body of the outer loop S_O. Our analysis thus computes loop transformers bottom-up, which is both attractive for conceptual as well computational reasons. As an example, consider the program in Fig. 2 (nested.c from [15]) with the sets of predicates defined as:

$$
\begin{aligned}
\Sigma_1 &= \{(y < 0), (y = 0), (y > 0)\} & \Sigma_4 &= \{(t < m), (t = m), (t > m)\} \\
\Sigma_2 &= \{(t < 0), (t = 0), (t > 0)\} & \Sigma_5 &= \{(y < m), (y = m), (y > m)\} \\
\Sigma_3 &= \{(t < y), (t = y), (t > y)\} &
\end{aligned}
$$

(1)	assume $y = 0$;	(1)	assume $y = 0$;
(2)	assume $m \geq 0$;	(2)	assume $m \geq 0$;
(3)	assume $t = 0$;	(3)	assume $t = 0$;
(4)	while $y < m$ do	(4)	while $y < m$ do
(5)	$\quad y := y + 1$;	(5)	$\quad y' := y + 1$;
(6)	$\quad t := 0$;	(6)	$\quad t' := 0$;
(7)	$\quad$ while $t < y$ do	(7)	$\quad$ if $y' < 0$ then assume $y'' < 0$ endif
(8)	$\quad\quad t := t + 1$;	(8)	$\quad$ if $y' = 0$ then assume $y'' = 0$ endif
(9)	$\quad$ endwhile	(9)	$\quad$ if $y' > 0$ then assume $y'' > 0$ endif
(10)	endwhile	(10)	$\quad$ if $t' = 0$ then assume $t'' \geq 0$ endif
(11)	assert $y = m$	(11)	$\quad$ if $t' > 0$ then assume $t'' > 0$ endif
		(12)	$\quad$ if $t' < y'$ then assume $t'' \leq y''$ endif
		(13)	$\quad$ if $t' = y'$ then assume $t'' = y''$ endif
		(14)	$\quad$ if $t' > y'$ then assume $t'' > y''$ endif
		(15)	$\quad$ assume $t'' \geq y''$
		(16)	endwhile
		(17)	assert $y = m$

Fig. 2. Bottom-up derivation of transformer for a nested loop from [15]

Applying our technique to the inner loop on predicates $\Sigma_1 \cup \Sigma_2 \cup \Sigma_3$, we compute the map f_I as follows:

$$f_I(y < 0) = (y < 0)$$
$$f_I(y = 0) = (y = 0)$$
$$f_I(y > 0) = (y > 0)$$
$$f_I(t < y) = (t < y) \vee (t = y)$$
$$f_I(t = y) = (t = y)$$
$$f_I(t > y) = (t > y)$$

$$f_I(t < 0) = (t < 0) \vee (t = 0)$$
$$f_I(t = 0) = (t = 0) \vee (t > 0)$$
$$f_I(t > 0) = (t > 0)$$

Then, as before, we compute the closure of f_I to give:

$$\uparrow\!f_I(y < 0) = (y < 0)$$
$$\uparrow\!f_I(y = 0) = (y = 0)$$
$$\uparrow\!f_I(y > 0) = (y > 0)$$
$$\uparrow\!f_I(t < 0) = \uparrow\!f_I(t < 0) \vee \uparrow\!f_I(t = 0) = (t < 0) \vee (t = 0) \vee (t > 0) = \text{true}$$
$$\uparrow\!f_I(t = 0) = (t = 0) \vee (t > 0)$$
$$\uparrow\!f_I(t > 0) = (t > 0)$$
$$\uparrow\!f_I(t < y) = \uparrow\!f_I(t < y) \vee \uparrow\!f_I(t = y) = (t < y) \vee (t = y)$$
$$\uparrow\!f_I(t = y) = (t = y)$$
$$\uparrow\!f_I(t > y) = (t > y)$$

To abstract the outer loop in Fig. 2, we replace the inner loop, defined at lines (7)–(9) on the left, by its summary. This gives the program on the right. Here, lines (7)–(14) encode an application of the closure, whereas line (15) models the loop exit condition of S_I. Note that lines 10 and 12 relax strict inequalities to non-strict inequalities to simultaneously express two predicates (which is merely for presentational purposes). Even though the transformed program appears to have multiple paths, it is not treated as such: lines (7)–(14) rather model auxiliary constraints imposed by the closure on a single path.

Next a predicate transformer f_O for the outer loop S_O is computed which amounts, like before, to reachability analysis over the predicates $\bigcup_{i=1}^{5} \Sigma_i$. We obtain a map $f_O : \Sigma \to \wp(\wp(\Sigma))$ defined as:

$$
\begin{aligned}
f_O(y < 0) &= ((y < 0) \vee (y = 0)) \wedge ((t = 0) \vee (t > 0)) \wedge ((t = y) \vee (t > y)) \\
f_O(y = 0) &= (y > 0) \wedge (t > 0) \wedge (t = y) \\
f_O(y > 0) &= (y > 0) \wedge ((t = 0) \vee (t > 0)) \wedge ((t = y) \vee (t > y)) \\
f_O(t < 0) &= ((t = 0) \vee (t > 0)) \wedge ((t = y) \vee (t > y)) \\
f_O(t = 0) &= ((t = 0) \vee (t > 0)) \wedge ((t = y) \vee (t > y)) \\
f_O(t > 0) &= ((t = 0) \vee (t > 0)) \wedge ((t = y) \vee (t > y)) \\
f_O(t < y) &= (t = y) \\
f_O(t = y) &= (t = y) \\
f_O(t > y) &= (t > y) \\
f_O(t < m) &= (t = y) \vee (t > y) \\
f_O(t = m) &= (t = y) \vee (t > y) \\
f_O(t > m) &= (t = y) \vee (t > y) \\
f_O(y < m) &= ((y < m) \vee (y = m)) \wedge ((t = 0) \vee (t > 0)) \wedge ((t = y) \vee (t > y)) \\
f_O(y = m) &= (y = m) \\
f_O(y > m) &= (y > m)
\end{aligned}
$$

Analogous to before, closure computation amounts to substituting the predicates in the image of f_O. In case of the predicate $(y = 0) \in \Sigma_1$, for example, computing the closure of $f_O(y = 0) = (y > 0) \wedge (t > 0) \wedge (t = y)$ amounts to substituting $(y > 0)$, $(t > 0)$ and $(t = y)$ by $\uparrow\!f_O(y > 0)$, $\uparrow\!f(t > 0)$ and $\uparrow\!f(t = y)$, respectively. By repeated substitution (with entailment checking), we obtain the following closures for $(y = 0) \in \Sigma_1$, $(t = 0) \in \Sigma_3$ and $(y < m) \in \Sigma_5$:

$$
\begin{aligned}
\uparrow\!f_O(y = 0) &= (y > 0) \wedge (t > 0) \wedge (t = y) \\
\uparrow\!f_O(t = 0) &= ((t = 0) \vee (t > 0)) \wedge ((t = y) \vee (t > y)) \\
\uparrow\!f_O(y < m) &= ((y < m) \vee (y = m)) \wedge ((t = 0) \vee (t > 0)) \wedge ((t = y) \vee (t > y))
\end{aligned}
$$

Likewise, we close f for the remaining predicates.

To illustrate the precision of this type of transformer for nested loops, suppose $(y = 0) \wedge (y < m) \wedge (t = 0)$ holds on enter into the outer loop. The loop transformer for $(y = 0) \wedge (y < m) \wedge (t = 0)$ is computed as $\uparrow\!f_O(y = 0) \wedge \uparrow\!f_O(y < m) \wedge \uparrow\!f_O(t = 0)$, which simplifies to give:

$$
\begin{aligned}
&\uparrow\!f_O(y = 0) \wedge \uparrow\!f_O(y < m) \wedge \uparrow\!f_O(t = 0) \\
&= \begin{cases} (y > 0) \wedge (t > 0) \wedge (t = y) & \wedge \\ ((t = 0) \vee (t > 0)) \wedge ((t = y) \vee (t > y)) & \wedge \\ ((y < m) \vee (y = m)) \wedge ((t = 0) \vee (t > 0)) \wedge ((t = y) \vee (t > y)) \end{cases} \\
&= (y > 0) \wedge (t > 0) \wedge (t = y) \wedge ((y < m) \vee (y = m))
\end{aligned}
$$

By conjoining this output of the outer loop with the exit-condition $(y \geq m)$, we obtain the post-state of the program after the loop:

$\Uparrow f_0((y=0) \wedge (y < m) \wedge (t=0))) \wedge (y \geq m)$
$= (y > 0) \wedge (t > 0) \wedge (t = y) \wedge ((y < m) \vee (y = m)) \wedge (y \geq m)$
$= (y > 0) \wedge (t > 0) \wedge (t = y) \wedge (y = m)$

Clearly, the assertion in line (11) of Fig. 2 follows, as is required.

3   Semantics

In this section we formalise our approach to predicate abstraction and demonstrate its correctness. The starting is a (countable) finite concrete domain B that is interpreted as the set of possible program states, for instance, $B = [-2^{31}, 2^{31} - 1]^2$ for a program with just two 32-bit signed integer variables. For generality the definition of B is left open. To illustrate the compositional nature of our analysis, the formal study focuses on a language $\mathcal{L}$ of structured statements S defined by

$$S ::= \mathsf{skip} \mid \mathsf{assume}(\rho) \mid \mathsf{transform}(\tau) \mid S; S \mid \mathsf{if}\ \rho\ \mathsf{then}\ S\ \mathsf{else}\ S \mid \mathsf{while}\ \rho\ \mathsf{do}\ S$$

where $\tau \subseteq B \times B$ is a relation between assignments and $\rho \subseteq B$ is a predicate. Since τ is a binary relation, rather than a function, the statement $\mathsf{transform}(\tau)$ can express non-determinism. If $\tau = \{\langle x, y \rangle \times \langle x', y' \rangle \in ([-2^{31}, 2^{31} - 1]^2)^2 \mid x' = x\}$, for instance, then the statement $\mathsf{transform}(\tau)$ preserves the value of x but assigns y to an arbitrary 32-bit value. For brevity of presentation, we define the composition of a unary relation $\rho \subseteq B$ with a binary relation $\tau \subseteq B \times B$ which is defined thus $\rho \circ \tau = \{b' \in B \mid b \in \rho \wedge \langle b, b' \rangle \in \tau\}$ (and should not be confused with function composition whose operands are sometimes written in the reverse order). We also define $\neg \rho = B \setminus \rho$ for $\rho \subseteq B$.

3.1   Concrete Semantics

Because of the non-deterministic nature of $\mathsf{transform}(\tau)$ the semantics that is used as the basis for abstraction operates on sets of values drawn from B. The semantics is denotational in nature, associating with each statement in a program with a mapping $\wp(B) \to \wp(B)$ that expresses its behaviour. The function space $\wp(B) \to \wp(B)$ is ordered pointwise by $f_1 \sqsubseteq f_2$ iff $f_1(\rho) \subseteq f_2(\rho)$ for all $\rho \subseteq B$. In fact $\langle \wp(B) \to \wp(B), \sqcap, \sqcup, \lambda\rho.\emptyset, \lambda\rho.B \rangle$ is a complete lattice where $f_1 \sqcap f_2 = \lambda\rho.f_1(\rho) \cap f_2(\rho)$ and likewise $f_1 \sqcup f_2 = \lambda\rho.f_1(\rho) \cup f_2(\rho)$. The complete lattice $\mathcal{L} \to \wp(B) \to \wp(B)$ is defined analogously. With this structure in place a semantics for statements can be defined:

Definition 1. The mapping $[\![\cdot]\!]_C : \mathcal{L} \to \wp(B) \to \wp(B)$ is the least solution to:

$$[\![\mathsf{skip}]\!]_C = \lambda\sigma.\sigma$$
$$[\![\mathsf{assume}(\rho)]\!]_C = \lambda\sigma.\sigma \cap \rho$$
$$[\![\mathsf{transform}(\tau)]\!]_C = \lambda\sigma.\sigma \circ \tau$$
$$[\![S_1; S_2]\!]_C = \lambda\sigma.[\![S_2]\!]_C([\![S_1]\!]_C(\sigma))$$
$$[\![\mathsf{if}\ \rho\ \mathsf{then}\ S_1\ \mathsf{else}\ S_2]\!]_C = \lambda\sigma.([\![S_1]\!]_C(\sigma \cap \rho)) \cup ([\![S_2]\!]_C(\sigma \cap \neg\rho))$$
$$[\![\mathsf{while}\ \rho\ \mathsf{do}\ S]\!]_C = \lambda\sigma.([\![\mathsf{while}\ \rho\ \mathsf{do}\ S]\!]_C([\![S]\!]_C(\sigma \cap \rho))) \cup (\sigma \cap \neg\rho)$$

3.2 Abstract Semantics

The correctness of the bottom-up analysis, the so-called closure semantics, is argued relative a top-down analysis, the abstract semantics, which, in turn, is proved correct relative to the concrete semantics. The abstract semantics is parametric in terms of a finite set of predicates $\Sigma = \{\sigma_1, \ldots, \sigma_n\}$ where $\sigma_1, \ldots, \sigma_n \subseteq B$ with $\sigma_i \neq \sigma_j$ if $i \neq j$ are distinct predicates. A set of predicates $\delta \in \Delta \subseteq \wp(\Sigma)$ is interpreted by the following:

Definition 2. The concretisation map $\gamma : \wp(\wp(\Sigma)) \to \wp(B)$ is defined:

$$\gamma(\Delta) = \bigcup_{\delta \in \Delta} \gamma(\delta) \quad \text{where} \quad \gamma(\delta) = \bigcap_{\sigma \in \delta} \sigma$$

Example 1. Suppose $\delta_0 = \emptyset$, $\delta_1 = \{\sigma_1\}$ and $\delta_2 = \{\sigma_1, \sigma_2\}$. Then $\gamma(\delta_0) = B$, $\gamma(\delta_1) = \sigma_1$ and $\gamma(\delta_2) = \sigma_1 \cap \sigma_2$.

The concretisation map γ induces an quasi-ordering on $\wp(\wp(\Sigma))$ by $\Delta_1 \sqsubseteq \Delta_2$ iff $\gamma(\Delta_1) \subseteq \gamma(\Delta_2)$. To obtain a poset an operator $\downarrow$ is introduced to derive a canonical representation for an arbitrary $\Delta \subseteq \wp(\Sigma)$ by forming its down-set. The down-set is defined $\downarrow\Delta = \{\delta' \subseteq \Sigma \mid \exists \delta \in \Delta . \gamma(\delta') \subseteq \gamma(\delta)\}$ from which we construct $D = \{\downarrow\Delta \mid \Delta \subseteq \wp(\Sigma)\}$. Observe that if $\Delta_1, \Delta_2 \in D$ then $\Delta_1 \cap \Delta_2 \in D$. To see that $\Delta_1 \cup \Delta_2 \in D$ let $\delta \in \Delta_1 \cup \Delta_2$ and suppose $\delta \in \Delta_i$. Then if $\gamma(\delta') \subseteq \gamma(\delta)$ it follows that $\delta' \in \Delta_i \subseteq \Delta_1 \cup \Delta_2$. Moreover $\langle D, \subseteq, \cup, \cap, \emptyset, \wp(\Sigma) \rangle$ is a complete lattice where $\cap$ is meet and $\cup$ is join.

Proposition 1. The maps $\alpha : \wp(B) \to D$ and $\gamma : D \to \wp(B)$ form a Galois connection between $\langle \wp(B), \subseteq \rangle$ and $\langle D, \subseteq \rangle$ where $\alpha(\sigma) = \cap\{\Delta \in D \mid \sigma \subseteq \gamma(\Delta)\}$

Example 2. Suppose $\Sigma = \{\sigma_1, \sigma_2\}$ where $\sigma_1 = (0 \leq i \leq 1)$ and $\sigma_2 = (1 \leq i \leq 2)$. Let $\Delta_1 = \{\{\sigma_1\}, \{\sigma_1, \sigma_2\}\}$ and $\Delta_2 = \{\{\sigma_2\}, \{\sigma_1, \sigma_2\}\}$. Note that $\downarrow\Delta_1 = \Delta_1$ and $\downarrow\Delta_2 = \Delta_2$ thus $\Delta_1, \Delta_2 \in D$. However $\{\{\sigma_1\}\} \notin D$ and $\{\{\sigma_2\}\} \notin D$. Observe $\gamma(\Delta_1) = \sigma_1$ and $\gamma(\Delta_2) = \sigma_2$. Moreover $\Delta_1 \cap \Delta_2 \in D$ and $\Delta_1 \cup \Delta_2 \in D$ with $\gamma(\Delta_1 \cap \Delta_2) = \sigma_1 \cap \sigma_2 = (i = 1)$ and $\gamma(\Delta_1 \cup \Delta_2) = \sigma_1 \cup \sigma_2 = (0 \leq i \leq 2)$. Furthermore $\alpha(i = 1) = \{\{\sigma_1, \sigma_2\}\}$ and $\alpha(0 \leq i \leq 2) = \{\{\sigma_1\}, \{\sigma_2\}, \{\sigma_1, \sigma_2\}\}$.

Example 3. Observe that if $\Delta = \emptyset$ then $\Delta \in D$ and $\gamma(\Delta) = \emptyset$. But if $\delta = \emptyset$, $\delta \in \Delta$ and $\Delta \in D$ then $\Delta = \wp(\Sigma)$ since $\gamma(\delta') \subseteq B = \gamma(\delta)$ for all $\delta' \subseteq \Sigma$.

Proposition 2. If $\sigma \in \Sigma$ then $\alpha(\sigma) = \downarrow\{\{\sigma\}\}$.

Both for brevity and for continuity of the exposition, the proofs are relegated to a technical report [5].

As before, the abstract semantics is denotational associating each statement with a mapping $D \to D$. The function space $D \to D$ is ordered point-wise by $f_1 \sqsubseteq f_2$ iff $f_1(\Delta) \subseteq f_2(\Delta)$ for all $\Delta \in D$. Also like before $\langle D \to D, \sqcap, \sqcup, \lambda\Delta.\emptyset, \lambda\Delta.\wp(\Sigma) \rangle$ is a complete lattice where $f_1 \sqcap f_2 = \lambda\Delta.f_1(\Delta) \sqcap f_2(\Delta)$ and likewise $f_1 \sqcup f_2 = \lambda\Delta.f_1(\Delta) \sqcup f_2(\Delta)$. Moreover, the point-wise ordering on $D \to D$ lifts to define a point-wise ordering on $\mathcal{L} \to D \to D$ in an analogous manner. Since $\mathcal{L} \to D \to D$ is a complete lattice the following is well-defined:

Definition 3. The mapping $[\![\cdot]\!]_A : \mathcal{L} \to D \to D$ is the least solution to:

$$
\begin{aligned}
[\![\mathsf{skip}]\!]_A &= \lambda \Delta. \Delta \\
[\![\mathsf{assume}(\rho)]\!]_A &= \lambda \Delta. \Delta \cap \alpha(\rho) \\
[\![\mathsf{transform}(\tau)]\!]_A &= \lambda \Delta. \alpha(\gamma(\Delta) \circ \tau) \\
[\![S_1; S_2]\!]_A &= \lambda \Delta. [\![S_2]\!]_A([\![S_1]\!]_A(\Delta)) \\
[\![\mathsf{if}\ \rho\ \mathsf{then}\ S_1\ \mathsf{else}\ S_2]\!]_A &= \lambda \Delta. ([\![S_1]\!]_A(\Delta \cap \alpha(\rho))) \cup ([\![S_2]\!]_A(\Delta \cap \alpha(\neg \rho))) \\
[\![\mathsf{while}\ \rho\ \mathsf{do}\ S]\!]_A &= \lambda \Delta. ([\![\mathsf{while}\ \rho\ \mathsf{do}\ S]\!]_A([\![S]\!]_A(\Delta \cap \alpha(\rho))) \cup (\Delta \cap \alpha(\neg \rho))
\end{aligned}
$$

Proposition 3. Let $S \in \mathcal{L}$. If $\rho \in \gamma(\Delta)$ then $[\![S]\!]_C(\rho) \subseteq \gamma([\![S]\!]_A(\Delta))$.

3.3 Closure Semantics

At the heart of the closure semantics are functions with signature $\Sigma \to D$. Join and meet lift point-wise to the function space $\Sigma \to D$ since if $f_1 : \Sigma \to D$ and $f_2 : \Sigma \to D$ then $f_1 \sqcup f_2 = \lambda \sigma. f_1(\sigma) \cup f_2(\sigma)$ and $f_1 \sqcap f_2 = \lambda \sigma. f_1(\sigma) \cap f_2(\sigma)$. The key idea is to construct a mapping $f : \Sigma \to D$ whose extension to $f : D \to D$ is a closure, that is, an operation which is monotonic, extensive and idempotent. A map $f : \Sigma \to D$ lifts to $f : \wp(\Sigma) \to D$ and then further lifts to $f : \wp(\wp(\Sigma)) \to D$ by $f(\delta) = \cap\{f(\sigma) \mid \sigma \in \delta\}$ and $f(\Delta) = \cup\{f(\delta) \mid \delta \in \Delta\}$ respectively. Observe that a lifting $f : D \to D$ is monotonic, irrespective of f, since if $\Delta_1 \subseteq \Delta_2$ then $f(\Delta_1) \subseteq f(\Delta_2)$. It also distributes over union, that is, $f(\Delta_1) \cup f(\Delta_2) = f(\Delta_1 \cup \Delta_2)$. We introduce $\Uparrow f : \Sigma \to D$ to denote the idempotent relaxation of $f : \Sigma \to D$ which is defined thus:

Definition 4. If $f : \Sigma \to D$ then

$$
\Uparrow f = \sqcap\{f' : \Sigma \to D \mid f \sqsubseteq f' \wedge \forall \sigma \in \Sigma. f'(\sigma) = f'(f'(\sigma))\}
$$

Note the use of overloading within the expression $f'(f'(\sigma))$: the inner f' has type $f' : \Sigma \to D$ whereas the outer f' has type $f' : \Sigma \to D$. Observe too that $\Uparrow f : \Sigma \to D$ is extensive if $f : \Sigma \to D$ is extensive. Although the above definition is not constructive, the idempotent relaxation can be computed in an iterative fashion using the following result:

Proposition 4. $\Uparrow f = \sqcup_{i=0} f_i$ where $f_0 = f$ and $f_{i+1} = f_i \sqcup \lambda \sigma. f_i(f_i(\sigma))$

With $\Uparrow f$ both defined and computable (by virtue of the finiteness of Σ), an analysis based on closures can be formulated thus:

Definition 5. The mapping $[\![\cdot]\!]_L : \mathcal{L} \to D \to D$ is the least solution to:

$$
\begin{aligned}
[\![\mathsf{skip}]\!]_L &= \lambda \Delta. \Delta \\
[\![\mathsf{assume}(\rho)]\!]_L &= \lambda \Delta. \Delta \cap \alpha(\rho) \\
[\![\mathsf{transform}(\tau)]\!]_L &= \lambda \Delta. \alpha(\gamma(\Delta) \circ \tau) \\
[\![S_1; S_2]\!]_L &= \lambda \Delta. [\![S_2]\!]_L([\![S_1]\!]_L(\Delta)) \\
[\![\mathsf{if}\ \rho\ \mathsf{then}\ S_1\ \mathsf{else}\ S_2]\!]_L &= \lambda \Delta. ([\![S_1]\!]_L(\Delta \cap \alpha(\rho))) \cup ([\![S_2]\!]_L(\Delta \cap \alpha(\neg \rho))) \\
[\![\mathsf{while}\ \rho\ \mathsf{do}\ S]\!]_L &= \lambda \Delta. \Uparrow f(\Delta) \cap \alpha(\neg \rho) \text{ where} \\
&\quad f = \lambda \sigma. \Downarrow\{\{\sigma\}\} \cup [\![S]\!]_L(\Downarrow\{\{\sigma\}\} \cap \alpha(\rho))
\end{aligned}
$$

Table 1. Experimental results

Program	$|\Sigma|$	Time	Input	Result
counter.c	12	0.1 s	$x = 0 \wedge n \geq 0$	$n \geq 0 \wedge x = n$
ex1a.c	12	0.1 s	$0 \leq x \leq 2 \wedge 0 \leq y \leq 2$	$x \geq 0 \wedge x \leq 2$
ex1b.c	20	0.1 s	$m = 0 \wedge x = 0$	$m \geq 0 \wedge n > m \wedge x = n \wedge x > 0$
ex3.c	25	0.6 s	$x \leq y \wedge x = 0 \wedge y = m$	$x \leq m \wedge x = n \wedge x = y \wedge y \geq m$
lockstep.c	12	0.1 s	$x \leq y \wedge x \geq y$	$x = y \wedge x = n$
nested.c	15	1.0 s	$t = 0 \wedge y = 0 \wedge m \geq 0$	$t > 0 \wedge t = y \wedge y = m \wedge y > 0$
two-loop.c	20	0.2 s	$x = 0 \wedge y = 0$	$x = n \wedge y = n$

Note that $\uparrow f$ is a closure since f is extensive by construction. Observe too that $[\![\text{while } \rho \text{ do } S]\!]_L$ is defined with a single call to $[\![S]\!]_L$ whereas $[\![\text{while } \rho \text{ do } S]\!]_A$ is defined in terms of possibly many calls to $[\![S]\!]_A$. Thus the closure semantics can be realised without auxiliary structures such as memo tables that are needed to intercept repeated calls.

Conceptually the closure semantics simulates the top-down flow of the abstract semantics from which it is derived, until a loop is encountered at which point the loop body is entered. The loop body is then evaluated, again top-down, for each of the predicates. The closure is then calculated, applied to the formula that holds on entry to the loop, and the result composed with the negation of the loop condition, to infer the formula that holds on exit from the loop. Yet because of the structured nature of the domain, the loop transformer can be represented as a straight-line block of conditional assumptions. Thus the transformer has the dual attributes of: closely mimicking the top-down abstract semantics, which aids in constructing a convincing correctness argument, whilst being fully compositional which is the key attribute in the bottom-up approach to loop summarisation.

Proposition 5. Let $S \in \mathcal{L}$ and $\Delta \in D$. Then $[\![S]\!]_A(\Delta) \subseteq [\![S]\!]_L(\Delta)$.

By composing propositions 3 and 5 the main correctness result is obtained:

Corollary 1. Let $S \in \mathcal{L}$. If $\rho \in \gamma(\Delta)$ then $[\![S]\!]_C(\rho) \subseteq \gamma([\![S]\!]_L(\Delta))$.

4 Experiments

A prototype analyser had been implemented in RUBY [13], with the express aim of evaluating the precision of our technique on some loops used elsewhere for benchmarking. The analyser faithfully realises the closure semantics as set out in Def. 5. In addition to the examples outlined in Sect. 2, we applied our prototype to the programs evaluated in [18] which are available from [15]. These sample programs test and mutate integers with loop structures are either single loops, nested loops, or sequences of loops.

The results our experiments are presented in Tab. 1. The column $|\Sigma|$ denotes the number of predicates used, followed by *Time* which indicates the runtime required to evaluate the whole program. The column *Input* gives the formula that input to the program (actually an assumption that was given in the benchmark). Likewise for Σ we chose those predicates which are listed in a comment in the benchmark itself. The *Result* column documents the formula obtained by running the program on this input (in a cleaned format as is explained below). The runtime for all tests where less than a second on a 2.6 GHz MacBook Pro equipped with 4 GiB RAM.

Interestingly, our implementation seems to outperform the invariant generation technique presented in [18] for speed in all except one benchmark (`nested.c`). This result is rather surprising as our prototype has been implemented naïvely in RUBY, more as a sanity check on the design rather than a tool for assessing performance. Considering that RUBY is interpreted, the runtimes of our proof-of-concept implementation are encouraging. It should be noted, however, that we generate the transformers for blocks off-line, prior to applying the analysis, rather than using a SMT solver to compute block transformers on-the-fly. Nevertheless the dominating time is the closure calculation since it needs to repeatedly combine formulae; pruning intermediate formulae should improve this.

In terms of precision, most output formulae are actually disjunctive, but the table gives conjunctive simplifications to make the presentation accessible. In case of `counter.c`, for instance, we write $n \geq 0 \wedge x = n$ instead of the disjunctive formula $(n = 0 \wedge x = n) \vee (n > 0 \wedge x = n)$. Manually we checked that each of the component cubes (conjunctions) were genuinely reachable on program exit. (It may not be feasible to infer invariants by hand but if Σ is small it is possible to manually verify that a cube is irredundant with a high degree of confidence.) We conclude that these invariants appear to be optimal even though the closure semantics can, in principle, lead to a sub-optimal transformer for loops.

5   Related Work

The key idea in predicate abstraction [3,12,14] is to describe a large, possibly infinite, set of states with a finite set of predicates. If the two predicates ρ_i and ρ_j describe, respectively, the sets of states $\gamma(\rho_i)$ and $\gamma(\rho_j)$, then all the transitions between a state in $\gamma(\rho_i)$ and a state in $\gamma(\rho_j)$ are described with a single abstract transition from ρ_i to ρ_j. The existence of a transition between $\gamma(\rho_i)$ and $\gamma(\rho_j)$, and hence an abstract one between ρ_i and ρ_j, can be determined by querying a SAT/SMT solver [8] or a theorem prover [14]. The domain of conjuncts of predicates is related to the domain of sets of states by a Galois connection [4], allowing the framework of abstract interpretation [9], as well as domain refinements such as disjunctive completion [4], to be applied to systematically derive loop invariants using iterative fixpoint computation.

5.1   Loop Summarisation

Motived by the desire to improve efficiency, a thread of work has emerged on compositional bottom-up analysis that strives to reorganise iterative fixed-point computation by applying loop summarisation [34]. The idea is to substitute a loop with a conservative abstraction of its behaviour, constructing abstract transformers for nested loops starting from the inner-most loop [2,22]. Various approaches have been proposed for loop summarisation, such as taking cues from the control structure to suggest candidate invariants that are subsequently checked for soundness [22, Sect. 3.3]. Inference rules have also been proposed for deriving summaries based on control structures [33]. Increasingly loop summarisation is finding application in termination analysis [2,36].

5.2 Quantifier Elimination

Existential quantification has also been applied to characterise inductive loop invariants. Kapur [19] uses a parameterised first-order formula as a template and specifies constraints on these parameters using quantification. Quantifiers are then eliminated to derive the loop invariants [19, Sect. 3] which, though attractive conceptually, inevitably presents a computational bottleneck [11]. Likewise Monniaux (see [25, Sect. 3.4] and [26, Sect. 3.4]) uses quantification to specify inductive loop invariants for linear templates [32].

5.3 Disjunctive Invariants

Gulwani et al. [18] derive loop invariants in bounded DNF using SAT by specifying constraints that model state on entry and exit of a loop as well as inductive relations. Monniaux and Bodin [28] apply predicate abstraction to compute automata (with a number of states that is bounded a priori) which represent the semantics of reactive nodes using predicates and an abstract transition relation. Rather than computing abstractions as arbitrary formulae over predicates, they consider disjunctions of a fixed number of cubes. The specification of loop invariants itself is not dissimilar to that in [25, Sect. 3.4]. However, bounding the problem allows for the application of incremental techniques to improve performance [28, Sect. 2.4]. Similar in spirit, though based on classical abstract interpretation rather than SMT-based predicate abstraction, is the work of Balakrishnan et al. [1] on control-structure refinement for loops in Lustre.

Disjunctive loop invariants have also been studied in other contexts, for instance, Gulwani et al. [16,17] apply auxiliary variables in the complexity analysis of multi-path loops, where disjunctive invariants describe the complexities over counter variables. Recent work by Sharma et al. [35] focusses on the structure of loops in general. The authors observed that loops, which require disjunctive invariants, often depend on a single phase-transition. They provide a technique that soundly detects whether a loop relies on such, and if so, rewrite the program so that conjunctive techniques can be applied. Such invariants are easier to handle than disjunctive ones. By way of contrast, Popeea and Chin [29] compute disjunctions of convex polyhedra using abstract interpretation. To determine whether a pair of two polyhedra shall be merged, they apply distance metrics so to balance expressiveness against computational cost.

6   Conclusions

This paper advocates a technique for leaping loops in predicate abstraction where the abstract domain is not merely a conjunction of predicates that simultaneously hold but rather a (possibly disjunctive) monotonic formula over the set of predicates. Each loop is summarised with a closure that enables each loop to be treated as if it were a straight-line block. Because the number of monotonic formulae grows rapidly with the number of predicates, the method, by design, does not compute a best transformer. Instead closures are derived solely for the atomic predicates and, as a result, each closure can be represented by just n monotonic formulae where n is the number of predicates. Applying the loop transformer then amounts to computing logical combinations of these n formulae. The compact nature of the loop transformers, their conceptual simplicity, as well as their accuracy which is demonstrated empirically, suggests that this notion of closure is a sweet-point in the design space for loop leaping on this domain. Future work will investigate adapting these loop leaping techniques to other abstract domains.

Acknowledgements. This work was supported, in part, by the DFG research training group 1298 *Algorithmic Synthesis of Reactive and Discrete-Continuous Systems* and by the DFG *Cluster of Excellence on Ultra-high Speed Information and Communication*, German Research Foundation grant DFG EXC 89. This cooperation was funded, in part, by a Royal Society Industrial Fellowship and the Royal Society Joint Project grant JP101405.

References

1. Balakrishnan, G., Sankaranarayanan, S., Ivancic, F., Gupta, A.: Refining the Control Structure of Loops using Static Analysis. In: EMSOFT 2009, pp. 49–58. ACM Press (2009)
2. Ball, T., Kupferman, O., Sagiv, M.: Leaping Loops in the Presence of Abstraction. In: Damm, W., Hermanns, H. (eds.) CAV 2007. LNCS, vol. 4590, pp. 491–503. Springer, Heidelberg (2007)
3. Ball, T., Majumdar, R., Millstein, T.D., Rajamani, S.K.: Automatic Predicate Abstraction of C Programs. In: PLDI, pp. 203–213 (2001)
4. Ball, T., Podelski, A., Rajamani, S.K.: Boolean and Cartesian Abstraction for Model Checking C Programs. In: Margaria, T., Yi, W. (eds.) TACAS 2001. LNCS, vol. 2031, pp. 268–283. Springer, Heidelberg (2001)
5. Biallas, S., Brauer, J., King, A., Kowalewski, S.: Proof Appendix for Loop Leaping with Closures. Technical Report 3-12, University of Kent, Canterbury, CT2 7NF, UK (June 2012), http://www.cs.kent.ac.uk/people/staff/amk/pubs.html
6. Brauer, J., King, A.: Transfer Function Synthesis without Quantifer Elimination. Logical Methods in Computer Science 8 (2012)
7. Brauer, J., King, A., Kriener, J.: Existential Quantification as Incremental SAT. In: Gopalakrishnan, G., Qadeer, S. (eds.) CAV 2011. LNCS, vol. 6806, pp. 191–207. Springer, Heidelberg (2011)

8. Clarke, E., Kroning, D., Sharygina, N., Yorav, K.: SATABS: SAT-Based Predicate Abstraction for ANSI-C. In: Halbwachs, N., Zuck, L.D. (eds.) TACAS 2005. LNCS, vol. 3440, pp. 570–574. Springer, Heidelberg (2005)

9. Cousot, P., Cousot, R.: Abstract Interpretation: A Unified Lattice model for Static Analysis of Programs by Construction or Approximation of Fixpoints. In: POPL, pp. 238–252. ACM Press (1977)

10. Cytron, R., Ferrante, J., Rosen, B.K., Wegman, M.N., Zadeck, F.K.: Effciently computing static single assignment form and the control dependence graph. ACM Transaction on Programming Languages and Systems, 451–590 (1991)

11. Davenport, J., Heintz, J.: Real Quantifier Elimination is Doubly Exponential. Journal of Symbolic Computation 5(1), 29–35 (1988)

12. Flanagan, C., Qadeer, S.: Predicate Abstraction for Software Verification. In: POPL, pp. 191–202 (2002)

13. Flanagan, D., Matsumoto, Y.: The Ruby Programming Language. O'Reilly (2008)

14. Graf, S., Saïdi, H.: Construction of Abstract State Graphs with PVS. In: Grumberg, O. (ed.) CAV 1997. LNCS, vol. 1254, pp. 72–83. Springer, Heidelberg (1997)

15. Gulwani, S.: Source Files and Invariants Generated (2009), http://research.microsoft.com/en-us/um/people/sumitg/benchmarks/pa.html

16. Gulwani, S.: SPEED: Symbolic Complexity Bound Analysis. In: Bouajjani, A., Maler, O. (eds.) CAV 2009. LNCS, vol. 5643, pp. 51–62. Springer, Heidelberg (2009)

17. Gulwani, S., Mehra, K.K., Chilimbi, T.M.: SPEED: precise and efficient static estimation of program computational complexity. In: POPL, pp. 127–139 (2009)

18. Gulwani, S., Srivastava, S., Venkatesan, R.: Constraint-Based Invariant Inference over Predicate Abstraction. In: Jones, N.D., Müller-Olm, M. (eds.) VMCAI 2009. LNCS, vol. 5403, pp. 120–135. Springer, Heidelberg (2009)

19. Kapur, D.: Automatically Generating Loop Invariants Using Quantifier Elimination. In: Deduction and Applications, vol. 05431. IBFI (2005)

20. Kettle, N., King, A., Strzemecki, T.: Widening ROBDDs with Prime Implicants. In: Hermanns, H. (ed.) TACAS 2006. LNCS, vol. 3920, pp. 105–119. Springer, Heidelberg (2006)

21. King, A., Søndergaard, H.: Automatic Abstraction for Congruences. In: Barthe, G., Hermenegildo, M. (eds.) VMCAI 2010. LNCS, vol. 5944, pp. 197–213. Springer, Heidelberg (2010)

22. Kroening, D., Sharygina, N., Tonetta, S., Tsitovich, A., Wintersteiger, C.M.: Loop Summarization Using Abstract Transformers. In: Cha, S(S.), Choi, J.-Y., Kim, M., Lee, I., Viswanathan, M. (eds.) ATVA 2008. LNCS, vol. 5311, pp. 111–125. Springer, Heidelberg (2008)

23. Kroening, D., Sharygina, N., Tonetta, S., Tsitovich, A., Wintersteiger, C.M.: Loopfrog: A Static Analyzer for ANSI-C Programs. In: ASE, pp. 668–670. IEEE Computer Society (2009)

24. Kroening, D., Strichman, O.: Decision Procedures. Springer (2008)

25. Monniaux, D.: Automatic Modular Abstractions for Linear Constraints. In: POPL, pp. 140–151. ACM Press (2009)

26. Monniaux, D.: Automatic Modular Abstractions for Template Numerical Constraints. Logical Methods in Computer Science 6(3) (2010)

27. Monniaux, D.: Quantifier Elimination by Lazy Model Enumeration. In: Touili, T., Cook, B., Jackson, P. (eds.) CAV 2010. LNCS, vol. 6174, pp. 585–599. Springer, Heidelberg (2010)

28. Monniaux, D., Bodin, M.: Modular Abstractions of Reactive Nodes Using Disjunctive Invariants. In: Yang, H. (ed.) APLAS 2011. LNCS, vol. 7078, pp. 19–33. Springer, Heidelberg (2011)

29. Popeea, C., Chin, W.-N.: Inferring Disjunctive Postconditions. In: Okada, M., Satoh, I. (eds.) ASIAN 2006. LNCS, vol. 4435, pp. 331–345. Springer, Heidelberg (2008)

30. Reps, T., Sagiv, M., Yorsh, G.: Symbolic Implementation of the Best Transformer. In: Steffen, B., Levi, G. (eds.) VMCAI 2004. LNCS, vol. 2937, pp. 252–266. Springer, Heidelberg (2004)

31. Rudeanu, S.: Boolean Functions and Equations. North-Holland (1974)

32. Sankaranarayanan, S., Sipma, H.B., Manna, Z.: Constraint-Based Linear-Relations Analysis. In: Giacobazzi, R. (ed.) SAS 2004. LNCS, vol. 3148, pp. 53–68. Springer, Heidelberg (2004)

33. Seghir, M.N.: A Lightweight Approach for Loop Summarization. In: Bultan, T., Hsiung, P.-A. (eds.) ATVA 2011. LNCS, vol. 6996, pp. 351–365. Springer, Heidelberg (2011)

34. Sharir, M., Pnueli, A.: Two Approaches to Interprocedural Data Flow Analysis. In: Program Flow Analysis: Theory and Applications, pp. 189–234. Prentice-Hall (1981)

35. Sharma, R., Dillig, I., Dillig, T., Aiken, A.: Simplifying Loop Invariant Generation Using Splitter Predicates. In: Gopalakrishnan, G., Qadeer, S. (eds.) CAV 2011. LNCS, vol. 6806, pp. 703–719. Springer, Heidelberg (2011)

36. Tsitovich, A., Sharygina, N., Wintersteiger, C.M., Kroening, D.: Loop Summarization and Termination Analysis. In: Abdulla, P.A., Leino, K.R.M. (eds.) TACAS 2011. LNCS, vol. 6605, pp. 81–95. Springer, Heidelberg (2011)

37. Wiedemann, D.: A computation of the eighth Dedekind number. Order 1(8), 5–6 (1991)

Path-Sensitive Backward Slicing

Joxan Jaffar[1], Vijayaraghavan Murali[1], Jorge A. Navas[2], and Andrew E. Santosa[3]

[1] National University of Singapore
[2] The University of Melbourne
[3] University of Sydney

Abstract. Backward slicers are typically path-insensitive (i.e., they ignore the evaluation of predicates at conditional branches) often producing too big slices. Though the effect of path-sensitivity is always desirable, the major challenge is that there are, in general, an exponential number of predicates to be considered. We present a *path-sensitive* backward slicer and demonstrate its practicality with real C programs. The crux of our method is a symbolic execution-based algorithm that excludes spurious dependencies lying on infeasible paths and avoids imprecise joins at merging points while reusing dependencies already computed by other paths, thus pruning the search space significantly.

1 Introduction

Weiser [19] defined the *backward slice* of a program with respect to a program location ℓ and a variable x, called the slicing criterion, as all statements of the program that might affect the value of x at ℓ, considering all possible executions of the program. Slicing was first developed to facilitate software debugging, but it has subsequently been used for performing diverse tasks such as parallelization, software testing and maintenance, program comprehension, reverse engineering, program integration and differencing, and compiler tuning.

Although static slicing has been successfully used in many software engineering applications, slices may be quite imprecise in practice - *"slices are bigger than expected and sometimes too big to be useful [2]"*. Two possible sources of imprecision are: inclusion of dependencies originated from *infeasible paths*, and merging abstract states (via join operator) along incoming edges of a *control flow merge*. A systematic way to avoid these inaccuracies is to perform path-sensitive analysis. An analysis is said to be *path-sensitive* if it keeps track of different state values based on the evaluation of the predicates at conditional branches. Although path-sensitive analyses are more precise than both flow-sensitive and context-sensitive analyses they are very rare due to the difficulty of designing efficient algorithms that can handle its combinatorial nature.

The main result of this paper is a practical path-sensitive algorithm to compute backward slices. *Symbolic execution (SE)* is the underlying technique that provides path-sensitiveness to our method. SE uses symbolic inputs rather than actual data and executes the program considering those symbolic inputs. During the execution of a path all its constraints are accumulated in a formula P. Whenever code of the form if(C) then S1 else S2 is reached the execution forks the current state and updates the two copies $P_1 \equiv P \wedge C$ and $P_2 \equiv P \wedge \neg C$, respectively. Then, it checks if either P_1 or P_2 is unsatisfiable. If yes, then the path is *infeasible* and hence, the execution stops and backtracks to

A. Miné and D. Schmidt (Eds.): SAS 2012, LNCS 7460, pp. 231–247, 2012.

the last choice point. Otherwise, the execution continues. The set of all paths explored by symbolic execution is called the *symbolic execution tree (SET)*.

Not surprisingly, a backward slicer can be easily adapted to compute slices on SETs rather than control flow graphs (CFGs) and then mapping the results from the SET to the original CFG. It is not difficult to see that the result would be a fully path-sensitive slicer. However, there are two challenges facing this idea. First, the *path explosion problem* in path-sensitive analyses that is also present in SE since the size of the SET is exponential in the number of conditional branches. The second challenge is the infinite length of symbolic paths due to unbounded loops. To overcome the latter we borrow from [17] the use of inductive invariants produced from an abstract interpreter to automatically compute *approximate loop invariants*. Because invariants are approximate our algorithm cannot be considered fully path-sensitive in the presence of loops. Nevertheless our results in Sec. 5 demonstrate that our approach can still produce significantly more precise slices than a path-insensitive slicer.

Therefore, the main technical contribution of this paper is how to tackle the path-explosion problem. We rely on the observation that *many symbolic paths have the same impact on the slicing criterion*. In other words, there is no need to explore all possible paths to produce the most precise slice. Our method takes advantage of this observation and explores the search space by dividing the problem into smaller sub-problems which are then solved recursively. Then, it is common for many sub-problems to be *"equivalent"* to others. When this is the case, those sub-problems can be skipped and the search space can be significantly reduced with exponential speedups. In order to successfully implement this search strategy we need to (a) store the solution of a sub-problem as well as the conditions that must hold for reusing that solution, (b) reuse a stored solution if a new encountered sub-problem is "equivalent" to one already solved.

Our approach symbolically executes the program in a depth-first search manner. This allows us to define a sub-problem as any subtree contained in the SET. Given a subtree, our method following Weiser's algorithm computes dependencies among variables that allow us to also infer which statements may affect the slicing criterion. The fundamental idea for reusing a solution is that when the set of feasible paths in a given subtree is *identical* to that of an already explored subtree, it is not possible to deduce more accurate dependencies from the given subtree. In such cases we can safely reuse dependencies from the explored subtree. However, this check is impractical because it is tantamount to actually exploring the given subtree, which defeats the purpose of reuse. Hence we define certain reusing conditions, the cornerstone of our algorithm, which are both sound and precise enough to allow reuse without exploring the given subtree.

First, we store a formula that succinctly captures all the infeasible paths detected during the symbolic execution of a subtree. We use efficient *interpolation* techniques to generate *interpolants* [5] for this purpose. Then, whenever a new subtree is encountered we check if the constraints accumulated *imply* in the logical sense the *interpolant* of an already solved subtree. If not, it means there are paths in the new subtree which were unexplored (infeasible) before, and so we need to explore the subtree in order to be sound. Otherwise, the set of paths in the new subtree is a *subset* of that of the explored subtree. However, being a subset is not sufficient for reuse since we need to know if they are *equivalent*, but the equivalence test, as mentioned before, is impractical. Here, we

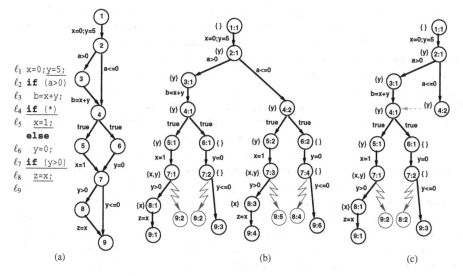

Fig. 1. (a) A program and its transition system, (b) its naive symbolic execution tree (SET) and (c) its interpolation-based SET, for slicing criterion $\langle \ell_9, \{z\} \rangle$. The final slice consists of the underlined statements.

make use of our intuition that only few paths contribute to the dependency information in every subtree. Hence, to check for equivalence of subtrees we need not check all paths, but only those few that contributed to the dependencies, what we call the *witness paths*. Now, if the previous implication succeeds we also check if the conjunctions of constraints along the witness paths of the explored subtree are satisfiable in the new subtree. If yes, we reuse dependencies. Otherwise, the equivalence test failed.

Finally, it is worth mentioning that some previous works have tackled the problem of path-sensitive backward slicing before as we will discuss them in Sec. 6. However, to the best of our knowledge either they suffer from the path-explosion problem or efficiency is achieved at the expense of losing some path-sensitiviness. One essential result of our method is that it produces *exact* slices for loop-free programs. By "exact" we mean that the algorithm guarantees to not produce dependencies from spurious[1] (i.e., non-executable) paths. In other words, it produces the *smallest* possible, *sound* slice of a loop-free program for any given slicing criterion.

2   Motivating Example

We first describe our approach through an example. Consider the program in Fig. 1(a) and assume we would like to slice it wrt location ℓ_9 and variable z. The assignment $x=0$ at ℓ_1 should not be included in the slice because any path that reaches ℓ_8 through ℓ_5 redefines x and any path that reaches ℓ_8 through ℓ_6 (without redefining x) is infeasible. Note that a path insensitive algorithm would not be able to infer this from the CFG.

---

[1] Of course, limited by theorem prover technology which decides whether a formula is unsatisfiable or not.

Fig. 1(b) shows the naive symbolic execution tree of the program. The nodes are labeled with $\ell : k$ (ℓ is a program location and k is an identifier to distinguish nodes with the same program location belonging to different symbolic paths) and edges between two locations are labeled by the intervening program operation. Solid (black) edges denote feasible transitions and zigzag (red) edges denote infeasible transitions. Each node is annotated with its *dependency set* between brackets (blue) obtained by running Weiser's [19] algorithm. Informally, a dependency set at location ℓ contains all variables that may affect the slicing criterion from any path reachable from ℓ. A statement at ℓ is included in the slice if the intersection between the dependency set and the set of variables both defined at ℓ (i.e., left-hand side of the assignment) is not empty. Note that the dependency set at 2:1 only contains y and therefore, the statement $x=0$ at ℓ_1 would not be included in the slice. Hence it is clear that the path-sensitive SET improves the accuracy of slices. The problem is that the size of the tree is exponential in the number of branches. However, consider now the tree[2] in Fig. 1(c) constructed by our method where dotted (green) edges denote reusing transitions. This tree contains the same relevant information needed to exclude $x=0$ from the slice but without some redundant paths present in Fig. 1(b). Let us see how our method generates the tree in Fig. 1(c).

Our algorithm performs symbolic execution guided by depth-first search exploring first the path $\ell_1 \cdot \ell_2 \cdot \ell_3 \cdot \ell_4 \cdot \ell_5 \cdot \ell_7 \cdot \ell_8 \cdot \ell_9$. As usual, it accumulates the constraints along the path in a formula Π, where variable redefinitions are denoted by primed versions. For the above path, $\Pi_{9:1} \equiv x = 0 \wedge y = 5 \wedge a > 0 \wedge b = x + y \wedge x' = 1 \wedge y > 0 \wedge z = x'$ is the formula built at 9:1, which is satisfiable. It then applies Weiser's algorithm to compute the dependency set at each node along the path. In addition, it also computes at each node one of the reusing conditions: the (smallest possible) set of paths from which the dependency set was generated. For example, at 7:1 the dependency set $\{x,y\}$ was obtained from the suffix path $\ell_7 \cdot \ell_8 \cdot \ell_9$, at 4:1 the dependency set $\{y\}$ was obtained from $\ell_4 \cdot \ell_5 \cdot \ell_7 \cdot \ell_8 \cdot \ell_9$, and so on. These paths are called the *witness paths* and they represent the paths along which each variable in the dependency set affects the slicing criterion.

Next our algorithm backtracks and explores the path $\ell_1 \cdot \ell_2 \cdot \ell_3 \cdot \ell_4 \cdot \ell_5 \cdot \ell_7 \cdot \ell_9$ with constraints $\Pi_{9:2} \equiv x = 0 \wedge y = 5 \wedge a > 0 \wedge b = x + y \wedge x' = 1 \wedge y \leq 0$. This formula is unsatisfiable and hence the path is infeasible. Now it generates another reusing condition: a formula called *interpolant* that captures the essence of the reason of infeasibility of the path. The main purpose of the interpolant is to exclude irrelevant facts pertaining to the infeasibility so that the reusing conditions are more likely to be reusable in future. For the above path a possible interpolant is $y = 5$ which is enough to capture its infeasibility and the infeasibility of any path that carries the constraint $y \leq 0$. In summary, our algorithm generates two kind of reusing conditions: witness paths from feasible paths and interpolants from infeasible paths.

Next it backtracks and explores the path $\ell_1 \cdot \ell_2 \cdot \ell_3 \cdot \ell_4 \cdot \ell_6 \cdot \ell_7$. At 7:2, it checks whether it can reuse the solution from 7:1 by checking first if the accumulated constraints $\Pi_{7:2} \equiv x = 0 \wedge y = 5 \wedge a > 0 \wedge b = x + y \wedge y' = 0$ *imply* the interpolant at 7:1,

---

[2] In fact, it is a Directed Acyclic Graph (DAG) due to the existence of reusing edges.

$y' = 5^3$. Since the implication fails, it has to explore 7:2 in order to be sound. The subtree after exploring this can be seen in Fig. 1(c). An important thing to note here is that while applying Weiser's algorithm, it has obtained a more accurate dependency set (empty set) at 7:2 than that which would have been obtained if it reused the solution from 7:1. Also note that at 4:1, the dependency set is still $\{y\}$ with witness path $\ell_4 \cdot \ell_5 \cdot \ell_7 \cdot \ell_8 \cdot \ell_9$ and interpolant $y = 5$.

Note what happens now. When our algorithm backtracks to explore the path $\ell_1 \cdot \ell_2 \cdot \ell_4$, it checks at 4:2 if it can reuse the solution from 4:1. This time, the accumulated constraints $x = 0 \wedge y = 5 \wedge a \leq 0$ imply the interpolant at 4:1, $y = 5$. In addition, the witness path at 4:1 is also feasible under 4:2. Hence, it simply reuses the dependency set $\{y\}$ from 4:1 both in a *sound* and *precise* manner, and backtracks without exploring 4:2. In this way, it prunes the search space while still maintaining as much as accuracy as the naive SET in Fig. 1(b). Now, when Weiser's algorithm propagates back the dependency set $\{y\}$ from 4:2, we get the dependency set $\{y\}$ again at 2:1, and the statement $x=0$ at 1:1 is not included in the slice.

3   Background

Syntax. We restrict our presentation to a simple imperative programming language where all basic operations are either assignments or assume operations, and the domain of all variables are integers. The set of all program variables is denoted by *Vars*. An *assignment* x = e corresponds to assign the evaluation of the expression e to the variable x. In the *assume* operator, assume(c), if the boolean expression c evaluates to *true*, then the program continues, otherwise it halts. The set of operations is denoted by *Ops*. We then model a program by a *transition system*. A transition system is a quadruple $\langle \Sigma, I, \longrightarrow, O \rangle$ where Σ is the set of states and $I \subseteq \Sigma$ is the set of initial states. $\longrightarrow \subseteq \Sigma \times \Sigma \times Ops$ is the transition relation that relates a state to its (possible) successors executing operations. This transition relation models the operations that are executed when control flows from one program location to another. We shall use $\ell \xrightarrow{\text{op}} \ell'$ to denote a transition relation from $\ell \in \Sigma$ to $\ell' \in \Sigma$ executing the operation op $\in Ops$. Finally, $O \subseteq \Sigma$ is the set of final states.

Symbolic Execution. A *symbolic state* υ is a triple $\langle \ell, s, \Pi \rangle$. The symbol $\ell \in \Sigma$ corresponds to the current program location (with special symbols for initial location, ℓ_{start}, and final location, ℓ_{end}). The symbolic store s is a function from program variables to terms over input symbolic variables. Each program variable is initialized to a fresh input symbolic variable. The *evaluation* $[\![c]\!]_s$ of a constraint expression c in a store s is defined recursively as usual: $[\![v]\!]_s = s(v)$ (if $c \equiv v$ is a variable), $[\![n]\!]_s = n$ (if $c \equiv n$ is an integer), $[\![e \; \text{op}_r \; e']\!]_s = [\![e]\!]_s \; \text{op}_r \; [\![e']\!]_s$ (if $c \equiv e \; \text{op}_r \; e'$ where e, e' are expressions and op_r is a relational operator $<, >, =, ! =, >=, <=$), and $[\![e \; \text{op}_a \; e']\!]_s = [\![e]\!]_s \; \text{op}_a \; [\![e']\!]_s$ (if $c \equiv e \; \text{op}_a \; e'$ where e, e' are expressions and op_a is an arithmetic operator $+, -, \times, \ldots$). Finally, Π is called *path condition* and it is a first-order formula over the symbolic inputs

---

[3] The variable versions used in the interpolants must be properly renamed to be consistent with the versions used in a formula Π. For instance, here we know that the interpolant at 7:1 must be $y' = 5$, where y' is the newest version of y used in $\Pi_{7:2}$.

and it accumulates constraints which the inputs must satisfy in order for an execution to follow the particular corresponding path. The set of first-order formulas and symbolic states are denoted by *FOL* and *SymStates*, respectively. Given a transition system $\langle \Sigma, I, \longrightarrow, O \rangle$ and a state $\upsilon \equiv \langle \ell, s, \Pi \rangle \in SymStates$, the symbolic execution of $\ell \xrightarrow{op} \ell'$ returns another symbolic state υ' defined as:

$$\upsilon' \triangleq \begin{cases} \langle \ell', s, \Pi \wedge [\![c]\!]_s \rangle & \text{if op} \equiv \text{assume(c) and } \Pi \wedge [\![c]\!]_s \text{ is satisfiable} \\ \langle \ell', s[x \mapsto [\![e]\!]_s], \Pi \rangle & \text{if op} \equiv x = e \end{cases} \quad (1)$$

Note that Eq. (1) queries a *theorem prover* for satisfiability checking on the path condition. We assume the theorem prover is sound but not necessarily complete. That is, the theorem prover must say a formula is unsatisfiable only if it is indeed so.

Abusing notation, given a symbolic state $\upsilon \equiv \langle \ell, s, \Pi \rangle$ we define $[\![\upsilon]\!] : SymStates \to FOL$ as the formula $(\bigwedge_{v \in Vars} [\![v]\!]_s) \wedge \Pi$ where *Vars* is the set of program variables.

A *symbolic path* $\pi \equiv \upsilon_0 \cdot \upsilon_1 \cdot \ldots \cdot \upsilon_n$ is a sequence of symbolic states such that $\forall i \bullet 1 \le i \le n$ the state υ_i is a *successor* of υ_{i-1}. A symbolic state $\upsilon' \equiv \langle \ell', \cdot, \cdot \rangle$ is a successor of another $\upsilon \equiv \langle \ell, \cdot, \cdot \rangle$ if there exists a transition relation $\ell \xrightarrow{op} \ell'$. A path $\pi \equiv \upsilon_0 \cdot \upsilon_1 \cdot \ldots \cdot \upsilon_n$ is *feasible* if $\upsilon_n \equiv \langle \ell, s, \Pi \rangle$ such that $[\![\Pi]\!]_s$ is satisfiable. If $\ell \in O$ and υ_n is feasible then υ_n is called *terminal* state. Otherwise, if $[\![\Pi]\!]_s$ is unsatisfiable the path is called *infeasible* and υ_n is called an *infeasible* state. If there exists a feasible path $\pi \equiv \upsilon_0 \cdot \upsilon_1 \cdot \ldots \cdot \upsilon_n$ then we say υ_k $(0 \le k \le n)$ is *reachable* from υ_0 in k *steps*. We say υ'' is reachable from υ if it is reachable from υ in some number of steps.

A *symbolic execution tree* contains all the execution paths explored during the symbolic execution of a transition system by triggering Eq. (1). The nodes represent symbolic states and the arcs represent transitions between states.

Program Slicing. The *backward slice* of a program wrt a program location ℓ and a set of variables $V \subseteq Vars$, called the *slicing criterion* $\langle \ell, V \rangle$, is all statements of the program that might affect the values of V at ℓ.[4] We follow the dataflow approach described by Weiser [19] reformulated as an abstract domain $\mathcal{D} \equiv \{\bot\} \cup \mathcal{P}(Vars)$ (where $\mathcal{P}(Vars)$ is the powerset of program variables) with a lattice structure $\langle \sqsubseteq, \bot, \sqcup, \sqcap, \top \rangle$, such that $\sqsubseteq \equiv \subseteq$, $\sqcup \equiv \cup$, and $\sqcap \equiv \cap$ are conveniently lifted to consider the element $\bot$.

We say $\sigma_\ell \in \mathcal{D}$ is the approximate set of variables at location ℓ that may affect the slicing criterion. We will abuse notation to denote the dependencies associated to a symbolic state υ also as σ_υ. *Backward data dependencies* can be formulated using this set, defining two kinds of dataflow information. Given a transition relation $\ell \xrightarrow{op} \ell'$ we define *def*(op) and *use*(op) as the sets of variables altered and used during the execution of op, respectively. Then,

$$\sigma_\ell \triangleq \begin{cases} (\sigma_{\ell'} \setminus def(\text{op})) \cup use(\text{op}) & \text{if } \sigma_{\ell'} \cap def(\text{op}) \neq \emptyset \\ \sigma_{\ell'} & \text{otherwise} \end{cases} \quad (2)$$

---

[4] W.l.o.g., we assume in this paper a single slicing criterion at ℓ_{end}.

where $\sigma_{\ell'} = V$ if $\ell' = \ell_{end}$. We say a transition relation $\ell \xrightarrow{op} \ell'$ where $op \equiv x = e$ is included in the slice if:

$$\sigma_{\ell'} \cap def(op) \neq \emptyset \qquad (3)$$

Backward control dependencies can also affect the slicing criterion. A transition relation $\delta \equiv \ell \xrightarrow{op} \ell'$ where $op \equiv \mathsf{assume}(c)$ is included in the slice if any transition under the range of influence of δ (any path between δ and its *nearest postdominator* [19] in the transition system) is included in the slice, and   (4)

$$\sigma_{\ell} \triangleq \sigma_{\ell'} \cup use(op) \qquad (5)$$

Finally, a function $\widehat{pre}_{\mathcal{D}}(\sigma_{\ell}, op)$ that returns the *pre-state* after executing backwards the operation op with the *post-state* σ_{ℓ} is defined using Eqs. (2), (3), (4), and (5).

4   Algorithm

A path-sensitive slicing algorithm over a symbolic execution tree (SET) can be defined as an *annotation* process which labels each symbolic state $\upsilon \equiv \langle \ell, \cdot, \cdot \rangle$ with $\sigma_{\ell} \in \mathcal{D}$ by computing a fixpoint (later formalized) over the tree, using Eqs. (2) and (5) described in Sec. 3. In an interleaved process, the final SET is obtained through Eqs. (3) and (4). Since the SET may have multiple instances of the same transition relation, we say that a transition relation is included in the final slice if at least one of its instances is included in the slice on the SET. It is easy to see that the path-sensitiveness comes from how symbolic execution builds the tree since no dependencies from a non-executable path can be considered.

Our algorithm performs symbolic execution in a depth-first search manner excluding all infeasible paths. Whenever the forward traversal of a path finishes due to a (a) terminal state, (b) infeasible state, or (c) reusing state (i.e., a state reusing a solution from another state), the algorithm halts and backtracks to the next path. During this backtracking each symbolic state υ is labelled with its *solution*, i.e., the set of variables σ_{υ} at υ that may affect the slicing criterion. Furthermore, the reusing conditions are computed at each state for future use. We first introduce formally the two key concepts which will decide whether a solution can be reused or not.

Definition 1 (Interpolant). *Given two first order logic (FOL) formulas A and B such that $A \wedge B$ is false a Craig interpolant [5] wrt A is another FOL formula $\overline{\Psi}$ such that (a) $A \models \overline{\Psi}$, (b) $\overline{\Psi} \wedge B$ is false, and (c) $\overline{\Psi}$ is formed using common variables of A and B.*

Interpolation allows us to remove irrelevant facts from A without affecting the unsatisfiability of $A \wedge B$. It is worth mentioning that efficient interpolation algorithms exist for quantifier-free fragments of theories such as linear real/integer arithmetic, uninterpreted functions, pointers and arrays (e.g., [4]) where interpolants can be extracted from the refutation proof in linear time on the size of the proof.

Definition 2 (Witness Paths and Formulas). *Given a symbolic state $\upsilon \equiv \langle \ell, \cdot, \cdot \rangle$ annotated with the set of variables σ_{υ} that affect the slicing criterion at ℓ_{end}, a witness path for a variable $v \in \sigma_{\upsilon}$ is a symbolic path $\pi \equiv \langle \ell, \cdot, \cdot \rangle \cdot \ldots \cdot \langle \ell_{end}, \cdot, \Pi_{end} \rangle$ with the final symbolic state $\upsilon' \equiv \langle \ell_{end}, \cdot, \Pi_{end} \rangle$ such that $[\![\upsilon']\!]$ is satisfiable (i.e., π is feasible). We call $[\![\upsilon']\!]$ the witness formula of v, denoted ω_v.*

- $\sqcup : \mathcal{D}^{\omega} \times \mathcal{D}^{\omega} \to \mathcal{D}^{\omega}$

$$\sigma^{\omega}{}_1 \sqcup \sigma^{\omega}{}_2 \triangleq \sigma^{\omega}{}_1 \cup \sigma^{\omega}{}_2$$

- $\sqsubseteq : \mathcal{D}^{\omega} \times \mathcal{D}^{\omega} \to Bool$

$$\sigma^{\omega}{}_1 \sqsubseteq \sigma^{\omega}{}_2 \text{ if and only if } \sigma^{\omega}{}_1 \subseteq \sigma^{\omega}{}_2$$

- $\widehat{pre} : \mathcal{D}^{\omega} \times (\Sigma \times \Sigma \times Ops) \times (Vars \to SymVars) \to \mathcal{D}^{\omega}.$

$$\widehat{pre}(\sigma^{\omega\prime}, \ell \xrightarrow{\text{op}} \ell', s) \triangleq \begin{cases} \textbf{let } \sigma^{\omega} = \widehat{pre}\_aux(\sigma^{\omega\prime}, \ell \xrightarrow{\text{op}} \ell', s) \\ \quad \textbf{foreach } \langle x, \omega_x \rangle \in \sigma^{\omega}, \langle x, \omega_{x'} \rangle \in \sigma^{\omega} \\ \quad \sigma^{\omega} = \sigma^{\omega} \setminus \{ \langle x, \omega_x \rangle, \langle x, \omega_{x'} \rangle \} \\ \quad \textbf{if } \omega_x \models \omega_{x'} \textbf{ then } \sigma^{\omega} = \sigma^{\omega} \cup \{ \langle x, \omega_{x'} \rangle \} \\ \quad \textbf{else } \sigma^{\omega} = \sigma^{\omega} \cup \{ \langle x, \omega_x \rangle \} \\ \quad \textbf{if } (\sigma^{\omega} \cap def(\text{op}) \textbf{ or } \mathsf{INFL}(\ell \to \ell') \cap S \neq \emptyset) \textbf{ then} \\ \quad \quad S = S \cup \{ \ell \to \ell' \} \\ \textbf{in } \sigma^{\omega} \end{cases}$$

where:

$$\widehat{pre}\_aux(\sigma^{\omega\prime}, \ell \xrightarrow{\text{op}} \ell', s) \triangleq$$
$$\begin{cases} \{ \langle x, \omega_x \wedge [\![y = e]\!]s \rangle \mid \langle x, \omega_x \rangle \in \sigma^{\omega\prime}, \text{op} \equiv y = e, x \notin def(\text{op}) \} \cup \\ \{ \langle v, \omega_x \wedge [\![y = e]\!]s \rangle \mid \langle x, \omega_x \rangle \in \sigma^{\omega\prime}, \text{op} \equiv y = e, x \in def(\text{op}), v \in use(\text{op}) \} \cup \\ \{ \langle x, \omega_x \wedge [\![c]\!]s \rangle \mid \langle x, \omega_x \rangle \in \sigma^{\omega\prime}, \text{op} \equiv \mathsf{assume}(c) \} \cup \\ \{ \langle x, [\![\Pi_{\pi}]\!]s \wedge [\![c]\!]s \rangle \mid \langle x, \cdot \rangle \notin \sigma^{\omega\prime}, \text{op} \equiv \mathsf{assume}(c), x \in use(\text{op}), \\ \quad \mathsf{INFL}(\ell \to \ell') \cap S \neq \emptyset, \exists \, \pi \equiv \ell' \cdot \ldots \cdot \ell_{end} \} \end{cases}$$

Fig. 2. Main Abstract Operations for $\mathcal{D}^{\omega}$

Intuitively, a witness path for a variable at a node is a path below the node along which the variable affects the slicing criterion at the end. A witness formula represents a condition sufficient for the variable to affect the slicing criterion along the witness path.

Prior to establishing the reusing conditions, we augment the abstract domain $\mathcal{D}$ to accommodate the witness formulas. Here, and in the rest of the paper, we will refer to the term "dependency" as the set of variables that may affect the slicing criterion together with their witnesses.

Definition 3 ($\mathcal{D}^{\omega}$). *We define a new abstract domain $\mathcal{D}^{\omega}$ as a lattice $\langle \sqsubseteq, \bot, \sqcup, \top \rangle$ such that $\mathcal{D}^{\omega} \triangleq \{\bot\} \cup \mathcal{P}(Vars \times FOL)$ (i.e., set of pairs of the form $\langle x, \omega_x \rangle$ where x is a variable and ω_x is its witness formula) and abstract operations described in Fig. 2.*[5]

Note that the witness formulas can be obtained only from (feasible) paths in the program. Therefore, the number of witness formulas is always finite. As we will see later, even with loops, the size of each witness formula is also finite because we make the symbolic subtree of the loop finite. That is, we perform symbolic execution on a finite

---

[5] For lack of space, trivial treatment of the element $\bot$ is omitted from operations in Fig. 2.

program once loop invariants are given. This ensures that the abstract domain $\mathcal{D}^{\omega}$ is finite and hence, termination is guaranteed for any fixpoint computation based on it.

In Fig. 2, the operator $\sqcup$ computes the least upper bound of the abstract states by simply applying the set union of the two set of states. The operator $\sqsubseteq$ simply tests whether one set is a subset of the other. $\widehat{pre}$ is a bit more elaborated but basically consists of the Eqs. (2), (3), (4), and (5) defined in Sec. 3 extended with witnesses formulas. We assume here and in the algorithm in Fig. 3 that $\widehat{pre}$ accesses **S** which is the set of transitions included in the slice so far. In function $\widehat{pre}\_aux$, there are four cases to handle different kinds of statements and dependencies:

- In the first two cases, if the operation is an assignment, the dependencies are propagated from the *defined* to the *used* variables and any dependency from a variable not *defined* is kept. In these cases, the pre-state witness formula is the conjunction of the post-state witness formula with the corresponding statement.
- In the third case, if the operation is an assume, any *used* variable is preserved, with its pre-state witness formula being the conjunction of the post-state witness formula and the corresponding guard.
- In the last case, for any variable x occurring in an assume statement without any dependency, if any transition under the range of influence [19] (computed by INFL) of the assume is already in the slice, then x is added (due to control dependency) and its witness formula is the conjunction of the guard and the path condition of any (feasible) path from the assume statement that leads to the end of the program.

In addition, in function $\widehat{pre}$ whenever two pairs from the set of dependencies computed by $\widehat{pre}\_aux$ refer to the same variable, we use an entailment test to choose the one with the weaker witness formula (which is more likely to be reused). In practice, the entailment test can be skipped by choosing arbitrarily one. Finally, a transition is included in the slice if one of the Eqs. (3) and (4) holds.

Definition 4 (Reusing Conditions). *Given a current symbolic state $\upsilon \equiv \langle \ell, \cdot, \Pi \rangle$ and an already solved symbolic state $\upsilon' \equiv \langle \ell, \cdot, \cdot \rangle$ such that $\overline{\Psi}$ is the interpolant generated for υ' and σ^{ω} are the dependencies together with their attached witnesses at υ', we say υ is equivalent to υ' (or υ can reuse the solution at υ') if the following conditions hold:*

$$(a)\ \ [\![\upsilon]\!] \models \overline{\Psi} \qquad (b)\ \ \forall \langle x, \cdot \rangle \in \sigma^{\omega} \bullet \exists \langle x, \omega_x \rangle \in \sigma^{\omega} \ such\ that\ [\![\upsilon]\!] \wedge \omega_x \ is\ satisfiable \qquad (6)$$

The condition (a) affects *soundness* and it ensures that the set of symbolic paths reachable from υ must be a subset of those from υ'. The condition (b) is the witness check which essentially states that for each variable x in the dependency set at υ', there must be at least one witness path with formula ω_x that is feasible from υ. This affects *accuracy* and ensures that the reuse of dependencies does not incur any loss of precision.

We now describe in detail the main features of our algorithm defined by the function BackwardDeps$_V$ in Fig. 3. The main purpose of BackwardDeps$_V$ is to keep track of the *backward dependencies* between the program variables and the slicing criterion by inferring for each state the set of variables that may affect the slicing criterion. From these dependencies it is straightforward to obtain the slice of the program as explained

BackwardDeps$_V$ ($\upsilon \equiv \langle \ell, s, \Pi \rangle, \sigma^\omega$)

1:    change = *false*
2:    **if** INFEASIBLE(υ) **then** $\langle \overline{\Psi}, \sigma^\omega \rangle = \langle false, \emptyset \rangle$ and **goto** 12
3:    **if** TERMINAL(υ) **then** $\langle \overline{\Psi}, \sigma^\omega \rangle = \langle true, \{ \langle v, true \rangle \mid v \in V \} \rangle$ and **goto** 12
4:    **if** $\exists \upsilon' \equiv \langle \ell, s, \cdot \rangle$ labelled with $\langle \overline{\Psi}, \sigma^\omega \rangle$ such that REUSE(υ, υ') **then goto** 12

5:    **if** ℓ is the header of a loop **then**
6:    $\overline{\upsilon}$ = invariant($\upsilon, \ell \to \ldots \to \ell$)
7:    $\langle \overline{\Psi}, \sigma^\omega, change \rangle$ = UnwindTree$_V$($\overline{\upsilon}, \sigma^\omega$) and **goto** 12
8:    **if** $\exists \ell'$ such that $\ell \to \ell'$ is a backedge of a loop **then**
9:    $\langle \cdot, \cdot, \overline{\Pi} \rangle$ = invariant($\upsilon, \ell' \to \ldots \to \ell$)
10:    $\langle \overline{\Psi}, \sigma^\omega \rangle = \langle \overline{\Pi}, \sigma^\omega \rangle$ and **goto** 12

11:    $\langle \overline{\Psi}, \sigma^\omega, change \rangle$ = UnwindTree$_V$(υ, σ^ω)
12:    let υ be annotated with $\langle \cdot, \sigma^\omega_{old} \rangle$
13:    label υ with $\langle \overline{\Psi}, \sigma^\omega \rangle$ and **return** $\langle \overline{\Psi}, \sigma^\omega, change \lor \neg(\sigma^\omega_{old} \sqsubseteq_{\mathcal{D}^\omega} \sigma^\omega) \rangle$

UnwindTree$_V$ ($\upsilon \equiv \langle \ell, s, \Pi \rangle, \sigma^\omega_{in}$)

1:    $\overline{\Psi} = true$, $\sigma^\omega = \sigma^\omega_{in}$, change = *false*
2:    **foreach** transition relation $\ell \xrightarrow{op} \ell'$

3:

$$\upsilon' \triangleq \begin{cases} \langle \ell', s, \Pi \land [\![c]\!]s \rangle & \text{if } op \equiv \text{assume}(c) \\ \langle \ell', s[x \mapsto S_x], \Pi \land [\![x = e]\!]s \rangle & \text{if } op \equiv x = e \text{ and } S_x \text{ fresh variable} \end{cases}$$

4:    $\langle \overline{\Psi}', \sigma^{\omega'}, c \rangle$ = BackwardDeps$_V$($\upsilon', \sigma^\omega_{in}$)
5:    $\overline{\Psi} = \overline{\Psi} \land \widehat{wlp}(op, \overline{\Psi}')$
6:    $\sigma^\omega = \sigma^\omega \sqcup_{\mathcal{D}^\omega} \widehat{pre}_{\mathcal{D}^\omega}(\sigma^{\omega'}, op, s)$
7:    change = change $\lor$ c
8:    **return** $\langle \overline{\Psi}, \sigma^\omega, change \rangle$

BackwardDepsLoop$_V$ (υ, σ^ω)

1:    $\sigma^{\omega'} = \sigma^\omega$, change = *false*
2:    **do** $\langle \cdot, \sigma^{\omega'}, change \rangle$ = BackwardDeps$_V$($\upsilon, \sigma^{\omega'}$) **while** (change)

Fig. 3. Path-Sensitive Backward Slicing Analysis

at the beginning of this section. For clarity of presentation, let us omit for now the content of the *grey* boxes and assume programs do not have loops, which we will come to later.

BackwardDeps$_V$: *SymStates* $\times \mathcal{D}^\omega \to FOL \times \mathcal{D}^\omega \times Bool$ requires the program to have been translated to a transition system $\langle \Sigma, I, \longrightarrow, O \rangle$ and taking an initial symbolic state $\upsilon \equiv \langle \ell \in I, \varepsilon, true \rangle$ and an initially empty σ^ω. V is the set of variables of the slicing criterion. The set of transitions included in the slice, **S**, is also empty. Recall that **S** is only modified by $\widehat{pre}_{\mathcal{D}^\omega}$, and hence, we omit it from the description of the algorithm defining it as a global variable. The returned value is a triple with the interpolant, dependencies (i.e., reusing conditions and solution) and a boolean flag representing whether any change occurred in a dependency set at any symbolic state during the algorithm's backward traversal (this is used mainly to handle loops later). The actual object of interest computed by the algorithm is the set of transitions S included in the slice.

BackwardDeps$_V$ implements a recursive algorithm whose objective is to generate a finite complete SET while reusing solutions whenever possible to avoid path explosion. Line 1 initializes the (local) variable change to *false*, which will be updated later. Next, the three base cases for symbolic states are handled - infeasible, terminal, and reuse:

- In line 2, the function INFEASIBLE($\langle \cdot, \cdot, \Pi \rangle$) checks whether Π is satisfiable. If not, the symbolic execution detects an infeasible path and halts, excluding any dependency which would have been inferred from the non-executable path. In addition, it produces an interpolant from Π and *false*, namely $\overline{\Psi} \equiv false$, which generalizes the current path condition ($\Pi \models \overline{\Psi}$ and $\overline{\Psi}$ is *false*). Since the path is not executable there is no variable that may affect the slicing criterion and hence, the set of dependencies returned is empty.

- In line 3, the function TERMINAL($\langle \ell, \cdot, \cdot \rangle$) checks if the symbolic state is a terminal node by checking if $\ell = \ell_{end}$. If yes, the execution has reached the end of a path. Since the path is feasible, it can be fully generalized returning the interpolant $\overline{\Psi} \equiv true$. Since ℓ is a terminal node, the set of dependencies is the set of variables in the slicing criterion, V. The witness formula for each variable from V is initially *true*.

- In line 4 the algorithm searches for another state υ' whose dependencies can be reused by the current state υ so that the symbolic execution can be stopped. For this, the function REUSE(υ, υ') tests the reusing conditions in Eq. 6. If the test holds, the state υ can reuse the dependencies computed by υ'. Note that the amount of search space pruned by our method depends on how often this case is triggered.

If all three base cases are not applicable, the algorithm unwinds the execution tree by calling the procedure UnwindTree$_V$ at line 11. UnwindTree$_V$, at line 3, executes one symbolic step [6] and calls the main procedure BackwardDeps$_V$ with the successor state (line 4). After the call, the two key remaining steps are to compute:

- the interpolant $\overline{\Psi}$ (UnwindTree$_V$ line 5) that generalizes the symbolic execution tree below υ while preserving its infeasible paths. The procedure $\widehat{wlp} : Ops \times FOL \rightarrow FOL$ ideally computes the *weakest liberal precondition (wlp)* [7] which is the weakest formula on the initial state ensuring the execution of op results in a final state $\overline{\Psi}'$. In practice, we approximate *wlp* following the algorithm described in [14].[7] The interpolant $\overline{\Psi}$ is an FOL formula consisting of the conjunction of the result of $\widehat{wlp}$ on each child's interpolant.

---

[6] Note that the rule described in line 3 is slightly different from the one described in Sec. 3 because no consistency check is performed. Instead, the consistency check is postponed and done by the first base case at line 2.

[7] Current SMT solvers (e.g. [4]) can produce (very efficiently) interpolants at each location along a path from a single query which can be used for approximating wlp's. However, those interpolants are often stronger than those generated by [14].

- the solution, σ^ω, for the current state υ at line 6 which is computed by executing $\widehat{pre}_{\mathcal{D}^\omega}$ on each child's solution and then combining all solutions using $\sqcup_{\mathcal{D}^\omega}$.

In addition, at line 7 it also records changes in any child's symbolic state (if any) and then returns a triple in the same format as BackwardDeps$_V$'s return value. In Backward-Deps$_V$, line 12 updates change to *true* if either it was set to *true* in UnwindTree$_V$ at line 11 or the current symbolic state is about to be updated with a more precise solution than that it already has. The final operation before returning from BackwardDeps$_V$ is to label the state υ with the reusing conditions and solution (line 13).

Now we continue describing our algorithm by discussing how it handles loops. The main issue is to produce a finite symbolic execution tree on which a fixpoint of the dependencies can be computed.

For this, the algorithm in Fig. 3 takes an annotated transition system in which program points are labelled with inductive invariants inferred automatically by an abstract interpreter using an abstract domain such as *octagons* or *polyhedra* (we borrow the ideas presented in [17] for this purpose). We assume the abstract interpreter provides a function getAssrt which, given a program location ℓ and a symbolic store s, returns an assertion in the form of an FOL formula renamed using s, which holds at ℓ. Note that when applied at loop headers, getAssrt will return a loop invariant. However, we would like to strengthen it using the constraints propagated from the symbolic execution. The function invariant performs this task as follows:

$$\text{invariant}(\langle \ell, s, \Pi \rangle, \ell_1 \to \ell_n) \triangleq \begin{cases} \mathbf{let}\ s' = \text{havoc}(s, \text{modifies}(\ell_1 \to \ell_n)) \\ \quad \overline{\Pi} = \text{getAssrt}(\ell, s') \wedge \Pi \\ \mathbf{in}\ \langle \ell, s', \overline{\Pi} \rangle \end{cases}$$

$\text{havoc}(s, \textit{Vars}) \triangleq \forall v \in \textit{Vars} \bullet s[v \mapsto z]$
where z is a fresh variable (implicitly $\exists$-quantified).

$\text{modifies}(\ell_1 \to \ldots \to \ell_n)$ takes a sequence of transitions and returns the set of variables that may be modified during its symbolic execution.

Intuitively, invariant clears the symbolic store of all variables modified in the loop (using the havoc function) and then enhances the path condition Π of the symbolic state with the invariants from the abstract interpreter.

Let us now explain the *grey* boxes in Fig. 3. Lines 5-7 in BackwardDeps$_V$ cover the case when a loop header has been encountered. The objective is to abstract the current symbolic state by using the loop invariant obtained from the abstract interpreter. The algorithm calls the function invariant (at line 6) with the transitions in the loop so as to obtain a copy of the current symbolic state annotated with the approximate loop invariant in its path condition. At line 7, the UnwindTree$_V$ procedure is called on the resulting abstracted symbolic state to explore the symbolic subtree associated with the loop.

If the symbolic execution encounters a loop backedge (lines 8-10) from ℓ to ℓ' it halts and backtracks. The reason is that the loop header at ℓ' has already been symbolically executed with a loop invariant. Hence there is no need to continue the loop since the invariant ensures that no new feasible paths will be encountered if it is explored again. This is our basic mechanism to make the symbolic execution of the loop finite.

Finally, the main algorithm to handle loops, BackwardDepsLoop$_V$, makes calls to the function BackwardDeps$_V$ until there is no change detected in the symbolic state of any program point. We present it in its simplest form, but it can be easily optimized to call BackwardDeps$_V$ only with those loop transitions affected by a change.

5 Results

We implemented a proof-of-concept prototype as an extension to TRACER [14]. TRACER is a software verifier for C programs from which we used mainly its symbolic execution interpreter and its capabilities for computing interpolants from infeasible paths.

Our prototype augmented TRACER in different ways. Given an operation that involves pointers our prototype updated the sets *def* and *use* to accommodate the points-to information correctly. For instance, given the statement *p =*q the set *def* contains everything that might be pointed to by p and the set *use* includes everything that might be pointed by q. Regarding loops, programs were first annotated with loop invariants[8] provided by the abstract intepreter InterProc [15] ensuring that symbolic execution is finite. Then, we implemented a fixpoint algorithm operating over symbolic execution trees that computes dependencies among variables following [19]. Witness paths were represented as formulas (conjunction of the constraints along the path) and stored efficiently in order to increase sharing among them. Functions were inlined and external functions were modeled as having no side effects and returning an unknown value.[9]

We used several instrumented device driver programs previously used as software model checking benchmarks: cdaudio, diskperf, floppy, and serial. In addition, we also considered mpeg, the mpeg-1 algorithm for compressing video, and fcron.2.9.5, a cron daemon. For the slicing criterion we consider variables that may be of interest during debugging tasks. For the instrumented software model checking programs, we choose as the slicing criterion the set of variables that appear in the safety conditions used for their verification in [10]. In the case of mpeg we choose a variable that contains the type of the video to be compressed. Finally, in fcron.2.9.5 we choose all the file descriptors opened and closed by the application.

Table 1 compares our path-sensitive slicer (columns labelled with Path-Sens) against the same slicer but without path-sensitivity (labelled with Path-Insens). Path-insensitivity is achieved by the following modifications in our slicer: (1) considering all paths as feasible, and (2) always forcing reuse. These changes have the same effect as always merging the abstract states along incoming edges in a control-flow merging node. In other words, they mimic running a path-insensitive slicer on the original CFG. We could have used a faster off-the-shelf path-insensitive program slicer (using e.g., [11]), however, our objective here is to isolate the impact of path-sensitivity and hence, we decided to perform the comparison on a common platform to produce the fairest results.

---

[8] We tried several numerical abstract domains with different tradeoffs between performance and precision (e.g., octagons and polyhedra) but obtained same results. As a limitation, those invariants cannot express properties about heap-allocated data structures.

[9] It is well-known that function inlining can be very inefficient and in fact, not possible in the presence of recursive functions. However, performing an interprocedural path-sensitive analysis is beyond the scope of this paper.

Table 1. Results on Intel 3.2Gz 2Gb evaluating path-sensitiveness

Program	LOC	Path-Insens		Path-Sens	
		Size Red	Time	Size Red	Time
mpeg	5K	4%	21s	8%	628s
diskperf	6K	32%	2s	57%	94s
floppy	8K	36%	9s	47%	263s
cdaudio	9K	23%	10s	52%	301s
serial	12K	39%	16s	50%	395s
fcron.2.9.5	12K	42%	32s	61%	832s
Mean		23%	15s	38%	418s

The column LOC represents the number of lines of program without comments. The column Size Red shows the reduction in slice size (in %) wrt the original program size. The reduction size is computed using the formula $(1 - \frac{size\ of\ slice}{size\ of\ original}) \times 100$. By *size* we mean all executable statements in the program, excluding type declarations, unused functions, comments, and blank lines. A minor complication here is that the SET may contain multiple *instances* of program points in the CFG, as can be seen in Fig. 1(c). To compare the reduction in slice sizes fairly, we use the rule mentioned at the beginning of Sec. 4 to compute slices: a transition in the original CFG is included in the slice if any of its instances in the SET is included in the slice. The column Time reflects the running time of the analysis in seconds excluding the external abstract interpreter. Finally, we summarize in row Mean the numbers of columns Size Red and Time by computing their *geometric* and *arithmetic* mean, respectively.

Our experimental evaluation shows that our path-sensitive slicer improves significantly in terms of size reduction over its path-insensitive counterpart. Roughly, slices produced by Path-Sens are 38% smaller than the original programs while only 23% in the case of Path-Insens. The mpeg program is an exception since the size of the slices in both Path-Insens and Path-Sens are quite big (i.e., very small reduction). The reason is that in mpeg all the computations depend on the type of video to be compressed which is our slicing criterion. On the other hand, the running times of Path-Sens (with a mean of 418 secs) are reasonable considering the size of the programs and the current status of our prototype implementation which has significant room for improvement. The analysis of mpeg is especially slow and it is due to the existence of many nested loops which are not supported efficiently by our naive fixpoint implementation.

To emphasize the importance of our reuse technique based on interpolation and witnesses we experimented with two variants of our algorithm. We first ran our path-sensitive slicer without reuse which mimics *Conditioned Slicing* [3] (see Sec. 6 for more details). Our second variant replaced interpolants with a syntactic method avoiding using the solver. Given formulas A and B (the inputs to the interpolation algorithm) the reusing condition is a formula formed from A such that any constraint *syntactically independent* from B is removed (taking into account the transitive closure of constraint dependencies). Then, the REUSE procedure can be implemented as a subset operation rather than an entailment test. Interestingly, neither of these two variants was able to finish with any program after a timeout of 1 hour or memory consumption of 2.5 Gb.

6 Related Work

Static slicing remains a very active area of research. We limit our discussion to the most relevant works that take into account path-sensitiveness. We also discuss pruning techniques that might have influenced our work.

Fully Path-Sensitive Methods. Conditioned slicing [3] also performs symbolic execution excluding infeasible paths before applying a static slicing algorithm, and hence it is fully path-sensitive (for loop-free programs) similar to us. However, even efficient implementations (e.g., [6]) still perform full path enumeration and essentially explore the search space of the naive SET suffering from the path explosion problem.

Partially Path-Sensitive Methods. A more scalable but not fully path-sensitive approach is described by Snelting et al. [18]. They compute the dependency between two program points y and x using the Program Dependence Graph (PDG) [11] and apply the following rule to remove spurious dependencies: $I(y,x) \Rightarrow \exists \bar{v} : PC(y,x)$, where $I(y,x)$ stands for y *influences* x (i.e., there is a dependency at x on y), $\bar{v}$ is some assignment of values to program variables and $PC(y,x)$ is the path condition from y to x. Essentially it means that if the path condition from y to x is found to be unsatisfiable, then there is definitely no influence from y to x. If there are multiple paths between two points, the path condition is computed as a disjunction of each path.

For the program in Fig. 1(a), Snelting et al. would proceed as follows. In the PDG there will be a dependency edge from ℓ_8 to ℓ_1, hence they would check to see if the path condition $PC(1,8)$ is unsatisfiable. First they calculate the path condition from ℓ_4 to ℓ_8 as $PC(4,8) \equiv (x = 1 \wedge y > 0 \wedge z = x) \vee (y = 0 \wedge y > 0 \wedge z = x) \equiv (x = 1 \wedge y > 0 \wedge z = x)$. Now they use this to calculate $PC(1,8) \equiv (x = 0 \wedge y = 5 \wedge ((a > 0 \wedge b = x+y \wedge PC(4,8)) \vee (a \le 0 \wedge PC(4,8))))$[10], which is not unsatisfiable. Hence the statement $x{=}0$ at ℓ_1 will be included in the slice. The fundamental reason for this is that for them, path conditions are only necessary and not sufficient, so false alarms in examples such as the above are possible. An important consequence of this is the fact that even for loop-free programs, their algorithm cannot be considered "exact" in the sense described at the end in Sec. 1. However, our algorithm guarantees to produce no false alarms for such programs.

Another slicer that takes into account path-sensitiveness up to some degree is Constrained slicing [8] which uses *graph rewriting* as the underlying technique. As the graph is rewritten, modified terms are tracked. As a result, terms in the final graph can be tracked back to terms in the original graph identifying the slice of the original graph that produced the particular term in the final graph. The rules described in [8] mainly perform constant propagation and dead code detection but not systematic detection of infeasible paths. More importantly, [8] does not define rules to prune the search space.

Interpolation and SAT. Interpolation has been used in software verification (e.g., [1,10,16,12,14]) as a technique to eliminate facts which are irrelevant to the proof. Similarly, SAT can explain and record failures in order to perform conflict analysis. By traversing a reverse implication graph it can build a *nogood* or conflict clause which

---

[10] We have simplified this formula since Snelting et al. use the SSA form of the program and add constraints for Φ-functions, but the essential idea is the same.

will avoid making the same wrong decision. Our algorithm has in common the use of interpolation that can be seen also as a form of *nogood learning* in order to prune the search space. But this is where the similarity ends. A fundamental distinction is that in program verification there is no solution (e.g., backward dependencies) to compute/discover and hence, there is no notion of reuse and the concept of witness paths does not exist. The work of [9] uses interpolation-based model checking techniques to improve the precision of dataflow analysis but still for the purpose of proving a safety property.

Finally, a recent work of the authors [13] has been a clear inspiration for this paper. [13] uses interpolation and witnesses as well to solve not an analysis problem, but rather, a *combinatorial optimization* problem: the Resource-Constrained Shortest Path (RCSP) problem. Moreover, there are other significant differences. First, [13] is totally defined in a finite setting. Second, [13] considers only the narrower problem of extraction of bounds of variables for loop-free programs while we present here a general-purpose program analysis like slicing. Third, this paper presents an implementation and demonstrates its practicality on real programs.

7   Conclusions

We presented a fully path-sensitive backward slicer limited only by solving capabilities and loop invariant technology. The main result is a symbolic execution algorithm which avoids imprecision due to infeasible paths and joins at merging points and halts execution of a path if certain conditions hold while reusing dependencies from already explored paths. The conditions are based on a notion of interpolation and witness paths with an aim to detect "a priori" whether the exploration of a path could improve the accuracy of the dependencies computed so far by other paths. We demonstrated the practicality of the approach with real medium-size C programs.

Finally, although this paper targets slicing, our approach can be generalized and applied to other backward program analyses (e.g., Live Variable, Very Busy Expressions, Worst-Case Execution Time analysis, etc.) providing them path-sensitiveness.

References

1. Ball, T., Majumdar, R., Millstein, T., Rajamani, S.K.: Automatic Predicate Abstraction of C Programs. In: PLDI 2001, pp. 203–213 (2001)
2. Bent, L., Atkinson, D.C., Griswold, W.G.: A Comparative Study of Two Whole Program Slicers for C. Technical report, University of California at San Diego, La Jolla (2001)
3. Canfora, G., Cimitile, A., De Lucia, A.: Conditioned Program Slicing. Information and Software Technology 40(11-12), 595–607 (1998)
4. Cimatti, A., Griggio, A., Sebastiani, R.: Efficient Interpolant Generation in Satisfiability Modulo Theories. In: Ramakrishnan, C.R., Rehof, J. (eds.) TACAS 2008. LNCS, vol. 4963, pp. 397–412. Springer, Heidelberg (2008)
5. Craig, W.: Three Uses of Herbrand-Gentzen Theorem in Relating Model Theory and Proof Theory. Journal of Symbolic Computation 22 (1955)
6. Daoudi, M., Ouarbya, L., Howroyd, J., Danicic, S., Harman, M., Fox, C., Ward, M.P.: Consus: A Scalable Approach to Conditioned Slicing. In: WCRE 2002, pp. 109–118 (2002)

7. Dijkstra, E.W.: A Discipline of Programming. Prentice-Hall Series in Automatic Computation. Prentice-Hall (1976)
8. Field, J., Ramalingam, G., Tip, F.: Parametric Program Slicing. In: POPL 1995, pp. 379–392 (1995)
9. Fischer, J., Jhala, R., Majumdar, R.: Joining Dataflow with Predicates. In: ESEC/FSE-13, pp. 227–236 (2005)
10. Henzinger, T.A., Jhala, R., Majumdar, R., McMillan, K.L.: Abstractions from Proofs. In: POPL 2004, pp. 232–244 (2004)
11. Horwitz, S., Reps, T., Binkley, D.: Interprocedural Slicing using Dependence Graphs. In: PLDI 1988, pp. 35–46 (1988)
12. Jaffar, J., Navas, J.A., Santosa, A.E.: Unbounded Symbolic Execution for Program Verification. In: Khurshid, S., Sen, K. (eds.) RV 2011. LNCS, vol. 7186, pp. 396–411. Springer, Heidelberg (2012)
13. Jaffar, J., Santosa, A.E., Voicu, R.: Efficient Memoization for Dynamic Programming with Ad-hoc Constraints. In: AAAI 2008, pp. 297–303 (2008)
14. Jaffar, J., Murali, V., Navas, J.A., Santosa, A.E.: TRACER: A Symbolic Execution Tool for Verification. In: Madhusudan, P., Seshia, S.A. (eds.) CAV 2012. LNCS, vol. 7358, pp. 758–766. Springer, Heidelberg (2012)
15. Lalire, G., Argoud, M., Jeannet, B.: The Interproc Analyzer (2009), http://pop-art.inrialpes.fr/people/bjeannet/bjeannet-forge/interproc
16. McMillan, K.L.: Lazy Annotation for Program Testing and Verification. In: Touili, T., Cook, B., Jackson, P. (eds.) CAV 2010. LNCS, vol. 6174, pp. 104–118. Springer, Heidelberg (2010)
17. Seo, S., Yang, H., Yi, K.: Automatic Construction of Hoare Proofs from Abstract Interpretation Results. In: Ohori, A. (ed.) APLAS 2003. LNCS, vol. 2895, pp. 230–245. Springer, Heidelberg (2003)
18. Snelting, G., Robschink, T., Krinke, J.: Efficient Path Conditions in Dependence Graphs for Software Safety Analysis. In: TOSEM 2006, vol. 15, pp. 410–457 (2006)
19. Weiser, M.: Program Slicing. In: ICSE 1981, pp. 439–449 (1981)

Symbolic Learning of Component Interfaces*

Dimitra Giannakopoulou[1], Zvonimir Rakamarić[2,**], and Vishwanath Raman[3]

[1] NASA Ames Research Center, USA
dimitra.giannakopoulou@nasa.gov
[2] School of Computing, University of Utah, USA
zvonimir.rakamaric@gmail.com
[3] Carnegie Mellon University, USA
vishwa.raman@sv.cmu.edu

Abstract. Given a white-box component $\mathscr{C}$ with specified unsafe states, we address the problem of automatically generating an interface that captures safe orderings of invocations of $\mathscr{C}$'s public methods. Method calls in the generated interface are guarded by constraints on their parameters. Unlike previous work, these constraints are generated automatically through an iterative refinement process. Our technique, named PSYCO (Predicate-based SYmbolic COmpositional reasoning), employs a novel combination of the L* automata learning algorithm with symbolic execution. The generated interfaces are three-valued, capturing whether a sequence of method invocations is safe, unsafe, or its effect on the component state is unresolved by the symbolic execution engine. We have implemented PSYCO as a new prototype tool in the JPF open-source software model checking platform, and we have successfully applied it to several examples.

1 Introduction

Component interfaces are at the heart of modular software development and reasoning techniques. Modern components are open building blocks that are reused or connected dynamically to form larger systems. As a result, component interfaces must step up, from being purely syntactic, to representing component aspects that are relevant to tasks such as dynamic component retrieval and substitution, or functional and non-functional reasoning about systems. This paper focuses on "temporal" interfaces, which capture ordering relationships between invocations of component methods. For example, for the NASA Crew Exploration Vehicle (CEV) model discussed in Sec. 7, an interface prescribes that a lunar lander cannot dock with a lunar orbiter without first jettisoning the launch abort sub-system. Temporal interfaces are well-suited for components that exhibit a protocol-like behavior. Control-oriented components, such as NASA control software, device drivers, and web-services, often fall into this category.

An ideal interface should precisely represent the component in all its intended usages. In other words, it should include all the good interactions, and exclude all problematic interactions. Previous work presented approaches for computing temporal interfaces using techniques such as predicate abstraction [16] and learning [2,11,25].

* This research was supported by the NASA CMU grant NNA10DE60C.
** The author did this work while at Carnegie Mellon University.

Our work studies a more general problem: automatic generation of precise temporal interfaces for components that include methods with parameters. Whether a method call is problematic or not may depend on the actual values passed for its formal parameters. Therefore, we target the generation of interfaces which, in addition to method orderings, also include method *guards* (i.e., constraints on the parameters of the methods), as illustrated in Fig. 2. We are not aware of any existing approaches that provide a systematic and automated way of introducing method guards for temporal interface generation.

Our proposed solution is based on a novel combination of learning with symbolic execution techniques. In particular, we use the L* [3,23] automata-learning algorithm to automatically generate a component interface expressed as a finite-state automaton over the public methods of the component. L* generates approximations of the component interface by interacting with a *teacher*. The teacher uses symbolic execution to answer queries from L* about the target component, and provides counterexamples to L* when interface approximations are not precise. The teacher may also detect a need for partitioning the space of input parameter values based on constraints computed by the underlying symbolic engine. The alphabet is then refined accordingly, and learning restarts on the refined alphabet. Several learn-and-refine cycles may occur during interface generation. The generated interfaces are three-valued, capturing whether a sequence of method invocations is safe, unsafe, or its effect on the component state is unresolved by the underlying symbolic execution engine.

We have implemented our approach within the JPF (Java Pathfinder) software verification toolset [20]. JPF is an open-source project developed at the NASA Ames Research Center. The presented technique is implemented as a new tool called PSYCO in the JPF project jpf-psyco. We have applied PSYCO to learn component interfaces of several realistic examples that could not be handled automatically and precisely using previous approaches. Our main contributions are summarized as follows:

- This work is the *first* to combine learning and symbolic techniques for temporal interface generation, including method guards. The automated generation and refinement of these guards is based on constraints that are computed by symbolic execution. A significant challenge, which our proposed algorithm addresses, is to develop a refinement scheme that guarantees progress and termination.
- We use three-valued automata to account for potential incompleteness of the underlying analysis technique. These automata record *precisely* whether a sequence of method invocations is safe, unsafe, or unresolved. As a result, subsequent alternative analyses can be targetted to unresolved paths.
- We implemented the approach in an *open-source* and *extensible* tool within JPF and successfully applied it to several realistic examples.

Related Work. Interface generation for white-box components has been studied extensively in the literature (e.g., [16,2,11,25]). However, as discussed, we are not aware of any existing approach that provides a systematic and automated way of refining the interface method invocations using constraints on their parameters.

Automatically creating component models for black-box components is a related area of research. For methods with parameters, abstractions are introduced that map alphabet symbols into sets of concrete argument values. A set of argument values represents a partition, and is used to invoke a component method. In the work by Aarts et al. [1], abstractions are user-defined. Hower et al. [18] discover such abstraction mappings through an automated refinement process. In contrast to these works, availability of the component source code enables us to generate guards that characterize precisely each method partition, making the generated automata more informative. MACE [8] combines black- and white-box techniques to discover concrete input messages that generate new system states. These states are then used as initial states for symbolic exploration on component binaries. The input alphabet is refined based on a user-provided abstraction of output messages. MACE focuses on increasing path coverage to discover bugs, rather than generating precise component interfaces, as targeted here.

Interface generation is also related to assumption generation for compositional verification, where several learning-based approaches have been proposed [22,15,7,6]. A type of alphabet refinement developed in this context is geared towards computing smaller assumption alphabets that guarantee compositional verification achieves conclusive results [10,5]. None of these works address the automatic generation of method guards in the computed interfaces/assumptions. Finally, recent work on the analysis of multi-threaded programs for discovering concurrency bugs involves computing traces and preconditions that aid component interface generation [4,19]. However, the data that these works generate is limited, and cannot serve the purpose of temporal interface generation, as presented in this paper.

2   Motivating Example

Our motivating example is the *PipedOutputStream* class taken from the *java.io* package. Similar to previous work [2,25], we removed unnecessary details from the example; Fig. 1 shows the simplified code. The example has one private field *sink* of type *Piped-InputStream*, and four public methods called *connect, write, flush,* and *close*. Throwing exceptions is modeled by asserting *false*, denoting an undesirable error state.

The class initializes field *sink* to *null*. Method *connect* takes a parameter *snk* of type *PipedInputStream*, and goes to an error state (i.e., throws an exception) either if *snk* is *null* or if one of the streams has already been connected; otherwise, it connects the input and output streams. Method *write* can be called only if *sink* is not *null*, otherwise an error state is reached. Methods *flush* and *close* have no effect when *sink* is *null*, i.e., they do not throw an exception.

Fig. 2 shows on the right the interface generated with PSYCO for this example. Note that, as described in Section 4, PSYCO currently only handles basic types. Therefore, we transformed the example in Figure 1 accordingly. The interface captures the fact that *flush* and *close* can be invoked unconditionally, whereas *write* can only occur after a successful invocation of *connect*. The guard $snk \neq null \wedge snk.connected = false$, over the parameter *snk* of the method *connect*, captures the condition for a successful connection. Without support for guards in our component interfaces, we would obtain the interface shown on the left. This interface allows only methods that can be invoked unconditionally, i.e., *close* and *flush*. Method *connect* is blocked from the interface since it cannot be called unconditionally. Since *connect* cannot be invoked, *write* is blocked as well. Clearly, the interface on the left, obtained using existing interface generation techniques, precludes several legal sequences of method invocations. In existing approaches, a user is expected to manually define a refinement of the component methods

```
class PipedOutputStream {
  PipedInputStream sink = null;              public void write() {
                                               if (sink == null) {
  public void connect(                           assert false;
      PipedInputStream snk) {                   } else {...}
    if (snk == null) {                        }
      assert false;
    } else if (sink != null ||               public void flush() {
        snk.connected) {                        if (sink != null) {...}
      assert false;                           }
    }
    sink = snk;                              public void close() {
    snk.connected = true;                       if (sink != null) {...}
  }                                          }
}                                          }
```

Fig. 1. Motivating example

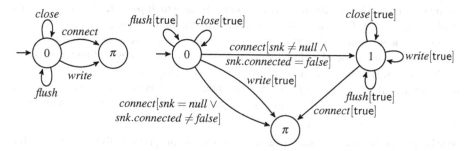

Fig. 2. Interfaces for our motivating example. On the left, there is no support for guards, while on the right, PSYCO is used to generate guards. Initial states are marked with arrows that have no origin; error states are marked with π. Edges are labelled with method names (with guards, when applicable).

to capture these additional legal behaviors. Our approach performs such a refinement automatically. Therefore, support for automatically generating guards enables PSYCO to generate richer and more precise component interfaces for components that have methods with parameters.

3 Preliminaries

Labeled Transition Systems (LTS). We use deterministic LTSs to express temporal component interfaces. Symbols π and υ denote a special *error* and *unknown* state, respectively. The former models unsafe states and the latter captures the lack of knowledge about whether a state is safe or unsafe. States π and υ have no outgoing transitions.

A deterministic LTS M is a four-tuple $\langle Q, \alpha M, \delta, q_0 \rangle$ where: 1) Q is a finite non-empty set of states, 2) αM is a set of observable actions called the *alphabet* of M,

3) $\delta : (Q \times \alpha M) \mapsto Q$ is a transition function, and 4) $q_0 \in Q$ is the initial state. LTS M is complete if each state except π and υ has outgoing transitions for every action in αM.

A *trace*, also called *execution* or *word*, of an LTS M is a finite sequence of observable actions that label the transitions that M can perform starting from its initial state. A trace is illegal if it leads M to state π, unknown if it leads M to state υ, and legal otherwise. The illegal (resp. unknown, legal) language of M, denoted as $\mathscr{L}_{illegal}(M)$ (resp. $\mathscr{L}_{unknown}(M)$, $\mathscr{L}_{legal}(M)$), is the set of illegal (resp. unknown, legal) traces of M.

Three-Valued Automata Learning with L*. We use an adaptation [7] of the classic L* learning algorithm [3,23], which learns a three-valued deterministic finite-state automaton (3DFA) over some alphabet Σ. In our setting, learning is based on partitioning the words over Σ into three unknown regular languages L_1, L_2, and L_3, with L* using this partition to infer an LTS with three values that is consistent with the partition. To infer an LTS, L* interacts with a teacher that answers two types of questions. The first type is a *membership query* that takes as input a string $\sigma \in \Sigma^*$ and answers *true* if $\sigma \in L_1$, *false* if $\sigma \in L_2$, and *unknown* otherwise. The second type is an *equivalence query* or *conjecture*, i.e., given a candidate LTS M whether or not the following holds: $\mathscr{L}_{legal}(M) = L_1$, $\mathscr{L}_{illegal}(M) = L_2$, and $\mathscr{L}_{unknown}(M) = L_3$. If the above conditions hold of the candidate M, then the teacher answers *true*, at which point L* has achieved its goal and returns M. Otherwise, the teacher returns a counterexample, which is a string σ that invalidates one of the above conditions. The counterexample is used by L* to drive a new round of membership queries in order to produce a new, refined, candidate. Each candidate M that L* constructs is smallest, meaning that any other LTS consistent with the information provided to L* up to that stage has at least as many states as M. Given a correct teacher, L* is guaranteed to terminate with a minimal (in terms of numbers of states) LTS for L_1, L_2, and L_3.

Symbolic Execution. Symbolic execution is a static program analysis technique for systematically exploring a large number of program execution paths [21]. It uses symbolic values as program inputs in place of concrete (actual) values. The resulting output values are then statically computed as symbolic expressions (i.e., constraints), over symbolic input values and constants, using a specified set of operators. A symbolic execution tree, or constraints tree, characterizes all program execution paths explored during symbolic execution. Each node in the tree represents a symbolic state of the program, and each edge represents a transition between two states. A symbolic state consists of a unique program location identifier, symbolic expressions for the program variables currently in scope, and a path condition defining conditions (i.e., constraints) that have to be satisfied in order for the execution path to this state to be taken. The path condition describing the current path through the program is maintained during symbolic execution by collecting constraints when conditional statements are encountered. Path conditions are checked for satisfiability using a constraint solver to establish whether the corresponding execution path is feasible.

4   Components and Interfaces

Components and Methods. A *component* is defined by the grammar in Fig. 3. A component $\mathscr{C}$ has a set of global variables representing internal state and a set of one or

Component ::=	**class** *Ident* { *Global* Method\+* }	*Stmt* ::=	*Stmt*; *Stmt*
Method ::=	*Ident* (*Parameters*) { *Stmt* }			*Ident* = *Expr*
Global ::=	*Type Ident*;			**assert** *Expr*
Arguments ::=	*Arguments, Expr*	ε			**if** *Expr* **then** *Stmt* **else** *Stmt*
Parameters ::=	*Pararameters, Parameter*	ε			**while** *Expr* **do** *Stmt*
Parameter ::=	*Type Ident*			**return** *Expr*

Fig. 3. Component grammar. *Ident*, *Expr*, and *Type* have the usual meaning.

more methods. Furthermore, components are sequential. For simplicity of exposition, we assume there is no recursion, and all method calls are inlined. Note, however, that our implementation handles calls without inlining. Moreover, as customary, our symbolic execution engine unrolls recursion to a bounded depth. We also assume the usual statement semantics. We expect that all unsafe states are implied by assert statements. Let Ids be the set of component method identifiers (i.e., names), Stmts the set of all component statements, and Prms the set of all input parameters of component methods. We define the signature Sig_m of a method m as a pair $\langle Id_m, P_m \rangle \in \text{Ids} \times 2^{\text{Prms}}$; we write $Id_m(P_m)$ for the signature Sig_m of the method m. A *method* m is then defined as a pair $\langle Sig_m, s_m \rangle$ where $s_m \in$ Stmts is its top-level statement.

Let $\mathcal{M}$ be the set of methods in a component $\mathcal{C}$ and G be the set of its global variables. For every method $m \in \mathcal{M}$, each parameter $p \in P_m$ takes values from a domain D_p based on its type; similarly for global variables. We expect that all method parameters are of basic types. Given a method $m \in \mathcal{M}$, an execution $\theta \in$ Stmts* of m is a finite sequence of visited statements $s_1 s_2 \ldots s_n$ where s_1 is the top-level method statement s_m. The set $\Theta_m \in 2^{\text{Stmts}^*}$ is the set of all unique executions of m. We assume that each execution $\theta \in \Theta_m$ of a method visits a bounded number of statements (i.e., $|\theta|$ is bounded), and also that the number of unique executions is bounded (i.e., $|\Theta_m|$ is bounded); in other words, the methods have no unbounded loops. Again, in our implementation, loops are unrolled to a bounded depth, as is customary in symbolic execution. A *valuation* over P_m, denoted $[P_m]$, is a function that assigns to each parameter $p \in P_m$ a value in D_p. We denote a valuation over variables in G with $[G]$. We take $[G_i]$ as the valuation representing the initial values of all global variables. Given valuations $[P_m]$ and $[G]$, we assume that the execution of m visits exactly the same sequence of statements; in other words, the methods are deterministic.

Symbolic Expressions. We interpret all method parameters symbolically, using the name of each parameter as its symbolic name; we abuse notation and take Prms to also denote the set of symbolic names. A *symbolic expression* e is defined as follows:

$$e ::= C \mid p \mid (e \circ e),$$

where C is a constant, $p \in$ Prms a parameter, and $\circ \in \{+, -, *, /, \%\}$ an arithmetic operator. The set of constants in an expression may include constants that are used in statements or the initial values of component state variables in $[G_i]$.

Constraints. We define a *constraint* φ as follows:

$$\varphi ::= \textit{true} \mid \textit{false} \mid e \oplus e \mid \varphi \wedge \varphi \mid \varphi \vee \varphi,$$

where $\oplus \in \{<, >, =, \leq, \geq\}$ is a comparison operator.

Guards. Given a method signature $m = \langle Id_m, P_m \rangle$, a guard γ_m is defined as a constraint that only includes parameters from P_m.

Interfaces. Previous work uses LTSs to describe temporal component interfaces. However, as described in Sec. 2, a more precise interface ideally also uses guards to capture constraints on method input parameters.

We define an *interface LTS*, or *iLTS*, to take into account guards, as follows. An iLTS is a tuple $A = \langle M, \mathscr{S}, \Gamma, \Delta \rangle$, where $M = \langle Q, \alpha M, \delta, q_0 \rangle$ is a deterministic and complete LTS, $\mathscr{S}$ a set of method signatures, Γ a set of guards for method signatures in $\mathscr{S}$, and $\Delta : \alpha M \mapsto \mathscr{S} \times \Gamma$ a function that maps each a $\in \alpha M$ into a method signature $m \in \mathscr{S}$ and a guard $\gamma_m \in \Gamma$. In addition, the mapping Δ is such that the set of all guards for a given method signature form a partition of the input space of the corresponding method. Let $\Gamma_m = \{\gamma \mid \exists a \in \alpha M.\Delta(a) = (m, \gamma)\}$ be the set of guards belonging to a method m. More formally, the guards for a method are (1) non-overlapping:

$$\forall a, b \in \alpha M, \ \gamma_a, \gamma_b \in \Gamma, \ m \in \mathscr{S} \ . \ a \neq b \wedge \Delta(a) = (m, \gamma_a) \wedge \Delta(b) = (m, \gamma_b) \Rightarrow \neg \gamma_a \vee \neg \gamma_b,$$

(2) cover all of the input space: $\forall m \in \mathscr{S} \ . \ \bigvee_{\gamma \in \Gamma_m} \gamma = \text{true}$, and (3) are non-empty.

Given an iLTS $A = \langle M, \mathscr{S}, \Gamma, \Delta \rangle$, an execution of A is a sequence of pairs $\sigma = (m_0, \gamma_{m_0}), (m_1, \gamma_{m_1}), \ldots, (m_n, \gamma_{m_n})$, where for $0 \leq i \leq n$, pair (m_i, γ_{m_i}) consists of a method signature $m_i \in \mathscr{S}$ and its corresponding guard γ_{m_i}. Every execution σ has a corresponding trace $a_0, a_1, \ldots, a_n$ in M such that for $0 \leq i \leq n$, $\Delta(a_i) = (m_i, \gamma_{m_i})$. Then σ is a legal (resp. illegal, unknown) execution in A, if its corresponding trace in M is legal (resp. illegal, unknown). Based on this distinction, we define $\mathscr{L}_{legal}(A)$, $\mathscr{L}_{illegal}(A)$, and $\mathscr{L}_{unknown}(A)$ as the sets of legal, illegal, and unknown executions of A, respectively.

An iLTS $A = \langle M, \mathscr{S}, \Gamma, \Delta \rangle$ is an interface for a component $\mathscr{C}$ if $\mathscr{S}$ is a subset of method signatures of the methods $\mathscr{M}$ in $\mathscr{C}$. However, not all such interfaces are acceptable and a notion of interface correctness also needs to be introduced. Traditionally, correctness of an interface for a component $\mathscr{C}$ is associated with two characteristics: *safety* and *permissiveness*, meaning that the interface blocks all erroneous and allows all good executions (i.e., executions that do not lead to an error) of $\mathscr{C}$, respectively. A *full* interface is then an interface that is both safe and permissive [16].

We extend this definition to iLTSs as follows. Let iLTS A be an interface for a component $\mathscr{C}$. An execution $\sigma = (m_0, \gamma_{m_0}), (m_1, \gamma_{m_1}), \ldots, (m_n, \gamma_{m_n})$ of A then represents every concrete sequence $\sigma_c = (m_0, [P_{m_0}]), (m_1, [P_{m_1}]), \ldots, (m_n, [P_{m_n}])$ such that for $0 \leq i \leq n$, $[P_{m_i}]$ satisfies γ_{m_i}. Each such concrete sequence defines an execution of the component $\mathscr{C}$. We say an execution of a component is illegal if it results in an assertion violation; otherwise, the execution is legal. Then, A is a *safe* interface for $\mathscr{C}$ if for every execution $\sigma \in \mathscr{L}_{legal}(A)$, we determine that all the corresponding concrete executions of component $\mathscr{C}$ are legal. It is *permissive* if for every execution $\sigma \in \mathscr{L}_{illegal}(A)$, we determine that all the corresponding concrete executions of component $\mathscr{C}$ are illegal. Finally, A is *tight* if for every execution $\sigma \in \mathscr{L}_{unknown}(A)$, we cannot determine whether

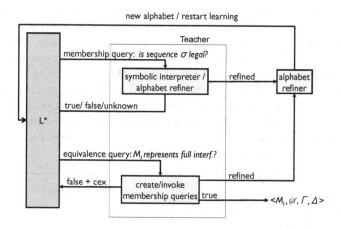

Fig. 4. PSYCO framework during iteration i of learning algorithm

the corresponding concrete executions of component $\mathscr{C}$ are legal or illegal; this explicitly captures possible incompleteness of the underlying analysis technique. To conclude, we say A is *full* if it is *safe, permissive,* and *tight*. Moreover, we say A is *k-full* for some $k \in \mathbb{N}$ if it is safe, permissive, and tight for all method sequences of length up to k.

5   Symbolic Interface Learning

Let $\mathscr{C}$ be a component and $\mathscr{S}$ the set of signatures of a subset of the methods $\mathscr{M}$ in $\mathscr{C}$. Our goal is to automatically compute an interface for $\mathscr{C}$ as an iLTS $A = \langle M, \mathscr{S}, \Gamma, \Delta \rangle$. We achieve this through a novel combination of L* to generate LTS M, and symbolic execution to compute the set of guards Γ and the mapping Δ. The termination criterion for symbolic execution is that all paths be characterized as either legal, illegal or unknown.

At a high level, our proposed framework operates as follows (see Fig. 4). It uses L* to learn an LTS over an alphabet that initially corresponds to a set of signatures $\mathscr{S}$ of the methods of $\mathscr{C}$. For our motivating example, we start with the alphabet $\alpha M = \{close, flush, connect, write\}$, set of signatures $\mathscr{S} = \{close(), flush(), connect(snk), write()\}$, and Δ such that $\Delta(close) = (close(), \text{true})$, $\Delta(flush) = (flush(), \text{true})$, $\Delta(connect) = (connect(snk), \text{true})$, and $\Delta(write) = (write(), \text{true})$. As mentioned earlier, L* interacts with a teacher that responds to its membership and equivalence queries. A membership query over the alphabet αM is a sequence $\sigma = a_0, a_1, \ldots, a_n$ such that for $0 \leq i \leq n$, $a_i \in \alpha M$. Given a query σ, the teacher uses symbolic execution to answer the query. The semantics of executing a query in this context corresponds to exercising all paths through the methods in the query sequence, subject to satisfying the guards returned by the map Δ. Whenever the set of all paths through the sequence can be partitioned into proper subsets that are safe, lead to assertion violations, or to limitations of symbolic execution that prevent further exploration, we refine guards to partition the input space of the methods in the query sequence. We call this process *alphabet refinement*.

For our motivating example, the sequence $\sigma = connect$ will trigger refinement of symbol *connect*. As illustrated in Fig. 2, the input space of method *connect* must be partitioned into the case where: (1) $snk \neq null \land snk.connected = false$, which leads to safe executions, and (2) the remaining inputs, which lead to unsafe executions. When a method is partitioned, we replace the symbol in αM corresponding to the refined method with a fresh symbol for each partition, and the learning process is restarted with the new alphabet. For example, we partition the symbol *connect* into *connect_1* and *connect_2*, corresponding to the two cases above, before we restart learning. The guards that define the partitions are stored in Γ, and the mapping from each new symbol to the corresponding method signature and guard is stored in Δ.

Algo. 1. Learning an iLTS for a component

Input: A set of method signatures $\mathscr{S}$ of a component $\mathscr{C}$.
Output: An iLTS $A = \langle M, \mathscr{S}, \Gamma, \Delta \rangle$.

```
 1:  αM ← ∅, Γ ← {true}
 2:  for all m ∈ 𝒮 do
 3:      a ← CreateSymbol()
 4:      αM ← αM ∪ {a}
 5:      Δ(a) ← (m, true)
 6:  loop
 7:      AlphabetRefiner.init(αM, Δ)
 8:      SymbolicInterpreter.init(
 9:          αM, AlphabetRefiner)
10:      Teacher.init(Δ, SymbolicInterpreter)
11:      Learner.init(αM, Teacher)
12:      M ← Learner.learnAutomaton()
13:      if M = null then
14:          (αM, Γ, Δ)
15:          ← AlphabetRefiner.getRefinement()
16:      else
17:          return A = ⟨M, 𝒮, Γ, Δ⟩
```

Algo. 1 is the top-level algorithm implemented by our interface generation framework. First, we initialize the alphabet αM and the set of guards Γ on line 1. Then, we create a fresh symbol a for every method signature m, and use it to populate the alphabet αM and the mapping Δ (lines 2–5). The main loop of the algorithm learns an interface for the current alphabet; the loop either refines the alphabet and reiterates, or produces an interface and terminates. In the loop, an alphabet refiner is initialized on line 7, and is passed as an argument for the initialization of the *SymbolicInterpreter* on line 9. The *SymbolicInterpreter* is responsible for invoking the symbolic execution engine and interpreting the obtained results. It may, during this process, detect the need for alphabet refinement, which will be performed through invocation of *AlphabetRefiner*. We initialize a teacher with the current alphabet and the *SymbolicInterpreter* on line 10, and finally a learner with this teacher on line 11. The learning process then takes place to generate a classical LTS M (line 12). When learning produces an LTS M that is not *null*, then an iLTS A is returned that consists of M and the current guards and mapping, at which point the framework terminates (line 17). If M is *null*, it means that refinement

```
void main(PipedInputStream snk) {
  assume true; close();
  assume snk != null && snk.connected == false; connect(snk);
  assume true; write();
}
```

Fig. 5. The generated program P_σ for the query sequence $\sigma = close, connect\_1, write$, where $\Delta(close) = (close(), true)$, $\Delta(connect\_1) = (connect(snk), snk \neq null \wedge snk.connected = false)$, and $\Delta(write) = (write(), true)$.

took place during learning. We obtain the new alphabet, guards, and mapping from the *AlphabetRefiner* (line 15) and start a new learn-refine iteration.

Teacher. As discussed in Sec. 3, the teacher responds to membership and equivalence queries produced by L*. Given a membership query $\sigma = a_0, a_1, \ldots, a_n$, the symbolic teacher first generates a program P_σ. For each symbol a_i in the sequence, P_σ invokes the corresponding method m_i while assuming its associated guard γ_{m_i} using an assume statement. The association is provided by the current mapping Δ, i.e., $\Delta(a_i) = (m_i, \gamma_{m_i})$. The semantics of statement **assume** *Expr* is that it behaves as skip if *Expr* evaluates to true; otherwise, it blocks the execution. This ensures that symbolic execution considers only arguments that satisfy the guard, and ignores all other values.

For the example of Fig. 1, let $\sigma = close, connect\_1, write$ be a query, where $\Delta(close) = (close(), true)$, $\Delta(connect\_1) = (connect(snk), snk \neq null \wedge snk.connected = false)$, and $\Delta(write) = (write(), true)$. Fig. 5 gives the generated program P_σ for this query. Such a program is then passed to the *SymbolicInterpreter* that performs symbolic analysis and returns one of the following: (1) TRUE corresponding to a *true* answer for learning, (2) FALSE corresponding to a *false* answer, (3) UNKNOWN corresponding to an *unknown* answer, and (4) REFINED, reflecting the fact that alphabet refinement took place, in which case the learning process must be interrupted, and the learner returns an LTS $M = null$.

An equivalence query checks whether the conjectured iLTS $A = \langle M, \mathscr{S}, \Gamma, \Delta \rangle$, with $M = \langle Q, \alpha M, \delta, q_0 \rangle$, is safe, permissive, and tight. One approach to checking these three properties would be to encode the interface as a program, similar to the program for membership queries. During symbolic execution of this program, we would check whether the conjectured iLTS correctly characterizes legal, illegal, and unknown uses of the component. However, conjectured interfaces have unbounded loops; symbolic techniques handle such loops through bounded unrolling. We follow a similar process, but rather than having the symbolic engine unroll loops, we reduce equivalence queries to membership queries of bounded depth. Note that this approach, similar to loop unrolling during symbolic execution, is not complete in general. However, even in cases where we face incompleteness, we provide useful guarantees of the generated iLTS.

In order to provide guarantees of the generated interface to some depth k, we proceed as follows. During a depth-first traversal of M to depth k, whenever we reach state π or υ, we generate the sequence σ that leads to this state, where $\sigma = a_0, a_1, \ldots, a_{n-1}, a_n$ in $\mathscr{L}_{illegal}(M)$ or $\mathscr{L}_{unknown}(M)$, respectively. Moreover, we generate the sub-sequence $\sigma_L = a_0, a_1, \ldots, a_{n-1}$, knowing $\sigma_L \in \mathscr{L}_{legal}(M)$, since π and υ have no outgoing transitions ($\mathscr{L}_{illegal}(M)$ and $\mathscr{L}_{unknown}(M)$ are suffix-closed). Whenever depth k is reached during traversal, and the state reached is not π and not υ, we generate the sequence $\sigma = a_0, a_1, \ldots, a_k$ (with $\sigma \in \mathscr{L}_{legal}(M)$) leading to this state. In other words, we generate all legal sequences in $\mathscr{L}_{legal}(M)$ of depth exactly k, all sequences in $\mathscr{L}_{illegal}(M)$ and $\mathscr{L}_{unknown}(M)$ of depth less than or equal to k, as well as the largest prefix of each generated illegal and unknown sequence that is in $\mathscr{L}_{legal}(M)$.

Every generated sequence σ is then queried using the algorithm for membership queries. Since $\mathscr{L}_{legal}(M)$ is prefix-closed, and $\mathscr{L}_{illegal}(M)$ and $\mathscr{L}_{unknown}(M)$ are suffix-closed, the generated queries are sufficient to check the conjectured interface to depth k, as shown in the technical memorandum [12]. If the membership query for σ returns REFINED, learning is restarted since the alphabet has been refined. Furthermore, if the membership query for a sequence $\sigma \in \mathscr{L}_{legal}(M)$ (resp. $\sigma \in \mathscr{L}_{illegal}(M)$, $\sigma \in \mathscr{L}_{unknown}(M)$) does not return TRUE (resp. FALSE, UNKNOWN), the corresponding interface is not full and σ is returned to L* as a counterexample to the equivalence query. Otherwise, the interface is guaranteed to be k-full, i.e., safe, permissive, and tight up to depth k.

Symbolic Interpreter. Algo. 2 shows the algorithm implemented in *SymbolicInterpreter* and called by the teacher. The algorithm invokes a symbolic execution engine, and interprets its results to determine answers to queries. The input to Algo. 2 is a program P_σ as defined above, and a set of symbols Σ. The output is either TRUE, FALSE, or UNKNOWN, if no alphabet refinement is needed, or REFINED, which reflects that alphabet refinement took place.

Algo. 2 starts by executing P_σ symbolically (line 1), treating main method parameters (e.g., *snk* in Fig. 5) as symbolic inputs. Every path through the program is then characterized by a *path constraint*, denoted by pc. A pc is a constraint over symbolic parameters, with each conjunct in the constraint stemming from a conditional statement encountered along the path; a path constraint precisely characterizes a path taken through the program. A constraint partitions the set of all valuations over input parameters of the program (i.e., input parameters of the called component methods) into the set of valuations that satisfy the constraint and the set of valuations that do not satisfy the constraint. We denote a set of path constraints as PC.

We define a map $\rho : PC \mapsto \{error, ok, unknown\}$ which, given a path constraint $pc \in PC$, returns error (resp. ok) if the corresponding path represents an erroneous (resp. good) execution of the program; otherwise, ρ returns unknown. Mapping pc to unknown represents a case when the path constraint cannot be solved by the underlying constraint solver used by the symbolic execution engine. Symbolic execution returns a set of path constraints PC and the mapping ρ, which are then interpreted by the algorithm to determine the answer to the query.

After invoking symbolic execution, the algorithm initializes three constraints (φ^{err} for error, φ^{ok} for good, and φ^{unk} for unknown paths) to false on line 2. The loop on lines 3–9 iterates over path constraints $pc \in PC$, and based on whether pc maps into error, ok, or unknown, adds pc as a disjunct to either φ^{err}, φ^{ok}, or φ^{unk}, respectively. Let $SAT : \Phi \mapsto \mathbb{B}$, where Φ is the universal set of constraints, be a predicate such that $SAT(\varphi)$ holds if and only if the constraint φ is satisfiable. In lines 10–15, the algorithm

Algo. 2. Symbolic interpreter

Input: Program P_σ and set of symbols Σ.
Output: TRUE, FALSE, UNKNOWN, or REFINED.
1: $(PC, \rho) \leftarrow SymbolicallyExecute(P_\sigma)$
2: $\varphi^{err} \leftarrow \varphi^{ok} \leftarrow \varphi^{unk} \leftarrow$ false
3: **for all** $pc \in PC$ **do**
4:    **if** $\rho(pc) =$ error **then**
5:       $\varphi^{err} \leftarrow \varphi^{err} \vee pc$
6:    **else if** $\rho(pc) =$ ok **then**
7:       $\varphi^{ok} \leftarrow \varphi^{ok} \vee pc$
8:    **else**
9:       $\varphi^{unk} \leftarrow \varphi^{unk} \vee pc$
10: **if** $\neg(SAT(\varphi^{err}) \vee SAT(\varphi^{unk}))$ **then**
11:    **return** TRUE
12: **else if** $\neg(SAT(\varphi^{ok}) \vee SAT(\varphi^{unk}))$ **then**
13:    **return** FALSE
14: **else if** $\neg(SAT(\varphi^{err}) \vee SAT(\varphi^{ok}))$ **then**
15:    **return** UNKNOWN
16: **else**
17:    $\Sigma_{new} \leftarrow AlphabetRefiner.refine(\varphi^{err}, \varphi^{unk})$
18:    **if** $|\Sigma_{new}| = |\Sigma|$ **then**
19:       **return** UNKNOWN
20:    **else**
21:       **return** REFINED

Algo. 3. Symbolic alphabet refinement

Input: Set of symbols Σ, mapping Δ, and constraints φ^{err}, φ^{unk}.
Output: Refinement $\Sigma_{new}, \Gamma_{new}, \Delta_{new}$.
1: $\Sigma_{new} \leftarrow \Gamma_{new} \leftarrow \emptyset$
2: **for all** $a \in \Sigma$ **do**
3:    $(m, \gamma) \leftarrow \Delta(a)$
4:    $\varphi_m^{err} \leftarrow \Pi_m(\varphi^{err})$
5:    $\varphi_m^{unk} \leftarrow \gamma \wedge \neg\varphi_m^{err} \wedge \Pi_m(\varphi^{unk})$
6:    **if** $\neg MP(\varphi_m^{err}) \wedge \neg MP(\varphi_m^{unk})$ **then**
7:       $\varphi_m^{ok} \leftarrow \gamma \wedge \neg\varphi_m^{err} \wedge \neg\varphi_m^{unk}$
8:       **if** $SAT(\varphi_m^{err})$ **then**
9:          $a_{err} \leftarrow CreateSymbol()$
10:          $\Sigma_{new} \leftarrow \Sigma_{new} \cup \{a_{err}\}$
11:          $\Gamma_{new} \leftarrow \Gamma_{new} \cup \{\varphi_m^{err}\}$
12:          $\Delta_{new}(a_{err}) \leftarrow (m, \varphi_m^{err})$
13:       **if** $SAT(\varphi_m^{unk})$ **then**
14:          $a_{unk} \leftarrow CreateSymbol()$
15:          $\Sigma_{new} \leftarrow \Sigma_{new} \cup \{a_{unk}\}$
16:          $\Gamma_{new} \leftarrow \Gamma_{new} \cup \{\varphi_m^{unk}\}$
17:          $\Delta_{new}(a_{unk}) \leftarrow (m, \varphi_m^{unk})$
18:       **if** $SAT(\varphi_m^{ok})$ **then**
19:          $a_{ok} \leftarrow CreateSymbol()$
20:          $\Sigma_{new} \leftarrow \Sigma_{new} \cup \{a_{ok}\}$
21:          $\Gamma_{new} \leftarrow \Gamma_{new} \cup \{\varphi_m^{ok}\}$
22:          $\Delta_{new}(a_{ok}) \leftarrow (m, \varphi_m^{ok})$
23:    **else**
24:       $\Sigma_{new} \leftarrow \Sigma_{new} \cup \{a\}$
25:       $\Gamma_{new} \leftarrow \Gamma_{new} \cup \{\gamma\}$
26:       $\Delta_{new}(a) \leftarrow (m, \gamma)$
27: **return** $\Sigma_{new}, \Gamma_{new}, \Delta_{new}$

returns TRUE if all paths are good paths (i.e., if there are no error and unknown paths), FALSE if all paths are error paths, or UNKNOWN if all paths are unknown paths.

Otherwise, alphabet refinement needs to be performed; method *refine* of the *AlphabetRefiner* is invoked, which returns the new alphabet Σ_{new} (line 17). If no new symbols have been added to the alphabet, no methods have been refined. This can only happen if all potential refinements involve *mixed-parameter* constraints. Informally, a constraint is considered mixed-parameter if it relates symbolic parameters from multiple methods. As explained in Algo. 3, dealing with mixed parameters precisely is beyond the scope of this work. Therefore, Algo. 2 returns UNKNOWN. Otherwise, refinement took place, and Algo. 2 returns REFINED.

Symbolic Alphabet Refinement. The *SymbolicInterpreter* invokes the refinement algorithm using method *refine* of the *AlphabetRefiner*. The current alphabet, mapping, and constraints φ^{err} and φ^{unk} computed by the *SymbolicInterpreter*, are passed as inputs. Method *refine* implements Algo. 3.

In Algo. 3, the new set of alphabet symbols Σ_{new} and guards Γ_{new} are initialized on line 1. The loop on lines 2–26 determines, for every alphabet symbol, whether it needs to be refined, in which case it generates the appropriate refinement. Let $\Delta(a) = (m, \gamma)$. An operator Π_m is then used to project φ^{err} on the parameters of m (line 4). When applied to a path constraint pc_i, Π_m erases all conjuncts that don't refer to a symbolic parameter of m. If no conjunct remains, then the result is false. For a disjunction of path constraints $\varphi = pc_1 \vee \ldots \vee pc_n$ (such as φ^{err} or φ^{unk}), $\Pi_m(\varphi) = \Pi_m(pc_1) \vee \ldots \vee \Pi_m(pc_n)$. For example, if $m = \langle foo, \{x,y\}\rangle$, then $\Pi_m((s = t) \vee (x < y) \vee (s \leq z \wedge y = z)) \mapsto$ false $\vee (x < y) \vee (y = z)$, which simplifies to $(x < y) \vee (y = z)$.

We compute φ_m^{unk} on line 5. At that point, we check whether either φ_m^{err} or φ_m^{unk} involve mixed-parameter constraints (line 6). This is performed using a predicate $MP : \Phi \mapsto \mathbb{B}$, where Φ is the universal set of constraints, defined as follows: $MP(\varphi)$ holds if and only if $|Mthds(\varphi)| > 1$. The map $Mthds : \Phi \mapsto 2^{\mathcal{M}}$ maps a constraint $\varphi \in \Phi$ into the set of all methods that have parameters occurring in φ. Dealing with mixed-parameter constraints in a precise fashion would require more expressive automata, and is beyond the scope of this paper. Therefore, refinement proceeds for a symbol only if mixed-parameter constraints are not encountered in φ_m^{err} and φ_m^{unk}. Otherwise, the current symbol is simply added to the new alphabet (lines 24–26).

We compute φ_m^{ok} on line 7 in terms of φ_m^{err} and φ_m^{unk}, so it does not contain mixed-parameter constraints either. Therefore, when the algorithm reaches this point, all of φ_m^{err}, φ_m^{unk}, φ_m^{ok} represent potential guards for the method refinement. Note that φ_m^{err}, φ_m^{unk}, and φ_m^{ok} are computed in such a way that they partition the input space of the method m, if it gets refined. A fresh symbol is subsequently created for each guard that is satisfiable (lines 8, 13, 18), We update Σ_{new}, Γ_{new}, and Δ_{new} with the fresh symbol and its guard. In the end, the algorithm returns the new alphabet. The computed guards and mapping are stored in local fields that can be accessed through the getter method getRefinement() of the AlphabetRefiner (see Algo. 1, line 15).

6   Correctness and Guarantees

Prior to the application of our framework, loops and recursion are unrolled a bounded number of times. Consequently, our correctness arguments assume that methods have a finite number of paths. Proofs of our theorems appear in the technical memorandum [12].

We begin by showing correctness of the teacher for L*. In the following lemma, we prove that the program P_σ that we generate to answer a query σ captures all possible concrete sequences for σ. The proof follows from the structure of P_σ.

Lemma 1. (Correctness of P_σ). *Given a component $\mathscr{C}$ and a query σ on $\mathscr{C}$, the set of executions of $\mathscr{C}$ driven by P_σ is equal to the set of concrete sequences for σ.*

The following theorem shows that the teacher correctly responds to membership queries. The proof follows from the finiteness of paths taken through a component and from an analysis of Algo. 2.

Theorem 1. (Correctness of Answers to Membership Queries). *Given a component $\mathscr{C}$ and a query σ, the teacher responds* TRUE *(resp.* FALSE, UNKNOWN*) if and only if all executions of $\mathscr{C}$ for σ are legal (resp. illegal, cannot be resolved by the analysis).*

Next, we show that the teacher correctly responds to equivalence queries up to depth k. The proof follows from our reduction of equivalence queries to membership queries that represent all sequences of length $\leq k$ of the conjectured iLTS.

Theorem 2. (Correctness to Depth k of Answers to Equivalence Queries). *Let M be an LTS conjectured by the learning process for some component $\mathscr{C}$, Γ the current set of guards, and Δ the current mapping. If an equivalence query returns a counterexample, $A = \langle M, \mathscr{S}, \Gamma, \Delta \rangle$ is not a full interface for $\mathscr{C}$. Otherwise, A is k-full.*

In proving progress and termination of our framework, we use Lemma 2, which is a property of L*, and Lemma 3, which is a property of our alphabet refinement.

Lemma 2. (Termination of Learning). *If the unknown languages are regular, then L* is guaranteed to terminate.*

Lemma 3. (Alphabet Partitioning). *Algo. 3 creates partitions for the alphabet symbols it refines.*

Given that the number of paths through a method is bounded, we can have at most as many guards for the method as the number of these paths, which is bounded. Furthermore, if alphabet refinement is required, Algo. 3 always partitions at least one method. This leads us to the following theorem.

Theorem 3. (Progress and Termination of Refinement). *Alphabet refinement strictly increases the alphabet size, and the number of possible refinements is bounded.*

Finally, we characterize the overall guarantees of our framework with the following theorem, whose proof follows from Theorem 2, Theorem 3, and Lemma 2.

Theorem 4. (Guarantees of PSYCO). *If the behavior of a component $\mathscr{C}$ can be characterized by an iLTS, then PSYCO terminates with a k-full iLTS for $\mathscr{C}$.*

7   Implementation and Evaluation

We implemented our approach in a tool called PSYCO within the Java Pathfinder (JPF) open-source framework [20]. PSYCO consists of three new, modular JPF extensions: (1) `jpf-learn` implements both the standard and the three-valued version of L*; (2) `jpf-jdart` is our symbolic execution engine that performs concolic execution [13,24]; (3) `jpf-psyco` implements the symbolic-learning framework, including the teacher for L*. For efficiency, our implementation of L* caches query results in a *MemoizedTable*, which is preserved after refinement to enable reuse of previous learning results. Programs P_σ are generated dynamically by invoking their corresponding methods using Java reflection. We evaluated our approach on the following examples:

SIGNATURE A class from the *java.security* package used in a paper by Singh et al. [25].
PIPEDOUTPUTSTREAM A class from the *java.io* package and our motivating example (see Fig. 1). Taken from a paper by Singh et al. [25].

Table 1. Experimental results. Time budget is set to one hour. "#Methods" is the number of component methods (and also the size of the initial alphabet); "*k-max*" the maximum value of k explored (i.e., the generated iLTS is *k-max*-full); "*k-min*" the smallest value of k for which our approach converges to the final iLTS that gets generated; "#Conjectures" the total number of conjectured iLTSs; "#Refinements" the total number of performed alphabet refinements; "#Alphabet" the size of the final alphabet; "#States" the number of states in the final iLTS.

Example	#Methods	k-max	k-min	#Conjectures	#Refinements	#Alphabet	#States
SIGNATURE	5	7	2	2	0	5	4
PIPEDOUTPUTSTREAM	4	8	2	2	1	5	3
INTMATH	8	1	1	1	7	16	3
ALTBIT	2	35	4	8	3	5	5
CEV-FLIGHTRULE	3	4	3	3	2	5	3
CEV	18	3	3	10	6	24	9

INTMATH A class from the Google Guava repository [14]. It implements arithmetic operations on integer types.

ALTBIT Implements a communication protocol that has an alternating bit style of behavior. Howar et al. [18] use it as a case study.

CEV NASA Crew Exploration Vehicle (CEV) 1.5 EOR-LOR example modeling flight phases of a space-craft; a Java state-chart model in the JPF distribution under `examples/jpfESAS`. We translated the example from state-charts to plain Java.

CEV-FLIGHTRULE Simplified version of the CEV example that exposes a flight rule.

For all experiments, `jpf-jdart` used the Yices SMT solver [9]. The experiments were performed on a 2GHz Intel Core i7 laptop with 8GB of memory running Mac OS X. We budgeted a total of one hour running time for each application, after which PSYCO was terminated. Using a simple static analysis, PSYCO first checks whether a component is stateless. For stateless components (e.g., INTMATH), a depth of one suffices, hence we fix $k = 1$. For such components, the interface generated by PSYCO still provides useful information in terms of method guards. The resulting interface automaton for INTMATH can reach state unknown due to the presence of non-linear constraints, that cannot be solved using Yices. For all other components, the depth k for equivalence queries gets incremented whenever no counterexample is obtained after exhausting exploration of the automaton to depth k. In this way, we are able to report the maximum depth *k-max* that we can guarantee for our generated interfaces within the allocated time of one hour.

Table 1 summarizes the obtained experimental results. The generated interfaces are shown in [12]. In addition, we inspected the generated interfaces to check whether or not they correspond to our expected component behavior. For all examples, except CEV, our technique converges, within a few minutes and with a relatively small k (see column *k-min* in the table), to the expected iLTS. The iLTS do not change between *k-min* and *k-max*. Our technique guarantees they are *k-max-full*. In general, users of our framework may increase the total time budget if they require additional guarantees, or may interrupt the learning process if they are satisfied with the generated interfaces. In all of our examples the majority of the time was spent in symbolic execution.

A characteristic of the examples for which PSYCO terminated with a smaller *k-max*, such as CEV, is that they involve methods with a significant degree of branching. On the other hand, PSYCO managed to explore ALTBIT to a large depth because branching is smaller. This is not particular to our approach, but inherent in any path-sensitive program analysis technique. If n is the number of branches in each method, and a program invokes m methods in sequence, then the number of paths in this program is, in the worst case, exponential in $m * n$. As a result, symbolic analysis of queries is expensive both in branching within each method as well as in the length of the query. Memoization and reuse of learning results after refinement helps ameliorate this problem; for CEV, 7800 out of 12002 queries were answered through memoization.

8   Conclusions and Future Work

We have presented the foundations of a novel approach for generating temporal component interfaces enriched with method guards. PSYCO produces three-valued iLTS, with an unknown state reflecting component behavior that was not covered by the underlying analysis. For compositional verification, unknown states can be interpreted conservatively as errors, or optimistically as legal states, thus defining bounds for the component interface. Furthermore, alternative analyses can be applied subsequently to target these unexplored parts. The interface could also be enriched during testing or usage of the component. Reuse of previous learning results, similar to what is currently performed, could make this process incremental.

In the future, we also intend to investigate ways of addressing mixed parameters more precisely. For example, we plan to combine PSYCO with a learning algorithm for register automata [17]. This would enable us to relate parameters of different methods through equality and inequality. Moreover, we will incorporate and experiment with heuristics both in the learning and the symbolic execution components of PSYCO. Finally, we plan to investigate interface generation in the context of compositional verification.

Acknowledgements. We would like to thank Peter Mehlitz for his help with Java PathFinder and Neha Rungta for reviewing a version of this paper.

References

1. Aarts, F., Jonsson, B., Uijen, J.: Generating models of infinite-state communication protocols using regular inference with abstraction. In: ICTSS, pp. 188–204 (2010)
2. Alur, R., Cerný, P., Madhusudan, P., Nam, W.: Synthesis of interface specifications for Java classes. In: POPL, pp. 98–109 (2005)
3. Angluin, D.: Learning regular sets from queries and counterexamples. Inf. Comput. 75(2), 87–106 (1987)
4. Burckhardt, S., Dern, C., Musuvathi, M., Tan, R.: Line-up: A complete and automatic linearizability checker. In: PLDI, pp. 330–340 (2010)
5. Chaki, S., Strichman, O.: Three optimizations for assume-guarantee reasoning with L*. FMSD 32(3), 267–284 (2008)

6. Chen, Y.-F., Clarke, E.M., Farzan, A., Tsai, M.-H., Tsay, Y.-K., Wang, B.-Y.: Automated Assume-Guarantee Reasoning through Implicit Learning. In: Touili, T., Cook, B., Jackson, P. (eds.) CAV 2010. LNCS, vol. 6174, pp. 511–526. Springer, Heidelberg (2010)
7. Chen, Y.-F., Farzan, A., Clarke, E.M., Tsay, Y.-K., Wang, B.-Y.: Learning Minimal Separating DFA's for Compositional Verification. In: Kowalewski, S., Philippou, A. (eds.) TACAS 2009. LNCS, vol. 5505, pp. 31–45. Springer, Heidelberg (2009)
8. Cho, C.Y., Babić, D., Poosankam, P., Chen, K.Z., Wu, E.X., Song, D.: MACE: Model-inference-assisted concolic exploration for protocol and vulnerability discovery. In: USENIX Security Symposium (2011)
9. Dutertre, B., Moura, L.D.: The Yices SMT solver. Technical report, SRI International (2006)
10. Gheorghiu, M., Giannakopoulou, D., Păsăreanu, C.S.: Refining Interface Alphabets for Compositional Verification. In: Grumberg, O., Huth, M. (eds.) TACAS 2007. LNCS, vol. 4424, pp. 292–307. Springer, Heidelberg (2007)
11. Giannakopoulou, D., Păsăreanu, C.S.: Interface Generation and Compositional Verification in JavaPathfinder. In: Chechik, M., Wirsing, M. (eds.) FASE 2009. LNCS, vol. 5503, pp. 94–108. Springer, Heidelberg (2009)
12. Giannakopoulou, D., Rakamarić, Z., Raman, V.: Symbolic learning of component interfaces. Technical report, NASA Ames Research Center (2012)
13. Godefroid, P., Klarlund, N., Sen, K.: DART: Directed automated random testing. SIGPLAN Not. 40(6), 213–223 (2005)
14. Guava: Google core libraries, `http://code.google.com/p/guava-libraries/`
15. Gupta, A., McMillan, K.L., Fu, Z.: Automated Assumption Generation for Compositional Verification. In: Damm, W., Hermanns, H. (eds.) CAV 2007. LNCS, vol. 4590, pp. 420–432. Springer, Heidelberg (2007)
16. Henzinger, T.A., Jhala, R., Majumdar, R.: Permissive interfaces. In: ESEC/FSE, pp. 31–40 (2005)
17. Howar, F., Steffen, B., Jonsson, B., Cassel, S.: Inferring Canonical Register Automata. In: Kuncak, V., Rybalchenko, A. (eds.) VMCAI 2012. LNCS, vol. 7148, pp. 251–266. Springer, Heidelberg (2012)
18. Howar, F., Steffen, B., Merten, M.: Automata Learning with Automated Alphabet Abstraction Refinement. In: Jhala, R., Schmidt, D. (eds.) VMCAI 2011. LNCS, vol. 6538, pp. 263–277. Springer, Heidelberg (2011)
19. Joshi, S., Lahiri, S.K., Lal, A.: Underspecified harnesses and interleaved bugs. In: POPL, pp. 19–30 (2012)
20. Java PathFinder (JPF), `http://babelfish.arc.nasa.gov/trac/jpf`
21. King, J.C.: Symbolic execution and program testing. Commun. ACM 19(7), 385–394 (1976)
22. Pasareanu, C.S., Giannakopoulou, D., Bobaru, M.G., Cobleigh, J.M., Barringer, H.: Learning to divide and conquer: applying the L* algorithm to automate assume-guarantee reasoning. FMSD 32(3), 175–205 (2008)
23. Rivest, R.L., Schapire, R.E.: Inference of finite automata using homing sequences. Inf. Comput. 103(2), 299–347 (1993)
24. Sen, K., Marinov, D., Agha, G.: CUTE: A concolic unit testing engine for C. In: ESEC/FSE, pp. 263–272 (2005)
25. Singh, R., Giannakopoulou, D., Păsăreanu, C.: Learning Component Interfaces with May and Must Abstractions. In: Touili, T., Cook, B., Jackson, P. (eds.) CAV 2010. LNCS, vol. 6174, pp. 527–542. Springer, Heidelberg (2010)

Liveness-Based Pointer Analysis

Uday P. Khedker[1], Alan Mycroft[2], and Prashant Singh Rawat[1]

[1] Indian Institute of Technology Bombay
{uday,prashantr}@cse.iitb.ac.in
[2] University of Cambridge
Alan.Mycroft@cl.cam.ac.uk

Abstract. Precise flow- and context-sensitive pointer analysis (FCPA) is generally considered prohibitively expensive for large programs; most tools relax one or both of the requirements for scalability. We argue that precise FCPA has been over-harshly judged—the vast majority of points-to pairs calculated by existing algorithms are never used by any client analysis or transformation because they involve dead variables. We therefore formulate a FCPA in terms of a joint points-to and liveness analysis which we call L-FCPA. We implemented a naive L-FCPA in GCC-4.6.0 using linked lists. Evaluation on SPEC2006 showed significant increase in the precision of points-to pairs compared to GCC's analysis. Interestingly, our naive implementation turned out to be faster than GCC's analysis for all programs under 30kLoC. Further, L-FCPA showed that fewer than 4% of basic blocks had more than 8 points-to pairs. We conclude that the usable points-to information and the required context information is small and sparse and argue that approximations (e.g. weakening flow or context sensitivity) are not only undesirable but also unnecessary for performance.

1 Introduction

Interprocedural data flow analysis extends an analysis across procedure boundaries to incorporate the effect of callers on callees and vice-versa. In order to compute *precise* information, such an analysis requires flow sensitivity (associating different information with distinct control flow points) and context sensitivity (computing different information for different calling contexts). The efficiency and scalability of such an analysis is a major concern and sacrificing precision for scalability is a common trend because the size of information could be large. Hence precise flow- and context-sensitive pointer analysis (FCPA) is considered prohibitively expensive and most methods employ heuristics that relax one or both of the requirements for efficiency.

We argue that the precision and efficiency in pointer analysis need not conflict and may actually be synergistic. We demonstrate this by formulating a liveness-based flow- and context-sensitive points-to analysis (referred to as L-FCPA): points-to information is computed only for the pointers that are live and the propagation of points-to information is restricted to live ranges of respective pointers. We use *strong liveness* to discover pointers that are directly used or are used in defining pointers that are strongly live. This includes the effect of dead code elimination and is more precise than simple liveness.

Fig. 1 provides a motivating example. Since *main* prints z, it is live at O_{12} (exit of node 12) and hence at I_{12} (entry of node 12). Thus w becomes live at O_9 and hence at

A. Miné and D. Schmidt (Eds.): SAS 2012, LNCS 7460, pp. 265–282, 2012.

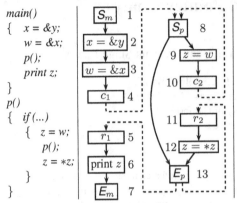

Let I_n/O_n denote the entry/exit point of node n. Let (a, b) at a program point u denote that a points-to b at u. Then,

- z is live at O_9 which make w live at O_3. Hence we should compute (w, x) in node 3 and thereby (z, x) in node 9. This causes x to be live because of $*z$ in node 12. Hence we should compute (x, y) in node 2 and (z, y) in node 12.
- (w, x) and (x, y) should not be propagated to nodes 5, 6, 7 because w, x are not live in these nodes.

Fig. 1. A motivating example for L-FCPA and its supergraph representation. The solid and dashed edges represent intraprocedural and interprocedural control flow respectively.

O_3 resulting in the points-to pair (w, x) at O_3. This pair reaches I_9 giving the pair (z, x) at O_9. When this information reaches I_{12}, x becomes live. This liveness is propagated to O_2 giving the pair (x, y). Finally, we get the pair (z, y) at O_{12}. Figures 6 and 7 give fuller detail of the solution after formulating L-FCPA. Here we highlight the following:

- *Use of liveness*: points-to pairs are computed only when the pointers become live.
- *Sparse propagation*: pairs (x, y) and (w, x) are not propagated beyond the call to p in *main* because they are not live.
- *Flow sensitivity*: points-to information is different for different control flow points.
- *Context sensitivity*: (z, x) holds only for the inner call to p made from within p but not for the outer call to p made from the main procedure. Thus in spite of z being live at I_6, (z, x) is not propagated to I_6 but (z, y) is.

We achieve this using a data flow framework (Section 3) that employs an interdependent formulation for discovering strongly live pointer variables and their pointees. We compute must-points-to information from may-points-to information without fixed-point computation. Section 4 uses value-based termination of call strings for precise interprocedural analysis without having to compute a prohibitively large number of call strings. Section 5 discusses how heap locations, stack locations, and records are handled. After Section 6 (related work), Section 7 details experimental results which suggest that the traditional FCPA is non-scalable because it computes and stores (a) an order of magnitude more points-to pairs than can ever be used by a client analysis (e.g. pairs for dead pointers), and (b) a prohibitively large number of redundant contexts.

2   Background

A procedure p is represented by a control-flow graph (CFG). It has a unique entry node S_p with no predecessor and a unique exit node E_p with no successor; every node n is reachable from S_p, and E_p is reachable from every n. At the interprocedural level, a

Forward Analysis (Out_n depends on In_n)	Backward Analysis (In_n depends on Out_n)

$$In_n = \begin{cases} BI & n = S_p \\ \displaystyle\bigcap_{m \in pred(n)} Out_m & \text{otherwise} \end{cases}$$

$$Out_n = f_n(In_n)$$

$$In_n = f_n(Out_n)$$

$$Out_n = \begin{cases} BI & n = E_p \\ \displaystyle\bigcap_{m \in succ(n)} In_m & \text{otherwise} \end{cases}$$

Fig. 2. Typical data flow equations for some procedure p.

program is represented by a *supergraph* (e.g. in Fig. 1) which connects the CFGs by *interprocedural edges*. A call to procedure p at call site i is split into a *call node c_i* and a *return node r_i* with a call edge $c_i \rightarrow S_p$ and a return edge $E_p \rightarrow r_i$.

Formulating Data Flow Analysis. Data flow variables In_n and Out_n associate data flow information with CFG node n (respectively for its entry point I_n and exit point O_n); they must satisfy data flow equations (Fig. 2) involving node transfer functions f_n. Data flow values are taken from a meet-semilattice (meet represents confluence and the initial data flow value is $\top$). The *boundary information BI* represents the data flow information at I_{S_p} for forward analysis and O_{E_p} for backward analysis. Its value is governed by the semantics of the information being discovered. Interprocedural analysis eliminates the need for a fixed *BI* (except for arguments to the *main* procedure) by computing it from the calling contexts during the analysis. *Flow-insensitive* approaches disregard intraprocedural control flow for efficiency; they effectively treat the flow-equations as inequations ($\sqsubseteq$) and constrain all the In_n to be equal (and similarly all the Out_n). *Flow-sensitive* analyses honour control flow and keep the data flow information separate for each program point. *Iterative methods* solve data flow equations by repeatedly refining the values at each program point n starting from a conservative initialisation of $\top$; there are various strategies for this including *round robin* sweeps and *work list* methods.

The most precise data flow information at the intraprocedural level is the *Meet over Paths* (MoP) solution [1, 2]. However, in general, an algorithm can at best compute the *Maximum Fixed Point* (MFP) solution [1, 2]; however this is possible only if it is flow-sensitive. For distributive frameworks, e.g. live-variable analysis, MFP and MoP coincide; for non-distributive frameworks such as points-to analysis, they may differ.

Pointer Analysis. Points-to relations are computed by identifying locations corresponding to the left- and right-hand sides of a pointer assignment and taking their cartesian product [3, 4]. The points-to pairs of locations that are modified are removed. May-points-to information at n contains the points-to pairs that hold along some path reaching n whereas must-points-to information contains the pairs that hold along every path reaching n (hence a pointer can have at most one pointee) [4]. Fig. 3 exemplifies flow-sensitive points-to analysis. By contrast an inclusion-based (Andersen) flow-insensitive analysis [5] associates (p, r), (p, s), (q, r), (r, s), (s, r) with all program points while the weaker equality-based (Steensgaard) analysis [6] further adds (q, s).

Interprocedural Data Flow Analysis. A supergraph contains control flow paths which violate nestings of matching call return pairs (e.g. 1-2-3-4-8-13-11 for the supergraph in

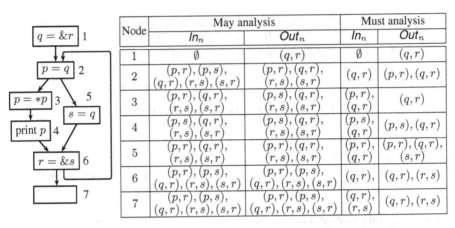

Node	May analysis		Must analysis	
	In_n	Out_n	In_n	Out_n
1	$\emptyset$	(q,r)	$\emptyset$	(q,r)
2	$(p,r),(p,s),$ $(q,r),(r,s),(s,r)$	$(p,r),(q,r),$ $(r,s),(s,r)$	(q,r)	$(p,r),(q,r)$
3	$(p,r),(q,r),$ $(r,s),(s,r)$	$(p,s),(q,r),$ $(r,s),(s,r)$	$(p,r),$ (q,r)	(q,r)
4	$(p,s),(q,r),$ $(r,s),(s,r)$	$(p,s),(q,r),$ $(r,s),(s,r)$	$(p,s),$ (q,r)	$(p,s),(q,r)$
5	$(p,r),(q,r),$ $(r,s),(s,r)$	$(p,r),(q,r),$ $(r,s),(s,r)$	$(p,r),$ (q,r)	$(p,r),(q,r),$ (s,r)
6	$(p,r),(p,s),$ $(q,r),(r,s),(s,r)$	$(p,r),(p,s),$ $(q,r),(r,s),(s,r)$	$(q,r),$	$(q,r),(r,s)$
7	$(p,r),(p,s),$ $(q,r),(r,s),(s,r)$	$(p,r),(p,s),$ $(q,r),(r,s),(s,r)$	$(q,r),$ (r,s)	$(q,r),(r,s)$

Fig. 3. An example of flow-sensitive intraprocedural points-to analysis

Fig. 1). Such paths correspond to infeasible contexts. An *interprocedurally valid path* is a feasible execution path containing a legal sequence of call and return edges.

A *context-sensitive* analysis retains sufficient information about calling contexts to distinguish the data flow information reaching a procedure along different call chains. This restricts the analysis to interprocedurally valid paths. A *context-insensitive* analysis does not distinguish between valid and invalid paths, effectively merging data flow information across calling contexts. Recursive procedures have potentially infinite contexts, yet context-sensitive analysis is decidable for data flow frameworks with finite lattices and it is sufficient to maintain a finite number of contexts for such frameworks. Since this number is almost always impractically large, most context-sensitive methods limit context sensitivity in some way.

At the interprocedural level, the most precise data flow information is the *Meet over Interprocedurally Valid Paths* (IMoP) and the *Maximum Fixed Point over Interprocedurally Valid Paths* (IMFP) [7–9]. For computing IMFP, an interprocedural method must be fully flow and context sensitive. Relaxing flow (context) sensitivity admits invalid intraprocedural (interprocedural) paths; since no path is excluded, the computed information is provably safe but could be imprecise. Some examples of fully flow- and context-sensitive methods are: the graph reachability method [8] and the more general functional and full call-strings methods [7]. We use a variant of the full call-strings method [10] and compute the IMFP giving the most precise computable solution for pointer analysis; the loss of precision due to non-distributivity is inevitable.

Call-Strings Method [1, 7, 10]. This is a flow- and context-sensitive approach that embeds context information in the data flow information and ensures the validity of interprocedural paths by maintaining a history of calls in terms of call strings. A *call string* at node n is a sequence $c_1 c_2 \ldots c_k$ of *call sites* corresponding to unfinished calls at n and can be viewed as a snapshot of the call stack. Call-string construction is governed by interprocedural edges. Let σ be a call string reaching procedure p. For an intraprocedural edge $m \rightarrow n$ in p, σ reaches n. For a call edge $c_i \rightarrow S_q$ where c_i

belongs to p, call string σc_i reaches S_q. For a return edge $E_p \rightarrow r_j$ where r_j belongs to a caller of p there are two cases: if $\sigma = \sigma' c_j$ then σ' reaches r_j; otherwise σ and its data flow value is not propagated to r_j. This ensures that data flow information is only propagated to appropriate call sites. In a backward analysis, the call string grows on traversing a return edge and shrinks on traversing a call edge. The interprocedural data flow information at node n is a function from call strings to data flow values. Merging ($\sqcap$) the data flow values associated with all call strings reaching n gives the overall data flow value at n.

The original full call-strings method [7] used a pre-calculated length resulting in an impractically large number of call strings. We use value-based termination of call-string construction [10]. For forward flow, call strings are partitioned at S_p based on equality of their data flow values, only one call string per partition is propagated, and all call strings of the partition are regenerated at E_p (and the other way round for backward flows). This constructs only the relevant call strings (i.e. call strings with distinct data flow values) reducing the number of call strings significantly. For finite data flow lattices, we require only a finite number of call strings even in the presence of recursion. Moreover, there is no loss of precision as all relevant call strings are constructed.

We briefly describe value-based termination of call strings for forward analysis. Let $df(\sigma, n)$ denote the data flow value for call string σ at the entry of node n. Let $df(\sigma_1, S_p) = df(\sigma_2, S_p) = v$. Since data flow values are propagated along the same set of paths from S_p to E_p, $df(\sigma_1, S_p) = df(\sigma_2, S_p) \Rightarrow df(\sigma_1, E_p) = df(\sigma_2, E_p)$. Thus, we can propagate only one of them (say $\langle \sigma_1, v \rangle$) through the body of p. Let it reach E_p as $\langle \sigma_1, v' \rangle$. Then we can regenerate $\langle \sigma_2, v' \rangle$ at E_p by using $df(\sigma_1, E_p)$ if we remember that σ_2 was represented by σ_1 at S_p.

Recursion creates *cyclic* call strings $\gamma \alpha^i$ where γ and α are non-overlapping call site sequences and α occurs i times. Since the lattice is finite and the flow functions are monotonic, some $k \geq 0$ must exist such that $df(\gamma \alpha^{k+m}, S_p) = df(\gamma \alpha^k, S_p)$ where m is the *periodicity*[1] of the flow function for α. Hence $\gamma \alpha^{k+m}$ is represented by $\gamma \alpha^k$. Since $df(\gamma \alpha^{k+i \cdot m}, S_p) = df(\gamma \alpha^k, S_p), i > 0$, call string $\gamma \alpha^{k+m}$ is constructed for representation but call strings $\gamma \alpha^{k+i \cdot m}, i > 1$ are not constructed. Let $df(\gamma \alpha^k, E_p)$ be v. Then we generate $\langle \gamma \alpha^{k+m}, v \rangle$ in Out_{E_p} which is propagated along the sequence of return nodes thereby removing one occurrence of α. Thus the call string reaches E_p as $\gamma \alpha^k$, once again to be regenerated as $\gamma \alpha^{k+m}$. This continues until the values change, effectively computing $df(\gamma \alpha^{k+i \cdot m}, E_p), i > 1$ without constructing the call strings.

3   Liveness-Based Pointer Analysis

We consider the four basic pointer assignment statements: $x = \&y, x = y, x = *y, *x = y$ using which other pointer assignments can be rewritten. We also assume a *use x* statement to model other uses of pointers (such as in conditions). Discussion of address-taken local variables and allocation (*new* or *malloc*) is deferred to Section 5.

Let V denote the set of variables (i.e. "named locations"). Some of these variables (those in $P \subset V$) can hold pointers to members of V. Other members of V hold

---

[1] x is a periodic point of f if $f^m(x) = x$ and $f^i(x) \neq x, 0 < i < m$. If $m = 1$, x is a fixed point of f. See Fig. 9.12 on page 316 in [1] for a points-to analysis example where $m = 2$.

non-pointer values. These include variables of non-pointer type such as int. NULL is similarly best regarded as a member of $V - P$; finally a special value '?' in $V - P$ denotes an undefined location (again Section 5 discusses this further).

Points-to information is a set of pairs (x, y) where $x \in P$ is the pointer of the pair and $y \in V$ is a pointee of x and is also referred to as the pointee of the pair. The pair $(x, ?)$ being associated with program point n indicates that x may contain an invalid address along some potential execution path from S_p to n.

The data flow variables Lin_n and $Lout_n$ give liveness information for statement n while Ain_n and $Aout_n$ give may-points-to information. Must-points-to information, Uin_n and $Uout_n$, is calculated from may-points-to. Note that liveness propagates backwards (transfer functions map *out* to *in*) while points-to propagates forwards.

The lattice of liveness information is $\mathcal{L} = \langle \mathcal{P}(P), \supseteq \rangle$ (we only track the data flow of pointer variables) and lattice of may-points-to information is $\mathcal{A} = \langle \mathcal{P}(P \times V), \supseteq \rangle$. The overall data flow lattice is the product $\mathcal{L} \times \mathcal{A}$ with partial order $\langle l_1, a_1 \rangle \sqsubseteq \langle l_2, a_2 \rangle \Leftrightarrow (l_1 \sqsubseteq l_2) \wedge (a_1 \sqsubseteq a_2) \Leftrightarrow (l_1 \supseteq l_2) \wedge (a_1 \supseteq a_2)$ and having $\top$ element $\langle \emptyset, \emptyset \rangle$ and $\bot$ element $\langle P, P \times V \rangle$. We use standard algebraic operations on points-to relations: given relation $R \subseteq P \times V$ and $X \subseteq P$, define relation *application* $R \ X = \{v \mid u \in X \wedge (u, v) \in R\}$ and relation *restriction* $R|_X = \{(u, v) \in R \mid u \in X\}$.

Data Flow Equations. Fig. 4 provides the data flow equations for liveness-based pointer analysis. They resemble the standard data flow equations of strong liveness analysis and pointer analyses [1] except that liveness and may-points-to analyses depend on each other (hence the combined data flow is bi-directional in a CFG) and must-points-to information is computed from may-points-to information.

Since we use the greatest fixpoint formulation, the initial value ($\top$ of the corresponding lattices) is $\emptyset$ for both liveness and may-points-to analyses. For liveness BI is $\emptyset$ and defines $Lout_{E_p}$; for points-to analysis, BI is $Lin_n \times \{?\}$ and defines Ain_{S_p}. This reflects that no pointer is live on exit or holds a valid address on entry to a procedure.

Extractor Functions. The flow functions occurring in Equations (3) and (5) use *extractor functions* Def_n, $Kill_n$, Ref_n and $Pointee_n$ which extract the relevant pointer variables for statement n from the incoming pointer information Ain_n. These extractor functions are inspired by similar functions in [3, 4].

Def_n gives the set of pointer variables which a statement may modify and $Pointee_n$ gives the set of pointer values which may be assigned. Thus the new may-points-to pairs generated for statement n are $Def_n \times Pointee_n$ (Equation 5). Ref_n computes the variables that become live in statement n. Condition $Def_n \cap Lout_n$ ensures that Ref_n computes strong liveness rather than simple liveness. As an exception to the general rule, x is considered live in statement $*x = y$ regardless of whether the pointees of x are live otherwise, the pointees of x would not be discovered. For example, given $\{x=\&a; \ y=3; \ *x=y; \ \text{return};\}$, (x, a) cannot be discovered unless x is marked live. Hence liveness of x cannot depend on whether the pointees of x are live. By contrast, statement $y = *x$ uses the liveness of y to determine the liveness of x.

$Kill_n$ identifies pointer variables that are definitely modified by statement n. This information is used to kill both liveness and points-to information. For statement $*x = y$,

Given relation $R \subseteq \boldsymbol{P} \times \boldsymbol{V}$ (either Ain_n or $Aout_n$) we first define an auxiliary extractor function

$$Must(R) = \bigcup_{x \in \boldsymbol{P}} \{x\} \times \begin{cases} \boldsymbol{V} & R\{x\} = \emptyset \vee R\{x\} = \{?\} \\ \{y\} & R\{x\} = \{y\} \wedge y \neq ? \\ \emptyset & \text{otherwise} \end{cases} \quad (1)$$

Extractor functions for statement n ($Def_n, Kill_n, Ref_n \subseteq \boldsymbol{P}$; $Pointee_n \subseteq \boldsymbol{V}$) Notation: we assume that $x, y \in \boldsymbol{P}$ and $a \in \boldsymbol{V}$. A abbreviates Ain_n.					
Stmt.	Def_n	$Kill_n$	Ref_n		$Pointee_n$
			if $Def_n \cap Lout_n \neq \emptyset$	Otherwise	
$use\ x$	$\emptyset$	$\emptyset$	$\{x\}$	$\{x\}$	$\emptyset$
$x = \&a$	$\{x\}$	$\{x\}$	$\emptyset$	$\emptyset$	$\{a\}$
$x = y$	$\{x\}$	$\{x\}$	$\{y\}$	$\emptyset$	$A\{y\}$
$x = *y$	$\{x\}$	$\{x\}$	$\{y\} \cup (A\{y\} \cap \boldsymbol{P})$	$\emptyset$	$A(A\{y\} \cap \boldsymbol{P})$
$*x = y$	$A\{x\} \cap \boldsymbol{P}$	$Must(A)\{x\} \cap \boldsymbol{P}$	$\{x, y\}$	$\{x\}$	$A\{y\}$
other	$\emptyset$	$\emptyset$	$\emptyset$	$\emptyset$	$\emptyset$

Data Flow Values: $Lin_n, Lout_n \subseteq \boldsymbol{P}$ $Ain_n, Aout_n \subseteq \boldsymbol{P} \times \boldsymbol{V}$

$$Lout_n = \begin{cases} \emptyset & n \text{ is } E_p \\ \bigcup_{s \in succ(n)} Lin_s & \text{otherwise} \end{cases} \quad (2)$$

$$Lin_n = (Lout_n - Kill_n) \cup Ref_n \quad (3)$$

$$Ain_n = \begin{cases} Lin_n \times \{?\} & n \text{ is } S_p \\ \left(\bigcup_{p \in pred(n)} Aout_p \right) \Big|_{Lin_n} & \text{otherwise} \end{cases} \quad (4)$$

$$Aout_n = ((Ain_n - (Kill_n \times \boldsymbol{V})) \cup (Def_n \times Pointee_n)) \big|_{Lout_n} \quad (5)$$

Fig. 4. Intraprocedural formulation of liveness-based pointer analysis

$Kill_n$ depends on Ain_n filtered using the function $Must$. When no points-to information for x is available, the statement $*x = y$ marks all pointers as killed; this theoretically reflects the need for $Kill_n$ to be anti-monotonic and practically that unreachable or C-undefined code is analysed liberally. When the points-to information for x is non-empty, $Must$ performs a *weak update* or a *strong update* according to the number of pointees[2]: when x has multiple pointees we employ weak update as we cannot be certain which one will be modified because x may point to different locations along different execution paths reaching n. By contrast, when x has a single pointee *other than* '?', it indicates that x points to the same location along all execution paths reaching n and a strong update can be performed. Having BI be $Lin_n \times \{?\}$ completes this: if there is a definition-free path from S_p to statement n, the pair $(x, ?)$ will reach n and so a pair (x, z) reaching n cannot be incorrectly treated as a must-points-to pair.

---

[2] Or whether x is a summary node (see Section 5). Here we ignore summary nodes.

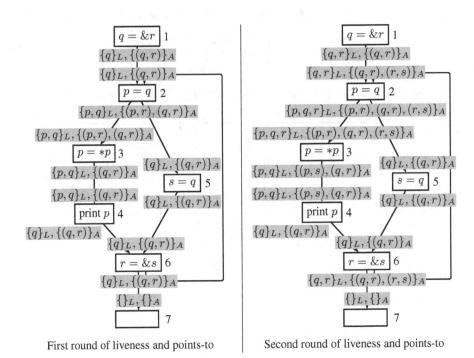

First round of liveness and points-to | Second round of liveness and points-to

Fig. 5. Intraprocedural liveness-based points-to analysis of the program in Fig. 3. Shaded boxes show the liveness and points-to information suffixed by L and A respectively.

The above discussion of $Kill_n$ and $Must$ justifies why must-points-to analysis need not be performed as an interdependent fixed-point computation [4, 1]. Given pointer x, a single points-to pair (x, y) with $y \neq ?$ in Ain_n or $Aout_n$, guarantees that x points to y. Conversely multiple may-points-to pairs associated with x means that its must-points-to information is empty.[3] Hence must-points-to information can be extracted from may-points-to information by $Uin_n = Must(Ain_n)$ and $Uout_n = Must(Aout_n)$. Note that generally $Uin_n \subseteq Ain_n$ and $Uout_n \subseteq Aout_n$; the only exception would be for nodes that are not reached by the analysis because no pointer has been found to be live. For such nodes Uin_n, $Uout_n$ are $\mathbf{P} \times \mathbf{V}$ whereas Ain_n, $Aout_n$ are $\emptyset$; this matches previous frameworks and corresponds to $Must$ being anti-monotonic (see above).

Motivating Example Revisited. Fig. 5 gives the result of liveness-based pointer analysis for our motivating example of Fig. 3. After the first round of liveness analysis followed by points-to analysis, we discover pair (p, r) in Ain_3. Thus r becomes live requiring a second round of liveness analysis. This then enables discovering the points-to pair (r, s) in node 6. A comparison with traditional may-points-to analysis (Fig. 3) shows that our analysis eliminates many redundant points-to pairs.

---

[3] This is more general than a similar concept for flow-sensitive kill in [11]. See Section 6.

Correctness. The following two claims are sufficient to establish soundness: (a) the flow functions in our formulation are monotonic (Theorem 1), and (b) for every use of a pointer, the points-to information defined by our formulation contains all addresses that it can hold at run time at a given program point (Theorem 2). Point (a) guarantees MFP computation at the intraprocedural level; at the interprocedural level, the full call-strings method ensures IMFP computation; point (b) guarantees that MFP (or IMFP) contains all usable pointer information.

Theorem 1. *The function* Must *is anti-monotonic hence the transfer functions* Lin_n, $Lout_n$, Ain_n *and* $Aout_n$ *in Fig. 4 are monotonic.*

Theorem 2. *If* $x \in P$ *holds the address of* $z \in (V - \{?\})$ *along some execution path reaching node* n, *then* $x \in Ref_n \Rightarrow (x, z) \in Ain_n$.

4 Interprocedural Liveness-Based Pointer Analysis

When our intraprocedural liveness-based points-to analysis is lifted to the interprocedural level using the call-strings method, Lin_n, $Lout_n$ and Ain_n, $Aout_n$ become functions of contexts written as sets of pairs $\langle \sigma, l \rangle, l \in L$ and $\langle \sigma, a \rangle, a \in A$ where σ is a call string reaching node n. Finally, the overall values of Ain_n, $Aout_n$ are computed by merging ($\sqcap$) the values along all call strings.

Matching Contexts for Liveness and Points-to Analysis. Since points-to information should be restricted to live ranges, it is propagated along the call strings constructed during liveness analysis. In the presence of recursion, we may need additional call strings for which liveness information may not yet be available. Such cases can be resolved by using the existing call strings as explained below. Let σ_a denote an acyclic call string and let $\sigma_c = \gamma\alpha^i$ be a cyclic call string (see Section 2). Then for liveness analysis:

- The partitioning information for every σ_a is available because either $\langle \sigma_a, x \rangle$ has reached node n in procedure p or σ_a has been represented by some other call string.
- Let $df(\gamma\alpha^i, n)$ differ for $0 \leq i \leq k$ but let $df(\gamma\alpha^k, n) = df(\gamma\alpha^{k+j}, n), j > 0$ (the periodicity m for liveness analysis is 1). Then the partitioning information is available for only $\gamma\alpha^k$ and $\gamma\alpha^{k+1}$ because $\gamma\alpha^{k+j}, j > 1$ are not constructed.

Consider a call string σ' reaching node n during points-to analysis. If σ' is an acyclic call string then its partitioning information and hence its liveness information is available. If σ' is a cyclic call string $\gamma\alpha^i$, its liveness information may not be available if it has not been constructed for liveness. In such a situation, it is sufficient to locate the longest $\gamma\alpha^l$, $l < i$ among the call strings that have been created and use its liveness information. This effect is seen below in our motivating example.

Motivating Example Revisited. For brevity, let I_n and O_n denote the entry and exit of node n. In the first round of liveness (Fig. 6), z becomes live at I_6 as $\langle \lambda, z \rangle_L$, reaches $O_{13}, I_{13}, O_{12}, I_{12}, O_{11}$ as $\langle c_1, z \rangle_L$, becomes $\langle c_1c_2, z \rangle_L$ at I_{11}, reaches O_{13} and gets represented by $\langle c_1, z \rangle_L$. Hence $\langle c_1c_2, z \rangle_L$ is not propagated within the body of p.

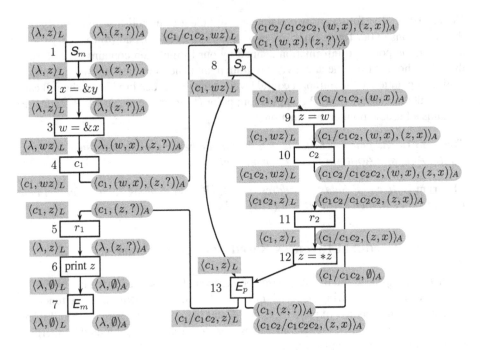

Fig. 6. Liveness and points-to information (subscripted with L and A) after the first round of interprocedural analysis. For brevity, set of live variables are represented as strings and '{' and '}' are omitted. Multiple call strings with the same data flow value are separated by a '/'.

$\langle c_1 c_2, z \rangle_L$ is regenerated at I_8, becomes $\langle c_1, z \rangle_L$ at I_{10}, becomes $\langle c_1, w \rangle_L$ at I_9. At O_8, it combines with $\langle c_1, z \rangle_L$ propagated from I_{13} and becomes $\langle c_1, w\ z \rangle_L$. Thus $c_1 c_2$ is regenerated as $\langle c_1 c_2, w\ z \rangle_L$ at I_8. $\langle c_1, w\ z \rangle_L$ reaches O_4 and becomes $\langle \lambda, w\ z \rangle_L$ at I_4.

In the first round of points-to analysis (Fig. 6), since z is live at I_1, $BI = \langle \lambda, (z, ?) \rangle_A$. $\langle \lambda, (w, x) \rangle_A$ is generated at O_3. Thus $\langle c_1, (w, x), (z, ?) \rangle_A$ reaches I_8. This becomes $\langle c_1, (w, x), (z, x) \rangle_A$ at O_9 and reaches as $\langle c_1 c_2, (w, x), (z, x) \rangle_A$ at I_8. Since z is not live at I_9, $\langle c_1 c_2, (w, x) \rangle_A$ is propagated to I_9. This causes $\langle c_1 c_2 c_2, (w, x), (z, x) \rangle_A$ to be generated at O_{10} which reaches I_9 and is represented by $\langle c_1 c_2, (w, x), (z, x) \rangle_A$. This is then regenerated as $\langle c_1 c_2 c_2, (z, x) \rangle_A$ at O_{13} because only z is live at O_{13}. Note that we do not have the liveness information along $c_1 c_2 c_2$ but we know (from above) that it is identical to that along $c_1 c_2$. We get $\langle c_1 c_2, (z, x) \rangle_A$ and $\langle c_1, (z, x) \rangle_A$ at O_{11}. Since we have no points-to information for x, we get $\langle c_1 c_2, \emptyset \rangle_A$ and $\langle c_1, \emptyset \rangle_A$ at O_{12}.

We leave it for the reader to verify that, in the second round (Fig. 7), x becomes live at I_{12} due to $z = *z$, reaches O_2 and causes $\langle \lambda, (x, y) \rangle_A$ to be generated. As a consequence, we get (z, y) at I_{12}. Note that (z, x) cannot reach I_6 along any interprocedurally valid path. The invocation graph method [3] which is generally considered the most precise flow- and context-sensitive method, *does* compute (z, x) at I_6. This shows that it is only partially context-sensitive. L-CFPA is more precise than [3] not only because of liveness but also because it is fully context-sensitive.

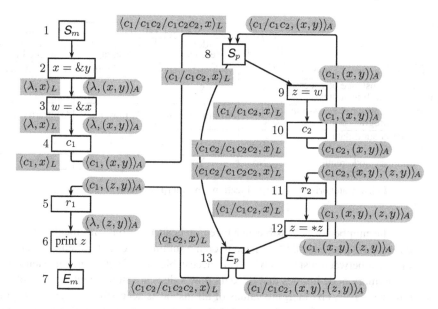

Fig. 7. Second round of liveness and points-to analysis to compute dereferencing liveness and the resulting points-to information. Only the additional information is shown.

5   Heaps, Escaping Locals and Records

Each data location statically specified in a program is an abstract location and may correspond to multiple actual locations. It may be explicitly specified by taking the address of a variable or implicitly specified as the result of *new* or *malloc*. For interprocedural analysis, we categorise all abstract locations as shown in Fig. 8.

Define *interprocedural locations* as those abstract locations which are accessible in multiple contexts reaching a given program point or whose data flow values depend (via a dataflow equation) on another interprocedural location. These are the locations for which interprocedural data flow analysis is required. Global variables and heap locations are interprocedural locations. For pointer analysis, a local variable x becomes an interprocedural location if its address escapes the procedure containing it, or there is an assignment $x = y$ or $x = *z$ with y, z or one of z's pointees being an interprocedural location. Interprocedural locations for liveness analysis are similarly identified.

It is easy to handle different instances of a local variable which is not an interprocedural location (even if its address is taken). To see how other local variables are handled, consider a local variable x which becomes interprocedural from assignment $x = y$ or $x = *z$ as in the previous paragraph. Since call strings store context-sensitive data flow values of y and z, they also distinguish between instances of x whose data flow values may differ. Thus, call strings inherently support precise interprocedural analysis of global variables and locals (even interprocedural locals) whose addresses do not escape (the entry "No*" for the latter category in Fig. 8 indicates that interprocedural analysis is either not required or is automatically supported by call-strings method without any special treatment).

Issue	Global Variable	Local Variable		Heap allocation at a given source line
		Address escapes	Address does not escape	
How many instances can exist?	Single	Arbitrarily many	Arbitrarily many	Arbitrarily many
Can a given instance be accessed in multiple calling contexts?	Yes	Yes	No	Yes
Number of instances accessible at a given program point?	At most one	Arbitrarily many	At most one	Arbitrarily many
Is interprocedural data flow analysis required?	Yes	Yes	No*	Yes
Is a summary node required?	No	Yes	No	Yes

Fig. 8. Categorisation of data locations for interprocedural pointer analysis

Since the number of accessible instances of heap locations and locals whose addresses escape is not bounded,[4] we need to create summary nodes for them. It is difficult to distinguish between instances which are accessible in different contexts. Hence creating a summary node implies that the data flow values are stored context insensitively (but flow sensitively) by merging values of all instances accessible at a given program point. A consequence of this decision is that strong updates on these abstract locations are prohibited; this is easily engineered by *Must* returning $\emptyset$ for summary-node pointees which is consistent with the requirements of $Uin_n/Uout_n$ computation.

Recall that Equation 1 does not treat '?' as a summary node. This depends on the language-defined semantics of indirect writes via uninitialised pointers. In C (because the subsequent program behaviour is undefined) or Java (because of 'NullPointerException') it is safe to regard *Must* as returning all possible values when only '?' occurs. Alternatively, were the semantics to allow subsequent code to be executed in a defined manner, then '?' needs to be treated as a summary node so that *Must* returns $\emptyset$ and indirect writes kill nothing (in general this results in reduced optimisation possibilities).

Our implementation treats an array variable as a single scalar variable with weak update (no distinction is made between different index values). Stack-allocated structures are handled field-sensitively by using the offsets of fields. Heap-allocated structures are also handled field sensitively where possible. Function pointers are handled as in [3].

6   Related Work

The reported benefits of flow and context sensitivity for pointer analysis have been mixed in literature [12–15] and many methods relax them for efficiency [5, 6, 11, 16]. It has also been observed that an increase in precision could increase efficiency [17, 11]. Both these aspects have been studied without the benefit of liveness, partially explaining marginal results. Some methods lazily compute pointer information on demand [18–21]. By contrast, L-FCPA does not depend on a client analysis and proactively computes the entire usable pointer information. If there are many demands, repeated incremental computations could be rather inefficient [22]. Efficient encoding of information by using BDDs [23] has been an orthogonal approach of achieving efficiency. Although the

---

[4] Local variables whose addresses escape may belong to recursive procedures.

usable pointer information discovered by L-FCPA is small, recording it flow sensitively in a large program may benefit from BDDs.

The imprecision caused by flow insensitivity can be partially mitigated by using SSA representation which enables a flow-insensitive method to compute flow-sensitive information for local scalar variables. For pointers, the essential properties of SSA can only be guaranteed for top-level pointers whose address is not taken. Some improvements are enabled by Factored SSA [24] or Hashed SSA [25]. In the presence of global pointer variables or multiple indirections, the advantages of SSA are limited unless interleaved rounds of SSA construction and pointer analysis are performed [26, 27]. A recent method introduces flow-sensitive kill in an otherwise flow-insensitive method [11].

Full context sensitivity can be relaxed in many ways: (a) using a context-insensitive approach, (b) using a context-sensitive approach for non-recursive portions of a program but merging data flow information in the recursive portions (e.g. [3, 27–29]), or (c) using limited depth of contexts in both recursive and non-recursive portions (e.g. the k-limited call-strings method [7] or [23]). Most context-sensitive approaches that we are aware of belong to category (b). Our fully context-sensitive approach generalises partially context-sensitive approaches such as *object-sensitivity* [30, 12, 17] as follows. For an object x and its method f, a (virtual) call $x.f(e_1, \ldots, e_n)$ is viewed as the call $(x.f\_in\_vtab)(\&x, e_1, \ldots, e_n)$. Thus object identification reduces to capturing the flow of values which is inherently supported by full flow and context sensitivity.

We highlight some key ideas that have not been covered above. A memoisation-based functional approach enumerates partial transfer functions [28] whereas an alternative functional approach constructs full transfer functions hierarchically in terms of pointer indirection levels [27]. The invocation-graph-based approach unfolds a call graph in terms of call chains [3]. Finally, a radically different approach begins with flow- and context-insensitive information which is refined systematically to restrict it to flow- and context-sensitive information [29]. These approaches merge points-to information in recursive contexts (category (b) above). Fig. 9.6 (page 305) in [1] contains an example for which a method belonging to category (b) or (c) above cannot compute precise result—the pointer assignments in the recursion unwinding part undo the effect of the pointer assignments in the part that builds up recursion and the overall function is an identity function. When all recursive calls receive the same (merged) information, the undo effect on the pointer information cannot be captured.

Finally, many investigations tightly couple analysis specification and implementation; by contrast our formulation maintains a clean separation between the two and does not depend on intricate procedural algorithms or ad-hoc implementation for efficiency.

7   Implementation and Empirical Measurements

We implemented L-FCPA and FCPA in GCC 4.6.0 using the GCC's Link Time Optimisation (LTO) framework.[5] We executed them on various programs from SPEC CPU2006 and CPU2000 Integer Benchmarks on a machine with 16 GB RAM with 8 64-bit Intel i7-960 CPUs running at 3.20GHz. We compared the performance of three

---

[5] They can be downloaded from
http://www.cse.iitb.ac.in/grc/index.php?page=lipta

Table 1. Time and unique points-to pairs measurements. For h264ref, FCPA ran out of memory.

Program	kLoC	Call Sites	Time in milliseconds				Unique points-to pairs		
			L-FCPA		FCPA	GPTA	L-FCPA	FCPA	GPTA
			Liveness	Points-to					
lbm	0.9	33	0.55	0.52	1.9	5.2	12	507	1911
mcf	1.6	29	1.04	0.62	9.5	3.4	41	367	2159
libquantum	2.6	258	2.0	1.8	5.6	4.8	49	119	2701
bzip2	3.7	233	4.5	4.8	28.1	30.2	60	210	8.8×10^4
parser	7.7	1123	1.2×10^3	145.6	4.3×10^5	422.12	531	4196	1.9×10^4
sjeng	10.5	678	858.2	99.0	3.2×10^4	38.1	267	818	1.1×10^4
hmmer	20.6	1292	90.0	62.9	2.9×10^5	246.3	232	5805	1.9×10^6
h264ref	36.0	1992	2.2×10^5	2.0×10^5	?	4.3×10^3	1683	?	1.6×10^7

methods: L-FCPA, FCPA and GPTA (GCC's points-to analysis). Both L-FCPA and FCPA are flow and context sensitive and use call strings with value-based termination. L-FCPA uses liveness whereas FCPA does not. GPTA is flow and context insensitive but acquires partial flow sensitivity through SSA.

Since our main goal was to find out if liveness increases the precision of points-to information, both L-FCPA and FCPA are naive implementations that use linked lists and linear searches within them. Our measurements confirm this hypothesis beyond doubt, but we were surprised by the overall implementation performance because we had not designed for time/space efficiency or scalability. We were able to run naive L-FCPA on programs of around 30kLoC but not on the larger programs.

Table 1 presents the computation time and number of points-to pairs whereas Tables 2 and 3 present measurements of points-to information and context information respectively. To measure the sparseness of information, we created four buckets of the numbers of points-to pairs and call strings: 0, 1–4, 5–8 and 9 or more. We counted the number of basic blocks for each bucket of points-to information and the number of functions for each bucket of context information. Our data shows that:

- The usable pointer information is (a) rather sparse (64% of basic blocks have 0 points-to pairs), and (b) rather small (four programs have at most 8 points-to pairs and in other programs, 9+ points-to pairs reach fewer than 4% basic blocks). In contrast, GPTA computes an order-of-magnitude-larger number of points-to pairs at each basic block (see the last column in Table 1).
- The number of contexts required for computing the usable pointer information is (a) rather sparse (56% or more basic blocks have 0 call strings), and (b) rather small (six programs have at most 8 call strings; in other programs, 9+ call strings reach less than 3% basic blocks). Thus, contrary to the common apprehension, context information need not be exponential in practice. Value-based termination reduces the number of call strings dramatically [10] and the use of liveness enhances this effect further by restricting the computation of data flow values to the usable information.

Table 2. Liveness restricts the analysis to usable pointer information which is small and sparse

Program	Total no. of BBs	No. and percentage of basic blocks (BBs) for points-to (pt) pair counts							
		0 pt pairs		1-4 pt pairs		5-8 pt pairs		9+ pt pairs	
		L-FCPA	FCPA	L-FCPA	FCPA	L-FCPA	FCPA	L-FCPA	FCPA
lbm	252	229 (90.9%)	61 (24.2%)	23 (9.1%)	82 (32.5%)	0	66 (26.2%)	0	43 (17.1%)
mcf	472	356 (75.4%)	160 (33.9%)	116 (24.6%)	2 (0.4%)	0	1 (0.2%)	0	309 (65.5%)
libquantum	1642	1520 (92.6%)	793 (48.3%)	119 (7.2%)	796 (48.5%)	3 (0.2%)	46 (2.8%)	0	7 (0.4%)
bzip2	2746	2624 (95.6%)	1085 (39.5%)	118 (4.3%)	12 (0.4%)	3 (0.1%)	12 (0.4%)	1 (0.0%)	1637 (59.6%)
		9+ pt pairs in L-FCPA: Tot 1, Min 12, Max 12, Mean 12.0, Median 12, Mode 12							
sjeng	6000	4571 (76.2%)	3239 (54.0%)	1208 (20.1%)	12 (0.2%)	221 (3.7%)	41 (0.7%)	0	2708 (45.1%)
hmmer	14418	13483 (93.5%)	8357 (58.0%)	896 (6.2%)	21 (0.1%)	24 (0.2%)	91 (0.6%)	15 (0.1%)	5949 (41.3%)
		9+ pt pairs in L-FCPA: Tot 6, Min 10, Max 16, Mean 13.3, Median 13, Mode 10							
parser	6875	4823 (70.2%)	1821 (26.5%)	1591 (23.1%)	25 (0.4%)	252 (3.7%)	154 (2.2%)	209 (3.0%)	4875 (70.9%)
		9+ pt pairs in L-FCPA: Tot 13, Min 9, Max 53, Mean 27.9, Median 18, Mode 9							
h264ref	21315	13729 (64.4%)	?	4760 (22.3%)	?	2035 (9.5%)	?	791 (3.7%)	?
		9+ pt pairs in L-FCPA: Tot 44, Min 9, Max 98, Mean 36.3, Median 31, Mode 9							

The significant increase in precision achieved by L-FCPA suggests that a pointer analysis need not compute exponentially large information. We saw this sub-exponential trend in programs of up to around 30kLoC and anticipate it might hold for larger programs too—because although reachable pointer information may increase significantly, usable information need not accumulate and may remain distributed in the program.

A comparison with GPTA shows that using liveness reduces the execution time too— L-FCPA outperforms GPTA for most programs smaller than 30kLoC. That a flow- and context-sensitive analysis could be faster than flow- and context-insensitive analysis came as a surprise to us. In hindsight, this is possible because the information that we can gainfully use is much smaller than commonly thought. Note that a flow- and context-insensitive analysis cannot exploit the small size of usable pointer information because it is small only when considered flow and context sensitively.

The hypothesis that our implementation suffers because of linear search in linked lists was confirmed by an accidental discovery: in order to eliminate duplicate pairs in GPTA, we used our linear list implementation of sets from L-FCPA which never adds duplicate entries. The resulting GPTA took more than an hour for the *hmmer* program instead of the original 246.3 milliseconds! Another potential source of inefficiency concerns the over-eager liveness computation to reduce the points-to pairs in L-CFPA: a new round of liveness is invoked when a new points-to pair for y is discovered for $x = *y$ putting on hold the points-to analysis. This explains the unusually large time spent in liveness analysis compared to points-to analysis for programs *parser* and *sjeng*.

Table 3. Context information for computing usable pointer information is small and sparse

Program	Total no. of functions	No. and percentage of functions for call-string counts							
		0 call strings		1-4 call strings		5-8 call strings		9+ call strings	
		L-FCPA	FCPA	L-FCPA	FCPA	L-FCPA	FCPA	L-FCPA	FCPA
lbm	22	16 (72.7%)	3 (13.6%)	6 (27.3%)	19 (86.4%)	0	0	0	0
mcf	25	16 (64.0%)	3 (12.0%)	9 (36.0%)	22 (88.0%)	0	0	0	0
bzip2	100	88 (88.0%)	38 (38.0%)	12 (12.0%)	62 (62.0%)	0	0	0	0
libquantum	118	100 (84.7%)	56 (47.5%)	17 (14.4%)	62 (52.5%)	1 (0.8%)	0	0	0
sjeng	151	96 (63.6%)	37 (24.5%)	43 (28.5%)	45 (29.8%)	12 (7.9%)	15 (9.9%)	0	54 (35.8%)
hmmer	584	548 (93.8%)	330 (56.5%)	32 (5.5%)	175 (30.0%)	4 (0.7%)	26 (4.5%)	0	53 (9.1%)
parser	372	246 (66.1%)	76 (20.4%)	118 (31.7%)	135 (36.3%)	4 (1.1%)	63 (16.9%)	4 (1.1%)	98 (26.3%)
	9+ L-FCPA call strings: Tot 4, Min 10, Max 52, Mean 32.5, Median 29, Mode 10								
h264ref	624	351 (56.2%)	?	240 (38.5%)	?	14 (2.2%)	?	19 (3.0%)	?
	9+ L-FCPA call strings: Tot 14, Min 9, Max 56, Mean 27.9, Median 24, Mode 9								

The number of rounds of analysis required for these programs was much higher than in other programs of comparable size. Finally, GCC's LTO framework has only two options: either to load no CFG or to load all CFGs at the same time. Since the size of the entire program could be large, this affects the locality and hence the cache behaviour.

8   Conclusions and Future Work

We have described a data flow analysis which jointly calculates points-to and liveness information. It is fully flow- and context-sensitive and uses recent refinements of the call-strings approach. One novel aspect of our approach is that it is effectively bi-directional (such analysis seem relatively rarely exploited).

Initial results from our naive prototype implementation were impressive: unsurprisingly our analysis produced much more precise results, but by an order of magnitude (in terms of the size of the calculated points-to information). The reduction of this size allowed our naive implementation also to run faster than GCC's points-to analysis at least for programs up to 30kLoC. This is significant because GCC's analysis compromises both on flow and context sensitivity. This confirms our belief that the usable pointer information is so small and sparse that we can achieve both precision and efficiency without sacrificing one for the other. Although the benefit of precision in efficiency has been observed before [17, 11], we are not aware of any study that shows the sparseness and small size of points-to information to this extent.

We would like to take our work further by exploring the following:

- Improving our implementation in ways such as: using efficient data structures (vectors or hash tables, or perhaps BDDs); improving GCC's LTO framework to allow on-demand loading of individual CFGs instead of loading the complete supergraph; and experimenting with less-eager strategies of invoking liveness analysis.
- Exploring the reasons for the 30kLoC speed threshold; perhaps there are ways in practice to partition most bigger programs (around loosely-coupled boundaries) without significant loss of precision.
- We note that data flow information often only slightly changes when revisiting a node compared to the information produced by the earlier visits. Hence, we plan to explore incremental formulations of L-FCPA.
- GCC passes hold alias information in a per-variable data structure thereby using the same information for every occurrence of the variable. We would like to change this to use point-specific information computed by L-FCPA and measure how client analyses/optimisations benefit from increased precision.

Acknowledgements. Prashant Singh Rawat was supported by GCC Resource Center funding as part of the Government of India's National Resource Center for Free and Open Source Software (NRCFOSS). Empirical measurements were carried out by Prachee Yogi and Aboli Aradhye. Prachee also implemented intraprocedural analysis in Prolog. Ashwin Paranjape was involved in initial explorations. We are grateful to the anonymous referee who requested more detail on our treatment of allocation and summary nodes (Section 5); this helped our presentation.

References

1. Khedker, U.P., Sanyal, A., Karkare, B.: Data Flow Analysis: Theory and Practice. CRC Press Inc. (2009)
2. Kildall, G.A.: A unified approach to global program optimization. In: Proc. of POPL 1973, pp. 194–206 (1973)
3. Emami, M., Ghiya, R., Hendren, L.J.: Context-sensitive interprocedural points-to analysis in the presence of function pointers. In: Proc. of PLDI 1994, pp. 242–256 (1994)
4. Kanade, A., Khedker, U.P., Sanyal, A.: Heterogeneous Fixed Points with Application to Points-To Analysis. In: Yi, K. (ed.) APLAS 2005. LNCS, vol. 3780, pp. 298–314. Springer, Heidelberg (2005)
5. Andersen, L.O.: Program Analysis and Specialization for the C Programming Language. PhD thesis, DIKU, University of Copenhagen (1994)
6. Steensgaard, B.: Points-to analysis in almost linear time. In: Proc. of POPL 1996, pp. 32–41 (1996)
7. Sharir, M., Pnueli, A.: Two approaches to interprocedural data flow analysis. In: Muchnick, S.S., Jones, N.D. (eds.) Program Flow Analysis: Theory and Applications. Prentice-Hall Inc. (1981)
8. Reps, T., Horwitz, S., Sagiv, M.: Precise interprocedural dataflow analysis via graph reachability. In: Proc. of POPL 1995, pp. 49–61 (1995)
9. Knoop, J., Steffen, B.: The Interprocedural Coincidence Theorem. In: Pfahler, P., Kastens, U. (eds.) CC 1992. LNCS, vol. 641, pp. 125–140. Springer, Heidelberg (1992)

10. Khedker, U.P., Karkare, B.: Efficiency, Precision, Simplicity, and Generality in Interprocedural Data Flow Analysis: Resurrecting the Classical Call Strings Method. In: Hendren, L. (ed.) CC 2008. LNCS, vol. 4959, pp. 213–228. Springer, Heidelberg (2008)

11. Lhoták, O., Chung, K.A.: Points-to analysis with efficient strong updates. In: Proc. of POPL 2011, pp. 3–16 (2011)

12. Lhoták, O., Hendren, L.: Context-Sensitive Points-to Analysis: Is It Worth It? In: Mycroft, A., Zeller, A. (eds.) CC 2006. LNCS, vol. 3923, pp. 47–64. Springer, Heidelberg (2006)

13. Ruf, E.: Context-insensitive alias analysis reconsidered. In: Proc. of PLDI 1995, pp. 13–22 (1995)

14. Shapiro, M., Horwitz, S.: The Effects of the Precision of Pointer Analysis. In: Van Hentenryck, P. (ed.) SAS 1997. LNCS, vol. 1302, pp. 16–34. Springer, Heidelberg (1997)

15. Hind, M., Pioli, A.: Assessing the Effects of Flow-Sensitivity on Pointer Alias Analyses. In: Levi, G. (ed.) SAS 1998. LNCS, vol. 1503, pp. 57–81. Springer, Heidelberg (1998)

16. Hardekopf, B.C., Lin, C.: The ant and the grasshopper: Fast and accurate pointer analysis for millions of lines of code. In: Proc. of PLDI 2007, pp. 290–299 (2007)

17. Smaragdakis, Y., Bravenboer, M., Lhoták, O.: Pick your contexts well: Understanding object-sensitivity. In: Proc. of POPL 2011, pp. 17–30 (2011)

18. Guyer, S.Z., Lin, C.: Client-Driven Pointer Analysis. In: Cousot, R. (ed.) SAS 2003. LNCS, vol. 2694, pp. 214–236. Springer, Heidelberg (2003)

19. Heintze, N., Tardieu, O.: Demand-driven pointer analysis. In: Proc. of PLDI 2001, pp. 24–34 (2001)

20. Sridharan, M., Gopan, D., Shan, L., Bodík, R.: Demand-driven points-to analysis for Java. In: Proc. of OOPSLA 2005, pp. 59–76 (2005)

21. Zheng, X., Rugina, R.: Demand-driven alias analysis for C. In: Proc. of POPL 2008, pp. 197–208 (2008)

22. Rosen, B.K.: Linear cost is sometimes quadratic. In: Proc. of POPL 1981, pp. 117–124 (1981)

23. Whaley, J., Lam, M.S.: Cloning-based context-sensitive pointer alias analysis using binary decision diagrams. In: Proc. of PLDI 2004, pp. 131–144 (2004)

24. Choi, J.D., Cytron, R., Ferrante, J.: On the efficient engineering of ambitious program analysis. IEEE Trans. Softw. Eng. 20, 105–114 (1994)

25. Chow, F.C., Chan, S., Liu, S.-M., Lo, R., Streich, M.: Effective Representation of Aliases and Indirect Memory Operations in SSA Form. In: Gyimóthy, T. (ed.) CC 1996. LNCS, vol. 1060, pp. 253–267. Springer, Heidelberg (1996)

26. Hasti, R., Horwitz, S.: Using static single assignment form to improve flow-insensitive pointer analysis. In: Proc. of PLDI 1998, pp. 97–105 (1998)

27. Yu, H., Xue, J., Huo, W., Feng, X., Zhang, Z.: Level by level: making flow- and context-sensitive pointer analysis scalable for millions of lines of code. In: Proc. of CGO 2010, pp. 218–229 (2010)

28. Wilson, R.P., Lam, M.S.: Efficient context-sensitive pointer analysis for C programs. In: Proc. of POPL 1995, pp. 1–12 (1995)

29. Kahlon, V.: Bootstrapping: a technique for scalable flow and context-sensitive pointer alias analysis. In: Proc. of PLDI 2008, pp. 249–259 (2008)

30. Milanova, A., Rountev, A., Ryder, B.G.: Parameterized object sensitivity for points-to analysis for Java. ACM Trans. Softw. Eng. Methodol. 14, 1–41 (2005)

Succinct Representations
for Abstract Interpretation[*]
Combined Analysis Algorithms
and Experimental Evaluation

Julien Henry[1,2], David Monniaux[1,3], and Matthieu Moy[1,4]

[1] VERIMAG laboratory, Grenoble, France
[2] Université Joseph Fourier
[3] CNRS
[4] Grenoble-INP

Abstract. Abstract interpretation techniques can be made more precise by distinguishing paths inside loops, at the expense of possibly exponential complexity. SMT-solving techniques and sparse representations of paths and sets of paths avoid this pitfall.

We improve previously proposed techniques for guided static analysis and the generation of disjunctive invariants by combining them with techniques for succinct representations of paths and symbolic representations for transitions based on static single assignment.

Because of the non-monotonicity of the results of abstract interpretation with widening operators, it is difficult to conclude that some abstraction is more precise than another based on theoretical local precision results. We thus conducted extensive comparisons between our new techniques and previous ones, on a variety of open-source packages.

1 Introduction

Static analysis by abstract interpretation is a fully automatic program analysis method. When applied to imperative programs, it computes an inductive invariant mapping each program location (or a subset thereof) to a set of states represented symbolically [8]. For instance, if we are only interested in scalar numerical program variables, such a set may be a convex polyhedron (the set of solutions of a system of linear inequalities) [10,16,2,4].

In such an analysis, information may flow *forward* or *backward*; forward program analysis computes super-sets of the states reachable from the initialization of the program, backward program analysis computes super-sets of the states co-reachable from some property of interest (for instance, the violation of an assertion). In forward analysis, control-flow joins correspond to convex hulls if using convex polyhedra (more generally, they correspond to least upper bounds in a lattice); in backward analysis, it is control-flow splits that correspond to convex hulls.

---

[*] ⟳ This work was partially funded by ANR project "ASOPT".

A. Miné and D. Schmidt (Eds.): SAS 2012, LNCS 7460, pp. 283–299, 2012.

It is a known limitation of program analysis by abstract interpretation that this convex hull, or more generally, least upper bound operation, may introduce states that cannot occur in the real program: for instance, the convex hull of the intervals $[-2, -1]$ and $[1, 2]$ is $[-2, 2]$, strictly larger than the union of the two. Such introduction may prevent proving desired program properties, for instance $\neq 0$. The alternative is to keep the union symbolic (e.g. compute using $[-2, -1] \cup [1, 2]$) and thus compute in the *disjunctive completion* of the lattice, but the number of terms in the union may grow exponentially with the number of successive tests in the program to analyze, not to mention difficulties for designing suitable widening operators for enforcing the convergence of fixpoint iterations [2,4,3]. The exponential growth of the number of terms in the union may be controlled by heuristics that judiciously apply least upper bound operations, as in the *trace partitioning domain* [29] implemented in the Astrée analyzer [7,9].

Assuming we are interested in a loop-free program fragment, the above approach of keeping symbolic unions gives the same results as performing the analysis separately over every path in the fragment. A recent method for finding disjunctive loop invariants [15] is based on this idea: each path inside the loop body is considered separately. Two recent proposals use SMT-solving [22] as a decision procedure for the satisfiability of first-order arithmetic formulas in order to enumerate only paths that are needed for the progress of the analysis [12,27]. They can equivalently be seen as analyses over a multigraph of transitions between some distinguished control nodes. This multigraph has an exponential number of edges, but is never explicitly represented in memory; instead, this graph is *implicitly* or *succinctly* represented: its edges are enumerated as needed as solutions to SMT problems.

An additional claim in favor of the methods that distinguish paths inside the loop body [15,27] is that they tend to generate better invariants than methods that do not, by behaving better with respect to the *widening operators* [8] used for enforcing convergence when searching for loop invariants by Kleene iterations. A related technique, *guided static analysis* [14], computes successive loop invariants for increasing subsets of the transitions taken into account, until all transitions are considered; again, the claim is that this approach avoids some gross over-approximation introduced by widenings.

All these methods improve the precision of the analysis by keeping the same abstract domain (say, convex polyhedra) but changing the operations applied and their ordering. An alternative is to change the abstract domain (e.g. octagons, convex polyhedra [25]), or the widening operator [1,17].

This article makes the following contributions:

1. We recast the guided static analysis technique from [14] on the expanded multigraph from [27], considering entire paths instead of individual transitions, using SMT queries and binary decision diagrams (See §3).
2. We improve the technique for obtaining disjunctive invariants from [15] by replacing the explicit exhaustive enumeration of paths by a sequence of SMT queries (See §4).
3. We implemented these techniques, in addition to "classical" iterations and the original guided static analysis, inside a prototype static analyzer. This

tool uses the LLVM bitcode format [23,24] as input, which can be produced by compilation from C, C++ and Fortran, enabling it to be run on many real-life programs. It uses the APRON library [21], which supports a variety of abstract domains for numerical variables, from which we can choose with minimal changes to our analyzer.

4. We conducted extensive experiments with this tool, on real-life programs.

2 Bases

2.1 Static Analysis by Abstract Interpretation

Let X be the set of possible states of the program variables; for instance, if the program has 3 unbounded integer variables, then $X = \mathbb{Z}^3$. The set $\mathcal{P}(X)$ of subsets of X, partially ordered by inclusion, is the *concrete domain*. An *abstract domain* is a set $X^\sharp$ equipped with a partial order $\sqsubseteq$ (the associated strict order being $\sqsubset$); for instance, it can be the domain of convex polyhedra in $\mathbb{Q}^3$ ordered by geometric inclusion. The concrete and abstract domains are connected by a monotone *concretization* function $\gamma : (X^\sharp, \sqsubseteq) \to (\mathcal{P}(X), \subseteq)$: an element $x^\sharp \in X^\sharp$ represents a set $\gamma(x^\sharp)$.

We also assume a join operator $\sqcup : X^\sharp \times X^\sharp \to X^\sharp$, with infix notation; in practice, it is generally a least upper bound operation, but we only need it to satisfy $\gamma(x^\sharp) \cup \gamma(y^\sharp) \subseteq \gamma(x^\sharp \sqcup y^\sharp)$ for all $x^\sharp, y^\sharp$.

Classically, one considers the control-flow graph of the program, with edges labeled with concrete transition relations (e.g. $x' = x + 1$ for an instruction x = x+1;), and attaches an abstract element to each control point. A concrete transition relation $\tau \subseteq X \times X$ is replaced by an abstract *forward abstract transformer* $\tau^\sharp : X^\sharp \to X^\sharp$, such that $\forall x^\sharp \in X^\sharp, x, x' \in X, \ x \in \gamma(x^\sharp) \wedge (x, x') \in \tau \implies x' \in \gamma \circ \tau^\sharp(x^\sharp)$. It is easy to see that if to any control point $p \in P$ we attach an abstract element $x_p^\sharp$ such that (i) for any p, $\gamma(x_p^\sharp)$ includes all initial states possible at control node p (ii) for any p, p', $\tau_{p,p'}^\sharp(x_p^\sharp) \sqsubseteq x_{p'}^\sharp$, noting $\tau_{p,p'}$ the transition from p to p', then $(\gamma(x_p^\sharp))_{p \in P}$ form an *inductive invariant*: by induction, when the control point is p, the program state always lies in $\gamma(x_p^\sharp)$.

Kleene iterations compute such an inductive invariant as the stationary limit, if it exists, of the following system: for each p, initialize $x_p^\sharp$ such that $\gamma(x_p^\sharp)$ is a superset of the initial states at point p; then iterate the following: if $\tau_{p,p'}^\sharp(x_p^\sharp) \not\sqsubseteq x_{p'}^\sharp$, replace $x_{p'}^\sharp$ by $x_{p'}^\sharp \sqcup \tau_{p,p'}^\sharp(x_p^\sharp)$. Such a stationary limit is bound to exist if $X^\sharp$ has no infinite ascending chain $a_1 \sqsubset a_2 \sqsubset \ldots$; this condition is however not met by domains such as intervals or convex polyhedra.

Widening-accelerated Kleene iterations proceed by replacing $x_{p'}^\sharp \sqcup \tau_{p,p'}^\sharp(x_p^\sharp)$ by $x_{p'}^\sharp \triangledown (x_{p'}^\sharp \sqcup \tau_{p,p'}^\sharp(x_p^\sharp))$ where $\triangledown$ is a *widening operator*: for all $x^\sharp, y^\sharp$, $\gamma(y^\sharp) \subseteq \gamma(x^\sharp \triangledown y^\sharp)$, and any sequence $u_1^\sharp, u_2^\sharp, \ldots$ of the form $u_{n+1}^\sharp = u_n^\sharp \triangledown v_n^\sharp$, where $v_n^\sharp$ is another sequence, become stationary. The stationary limit $(x_p^\sharp)_{p \in P}$, defines an inductive invariant $(\gamma(x_p^\sharp))_{p \in P}$. Note that this invariant is not, in general, the least one expressible in the abstract domain, and may depend on the iteration ordering (the successive choices p, p').

Once an inductive invariant $\gamma((x_p^\#)_{p \in P})$ has been obtained, one can attempt *decreasing* or *narrowing* iterations to reduce it. In their simplest form, this just means running the following operation until a fixpoint or a maximal number of iterations are reached: for any p', replace $x_{p'}^\#$ by $x_{p'}^\# \cap \left(\bigsqcup_{p \in P} \tau_{p,p'}^\#(x_p^\#) \right)$. The result also defines an inductive invariant. These decreasing iterations are indispensable to recover properties from guards (tests) in the program in most iteration settings; unfortunately, certain loops, particularly those involving identity (no-operation) transitions, may foil them: the iterations immediately reach a fixpoint and do not decrease further (see example in §2.3). Sections 2.4 and 2.5 describe techniques that work around this problem.

2.2   SMT-Solving

Boolean satisfiability (SAT) is the canonical NP-complete problem: given a propositional formula (e.g. $(a \vee \neg b) \wedge (\neg a \vee b \vee \neg c)$), decide whether it is satisfiable — and, if so, output a satisfying assignment. Despite an exponential worst-case complexity, the DPLL algorithm [22,6] solves many useful SAT problems in practice.

SAT was extended to *satisfiability modulo theory* (SMT): in addition to propositional literals, SMT formulas admit atoms from a theory. For instance, the theories of linear integer arithmetic (LIA) and linear real arithmetic (LRA) have atoms of the form $a_1 x_1 + \cdots + a_n x_n \bowtie C$ where $a_1, \ldots, a_n, C$ are integer constants, $x_1, \ldots, x_n$ are variables (interpreted over $\mathbb{Z}$ for LIA and $\mathbb{R}$ or $\mathbb{Q}$ for LRA), and $\bowtie$ is a comparison operator $=, \neq, <, \leq, >, \geq$. Satisfiability for LIA and LRA is NP-complete, yet tools based on DPLL(T) approach [22,6] solve many useful SMT problems in practice. All these tools provide a *satisfying assignment* if the problem is satisfiable.

2.3   A Simple, Motivating Example

Consider the following program, adapted from [27], where input(a, b) stands for a nondeterministic input in $[a, b]$ (the control-flow graph on the right depicts the loop body, s is the start node and e the end node):

```
1 void rate_limiter() {
2    int x_old = 0;
3    while (1) {
4       int x = input(-100000, 100000);
5       if (x > x_old+10) x = x_old+10;
6       if (x < x_old-10) x = x_old-10;
7       x_old = x;
8 } }
```

This program implements a construct commonly found in control programs (in e.g. automotive or avionics): a rate or slope limiter.

The expected inductive invariant is x_old $\in [-100000, 100000]$, but classical abstract interpretation using intervals (or octagons or polyhedra) finds x_old $\in (-\infty, +\infty)$ [9]. Let us briefly see why.

Widening iterations converge to x_old $\in (-\infty, +\infty)$; let us now see why decreasing iterations fail to recover the desired invariant. The x > x_old+10 test at line 6, if taken, yields x_old $\in (-\infty, 99990)$; followed by x = x_old+10, we obtain x $\in (-\infty, 100000)$, and the same after union with the no-operation "else" branch. Line 7 yields x $\in (-\infty, +\infty)$.

We could use "widening up to" or "widening with thresholds", propagating the "magic values" ± 100000 associated to x into x_old, but these syntactic approaches cannot directly cope with programs for which x $\in [-100000, +100000]$ is itself obtained by analysis. The guided static analysis of [14] does not perform better, and also obtains x_old $\in (-\infty, +\infty)$.

In contrast, let us distinguish all four possible execution paths through the tests at lines 6 and 7. The path through both "else" branches is infeasible; the program is thus equivalent to a program with 3 paths:

```
1 void rate_limiter() {
2   int x_old = 0;
3   while (1) {
4     int x = input(-100000, 100000);
5     if (x > x_old+10) x_old = x_old+10;
6     else if (x < x_old-10) x_old = x_old-10;
7     else x_old = x;
8 } }
```

Classical interval analysis on this program yields x_old $\in [-100000, 100000]$. We have transformed the program, manually pruning out infeasible paths; yet in general the resulting program could be exponentially larger than the first, even though not all feasible paths are needed to compute the invariant.

Following recent suggestions [12,27], we avoid this space explosion by keeping the second program implicit while simulating its analysis. This means we work on an implicitly represented transition multigraph ; it is succinctly represented by the transition graph of the first program. Our first contribution (§3) is to recast the "guided analysis" from [14] on such a succinct representation of the paths in lieu of the individual transitions. A similar explosion occurs in disjunctive invariant generation, following [15]; our second contribution (§4) applies our implicit representation to their method.

2.4   Guided Static Analysis

Guided static analysis was proposed by [14] as an improvement over classical upward Kleene iterations with widening. Consider the program in Fig. 1, taken from [14].

Classical iterations on the domain of convex polyhedra [10,1] or octagons [25] start with $x = 0 \wedge x = 0$, then continue with $x = y \wedge 0 \leq x \leq 1$. The widening operator extrapolates from these two iterations and yields $x = y \wedge x \geq 0$. From

```
1 int x = 0, y = 0;
2 while (1) {
3    if (x <= 50) y++;
4    else y--;
5    if (y < 0) break;
6    x++;
7 }
```

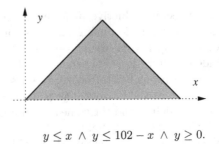

$$y \leq x \;\wedge\; y \leq 102 - x \;\wedge\; y \geq 0.$$

Fig. 1. Example program and its invariant: the piecewise linear, solid line is the strongest invariant, the grayed polyhedron is its convex hull

there, the "else" branch at line 4 may be taken; with further widening, $0 \leq y \leq x$ is obtained as a loop invariant, and thus the computed loop postcondition is $x \geq 0 \wedge y = 0$. Yet the strongest invariant is $(0 \leq x \leq 51 \wedge y = x) \vee (51 \leq x \leq 102 \wedge x + y = 102)$, and its convex hull, a convex polyhedron (Fig. 1).

Intuitively, this disappointing result is obtained because widening extrapolates from the first iterations of the loop, but the loop has two different phases ($x \leq 50$ and $x > 50$) with different behaviors, thus the extrapolation from the first phase is not valid for the second.

Gopan and Reps' idea is to analyze the first phase of the loop with a widening and narrowing sequence, and thus obtain $0 \leq x \leq 50 \wedge y = x$, and then analyze the second phase, finally obtaining invariant (2.4); each phase is identified by the tests taken or not taken.

The analysis starts by identifying the tests taken and not taken during the first iteration of the loop, starting in the loop initialization. The branches not taken are pruned from the loop body, yielding:

```
while(1) {
    if(x <= 50) y++;
    else break; /* not taken in phase 1 */
    if(y < 0) break;
    x++;
}
```

Analyzing this loop using widening and narrowing on convex polyhedra or octagons yields the loop invariant $0 \leq x \leq 51 \wedge y = x$. Now, the transition at line 4 becomes feasible; and we analyze the full loop, starting iterations from $0 \leq x \leq 51 \wedge y = x$, and obtain invariant (2.4) in Fig 1.

More generally, this analysis method considers an ascending sequence of subsets of the transitions in the loop body ; for each subset, an inductive invariant is computed for the program restricted to it. The starting subset consists in the transitions reachable in one step from the loop initialization. If for a given subset S in the sequence, no transitions outside S are reachable from the inductive invariant attached to S, then iterations stop; otherwise, add these transitions to S and iterate more. Termination ensues from the finiteness of the control-flow graph.

2.5   Path-focusing

Monniaux & Gonnord's *path-focusing* [27] technique distinguishes the different paths in the program in order to avoid loss of precision due to merge operations. Since the number of paths may be exponential, the technique keeps them implicit and computes them when needed using SMT-solving. The (accelerated) Kleene iterations (§2.1) are computed over a reduced multigraph instead of the classical transition graph.

Let P be the set of control points in the transition graph, $P_W \subseteq P$ the set of widening points such that removing the points in P_W gives an acyclic graph. One can choose a set P_R such that $P_W \subseteq P_R \subseteq P$.

The set of paths is kept implicit by an SMT formula ρ expressing the semantics of the program, assuming that the transition semantics can be expressed within a decidable theory. For an easy construction of ρ, we also assume that the program is expressed in SSA form, meaning that each variable is only assigned once in the transition graph. This is not a restriction, since there exists standard algorithms that transform a program into an SSA format.

This formula contains Boolean *reachability predicates* b_i for each control points $p_i \notin P_R$, b_i^s and b_i^d for each $p_i \in P_R$, so that a path $p_{i_1} \to p_{i_2} \to \cdots \to p_{i_n}$ between two points $p_{i_1}, p_{i_n} \in P_R$ can easily be expressed as the conjunction $b_{i_1}^s \wedge \bigwedge_{2 \leq k < n} b_{i_k} \wedge b_{i_n}^d$. The Boolean b_i^s is *true* when the path starts at point p_i, whereas b_i^d is *true* when the path arrives at p_i. In other words, we split the points in P_R into a *source* point, with only outgoing transitions, and a *destination* point, with only incoming transitions, so that the resulting graph is acyclic and there are no paths going through control points in P_R.

In order to find focus paths, we solve an SMT formula which is satisfiable when there exists a path starting at a point $p_i \in P_R$ in a state included in the current invariant candidate X_i, and arriving at a point $p_j \in P_R$ in a state outside X_j. In this case, we construct this path using the model and update X_j. When $p_i = p_j$, meaning that the path is actually a self-loop, we can apply a widening/narrowing sequence, or even compute the transitive closure of the loop (or an approximation thereof, or its application to X_i) using abstract acceleration [13].

We assume that we can encode the concrete semantics of the program into the SMT formula, or at least an abstraction thereof at least as precise as the one applied by the abstract interpreter (in simple terms: we want to avoid the case where the SMT solver exhibits a possible path, but the static analyzer realizes that this path is infeasible; this would lead to nontermination, because the SMT solver would exhibit the same path on the next iteration). A workaround would be to apply *satisfiability modulo path programs* [18]: from each path ruled infeasible by abstract interpretation, extract a blocking clause for the SAT solver underlying the SMT-solver.

3   Guided Analysis over the Paths

Guided static analysis, as proposed by [14], applies to the transition graph of the program. We now present a new technique applying this analysis on the implicit multigraph from [27], thus avoiding control flow merges with unfeasible paths. In this section, we use the same notations as §2.5.

The combination of these two techniques aims at first discovering a precise inductive invariant for a subset of paths between two points in P_R, by the mean of ascending and narrowing iterations. When an inductive invariant has been found, we add new feasible paths to the subset and compute an inductive invariant for this new subset, starting with the results from the previous analysis. In other words, our technique considers an ascending sequence of subsets of the paths between two points in P_R. We iterate the operations until the whole program (i.e all the feasible paths) has been considered. The result will then be an inductive invariant of the entire program.

The ascending iteration applies path-focusing [27] to a subset of the multigraph. As [14], we do some narrowing, to recover precision lost by widening, *before* computing and taking into account new feasible paths. Thus, our technique combines the advantages of *Guided Static Analysis* and *Path-focusing*.

Algorithm 1 performs Guided static analysis on the implicitly represented multigraph. I_p denotes a set of initial states at program point p (thus $\emptyset$ for most p). The current working subset of paths, noted P and initially empty, is stored using a compact representation, such as binary decision diagrams. We also maintain two sets of control points:

- A' : points in P_R that may be the starting points of new feasible paths.
- A : points in P_R on which we apply the ascending iterations. When the abstract value of a control point p is updated, p is added to both A and A'.

Algorithm 1. Guided static analysis on implicit multigraph

1: $A' \leftarrow \{p|P_R/I_p \neq \emptyset\}$
2: $A \leftarrow \emptyset$
3: $P \leftarrow \emptyset$ // Paths in the current subset
4: **for all** $p_i \in P_R$ **do**
5:     $X_i \leftarrow I_{p_i}$
6: **end for**
7: **while** $A' \neq \emptyset$ **do**
8:     **while** $A' \neq \emptyset$ **do**
9:         Select $p_i \in A'$
10:         $A' \leftarrow A' \setminus \{p_i\}$
11:         ComputeNewPaths(p_i) // Update A, A' and P
12:     **end while**
13:     // ascending iterations on P
14:     **while** $A \neq \emptyset$ **do**
15:         Select $p_i \in A$
16:         $A \leftarrow A \setminus \{p_i\}$
17:         PathFocusing(p_i) // Update A and A'
18:     **end while**
19:     Narrow
20: **end while**
21: **return** $\{X_i, i \in P_R\}$

We distinguish three phases in the main loop of the analysis:

1. We start finding a new relevant subset P of the graph. Either the previous iteration or the initialization led us to a state where there are no more paths in the previous subset P, starting at p_i, that make the abstract values of the successors grow (otherwise, the SMT solver would not have answered "*unsat*"). Narrowing iterations preserve this property. However, there may exist such paths in the entire multigraph, that are not in P. This phase computes these paths and adds them to the subset. This phase is described in 3.2 and corresponds to lines in 8 to 12 in Algorithm 1.

2. Given a new subset P, we search for paths starting at point $p_i \in P_R$, such that these paths are in P, i.e are included in the working subgraph. Each time we find a path, we update the abstract value of the destination point of the path. This is the phase explained in 3.1, and corresponds to lines 14 to 18 in Algorithm 1.

3. We perform narrowing iterations the usual way (line 19 in algorithm 1) and reiterate from step 1 unless there are no more points to explore, i.e. $A' = \emptyset$.

The order of steps is important: narrowing has to be performed before adding new paths, or spurious new paths would be added to P. Starting with the addition of new paths avoids doing the ascending iterations on an empty graph.

3.1   Ascending Iterations by Path-focusing

For computing an inductive invariant over a subgraph, we use the Path-focusing algorithm from [27] with special treatment for self loops (line 17 in algorithm 1).

In order to find which path to focus on, we construct an SMT formula $f(p_i)$, whose model when satisfiable is a path that starts in p_i, goes to a successor $p_j \in P_R$ of p_i, such that the image of X_i by the path transformation is not included in the current X_j. Intuitively, such a path makes the abstract value X_j grow, and thus is an interesting path to focus on. We loop until the formula becomes unsatisfiable, meaning that the analysis of p_i is finished.

If we note $Succ(i)$ the set of indices j such that $p_j \in P_R$ is a successor of p_i in the expanded multigraph, and X_i the abstract value associated to p_i :

$$f(p_i) = \rho \wedge b_i^s \wedge \bigwedge_{\substack{j \in P_R \\ j \neq i}} \neg b_j^s \wedge X_i \wedge \bigvee_{j \in Succ(i)} (b_j^d \wedge \neg X_j)$$

The difference with [27] is that we do not work on the entire transition graph but on a subset of it. Therefore we conjoin the formula $f(p_i)$ with the actual set of working paths, noted P, expressed as a Boolean formula, where the Boolean variables are the *reachability predicates* of the control points. We can easily construct this formula from the binary decision diagram using dynamic programming, and avoiding an exponentially sized formula. In other words, we force the SMT solver to give us a path included in P. Each time the invariant candidate of a point p_j has been updated, p_j is inserted into A' since it may be the start of a new feasible paths.

3.2 Adding New Paths

Our technique computes the fixpoint iterations on an ascending sequence of subgraphs, until the complete graph is reached. When the analysis of a subgraph is finished, meaning that the abstract values for each control point has converged to an inductive invariant for this subgraph, the next subgraph to work on has to be computed.

This new subgraph contains all the paths from the previous one, and also new paths that become feasible regarding the current abstract values. The new paths in P are computed one after another, until no more path can make the invariant grow. This is line 11 in Algorithm 1, which corresponds to Algorithm 2. We also use SMT solving to discover these new paths, but we subtly change the SMT formula given to the SMT solver: we now try to find a path that is not yet in P, but is feasible and makes the invariant candidate of its destination grow. We thus check the satisfiability of the formula $f'(p_i)$, where:

$$f'(p_i) = f(p_i) \land \neg P$$

X_j is updated using an abstract union when the point p_j is the target of a new path. This way, further SMT queries do not compute other paths with the same source and destination if it is not needed (because these new paths would not make X_j grow, hence would not be returned by the SMT solver).

Algorithm 2. ComputeNewPaths

1: **while** true **do**
2:    $res \leftarrow SmtSolve\,[f'(p_i)]$
3:    **if** $res = unsat$ **then**
4:        **break**
5:    **end if**
6:    Compute the path e from the model
7:    $X_j \leftarrow X_j \sqcup \tau_e(X_i)$
8:    $P \leftarrow P \cup \{e\}$
9:    $A \leftarrow A \cup \{p_i\}$
10:    $A' \leftarrow A' \cup \{p_i\}$
11: **end while**

When a new path has been found, it is immediately added into P. We then have to add p_i and p_j into A (since we do not apply widening in this section) and p_j into A', since p_j may be the starting point of a new feasible path.

3.3 Termination

Termination of this algorithm is guaranteed, because: 1. the subset of paths P strictly increases at each loop iteration, and is bounded by the finite set of paths in the entire graph. 2. when computing new paths, we cunjunct our formula with $\neg P$, meaning that we obtain each possible path only once. The number of path is finite, so this computation always terminates. 3. the Path-focusing iterations terminate because of the properties of widening.

3.4   Example

We revise the rate limiter described in 2.3. In this example, *Path-focusing* works
well because all the paths starting at the loop header are actually self loops. In
such a case, the technique performs a widening/narrowing sequence or acceler-
ates the loop, thus leading to a precise invariant. However, in some cases, there
also exists paths that are not self loops, in which case *Path-focusing* applies
widening. This widening may induce unrecoverable loss of precision.

Suppose the main loop of the rate limiter contains a nested loop like:

```
1 void rate_limiter() {
2   int x_old = 0;
3   while (1) {
4     int x = input(-100000, 100000);
5     if (x > x_old+10) x = x_old+10;
6     if (x < x_old-10) x = x_old-10;
7     x_old = x;
8     while (wait()) {}
9 } }
```

We choose P_R as the set of loop headers of the function, plus the initial state.
In this case, we have three elements in P_R.

The main loop in the expanded multigraph has then 4 distinct paths going to
the header of the nested loop.

Guided static analysis from [14] yields, at line 3, x_old $\in (-\infty, +\infty)$. Path-
focusing [27] also finds x_old $\in (-\infty, +\infty)$. Now, let us see how our technique
performs on this example.

Figure 2 shows the sequence of subset of paths during the analysis. The points
in P_R are noted p_i, where i is the corresponding line in the code: for instance,
p_3 corresponds to the header of the main loop.

1. The starting subgraph is depicted on Figure 2 Step 1. At the beginning, this
   graph has no transitions.
2. We compute the new feasible paths that have to be added into the subgraph.
   We first find the path from p_1 to p_3 and obtain at p_3 x_old $= 0$.

   The image of x_old $= 0$ by the path that goes from p_3 to p_8, and that goes
   through the *else* branch of each *if-then-else*, is $-10 \le$ x_old ≤ 10. This path
   is then added to our subgraph.

   Moreover, there is no other path starting at p_3 whose image is not in
   $-10 \le$ x_old ≤ 10.

   Finally, since the abstract value associated to p_8 is $-10 \le$ x_old ≤ 10, the
   path from p_8 to p_3 is feasible and is added into P. The final subgraph is
   depicted on Figure 2 Step 2.
3. We then compute the ascending iterations by path-focusing. At the end of
   these iterations, we obtain $-\infty \le$ x_old $\le +\infty$ for both p_3 and p_8.
4. We now can apply narrowing iterations, and recover the precision lost by
   widening: we obtain $-10000 \le$ x_old ≤ 10000 at points p_3 and p_8.
5. Finally, we compute the next subgraph. The SMT-solver does not find any
   new path that makes the abstract values grow, and the algorithm terminates.

Our technique gives us the expected invariant x_old $\in$ $[-10000, 10000]$. Here, only 3 paths out of the 6 have been computed during the analysis. In practice, depending on the order the SMT-solver returns the paths, other feasible paths could have been added during the analysis.

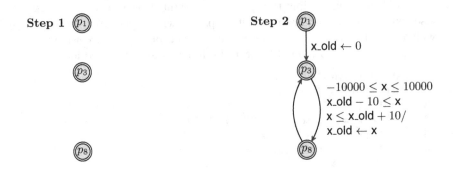

Fig. 2. Ascending sequence of subgraphs

In this example, we see that our technique actually combines best of *Guided Static Analysis* and *Path Focusing*.

4   Disjunctive Invariants

While many (most?) useful program invariants on numerical variables can be expressed as conjunctions of inequalities and congruences, it is sometimes necessary to introduce disjunctions. For instance, the loop **for** (**int** i=0; i<n; i++) {...} has head invariant $0 \le i \le n \lor (i = 0 \land n < 0)$. For this very simple example, a simple syntactic transformation of the control structure (into i=0; **if** (i<n)**do** {...} **while** (i<n)) is sufficient, but in more complex cases more advanced analyses are necessary [5,20,30,26]; in intuitive terms, they discover *phases* or *modes* in loops.

Gulwani & Zuleger [15] proposed a technique for computing disjunctive invariants, by distinguishing all the paths inside a loop. In this section, we propose to improve this technique by using SMT queries to find interesting paths, the objective being to avoid an explicit exhaustive enumeration of an exponential number of paths.

For each control point p_i, we compute a disjunctive invariant $\bigvee_{1 \le j \le m_i} X_{i,j}$. We denote by n_i the number of distinct paths starting at p_i. To perform the analysis, one chooses an integer $\delta_i \in [1, m_i]$, and a mapping function $\sigma_i : [1, m_i] \times [1, n_i] \mapsto [1, m_i]$. The k-th path starting fom p_i is denoted $\tau_{i,k}$. The image of the j-th disjunct $X_{i,j}$ by the path $\tau_{i,k}$ is then joined with $X_{i,\sigma(j,k)}$. Initially, the δ_i-th abstract value contains the initial states of p_i, and all other abstract values contain $\emptyset$.

For each control point $p_i \in P_R$, m_i, δ_i and σ_i can be defined heuristically. For instance, one could define σ_i so that $\sigma_i(j, k)$ only depends on the last transition of the path, or else construct it dynamically during the analysis.

Our method improves this technique in two ways :

- Instead of enumerating the whole set of paths, we keep them implicit and compute them only when needed.
- At each loop iteration of the original algorithm [15], an image by each path inside the loop is computed for each disjunct of the invariant candidate. Yet, many of these images may be redundant: for instance, if our invariant candidate is $(0 \leq x \leq 10 \wedge 0 \leq y \leq 1000) \vee (x < -10 \wedge y < -10)$, then there is no point enumerating paths whose image is included in this invariant candidate. In our approach, we compute such an image only if it makes the resulting abstract value grow.

Our improvement consists in a modification of the SMT formula we solve in 3. We introduce in this formula Boolean variables $\{d_j, 1 \leq j \leq m\}$, so that we can easily find in the model which abstract value of the disjunction of the source point has to be chosen to make the invariant of the destination grow. The resulting formula that is given to the SMT solver is defined by $g(p_i)$. When the formula is satisfiable, we know that the index j of the starting disjunct that has to be chosen is the one for which the associate Boolean value d_j is *true* in the model. Then, we can easily compute the value of $\sigma_i(j, k)$, thus know the index of the disjunct to join with.

$$g(p_i) = \rho \wedge b_i^s \wedge \bigwedge_{\substack{j \in P_R \\ j \neq i}} \neg b_j^s \wedge \bigvee_{1 \leq k \leq m_i} (d_k \wedge X_{i,k} \wedge \bigwedge_{l \neq k} \neg d_l) \wedge \bigvee_{j \in Succ(i)} (b_j^d \wedge \bigwedge_{1 \leq k \leq m_i} (\neg X_{j,k}))$$

In our algorithm, the initialization of the abstract values slightly differs from algorithm 1 line 5, since we now have to initialize each disjunct. Instead of Line 5, we initialize $X_{i,k}$ with $\bot$ for all $k \in \{1, .., m_i\} \setminus \{\delta_i\}$, and X_{i,δ_i} with $\leftarrow I_{p_i}$.

Furthermore, the Path-focused algorithm (line 17 from algorithm 1) is enhanced to deal with disjunctive invariants, and is detailed in algorithm 3.

The *Update* function can classically assign $X_{i,\sigma_i(j,k)} \nabla (X_{i,\sigma_i(j,k)} \sqcup \tau_{i,k}(X_{i,j}))$ to $X_{i,\sigma_i(j,k)}$, or can integrate the special treatment for self loops proposed by [27], with widening/narrowing sequence or acceleration.

We experimented with a heuristic of dynamic construction of the σ_i functions, adapted from [15]. For each control point $p_i \in P_R$, we start with one single disjunct ($m_i = 1$) and define $\delta_i = 1$. M denotes an upper bound on the number of disjuncts per control point.

The σ_i functions take as parameters the index of the starting abstract value, and the path we focus on. Since we dynamically construct these functions during the analysis, we store their already computed image into a compact representation, such as Algebraic Decision Diagrams. $\sigma_i(j, k)$ is then constructed on the fly only when needed, and computed only once. When the value of $\sigma_i(j, k)$ is required but undefined, we first compute the image of the abstract value $X_{i,j}$ by the path indexed by k, and try to find an existing disjunct of index j' so that the least upper bound of the two abstract values is exactly their union (using SMT-solving). If such an index exists, then we set $\sigma_i(j, k) = j'$. Otherwise:

Algorithm 3. Disjunctive invariant computation with implicit paths

```
1: while true do
2:    res ← SmtSolve [g(pᵢ)]
3:    if res = unsat then
4:       break
5:    end if
6:    Compute the path τᵢ,ₖ from res
7:    Take j ∈ {l|dₗ = true}
8:    Update(Xᵢ,σᵢ(j,k))
9: end while
```

- if $m_i < M$, we increase m_i by 1 and define $\sigma_i(j, k) = m_i$
- if $m_i = M$, we define $\sigma_i(j, k) = M$

The main difference with the original algorithm [15] is that we construct $\sigma_i(j, k)$ using SMT queries instead of enumerating a possibly exponential number of paths to find a solution.

5   Implementation and Experimental Comparisons

We have implemented our proposed solutions inside a prototype of intraprocedural static analyzer called PAGAI, as well as the classical abstract interpretation algorithm, and the state-of-the-art techniques *Path Focusing* [27] and *Guided Static Analysis* [14]. It is available online at https://forge.imag.fr/projects/pagai/. The implementation is documented in [19].

PAGAI operates over LLVM bitcode [24,23], which is a target for several compilers, most notably Clang (supporting C and C++) and llvm-gcc (supporting C, C++, Fortran and Ada). Abstract domains are provided by the APRON library [21], and include convex polyhedra (from the builtin Polka "PK" library), octagons, intervals, and linear congruences. For SMT-solving, our analyzer uses Yices [11] or Microsoft Z3 [28].

PAGAI currently neither models the memory heap nor performs interprocedural analysis. Instead, LLVM optimization phases are applied prior to analysis, in order to inline non-recursive function calls and lift certain memory accesses to operations on explicit numerical variables (e.g. y=t[0]*t[0]; preceded by t[0]=x; without any aliased write in between is replaced by y=x*x;). The remaining memory reads are considered as indeterminates, and memory writes are ignored; this is a sound abstraction.

We conducted extensive experiments on real-life programs in order to compare the different techniques, mostly on open-source projects (Fig. 3) written in C, C++ and Fortran. These results confirm that our combined technique improve the analysis in comparison with the two techniques taken individually, at a reasonable cost. The extension with disjunctive invariants increases precision in many cases, but with higher cost in terms of execution time.

Table 1. Execution times for various techniques

Name	Size		Execution time (seconds)				
	kLOC	$|P_R|$	S	G	PF	G+PF	DIS
a2ps-4.14	55	2012	23	74	34	115	162
gawk-4.0.0	59	902	15	46	12	40	50
gnuchess-6.0.0	38	1222	50	220	81	312	351
gnugo-3.8	83	2801	77	159	92	766	1493
grep-2.9	35	820	41	85	22	65	122
gzip-1.4	27	494	22	268	91	303	230
lapack-3.3.1	954	16422	294	3740	3773	8159	10351
make-3.82	34	993	67	108	53	109	257
tar-1.26	73	1712	37	218	115	253	396

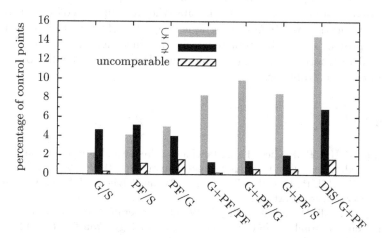

Fig. 3. Comparison of the abstract values obtained on several open-source projects. The table shows their respective number of lines of code, number of control points in P_R, and execution time on various techniques. Techniques are classical abstract interpretation (S), *Guided Static Analysis* (G), *Path-focused* technique (PF), our combined technique (G+PF), and its version with disjunctive invariants (DIS). The $\subsetneq$ bars (resp. $\supsetneq$) gives the percentage of invariants stronger (more precise; smaller with respect to inclusion) with the left-side (resp. right-side) technique, and "uncomparable" gives the percentage of invariants that are uncomparable, i.e neither greater nor smaller; the code points where both invariants are equal make up the remaining percentage.

6   Conclusion and Future Prospects

Roughly, an analysis by abstract interpretation is defined by the choice of an iteration strategy and an abstract domain. In this article, we demonstrated that changes in the iteration algorithm can significantly improve precision, sometimes while improving analysis times.

A common criticism of analysis techniques based on SMT-solving is that they do not scale up. Yet, our experiments show that, for numerical properties, they scale up to the size of typical functions and loops. It is however quite certain that, naively applied, they cannot scale to the kind of programs targeted by e.g. the Astrée tool, that is, a dozens or hundreds of thousands of lines of code in a single loop operating over similar numbers of remanent variables. Actually, for such applications, only (quasi-)linear algorithms scale up, and "cheap" abstract domains such as octagons ($O(n^3)$ where n is the number of variables) are not applied to the full variable set, but to restricted subsets thereof. It thus seems reasonable that techniques such as considering "packs" of related variables, slicing, etc. may similarly help SMT-based techniques to scale to global analyses.

We compared the precision of different techniques and abstract domains by comparing the invariants for the inclusion ordering. A better metric is perhaps to take a client analysis — such as the detection of overflows and array bound violations — and compare the rates of alarms.

We focused on numerical properties, because they are supported by easily available abstract libraries. Yet, in most programs, properties of data structures are important for proving interesting properties. Further investigations are needed not only on good abstractions for pointers (many are already known) but also on their conversion to SMT problems.

References

1. Bagnara, R., Hill, P.M., Ricci, E., Zaffanella, E.: Precise widening operators for convex polyhedra. Science of Computer Programming 58(1-2), 28–56 (2005)
2. Bagnara, R., Hill, P.M., Zaffanella, E.: The Parma Polyhedra Library, version 0.9, http://www.cs.unipr.it/ppl
3. Bagnara, R., Hill, P.M., Zaffanella, E.: Widening operators for powerset domains. International Journal on Software Tools for Technology Transfer (STTT) 8(4-5), 449–466 (2006)
4. Bagnara, R., Hill, P.M., Zaffanella, E.: The Parma Polyhedra Library: Toward a complete set of numerical abstractions for the analysis and verification of hardware and software systems. Science of Computer Programming 72(1-2), 3–21 (2008)
5. Balakrishnan, G., Sankaranarayanan, S., Ivancic, F., Gupta, A.: Refining the control structure of loops using static analysis. In: EMSOFT, pp. 49–58. ACM (2009)
6. Biere, A., Heule, M., van Maaren, H., Walsh, T. (eds.): Handbook of satisfiability. Frontiers in Artificial Intelligence and Applications, vol. 185. IOS Press, Amsterdam (2009)
7. Blanchet, B., Cousot, P., Cousot, R., Feret, J., Mauborgne, L., Miné, A., Monniaux, D., Rival, X.: A static analyzer for large safety-critical software. In: Programming Language Design and Implementation (PLDI), pp. 196–207. ACM (2003)
8. Cousot, P., Cousot, R.: Abstract interpretation frameworks. J. of Logic and Computation, 511–547 (August 1992)
9. Cousot, P., Cousot, R., Feret, J., Mauborgne, L., Miné, A., Monniaux, D., Rival, X.: The ASTREÉ Analyzer. In: Sagiv, M. (ed.) ESOP 2005. LNCS, vol. 3444, pp. 21–30. Springer, Heidelberg (2005)
10. Cousot, P., Halbwachs, N.: Automatic discovery of linear restraints among variables of a program. In: Principles of Programming Languages (POPL), pp. 84–96. ACM (1978)

11. Dutertre, B., de Moura, L.: A Fast Linear-Arithmetic Solver for DPLL(T). In: Ball, T., Jones, R.B. (eds.) CAV 2006. LNCS, vol. 4144, pp. 81–94. Springer, Heidelberg (2006)
12. Gawlitza, T., Monniaux, D.: Improving Strategies via SMT Solving. In: Barthe, G. (ed.) ESOP 2011. LNCS, vol. 6602, pp. 236–255. Springer, Heidelberg (2011)
13. Gonnord, L., Halbwachs, N.: Combining Widening and Acceleration in Linear Relation Analysis. In: Yi, K. (ed.) SAS 2006. LNCS, vol. 4134, pp. 144–160. Springer, Heidelberg (2006)
14. Gopan, D., Reps, T.W.: Guided Static Analysis. In: Riis Nielson, H., Filé, G. (eds.) SAS 2007. LNCS, vol. 4634, pp. 349–365. Springer, Heidelberg (2007)
15. Gulwani, S., Zuleger, F.: The reachability-bound problem. In: PLDI, pp. 292–304. ACM (2010)
16. Halbwachs, N.: Détermination automatique de relations linéaires vérifiées par les variables d'un programme. Ph.D. thesis, Grenoble University (1979)
17. Halbwachs, N., Proy, Y.E., Roumanoff, P.: Verification of real-time systems using linear relation analysis. Formal Methods in System Design 11(2), 157–185 (1997)
18. Harris, W.R., Sankaranarayanan, S., Ivancic, F., Gupta, A.: Program analysis via satisfiability modulo path programs. In: POPL, pp. 71–82. ACM (2010)
19. Henry, J.: Static Analysis by Path Focusing. Master's thesis, Grenoble INP (2011), http://www-verimag.imag.fr/~jhenry/pdf/M2R_report.pdf
20. Jeannet, B.: Dynamic partitioning in linear relation analysis: Application to the verification of reactive systems. Formal Methods in System Design 23(1), 5–37 (2003)
21. Jeannet, B., Miné, A.: APRON: A Library of Numerical Abstract Domains for Static Analysis. In: Bouajjani, A., Maler, O. (eds.) CAV 2009. LNCS, vol. 5643, pp. 661–667. Springer, Heidelberg (2009)
22. Kroening, D., Strichman, O.: Decision procedures. Springer (2008)
23. Lattner, C., Adve, V.: LLVM: A compilation framework for lifelong program analysis & transformation. In: CGO, pp. 75–86. IEEE Computer Society, Washington, DC (2004)
24. LLVM team: LLVM Language Reference Manual (2011), http://llvm.org/docs/LangRef.html
25. Miné, A.: The octagon abstract domain. Higher-Order and Symbolic Computation 19(1), 31–100 (2006)
26. Monniaux, D., Bodin, M.: Modular Abstractions of Reactive Nodes Using Disjunctive Invariants. In: Yang, H. (ed.) APLAS 2011. LNCS, vol. 7078, pp. 19–33. Springer, Heidelberg (2011)
27. Monniaux, D., Gonnord, L.: Using Bounded Model Checking to Focus Fixpoint Iterations. In: Yahav, E. (ed.) SAS 2011. LNCS, vol. 6887, pp. 369–385. Springer, Heidelberg (2011)
28. de Moura, L., Bjørner, N.: Z3: An Efficient SMT Solver. In: Ramakrishnan, C.R., Rehof, J. (eds.) TACAS 2008. LNCS, vol. 4963, pp. 337–340. Springer, Heidelberg (2008)
29. Rival, X., Mauborgne, L.: The trace partitioning abstract domain. Transactions on Programming Languages and Systems (TOPLAS) 29(5), 26 (2007)
30. Sharma, R., Dillig, I., Dillig, T., Aiken, A.: Simplifying Loop Invariant Generation Using Splitter Predicates. In: Gopalakrishnan, G., Qadeer, S. (eds.) CAV 2011. LNCS, vol. 6806, pp. 703–719. Springer, Heidelberg (2011)

Craig Interpretation

Aws Albarghouthi[1], Arie Gurfinkel[2], and Marsha Chechik[1]

[1] Department of Computer Science, University of Toronto, Canada
[2] Software Engineering Institute, Carnegie Mellon University, USA

Abstract. Abstract interpretation (AI) is one of the most scalable automated approaches to program verification available today. To achieve efficiency, many steps of the analysis, e.g., joins and widening, lose precision. As a result, AI often produces false alarms, coming from the inability to find a safe inductive invariant even when it exists in a chosen abstract domain.

To tackle this problem, we present VINTA, an iterative algorithm that uses *Craig interpolants* to refine and guide AI away from false alarms. VINTA is based on a novel refinement strategy that capitalizes on recent advances in SMT and interpolation-based verification to (a) find counterexamples to justify alarms produced by AI, and (b) to strengthen an invariant to exclude alarms that cannot be justified. The refinement process continues until either a safe inductive invariant is computed, a counterexample is found, or resources are exhausted. This strategy allows VINTA to recover precision lost in many AI steps, and even to compute inductive invariants that are inexpressible in the chosen abstract domain (e.g., by adding disjunctions and new terms).

We have implemented VINTA and compared it against top verification tools from the recent software verification competition. Our results show that VINTA outperforms state-of-the-art verification tools.

1 Introduction

Abstract interpretation (AI) is one of the most scalable automated approaches to program verification available today. AI iteratively computes an *inductive invariant* I of a given program P in a chosen abstract domain D. P is *safe*, i.e., it cannot reach an error location e, if I is *safe*, i.e., it does not include e. The price of AI's efficiency is false alarms (i.e., inability to find a safe I even when it exists in D), that are introduced through imprecision inherent in many steps of the analysis (e.g., join and widening).

In this paper, we present VINTA[1], an iterative algorithm that uses *Craig interpolants* [8] to refine and guide AI away from false alarms. VINTA marries the efficiency of AI with the precision of Bounded Model Checking (BMC) [6] and the ability to generalize from concrete executions of interpolation-based software verification [15,1].

---

[1] Verification with INTerpolation and Abstract interpretation.

A. Miné and D. Schmidt (Eds.): SAS 2012, LNCS 7460, pp. 300–316, 2012.
© Springer-Verlag Berlin Heidelberg 2012

The main phases of the algorithm are shown in Fig. 1. Given a program P and a safety property φ, VINTA starts by computing an inductive invariant I of P using an abstract domain D (the AI phase). If I is safe (i.e., $I \Rightarrow \varphi$), then P is safe as well. Otherwise, VINTA goes to a novel refinement phase. First, refinement uses BMC to check for a counterexample in the explored part of P. Second, if BMC fails to find a counterexample, it uses an interpolation-based procedure to strengthen I to I'. If I' is not inductive (checked in the "Is Inductive?" phase), the AI phase is repeated to weaken I' to include all reachable states of P. This process continues until either a safe inductive invariant or a counterexample is found, or resources (i.e., time or memory) are exhausted.

In our experience, VINTA is able to recover precision lost due to widening, join, imprecise post-image, and inexpressiveness of the chosen domain D. Furthermore, unless aborted, it never produces false alarms. While we present VINTA as a refinement strategy for AI, it can equivalently be seen as an interpolation-based verification algorithm guided by AI. Indeed, we show that both the BMC and interpolation phases benefit greatly from the invariants discovered by AI. We have implemented VINTA in UFO [2,1], our software verification framework built on top of the LLVM compiler [14]. For evaluation, we used benchmarks from the recent Software Verification Competition (SV-COMP) [4]. We have compared several configurations of VINTA with our prior tool, UFO [1], and with the top two tools from SV-COMP, CPACHECKER-ABE and CPACHECKER-MEMO. The results show that VINTA outperforms these state-of-the-art approaches.

This paper makes several contributions. First, the AI phase is a novel AI-based invariant computation algorithm. It works on a summary of a Control Flow Graph (CFG) that contains only loop-heads. It efficiently maintains disjunctive loop invariants. Finally, it provides counterexamples to justify alarms. Second, we present a new widening strategy that extends widening from a given domain D to its finite powerset $\mathcal{P}_f(D)$. Third, we present a novel refinement strategy for strengthening invariants and eliminating potential false alarms. Unlike existing work on interpolation-based refinement (e.g., [1,15]), our strategy is both guided and bounded by the invariants discovered by AI. Finally, we show empirically that the new approach outperforms other state-of-the-art techniques on a collection of software verification benchmarks.

Related Work. Our approach is closely related to the DAGGER tool of Gulavani et al. [10] that is also based on refining AI, and to our earlier tool UFO [1] that combines predicate abstraction with interpolation-based verification. The key differences between VINTA and DAGGER are: (1) DAGGER can only refine imprecision caused by widening and join. VINTA can refine imprecision up to the concrete semantics of the program (as modeled in SMT). (2) DAGGER refines joins explicitly, which may result in an exponential increase in the number of abstract states compared to the size of the program. VINTA refines joins implicitly using interpolants and SMT. (3) DAGGER requires a specialized interpolation procedure, which, so far, has only been developed for the octagon and the polyhedra domains. VINTA can use any off-the-shelf interpolating SMT solver, immediately benefiting from any advances in the field.

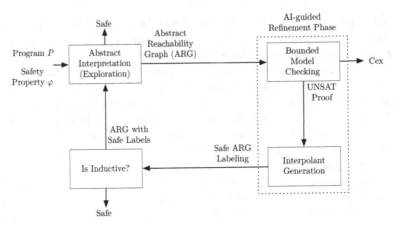

Fig. 1. High-level overview of VINTA

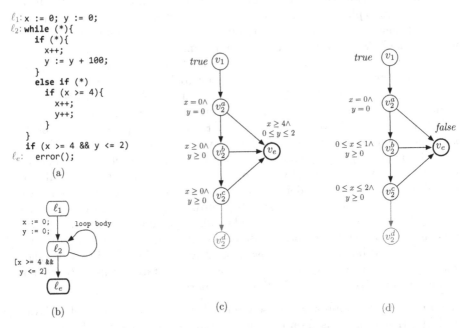

Fig. 2. (a) A safe program P ('*' denotes a nondeterministic choice). (b) A cutpoint graph of P. An ARG of P after (c) the first and (d) after the second AI step.

Compared to UFO, VINTA improves both the exploration algorithm (by extending it to an arbitrary abstract domain) and the refinement procedure (by extending it to use intermediate invariants computed by AI). Both of these extensions are important for VINTA's success, as shown in the experiments in Sec. 5.

The rest of the paper is organized as follows: Sec. 2 gives a general overview of VINTA. Sec. 3 provides the notation and definitions required for the paper. Sec. 4 formally presents our algorithm. Sec. 5 describes our implementation, optimizations and experimental results. Finally, Sec. 6 concludes the paper.

2 Example

In this section, we illustrate VINTA on proving safety (i.e., unreachability of ℓ_e) of program P from [10], shown in Fig. 2(a). P is known to be hard to analyze without refinement, and even the refinement approaches of [9] and [17] fail to solve it (see [10] for details). DAGGER [10] (the state-of-the-art in AI-refinement) solves it using the domain of polyhedra by computing the safe invariant $x \leq y \leq 100x$. Here, we show how VINTA solves the problem using the BOX domain and refinement to compute an alternative safe invariant: $x \geq 4 \Rightarrow y > 100$. In this example, the refinement must recover imprecision lost due to widening and join, and extend the base-domain with disjunction. All of this is done automatically via an SMT-based interpolation procedure. Due to space limitations, we show only the first few iterations of the analysis.

Step 1.1: AI. VINTA works on a *cutpoint graph* (CPG) of a program: a collapsed CFG where the only nodes are cutpoints (loop-heads), entry, and error locations. A CPG for P is shown in Fig. 2(b).

VINTA uses a typical AI-computation following the *recursive iteration strategy* [7] and widening at every loop unrolling. Additionally, it records the finite traces explored by AI in an *Abstract Reachability Graph* (ARG). An ARG is an unrolling of the CPG. Each node u of an ARG corresponds to some node v of a CPG, and is labeled with an over-approximation of the set of states reachable at that point.

Fig. 2(c) shows the ARG from the first AI-computation on P. Each node v_i in the ARG refers to node ℓ_i in the CPG. The superscript in nodes v_2^a, v_2^b, v_2^c, and v_2^d is used to distinguish between the different unrollings of the loop at ℓ_2. The labels of the nodes v_2^a, v_2^b, and v_2^c over-approximate the states reachable before the first, second, and third iterations of the loop, respectively. The node v_2^c is said to be *covered* (i.e., subsumed) by $\{v_2^a, v_2^b\}$. The labels of the set $\{v_2^a, v_2^b\}$ form an inductive invariant $\mathcal{I}_1 \equiv (x \geq 0 \wedge y \geq 0)$. The node v_2^d is called an *unexplored child*, and has no label and no children. It is used later when AI-computation is restarted. Finally, note that $\mathcal{I}_1$ is not safe (the error location v_e is not labeled by *false*), and thus refinement is needed.

Step 1.2: AI-guided Refinement. First, VINTA uses a BMC-style technique [11] to check using an SMT-solver whether the current ARG has a feasible execution to the error node ℓ_e. There is no such execution in our example (see Fig. 2(c)) and the algorithm moves to the next phase.

The second phase of refinement is based on a novel interpolation-based procedure that is described in detail in Sec. 4. Specifically, the procedure takes the current ARG (Fig. 2(c)) and its labeling and produces a new safe (but not necessarily inductive) labeling shown in Fig. 2(d). Here, refinement reversed the effects of widening by restoring the upper bounds on x. Note that the new labels are stronger than the original ones – this is guaranteed by the procedure and the original labels are used to guide it.

Step 1.3: Is Inductive? The new ARG labeling (Fig. 2(d)) is not inductive since the label of v_2^c is not contained in the label of v_2^b (checked by an SMT-solver), and another AI phase is started.

Step 2.1: AI (again). AI is restarted "lazily" from the nodes that have unexplored children. Here, v_2^c is the only such node. This ensures that AI is restarted from the inner-most loop where the invariant is no longer inductive. First, the label of v_2^c is converted into an element of an abstract domain by a given abstraction function. In our example, the label is immediately expressible in Box, so this step is trivial. Then, AI-computation is restarted as usual.

In the following four iterations (omitted here), refinement works with the AI-based exploration to construct a safe inductive invariant $x \geq 4 \Rightarrow y > 100$. Note that since the invariant contains a disjunction, this means refinement had to recover from imprecision of join (as well as recovering from imprecision due to widening shown above).

This example is simple enough to be solved with other interpolation-based techniques, but they require more iterations. UFO [1], our prior approach without AI-based exploration and refinement, needs nine iterations, and a version of VINTA with unguided refinement from UFO needs seven. Our experiments suggest that this translates into a significant performance difference on bigger programs.

3   Definitions

In this section, we present the definitions and notation used in the rest of the paper.

Programs as Cutpoint Graphs. We represent a program by a *cutpoint graph* (CPG), a collapsed form of a CFG where each node is a loop-head and each edge is a loop-free path between two loop-heads. Formally, a *program* P is a tuple $(\mathcal{CP}, \delta, \mathsf{en}, \mathsf{err}, \mathsf{Var})$, where $\mathcal{CP}$ is a finite set of cutpoints, δ is a finite set of actions, $\mathsf{en} \in \mathcal{CP}$ is a special cutpoint denoting the entry location of P, $\mathsf{err} \in \mathcal{CP}$ is the error cutpoint, and Var is the set of variables of program P. An *action* $(\ell_1, T, \ell_2) \in \delta$ represents loop-free paths between ℓ_1 and ℓ_2, where $\ell_1, \ell_2 \in \mathcal{CP}$ and T is the set of statements along the paths. We assume that there does not exist an action $(\ell_1, T, \ell_2) \in \delta$ s.t. $\ell_1 = \mathsf{err}$. T can be viewed as a transition relation over the variables $\mathsf{Var} \cup \mathsf{Var}'$, where Var' is the set of primed versions of variables in Var. We write $[\![T]\!]$ for the standard semantics of a statement T. For example, if T is if x = 0 then x := 1 else x := 2, then $[\![T]\!] \equiv (x = 0 \Rightarrow x' = 1) \wedge (x \neq 0 \Rightarrow x' = 2)$.

A program P is *safe* iff there does not exist an execution that starts in en and reaches err through the actions in δ.

Weak Topological Ordering. A *Weak Topological Ordering* (WTO) [7] of a directed graph $G = (V, E)$ is a well-parenthesized total-order, denoted $\prec$, of V without two consecutive "(" s.t. for every edge $(u, v) \in E$:

$$(u \prec v \wedge v \notin \omega(u)) \vee (v \preceq u \wedge v \in \omega(u)),$$

where elements between two matching parentheses are called a *(wto-)component*, the first element of a component is called a *head*, and $\omega(v)$ is the set of heads of all components containing v.

Let $v \in V$, and U be the innermost component that contains v in the WTO. We write $\text{WTONEXT}(v)$ for an element $u \in U$ that immediately follows $\cdot v$, if it exists, and for the head of U otherwise.

Let U_v be a component with head v. First, suppose that U_v is a subcomponent of some component U. If there exists a $u \in U$ s.t. $u \notin U_v$ and u is the first element in the total-order s.t. $v \prec u$, then $\text{WTOEXIT}(v) = u$. Otherwise, $\text{WTOEXIT}(v) = w$, where w is the head of U. Second, suppose that U_v is not a subcomponent of any other component, then $\text{WTOEXIT}(v) = u$, where u is the first element in the total-order s.t. $u \notin U_v$ and $v \prec u$. Intuitively, if the WTO represented program locations, then $\text{WTOEXIT}(v)$ is the first control location visited after exiting the loop headed by v. For example, for the program in Fig. 2(b), a WTO of the control locations is $\ell_1(\ell_2)\ell_3$, where ℓ_2 is the head of the component comprising the while loop. $\text{WTONEXT}(\ell_2) = \ell_2$ and $\text{WTOEXIT}(\ell_2) = \ell_3$. Note that WTONEXT and WTOEXIT are partial functions and we only use them where they have been defined.

Abstract Reachability Graphs (ARGs). Let $P = (\mathcal{CP}, \delta, \text{en}, \text{err}, \text{Var})$ be a program. An *Abstract Reachability Graph* (ARG) of P is a tuple $(V, E, v_{\text{en}}, \nu, \tau, \psi)$, where (V, E, v_{en}) is a directed acyclic graph (DAG) rooted at the *entry node* $v_{\text{en}} \in V$, $\nu : V \to \mathcal{CP}$ is a map from nodes to cutpoints of P where $\nu(v_{\text{en}}) = \text{en}$, $\tau : E \to \delta$ is a map from edges to actions of P s.t. for every edge $(u, v) \in E$ there exists an action $(\nu(u), \tau(u, v), \nu(v)) \in \delta$, and $\psi : V \to B$ is a map from nodes V to Boolean formulas over Var. A node v s.t. $\nu(v) = \text{err}$ is called an *error node*.

A node $v \in V$ is *covered* iff there exists a node $u \in V$ that dominates v and there exists a set of nodes $X \subseteq V$, s.t. $\psi(u) \Rightarrow \bigvee_{x \in X} \psi(x)$ and $\forall x \in X \cdot \nu(u) = \nu(x) \wedge u \npreceq x$, where $\preceq$ is the ancestor relation on nodes and all $x \in X$ are less than u according to some fixed total order on nodes V. A node u *dominates* v iff all paths from v_{en} to v pass through u. By convention, every node dominates itself.

Definition 1 (Well-labeledness of ARGs). *Given an ARG $\mathcal{A} = (V, E, v_{\text{en}}, \nu, \tau, \psi)$ of a program $P = (\mathcal{CP}, \delta, \text{en}, \text{err}, \text{Var})$ and a map $\mathcal{L}$ from every $v \in V$ to a Boolean formula over Var, we say that $\mathcal{L}$ is a well-labeling of $\mathcal{A}$ iff (1) $\mathcal{L}(v_{\text{en}}) \equiv \text{true}$; and (2) $\forall (u, v) \in E \cdot \mathcal{L}(u) \wedge [\![\tau(u, v)]\!] \Rightarrow \mathcal{L}(v)'$. If ψ is a well-labeling of $\mathcal{A}$, we say that $\mathcal{A}$ is* well-labeled.

An ARG is *safe* iff for all $v \in V$ s.t. $\nu(v) = \text{err}$, $\psi(v) \equiv \text{false}$. An ARG is *complete* iff for all uncovered nodes u, for all $(\nu(u), T, \ell) \in \delta$, there exists an edge $(u, v) \in E$ s.t. $\nu(v) = \ell$ and $\tau(u, v) = T$.

Theorem 1 (Program Safety [1]). *If there exists a safe, complete, and well-labelled ARG for a program P, then P is safe.*

Abstract Domain. Abstract and concrete domains are often presented as Galois-connected lattices. In this paper, we use a more operational presentation. Without loss of generality, we restrict the concrete domain to a set B

```
 1: func VINTAMAIN (Program P) :          29: func EXPANDARG () :
 2:    create nodes v_en, v_err              30:    vis ← ∅ ; FN ← ∅
 3:    ψ(v_en) ← true ; ν(v_en) ← en         31:    FN(err) ← v_err ; v ← v_en
 4:    ψ(v_err) ← false ; ν(v_err) ← err     32:    while true do
 5:    marked(v_en) ← true                   33:       ℓ ← ν(v)
 6:    labels ← ∅                            34:       EXPANDNODE(v)
 7:    while true do                         35:       if marked(v) then
 8:       EXPANDARG()                        36:          marked(v) ← false
 9:       if ψ(v_err) is UNSAT then          37:          ψ(v) ← COMPUTEPOST(v)
10:          return SAFE                     38:          ψ(v) ← WIDENWITH({ψ(u) | u ∈ vis(ℓ)}, ψ(v))
11:       labels ← REFINE(A)                 39:          for all (v, w) ∈ E do marked(w) ← true
12:       if labels = ∅ then                 40:       else if labels(v) is defined then
13:          return UNSAFE                   41:          ψ(v) ← labels(v)
                                             42:          for all {(v, w) ∈ E | labels(w) is undefined} do
14: func GETFUTURENODE (ℓ ∈ CP) :           43:             marked(w) ← true
15:    if FN(ℓ) is defined then              44:       vis(ℓ) ← vis(ℓ) ∪ {v}
16:       return FN(ℓ)                       45:       if v = v_err then break
17:    create node v                        46:       if SMT.ISVALID(ψ(v) ⇒ ⋁_{u∈vis(ℓ),u≠v} ψ(u)) then
18:    ψ(v) ← true ; ν(v) ← ℓ               47:          erase FN(ℓ)
19:    FN(l) ← v                            48:          repeat ℓ ← WTOEXIT(ℓ) until FN(ℓ) is defined
20:    return v                             49:          v ← FN(ℓ) ; erase FN(ℓ)
                                             50:          for all {(v, w) ∈ E | ∄u ≠ v · (u, w) ∈ E} do
21: func EXPANDNODE (v ∈ V) :               51:             erase FN(ν(w))
22:    if v has children then               52:       else
23:       for all (v, w) ∈ E do             53:          ℓ ← WTONEXT(ℓ)
24:          FN(ν(w)) ← w                    54:          v ← FN(ℓ) ; erase FN(ℓ)
25:    else
26:       for all (ν(v), T, ℓ) ∈ δ do
27:          w ← GETFUTURENODE(ℓ)
28:          E ← E ∪ {(v, w)} ; τ(v, w) ← T
```

Fig. 3. VINTA algorithm

of all Boolean expressions over program variables (as opposed to the powerset of concrete program states). We define an abstract domain as a tuple $\mathcal{D} = (D, \top, \bot, \sqcup, \nabla, \alpha, \gamma)$, where D is the set of abstract elements with two designated elements $\top, \bot \in D$, called *top* and *bottom*, respectively; two binary functions $\sqcup, \nabla : D \times D \to D$, called *join* and *widen*, respectively; and two functions: an *abstraction* $\alpha : B \to D$ and a *concretization* $\gamma : D \to B$. The functions respect the expected properties: $\alpha(true) = \top$, $\gamma(\bot) = false$, for $x, y, z \in D$. if $z = x \sqcup y$ then $\gamma(x) \vee \gamma(y) \Rightarrow \gamma(z)$, etc. Note that D has no meet and no abstract order – we do not use them. Finally, we assume that for every action T, there is a sound abstract transformer $\text{POST}_\mathcal{D}$ s.t. if $d_2 = \text{POST}_\mathcal{D}(T, d_1)$ then $\gamma(d_1) \wedge \llbracket T \rrbracket \Rightarrow \gamma(d_2)'$, where $d_1, d_2 \in D$, and for a formula X, X' is X with all variables primed.

4 Vinta

In this section, we formally describe VINTA and discuss its properties.

4.1 Main Algorithm

VintaMain. Function VINTAMAIN in Fig. 3 implements the loop in Fig. 1. It takes a program $P = (\mathcal{CP}, \delta, \text{en}, \text{err}, \text{Var})$ and checks whether the error location err is reachable. Without loss of generality, we assume that every location in $\mathcal{CP}$ is reachable from en and can reach err (ignoring the semantics of actions). VINTAMAIN maintains a globally accessible ARG $\mathcal{A} = (V, E, v_{en}, \nu, \tau, \psi)$. If VINTAMAIN returns SAFE, then $\mathcal{A}$ is safe, complete, and well-labeled (thus proving safety of P by Theorem 1).

VINTAMAIN is parameterized by (1) the abstract domain $\mathcal{D}$, and (2) the refinement function REFINE. First, an ARG is constructed by EXPANDARG using an abstract transformer POST$_\mathcal{D}$. For simplicity of presentation, we assume that all labels are Boolean expressions that are implicitly converted to and from $\mathcal{D}$ using functions α and γ, respectively. EXPANDARG always returns a complete and well-labeled ARG. So, on line 9, VINTAMAIN only needs to check whether the current ARG is safe. If the check fails, REFINE is called to find a counterexample and remove false alarms. We describe our implementation of REFINE in Sec. 4.3, but the correctness of the algorithm depends only on the following abstract specification:

Definition 2 (Specification of Refine [1]). REFINE *returns an empty map* (labels = $\emptyset$) *if there exists a feasible execution from* v_{en} *to* v_{err} *in* $\mathcal{A}$*. Otherwise, it returns a map* labels *from nodes to Boolean expressions s.t. (1)* labels(v_{en}) $\equiv$ true *and* labels(v_{err}) $\equiv$ false*, and (2)* $\forall (u, v) \in E \cdot$ labels(u) $\wedge [\![\tau(u,v)]\!] \Rightarrow$ labels(v)$'$.

In our case, refinement uses BMC and interpolation through an SMT solver to compute labels, therefore, if no labels are found, refinement produces a counterexample as a side-effect.

Whenever REFINE returns a non-empty labeling (i.e., false alarms were removed), VINTAMAIN calls EXPANDARG again. EXPANDARG uses *labels* to relabel the existing ARG nodes and uses POST$_\mathcal{D}$ to expand the ARG further, as necessary.

ExpandArg. EXPANDARG constructs the ARG in a *recursive iteration strategy* [7], It assumes existence of a *weak topological ordering* (WTO) [7] of the CPG and two functions, WTONEXT and WTOEXIT as described in Sec. 3.

EXPANDARG maintains two local maps: vis and FN. vis maps a cutpoint ℓ to the set of visited nodes corresponding to ℓ, and FN maps a cutpoint ℓ to the first unexplored node $v \in V$ s.t. $\nu(v) = \ell$. The predicate *marked* specifies whether a node is labeled using AI (*marked* is *true*) or it gets a label from the map *labels* produced by REFINE (*marked* is *false*). Marks are propagated from a node to children (lines 39 and 42). Initially, the entry node is marked (line 5), which causes all of its descendants to be marked as well. AI over all incoming edges of a node v is done using COMPUTEPOST(v) that over-approximates POST$_\mathcal{D}$ computations over all predecessors of a node v (that are in vis).

Note that VINTA uses an ARG as an efficient representation of a disjunctive invariant: for each cutpoint $\ell \in \mathcal{CP}$, the disjunction $\bigvee_{v \in \text{vis}(\ell)} \psi(v)$ is an inductive invariant. The key to efficiency is two-fold. First, a possibly expensive abstract subsumption check is replaced by an SMT-check (line 46). Second, inspired by [10], an expensive powerset widening is replaced by a simple widening scheme, WIDENWITH, that lifts base domain widening $\triangledown$ to a widening between a set and a *single* abstract element. We describe WIDENWITH in detail in Sec. 4.2.

VINTA is based on UFO [1], but improves it in two directions: (1) it extends UFO to arbitrary abstract domains using widening and (2) it employs a more efficient covering strategy (line 46). While in theory VINTA is compatible with the refinement strategy of UFO, in Sec. 4.3 we describe the shortcomings of UFO's refinement in our setting and present a new refinement strategy.

4.2 Widening

In this section, we describe the powerset widening operator WIDENWITH used by VINTA.

Definition 3 (Specification of WIDENWITH). *Let $\mathcal{D} = (D, \top, \bot, \sqcup, \nabla, \alpha, \gamma)$ be an abstract domain. An operator $\nabla_W : \mathcal{P}_f(D) \times D \to D$ is a WIDENWITH operator iff it satisfies the following two conditions:*

1. *(soundness) for any $X \subseteq D$ and $y \in D$, $(\gamma(X) \vee \gamma(y)) \Rightarrow (\gamma(X) \vee \gamma(X \nabla_W y))$;*
2. *(termination) for any $X \subseteq D$, and a sequence $\{y_i\}_i \in D$, the sequence $\{Z_i\}_i \subseteq D$, where $Z_0 = X$, and $Z_i = Z_{i-1} \cup \{Z_{i-1} \nabla_W y_i\}$ converges, i.e., $\exists i \cdot \gamma(Z_i) \Leftarrow \gamma(Z_{i+1})$,*

where $\gamma(X) \equiv \bigvee_{x \in X} \gamma(x)$, for some set of abstract elements X.

Note that unlike traditional powerset widening operators (e.g., [3]), WIDENWITH is defined for a pair of a set and an element (and not a pair of sets). It is inspired by the widening operator ∇_T^p of Gulavani et al. [10], but differs from it in three important aspects. First, we do not require that if $z = \text{WIDENWITH}(X, y)$, then z is "bigger" than y, i.e., $\gamma(y) \Rightarrow \gamma(z)$. Intuitively, if X and y approximate sets of reachable states, then z over-approximates the *frontier* of y (i.e., states in y but not in X). Second, our termination condition is based on concrete implication (and not on an abstract order). Third, we do not require that X or the sets $\{Z_i\}_i$ in Def. 3 contain only "maximal" elements [10]. These differences give us more freedom in designing the operator and significantly simplify the implementation.

We now describe two implementations of WIDENWITH: the first, $\text{WIDENWITH}_\sqcup$, is based on ∇_T^p from [10] and applies to any abstract domain while the second, $\text{WIDENWITH}_\vee$, requires an abstract domain that supports disjunction ($\vee$) and set difference ($\backslash$). One example of such a domain is BOXES [12]. The operators are defined as follows:

$$\text{WIDENWITH}_\sqcup(\emptyset, y) = y \qquad\qquad \text{WIDENWITH}_\vee(\emptyset, y) = y \qquad (1)$$

$$\text{WIDENWITH}_\sqcup(X, y) = x \nabla (x \sqcup y) \qquad (2)$$

$$\text{WIDENWITH}_\vee(X, y) = \left(\left(\bigvee X \right) \nabla \left(\bigvee X \vee y \right) \right) \backslash \bigvee X \qquad (3)$$

where $x \in X$ is picked non-deterministically from X.

Theorem 2 (WIDENWITH$_{\{\vee, \sqcup\}}$ Correctness). $\text{WIDENWITH}_\sqcup$ *and* $\text{WIDENWITH}_\vee$ *satisfy the two conditions of Def. 3.*

1: **func** UFOREF (ARG $\mathcal{A} = (V, E, v_{\text{en}}, \nu, \tau, \psi)$) :
2:     $\mathcal{L}_E \leftarrow \text{ENCODEBMC}(\mathcal{A}); \mathcal{I} \leftarrow \text{DAGITP}((V, E, v_{\text{en}}, v_{\text{err}}), \mathcal{L}_E); \textbf{return} \text{DECODEBMC}(\mathcal{I})$

Fig. 4. UFO refinement procedure

4.3 Refinement

In this section, we formalize our refinement strategy. We start by reviewing the strategy used by UFO and based on a concept of a *Restricted DAG Interpolant* (RDI) – an extension of a *path interpolant* [13,15] to DAGs. In the rest of this section, we write F for a set of formulas; $G = (V, E, v^{en}, v^{ex})$ for a DAG with an entry node $v^{en} \in V$ and an exit node $v^{ex} \in V$, where v^{en} has no predecessors, v^{ex} has no successors, and every node $v \in V$ lies on a (v^{en}, v^{ex})-path. We also write $desc(v)$ and $anc(v)$ for the sets of descendants and ancestors of a node $v \in V$, respectively; $\mathcal{L}_E : E \to F$ and $\mathcal{L}_V : V \to F$ for maps from edges and vertices to formulas, respectively; and $FV(\varphi)$ for the set of free variables in a given formula φ.

Definition 4 (Restricted DAG Interpolant (RDI)). *Let G, $\mathcal{L}_E$, and $\mathcal{L}_V$ be as defined above. An RDI is a map $\mathcal{I} : V \to F$ s.t.*

1. $\forall e = (v_i, v_j) \in E \cdot \big(\mathcal{I}(v_i) \wedge \mathcal{L}_V(v_i) \wedge \mathcal{L}_E(e)\big) \implies \mathcal{I}(v_j) \wedge \mathcal{L}_V(v_j),$
2. $\mathcal{I}(v^{en}) \equiv \text{true, and } \big(\mathcal{I}(v^{ex}) \wedge \mathcal{L}_V(v^{ex})\big) \equiv \text{false, and}$
3. $\forall v_i \in V \cdot FV(\mathcal{I}(v_i)) \subseteq \big(\bigcup_{u \in desc(v_i)} FV(\mathcal{I}(u))\big) \cap \big(\bigcup_{u \in anc(v_i)} FV(\mathcal{I}(u))\big).$

Whenever $\forall v \cdot \mathcal{L}_V(v) = true$, we say that an RDI is *unrestricted* or simply a DAG Interpolant (DI). Intuitively, a DI $\mathcal{I}$ is a labeling of G such that for every path $v^{en}, \ldots, v^{ex}$, the sequence $\mathcal{I}(v^{en}), \ldots, \mathcal{I}(v^{ex})$ is a path interpolant [13,15]. In general, in a proper RDI $\mathcal{I}$ (i.e., when $\exists v \cdot \mathcal{L}_V(v) \neq true$), $\mathcal{I}(v)$ is not an interpolant by itself, but is a projection of an interpolant to $\mathcal{L}_V(v)$. That is, $\mathcal{I}(v)$ is the restriction needed to turn $\mathcal{L}_V(v)$ into an interpolant. Thus, an RDI can be weaker (and possibly easier to compute) than a DI.

UFO **Refinement.** UFO's refinement procedure is shown in Fig. 4. It uses the procedure DAGITP from [1][2] to compute a DI. Given an ARG $\mathcal{A} = (V, E, v_{\text{en}}, \nu, \tau, \psi)$ with an error node v_{err}, it first constructs an edge labeling $\mathcal{L}_E$ using a BMC-encoding such that for each ARG edge e, $\mathcal{L}_E(e)$ is the semantics of the corresponding action $\tau(e)$ (i.e., $[\![\tau(e)]\!]$), with variables renamed and added as necessary, and such that for any path $v_1, \ldots, v_k$, the formula $\bigwedge_{i \in [1,k)} \mathcal{L}_E(v_i, v_{i+1})$ encodes all executions from v_1 to v_k. Many BMC-encodings can be used for this step, and we use the approach of [11]. For example, for the three edges (v_1, v_2^a), (v_2^a, v_e), (v_2^a, v_2^b) of the ARG in Fig. 2(c), the $\mathcal{L}_E$ map is

---

[2] [1] used a different terminology. DAGITP refers to the procedure in Thm. 3 of [1].

$$\mathcal{L}_E(v_1, v_2^a) \equiv x_0 = 0 \wedge y_0 = 0 \tag{4}$$

$$\mathcal{L}_E(v_2^a, v_e) \equiv x_\phi \geq 4 \wedge y_\phi \leq 2 \wedge x_\phi = x_0 \wedge y_\phi = y_0 \tag{5}$$

$$\mathcal{L}_E(v_2^a, v_2^b) \equiv (x_1 = x_0 + 1 \wedge y_1 = y_0 + 1) \vee \tag{6}$$
$$(x_0 \geq 4 \wedge x_1 = x_0 + 1 \wedge y_1 = y_0 + 1) \vee$$
$$(x_1 = x_0 \wedge y_1 = y_0)$$

where, in addition to renaming, two extra variables x_ϕ and y_ϕ were added for the SSA encoding since node v_e has multiple edges incident on it. $\mathcal{L}_E(v_1, v_2^a) \wedge \mathcal{L}_E(v_2^a, v_e)$ encodes all executions on the path v_1, v_2^a, v_e, and $\mathcal{L}_E(v_1, v_2^a) \wedge \mathcal{L}_E(v_2^a, v_2^b)$ encodes all executions on the path v_1, v_2^a, v_2^b. Second, the refined labels are computed as a DI $\mathcal{I} = \text{DAGITP}((V, E, v_{en}, v_{err}), \mathcal{L}_E)$. Note that after reversing the renaming done by BMC-encoding (i.e., removing the subscripts), the DI $\mathcal{I}$ is a safe (by condition 2 of Def. 4) well-labeling (by condition 1 of Def. 4) of the ARG $\mathcal{A}$. Furthermore, $\mathcal{I}(v)$ is expressed completely in terms of variables defined before and used after $v \in V$. The result of refinement on our running example is shown in Fig. 2(d).

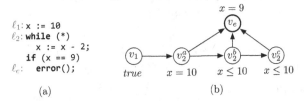

```
ℓ₁: x := 10
ℓ₂: while (*)
        x := x - 2;
        if (x == 9)
ℓₑ:     error();
```

(a)

(b)

Fig. 5. (a) A program and (b) its ARG

Using UFO Refinement with VINTA. While VINTA can use UFO's refinement since it satisfies the specification of REFINE in Def. 2, we found that it does not scale in practice. We believe there are two key reasons for this.

The first reason is that the DI-based refinement uses just the ARG while completely ignoring its node labeling (i.e., the set of reachable states discovered by AI). Thus, while the DI-based refinement recovers from imprecision to remove false alarms, it may introduce imprecision for further exploration steps. For example, consider the program in Fig. 5(a) and its ARG in Fig. 5(b) produced by AI using the BOX domain.

The ARG has a false alarm (in reality, v_e is unreachable). A possible DI-based refinement changes the labels of v_2^b, v_2^c, and v_e to $x \leq 10 \wedge x \neq 9$, $x \neq 9$, and *false*, respectively. While this is sufficient to eliminate the false alarm, the new labels do not form an inductive invariant – thus further unrolling of the ARG is required. Note that the refinement "improved" the label of v_2^c to $x \neq 9$, but "lost" an important fact $x \leq 10$. Instead, we propose to restrict refinement to produce new labels that are stronger than the existing ones. In this example, such a restricted refinement would change the labels of v_2^b, v_2^c, and v_e to $x \leq 10 \wedge x \neq 9$, $x \leq 10 \wedge x \neq 9$, and *false*, thus completing the verification.

```
1: func VintaRef (ARG 𝒜 = (V, E, v_en, ν, τ, ψ)) :        Require: ℒ_V is a well-labeling of G
2:    ℒ_E ← EncodeBmc(𝒜) ; ℒ_V ← Encode(ψ)              7: func VintaRdi (G, ℒ_E, ℒ_V) :
3:    ℐ ← VintaRdi((V, E, v_en, v_err), ℒ_E, ℒ_V)        8:    for all e = (u, v) ∈ E do
4:    if ℐ = ∅ then return ℐ                            9:       ℒ_E(e) ← ℒ_V(u) ∧ ℒ_E(e)
5:    for all v ∈ V do ℐ(v) ← ℐ(v) ∧ ℒ_V(v)            10:    ℐ ← DagItp(G, ℒ_E)
6:    return DecodeBmc(ℐ)                             11:    return ℐ
```

Fig. 6. VintaRef refinement procedure

The second reason is that ARGs produced by AI are large, and generating interpolants directly from them takes too long. Here, again, part of the problem is that refinement does not use the existing labeling to simplify the constraints. Instead of computing a DI of the ARG, we propose to compute an RDI restricted by the current labeling. Since an RDI is simpler (i.e., weaker, has fewer connectives, etc.) than a corresponding DI, the hope is that it is also easier to compute.

Vinta **Refinement.** Vinta's refinement procedure VintaRef is shown in Fig. 6. It takes a labeled ARG 𝒜 and returns a new safe well-labeling *labels* of 𝒜. First, it encodes the edges of 𝒜 using BMC-encoding as described above (line 2). Second, the current labeling ψ of 𝒜 is encoded to match the renaming introduced by the BMC-encoding. For example, for v_2^a in our running example, $\psi(v_2^a) \equiv x = 0 \wedge y = 0$, and the encoding $\mathcal{L}_V(v_2^a) \equiv x_0 = 0 \wedge y_0 = 0$. Third, it uses VintaRdi (shown in Fig. 6) to compute an RDI of 𝒜 restricted by $\mathcal{L}_V$. Fourth, it turns the RDI into a DI by conjoining it with $\mathcal{L}_V$ (line 5). Finally, it decodes the labels by undoing the BMC-encoding (line 6).

The function VintaRdi computes an RDI by reducing it to computing a DI using the DagItp procedure from [1] described earlier. Note that it requires that $\mathcal{L}_V$ is a well-labeling, i.e., for all $(u, v) \in E$, $\mathcal{L}_V(u) \wedge \mathcal{L}_E(u, v) \Rightarrow \mathcal{L}_V(v)$. The idea is to "communicate" to the SMT-solver the restriction of node u by conjoining $\mathcal{L}_V(u)$ to every edge from u. This information might be helpful to the SMT-solver for simplifying its proofs and the resulting interpolants.

Theorem 3 (Correctness of VintaRef). VintaRef *satisfies the specification of* Refine *in Def. 2.*

There is a simple generalization of VintaRef: ψ on line 2 can be replaced by any over-approximation U of reachable states. The current invariant represented by the ARG is a good candidate and so are invariants computed by other techniques. The only restriction is that VintaRdi requires U to be a well-labeling. Removing this restriction from VintaRdi remains an open problem.

5   Implementation and Evaluation

5.1   Implementation

We have implemented Vinta in the Ufo framework [2] for verifying C programs, which is built on top of the LLVM compiler infrastructure [14]. Our modular implementation of Vinta allows abstract domains to be easily plugged in and experimented with. Currently, the abstract domains used by VINTA are BOX and BOXES, defined in [12]. For SMT-solving and interpolation, VINTA uses Z3 [16] and MATHSAT5[3], respectively. In the rest of this section, we highlight the technical challenges addressed by our implementation. Specifically, we discuss our implementation of abstraction functions from Boolean expressions to BOX and BOXES elements, and describe key SMT-solving techniques that are instrumental to VINTA's efficiency. Our implementation and complete experimental results are available at http://www.cs.toronto.edu/~aws/vinta.

Abstraction Functions. We are using a simple abstraction function to convert between Boolean expressions and BOXES and BOX abstract domains. Given a formula φ, we first convert it to NNF. Then, we replace all literals involving more than one variable (e.g., $x + y = 0$) with *true*, thus over-approximating φ and removing all terms not expressible in BOX. Finally, for BOX, we additionally use join to approximate disjunction. This naive approach is very imprecise in general, but works well on our benchmarks.

Incremental Solving for Covering. Recall that EXPANDARG in Fig. 3 uses an SMT call at every cover check (line 46 in Fig. 3). This is highly inefficient. In practice, we exploit Z3's incremental interface (using **push** and **pop** commands) as follows. For each cutpoint ℓ, we maintain a separate SMT context ctx_ℓ. Every time a node v s.t. $\nu(v) = \ell$ is not covered (i.e., the check on line 46 in Fig. 3 fails), $\neg\psi(v)$ is added to ctx_ℓ. To check whether a node u with $\nu(u) = \ell$ is covered, we check whether $\psi(u)$ is satisfiable in ctx_ℓ. If the result is UNSAT, then u is covered; otherwise, it is not covered and $\neg\psi(u)$ is added to ctx_ℓ. Effectively, this is the same as checking whether $\psi(u) \wedge \bigwedge_{v \in \text{vis}(\nu(u)), v \neq u} \neg\psi(v)$ is UNSAT, which is equivalent to line 46 of EXPANDARG.

Using Post Computations for Simplification. In our implementation, we keep track of those ARG edges for which $\text{POST}_\mathcal{D}$ computations returned $\perp$. For each such edge e, we can replace $\mathcal{L}_E(e)$ in VINTARDI with *false*, thus reducing the size of the formula.

Improving Interpolation with UNSAT Cores. One technical challenge we faced is that MATHSAT5's performance degrades significantly when interpolation support is turned on, particularly on large formulas. To reduce the size of the formula given to MATHSAT5, we use the *assumptions* feature in the highly efficient but lacking interpolation support Z3. Let a formula $\varphi_1 \wedge \ldots \wedge \varphi_n$ and a set $X = \{b_i\}_{i=1}^n$ of Boolean *assumptions* variables be given. When Z3 is passed a formula $\Phi = (b_1 \Rightarrow \varphi_1) \wedge \ldots \wedge (b_n \Rightarrow \varphi_n)$, it returns a subset of X, called UNSAT core, that has to be *true* to make Φ UNSAT. In our case, we add an assumption for each literal appearing in formulas in $\mathcal{L}_E$, and use Z3 to find unnecessary literals, i.e., those not in the UNSAT core. Since Z3 does not produce a minimal core, we repeat the minimization process three times. Finally, we set unnecessary literals to *true* and use MATHSAT5 to interpolate over the simplified formula.

---

[3] http://mathsat.fbk.eu

Table 1. Summary of results on 93 C programs. Numbers in bold indicate the best result.

Algorithm	#Solved	#Safe	#Unsafe	Total Time (s)
vBox	**71**	20	**51**	**580** (539/**41**)
uBox	68	19	49	1,240 (1,162/78)
vBoxes	67	25	42	1,782 (596/1,186)
uBoxes	60	18	42	2,731 (808/1,923)
CpaAbe	65	**29**	36	1,167 (707/460)
CpaMemo	64	24	40	1,794 (**454**/1,341)
uInterp	70	20	50	1,535 (1,457/78)
uCp	69	19	50	1,687 (1,509/178)
uBp	64	15	49	1,062 (57/1,006)

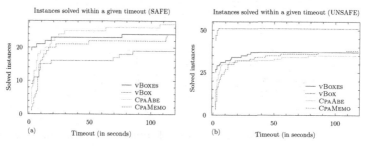

Fig. 7. Number of solved instances vs. timeout: (a) safe benchmarks; (b) unsafe benchmarks

5.2 Evaluation

For evaluation, we used `ntdrivers-simplified`, `ssh-simplified`, and `systemc` benchmarks from the 2012 Software Verification Competition (SV-COMP 2012) [4]. In total, we had 93 C programs (41 safe and 52 buggy).

We implemented several instantiations of VINTA: vBox, vBoxes, uBox, and uBoxes, using the Box and Boxes domains, and VINTAREF and UFOREF refinements, respectively. For Box and Boxes, we used the widening operators WIDENWITH$_\sqcup$ and WIDENWITH$_\lor$ from Sec. 4.2, respectively. In all cases, we applied widening on every third unrolling of each loop. We compared VINTA against the top two tools from SV-COMP 2012: CPACHECKER-ABE (CPAABE) and CPACHECKER-MEMO (CPAMEMO), which are two variations of the predicate-abstraction-based software model checker CPACHECKER [5]. For both tools, we used the same version and configuration as in the competition. We also compared against several instantiations of our UFO framework: uINTERP, uCP, and uBP, using interpolation-based verification by itself and in combination with Cartesian and Boolean predicate abstractions, respectively.

The overall results are summarized in Table 1. All experiments were conducted on a 3.40GHz Intel Core i7 processor with 8GB of RAM running Ubuntu Linux v11.10. We imposed a time limit of 500 seconds and a memory limit of 4GB per program. For each tool, we show the number of safe and unsafe instances solved and the total time taken. For example, vBox solved 20 safe and 51 unsafe

Table 2. Time of running VINTA, CPAABE, and CPAMEMO on 21 safe benchmarks. '–' indicates a timeout.

PROGRAM	vBOXES	uBOXES	vBOX	uBOX	CPAABE	CPAMEMO
s3_clnt_1	**0.30**	**0.30**	8.61	13.67	7.34	11.63
s3_clnt_2	**0.3**	**0.30**	8.79	13.45	6.72	8.53
s3_clnt_3	0.30	**0.29**	9.01	6.80	9.72	7.10
s3_clnt_4	**0.30**	**0.30**	9.55	8.52	6.33	12.43
s3_srvr_1a	**0.15**	–	1.08	–	2.86	4.344
s3_srvr_1b	**0.02**	**0.02**	–	–	1.49	1.64
s3_srvr_1	**0.00**	**0.00**	**0.00**	**0.00**	21.21	8.63
s3_srvr_2	**0.64**	115.48	–	115.13	63.44	113.07
s3_srvr_3	**0.75**	123.57	69.70	123.61	17.23	22.55
s3_srvr_4	**0.59**	168.44	85.81	168.08	7.50	14.57
s3_srvr_6	473.15	319.00	**74.87**	359.39	181.82	–
s3_srvr_7	**13.82**	–	–	274.12	24.84	112.53
s3_srvr_8	**0.69**	78.53	245.52	76.12	18.48	8.82
token_ring.01	**0.94**	–	4.05	–	4.13	8.04
token_ring.02	**2.53**	–	18.29	–	6.69	49.11
token_ring.03	**6.06**	–	–	–	29.55	–
token_ring.04	**18.22**	–	–	–	146.43	–
token_ring.05	**76.29**	–	–	–	–	–
token_ring.06	–	–	–	–	–	–
token_ring.07	–	–	–	–	–	–
token_ring.08	–	–	–	–	–	–

examples in 580 seconds, spending 539s on safe ones and 41s on unsafe ones (time spent in unsolved instances is not counted). vBox is an overall winner, and is able to solve the most unsafe instances in the least amount of time. CPAABE is the winner on the safe instances, with vBOXES coming in second. In the rest of this section, we examine these results in more detail.

Instances Solved vs. Timeout. Fig. 7 shows the number of instances solved in a given timeout for (a) safe and (b) unsafe benchmarks, respectively. To avoid clutter, we omit uINTERP, uBP, and uCP from the graphs and restrict the timeout to 120s, since only a few instances took more time. For the safe cases, vBOXES is a clear winner for the timeout of ≤ 10s. Indeed, on most safe benchmarks, vBOXES takes a lot less time to complete than CPAABE, CPAMEMO, and all other instantiations of UFO and VINTA. For the unsafe cases, vBOX is a clear winner for all timeouts. Interestingly, the extra precision of BOXES makes vBOXES perform poorly on unsafe instances: it either solves an unsafe instance in one iteration (i.e., no refinement), or runs out of time in the first AI- or refinement-phase.

Detailed Comparison. We now examine a portion of the benchmark suite in more detail, specifically, safe ssh-simplified benchmarks and safe token_ring benchmarks (from systemc). Table 2 shows the time taken by the different instantiations of VINTA, CPAABE, and CPAMEMO. On these benchmarks, we observe that vBOXES outperforms all other approaches.

Compared with CPAABE and CPAMEMO, vBOXES is able to solve almost all instances in much less time. For example, on token_ring.05, both CPAABE and CPAMEMO fail to return a result, but vBOXES proves safety in 76 seconds. Similarly, vBOXES is superior on most ssh-simplified examples.

To understand the importance of the refinement strategy, consider the `ssh-simplified` benchmarks. The invariant for most `ssh-simplified` instances is computable using BOXES with an appropriate widening strategy ("widen on every fourth unrolling"). The results in the table show how VINTA's refinement strategy is able to recover precision when an inadequate refinement strategy is used (i.e., "widen on every third unrolling"). Using UFO's refinement, uBOXES takes substantially more time and more iterations or fails to return a result within the allotted time limit. For example, on `s3_srvr_2`, vBOXES requires a single refinement, whereas uBOXES requires 38. Positive effects of VINTA's AI-guided refinement are also visible in vBOX vs. uBOX.

In summary, our results demonstrate the power of VINTA's refinement strategy and show how basic instantiations of VINTA can compete and outperform highly-optimized verification tools like CPACHECKER. To further improve VINTA's performance, it would be interesting to experiment with other abstract domains as well as with different automatic strategies for choosing an appropriate domain. For example, we saw that BOXES, in comparison with BOX, generates very large ARGs for unsafe examples. One strategy would be to keep track of ARG size and time spent in refinement and revert to a less precise abstract domain like BOX when they become too large.

6 Conclusion

In this paper, we presented VINTA, an iterative algorithm that uses Craig interpolants to refine invariants produced by abstract interpretation and eliminate false alarms. VINTA's verification technique marries the efficiency of abstract interpretation with the precision of bounded model checking and the ability to "guess" invariants of interpolation-based verification.

Our evaluation of VINTA against state-of-the-art verification tools demonstrates the power of our approach and calls for further experimentation with our refinement strategy on different abstract domains.

References

1. Albarghouthi, A., Gurfinkel, A., Chechik, M.: From Under-Approximations to Over-Approximations and Back. In: Flanagan, C., König, B. (eds.) TACAS 2012. LNCS, vol. 7214, pp. 157–172. Springer, Heidelberg (2012)
2. Albarghouthi, A., Gurfinkel, A., Chechik, M.: UFO: A Framework for Abstraction- and Interpolation-Based Software Verification. In: Madhusudan, P., Seshia, S.A. (eds.) CAV 2012. LNCS, vol. 7358, pp. 672–678. Springer, Heidelberg (2012)
3. Bagnara, R., Hill, P.M., Zaffanella, E.: Widening Operators for Powerset Domains. STTT 8(4-5), 449–466 (2006)
4. Beyer, D.: Competition on Software Verification - (SV-COMP). In: Flanagan, C., König, B. (eds.) TACAS 2012. LNCS, vol. 7214, pp. 504–524. Springer, Heidelberg (2012), http://sv-comp.sosy-lab.org/
5. Beyer, D., Keremoglu, M.E.: CPACHECKER: A Tool for Configurable Software Verification. In: Gopalakrishnan, G., Qadeer, S. (eds.) CAV 2011. LNCS, vol. 6806, pp. 184–190. Springer, Heidelberg (2011)

6. Biere, A., Cimatti, A., Clarke, E., Zhu, Y.: Symbolic Model Checking without BDDs. In: Cleaveland, W.R. (ed.) TACAS 1999. LNCS, vol. 1579, pp. 193–207. Springer, Heidelberg (1999)
7. Bourdoncle, F.: Efficient Chaotic Iteration Strategies with Widenings. In: Bjøcrner, D., Broy, M., Pottosin, I.V. (eds.) Proc. of FMPA 1993. LNCS, vol. 735, pp. 128–141. Springer, Heidelberg (1993)
8. Craig, W.: Three Uses of the Herbrand-Gentzen Theorem in Relating Model Theory and Proof Theory. J. of Symbolic Logic 22(3), 269–285 (1957)
9. Gulavani, B., Henzinger, T., Kannan, Y., Nori, A., Rajamani, S.: SYNERGY: A New Algorithm for Property Checking. In: Proc. of FSE 2006, pp. 117–127 (2006)
10. Gulavani, B.S., Chakraborty, S., Nori, A.V., Rajamani, S.K.: Automatically Refining Abstract Interpretations. In: Ramakrishnan, C.R., Rehof, J. (eds.) TACAS 2008. LNCS, vol. 4963, pp. 443–458. Springer, Heidelberg (2008)
11. Gurfinkel, A., Chaki, S., Sapra, S.: Efficient Predicate Abstraction of Program Summaries. In: Bobaru, M., Havelund, K., Holzmann, G.J., Joshi, R. (eds.) NFM 2011. LNCS, vol. 6617, pp. 131–145. Springer, Heidelberg (2011)
12. Gurfinkel, A., Chaki, S.: BOXES: A Symbolic Abstract Domain of Boxes. In: Cousot, R., Martel, M. (eds.) SAS 2010. LNCS, vol. 6337, pp. 287–303. Springer, Heidelberg (2010)
13. Henzinger, T.A., Jhala, R., Majumdar, R., McMillan, K.L.: Abstractions from Proofs. In: Proc. of POPL 2004, pp. 232–244 (2004)
14. Lattner, C., Adve, V.: LLVM: A Compilation Framework for Lifelong Program Analysis & Transformation. In: Proc. of CGO 2004, pp. 75–88 (2004)
15. McMillan, K.L.: Lazy Abstraction with Interpolants. In: Ball, T., Jones, R.B. (eds.) CAV 2006. LNCS, vol. 4144, pp. 123–136. Springer, Heidelberg (2006)
16. de Moura, L., Bjørner, N.: Z3: An Efficient SMT Solver. In: Ramakrishnan, C.R., Rehof, J. (eds.) TACAS 2008. LNCS, vol. 4963, pp. 337–340. Springer, Heidelberg (2008)
17. Wang, C., Yang, Z., Gupta, A., Ivančić, F.: Using Counterexamples for Improving the Precision of Reachability Computation with Polyhedra. In: Damm, W., Hermanns, H. (eds.) CAV 2007. LNCS, vol. 4590, pp. 352–365. Springer, Heidelberg (2007)

Satisfiability Solvers Are Static Analysers*

Vijay D'Silva**, Leopold Haller, and Daniel Kroening

Department of Computer Science, Oxford University
`firstname.surname@cs.ox.ac.uk`

Abstract. This paper shows that several propositional satisfiability algorithms compute approximations of fixed points using lattice-based abstractions. The Boolean Constraint Propagation algorithm (BCP) is a greatest fixed point computation over a lattice of partial assignments. The original algorithm of Davis, Logemann and Loveland refines BCP by computing a set of greatest fixed points. The Conflict Driven Clause Learning algorithm alternates between overapproximate deduction with BCP, and underapproximate abduction, with conflict analysis. Thus, in a precise sense, satisfiability solvers are abstract interpreters. Our work is the first step towards a uniform framework for the design and implementation of satisfiability algorithms, static analysers and their combination.

1 How I Learned to Stop SAT Solving and Love Abstract Interpretation

The abstract interpretation approach to program analysis is to compute properties of programs using lattices, transformers and fixed points [5]. The satisfiability approach is to encode programs as formulae that can be analysed with theorem provers [17]. The satisfiability approach has gained popularity in recent years due to dramatic improvements in the performance of propositional satisfiability solvers. The goal of much current research is to combine techniques based on abstract interpretation and based on satisfiability.

This paper shows that propositional satisfiability algorithms compute approximations of fixed points using lattices. Thus, analyses traditionally formulated over lattices and those formulated in terms of satisfiability can both be understood in terms of abstract interpretation. To appreciate the significance of such understanding, consider the program below, where φ is a formula with Boolean variables initialised to arbitrary values.

`if ( `φ` ) { assert( false ) }`

If φ is unsatisfiable, a program verifier that uses a SAT solver will conclude that the assertion is not violated. In contrast, a static analysis like constant propagation (or its conditional variant [26]) cannot always prove the absence of

---

* Supported by the Toyota Motor Corporation, EPSRC project EP/H017585/1 and ERC project 280053.

** Supported by a Microsoft Research European PhD Scholarship.

A. Miné and D. Schmidt (Eds.): SAS 2012, LNCS 7460, pp. 317–333, 2012.

assertion violations if a formula is unsatisfiable. This result is surprising because we show that all SAT solvers derived from the DPLL procedure use the same lattice as constant propagation. The insight of SAT algorithms is that we can use imprecise abstract domains to gain efficiency, and techniques like decisions and clause-learning to improve precision.

Contribution. This paper demonstrates that a broad range of propositional satisfiability algorithms have natural abstract interpretation descriptions. Our contributions include the following characterisations.

1. Propositional satisfiability as a property of fixed points of transformers over the lattice of truth assignments.
2. Boolean Constraint Propagation (BCP) as a greatest fixed point computation over the same lattice as constant propagation.
3. The Davis Putnam Logemann and Loveland algorithm (DPLL) as a refinement of BCP that uses value-based trace partitioning.
4. The conflict driven clause learning algorithm (CDCL) as a combination of overapproximate deduction with underapproximate abduction.

In separate work, we used the formalisation presented here to embed the interval abstract domain inside CDCL and verify programs that are beyond the scope of existing techniques [12]. This paper is organised as follows: We give fixed point semantics to propositional formulae in § 2. To illustrate our approach on simple examples, we formalise truth tables and resolution in § 3. The DPLL algorithm and CDCL are covered in § 4 and § 5.

2   Propositional Satisfiability via Transformers

This section contains a new characterisation of propositional satisfiability using fixed points. We first recall background on propositional logic and lattices.

Propositional Logic. Fix a set *Prop* of propositional variables. A *literal* is a variable or its negation. A *clause* is a disjunction of literals and a *cube* is a conjunction of literals. A formula in *conjunctive normal form* (CNF) is a conjunction of clauses, and a formula in *disjunctive normal form* (DNF) is a disjunction of cubes. Note that the negation of a cube is a clause and vice versa.

The set of truth values is $\mathbb{B} \doteq \{t, f\}$. An *assignment* $\sigma : Prop \to \mathbb{B}$ maps variables to truth values. An assignment σ is a *model* of φ, denoted $\sigma \models \varphi$, if σ satisfies φ and is a *countermodel* of φ otherwise. A formula is *satisfiable* if it has a model and is *unsatisfiable* otherwise.

Lattices A *lattice* $(L, \sqsubseteq, \sqcup, \sqcap)$ is a partially ordered set with a meet and a join. Two functions $f, g : Q \to L$ from a set Q to L can be *ordered pointwise*, denoted $f \sqsubseteq g$, if $f(x) \sqsubseteq g(x)$ holds for all x in Q. All functions over L can similarly be lifted pointwise to $Q \to L$. The least and greatest fixed points of a monotone function F on a complete lattice will be denoted $\mathsf{lfp}(F)$ and $\mathsf{gfp}(F)$, respectively.

Let id_S be the identity function. A *Galois connection* between posets $(C, \sqsubseteq)$ and $(A, \preccurlyeq)$, written $C \xleftrightarrow[\alpha]{\gamma} A$, is a pair of monotone functions $\alpha : C \to A$ and $\gamma : A \to C$ that satisfy the pointwise constraints $\alpha \circ \gamma \preccurlyeq id_A$ and $id_C \sqsubseteq \gamma \circ \alpha$.

We identify a few lattices of particular interest. The *lattice of truth values* $(\mathbb{B}, \Rightarrow, \vee, \wedge)$ consists of truth values with the implication order $\mathsf{f} \Rightarrow \mathsf{t}$. Disjunction is the join and conjunction is the meet of truth values. The *powerset lattice* over a set X, written $(\mathscr{P}(S), \subseteq, \cup, \cap)$, consists of all subsets of S order by inclusion. Let $(S, \sqsubseteq)$ be a poset. A set $Q \subseteq S$ is *downwards closed* if for every x in Q and y in S, $y \sqsubseteq x$ implies that y is in Q. A downwards closed set is called a *downset*. The *downset lattice* over $(S, \sqsubseteq)$, written $(\mathscr{D}(S), \subseteq, \cap, \cup)$, is the set of downsets of S ordered by inclusion. Downsets strictly generalise powersets because the powerset lattice of S is the downset lattice of S with the identity relation.

2.1   Concrete Semantics of Propositional Formulae

We present new, fixed point characterisations of the models and countermodels of a formula. Satisfiability and validity are properties of such fixed points.

Let $Asg \triangleq Prop \to \mathbb{B}$ be the set of assignments. The *concrete domain of assignments* is $(\mathscr{P}(Asg), \subseteq, \cup, \cap)$. A formula φ defines four *assignment transformers*. The name assignment transformers is used by analogy to state transformers and predicate transformers. Let X be a set of assignments. The *model transformer* mod_φ removes all countermodels of φ from X, the *countermodel transformer* $cmod_\varphi$ removes all models of φ from X, the *universal model transformer* $umod_\varphi$ adds all models of φ to X, and the *universal countermodel transformer* $ucmod_\varphi$ adds all countermodels of φ to X.

$$mod_\varphi(X) \triangleq \{\sigma \in X \mid \sigma \models \varphi\} \qquad umod_\varphi(X) \triangleq \{\sigma \in Asg \mid \sigma \models \varphi \text{ or } \sigma \in X\}$$
$$cmod_\varphi(X) \triangleq \{\sigma \in X \mid \sigma \not\models \varphi\} \qquad ucmod_\varphi(X) \triangleq \{\sigma \in Asg \mid \sigma \not\models \varphi \text{ or } \sigma \in X\}$$

Properties of a formula can be expressed with transformers. The set of models of φ is $mod_\varphi(Asg)$, or equivalently, $umod_\varphi(\emptyset)$. The set of countermodels of φ is $cmod_\varphi(Asg)$, or equivalently, $ucmod_\varphi(\emptyset)$. Algebraic properties of assignment transformers aid in deriving fixed point characterisations of satisfiability. The *De Morgan dual* of a function f on $\mathscr{P}(Asg)$ is the function $\neg \circ f \circ \neg$.

Theorem 1. *The assignment transformers have the following properties.*

1. *The pairs $(mod_\varphi, ucmod_\varphi)$ and $(cmod_\varphi, umod_\varphi)$ are De Morgan duals.*
2. *There are two Galois connections as below.*

$$\mathscr{P}(Asg) \xleftrightarrow[mod_\varphi]{ucmod_\varphi} \mathscr{P}(Asg) \qquad \mathscr{P}(Asg) \xleftrightarrow[cmod_\varphi]{umod_\varphi} \mathscr{P}(Asg)$$

Consider the statement $\mathsf{assume}(\varphi)$. The strongest postcondition is equivalent to mod_φ and the weakest liberal precondition is equivalent to $ucmod_\varphi$. Sound approximations of these transformers are available in abstract domain libraries. Since our characterisation use these transformers, the overhead of lifting satisfiability algorithms to new domains is low. Theorem 2 provides several fixed point characterisations of satisfiability.

Theorem 2. *The following statements are equivalent.*

1. *A formula φ is unsatisfiable.*
2. *The set of assignments $mod_\varphi(Asg)$ is empty.*
3. *The set of assignments $umod_\varphi(\emptyset)$ is empty.*
4. *The set $cmod_\varphi(Asg)$ contains all assignments.*
5. *The set $ucmod_\varphi(\emptyset)$ contains all assignments.*
6. *The greatest fixed point $\mathsf{gfp}(mod_\varphi)$ contains no assignments.*
7. *The least fixed point $\mathsf{lfp}(umod_\varphi)$ contains no assignments.*
8. *The greatest fixed point $\mathsf{gfp}(cmod_\varphi)$ contains all assignments.*
9. *The least fixed point $\mathsf{lfp}(ucmod_\varphi)$ contains all assignments.*

Proof. Due to space restrictions, we do not prove all cases.

(1 iff 2) The formula φ is unsatisfiable exactly if it has no models. An assignment σ is in $mod_\varphi(Asg)$ exactly if σ is a model of φ. The set $mod_\varphi(Asg)$ is empty exactly if φ is unsatisfiable.

(2 iff 5) Recall that $ucmod_\varphi(X)$ is the De Morgan dual of mod_φ. If $mod_\varphi(Asg)$ is the emptyset, $ucmod_\varphi(\emptyset)$ equals $\neg mod_\varphi(\neg\emptyset)$, which equals Asg.

(2 iff 4) The function mod_φ is idempotent, meaning that $mod_\varphi(X)$ is equal to $mod_\varphi(mod_\varphi(X))$ for all X. Since mod_φ is monotone, $mod_\varphi(Asg)$ equals $mod_\varphi(mod_\varphi(Asg))$, so the greatest fixed point of mod_φ is $mod_\varphi(Asg)$. Thus $mod_\varphi(Asg)$ is empty exactly if $\mathsf{gfp}(mod_\varphi)$ is empty.

The argument for the remaining equivalences is similar.

Since all the transformers are idempotent, the fixed points in Theorem 2 may seem superfluous. A sound abstraction of an idempotent function is not necessarily idempotent, so iterating an abstract transformer can provide strictly better results than applying it once. This intuition is formalised by the method of *locally decreasing iterations* [13].

2.2   Abstract Satisfaction

We use the term *abstract satisfaction* for the application of abstract interpretation to design satisfiability algorithms. Abstract interpretation is typically used to overapproximate a least fixed point (such as reachable states), or to underapproximate a greatest fixed point (such as the set of dead variables at a program location). In contrast, we will overapproximate the greatest fixed point $\mathsf{gfp}(mod_\varphi)$ or underapproximate the least fixed point $\mathsf{lfp}(ucmod_\varphi)$. If an overapproximation of $\mathsf{gfp}(mod_\varphi)$ is the emptyset, φ is unsatisfiable. If an underapproximation of $\mathsf{lfp}(ucmod_\varphi)$ contains all assignments, φ is unsatisfiable. Combining information from different approximations yields better results than using either in isolation.

Abstract Interpretation. Assume a Galois connection $C \xleftarrow{\gamma}\xrightarrow{\alpha} A$. The lattice C is called the *concrete domain* and A is called the *abstract domain*. If C is a powerset lattice, an abstract domain with respect to the subset order satisfies $x \subseteq \gamma(\alpha(x))$

and is called an overapproximation. An abstract domain with respect to the superset order satisfies $x \supseteq \gamma(\alpha(x))$ and is called an underapproximation.

Functions on a concrete domain are called *concrete transformers* and those on abstract domains are *abstract transformers*. The abstract transformer G soundly approximates F if $F \circ \gamma \sqsubseteq \gamma \circ G$ holds. The *best abstract transformer* $\alpha \circ F \circ \gamma$ represents the maximum precision that can be derived from an abstraction.

Abstract Interpretation of Satisfiability. This section presents new, fixed point approximations of satisfiability.

Let $(O, \sqsubseteq, \sqcup, \sqcap)$ be an overapproximation of the domain of assignments and $(U, \preccurlyeq, \curlyvee, \curlywedge)$ be underapproximation. The approximation is formalised by the Galois connections below. The orders $\sqsubseteq$ and $\preccurlyeq$ both refine the subset order on assignments. That is, $a \sqsubseteq b$ implies $\gamma(a) \subseteq \gamma(b)$, and $x \preccurlyeq y$ implies $\gamma(x) \subseteq \gamma(y)$.

$$(\mathscr{P}(Asg), \subseteq) \xrightleftharpoons[\alpha_O]{\gamma_O} (O, \sqsubseteq) \qquad (\mathscr{P}(Asg), \supseteq) \xrightleftharpoons[\alpha_U]{\gamma_U} (U, \succcurlyeq)$$

Abstract transformers can be defined for over- or underapproximating abstractions. We use an overapproximation of the model transformer and underapproximations of the countermodel and universal countermodel transformers. An *abstract model transformer* $amod_\varphi^O : O \to O$, an *abstract countermodel transformer* $acmod_\varphi^U : U \to U$, and an *abstract universal countermodel transformer* $aucmod_\varphi^U : U \to U$ are monotone functions satisfying the constraints below.

$$mod_\varphi \circ \gamma_O \sqsubseteq \gamma_O \circ amod_\varphi^O \qquad ucmod_\varphi \circ \gamma_U \supseteq \gamma_U \circ aucmod_\varphi^U$$
$$cmod_\varphi \circ \gamma_U \supseteq \gamma_U \circ acmod_\varphi^U$$

Theorem 3 provides sound and possibly incomplete characterisations of unsatisfiability. In contrast to concrete fixed points, the characterisations below are not equivalent because the domains and transformers may have different precision.

Theorem 3. *A propositional formula φ is unsatisfiable if at least one of the conditions below hold.*

1. *The set $\gamma_O(\mathsf{gfp}(amod_\varphi^O))$ is empty.*
2. *The set $\gamma_U(\mathsf{lfp}(aucmod_\varphi^U))$ contains all assignments.*
3. *The set $\gamma_O(x) \cap \neg\gamma_U(y)$ is empty in $(x, y) = \gamma_{OU}(\mathsf{gfp}(amc_\varphi^{OU}))$.*

Theorem 3 follows from the soundness of abstract interpretation. The rest of the paper shows that satisfiability algorithms compute these abstract fixed points.

3   Sound and Complete Abstractions

In this section, we formalise the construction of truth tables and resolution proofs in the abstract satisfaction framework. Truth table construction is abstract transformer application and the resolution rule is a sound abstract transformer. Repeated application of the resolution rule is abstract transformer iteration.

Truth Tables. A truth table is an enumeration that represents whether each truth assignment satisfies a formula. In abstract satisfaction, truth tables are a representation of the domain of assignments and truth table construction is application of the best abstract transformer for a formula. Binary Decision Diagrams are semantically equivalent but have a more efficient representation.

Example 1. This example illustrates the order on truth tables. Consider the formula $\varphi = p \wedge \neg q$. The set of assignments $\{p, q\} \to \mathbb{B}$ is shown in gray below. The truth tables for the formulae p and $\neg q$ are shown below.

p	q		p		$\neg q$		$p \wedge \neg q$
f	f		f		t		f
f	t		f	$\sqcap$	f	$=$	f
t	f		t		t		t
t	t		t		f		f

If the implication order on $\mathbb{B}$ is lifted to truth tables, the truth table for $p \wedge \neg q$ is the pointwise meet of the truth tables for p and $\neg q$.   ◁

A *truth table* is a function in *Table* $\hat{=} Asg \to \mathbb{B}$. The domain of truth tables (*Table*, $\sqsubseteq, \sqcup, \sqcap$) is ordered by pointwise lifting of the implication order on truth values. Specifically, $T_1 \sqsubseteq T_2$ if $T_1(\sigma) \Rightarrow T_2(\sigma)$ for every assignment σ. A set of assignments X abstracts to the truth table T that maps assignments in X to t and all other assignments to f. The functions α and γ below form a Galois connection, are bijections and satisfy that $\gamma \circ \alpha$ and $\alpha \circ \gamma$ are identity functions. That is, the Galois connection is a Galois isomorphism, meaning that truth tables do not abstract information.

$$\alpha(X) \hat{=} \{\sigma \mapsto \mathsf{t} \mid \sigma \in X\} \cup \{\sigma \mapsto \mathsf{f} \mid \sigma \notin X\} \qquad \gamma(T) \hat{=} \{\sigma \mid T(\sigma) = \mathsf{t}\}$$

Consider the best abstract transformer for mod_φ, denoted $amod_\varphi$. Observe that $amod_\varphi(\top)$ represents the truth table for φ. Thus, truth table construction can be viewed as transformer application. The completeness of truth-table construction is expressed as $mod_\varphi \circ \gamma = \gamma \circ amod_\varphi$.

Resolution. The *resolution principle* states that an assignment satisfying the clauses $C \vee p$ and $\neg p \vee D$ also satisfies $C \vee D$ [21]. The variable p is the *pivot* and $C \vee D$ is the *resolvent*. Resolution is sound but is not complete for deriving arbitrary implications. For example, the formula $p \wedge q$ implies $p \vee \neg q$, but this implication cannot be derived by resolution. Resolution is refutation complete: a formula is unsatisfiable exactly if the empty clause can be derived by resolution.

In abstract satisfaction, CNF formulae, with the superset order, are an abstract domain, and resolution defines an abstract transformer. The abstract transformer is a sound but incomplete abstraction.

Let *Lit* be the set of literals over the propositional variables *Prop*, and *Clause* $\hat{=} \mathscr{P}(Lit)$ be the set of clauses. The CNF *domain CNF* $\hat{=} \mathscr{P}(Clause)$ contains sets of clauses with the superset order (*CNF*, $\supseteq, \cap, \cup$). The superset order underapproximates implication because $\varphi \supseteq \psi$ entails $\varphi \Rightarrow \psi$ but the converse is not true. The functions below are related by the Galois connection $(\mathscr{P}(Asg), \subseteq)$ $\xleftrightarrow[\alpha]{\gamma} (CNF, \supseteq)$.

$$\alpha(X) \stackrel{\scriptscriptstyle\wedge}{=} \{C \mid X \subseteq mod_C(Asg)\} \qquad \gamma(\varphi) \stackrel{\scriptscriptstyle\wedge}{=} mod_\varphi(Asg)$$

We formalise resolution with a transformer. The resolvents derived from φ with pivot x are denoted $res(x, \varphi)$. The *resolution transformer* $Res_\varphi : CNF \to CNF$ adds all possible resolvents to a set of clauses.

$$res(x, \varphi) \stackrel{\scriptscriptstyle\wedge}{=} \{C \vee D \mid x \vee C \text{ and } \neg x \vee D \text{ are in } \varphi\}$$
$$Res_\varphi(\psi) \stackrel{\scriptscriptstyle\wedge}{=} \varphi \cup \psi \cup \bigcup_{x \in Prop} res(x, \varphi)$$

We express properties of resolution next. Logical soundness stating that every clause derived by resolution is implied by φ becomes the condition $\alpha \circ mod_\varphi \supseteq Res_\varphi \circ \alpha$. Res_φ is not idempotent, so multiple applications of resolution yield more resolvents than a single application. The set of clauses derived by resolution is the fixed point $\mathsf{gfp}(Res_\varphi)$. Resolution is not complete for arbitrary implications, so in general, $\alpha(\mathsf{gfp}(mod_\varphi))$ is a strict superset of $\mathsf{gfp}(Res_\varphi)$. The refutation completeness of resolution becomes the condition that $\gamma(\mathsf{gfp}(Res_\varphi))$ is the empty set exactly if $\mathsf{gfp}(Res_\varphi)$ contains the empty clause.

4 Fixed Point Refinement

In this section, we formalise the classic DPLL procedure. We first characterise Boolean Constraint Propagation as abstract fixed point iteration.

4.1 Boolean Constraint Propagation

The workhorse of all solvers based on DPLL is the Boolean Constraint Propagation (BCP) routine. BCP repeatedly applies a transformation called the *unit rule* to a data structure called a *partial assignment*. In abstract satisfaction, partial assignments are an abstract domain, the unit rule is the best abstract transformer for a clause, and BCP computes a greatest fixed point.

Example 2. We illustrate BCP with the formula below.

$$\varphi \stackrel{\scriptscriptstyle\wedge}{=} p \wedge (\neg p \vee \neg q) \wedge (q \vee r \vee \neg s) \wedge (q \vee r \vee s)$$

Initially, nothing is known about the formula, encoded by the empty set. Then, BCP concludes that p must be true in every satisfying assignment. Since p must be true, BCP concludes that q must be false to satisfy the clause $\neg p \vee \neg q$.

$$\pi_0 \stackrel{\scriptscriptstyle\wedge}{=} \top \qquad \pi_1 \stackrel{\scriptscriptstyle\wedge}{=} \langle p{:}t \rangle \qquad \pi_2 \stackrel{\scriptscriptstyle\wedge}{=} \langle p{:}t, q{:}f \rangle$$

All the remaining clauses have more than one literal unassigned, so BCP terminates. BCP is a sound but incomplete deduction procedure. BCP need not begin

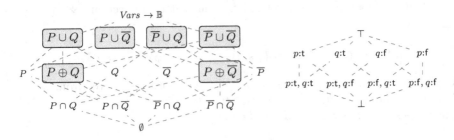

Fig. 1. Domains for assignments over p and q. The concrete domain $\mathscr{P}(Asg)$ is on the left. The set P contains assignments that map p to true. Partial assignments are on the right. The shaded elements of $\mathscr{P}(Asg)$ cannot be represented as partial assignments.

with π_0 as above. We can begin by assuming p is true, q is false, and r is false, written $\pi \;\hat{=}\; \langle p{:}t, q{:}f, r{:}f \rangle$. Given π, BCP concludes, from $(q \vee r \vee \neg s)$, that s must be false and from $(q \vee r \vee s)$ that s must be true. This situation, denoted $\bot$, is a *conflict*. No assignment extending π satisfies φ.   ◁

We show that partial assignments are an abstract domain. A *partial assignment* is a partial function in $Prop \to \mathbb{B}$. Consider the set $\{t, f, \top\}$ with the *information order* $t \sqsubseteq \top$ and $f \sqsubseteq \top$. We model a partial assignment as a total function $\pi : Prop \to \{t, f, \top\}$, where for each variable p, $\pi(x)$ is $\top$ if π is undefined on p. The *domain of partial assignments* $(PAsg, \sqsubseteq)$ contains a set $PAsg \;\hat{=}\; (Prop \to \{t, f, \top\}) \cup \{\bot\}$, of partial assignments extended with a least element $\bot$, called a *conflict*. The order between non-$\bot$ elements is the pointwise lifting of the information order. A partial assignment in which p is t and other variables map to $\top$ is written $\langle p{:}t \rangle$. Figure 1 depicts partial assignments over two variables.

A variant of the partial assignments domain is used for constant propagation [16] and is equivalent to the Cartesian abstraction [4]. In abstract interpretation parlance, partial assignments as presented here are a reduction of the Cartesian abstraction domain in which the empty set has a unique representation. The abstraction and concretisation functions $\alpha_{PAsg} : \mathscr{P}(Asg) \to PAsg$ and $\gamma_{PAsg} : PAsg \to \mathscr{P}(Asg)$ below are standard and are known to form a Galois connection.

$$\alpha_{PAsg}(\emptyset) \;\hat{=}\; \bot \quad \alpha_{PAsg}(S) \;\hat{=}\; \left\{ x \mapsto \bigsqcup \{ \sigma(x) \mid \sigma \in S \} \mid x \in Prop \right\}, \text{ for } S \neq \emptyset$$

$$\gamma_{PAsg}(\bot) \;\hat{=}\; \emptyset \quad \gamma_{PAsg}(\pi) \;\hat{=}\; \{ \sigma \in Asg \mid \text{ for all } x \text{ in } Prop, \sigma(x) \sqsubseteq \pi(x) \}$$

We formalise the unit rule. The *unit rule* states that if all but one literals in a clause are false under a partial assignment, the remaining literal must be true. It is defined by a function unit : $Clause \times PAsg \to PAsg$. The image of a clause θ under a partial assignment π is false if π and makes all literals in θ false.

$$\mathsf{unit}(\theta, \pi) \stackrel{\scriptscriptstyle\triangle}{=} \begin{cases} \bot & \text{if } \pi(\theta) \text{ is } \mathsf{f} \\ \pi \cup \{p \mapsto \mathsf{t}\} & \text{if } \theta \text{ is } \psi \vee p \text{ and } \pi(\psi) = \mathsf{f} \\ \pi \cup \{p \mapsto \mathsf{f}\} & \text{if } \theta \text{ is } \psi \vee \neg p \text{ and } \pi(\psi) = \mathsf{f} \\ \pi & \text{otherwise} \end{cases}$$

Example 3. We illustrate the unit rule with $\varphi \stackrel{\scriptscriptstyle\triangle}{=} \neg p \wedge (p \vee \neg q)$. Assume we have best abstract transformers for literals. The abstract transformer for φ is derived by replacing conjunction and disjunction by pointwise meet and join.

$$amod_\varphi \stackrel{\scriptscriptstyle\triangle}{=} amod_{\neg p} \sqcap (amod_p \sqcup amod_{\neg q})$$

We compute a greatest fixed point in the partial assignments domain.

$$\pi_0 \stackrel{\scriptscriptstyle\triangle}{=} \langle p{:}\top, q{:}\top\rangle \qquad \pi_1 \stackrel{\scriptscriptstyle\triangle}{=} \langle p{:}\mathsf{f}, q{:}\top\rangle \qquad \pi_2 \stackrel{\scriptscriptstyle\triangle}{=} \langle p{:}\mathsf{f}, q{:}\mathsf{f}\rangle \qquad \pi_3 \stackrel{\scriptscriptstyle\triangle}{=} \langle p{:}\mathsf{f}, q{:}\mathsf{f}\rangle$$

Applying the unit rule generates the same sequence. ◁

Lemma 1. *For a fixed clause θ, the unit rule is equivalent to the best abstract transformer:* $\mathsf{unit}(\theta, \pi) = \alpha_{PAsg} \circ mod_\theta \circ \gamma_{PAsg}(\pi)$.

Proof. Consider a partial assignment π and the best abstract transformer $amod_\theta \stackrel{\scriptscriptstyle\triangle}{=} \alpha_{PAsg} \circ mod_\theta \circ \gamma_{PAsg}$. We distinguish the cases in the definition of unit.

($\pi(\theta)$ *is* f) If π makes every literal in θ false, $\mathsf{unit}(\theta, \pi) = \bot$. No assignment in $\gamma_{PAsg}(\pi)$ will θ, so $mod_\theta(\gamma_{PAsg}(\pi))$ is the empty set and by definition of α_{PAsg}, from $amod_\theta(\pi) = \bot$.

($\theta = \psi \vee p$ *and* $\pi(\psi) = \mathsf{f}$) Here, $\mathsf{unit}(\theta, \pi) = \pi \cup \{p \mapsto \mathsf{t}\}$. Since p is unassigned, $\pi(p) = \top$, and $\gamma(\pi)$ contains assignments in which every p is true and false and all in φ are false. The set $mod_\theta(\gamma_\pi(\pi))$ only includes assignments that satisfy p because no other literal is satisfied. All other variables are unaffected. Thus, $\alpha_{PAsg}(mod_\theta(\gamma_\pi(\pi)))$ equals $\pi \cup \{p \mapsto \mathsf{t}\}$.

(π *undefined for multiple variables in* θ) The unit rule leaves π unchanged. At least two literals in θ are undefined in π, so $mod_\theta(\gamma_{PAsg}(\pi))$ contains an assignment that makes one true and the other false and vice-versa. Consequently, the variables for both literals map to $\top$ in $\alpha_{PAsg}(mod_\theta(\gamma_{PAsg}(\pi)))$ and π is unchanged, as required.

BCP maps a formula φ and a partial assignment π representing an assumption to the result of applying the unit rule repeatedly with all clauses till no changes are observed. Formally, BCP is a function $\mathsf{bcp} : CNF \times PAsg \rightarrow PAsg$.

Let φ be a formula, θ represent a clause, and $amod_\theta$ be the best abstract transformer for mod_θ. We model the effect of *concrete deduction* from a partial assignment Δ with the concrete transformer $mod_{\varphi,\Delta}$.

$$mod_\varphi : PAsg \times \mathscr{P}(Asg) \rightarrow \mathscr{P}(Asg) \qquad mod_{\varphi,\Delta}(x) \stackrel{\scriptscriptstyle\triangle}{=} mod_\varphi(x \cap \gamma(\Delta))$$

The abstract *deduction transformer* below overapproximates $mod_{\varphi,\Delta}$.

$$ded_\varphi : PAsg \times PAsg \to PAsg \quad ded_{\varphi,\Delta}(\pi) \mathrel{\hat=} \bigsqcap \{amod_\theta(\pi \sqcap \Delta) \mid \theta \text{ is in } \varphi\}$$

The soundness constraint $mod_{\varphi,\Delta} \circ \gamma_{PAsg} \subseteq \gamma_{PAsg} \circ ded_{\varphi,\Delta}$ implies that all conclusions derived by $ded_{\varphi,\Delta}$ are satisfied by all models of φ in Δ. Example 4 shows that the deduction transformer is not complete.

Example 4. The formula $\varphi \mathrel{\hat=} (\neg p \vee q) \wedge (p \vee \neg q) \wedge (\neg p \vee \neg q) \wedge (p \vee q)$ is unsatisfiable. The best abstract transformer satisfies $\alpha_{PAsg}(mod_{\varphi,\top}(\gamma_{PAsg}(\top))) = \bot$ whereas the deduction transformer satisfies $\alpha_{PAsg}(mod_{\varphi,\top}(\gamma_{PAsg}(\top))) = \top$. Thus, the abstract deduction transformer is incomplete.   ◁

Theorem 4. *The result of Boolean Constraint Propagation* $\mathsf{bcp}(\varphi, \Delta)$ *is equivalent to the greatest fixed point* $\mathsf{gfp}(ded_{\varphi,\Delta})$.

In abstract interpretation terms, BCP is bottom-up abstract interpretation of Boolean expressions with locally decreasing iterations [13,4].

4.2   The Classic DPLL Algorithm

We say classic DPLL, or DPLL, for the algorithm of Davis, Logemann, and Loveland [10]. The DPLL algorithm simplifies the algorithm of Davis and Putnam [11] by eliminating the resolution and pure literal rules. If BCP is viewed as a static analysis, DPLL can be understood as running BCP on the sequence of programs below. In abstract satisfaction terms, DPLL dynamically restricts the range of values a variable can take to improve precision. It is a procedure to dynamically discover value-based trace partitions [20].

$$P_0 \mathrel{\hat=} \begin{array}{l} \texttt{if}(\varphi) \\ \quad \texttt{assert(f)} \end{array} \qquad P_1 \mathrel{\hat=} \begin{array}{l} \texttt{if}(p)\ P_0 \\ \texttt{else}\ P_0 \end{array} \qquad P_2 \mathrel{\hat=} \begin{array}{l} \texttt{if}(q)\ P_1 \\ \texttt{else}\ P_1 \end{array}$$

Example 5. Revisit the formula $\varphi \mathrel{\hat=} (\neg p \vee q) \wedge (p \vee \neg q) \wedge (\neg p \vee \neg q) \wedge (p \vee q)$ which could not be refuted by BCP. Since $\mathsf{gfp}(ded_{\varphi,\top})$ is $\top$, DPLL concludes that precision was lost and computes two fixed points $\mathsf{gfp}(ded_{\varphi,\langle p:t \rangle})$ and $\mathsf{gfp}(ded_{\varphi,\langle p:f \rangle})$. Both fixed points are $\bot$, so DPLL concludes that φ is unsatisfiable.   ◁

DPLL operates in two phases, using two abstract domains. One phase consists of deduction under assumptions and uses BCP. The other phase refines assumptions and is formalised next. DPLL only considers assumptions that can be represented by partial assignments, but such a restriction is not necessary.

Example 6. Figure 2 illustrates partitions of two variable assignments. An element $\cdots / \mathsf{f}, \mathsf{f}$ represents a partition in which one block contains the assignment $\{p \mapsto \mathsf{f}, q \mapsto \mathsf{f}\}$ and the other block contains all other assignments. DPLL can be run using the assignments in each partition as assumptions. The partition lattice is large, with the size given by the *Bell number*.

An abstract lattice of partitions reduces the cases that must be considered. Figure 2 depicts partitions that can be expressed as partial assignments.

$$Asg$$

$$\cdots /f, f \qquad \cdots /f, t \qquad \cdots /t, f \qquad \cdots /t, t$$

$$\cdots /t, f/f, f \quad \cdots /t, f/f, t \quad t, t/\cdots /f, f \quad t, t/\cdots /f, t$$

$$t, t/t, f/f, t/f, f$$

$$\top, \top$$

$$t, \top/f, \top \qquad \top, t/\top, f$$

$$t, t/t, f/f, t/f, f$$

Fig. 2. The concrete domain for case-based reasoning is the lattice of partitions over assignments. The abstract domain only contains partitions that can be expressed as partial assignments.

The partition consisting of the two sets represented by $p \iff q$ and $p \iff \neg q$ cannot be expressed with partial assignments but the partition consisting of $p \iff f$ and $p \iff t$ can. ◁

An *abstract partition* is a set $\chi \subseteq A$ of elements from an abstract domain satisfying that $\{\gamma(a) \mid a \in \chi\}$ is a partition. Given two abstract partitions, χ_1 *refines* χ_2, denoted $\chi_1 \preccurlyeq \chi_2$, if for every a_2 in χ_2, there is an a_1 in χ_1 such that $a_1 \sqsubseteq a_2$. An abstract partition represents cases used in deduction. Let $(Cases(PAsg), \preccurlyeq)$ be the set of abstract partitions over partial assignments ordered by refinement.

Let χ be an abstract partition. The *case deduction* transformer models the effect of using each block of a partition as an assumption.

$$acase_\varphi : \chi \to PAsg \qquad acase_\varphi \mathrel{\hat=} \{\Delta \mapsto \mathsf{gfp}(ded_{\varphi, \Delta}) \mid \Delta \in \chi\}$$

In the refinement step, a variable that is currently undefined is used to refine a block of the partition. We model selection of an unassigned variable with a function $pick : PAsg \to Prop$ that maps a partial assignment π to a variable p for which $\pi(p) = \top$. The *case split* function $split : PAsg \to \mathscr{P}(PAsg)$ formalises refinement of a partition based on deduction.

$$split(\pi) \mathrel{\hat=} \{\pi \sqcap \langle p{:}t \rangle, \pi \sqcap \langle p{:}f \rangle \mid p = pick(\mathsf{gfp}(ded_{\varphi, \pi}))\}$$

DPLL runs until the formula is shown to be unsatisfiable or a satisfying assignment is found. Satisfying assignments are formalised using covering. An element a in a lattice *covers* $\bot$ if there is no distinct a' satisfying $\bot \sqsubseteq a' \sqsubseteq a$. Elements of $PAsg$ covering $\bot$ are assignments. If deduction under every block of a partition yields $\bot$, the formula is unsatisfiable.

Algorithm 1 presents an abstract interpretation perspective of DPLL. Since every function $acase_\varphi$ represents a trace partition [20], DPLL can be understood as a procedure to dynamically discover a trace partition.

5   Conflict Driven Clause Learning

This section formalises the Conflict Driven Clause Learning (CDCL) algorithm. Though CDCL historically derives from DPLL, DPLL can naturally be viewed as a

Abstract-DPLL(φ, χ)
  Compute $acase_\varphi$
  if $acase_\varphi(\Delta) = \bot$ *for all Δ in χ then* return UNSAT
  if $acase_\varphi(\Delta)$ *covers $\bot$ for some Δ in χ then* return SAT
  else
    $\chi \leftarrow (\chi \setminus \{\Delta\}) \cup split(\Delta)$
  Abstract-DPLL(φ, χ)

Algorithm 1: DPLL as fixed point computation with dynamic refinement

recursive search procedure, while the search pattern of CDCL is more intricate. DPLL uses case based reasoning to refine an analysis. CDCL uses clause learning to refine the transformers used to compute a fixed point. In terms of programs, every iteration of CDCL generates and analyses a program of the form below.

$$P_0 \mathrel{\hat{=}} \texttt{if}(\varphi) \; \texttt{assert}(f) \qquad P_1 \mathrel{\hat{=}} \texttt{if}(\theta_1) \; P_0 \qquad P_2 \mathrel{\hat{=}} \texttt{if}(\theta_2) \; P_1$$

Example 7. This example illustrates a run of CDCL on a formula φ.

$$\varphi \mathrel{\hat{=}} \{ \; \{\neg u, v, w\}, \{\neg w, \neg x\}, \{\neg w, y\}, \{x, \neg y, z\}, \{x, \neg z\}, \{x, y\}, \{\neg y, \neg x\} \; \}$$

CDCL initially proceeds like DPLL and alternates BCP and decisions. The steps in BCP are recorded by an implication graph shown below. A directed edge from u to w and from $\neg v$ to w indicates that BCP deduced that w is true if u is true and v is false. A cut in the graph represents a conjunction of literals. A cut that separates u and $\neg v$ from $\bot$ represents a sufficient condition for a conflict. The disjunction of formulae represented by a set of cuts is also sufficient for a conflict.

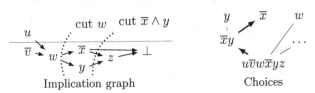

Implication graph   Choices

The first step of conflict analysis is to heuristically choose a cut. A single cut is used rather than a set to save space. Suppose the solver chooses the cut $\neg x \wedge y$.

The second step is to generalise the cut. Observe that if $\neg x$ holds, the unit rule and the clause $\{x, y\}$ imply y. Similarly, the solver can use y and $\{\neg x, \neg y\}$ to deduce $\neg x$. The conflict can be generalised to either or $\neg x$ or y. If $\neg x$ is sufficient for a conflict, its negation x must be satisfied by all models of φ. The solver *learns* the clause $\{x\}$ and continues with model search. $\triangleleft$

We view CDCL as operating in two phases. In the *model search* phase, CDCL uses BCP to draw conclusions about all models of φ. Since $\varphi \Rightarrow \psi$ if all models of φ satisfy ψ, we say that BCP *overapproximates deduction*. The incompleteness of BCP translates into imprecision in an abstract transformer. CDCL uses decisions to gain precision. That is, CDCL makes assumptions (that we write as a formula Δ) until

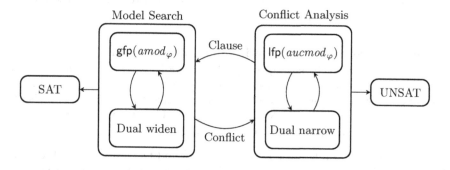

Fig. 3. Abstract Interpretation view of CDCL

it finds a satisfying assignment, or until $\varphi \wedge \Delta \Rightarrow$ f. Unlike in DPLL, only one assumption is made, so the use of assumptions is unsound.

After a conflict is found, CDCL enters the *conflict analysis* phase. The goal of conflict analysis is to derive a formula θ such that $\varphi \wedge \theta$ implies f. Given formulae φ and ψ, the task of deriving θ such that $\varphi \wedge \theta \Rightarrow \psi$ is called abduction. Conflict analysis only derives those θ that can be expressed as a cube, so this step underapproximates abduction. The abstract interpretation view of CDCL is illustrated in Figure 3 and formalised next.

Model Search and Extrapolation. As before, BCP is a greatest fixed point computation with the abstract transformer $amod_\varphi$. Decisions are used to increase precision by iterating below the greatest fixed point $\mathsf{gfp}(ded_{\varphi,\top})$. Recall that widening operators are used to ascend up a lattice in a least fixed point computation. Decisions underapproximate the greatest fixed point computed by BCP and are dual widening operators [8]. Widening is typically used to enforce convergence. The goal of decisions is not convergence, so we use the term *extrapolation*, suggested in [8] for a weakening of widening without a convergence requirement.

A *downwards extrapolation* on a lattice is a function $f : L \to L$ satisfying $f(a) \sqsubseteq a$ for all a. Such a function is usually called *reductive* or *decreasing*, but we prefer extrapolation to emphasise the connection to widening. We model decisions with the downwards extrapolation function below.

$$ext\!\downarrow : PAsg \twoheadrightarrow PAsg$$
$$ext\!\downarrow(\pi) \mathrel{\hat{=}} \pi \sqcap \langle p{:}b \rangle \text{ where } p = pick(\pi) \text{ and } b \in \mathbb{B}$$

The model search phase of CDCL computes $\pi = \mathsf{gfp}(ded_{\varphi,\top})$. If π is $\bot$, the formula is unsatisfiable. If π covers $\bot$, the formula is satisfiable. In other cases, extrapolation is used to derive a partial assignment $\Delta = ext\!\downarrow(\pi)$. This partial assignment represents the new assumptions that will be used. Model search continues by computing $\mathsf{gfp}(ded_{\varphi,\Delta})$. Extrapolation is typically used to accelerate convergence of a fixed point computation by losing precision while preserving soundness. The application of extrapolation to gain precision at the cost of soundness in CDCL is unusual.

Conflict Analysis and Interpolation. If model search with extrapolation discovers an element Δ such that $\mathsf{gfp}(ded_{\varphi,\Delta})$ is $\bot$ CDCL enters the conflict analysis phase. The goal of conflict analysis is to generalise the reason for the conflict. In terms of concrete transformers, we have that $mod_\varphi(\gamma(\Delta))$ is empty and wish to compute the set of countermodels $ucmod_\varphi(\gamma(\Delta))$. This set is underapproximated using an underapproximate domain and transformer.

Example 8. This example illustrates the domain and transformers used for conflict analysis. Revisit the implication graph in Example 7. Every cut in the graph that separates the vertices u and $\neg v$ from $\bot$ is a reason for a conflict. Such cuts can be computed by traversing the graph starting from $\bot$.

$$C_0 = \{\{\bot\}\} \qquad C_1 = \{\{\bot\}, \{\neg x, z\}\} \qquad C_2 = \{\{\bot\}, \{\neg x, z\}, \{\neg x, y\}\}$$

Note that a graph cut is a set of vertices, so the set of graph cuts is a set of sets of vertices. Unlike breadth-first reachability, which only maintains a set of vertices, the iteration above maintains a set of sets of vertices.   ◁

We formalise the domain and transformer for conflict analysis. A cut in the implication graph represents a conjunction of literals, so every cut c can be represented by a partial assignment π_c. A set of cuts is a set of partial assignments. If c is a set of vertices representing a cut every set of vertices d that contains c also represents a cut. If c is contained in d, the corresponding partial assignments satisfy $\pi_d \sqsubseteq \pi_c$. The domain for conflict analysis is downwards closed sets (downsets) of partial assignments.

Let $(\mathscr{D}(PAsg), \subseteq)$ be the family of downsets of partial assignments. We make the standard assumption that downsets are represented by their maximal elements. The lattice of downsets is an underapproximating abstract domain with the following abstraction and concretisation functions [7].

$$\alpha_\mathscr{D}(X) = \bigcup \{\pi{\downarrow} \mid \gamma_{PAsg}(\pi) \subseteq X\} \qquad \gamma_\mathscr{D}(Y) = \{\gamma_{PAsg}(\pi) \mid \pi \in Y\}$$

Since every set of assignments is also a set of partial assignments, this abstract domain can represent all sets of assignments. We also note that the downset lattice is called the *disjunctive completion* of an abstract domain.

We model *concrete abduction* with the transformer below.

$$ucmod_\varphi : PAsg \times \mathscr{P}(Asg) \to \mathscr{P}(Asg) \qquad ucmod_{\varphi,\Delta}(x) \mathrel{\hat{=}} ucmod_\varphi(x \cup \gamma_{PAsg}(\Delta))$$

An *abstract abduction* transformer $abd_\varphi : PAsg \times \mathscr{D}(PAsg) \to \mathscr{D}(PAsg)$ underapproximates concrete abduction and maps a partial assignment Δ and set Q to a set of partial assignments derived from Q.

We describe an instance of abduction which formalises clause minimisation [23]. In general, other techniques such as cutting a conflict graph [22] may also be used.

$$minimise_{\varphi,\Delta}(P) \mathrel{\hat{=}} \{\pi \in PAsg \mid \exists \theta \in Form. \; amod_\theta(\pi) \sqsubseteq \pi', \pi' \in P \cup \{\Delta\}\}$$

The conflict minimisation transformer $minimise_{\varphi,\Delta}$ finds all partial assignments from which a known conflict can be deduced with the unit rule. Applying abduction may produce a set of partial assignments. Conflict analysis is expensive, so solvers heuristically choose a single partial assignment and return to model search.

In a dual manner to deduction, underapproximating the set of reasons for a conflict can be viewed as a least fixed point computation. Recall that narrowing operators are used to overapproximate the limit of a decreasing iteration sequence [8]. A dual narrowing operator can be used to underapproximate the limit of an increasing iteration sequence. Choosing a reason for a conflict can be viewed as dual narrowing. For similar reasons to our use of extrapolation, the term *interpolation* is more appropriate because convergence is not an issue. The use of the term interpolation should not be confused with Craig interpolants.

An *upwards interpolation* on a lattice is a function $f : L \times L \to L$ satisfying that $a \sqsubseteq b \Rightarrow a \sqsubseteq f(a,b) \sqsubseteq b$ for all a, b. We model heuristic choice among candidates as the upwards interpolation function below.

$$int\!\upharpoonright : \mathscr{D}(PAsg) \times \mathscr{D}(PAsg) \to \mathscr{D}(PAsg)$$
$$\text{For } P \subseteq Q, \ int\!\upharpoonright(P,Q) \triangleq \{choose(p,Q) \mid p \text{ is maximal in } P\}$$

The statement $choose(p, Q)$ above is defined when p is an element of Q and returns a maximal element q of Q with $p \sqsubseteq q$.

Example 9. In Example 8, the initial conflict is $p = \langle u : \mathsf{t}, v : \mathsf{f}, w : \mathsf{t}, x : \mathsf{f}, y : \mathsf{t}, z : \mathsf{f}\rangle$. The two graph cuts produce the set of candidates $Q = \{\langle w : \mathsf{t}\rangle, \langle x : \mathsf{f}, y : \mathsf{t}\rangle\}$. The second element of the set is chosen. This corresponds to the application of upwards interpolation $int\!\upharpoonright(\{p\}, Q) = \{\langle x : \mathsf{f}, y : \mathsf{t}\rangle\}$. ◁

6   Related Work and Discussion

Standard static analysis is, of necessity, incomplete and computes approximations. A surprising insight of our work is that satisfiability procedures operate over imprecise abstractions but obtain sound and complete results. The main reason is that SAT solvers use techniques to refine the precision of an analysis.

The verification literature contains numerous examples of domain refinement, originating in [6]. A very popular refinement technique at present is Counterexample Guided Abstraction Refinement (CEGAR) [3]. We believe the refinement in SAT solvers is very different from CEGAR. Each iteration of the CEGAR loop requires constructing a new abstraction and new transformers. In stark contrast, SAT solvers never change the domain. This immutability is crucial for efficiency as abstract domain implementations can be highly optimised. In fact, SAT algorithms can be understood as a portfolio of techniques for refinement without domain manipulation.

The refinement in BCP is to compute a fixed point instead of applying a transformer. BCP uses locally decreasing iterations [13] to refine conditional constant propagation [26], which in turn refines constant propagation [16]. The refinement in DPLL is to compute a set of fixed points instead of a single fixed point. A run of DPLL can be understood as a search for a sufficiently precise set of fixed points or as a search for a trace partition [15,20]. CDCL uses two types of refinements. Decisions refine the starting element for fixed point iteration to eliminate precision loss. Conflict analysis refines the input constraints.

We are not aware of existing program analysis techniques that generalise CDCL in a strict mathematical sense but there are several tantalizing similarities that deserve closer study. Transformer refinement in predicate abstraction [1] achieves a similar effect to clause learning. Counterexample DAGs in [14] play a similar role to implication graphs, while the combination of testing with weakest preconditions in Yogi [2] and with interpolants in lazy annotation [18] resembles the interplay between decisions and conflict analysis.

The breadth and diversity of the satisfiability literature made it infeasible to cover all but a few *propositional satisfiability* procedures in this paper. Stålmarck's method is not covered in this paper but can naturally be understood as an extension of BCP that combines case-based refinement with joins. Thakur and Reps [24,25] have recently applied abstract interpretation to generalise Stålmarck's method and shown that this generalisation has applications beyond SAT solving.

We conjecture that algorithms for solving satisfiability in a theory (SMT) have abstract interpretation characterisations and may independently exist in the static analysis literature. The analysis of a formula based on its propositional structure in DPLL(T) [19] is remarkably similar to the program analysis using control flow paths. The Nelson-Oppen combination procedure was recently shown to be an instance of the iterative reduced product [9]. We believe that these are but a few directions that must be explored en route to an exciting unification of the theory and practice of decision procedures and static analysers.

Acknowledgements. We are deeply indebted to the French static analysis community, and Patrick and Radhia Cousot in particular, for their encouragement and support.

References

1. Ball, T., Majumdar, R., Millstein, T.D., Rajamani, S.K.: Automatic predicate abstraction of C programs. In: PLDI, pp. 203–213. ACM Press (2001)
2. Beckman, N.E., Nori, A.V., Rajamani, S.K., Simmons, R.J.: Proofs from tests. In: Proc. of Software Testing and Analysis, pp. 3–14. ACM Press (2008)
3. Clarke, E., Grumberg, O., Jha, S., Lu, Y., Veith, H.: Counterexample-guided abstraction refinement for symbolic model checking. JACM 50, 752–794 (2003)
4. Cousot, P.: Abstract interpretation. MIT Course 16.399 (February-May 2005)
5. Cousot, P., Cousot, R.: Abstract interpretation: a unified lattice model for static analysis of programs by construction or approximation of fixpoints. In: POPL, pp. 238–252. ACM Press (1977)
6. Cousot, P., Cousot, R.: Systematic design of program analysis frameworks. In: POPL, pp. 269–282. ACM Press (1979)

7. Cousot, P., Cousot, R.: Abstract interpretation and application to logic programs. Journal of Logic Programming 13(2-3), 103–179 (1992)
8. Cousot, P., Cousot, R.: Abstract interpretation frameworks. Journal of Logic and Computation 2(4), 511–547 (1992)
9. Cousot, P., Cousot, R., Mauborgne, L.: The Reduced Product of Abstract Domains and the Combination of Decision Procedures. In: Hofmann, M. (ed.) FOSSACS 2011. LNCS, vol. 6604, pp. 456–472. Springer, Heidelberg (2011)
10. Davis, M., Logemann, G., Loveland, D.: A machine program for theorem-proving. CACM 5, 394–397 (1962)
11. Davis, M., Putnam, H.: A computing procedure for quantification theory. JACM 7, 201–215 (1960)
12. D'Silva, V., Haller, L., Kroening, D., Tautschnig, M.: Numeric Bounds Analysis with Conflict-Driven Learning. In: Flanagan, C., König, B. (eds.) TACAS 2012. LNCS, vol. 7214, pp. 48–63. Springer, Heidelberg (2012)
13. Granger, P.: Improving the Results of Static Analyses Programs by Local Decreasing Iteration (Extended Abstract). In: Shyamasundar, R. (ed.) FSTTCS 1992. LNCS, vol. 652, pp. 68–79. Springer, Heidelberg (1992)
14. Gulavani, B.S., Chakraborty, S., Nori, A.V., Rajamani, S.K.: Automatically Refining Abstract Interpretations. In: Ramakrishnan, C.R., Rehof, J. (eds.) TACAS 2008. LNCS, vol. 4963, pp. 443–458. Springer, Heidelberg (2008)
15. Holley, L.H., Rosen, B.K.: Qualified data flow problems. In: POPL, pp. 68–82. ACM Press, New York (1980)
16. Kildall, G.A.: A unified approach to global program optimization. In: POPL, pp. 194–206. ACM, New York (1973)
17. King, J.C.: A Program Verifier. PhD thesis (1969)
18. McMillan, K.L.: Lazy Annotation for Program Testing and Verification. In: Touili, T., Cook, B., Jackson, P. (eds.) CAV 2010. LNCS, vol. 6174, pp. 104–118. Springer, Heidelberg (2010)
19. Nieuwenhuis, R., Oliveras, A., Tinelli, C.: Solving SAT and SAT modulo theories: From an abstract Davis–Putnam–Logemann–Loveland procedure to DPLL(T). JACM 53, 937–977 (2006)
20. Rival, X., Mauborgne, L.: The trace partitioning abstract domain. TOPLAS 29(5), 26 (2007)
21. Robinson, J.A.: A machine-oriented logic based on the resolution principle. JACM 12(1), 23–41 (1965)
22. Silva, J.P.M., Sakallah, K.A.: GRASP – a new search algorithm for satisfiability. In: ICCAD, pp. 220–227 (1996)
23. Sörensson, N., Biere, A.: Minimizing Learned Clauses. In: Kullmann, O. (ed.) SAT 2009. LNCS, vol. 5584, pp. 237–243. Springer, Heidelberg (2009)
24. Thakur, A., Reps, T.: A Generalization of Stålmarck's Method. In: SAS. Springer (2012)
25. Thakur, A., Reps, T.: A Method for Symbolic Computation of Abstract Operations. In: Madhusudan, P., Seshia, S.A. (eds.) CAV 2012. LNCS, vol. 7358, pp. 174–192. Springer, Heidelberg (2012)
26. Wegman, M.N., Zadeck, F.K.: Constant propagation with conditional branches. TOPLAS 13, 181–210 (1991)

A Generalization of Stålmarck's Method[*]

Aditya Thakur[1] and Thomas Reps[1,2,**]

[1] University of Wisconsin, Madison, WI, USA
[2] GrammaTech., Inc., Ithaca, NY, USA

Abstract. This paper gives an account of Stålmarck's method for validity checking of propositional-logic formulas, and explains each of the key
components in terms of concepts from the field of abstract interpretation.
We then use these insights to present a framework for propositional-logic
validity-checking algorithms that is parametrized by an abstract domain
and operations on that domain. Stålmarck's method is one instantiation
of the framework; other instantiations lead to new decision procedures
for propositional logic.

1 Introduction

A tool for validity checking of propositional-logic formulas (also known as a
tautology checker) determines whether a given formula φ over the propositional
variables $\{p_i\}$ is true for all assignments of truth values to $\{p_i\}$. Validity is dual
to satisfiability: validity of φ can be determined using a SAT solver by checking
the satisfiability of $\neg\varphi$ and complementing the answer: $\text{VALID}(\varphi) = \neg\text{SAT}(\neg\varphi)$.

With the advent of SAT-solvers based on conflict-directed clause learning (i.e.,
CDCL SAT solvers) [11] and their use in a wide range of applications, SAT meth-
ods have received increased attention during the last twelve years. Previous to
CDCL, a fast validity checker (and hence a fast SAT solver) already existed, due
to Stålmarck [13]. Stålmarck's method was protected by Swedish, European, and
U.S. patents [15], which may have discouraged experimentation by researchers.
Indeed, one finds relatively few publications that concern Stålmarck's method—
some of the exceptions are by Harrison [9], Cook and Gonthier [2], and Björk [1].
(Kunz and Pradhan [10] discuss a closely related method.)

In this paper, we give a new account of Stålmarck's method by explaining
each of the key components in terms of concepts from the field of abstract interpretation [3]. In particular, we show that Stålmarck's method is based on a

[*] Supported, in part, by NSF under grants CCF-{0810053, 0904371}, by ONR under
grants N00014-{09-1-0510, 10-M-0251, 11-C-0447}, by ARL under grant W911NF-
09-1-0413, and by AFRL under grants FA9550-09-1-0279 and FA8650-10-C-7088.
Any opinions, findings, and conclusions or recommendations expressed in this publication are those of the authors, and do not necessarily reflect the views of the
sponsoring agencies.

[**] T. Reps has an ownership interest in GrammaTech, Inc., which has licensed elements
of the technology discussed in this publication.

A. Miné and D. Schmidt (Eds.): SAS 2012, LNCS 7460, pp. 334–351, 2012.
© Springer-Verlag Berlin Heidelberg 2012

certain *abstract domain* and a few *operations* on that domain. For the program-analysis community, the abstract-interpretation account explains the principles behind Stålmarck's method in terms of familiar concepts. In the long run, our hope is that a better understanding of Stålmarck's method will lead to

- better program-analysis tools that import principles found in Stålmarck's method into program analyzers
- improvements to Stålmarck-based validity checkers by (i) incorporating domains other than the ones that have been used (implicitly) in previous implementations of the method, or (ii) improving the method in other ways by incorporating additional techniques from the field of abstract interpretation.

There has been one payoff already: in [18], we describe ways in which ideas from Stålmarck's method can be adopted for use in program analysis. The techniques described in [18] are quite different from the huge amount of recent work based on reducing a program path π to a formula φ_π via symbolic execution, and then passing φ_π to a decision procedure to determine whether π is feasible. Instead, we adopted—and adapted—the key ideas from Stålmarck's method to create new algorithms for key program-analysis operations.

In this paper, we use the vantage point of abstract interpretation to describe the elements of the Dilemma Rule—the inference rule that distinguishes Stålmarck's method from other propositional-reasoning approaches—as follows:

Branch of a Proof: In Stålmarck's method, each proof-tree branch is associated with a so-called *formula relation* [13]. In abstract-interpretation terms, each branch is associated with an abstract-domain element.

Splitting: The step of splitting the current goal into sub-goals can be expressed in terms of meet ($\sqcap$).

Application of Simple Deductive Rules: Stålmarck's method applies a set of simple deductive rules after each split. In abstract-interpretation terms, the rules perform a *semantic reduction* [4] by means of a technique called *local decreasing iterations* [8].

"Intersecting" results: The step of combining the results obtained from an earlier split are described as an "intersection" in Stålmarck's papers. In the abstract-interpretation-based framework, the combining step is the *join* ($\sqcup$) of two abstract-domain values.

This more general view of Stålmarck's method furnishes insight on when an invocation of the Dilemma Rule fails to make progress in a proof. In particular, both branches of a Dilemma may each succeed (locally) in advancing the proof, but the abstract domain used to represent proof states may not be precise enough to represent the common information when the join of the two branches is performed; consequently, the global state of the proof is not advanced.

We use these insights to present a parametric framework for propositional validity-checking algorithms. The advantages of our approach are

- We prove correctness at the framework level, once and for all, instead of for each instantiation.
- Instantiations that use different abstract domains lead to different decision procedures for propositional logic. Stålmarck's method is the instantiation of our framework in which the abstract domain tracks equivalence relations between subformulas—or, equivalently, 2-variable Boolean affine relations (2-BAR). By instantiating the framework with other abstract domains, such as k-variable Boolean affine relations (k-BAR) and 2-variable Boolean inequality relations (2-BIR), we obtain more powerful decision procedures.

Contributions. The contributions of the paper can be summarized as follows:
- We explain Stålmarck's method in terms of abstract interpretation [3]—in particular, we show that it is one instance of a more general algorithm.
- The vantage point of abstract interpretation provides new insights on the existing Stålmarck method.
- Adopting the abstract-interpretation viewpoint leads to a parametric framework for validity checking, parameterized by an abstract domain that supports a small number of operations.

Organization. The remainder of the paper is organized as follows: §2 reviews Stålmarck's algorithm, and presents our generalized framework at a semi-formal level. §3 defines terminology and notation. §4 describes Stålmarck's method using abstract-interpretation terminology and presents the general framework. §5 describes instantiations of the framework that result in new decision procedures. §6 presents preliminary experimental results. §7 discusses related work. Proofs and a discussion of efficiency issues are presented in [17].

2   Overview

In this section, we first review Stålmarck's method with the help of a few examples. We then present our generalized framework at a semi-formal level. The algorithms that we give are intended to clarify the principles behind Stålmarck's method, rather than represent the most efficient implementation.

2.1   Stålmarck's Method

Consider the tautology $\varphi = (a \wedge b) \vee (\neg a \vee \neg b)$. Ex. 1 below shows that the simpler component of the two components of Stålmarck's method (application of "simple deductive rules") is sufficient to establish that φ is valid.

Example 1. We use **0** and **1** to denote the propositional constants false and true, respectively. Propositional variables, negations of propositional variables, and propositional constants are referred to collectively as *literals*. Stålmarck's method manipulates *formula relations*, which are equivalence relations over literals. A formula relation R will be denoted by $\equiv_R$, although we generally omit the subscript when R is understood. We use $\mathbf{0} \equiv \mathbf{1}$ to denote the universal (and contradictory) equivalence relation $\{l_i \equiv l_j \mid l_i, l_j \in \text{Literals}\}$.

$$v_1 \Leftrightarrow (v_2 \vee v_3) \qquad (1)$$

$$v_2 \Leftrightarrow (a \wedge b) \qquad (2)$$

$$v_3 \Leftrightarrow (\neg a \vee \neg b) \qquad (3)$$

Fig. 1. Integrity constraints corresponding to the formula $\varphi = (a \wedge b) \vee (\neg a \vee \neg b)$. The root variable of φ is v_1.

$$\frac{p \Leftrightarrow (q \vee r) \qquad p \equiv 0}{q \equiv 0 \qquad r \equiv 0} \text{ OR1}$$

$$\frac{p \Leftrightarrow (q \wedge r) \qquad q \equiv 1 \qquad r \equiv 1}{p \equiv 1} \text{ AND1}$$

Fig. 2. Propagation rules

Stålmarck's method first assigns to every subformula of φ a unique Boolean variable in a set of propositional variables $\mathcal{V}$, and generates a list of *integrity constraints* as shown in Fig. 1. An *assignment* is a function in $\mathcal{V} \to \{0, 1\}$. The integrity constraints limit the set of assignments in which we are interested. Here the integrity constraints encode the structure of the formula.

Stålmarck's method establishes the validity of the formula φ by showing that $\neg \varphi$ leads to a contradiction (which means that $\neg \varphi$ is unsatisfiable). Thus, the second step of Stålmarck's method is to create a formula relation that contains the assumption $v_1 \equiv 0$. Fig. 2 lists some *propagation rules* that enable Stålmarck's method to refine a formula relation by inferring new equivalences. For instance, rule OR1 says that if $p \Leftrightarrow (q \vee r)$ is an integrity constraint and $p \equiv 0$ is in the formula relation, then $q \equiv 0$ and $r \equiv 0$ can be added to the formula relation.

Fig. 3 shows how, starting with the assumption $v_1 \equiv 0$, the propagation rules derive the explicit contradiction $0 \equiv 1$, thus proving that φ is valid. □

Alg. 1 (Fig. 4) implements the propagation rules of Fig. 2. Given an integrity constraint $J \in \mathcal{I}$ and a set of equivalences $R_1 \subseteq R$, line 1 calls the function ApplyRule, which instantiates and applies the derivation rules of Fig. 2 and returns the deduced equivalences in R_2. The new equivalences in R_2 are incorporated into R and the transitive closure of the resulting equivalence relation is returned. We implicitly assume that if Close derives a contradiction then it returns $0 \equiv 1$. Alg. 2 (Fig. 4) describes *0-saturation*, which calls propagate repeatedly until no new information is deduced, or a contradiction is derived. If a contradiction is derived, then the given formula is proved to be valid.

Unfortunately, 0-saturation is not always sufficient.

$$
\begin{array}{ll}
v_1 \equiv 0 & \dots \text{ by assumption} \\
v_2 \equiv 0, \ v_3 \equiv 0 & \dots \text{ by rule OR1 using Eqn. (1)} \\
\neg a \equiv 0, \ \neg b \equiv 0 & \dots \text{ by rule OR1 using Eqn. (3)} \\
a \equiv 1, \quad b \equiv 1 & \dots \text{ interpretation of logical negation} \\
v_2 \equiv 1 & \dots \text{ by rule AND1 using Eqn. (2)} \\
0 \equiv 1 & \dots v_2 \equiv 0, v_2 \equiv 1
\end{array}
$$

Fig. 3. Proof that φ is valid

Algorithm 1. propagate($J, R_1, R, \mathcal{I}$)

1   $R_2 = \text{ApplyRule}[\mathcal{I}](J, R_1)$
2   **return** $Close(R \cup R_2)$

Algorithm 2. 0-saturation($R, \mathcal{I}$)

1   **repeat**
2     $R' \leftarrow R$
3   **foreach** $J \in I, R_1 \subseteq R$ **do**
4       $R \leftarrow \text{propagate}(J, R_1, R, \mathcal{I})$
5   **until** $(R = R') \parallel \text{contradiction}(R)$
6   **return** R

Algorithm 3. 1-saturation($R, \mathcal{I}$)

1   **repeat**
2     $R' \leftarrow R$
3   **foreach** v_i, v_j **such that**
      $v_i \equiv v_j \notin R$ **and** $v_i \equiv \neg v_j \notin R$
      do
4       $R_1 \leftarrow \text{Close}(R \cup \{v_i \equiv v_j\})$
5       $R_2 \leftarrow \text{Close}(R \cup \{v_i \equiv \neg v_j\})$
6       $R'_1 \leftarrow \text{0-saturation}(R_1)$
7       $R'_2 \leftarrow \text{0-saturation}(R_2)$
8       $R \leftarrow R'_1 \cap R'_2$
9   **until** $(R = R') \parallel \text{contradiction}(R)$
10 **return** R

Algorithm 4. k-saturation($R, \mathcal{I}$)

1   **repeat**
2     $R' \leftarrow R$
3   **foreach** v_i, v_j **such that**
      $v_i \equiv v_j \notin R$ **and** $v_i \equiv \neg v_j \notin R$
      do
4       $R_1 \leftarrow \text{Close}(R \cup \{v_i \equiv v_j\})$
5       $R_2 \leftarrow \text{Close}(R \cup \{v_i \equiv \neg v_j\})$
6       $R'_1 \leftarrow \text{(k–1)-saturation}(R_1, \mathcal{I})$
7       $R'_2 \leftarrow \text{(k–1)-saturation}(R_2, \mathcal{I})$
8       $R \leftarrow R'_1 \cap R'_2$
9   **until** $(R = R') \parallel \text{contradiction}(R)$
10 **return** R

Algorithm 5. k-Stålmarck(φ)

1   $(v_\varphi, \mathcal{I}) \leftarrow \text{integrity}(\varphi)$
2   $R \leftarrow \{v_\varphi \equiv \mathbf{0}\}$
3   $R' \leftarrow \text{k-saturation}(R, \mathcal{I})$
4   **if** $R' = 0 \equiv 1$ **then return** *valid*
5   **else return** *unknown*

Fig. 4. Stålmarck's method. The operation Close performs transitive closure on a formula relation after new tuples are added to the relation.

Example 2. Consider the tautology $\psi = (a \wedge (b \vee c)) \Leftrightarrow ((a \wedge b) \vee (a \wedge c))$, which expresses the distributivity of $\wedge$ over $\vee$. The integrity constraints for ψ are:

$$u_1 \Leftrightarrow (u_2 \Leftrightarrow u_3) \qquad u_2 \Leftrightarrow (a \wedge u_4) \qquad u_3 \Leftrightarrow (u_5 \vee u_6)$$
$$u_4 \Leftrightarrow (b \vee c) \qquad u_5 \Leftrightarrow (a \wedge b) \qquad u_6 \Leftrightarrow (a \wedge c)$$

The root variable of ψ is u_1. Assuming $u_1 \equiv \mathbf{0}$ and then performing 0-saturation does not result in a contradiction; all we can infer is $u_2 \equiv \neg u_3$.

To prove that ψ is a tautology, we need to use the Dilemma Rule, which is a special type of branching and merging rule. It is shown schematically in Fig. 5. After two literals v_i and v_j are chosen, the current formula relation R is split into two formula relations, based on whether we assume $v_i \equiv v_j$ or $v_i \equiv \neg v_j$, and transitive closure is performed on each variant of R. Next, the two relations are 0-saturated, which produces the two formula relations R'_1 and R'_2. Finally, the two proof branches are merged by intersecting the set of tuples in R'_1 and R'_2. The correctness of the Dilemma Rule follows from the fact that equivalences derived from *both* of the (individual) assumptions $v_i \equiv v_j$ and $v_i \equiv \neg v_j$ hold irrespective of whether $v_i \equiv v_j$ holds or whether $v_i \equiv \neg v_j$ holds.

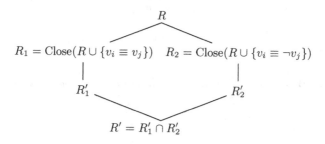

Fig. 5. The Dilemma Rule

The Dilemma Rule is applied repeatedly until no new information is deduced by a process called *1-saturation*, shown in Alg. 3 (Fig. 4). 1-saturation uses two literals v_i and v_j, and splits the formula relation with respect to $v_i \equiv v_j$ and $v_i \equiv \neg v_j$ (lines 4 and 5). 1-saturation finds a contradiction when both 0-saturation branches identify contradictions (in which case $R = R_1' \cap R_2'$ equals $0 \equiv 1$). The formula ψ in Ex. 2 can be proved valid using 1-saturation, as shown in Fig. 6. The first application of the Dilemma Rule, which splits on the value of b, does not make any progress; i.e., no new information is obtained after the intersection. The next two applications of the Dilemma Rule, which split on the values of a and c, respectively, each deduce a contradiction on one of their branches. Each contradictory branch is eliminated because the (universal) relation $0 \equiv 1$ is the identity element for intersection, and hence the intersection result is the equivalence relation from the non-contradictory branch. We illustrate this fact in Fig. 6 by eliding the merges with contradictory branches. Finally, splitting on the variable b leads to a contradiction on both branches.   □

Unfortunately 1-saturation may not be sufficient to prove certain tautologies. The 1-saturation procedure can be generalized to the k-saturation procedure shown in Alg. 4 (Fig. 4). Stålmarck's method (Alg. 5 of Fig. 4) is structured as a semi-decision procedure for validity checking. The actions of the algorithm are parameterized by a certain parameter k that is fixed by the user. For a given tautology, if k is large enough Stålmarck's method can prove validity, but if k is too small the answer returned is "unknown". In the latter case, one can increment k and try again. However, for each k, $(k+1)$-saturation is significantly more expensive than k-saturation: the running time of Alg. 5 as a function of k is $O(|\varphi|^k)$ [13].

Each equivalence relation that arises during Stålmarck's method can be viewed as an *abstraction* of a set of variable assignments. More precisely, at any moment during a proof there are some number of open branches. Each branch B_i has its own equivalence relation R_i, which represents a set of variable assignments A_i that might satisfy $\neg \varphi$. In particular, the contradictory equivalence relation $0 \equiv 1$ represents the empty set of assignments. Overall, the proof represents the set of assignments $\bigcup_i A_i$, which is a superset of the set of assignments that might satisfy $\neg \varphi$. Validity of φ is established by showing that the set $\bigcup_i A_i$ equals $\emptyset$.

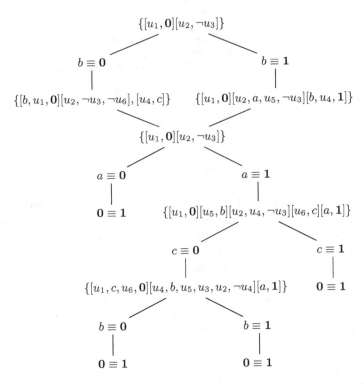

Fig. 6. Sequence of Dilemma Rules in a 1-saturation proof that ψ is valid. (Details of 0-saturation steps omitted.)

2.2 Generalizing Stålmarck's Method

Instead of computing an equivalence relation $\equiv$ on literals, let us compute an inequality relation $\leq$ between literals. Fig. 7 shows a few of the propagation rules that deduce inequalities. Because (i) an equivalence $a \equiv b$ can be represented using two inequality constraints, $a \leq b$ and $b \leq a$, (ii) an inequivalence $a \not\equiv b$ can be treated as an equivalence $a \equiv \neg b$, and (iii) $a \leq b$ cannot be represented with any number of equivalences, inequality relations are a strictly more expressive method than equivalence relations for abstracting a set of variable assignments. Moreover, Ex. 3 shows that, for some tautologies, replacing equivalence relations with inequality relations enables Stålmarck's method to be able to find a k-saturation proof with a strictly lower value of k.

Example 3. Consider the formula $\chi = (p \Rightarrow q) \Leftrightarrow (\neg q \Rightarrow \neg p)$. The corresponding integrity constraints are $w_1 \Leftrightarrow (w_2 \Leftrightarrow w_3)$, $w_2 \Leftrightarrow (p \Rightarrow q)$, and $w_3 \Leftrightarrow (\neg q \Rightarrow \neg p)$. The root variable of χ is w_1. Using formula relations (i.e., equivalence relations over literals), Stålmarck's method finds a 1-saturation proof that χ is valid. In contrast, using inequality relations, a Stålmarck-like algorithm finds a 0-saturation proof. The proof starts by assuming that $w_1 \leq \mathbf{0}$. 0-saturation using the propagation rules of Fig. 7 results in the contradiction $\mathbf{1} \leq \mathbf{0}$, as shown in Fig. 8. □

$$\frac{a \Leftrightarrow (b \Rightarrow c)}{c \leq a \quad \neg a \leq b} \; \text{IMP1} \qquad\qquad \frac{a \Leftrightarrow (b \Leftrightarrow c) \quad a \leq \mathbf{0}}{b \leq \neg c \quad \neg c \leq b} \; \text{IFF1}$$

$$\frac{a \Leftrightarrow (b \Rightarrow c) \quad \mathbf{1} \leq b \quad c \leq \mathbf{0}}{a \leq \mathbf{0}} \; \text{IMP2}$$

Fig. 7. Examples of propagation rules for inequality relations on literals

$w_1 \leq \mathbf{0}$	. . . by assumption
$w_2 \leq \neg w_3, \; \neg w_3 \leq w_2$	. . . Rule IFF1 on $w_1 \Leftrightarrow (w_2 \Leftrightarrow w_3)$
$q \leq w_2, \quad \neg w_2 \leq p$	. . . Rule IMP1 on $w_2 \Leftrightarrow (p \Rightarrow q)$
$q \leq \neg w_3$	. . . $q \leq w_2, w_2 \leq \neg w_3$
$w_3 \leq p$	. . . $w_2 \leq \neg w_3$ implies $w_3 \leq \neg w_2, \neg w_2 \leq p$
$\neg p \leq w_3, \; \neg w_3 \leq \neg q$	. . . Rule IMP1 on $w_3 \Leftrightarrow (\neg q \Rightarrow \neg p)$
$q \leq \mathbf{0}$	. . . $\neg w_3 \leq \neg q$ implies $q \leq w_3, q \leq \neg w_3$
$\mathbf{1} \leq p$	. . . $w_3 \leq p, \neg p \leq w_3$ implies $\neg w_3 \leq p$
$w_2 \leq \mathbf{0},$	. . . Rule IMP2 on $w_2 \Leftrightarrow (p \Rightarrow q)$
$w_3 \leq \mathbf{0}$	. . . Rule IMP2 on $w_3 \Leftrightarrow (\neg q \Rightarrow \neg p)$
$\mathbf{1} \leq \mathbf{0}$	. . . $w_2 \leq \neg w_3, \neg w_3 \leq w_2, w_2 \leq \mathbf{0}, w_3 \leq \mathbf{0}$

Fig. 8. 0-saturation proof that χ is valid, using inequality relations on literals

We say that the instantiation of Stålmarck's method with inequality relations is *more powerful than* the instantiation with equivalence relations. In general, Stålmarck's method can be made more powerful by using a more expressive abstraction: when you plug in a more expressive abstraction, a proof may be possible with a lower value of k. This observation raises the following questions:

1. What other abstractions can be used to create more powerful instantiations?
2. Given an abstraction, how do we come up with the propagation rules?
3. How do we split the current abstraction at the start of the Dilemma Rule?
4. How do we perform the merge at the end of the Dilemma Rule?
5. How do we guarantee that the above operations result in a sound and complete decision procedure?

Abstract interpretation provides the appropriate tools to answer these questions.

3 Terminology and Notation

3.1 Propositional Logic

We write propositional formulas over a set of propositional variables $\mathcal{V}$ using the propositional constants $\mathbf{0}$ and $\mathbf{1}$, the unary connective $\neg$, and the binary connectives $\wedge$, $\vee$, $\Rightarrow$, $\Leftrightarrow$, and $\oplus$ (xor). Propositional variables, negations of propositional variables, and propositional constants are referred to collectively as *literals*. $\text{voc}(\varphi)$ denotes the subset of $\mathcal{V}$ that occurs in φ.

The semantics of propositional logic is defined in the standard way:

Definition 1. *An* **assignment** *σ is a (finite) function in $\mathcal{V} \to \{0,1\}$. Given a formula φ over the propositional variables $x_1, \ldots, x_n$ and an assignment σ that is defined on (at least) $x_1, \ldots, x_n$, the* **meaning** *of φ with respect to σ, denoted by $[\![\varphi]\!](\sigma)$, is the truth value in $\{0,1\}$ defined inductively as follows:*

$$
\begin{array}{lll}
[\![0]\!](\sigma) = 0 & [\![\neg\varphi]\!](\sigma) = 1 - [\![\varphi]\!](\sigma) & [\![\varphi_1 \Rightarrow \varphi_2]\!](\sigma) = ([\![\varphi_1]\!](\sigma) \leq [\![\varphi_2]\!](\sigma)) \\
[\![1]\!](\sigma) = 1 & [\![\varphi_1 \wedge \varphi_2]\!](\sigma) = \min([\![\varphi_1]\!](\sigma), [\![\varphi_2]\!](\sigma)) & [\![\varphi_1 \Leftrightarrow \varphi_2]\!](\sigma) = ([\![\varphi_1]\!](\sigma) = [\![\varphi_2]\!](\sigma)) \\
[\![x_i]\!](\sigma) = \sigma(x_i) & [\![\varphi_1 \vee \varphi_2]\!](\sigma) = \max([\![\varphi_1]\!](\sigma), [\![\varphi_2]\!](\sigma)) & [\![\varphi_1 \oplus \varphi_2]\!](\sigma) = ([\![\varphi_1]\!](\sigma) \neq [\![\varphi_2]\!](\sigma))
\end{array}
$$

Assignment σ **satisfies** *φ, denoted by $\sigma \models \varphi$, iff $[\![\varphi]\!](\sigma) = 1$. Formula φ is* **satisfiable** *if there exists σ such that $\sigma \models \varphi$; φ is* **valid** *if for all σ, $\sigma \models \varphi$.*

We overload the notation $[\![\cdot]\!]$ as follows: $[\![\varphi]\!]$ means $\{\sigma \mid \sigma : \mathcal{V} \to \{0,1\} \wedge \sigma \models \varphi\}$. Given a finite set of formulas $\Phi = \{\varphi_i\}$, $[\![\Phi]\!]$ means $\bigcap_i [\![\varphi_i]\!]$. □

3.2 Abstract Domains

In this paper, the concrete domain $\mathcal{C}$ is $\mathbb{P}(\mathcal{V} \to \{0,1\})$. We will work with several abstract domains $\mathcal{A}$, each of which abstracts $\mathcal{C}$ by a Galois connection $\mathcal{C} \xleftrightarrow[\alpha]{\gamma} \mathcal{A}$. We assume that the reader is familiar with the basic terminology of abstract interpretation [3] ($\bot$, $\top$, $\sqcup$, $\sqcap$, $\sqsubseteq$, α, γ, monotonicity, distributivity, etc.), as well as with the properties of a Galois connection $\mathcal{C} \xleftrightarrow[\alpha]{\gamma} \mathcal{A}$.

Definition 2. *An element R of the domain of* **equivalence relations** *(Equiv) over the set $Literals[\mathcal{V}]$ formed from Boolean variables $\mathcal{V}$, their negations, and Boolean constants represents a set of assignments in $\mathbb{P}(\mathcal{V} \to \{0,1\})$. The special value $\bot_{Equiv}$ represents the empty set of assignments, and will be denoted by "$0 \equiv 1$". Each other value $R \in Equiv$ is an equivalence relation on $Literals[\mathcal{V}]$; the concretization $\gamma(R)$ is the set of all assignments that satisfy all the equivalences in R. The ordering $a_1 \sqsubseteq_{Equiv} a_2$ means that equivalence relation a_1 is a coarser partition of $Literals[\mathcal{V}]$ than a_2. The value $\top_{Equiv}$ is the identity relation, $\{(v,v) | v \in \mathcal{V}\}$, and thus represents the set of all assignments. $R_1 \sqcup R_2$ is the coarsest partition that is finer than both R_1 and R_2.*

An alternative way to define the same domain is to consider it as the domain of **two-variable Boolean affine relations** *(2-BAR) over $\mathcal{V}$. Each element $R \in$ 2-BAR is a conjunction of Boolean affine constraints, where each constraint has one of the following forms:*

$$v_i \oplus v_j = 0 \quad v_i \oplus v_j \oplus 1 = 0 \quad v_i = 0 \quad v_i \oplus 1 = 0,$$

which correspond to the respective equivalences

$$v_i \equiv v_j \quad v_i \equiv \neg v_j \quad v_i \equiv 0 \quad v_i \equiv 1.$$

The value $\bot_{2\text{-}BAR}$ is any set of unsatisfiable constraints. The value $\top_{2\text{-}BAR}$ is the empty set of constraints. The concretization function $\gamma_{2\text{-}BAR}$, and abstraction function $\alpha_{2\text{-}BAR}$ are:

$$
\gamma_{2\text{-}BAR}(R) = \{c \in (\mathcal{V} \to \{0,1\}) \mid R = \bigwedge_i r_i \text{ and for all } i, c \models r_i\}
$$
$$
\alpha_{2\text{-}BAR}(C) = \bigwedge\{r \mid \text{ for all } c \in C, c \models r\}
$$

For convenience, we will continue to use equivalence notation ($\equiv$) in examples that use 2-BAR, rather than giving affine relations ($\oplus$).   □

Definition 3. *An element of the* **Cartesian domain** *represents a set of assignments in* $\mathbb{P}(\mathcal{V} \to \{0,1\})$. *The special value* $\perp_{Cartesian}$ *denotes the empty set of assignments; all other values can be denoted via a 3-valued assignment in* $\mathcal{V} \to \{0,1,*\}$. *The third value "*$*$*" denotes an unknown value, and the values 0, 1, * are ordered so that* $0 \sqsubseteq *$ *and* $1 \sqsubseteq *$.

The partial ordering $\sqsubseteq$ *on 3-valued assignments is the pointwise extension of* $0 \sqsubseteq *$ *and* $1 \sqsubseteq *$, *and thus* $\top_{Cartesian} = \lambda w.*$ *and* $\sqcup_{Cartesian}$ *is pointwise join. The concretization function* $\gamma_{Cartesian}$, *and abstraction function* $\alpha_{Cartesian}$ *are:*
$$\gamma_{Cartesian}(A) = \{c \in (\mathcal{V} \to \{0,1\}) \mid c \sqsubseteq A\}$$
$$\alpha_{Cartesian}(C) = \lambda w. \bigsqcup \{c(w) \mid c \in C\}$$
We will denote an element of the Cartesian domain as a mapping, e.g., $[p \mapsto 0, q \mapsto 1, r \mapsto *]$, *or* $[0,1,*]$ *if* p, q, *and* r *are understood.*   □

Local Decreasing Iterations. Local decreasing iterations [8] is a technique that is ordinarily used for improving precision during the abstract interpretation of a program. During an iterative fixed-point-finding analysis, the technique of local decreasing iterations is applied at particular points in the program, such as, e.g., the interpretation of the true branch of an if-statement whose branch condition is φ. The operation that needs to be performed is the application of the abstract transformer for assume(φ). As the name "local decreasing iterations" indicates, a purely local iterative process repeatedly applies the operator assume(φ) either until some precision criterion or resource bound is attained, or a (local) fixed point is reached. The key theorem is stated as follows:

Theorem 1. *([8, Thm. 2]) An operator* τ *is a* **lower closure operator** *if it is monotonic, idempotent* ($\tau \circ \tau = \tau$), *and reductive* ($\tau \sqsubseteq \lambda x.x$). *Let* τ *be a lower closure operator on* $\mathcal{A}$; *let* $(\tau_1, \ldots, \tau_k)$ *be a k-tuple of reductive operators on* $\mathcal{A}$, *each of which over-approximates* ($\sqsupseteq$) τ; *and let* $(u_n)_{n \in N}$ *be a sequence of elements in* $[1, \ldots, k]$. *Then the sequence of reductive operators on* $\mathcal{A}$ *defined by*
$$\eta_0 = \tau_{u_0} \qquad \eta_{n+1} = \tau_{u_{n+1}} \circ \eta_n$$
is decreasing and each of its elements over-approximates τ.   □

Example 4. The propagation rules of Fig. 2 can be recast in terms of reductive operators that refine an element R of the 2-BAR domain as follows:

Operator	Derived from
$\tau_1(R) = R \cup ((v_1 \equiv \mathbf{0} \in R)\,?\,\{v_2 \equiv \mathbf{0}, v_3 \equiv \mathbf{0}\} : \emptyset)$	$v_1 \Leftrightarrow (v_2 \vee v_3) \in \mathcal{I}$
$\tau_2(R) = R \cup ((\{a \equiv \mathbf{1}, b \equiv \mathbf{1}\} \subseteq R)\,?\,\{v_2 \equiv \mathbf{1}\} : \emptyset)$	$v_2 \Leftrightarrow (a \wedge b) \in \mathcal{I}$
$\tau_3(R) = R \cup ((\{v_3 \equiv \mathbf{0}\} \in R)\,?\,\{a \equiv \mathbf{1}, b \equiv \mathbf{1}\} : \emptyset)$	$v_3 \Leftrightarrow (\neg a \wedge \neg b) \in \mathcal{I}$
$\tau_4(R) = (\{v_2 \equiv \mathbf{0}, v_2 \equiv \mathbf{1}\} \subseteq R)\,?\,\mathbf{0} \equiv \mathbf{1} : R$	

Table 1. Abstract-interpretation account of Stålmarck's method

Stålmarck's Method	Abstract-Interpretation Concept
Equivalence relation	Abstract-domain element
Propagation rule	Sound reductive operator
0-saturation	Local decreasing iterations
Split	Meet ($\sqcap$) in each proof-tree branch: one with a splitting-set element a and one with a's companion
Intersection ($\cap$)	Join ($\sqcup$)

The operators τ_1, τ_2, and τ_3 instantiate the rules of Fig. 2 for the three integrity constraints shown in Fig. 1. The derivation described in Fig. 3 can now be stated as $\tau_4(\tau_2(\tau_3(\tau_1(\{v_1 \equiv \mathbf{0}\})))) = (\tau_4 \circ \tau_2 \circ \tau_3 \circ \tau_1)(\{v_1 \equiv \mathbf{0}\})$, which results in the abstract state $\mathbf{0} \equiv \mathbf{1}$. $\square$

4   The Generalized Framework

In this section, we map the concepts used in Stålmarck's method to concepts used in abstract interpretation, as summarized in Tab. 1. The payoff is that we obtain a parametric framework for propositional validity-checking algorithms (Alg. 9) that can be instantiated in different ways by supplying different abstract domains. The proofs of all theorems stated in this section are found in [17].

Definition 4. *Given a Galois connection* $C \xleftarrow[\alpha]{\gamma} A$ *between abstract domain* A *and concrete domain* $C = \mathbb{P}(V \to \{0,1\})$, *an* ***acceptable splitting set*** S *for* A *satisfies*

1. $S \subseteq A$
2. *For every* $a \in S$, *there exists* $b \in S$ *such that* $\gamma(a) \cup \gamma(b) = \gamma(\top)$. *Two elements* $a, b \in S$ *such that* $\gamma(a) \cup \gamma(b) = \gamma(\top)$ *are called* ***companions***.
3. *For every assignment* $C \in V \to \{0,1\}$ *there exists* $M_C \subseteq S$ *such that* $\gamma(\sqcap M_C) = C$. *We call* M_C *the* ***cover*** *of* C. $\square$

Example 5. The set of "single-point" partial assignments $\{\top[v \leftarrow 0]\} \cup \{\top[v \leftarrow 1]\}$ is an acceptable splitting set for both the Cartesian domain and the 2-BAR domain. Another acceptable splitting set for the 2-BAR domain is the set consisting of all 2-BAR elements that consist of a single constraint. $\square$

The assumptions of our framework are rather minimal:

1. There is a Galois connection $C \xleftarrow[\alpha]{\gamma} A$ between A and the concrete domain of assignments $C = \mathbb{P}(V \to \{0,1\})$.
2. A is at least as expressive as the Cartesian domain (Defn. 3); that is, for all $A_c \in$ Cartesian, there exists $A \in A$ such that $\gamma_{\text{Cartesian}}(A_c) = \gamma_A(A)$.
3. There is an algorithm to perform the join of arbitrary elements of the domain; that is, for all $A_1, A_2 \in A$, there is an algorithm that produces $A_1 \sqcup A_2$.

Algorithm 6. propagate$_\mathcal{A}(J, A_1, A, \mathcal{I})$

1 requires($J \in \mathcal{I} \wedge A_1 \sqsupseteq A$)
2 **return** $A \sqcap \alpha(\llbracket J \rrbracket \cap \gamma(A_1))$

Algorithm 7. 0-saturation$_\mathcal{A}(A, \mathcal{I})$

1 **repeat**
2    $A' \leftarrow A$
3   **foreach** $J \in I, A_1 \sqsupseteq A$ **such that** $|\text{voc}(J) \cup \text{voc}(A_1)| < \epsilon$) **do**
4       $A \leftarrow$ propagate$_\mathcal{A}(J, A_1, A, \mathcal{I})$
5 **until** ($A = A'$) $\parallel A = \perp_\mathcal{A}$
6 **return** A

Algorithm 8. k-saturation$_\mathcal{A}(A, \mathcal{I})$

1 **repeat**
2    $A' \leftarrow A$
3   **foreach** a, b *that are companions* **such that** $a \not\sqsupseteq A$ **and** $b \not\sqsupseteq A$ **do**
4       $A_1 \leftarrow A \sqcap a$
5       $A_2 \leftarrow A \sqcap b$
6       $A'_1 \leftarrow$ (k–1)-saturation$_\mathcal{A}(A_1, \mathcal{I})$
7       $A'_2 \leftarrow$ (k–1)-saturation$_\mathcal{A}(A_2, \mathcal{I})$
8       $A \leftarrow A'_1 \sqcup A'_2$
9 **until** ($A = A'$) $\parallel A = \perp_\mathcal{A}$
10 **return** A

---

4. There is an algorithm to perform the meet of arbitrary elements of the domain; that is, for all $A_1, A_2 \in \mathcal{A}$, there is an algorithm that produces $A_1 \sqcap A_2$.
5. There is an acceptable splitting set S for $\mathcal{A}$ (Defn. 4).

Assumption 2 ensures that any instantiation that satisfies assumptions 1–4 will satisfy assumption 5: the set of "single-point" partial assignments inherited from the Cartesian domain (Ex. 5) is always an acceptable splitting set.

Note that because the concrete domain $\mathcal{C}$ is over a finite set of Boolean variables, the abstract domain $\mathcal{A}$ has no infinite descending chains. It is not hard to show that 2-BAR meets assumptions (1)–(5). The standard version of Stålmarck's method (§2.1) is the instantiation of the framework presented in this section with the abstract domain 2-BAR.

At any moment during our generalization of Stålmarck's method, each open branch B_i represents a set of variable assignments $C_i \in \mathcal{C}$ such that $\bigcup_i C_i \supseteq \llbracket \neg\varphi \rrbracket$. That is, each branch B_i represents an abstract state $A_i \in \mathcal{A}$ such that $\bigcup_i \gamma(A_i) \supseteq \llbracket \neg\varphi \rrbracket$. Let $\bar{A} = \bigsqcup_i A_i$. Then $\bar{A}$ is sound, i.e., $\gamma(\bar{A}) \supseteq \bigcup_i \gamma(A_i) \supseteq \llbracket \neg\varphi \rrbracket$. The net result of the proof rules is to derive a *semantic reduction* $\bar{A}'$ of $\bar{A}$ with respect to the integrity constraints $\mathcal{I}$; that is, $\gamma(\bar{A}') \cap \llbracket \mathcal{I} \rrbracket = \gamma(\bar{A}) \cap \llbracket \mathcal{I} \rrbracket$, and $\bar{A}' \sqsubseteq \bar{A}$. If the algorithm derives that $\bar{A}' = \perp_\mathcal{A}$, then the formula φ is proved valid.

Generalized Propagation Rules. The propagation rules aim to refine the abstract state by assuming a single integrity constraint $J \in \mathcal{I}$. It is possible to list all the propagation rules in the style of Fig. 2 for the 2-BAR domain; for brevity, Alg. 6 is stated in terms of the semantic properties that an individual propagation rule satisfies, expressed using the operations α, γ, and $\sqcap$ of abstract domain $\mathcal{A}$. This procedure is sound if the abstract value $\bar{A}$ returned satisfies $\gamma(\bar{A}) \supseteq \llbracket \mathcal{I} \rrbracket \cap \gamma(A)$. Furthermore, to guarantee progress we have to show that Alg. 6 implements a reductive operator, i.e., $\bar{A} \sqsubseteq A$.

Theorem 2. [Soundness of Alg. 6] *Let* $\bar{A} :=$ propagate$_\mathcal{A}(J, A_1, A, \mathcal{I})$ *with* $J \in \mathcal{I}$ *and* $A_1 \sqsupseteq A$. *Then* $\gamma(\bar{A}) \supseteq \llbracket \mathcal{I} \rrbracket \cap \gamma(A)$ *and* $\bar{A} \sqsubseteq A$. □

Example 6. Let us apply Alg. 6 with $J = v_1 \Leftrightarrow (v_2 \vee v_3)$, $A_1 = \{v_1 \equiv \mathbf{0}\}$ and $A = \{v_1 \equiv \mathbf{0}, v_4 \equiv \mathbf{0}\}$. To save space, we use 3-valued assignments to represent the concrete states of assignments to $v_1, \ldots, v_4$.

$$\llbracket J \rrbracket = \{(1,0,1,*), (1,1,0,*), (1,1,1,*), (0,0,0,*)\}$$
$$\gamma(A_1) = \{(0,*,*,*)\}$$
$$C = \llbracket J \rrbracket \cap \gamma(A_1) = \{(0,0,0,*)\}$$
$$\alpha(C) = \{v_1 \equiv \mathbf{0}, v_2 \equiv \mathbf{0}, v_3 \equiv \mathbf{0}\}$$
$$\bar{A} = A \sqcap \alpha(C) = \{v_1 \equiv \mathbf{0}, v_2 \equiv \mathbf{0}, v_3 \equiv \mathbf{0}, v_4 \equiv \mathbf{0}\}$$

Thus, the value $\bar{A}$ computed by Alg. 6 is exactly the abstract value that can be deduced by propagation rule OR1 of Fig. 2. □

Generalized 0-Saturation. Alg. 7 shows the generalized 0-saturation procedure that repeatedly applies the propagation rules (line 4) using a single integrity constraint (line 3), until no new information is derived or a contradiction is found (line 5); $\mathrm{voc}(\varphi)$ denotes the set of φ's propositional variables.

To improve efficiency the quantities J and A_1 are chosen so that $|\mathrm{voc}(J) \cup \mathrm{voc}(A_1)|$ is small (line 3). Such a choice enables efficient symbolic implementations of the operations used in Alg. 6, viz., implementing truth-table semantics on the limited vocabulary of size ϵ. Because J in Alg. 6 is a single integrity constraint, there are only a bounded number of Boolean operators involved in each propagation step. By limiting the size of $\mathrm{voc}(J) \cup \mathrm{voc}(A_1)$ (line 3 of Alg. 7), it is possible to generate automatically a bounded number of propagation-rule schemas to implement line 2 of Alg. 6.

To prove soundness we show that the abstract value $\bar{A}$ returned by Alg. 7 satisfies $\gamma(\bar{A}) \supseteq \llbracket \mathcal{I} \rrbracket \cap \gamma(A)$.

Theorem 3. [Soundness of Alg. 7]
For all $A \in \mathcal{A}$, $\gamma(\text{0-saturation}_{\mathcal{A}}(A, \mathcal{I})) \supseteq \llbracket \mathcal{I} \rrbracket \cap \gamma(A)$.   □

Generalized k-Saturation. Alg. 8 describes the generalized k-saturation procedure that repeatedly applies the generalized Dilemma Rule. By requirement 5, there is an acceptable splitting set S for $\mathcal{A}$. The generalized Dilemma Rule, shown schematically in Fig. 9, splits the current abstract state A into two abstract states A_1 and A_2 using companions $a, b \in S$. Using the fact that $\gamma(a) \cup \gamma(b) = \gamma(\top)$ (Defn. 4), we can show that $\gamma(A_1) \cup \gamma(A_2) = \gamma(A)$. This fact is essential for proving the soundness of the generalized Dilemma Rule. To merge the two branches of the generalized Dilemma Rule, we perform a join of the abstract states derived in each branch. The dashed arrows from A to A', A_1 to A_1', and A_2 to A_2' in Fig. 9 indicate that, in each case, the target value is a semantic reduction of the source value. The next theorem proves that Alg. 8, which utilizes the generalized Dilemma Rule, is sound.

Theorem 4. [Soundness of Alg. 8]
For all $A \in \mathcal{A}$, $\gamma(\text{k-saturation}_{\mathcal{A}}(A, \mathcal{I})) \supseteq \llbracket \mathcal{I} \rrbracket \cap \gamma(A)$.   □

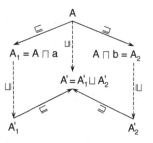

Fig. 9. Generalized Dilemma Rule

Algorithm 9. k-Stålmarck$_\mathcal{A}(\varphi)$

---

1   $(v_\varphi, \mathcal{I}) \leftarrow$ integrity(φ)
2   $A \leftarrow \top_\mathcal{A}[v_\varphi \leftarrow 0]$
3   $A' \leftarrow$ k-saturation$_\mathcal{A}(A, \mathcal{I})$
4   **if** $A' = \perp_\mathcal{A}$ **then return** *valid*
5   **else return** *unknown*

Generalized k-Stålmarck. Alg. 9 describes our generalization of Stålmarck's method, which is parameterized by an abstract domain $\mathcal{A}$. Line 1 converts the formula φ into the integrity constraints $\mathcal{I}$, with v_φ representing φ. We have to prove that Alg. 9 returns *valid* when the given formula φ is indeed valid.

Theorem 5. [Soundness of Alg. 9]
If k-Stålmarck$_\mathcal{A}(\varphi)$ returns valid, then $[\![\neg\varphi]\!] = \emptyset$. □

Completeness. As we saw in §2, Alg. 9 is not complete for all values of k. However, Alg. 9 is complete if k is large enough. To prove completeness we make use of item 3 of Defn. 4. After performing k-saturation, Alg. 9 has considered all assignments C that have a cover of size k. Let MinCover$[C] = \min\{|M| \mid M \subseteq S$ is a cover of $C\}$, and let $m = \max_{C \in \mathcal{C}}$MinCover$[C]$. m-Stålmarck$_\mathcal{A}(\varphi)$ will consider all assignments, and thus is complete; that is, if m-Stålmarck$_\mathcal{A}(\varphi)$ returns *unknown*, then φ is definitely not valid. The efficiency of our generalization of Stålmarck's Method is discussed in [17].

5 Instantiations

Stålmarck's method is the instantiation of the framework from §4 with the abstract domain 2-BAR. In this section, we present the details for a few other instantiations of the framework from §4. As observed in §4, any instantiation that satisfies the first four assumptions of the framework has an acceptable splitting set; hence, we only consider the first four assumptions in the discussion below.

Cartesian Domain. The original version of Stålmarck's method [16] did not use equivalence classes of propositional variables (i.e., the abstract domain 2-BAR). Instead, it was based on a weaker abstract domain of partial assignments, or equivalently, the Cartesian domain. It is easy to see that the Cartesian domain meets the requirements of the framework.

Three-Variable Boolean Affine Relations (3-BAR). The abstract domain 3-BAR is defined almost identically to 2-BAR (Defn. 2). In general, a non-bottom element of 3-BAR is a satisfiable conjunction of constraints of the form $\bigoplus_{i=1}^{3}(a_i \wedge x_i) \oplus b = \mathbf{0}$, where $a_i, b \in \{\mathbf{0}, \mathbf{1}\}$.

$$R_1 : \{z \oplus 1 = 0, x \oplus y = 0\} \quad R_2 : \{z = 0, x \oplus y \oplus 1 = 0\} \qquad\qquad R_1 : \{z \equiv 1, x \equiv y\} \quad R_2 : \{z \equiv 0, x \equiv \neg y\}$$

$$R_1 \sqcup R_2 = \{x \oplus y \oplus z \oplus 1 = 0\} \qquad\qquad\qquad R_1 \sqcup R_2 = \top_{\text{2-BAR}}$$

(a)   (b)

Fig. 10. 3-BAR (a) retains more information at the join than 2-BAR (b)

1. The definitions of the γ and α functions of the Galois connection $\mathbb{P}(\mathcal{V} \to \{0,1\}) \underset{\alpha}{\overset{\gamma}{\longleftrightarrow}}$ 3-BAR are identical to those stated in Defn. 2.
2. 3-BAR generalizes 2-BAR, and so is more precise than the Cartesian domain.
3. $A_1 \sqcup A_2$ can be implemented by first extending A_1 and A_2 with all implied constraints, and then intersecting the extended sets.
4. $A_1 \sqcap A_2$ can be implemented by unioning the two sets of constraints.

Example 7. Fig. 10 presents an example in which 2-BAR and 3-BAR start with equivalent information in the respective branches, but 2-BAR loses all information at a join, whereas 3-BAR retains an affine relation. Consequently, the instantiation of our framework with the 3-BAR domain provides a more powerful proof procedure than the standard version of Stålmarck's method.   □

Two-Variable Boolean Inequality Relations (2-BIR). 2-BIR is yet another constraint domain, and hence defined similarly to 2-BAR and 3-BAR. A non-bottom element of 2-BIR is a satisfiable conjunction of constraints of the form $x \leq y$, $x \leq b$, or $b \leq x$, where $x, y \in \mathcal{V}$ and $b \in \{\mathbf{0}, \mathbf{1}\}$.

1. The definitions of γ and α are again identical to those given in Defn. 2.
2. An equivalence $a \equiv b$ can be represented using two inequality constraints, $a \leq b$ and $b \leq a$, and hence 2-BIR is more precise than 2-BAR, which in turn is more precise than the Cartesian domain.
3. $A_1 \sqcup A_2$ can be implemented by first extending A_1 and A_2 with all implied constraints, and then intersecting the extended sets.
4. $A_1 \sqcap A_2$ can be implemented by unioning the two sets of constraints.

Example 8. Fig. 11 presents an example in which 2-BAR and 2-BIR start with equivalent information in the respective branches, but 2-BAR loses all information at a join, whereas 2-BIR retains a Boolean inequality. Consequently, the instantiation of our framework with the 2-BIR domain provides a more powerful proof procedure than the standard version of Stålmarck's method.   □

$$R_1 : \{a \leq \mathbf{0}, a \leq b\} \quad R_2 : \{\mathbf{1} \leq a, 1 \leq b, a \leq b, b \leq a\} \qquad R_1 : \{a \equiv \mathbf{0}\} \quad R_2 : \{a \equiv \mathbf{1}, b \equiv \mathbf{1}, a \equiv b\}$$

$$R_1 \sqcup R_2 = \{a \leq b\} \qquad\qquad\qquad\qquad R_1 \sqcup R_2 = \top_{\text{2-BAR}}$$

(a)   (b)

Fig. 11. 2-BIR (a) retains more information at the join than 2-BAR (b)

6 Experiments

As discussed in §1, a validity-checking algorithm can be used for checking satisfiability. In this section, we present preliminary experimental results for the following instantiations of our parametric framework:

- *1*-Stålmarck[Cartesian]: uses 1-saturation and the Cartesian domain.
- *1*-Stålmarck[2-BAR]: uses 1-saturation and the 2-BAR domain.
- *1*-Stålmarck[2-BIR]: uses 1-saturation and the 2-BIR domain.
- *2*-Stålmarck[Cartesian]: uses 2-saturation and the Cartesian domain.

We compared the above algorithms with the mature SAT solver, MiniSat (v2.2.0) solver [7]. For our evaluation, we used the Small, Difficult Satisfiability Benchmark (SDSB) suite, which contains 3,608 satisfiability benchmarks that have up to 800 literals, and have been found to be difficult for solvers [14]. We used a time-out limit of 500 seconds. If an algorithm could not determine whether a benchmark was satisfiable or unsatisfiable, then the solver is recorded as taking the full 500 seconds for that benchmark.

For each of the five algorithms, Fig. 12(a) is a semi-log plot in which each point (n, t) means that there were n benchmarks that were each solved correctly in no more than t seconds. Fig. 12(b) and Fig. 13 give log-log scatter plots of the time taken (in seconds) for each of the benchmarks, for several combinations of the five algorithms. As seen in Fig. 12(a), MiniSat correctly solves 3,484 of 3,608 benchmarks, and is significantly faster than *1*-Stålmarck[2-BAR] (Fig. 12(b)).

When comparing among the instantiations of our framework, we expect more benchmarks to be solved correctly as we move to more expressive abstract

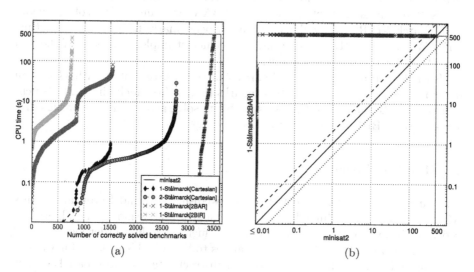

(a)   (b)

Fig. 12. (a) Semi-log plot showing the number of benchmarks that were each solved correctly in no more than t seconds. (b) Log-log scatter plot of the time taken (in seconds) by MiniSat versus *1*-Stålmarck[2-BAR].

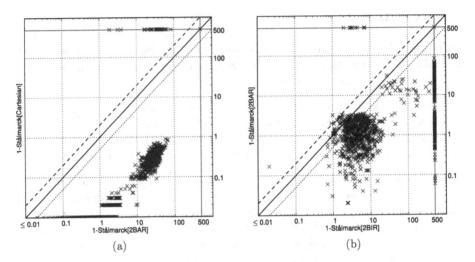

Fig. 13. Log-log scatter plots of the time taken (in seconds) by (a) *1*-Stålmarck[2-BAR] versus *1*-Stålmarck[Cartesian], and (b) *1*-Stålmarck[2-BIR] versus *1*-Stålmarck[2-BAR].

domains. For instance, *1*-Stålmarck[2-BAR] (1,545 benchmarks) solves 36 benchmarks that *1*-Stålmarck[Cartesian] (1,509 benchmarks) was unable to solve. On the other hand, *1*-Stålmarck[2-BAR] is slower than *1*-Stålmarck[Cartesian], as seen in Fig. 13(a), because the join operation of the 2-BAR domain is more expensive than that of the Cartesian domain. The complexity of the join operation plays an even greater role for the 2-BIR domain: although *1*-Stålmarck[2-BIR] solves 9 benchmarks that *1*-Stålmarck[2-BAR] was unable to solve, overall *1*-Stålmarck[2-BIR] is only able to solve 754 benchmarks in the 500-second time limit. We are currently investigating more efficient implementations of the join algorithms for the various domains.

Using 2-saturation allows Stålmarck's method instantiated with Cartesian domain to correctly solve 2,758 benchmarks (Fig. 12(a)), including 1,213 benchmarks that *1*-Stålmarck[2-BAR] was unable to solve and 1,774 benchmarks that *1*-Stålmarck[2-BIR] was unable to solve.

7   Related Work

Stålmarck's method was patented under Swedish, U.S., and European patents [15]. Sheeran and Stålmarck [13] give a lucid presentation of the algorithm. Björk [1] explored extensions of Stålmarck's method to first-order logic.

CDCL/DPLL solvers [12] are alternatives to Stålmarck's method for validity checking and SAT. D'Silva et al. [5] give an abstract-interpretation-based account of CDCL/DPLL SAT solvers. Thus, though having similar goals, our work and that of D'Silva et al. are complementary. Our work and that of D'Silva et al. were performed independently and contemporaneously. They have also lifted their technique from a propositional SAT solver to a floating-point decision procedure that makes use of floating-point intervals [6].

References

1. Björk, M.: First order Stålmarck. J. Autom. Reasoning 42(1), 99–122 (2009)
2. Cook, B., Gonthier, G.: Using Stålmarck's Algorithm to Prove Inequalities. In: Lau, K.-K., Banach, R. (eds.) ICFEM 2005. LNCS, vol. 3785, pp. 330–344. Springer, Heidelberg (2005)
3. Cousot, P., Cousot, R.: Abstract interpretation: A unified lattice model for static analysis of programs by construction or approximation of fixpoints. In: POPL (1977)
4. Cousot, P., Cousot, R.: Systematic design of program analysis frameworks. In: POPL (1979)
5. D'Silva, V., Haller, L., Kroening, D.: Satisfiability solvers are static analyzers. In: SAS (2012)
6. D'Silva, V., Haller, L., Kroening, D., Tautschnig, M.: Numeric Bounds Analysis with Conflict-Driven Learning. In: Flanagan, C., König, B. (eds.) TACAS 2012. LNCS, vol. 7214, pp. 48–63. Springer, Heidelberg (2012)
7. Eén, N., Sjørensson, N.: The MiniSat solver (2006), minisat.se/MiniSat.html
8. Granger, P.: Improving the Results of Static Analyses Programs by Local Decreasing Iteration (Extended Abstract). In: Shyamasundar, R. (ed.) FSTTCS 1992. LNCS, vol. 652, pp. 68–79. Springer, Heidelberg (1992)
9. Harrison, J.: Stålmarck's Algorithm as a HOL Derived Rule. In: von Wright, J., Grundy, J., Harrison, J. (eds.) TPHOLs 1996. LNCS, vol. 1125, pp. 221–234. Springer, Heidelberg (1996)
10. Kunz, W., Pradhan, D.: Recursive learning: A new implication technique for efficient solutions to CAD problems–test, verification, and optimization. IEEE Trans. on CAD of Integrated Circuits and Systems 13(9), 1143–1158 (1994)
11. Marques Silva, J., Sakallah, K.: GRASP – a new search algorithm for satisfiability. In: ICCAD (1996)
12. Moskewicz, M., Madigan, C., Zhao, Y., Zhang, L., Malik, S.: Chaff: Engineering an efficient SAT solver. In: DAC (2001)
13. Sheeran, M., Stålmarck, G.: A tutorial on Stålmarck's proof procedure for propositional logic. FMSD 16(1), 23–58 (2000)
14. Spence, I.: tts: A SAT-solver for small, difficult instances. Journal on Sat., Boolean Modeling and Computation (2008), Benchmarks http://www.cs.qub.ac.uk/~i.spence/sdsb
15. Stålmarck, G.: A system for determining propositional logic theorems by applying values and rules to triplets that are generated from a formula (1989), Swedish Patent No. 467,076 (approved 1992); U.S. Patent No. 5,276,897 (approved 1994); European Patent No. 403,454 (approved 1995)
16. Stålmarck, G., Säflund, M.: Modeling and verifying systems and software in propositional logic. In: Int. Conf. on Safety of Computer Controls Systems (1990)
17. Thakur, A., Reps, T.: A generalization of Stålmarck's method. TR 1699 (revised), CS Dept., Univ. of Wisconsin, Madison, WI (June 2012), www.cs.wisc.edu/wpis/papers/tr1699r.pdf
18. Thakur, A., Reps, T.: A Method for Symbolic Computation of Abstract Operations. In: Madhusudan, P., Seshia, S.A. (eds.) CAV 2012. LNCS, vol. 7358, pp. 174–192. Springer, Heidelberg (2012)

A Structural Soundness Proof for Shivers's Escape Technique
A Case for Galois Connections

Jan Midtgaard[1], Michael D. Adams[2], and Matthew Might[3]

[1] Aarhus University, Denmark
[2] Portland State University, USA
[3] University of Utah, USA

Abstract. Shivers's escape technique enables one to analyse the control flow of higher-order program fragments. It is widely used, but its soundness has never been proven. In this paper, we present the first soundness proof for the technique. Our proof is structured as a composition of Galois connections and thus rests on the foundations of abstract interpretation.

1 Introduction

Control-flow analysis is traditionally a *whole program analysis* [Nielson et al., 1999] meaning that it needs access to the entire program text. As flow-analysis algorithms such as 0CFA require cubic time in the size of the program,[1] this limits their applicability to large programs.

Techniques exist, however, for analysing only a part of a program (e.g., an independent module). One such technique is Shivers's escape technique [Shivers, 1991, Sec. 3.8.2]:

> *"Our abstract analysis can handle this by defining two special tokens: the external procedure* xproc, *and the external call* xcall. *The* xproc *represents unknown procedures that are passed into our program from the outside world at run time. The* xcall *represents calls to procedures that happen external to the program text.*
>
> . . .
>
> *We maintain a set* ESCAPED *of escaped procedures, which initially contains* xproc *and the top-level lambda of the program. The rules for the external call, the external procedure and escaped functions are simple:*
> 1. *Any procedure passed to the external procedure escapes.*
> 2. *Any escaped procedure can be called from the external call.*
> 3. *When a procedure is called from the external call, it may be applied to any escaped procedure."*

---

[1] For *typed* programs the complexity is usually not that bad [Heintze and McAllester, 1997].

A. Miné and D. Schmidt (Eds.): SAS 2012, LNCS 7460, pp. 352–369, 2012.

$$SExp \ni s ::= (t_0\ t_1 \ldots t_n)^\ell \qquad \text{(application)}$$

$$TExp \ni t ::= x^\ell \qquad \text{(variable)}$$

$$| \ (\lambda\,x_1 \ldots x_n.\ s)^\ell \qquad \text{(function)}$$

Fig. 1. CPS language

Shivers does not prove his technique to be sound, however. In this paper, we show how his technique can be derived using abstract interpretation by composing a number of well-known Galois connections.

We wish to stress that the escape technique presented in this paper is applicable to any higher-order program analysis even though we present it in terms of a higher-order language in continuation-passing style. It is thus as relevant to a higher-order language like JavaScript as it is to a higher-order language like Scheme. This proof technique grew out of an unpublished soundness proof for the fast type-recovery of Adams et al. [2011].

2   Control-Flow Analysis

To focus on the topic at hand, namely modularity, we limit ourselves to a core language consisting of the lambda calculus in *continuation-passing style* (CPS). The grammar of the language is presented in Figure 1. Following Reynolds [1998] the grammar distinguishes *serious* expressions (*SExp*) whose evaluation may diverge from *trivial* expressions (*TExp*) whose evaluation is guaranteed to terminate. As is standard [Nielson et al., 1999], we label all sub-expressions with a unique label ℓ to distinguish different occurrences of the same sub-expression. For the remainder of this paper, we let labels on variables be implicit to ease the syntactic overhead.

There are a number of advantages to the small-step CPS framework. First, since all intermediate results are bound to a variable, an analysis can be characterized in terms of computing an abstract environment or store. One would otherwise need to compute an *abstract cache* that maps labels to abstract values [Nielson et al., 1999]. Second, since all calls are *tail calls*, the analysis does not need special measures to propagate *return flow*. This is instead handled by bindings to continuation variables. CPS therefore makes for a simple, uniform analysis.

The control-flow analysis is formulated in terms of the curried transfer function T defined in Figure 2. For a given program P, the analysis is defined as the least fixed point of $T(P)$. The analysis computes an abstract environment, $\rho : Var \to Val$, which approximates the bindings of an actual program run. T relies on a helper function E for analysing trivial expressions. We furthermore use the shorthand notation $[\overline{x} \mapsto E(\overline{t}, \rho)]$ to mean $[x_1 \mapsto E(t_1, \rho), \ldots, x_n \mapsto E(t_n, \rho)]$. T considers all call sites $(t_0\ t_1 \ldots t_n)^\ell$ of the program P in each iteration. This is easily accomplished by a traversal of P's abstract syntax tree. Here we simply

$$T \ : \ \wp(SExp) \to (Var \to Val) \to (Var \to Val)$$

$$T(P)(\rho) = \bigsqcup_{\substack{(t_0 \ t_1 \ldots t_n)^\ell \in P \\ (\lambda x_1 \ldots x_n. \ s)^{\ell'} \in E(t_0, \rho)}} \rho \sqcup [\overline{x} \mapsto E(\overline{t}, \rho)]$$

where
$$E(x, \rho) = \rho(x)$$
$$E((\lambda x_1 \ldots x_n. \ s)^\ell, \rho) = \{(\lambda x_1 \ldots x_n. \ s)^\ell\}$$

Fig. 2. CPS analysis

$$Var = XVar + IVar \quad \text{(variables)}$$
$$Lam = XLam + ILam \quad \text{(functions)}$$
$$Val = \wp(Lam) \quad \text{(values)}$$

$$TExp = XTExp + ITExp \quad \text{(trivial exprs)}$$
$$SExp = XSexp + ISexp \quad \text{(serious exprs)}$$

Fig. 3. Syntactic and analysis domains

express P in terms of a set of call sites. For each possible receiver of a call, the analysis binds the (analysis result of the) actual parameters to the formals. This analysis agrees with the 0CFAs of Midtgaard and Jensen [2008] and Might [2010] (sans reachability) and is therefore known to be sound.

We define the domains for the refined analysis in Figure 3. To pave the way for a CFA over open programs, we split the domains into disjoint *external* and *internal* sets and assume some basic consistencies among them. Variables bound in an internal lambda are all internal variables. An analogous constraint applies to external variables and external lambdas. Similarly, trivial sub-expressions of an internal serious expression are all internal trivial expressions. However, the trivial sub-expressions of an external serious expression may be either internal or external.

For example, consider an analysis restricted to the boxed expression below. The sub-expressions outside the box are external while those inside the box are internal. Note that, inside the box, the variable occurrence of k is an internal expression but refers to the external variable k.

$$(\lambda k. \ (k \ \boxed{(\lambda x. \ (k \ x))} \ ))$$

Finally, we assume that internal variables must be located inside an internal lambda. Hence, for an external call site $(t_0 \ t_1 \ldots t_n)$ none of the t_j can be internal variables. If t_j is an internal lambda located immediately inside such an external call site, we include it in a dedicated set $Toplevel \subset ILam$.

3   Abstract Interpretation

A Galois connection is a pair of functions (the *adjoints*) $\alpha : C \to A$ and $\gamma : A \to C$ which connect two partially ordered sets $\langle C; \sqsubseteq \rangle$ and $\langle A; \leq \rangle$ such that:

$$\forall c \in C, a \in A \; : \; \alpha(c) \leq a \iff c \sqsubseteq \gamma(a)$$

Following abstract interpretation tradition [Cousot and Cousot, 1994], we type-set Galois connections as $\langle C; \sqsubseteq \rangle \xleftrightarrow[\alpha]{\gamma} \langle A; \leq \rangle$.

Galois connections enjoy a number of properties. First, α and γ are necessarily monotone. Second, the composition $\gamma \circ \alpha$ is extensive ($\forall c \in C : c \sqsubseteq \gamma \circ \alpha(c)$) and the composition $\alpha \circ \gamma$ is reductive ($\forall a \in A : \alpha \circ \gamma(a) \leq a$). For Galois connections with a surjective α (or equivalently with an injective γ), the latter composition yields the identity $\alpha \circ \gamma = 1$. These are called Galois surjections (or Galois insertions) and are typeset as $\langle C; \sqsubseteq \rangle \xleftrightarrow[\alpha]{\gamma} \langle A; \leq \rangle$. When both α and γ are surjective, the Galois connection is an isomorphism and is typeset as $\langle C; \sqsubseteq \rangle \xleftrightarrow[\alpha]{\gamma} \langle A; \leq \rangle$.

Galois connections that connect complete lattices have even more properties. For example, α is a complete join morphism (CJM) and thus preserves joins (i.e., $\alpha(\sqcup_i S_i) = \vee_i \alpha(S_i)$), and γ is a complete meet morphism and thus preserves meets (i.e., $\gamma(\wedge_i S_i) = \sqcap_i \gamma(S_i)$). For easy reference, we summarize in Figure 4 the Galois connections relevant to this paper. Following Might [2010] we typeset them as inference rules. For the purposes of this paper they all connect complete lattices.

Galois connections interact nicely with fixed points. Given a Galois connection between complete lattices and a monotone function F, the *fixed-point transfer theorem* [Cousot and Cousot, 1979] provides an approximation of lfp F:

$$\alpha(\text{lfp}\, F) \leq \text{lfp}(\alpha \circ F \circ \gamma) \leq \text{lfp}\, F^\sharp$$

Here, $F^\sharp$ is a monotone function such that $\alpha \circ F \circ \gamma \dot{\leq} F^\sharp$. Whereas any $F^\sharp$ satisfying these requirements will do, the *best abstraction* satisfying $F^\sharp = \alpha \circ F \circ \gamma$ represents the best possible function over the chosen abstract domain [Cousot and Cousot, 1992]. In the calculational approach to abstract interpretation, Cousot [1999] advocates simple algebraic manipulation to find such a function (if it exists) or a sound approximation thereof.

When F expresses an execution step in the formal semantics for a program, lfp F describes the *collecting semantics* of the program: an ideal but generally uncomputable exploration of program paths that is subject to over approximation.

4   Abstracting the Domains

We derive Shivers's escape technique in two steps. In this section, we define Galois connections that abstract over the domains of our analysis. Then, in

Transitive abstraction [Cousot and Cousot, 1994]

$$\frac{\langle D_0; \sqsubseteq_0 \rangle \xleftarrow[\alpha_1]{\gamma_1} \langle D_1; \sqsubseteq_1 \rangle \qquad \langle D_1; \sqsubseteq_1 \rangle \xleftarrow[\alpha_2]{\gamma_2} \langle D_2; \sqsubseteq_2 \rangle}{\langle D_0; \sqsubseteq_0 \rangle \xleftarrow[\alpha_2 \circ \alpha_1]{\gamma_1 \circ \gamma_2} \langle D_2; \sqsubseteq_2 \rangle} \text{ Trans}$$

Elementwise abstraction [Cousot and Cousot, 1997]

$$\frac{@ : C \to A}{\langle \wp(C); \subseteq \rangle \xleftarrow[\alpha_@ = \lambda P. \{@(p) \mid p \in P\}]{\gamma_@ = \lambda Q. \{p \mid @(p) \in Q\}} \langle \wp(A); \subseteq \rangle} \text{ Element}$$

Isomorphic maps

$$\frac{}{\langle (A+B) \to C; \dot{\sqsubseteq} \rangle \xleftarrow[\alpha_\sim = \lambda f. (f|_A, f|_B)]{\gamma_\sim = \lambda (g,h). \lambda x. \begin{cases} g(x) & x \in A \\ h(x) & x \in B \end{cases}} \langle (A \to C) \times (B \to C); \dot{\sqsubseteq} \times \dot{\sqsubseteq} \rangle} \text{ Iso}$$

Collapsing abstraction

$$\frac{}{\langle D \to \wp(C); \dot{\subseteq} \rangle \xleftarrow[\alpha_\cup = \lambda f. \cup_{x \in Dom(f)} f(x)]{\gamma_\cup = \lambda s. \lambda x. \, s} \langle \wp(C); \subseteq \rangle} \text{ Collapse}$$

Pointwise abstraction [Cousot and Cousot, 1994]

$$\frac{\langle \wp(C); \subseteq \rangle \xleftarrow[\alpha_1]{\gamma_1} \langle A; \sqsubseteq \rangle}{\langle D \to \wp(C); \dot{\subseteq} \rangle \xleftarrow[\alpha. = \lambda f. \lambda x. \, \alpha_1(f(x))]{\gamma. = \lambda f. \lambda x. \, \gamma_1(f(x))} \langle D \to A; \dot{\sqsubseteq} \rangle} \text{ Pointwise}$$

Product abstraction [Cousot and Cousot, 1994]

$$\frac{\langle C_1; \sqsubseteq_1 \rangle \xleftarrow[\alpha_1]{\gamma_1} \langle A_1; \leq_1 \rangle \qquad \langle C_2; \sqsubseteq_2 \rangle \xleftarrow[\alpha_2]{\gamma_2} \langle A_2; \leq_2 \rangle}{\langle C_1 \times C_2; \sqsubseteq_1 \times \sqsubseteq_2 \rangle \xleftarrow[\alpha_\times = \lambda (c_1,c_2). (\alpha_1(c_1), \alpha_2(c_2))]{\gamma_\times = \lambda (a_1,a_2). (\gamma_1(a_1), \gamma_2(a_2))} \langle A_1 \times A_2; \leq_1 \times \leq_2 \rangle} \text{ Component}$$

Subset abstraction [Cousot and Cousot, 1997]

$$\frac{S \subset C}{\langle \wp(C); \subseteq \rangle \xleftarrow[\alpha_C = \lambda c. \, c \cap S]{\gamma_C = \lambda s. \, s \cup (C \setminus S)} \langle \wp(S); \subseteq \rangle} \text{ Subset}$$

Fig. 4. Galois connection reference

Section 5, we use these abstractions to derive the transfer function of an analysis incorporating Shivers's escape technique.

Figure 5 provides an overview of the Galois connections defined in this section using the judgments defined in Figure 4.

4.1   Abstracting Values

The operator $@ : Lam \rightarrow ILam + \{\mathbf{xproc}\}$ maps lambdas to either internal lambdas or the dedicated token $\mathbf{xproc}$ representing all external procedures:

$$@((\lambda\, x_1 \ldots x_n.\ s)^{\ell}) = \begin{cases} (\lambda\, x_1 \ldots x_n.\ s)^{\ell} & (\lambda\, x_1 \ldots x_n.\ s)^{\ell} \in ILam \\ \mathbf{xproc} & (\lambda\, x_1 \ldots x_n.\ s)^{\ell} \in XLam \end{cases}$$

Using $@$, both ELEMENT judgments in Figure 5 build an elementwise abstraction on values. Since $@$ is surjective, the resulting Galois connection is a Galois surjection:

$$\wp(Lam) \xleftrightarrow[\alpha_@]{\gamma_@} \wp(ILam + \{\mathbf{xproc}\})$$

4.2   Abstracting the Store

We abstract the store by, first, mapping the store to an isomorphic representation containing two stores: one for external bindings and one for internal bindings. Then, we abstract each component individually. By transitivity, the resulting abstraction is a Galois connection.

The ISO judgment in Figure 5 uses the fact that $Var = XVar + IVar$ and an isomorphic representation of the store to build the following Galois connection:

$$(XVar + IVar) \rightarrow Val \xleftrightarrow[\alpha_\sim]{\gamma_\sim} (XVar \rightarrow Val) \times (IVar \rightarrow Val)$$

This isomorphism is well-known within set theory [Winskel, 2010], semantics, and functional programming [Wand and Vaillancourt, 2004]. It allows us to abstract the external bindings separately from the internal bindings.

Next, the COLLAPSE judgment in Figure 5 abstracts the external bindings with a collapsing abstraction $\alpha_\cup$ that join all bindings and aliases them into a single set of values:

$$XVar \rightarrow \wp(Lam) \xleftrightarrow[\alpha_\cup]{\gamma_\cup} \wp(Lam)$$

The POINTWISE judgment in Figure 5 abstracts the internal bindings using a standard pointwise lifting of the value abstraction:

$$IVar \rightarrow \wp(Lam) \xleftrightarrow[\alpha_.]{\gamma_.} IVar \rightarrow \wp(ILam + \{\mathbf{xproc}\})$$

Finally, the COMPONENT judgment composes the two abstractions to form a product abstraction of both external and internal bindings:

$$(XVar \rightarrow Val) \times (IVar \rightarrow Val) \xleftrightarrow[\alpha_\times]{\gamma_\times} \wp(ILam + \{\mathbf{xproc}\}) \times (IVar \rightarrow \wp(ILam + \{\mathbf{xproc}\}))$$

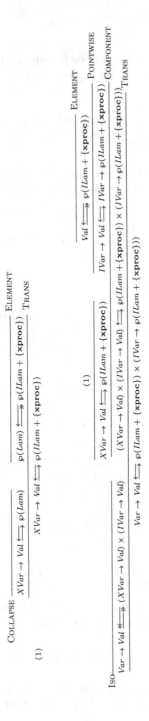

Fig. 5. Galois connection inference tree

4.3   Abstracting Programs

The analysis in Figure 2 computes a join for each call site of the input program P. When only a part of the program is available, we represent the information loss as an abstraction of the set of call sites. This is formulated as a subset abstraction where P omits $XSexp$ and keeps only $ISexp$:

$$\wp(SExp) \xleftrightarrow[\alpha_C]{\gamma_C} \wp(ISexp)$$

5   Abstracting the Analysis

In this section, we use the Galois connections defined in Section 4 to abstract T and derive a new transfer function, $T^\sharp$, that is sound with respect to T. By the fixed-point transfer theorem [Cousot and Cousot, 1979], the fixed point of $T^\sharp$ is a sound approximation of the fixed point of T.

5.1   Abstracting the Helper Function

We calculate a sound approximation of E, the helper function defined in Figure 2, by composing it with the adjoints of the Galois connections.

$$\alpha_@ \circ E(t, \gamma_\sim \circ \gamma_\times(\rho_e, \rho_i)) \hspace{3cm} \text{(def. of } E)$$

$$= \begin{cases} \alpha_@((\gamma_\sim \circ \gamma_\times(\rho_e, \rho_i))(x)) & t = x \\ \alpha_@(\{(\lambda x_1 \ldots x_n.\, s)^\ell\}) & t = (\lambda x_1 \ldots x_n.\, s)^\ell \end{cases} \hspace{1cm} \text{(def. of } \gamma_\times)$$

$$= \begin{cases} \alpha_@((\gamma_\sim(\gamma_\cup \circ \gamma_@(\rho_e), \gamma.(\rho_i)))(x)) & t = x \\ \alpha_@(\{(\lambda x_1 \ldots x_n.\, s)^\ell\}) & t = (\lambda x_1 \ldots x_n.\, s)^\ell \end{cases} \hspace{1cm} \text{(def. of } \gamma_\sim)$$

$$= \begin{cases} \alpha_@((\gamma_\cup \circ \gamma_@(\rho_e))(x)) & t = x \in XVar \\ \alpha_@((\gamma.(\rho_i))(x)) & t = x \in IVar \\ \alpha_@(\{(\lambda x_1 \ldots x_n.\, s)^\ell\}) & t = (\lambda x_1 \ldots x_n.\, s)^\ell \end{cases} \hspace{1cm} \text{(def. of } \gamma_\cup)$$

$$= \begin{cases} \alpha_@(\gamma_@(\rho_e)) & t = x \in XVar \\ \alpha_@((\gamma.(\rho_i))(x)) & t = x \in IVar \\ \alpha_@(\{(\lambda x_1 \ldots x_n.\, s)^\ell\}) & t = (\lambda x_1 \ldots x_n.\, s)^\ell \end{cases} \hspace{1cm} \text{(def. of } \gamma.)$$

$$= \begin{cases} \alpha_@(\gamma_@(\rho_e)) & t = x \in XVar \\ \alpha_@(\gamma_@(\rho_i(x))) & t = x \in IVar \\ \alpha_@(\{(\lambda x_1 \ldots x_n.\, s)^\ell\}) & t = (\lambda x_1 \ldots x_n.\, s)^\ell \end{cases} \hspace{1cm} \text{(Galois surjection)}$$

$$= \begin{cases} \rho_e & t = x \in XVar \\ \rho_i(x) & t = x \in IVar \\ \alpha_@(\{(\lambda x_1 \ldots x_n.\, s)^\ell\}) & t = (\lambda x_1 \ldots x_n.\, s)^\ell \end{cases} \hspace{1cm} \text{(def. of } \alpha_@)$$

$$= \begin{cases} \rho_e & t = x \in XVar \\ \rho_i(x) & t = x \in IVar \\ \{\mathbf{xproc}\} & t = (\lambda x_1 \ldots x_n.\, s)^\ell \in XLam \\ \{(\lambda x_1 \ldots x_n.\, s)^\ell\} & t = (\lambda x_1 \ldots x_n.\, s)^\ell \in ILam \end{cases}$$

Hence by defining $\widehat{E}$ as:

$$\widehat{E}(t, \rho_e, \rho_i) = \begin{cases} \rho_e & t = x \in XVar \\ \rho_i(x) & t = x \in IVar \\ \{\mathbf{xproc}\} & t = (\lambda\, x_1 \ldots x_n.\ s)^\ell \in XLam \\ \{(\lambda\, x_1 \ldots x_n.\ s)^\ell\} & t = (\lambda\, x_1 \ldots x_n.\ s)^\ell \in ILam \end{cases}$$

the following lemma holds by construction.

Lemma 1 ($\widehat{E}$ is the best abstraction of E)

$$\forall t, \rho_e, \rho_i\ :\ \alpha_@ \circ E(t, \gamma_\sim \circ \gamma_\times(\rho_e, \rho_i)) = \widehat{E}(t, \rho_e, \rho_i)$$

While $\widehat{E}$ is not an operator from a domain to itself, it nevertheless represents the best abstraction of the operator E in terms of the abstract arguments ρ_e and ρ_i.

By inspecting $\widehat{E}$ applied to external expressions, we have the following bound.

Lemma 2 (Upper bound on $\widehat{E}$)

$$\forall t \in XTExp, \rho_e, \rho_i\ :\ \widehat{E}(t, \rho_e, \rho_i) \subseteq \rho_e \cup \{\mathbf{xproc}\}$$

By a simple case analysis on t, we furthermore discover that $\widehat{E}$ is monotone in its environment arguments, ρ_e and ρ_i.

Lemma 3 ($\widehat{E}$ is monotone in environment arguments)

$$\forall t, \rho_e, \rho_e', \rho_i, \rho_i'\ :\ (\rho_e, \rho_i) \sqsubseteq (\rho_e', \rho_i') \implies \widehat{E}(t, \rho_e, \rho_i) \subseteq \widehat{E}(t, \rho_e', \rho_i')$$

5.2 Abstracting the Transfer Function

We now construct the abstract transfer function $T^\sharp$ by composing T with the adjoints of the Galois connections. Given P_i, ρ_e, and ρ_i, we have:

$$\alpha_\times \circ \alpha_\sim \circ (T(\gamma_\subset(P_i))) \circ \gamma_\sim \circ \gamma_\times(\rho_e, \rho_i)$$

$$= \ldots$$

$$\sqsubseteq (\rho_e \cup \{\mathbf{xproc}\} \cup Toplevel, \rho_i)$$

$$\sqcup \bigsqcup_{\substack{\{(t_0\ t_1 \ldots t_n)^\ell\} \subseteq P_i \\ \mathbf{xproc} \in \widehat{E}(t_0, \rho_e, \rho_i)}} (\rho_e \cup \bigcup_{j \in [1;n]} \widehat{E}(t_j, \rho_e, \rho_i), \rho_i)$$

$$\sqcup \bigsqcup_{(\lambda\, x_1 \ldots x_n.\ s)^\ell \in \rho_e \cup Toplevel} (\rho_e, \rho_i \,\dot{\cup}\, [\overline{x} \mapsto (\rho_e \cup \{\mathbf{xproc}\} \cup Toplevel)])$$

$$\sqcup \bigsqcup_{\substack{\{(t_0\ t_1 \ldots t_n)^\ell\} \subseteq P_i \\ (\lambda\, x_1 \ldots x_n.\ s)^{\ell'} \in \widehat{E}(t_0, \rho_e, \rho_i)}} (\rho_e, \rho_i \,\dot{\cup}\, [\overline{x} \mapsto \widehat{E}(\overline{t}, \rho_e, \rho_i)])$$

The full calculation is lengthy and is therefore deferred to Appendix A. Nonetheless, it proceeds from simple algebraic rewritings relying only on standard Galois-connection reasoning.

By defining the abstract transfer function $T^\sharp$ as:

$$T^\sharp : \wp(ISexp) \to \widehat{Env} \to \widehat{Env}$$

$$T^\sharp(P_i)(\rho_e, \rho_i) = (\rho_e \cup \{\mathbf{xproc}\} \cup Toplevel, \rho_i)$$

$$\sqcup \bigsqcup_{\substack{\{(t_0\ t_1...t_n)^\ell\}\subseteq P_i \\ \mathbf{xproc} \in \widehat{E}(t_0, \rho_e, \rho_i)}} (\rho_e \cup \bigcup_{j \in [1;n]} \widehat{E}(t_j, \rho_e, \rho_i), \rho_i)$$

$$\sqcup \bigsqcup_{(\lambda x_1...x_n.\ s)^\ell \in \rho_e \cup Toplevel} (\rho_e, \rho_i \mathbin{\dot\cup} [\overline{x} \mapsto (\rho_e \cup \{\mathbf{xproc}\} \cup Toplevel)])$$

$$\sqcup \bigsqcup_{\substack{\{(t_0\ t_1...t_n)^\ell\}\subseteq P_i \\ (\lambda x_1...x_n.\ s)^{\ell'} \in \widehat{E}(t_0, \rho_e, \rho_i)}} (\rho_e, \rho_i \mathbin{\dot\cup} [\overline{x} \mapsto \widehat{E}(\overline{t}, \rho_e, \rho_i)])$$

where $\widehat{Env} = \wp(ILam + \{\mathbf{xproc}\}) \times (IVar \to \wp(ILam + \{\mathbf{xproc}\}))$ the following lemma holds by construction.

Lemma 4 ($T^\sharp$ is a sound approximation of T)

$$\forall P_i, \rho_e, \rho_i\ :\ \alpha_\times \circ \alpha_\sim \circ (T(\gamma_\sqsubset(P_i))) \circ \gamma_\sim \circ \gamma_\times(\rho_e, \rho_i) \sqsubseteq T^\sharp(P_i)(\rho_e, \rho_i)$$

By a sequence of upward judgments ($\sqsubseteq$) from ρ_e to ρ'_e, and from ρ_i to ρ'_i and by appeal to Lemma 3 we can furthermore verify that the derived transfer function is monotone.

Lemma 5 ($T^\sharp$ is monotone)

$$\forall P_i, \rho_e, \rho'_e, \rho_i, \rho'_i\ :\ (\rho_e, \rho_i) \sqsubseteq (\rho'_e, \rho'_i) \implies T^\sharp(P_i)(\rho_e, \rho_i) \sqsubseteq T^\sharp(P_i)(\rho'_e, \rho'_i)$$

Finally, the soundness of the derived analysis follows from the fixed-point transfer theorem [Cousot and Cousot, 1979]:

Theorem 1 (Soundness of the analysis with Shivers's escape technique)

$$\forall P_i\ :\ \alpha_\times \circ \alpha_\sim(\operatorname{lfp} T(\gamma_\sqsubset(P_i))) \sqsubseteq \operatorname{lfp} T^\sharp(P_i)$$

5.3 Proof Summary

The soundness of the analysis (Theorem 1) is proven using the fixed-point transfer theorem. In order to use the fixed-point transfer theorem, we construct a Galois connection between the domains of T and $T^\sharp$ (Section 4), prove that $T^\sharp$ is a sound approximation of T (Lemma 4) and prove that $T^\sharp$ is monotone (Lemma 5).

Since T includes a helper function, E, we also abstract E to $E^\sharp$. Lemmas 1 and 2 simplify the calculations relating to $E^\sharp$ in the proof of Lemma 4. We use the fact that $E^\sharp$ is monotone (Lemma 3) in the proof that $T^\sharp$ is monotone (Lemma 5).

$$\text{XPROC} \frac{}{(\{\mathbf{xproc}\} \cup \mathit{Toplevel}) \subseteq \rho_e} \qquad \frac{(t_0\ t_1 \ldots t_n)^\ell \in P_i \qquad \mathbf{xproc} \in \widehat{E}(t_0, \rho_e, \rho_i)}{\widehat{E}(t_j, \rho_e, \rho_i) \subseteq \rho_e, \qquad j \in [1; n]} \text{ESCAPE}$$

$$\text{XCALL} \frac{(\lambda\, x_1 \ldots x_n.\ s)^\ell \in (\rho_e \cup \mathit{Toplevel})}{(\rho_e \cup \{\mathbf{xproc}\} \cup \mathit{Toplevel}) \subseteq \rho_i(\overline{x})}$$

$$\frac{(t_0\ t_1 \ldots t_n)^\ell \in P_i \qquad (\lambda\, x_1 \ldots x_n.\ s)^{\ell'} \in \widehat{E}(t_0, \rho_e, \rho_i)}{\widehat{E}(\overline{t}, \rho_e, \rho_i) \subseteq \rho_i(\overline{x})} \text{ICALL}$$

Fig. 6. CFA constraints

6 Extracting Constraints

Given the transfer function $T^\sharp$, we are now in a position to take a step backwards and extract constraints equivalent to $T^\sharp$ [Cousot and Cousot, 1995]. For any post-fixed point (ρ_e, ρ_i) of $T^\sharp$, it holds that $T^\sharp(P_i)(\rho_e, \rho_i) \sqsubseteq (\rho_e, \rho_i)$. This is equivalent to the constraint rules in Figure 6.

The XCALL constraint is needlessly complex, however, as XPROC guarantees that both $\{\mathbf{xproc}\}$ and $\mathit{Toplevel}$ are already subsets of ρ_e. Hence we can simplify XCALL to:

$$\text{XCALL'} \frac{(\lambda\, x_1 \ldots x_n.\ s)^\ell \in \rho_e}{\rho_e \subseteq \rho_i(\overline{x})}$$

The resulting constraints can be understood as follows.

- XPROC: External procedures and top-level procedures may escape.
- ESCAPE: If a call-site may target an external procedure, all of the actual parameters escape.
- XCALL': If a procedure escapes, then its formal parameters may take any escaped value.
- ICALL: For internal call-sites and procedures, values flow from the actual parameters to the formal parameters (as in the base analysis).

It is striking how close these constraints are to Shivers's original description as quoted in Section 1. In our characterization, the external environment ρ_e plays the role of Shivers's ESCAPED set. The two descriptions differ in that we have not found the need to abstract external call-sites into a dedicated $\mathbf{xcall}$ token. Doing so can be achieved by replacing the subset abstraction by another elementwise abstraction over call sites. In his description, Shivers also omits the detail that external (free) variables should be looked up in ESCAPED (i.e., ρ_e).

An implementation of the analysis can be realized as a direct implementation of the transfer function $T^\sharp$ by performing Kleene iteration or by outputting *conditional constraints* based on Figure 6 in the style of Palsberg and Schwartzbach [1995] and subsequently solving them in $O(n^3)$ time.

7   Related Work

This work derives from the Galois-connection school of abstract interpretation [Cousot and Cousot, 1979]. Previous work by the present authors investigate derivations of CFAs using Galois connections [Midtgaard and Jensen, 2008, 2012; Might, 2010].

Shivers [1991, Sec. 3.8.2] conceived of the escaping-lambdas technique using **xproc** to denote an external procedure, **xcall** to denote an external call, and ESCAPED to denote the set of escaping procedures. However, he did not prove the soundness of the technique. Serrano and Feeley [1996] used a similar concept of escaping to the top of the lattice in their development of modular analyses for both first-order and higher-order languages. Ashley and Dybvig [1998] later used the escaping-to-top idea to formulate a sub-cubic CFA by jumping to top if more than a constant number of procedures flow to a particular variable. The implementation described in Ashley's dissertation [Ashley, 1996, Sec. 6.1.1] furthermore uses an escape set to accommodate free variables. However, Ashley's soundness proof assumes programs are closed. The present authors [Adams et al., 2011] have recently combined the escaping-to-top idea with novel algorithms and data structures to develop a fast, flow-sensitive type-recovery analysis. We did not prove soundness of the escape technique in that work.

Flanagan and Felleisen [1999] developed a *componential* set-based analysis. Their approach extends the set-based analysis by Heintze [1992] by avoiding re-extracting constraints from unmodified program modules upon later re-analysis. As a consequence, they achieve substantial speed-ups in their interactive setting of a static debugger [Flanagan, 1997]. In a follow-up paper, Meunier et al. [2006] develop a set-based analysis for program modules with *contracts*. The contracts enable their analysis to statically detect and pin-point possible breaches (i.e., "blame" in the terminology of the contract literature).

Lee et al. [2002] construct 0CFA/m, a 0CFA variant extended to modules, which analyses a program's modules in order of dependence. The precision of their 0CFA/m is better than a standard 0CFA as it avoids some of the spurious flows of a standard 0CFA. In an accompanying technical report, they prove it sound with respect to *module-variant 0CFA*, an instantiation of Nielson and Nielson's infinitary collecting semantics [Nielson and Nielson, 1997]. Whereas the overall goal of our work agrees with that of Lee et al. [2002], it differs in that our reconstruction of Shivers's escape technique is a sound approximation of the base analysis, 0CFA. As such, it is still monovariant, whereas 0CFA/m is not.

The present paper and the above work focus on untyped programs, but others have investigated modular CFA for typed programs. Banerjee and Jensen [2003] developed a modular and polyvariant CFA based on intersection types for simply-typed programs with recursive function definitions. Like Shivers's untyped escape technique, it handles sub-expressions with free variables. Banerjee and Jensen's analysis is furthermore *compositional* in that the analysis of an expression can be calculated by combining the analysis results of its sub-expressions without re-analysing any of them. Reppy [2006] uses ML's type abstraction to improve the precision of a flow analysis by approximating the arguments of an abstract type with results computed earlier for the same abstract type. For a broader survey of CFA, we refer the reader to Midtgaard [2012].

Cousot and Cousot [2002] present four strategies for modular program analysis to debunk the myth that abstract interpretation is inherently a whole-program analysis technique. One of these is a *worst-case separate analysis*, which analyses external objects based on no information (i.e, $\top$ in the lattice). Shivers's escape technique goes beyond that approach, by keeping track of previously escaped procedures in the ESCAPED set.

8   Conclusion

Both abstract interpretation and (untyped) control-flow analysis are often presented as inherently whole-program analyses. By characterizing Shivers's CFA escape technique in terms of Galois connections, we show how to extend these to open programs. In doing so, we systematically derive an analysis which is provably sound by construction. Our soundness proof is modular in that the abstraction is structured as a combination of Galois connections. It is furthermore economical in that these Galois connections are well known from the literature. The structure of our approach indicates that staged proofs are a viable way forward for future higher-order analyses. After a base analysis is defined and proven sound, the escape technique can be added and the combination proven sound.

Whereas CPS allows us to focus on the task at hand, one can imagine a number of extensions. For one, our base CFA does not track the reachability of the individual serious expressions. Instead, it conservatively assumes that all sub-expressions are reachable. Adding an additional set to track reachability in the style of Midtgaard and Jensen [2008] and performing a subset abstraction thereof is straightforward. Another extension is to abstract external call-sites to **xcall** as outlined in Section 6 to pave the way for a modular kCFA soundness proof. In such a setting the modularized contours would consist of mixed strings of internal call sites and **xcall** tokens. Characterizing the flat-lattice sub-0CFA [Ashley and Dybvig, 1998] as an abstract interpretation and subsequently its open program extension would be another interesting endeavor.

Acknowledgement. We thank Peter A. Jonsson for comments on an earlier version of this paper.

References

Adams, M.D., Keep, A.W., Midtgaard, J., Might, M., Chauhan, A., Dybvig, R.K.: Flow-sensitive type recovery in linear-log time. In: Object-Oriented Programming, Systems, Languages and Applications (OOPSLA 2011), Portland, Oregon (October 2011)

Ashley, J.M.: Flexible and Practical Flow Analysis for Higher-Order Programming Languages. PhD thesis, Department of Computer Science, Indiana University, Bloomington, Indiana (May 1996)

Ashley, J.M., Dybvig, R.K.: A practical and flexible flow analysis for higher-order languages. ACM Transactions on Programming Languages and Systems 20(4), 845–868 (1998)

Banerjee, A., Jensen, T.: Modular control-flow analysis with rank 2 intersection types. Mathematical Structures in Computer Science 13(1), 87–124 (2003)

Cousot, P.: The calculational design of a generic abstract interpreter. In: Broy, M., Steinbrüggen, R. (eds.) Calculational System Design. NATO ASI Series. IOS Press, Amsterdam (1999)

Cousot, P., Cousot, R.: Systematic design of program analysis frameworks. In: Rosen, B.K. (ed.) Proc. of the Sixth Annual ACM Symposium on Principles of Programming Languages, San Antonio, Texas, pp. 269–282 (January 1979)

Cousot, P., Cousot, R.: Abstract interpretation and application to logic programs. Journal of Logic Programming 13(2-3), 103–179 (1992)

Cousot, P., Cousot, R.: Higher-order abstract interpretation (and application to comportment analysis generalizing strictness, termination, projection and PER analysis of functional languages). In: Bal, H. (ed.) Proc. of the Fifth IEEE International Conference on Computer Languages, Toulouse, France, pp. 95–112 (May 1994) (invited paper)

Cousot, P., Cousot, R.: Compositional and Inductive Semantic Definitions in Fixpoint, Equational, Constraint, Closure-condition, Rule-based and Game-Theoretic Form (Invited Paper). In: Wolper, P. (ed.) CAV 1995. LNCS, vol. 939, pp. 293–308. Springer, Heidelberg (1995)

Cousot, P., Cousot, R.: Abstract Interpretation of Algebraic Polynomial Systems. In: Johnson, M. (ed.) AMAST 1997. LNCS, vol. 1349, pp. 138–154. Springer, Heidelberg (1997)

Cousot, P., Cousot, R.: Modular Static Program Analysis. In: Horspool, R.N. (ed.) CC 2002. LNCS, vol. 2304, pp. 159–179. Springer, Heidelberg (2002)

Flanagan, C.: Effective Static Debugging via Componential Set-Based Analysis. PhD thesis, Rice University, Houston, Texas (May 1997)

Flanagan, C., Felleisen, M.: Componential set-based analysis. ACM Transactions on Programming Languages and Systems 21(2), 370–416 (1999)

Heintze, N.: Set-Based Program Analysis. PhD thesis, School of Computer Science, Carnegie Mellon University, Pittsburgh, Pennsylvania (October 1992)

Heintze, N., McAllester, D.: Linear-time subtransitive control flow analysis. In: Cytron, R.K. (ed.) Proc. of the ACM SIGPLAN 1997 Conference on Programming Languages Design and Implementation, Las Vegas, Nevada, pp. 261–272 (June 1997)

Lee, O., Yi, K., Paek, Y.: A proof method for the correctness of modularized 0CFA. Information Processing Letters 81(4), 179–185 (2002)

Meunier, P., Findler, R.B., Felleisen, M.: Modular set-based analysis from contracts. In: Peyton Jones, S. (ed.) Proc. of the 33rd Annual ACM Symposium on Principles of Programming Languages, Charleston, South Carolina, pp. 218–231 (January 2006)

Midtgaard, J.: Control-flow analysis of functional programs. ACM Computing Surveys 44(3) (2012)

Midtgaard, J., Jensen, T.: A Calculational Approach to Control-Flow Analysis by Abstract Interpretation. In: Alpuente, M., Vidal, G. (eds.) SAS 2008. LNCS, vol. 5079, pp. 347–362. Springer, Heidelberg (2008)

Midtgaard, J., Jensen, T.P.: Control-flow analysis of function calls and returns by abstract interpretation. Information and Computation 211, 49–76 (2012); a preliminary version was presented at the 2009 ACM SIGPLAN International Conference on Functional Programming (ICFP 2009)

Might, M.: Abstract Interpreters for Free. In: Cousot, R., Martel, M. (eds.) SAS 2010. LNCS, vol. 6337, pp. 407–421. Springer, Heidelberg (2010)

Nielson, F., Nielson, H.R.: Infinitary control flow analysis: a collecting semantics for closure analysis. In: Jones, N.D. (ed.) Proc. of the 24th Annual ACM Symposium on Principles of Programming Languages, Paris, France, pp. 332–345 (January 1997)

Nielson, F., Nielson, H.R., Hankin, C.: Principles of Program Analysis. Springer (1999)

Palsberg, J., Schwartzbach, M.I.: Safety analysis versus type inference. Information and Computation 118(1), 128–141 (1995)

Reppy, J.: Type-sensitive control-flow analysis. In: Kennedy, A., Pottier, F. (eds.) ML 2006: Proc. of the ACM SIGPLAN 2006 Workshop on ML, pp. 74–83 (September 2006)

Reynolds, J.C.: Definitional interpreters for higher-order programming languages. Higher-Order and Symbolic Computation 11(4), 363–397 (1998); reprinted from the proceedings of the 25th ACM National Conference (1972)

Serrano, M., Feeley, M.: Storage use analysis and its applications. In: Dybvig, R.K. (ed.) Proc. of the First ACM SIGPLAN International Conference on Functional Programming, Philadelphia, Pennsylvania, pp. 50–61 (May 1996)

Shivers, O.: Control-Flow Analysis of Higher-Order Languages or Taming Lambda. PhD thesis, School of Computer Science, Carnegie Mellon University, Pittsburgh, Pennsylvania, Technical Report CMU-CS-91-145 (May 1991)

Wand, M., Vaillancourt, D.: Relating models of backtracking. In: Fisher, K. (ed.) Proc. of the Ninth ACM SIGPLAN International Conference on Functional Programming (ICFP 2004), Snowbird, Utah, pp. 54–65 (September 2004)

Winskel, G.: Set theory for computer science. Unpublished lecture notes (2010), http://www.cl.cam.ac.uk/~gw104/STfCS2010.pdf

A   Calculating the Abstract Transfer Function

Let P_i, ρ_e, and ρ_i be given.

$$\alpha_\times \circ \alpha_\sim \circ (T(\gamma_\subset(P_i))) \circ \gamma_\sim \circ \gamma_\times(\rho_e, \rho_i) \qquad \text{(def. of } T)$$

$$= \alpha_\times \circ \alpha_\sim \Big(\bigsqcup_{\substack{(t_0\ t_1...t_n)^\ell \in \gamma_\subset(P_i) \\ (\lambda x_1...x_n.\ s)^{\ell'} \in E(t_0, \gamma_\sim \circ \gamma_\times(\rho_e, \rho_i))}} \gamma_\sim \circ \gamma_\times(\rho_e, \rho_i) \ \sqcup\ [\overline{x} \mapsto E(\overline{t}, \gamma_\sim \circ \gamma_\times(\rho_e, \rho_i))] \Big)$$

$$\qquad\qquad (\alpha_\times \circ \alpha_\sim \text{ a CJM})$$

$$= \bigsqcup_{\substack{(t_0\ t_1...t_n)^\ell \in \gamma_\subset(P_i) \\ (\lambda x_1...x_n.\ s)^{\ell'} \in E(t_0, \gamma_\sim \circ \gamma_\times(\rho_e, \rho_i))}} \alpha_\times \circ \alpha_\sim(\gamma_\sim \circ \gamma_\times(\rho_e, \rho_i) \ \sqcup\ [\overline{x} \mapsto E(\overline{t}, \gamma_\sim \circ \gamma_\times(\rho_e, \rho_i))])$$

$$\qquad\qquad (\alpha_\times \circ \alpha_\sim \text{ a CJM})$$

$$= \bigsqcup_{\substack{(t_0\ t_1...t_n)^\ell \in \gamma_\subset(P_i) \\ (\lambda x_1...x_n.\ s)^{\ell'} \in E(t_0, \gamma_\sim \circ \gamma_\times(\rho_e, \rho_i))}} \alpha_\times \circ \alpha_\sim \circ \gamma_\sim \circ \gamma_\times(\rho_e, \rho_i) \ \sqcup\ \alpha_\times \circ \alpha_\sim([\overline{x} \mapsto E(\overline{t}, \gamma_\sim \circ \gamma_\times(\rho_e, \rho_i))])$$

$$\qquad\qquad \text{(Galois surjection)}$$

$$= \bigsqcup_{\substack{(t_0\ t_1...t_n)^\ell \in \gamma_\subset(P_i) \\ (\lambda x_1...x_n.\ s)^{\ell'} \in E(t_0, \gamma_\sim \circ \gamma_\times(\rho_e, \rho_i))}} (\rho_e, \rho_i) \ \sqcup\ \alpha_\times \circ \alpha_\sim([\overline{x} \mapsto E(\overline{t}, \gamma_\sim \circ \gamma_\times(\rho_e, \rho_i))]) \qquad \text{(case analysis)}$$

$$= \bigsqcup_{\substack{(t_0\ t_1...t_n)^\ell \in \gamma_C(P_i) \\ (\lambda\, x_1...x_n.\ s)^{\ell'} \in E(t_0,\gamma_\sim \circ \gamma_\times(\rho_e,\rho_i))\cap XLam}} (\rho_e,\rho_i) \sqcup \alpha_\times \circ \alpha_\sim([\overline{x} \mapsto E(\overline{t},\gamma_\sim \circ \gamma_\times(\rho_e,\rho_i))])$$

$$\sqcup \bigsqcup_{\substack{(t_0\ t_1...t_n)^\ell \in \gamma_C(P_i) \\ (\lambda\, x_1...x_n.\ s)^{\ell'} \in E(t_0,\gamma_\sim \circ \gamma_\times(\rho_e,\rho_i))\cap ILam}} (\rho_e,\rho_i) \sqcup \alpha_\times \circ \alpha_\sim([\overline{x} \mapsto E(\overline{t},\gamma_\sim \circ \gamma_\times(\rho_e,\rho_i))]) \qquad \text{(def. of } \alpha_\sim)$$

$$= \bigsqcup_{\substack{(t_0\ t_1...t_n)^\ell \in \gamma_C(P_i) \\ (\lambda\, x_1...x_n.\ s)^{\ell'} \in E(t_0,\gamma_\sim \circ \gamma_\times(\rho_e,\rho_i))\cap XLam}} (\rho_e,\rho_i) \sqcup \alpha_\times([\overline{x} \mapsto E(\overline{t},\gamma_\sim \circ \gamma_\times(\rho_e,\rho_i))], \lambda x.\emptyset)$$

$$\sqcup \bigsqcup_{\substack{(t_0\ t_1...t_n)^\ell \in \gamma_C(P_i) \\ (\lambda\, x_1...x_n.\ s)^{\ell'} \in E(t_0,\gamma_\sim \circ \gamma_\times(\rho_e,\rho_i))\cap ILam}} (\rho_e,\rho_i) \sqcup \alpha_\times(\lambda x.\emptyset, [\overline{x} \mapsto E(\overline{t},\gamma_\sim \circ \gamma_\times(\rho_e,\rho_i))]) \qquad \text{(def. of } \alpha_\times)$$

$$= \bigsqcup_{\substack{(t_0\ t_1...t_n)^\ell \in \gamma_C(P_i) \\ (\lambda\, x_1...x_n.\ s)^{\ell'} \in E(t_0,\gamma_\sim \circ \gamma_\times(\rho_e,\rho_i))\cap XLam}} (\rho_e,\rho_i) \sqcup (\alpha_@ \circ \alpha_\cup([\overline{x} \mapsto E(\overline{t},\gamma_\sim \circ \gamma_\times(\rho_e,\rho_i))]), \alpha.(\lambda x.\emptyset))$$

$$\sqcup \bigsqcup_{\substack{(t_0\ t_1...t_n)^\ell \in \gamma_C(P_i) \\ (\lambda\, x_1...x_n.\ s)^{\ell'} \in E(t_0,\gamma_\sim \circ \gamma_\times(\rho_e,\rho_i))\cap ILam}} (\rho_e,\rho_i) \sqcup (\alpha_@ \circ \alpha_\cup(\lambda x.\emptyset), \alpha.([\overline{x} \mapsto E(\overline{t},\gamma_\sim \circ \gamma_\times(\rho_e,\rho_i))]))$$

$$\text{(def. of } \alpha_\cup)$$

$$= \bigsqcup_{\substack{(t_0\ t_1...t_n)^\ell \in \gamma_C(P_i) \\ (\lambda\, x_1...x_n.\ s)^{\ell'} \in E(t_0,\gamma_\sim \circ \gamma_\times(\rho_e,\rho_i))\cap XLam}} (\rho_e,\rho_i) \sqcup (\alpha_@(\bigcup_{j\in[1;n]} E(t_j,\gamma_\sim \circ \gamma_\times(\rho_e,\rho_i))), \alpha.(\lambda x.\emptyset))$$

$$\sqcup \bigsqcup_{\substack{(t_0\ t_1...t_n)^\ell \in \gamma_C(P_i) \\ (\lambda\, x_1...x_n.\ s)^{\ell'} \in E(t_0,\gamma_\sim \circ \gamma_\times(\rho_e,\rho_i))\cap ILam}} (\rho_e,\rho_i) \sqcup (\alpha_@(\emptyset), \alpha.([\overline{x} \mapsto E(\overline{t},\gamma_\sim \circ \gamma_\times(\rho_e,\rho_i))])) \qquad (\alpha_@ \text{ a CJM})$$

$$= \bigsqcup_{\substack{(t_0\ t_1...t_n)^\ell \in \gamma_C(P_i) \\ (\lambda\, x_1...x_n.\ s)^{\ell'} \in E(t_0,\gamma_\sim \circ \gamma_\times(\rho_e,\rho_i))\cap XLam}} (\rho_e,\rho_i) \sqcup (\bigcup_{j\in[1;n]} \alpha_@ \circ E(t_j,\gamma_\sim \circ \gamma_\times(\rho_e,\rho_i)), \alpha.(\lambda x.\emptyset))$$

$$\sqcup \bigsqcup_{\substack{(t_0\ t_1...t_n)^\ell \in \gamma_C(P_i) \\ (\lambda\, x_1...x_n.\ s)^{\ell'} \in E(t_0,\gamma_\sim \circ \gamma_\times(\rho_e,\rho_i))\cap ILam}} (\rho_e,\rho_i) \sqcup (\alpha_@(\emptyset), \alpha.([\overline{x} \mapsto E(\overline{t},\gamma_\sim \circ \gamma_\times(\rho_e,\rho_i))])) \qquad \text{(def. of } \alpha.)$$

$$= \bigsqcup_{\substack{(t_0\ t_1...t_n)^\ell \in \gamma_C(P_i) \\ (\lambda\, x_1...x_n.\ s)^{\ell'} \in E(t_0,\gamma_\sim \circ \gamma_\times(\rho_e,\rho_i))\cap XLam}} (\rho_e,\rho_i) \sqcup (\bigcup_{j\in[1;n]} \alpha_@ \circ E(t_j,\gamma_\sim \circ \gamma_\times(\rho_e,\rho_i)), \lambda x.\alpha_@(\emptyset))$$

$$\sqcup \bigsqcup_{\substack{(t_0\ t_1...t_n)^\ell \in \gamma_C(P_i) \\ (\lambda\, x_1...x_n.\ s)^{\ell'} \in E(t_0,\gamma_\sim \circ \gamma_\times(\rho_e,\rho_i))\cap ILam}} (\rho_e,\rho_i) \sqcup (\alpha_@(\emptyset), [\overline{x} \mapsto \alpha_@ \circ E(\overline{t},\gamma_\sim \circ \gamma_\times(\rho_e,\rho_i))]) \qquad \text{(Lemma 1)}$$

$$= \bigsqcup_{\substack{(t_0\ t_1...t_n)^\ell \in \gamma_C(P_i) \\ (\lambda\, x_1...x_n.\ s)^{\ell'} \in E(t_0,\gamma_\sim \circ \gamma_\times(\rho_e,\rho_i))\cap XLam}} (\rho_e,\rho_i) \sqcup (\bigcup_{j\in[1;n]} \widehat{E}(t_j,\rho_e,\rho_i), \lambda x.\alpha_@(\emptyset))$$

$$\sqcup \bigsqcup_{\substack{(t_0\ t_1...t_n)^\ell \in \gamma_C(P_i) \\ (\lambda\, x_1...x_n.\ s)^{\ell'} \in E(t_0,\gamma_\sim \circ \gamma_\times(\rho_e,\rho_i))\cap ILam}} (\rho_e,\rho_i) \sqcup (\alpha_@(\emptyset), [\overline{x} \mapsto \widehat{E}(\overline{t},\rho_e,\rho_i)]) \qquad \text{(def. of } \alpha_@)$$

$$= \bigsqcup_{\substack{(t_0\ t_1...t_n)^\ell \in \gamma_\subset(P_i) \\ (\lambda\, x_1...x_n.\ s)^{\ell'} \in E(t_0, \gamma_\sim \circ \gamma_\times(\rho_e, \rho_i)) \cap XLam}} (\rho_e, \rho_i) \sqcup (\bigsqcup_{j \in [1;n]} \widehat{E}(t_j, \rho_e, \rho_i), \lambda x.\emptyset)$$

$$\sqcup \bigsqcup_{\substack{(t_0\ t_1...t_n)^\ell \in \gamma_\subset(P_i) \\ (\lambda\, x_1...x_n.\ s)^{\ell'} \in E(t_0, \gamma_\sim \circ \gamma_\times(\rho_e, \rho_i)) \cap ILam}} (\rho_e, \rho_i) \sqcup (\emptyset, [\overline{x} \mapsto \widehat{E}(\overline{t}, \rho_e, \rho_i)]) \qquad \text{(def. of } \sqcup)$$

$$= \bigsqcup_{\substack{(t_0\ t_1...t_n)^\ell \in \gamma_\subset(P_i) \\ (\lambda\, x_1...x_n.\ s)^{\ell'} \in E(t_0, \gamma_\sim \circ \gamma_\times(\rho_e, \rho_i)) \cap XLam}} (\rho_e \cup \bigsqcup_{j \in [1;n]} \widehat{E}(t_j, \rho_e, \rho_i), \rho_i)$$

$$\sqcup \bigsqcup_{\substack{(t_0\ t_1...t_n)^\ell \in \gamma_\subset(P_i) \\ (\lambda\, x_1...x_n.\ s)^{\ell'} \in E(t_0, \gamma_\sim \circ \gamma_\times(\rho_e, \rho_i)) \cap ILam}} (\rho_e, \rho_i \dot{\cup} [\overline{x} \mapsto \widehat{E}(\overline{t}, \rho_e, \rho_i)]) \qquad \text{(def. of } \alpha_@)$$

$$= \bigsqcup_{\substack{(t_0\ t_1...t_n)^\ell \in \gamma_\subset(P_i) \\ (\lambda\, x_1...x_n.\ s)^{\ell'} \in E(t_0, \gamma_\sim \circ \gamma_\times(\rho_e, \rho_i)) \cap XLam}} (\rho_e \cup \bigsqcup_{j \in [1;n]} \widehat{E}(t_j, \rho_e, \rho_i), \rho_i)$$

$$\sqcup \bigsqcup_{\substack{(t_0\ t_1...t_n)^\ell \in \gamma_\subset(P_i) \\ (\lambda\, x_1...x_n.\ s)^{\ell'} \in \alpha_@ \circ E(t_0, \gamma_\sim \circ \gamma_\times(\rho_e, \rho_i))}} (\rho_e, \rho_i \dot{\cup} [\overline{x} \mapsto \widehat{E}(\overline{t}, \rho_e, \rho_i)]) \qquad \text{(Lemma 1)}$$

$$= \bigsqcup_{\substack{(t_0\ t_1...t_n)^\ell \in \gamma_\subset(P_i) \\ (\lambda\, x_1...x_n.\ s)^{\ell'} \in E(t_0, \gamma_\sim \circ \gamma_\times(\rho_e, \rho_i)) \cap XLam}} (\rho_e \cup \bigsqcup_{j \in [1;n]} \widehat{E}(t_j, \rho_e, \rho_i), \rho_i)$$

$$\sqcup \bigsqcup_{\substack{(t_0\ t_1...t_n)^\ell \in \gamma_\subset(P_i) \\ (\lambda\, x_1...x_n.\ s)^{\ell'} \in \widehat{E}(t_0, \rho_e, \rho_i)}} (\rho_e, \rho_i \dot{\cup} [\overline{x} \mapsto \widehat{E}(\overline{t}, \rho_e, \rho_i)]) \qquad (\alpha_@ \text{ monotone})$$

$$\sqsubseteq \bigsqcup_{\substack{(t_0\ t_1...t_n)^\ell \in \gamma_\subset(P_i) \\ \mathbf{xproc} \in \alpha_@ \circ E(t_0, \gamma_\sim \circ \gamma_\times(\rho_e, \rho_i))}} (\rho_e \cup \bigsqcup_{j \in [1;n]} \widehat{E}(t_j, \rho_e, \rho_i), \rho_i)$$

$$\sqcup \bigsqcup_{\substack{(t_0\ t_1...t_n)^\ell \in \gamma_\subset(P_i) \\ (\lambda\, x_1...x_n.\ s)^{\ell'} \in \widehat{E}(t_0, \rho_e, \rho_i)}} (\rho_e, \rho_i \dot{\cup} [\overline{x} \mapsto \widehat{E}(\overline{t}, \rho_e, \rho_i)]) \qquad \text{(Lemma 1)}$$

$$= \bigsqcup_{\substack{(t_0\ t_1...t_n)^\ell \in \gamma_\subset(P_i) \\ \mathbf{xproc} \in \widehat{E}(t_0, \rho_e, \rho_i)}} (\rho_e \cup \bigsqcup_{j \in [1;n]} \widehat{E}(t_j, \rho_e, \rho_i), \rho_i)$$

$$\sqcup \bigsqcup_{\substack{(t_0\ t_1...t_n)^\ell \in \gamma_\subset(P_i) \\ (\lambda\, x_1...x_n.\ s)^{\ell'} \in \widehat{E}(t_0, \rho_e, \rho_i)}} (\rho_e, \rho_i \dot{\cup} [\overline{x} \mapsto \widehat{E}(\overline{t}, \rho_e, \rho_i)]) \qquad \text{(Galois connection)}$$

$$= \bigsqcup_{\substack{\alpha_\subset(\{(t_0\ t_1...t_n)^\ell\}) \subseteq P_i \\ \mathbf{xproc} \in \widehat{E}(t_0, \rho_e, \rho_i)}} (\rho_e \cup \bigsqcup_{j \in [1;n]} \widehat{E}(t_j, \rho_e, \rho_i), \rho_i)$$

$$\sqcup \bigsqcup_{\substack{\alpha_\subset(\{(t_0\ t_1...t_n)^\ell\}) \subseteq P_i \\ (\lambda\, x_1...x_n.\ s)^{\ell'} \in \widehat{E}(t_0, \rho_e, \rho_i)}} (\rho_e, \rho_i \dot{\cup} [\overline{x} \mapsto \widehat{E}(\overline{t}, \rho_e, \rho_i)]) \qquad \text{(def. of } \alpha_\subset)$$

$$= \bigsqcup_{\substack{\{(t_0 \ t_1 \ldots t_n)^\ell\} \subseteq XSexp \\ \mathbf{xproc} \in \widehat{E}(t_0, \rho_e, \rho_i)}} (\rho_e \cup \bigcup_{j \in [1;n]} \widehat{E}(t_j, \rho_e, \rho_i), \rho_i)$$

$$\sqcup \bigsqcup_{\substack{\{(t_0 \ t_1 \ldots t_n)^\ell\} \subseteq P_i \\ \mathbf{xproc} \in \widehat{E}(t_0, \rho_e, \rho_i)}} (\rho_e \cup \bigcup_{j \in [1;n]} \widehat{E}(t_j, \rho_e, \rho_i), \rho_i)$$

$$\sqcup \bigsqcup_{\substack{\{(t_0 \ t_1 \ldots t_n)^\ell\} \subseteq XSexp \\ (\lambda x_1 \ldots x_n . \ s)^{\ell'} \in \widehat{E}(t_0, \rho_e, \rho_i)}} (\rho_e, \rho_i \ \dot{\cup} \ [\overline{x} \mapsto \widehat{E}(\overline{t}, \rho_e, \rho_i)])$$

$$\sqcup \bigsqcup_{\substack{\{(t_0 \ t_1 \ldots t_n)^\ell\} \subseteq P_i \\ (\lambda x_1 \ldots x_n . \ s)^{\ell'} \in \widehat{E}(t_0, \rho_e, \rho_i)}} (\rho_e, \rho_i \ \dot{\cup} \ [\overline{x} \mapsto \widehat{E}(\overline{t}, \rho_e, \rho_i)]) \qquad \text{(Lemma 2)}$$

$$\sqsubseteq \bigsqcup_{\substack{\{(t_0 \ t_1 \ldots t_n)^\ell\} \subseteq XSexp \\ \mathbf{xproc} \in (\rho_e \cup \{\mathbf{xproc}\} \cup Toplevel)}} (\rho_e \cup (\rho_e \cup \{\mathbf{xproc}\} \cup Toplevel), \rho_i)$$

$$\sqcup \bigsqcup_{\substack{\{(t_0 \ t_1 \ldots t_n)^\ell\} \subseteq P_i \\ \mathbf{xproc} \in \widehat{E}(t_0, \rho_e, \rho_i)}} (\rho_e \cup \bigcup_{j \in [1;n]} \widehat{E}(t_j, \rho_e, \rho_i), \rho_i)$$

$$\sqcup \bigsqcup_{\substack{\{(t_0 \ t_1 \ldots t_n)^\ell\} \subseteq XSexp \\ (\lambda x_1 \ldots x_n . \ s)^{\ell'} \in (\rho_e \cup \{\mathbf{xproc}\} \cup Toplevel)}} (\rho_e, \rho_i \ \dot{\cup} \ [\overline{x} \mapsto (\rho_e \cup \{\mathbf{xproc}\} \cup Toplevel)])$$

$$\sqcup \bigsqcup_{\substack{\{(t_0 \ t_1 \ldots t_n)^\ell\} \subseteq P_i \\ (\lambda x_1 \ldots x_n . \ s)^{\ell'} \in \widehat{E}(t_0, \rho_e, \rho_i)}} (\rho_e, \rho_i \ \dot{\cup} \ [\overline{x} \mapsto \widehat{E}(\overline{t}, \rho_e, \rho_i)]) \qquad \text{(simplify)}$$

$$= (\rho_e \cup \{\mathbf{xproc}\} \cup Toplevel, \rho_i)$$

$$\sqcup \bigsqcup_{\substack{\{(t_0 \ t_1 \ldots t_n)^\ell\} \subseteq P_i \\ \mathbf{xproc} \in \widehat{E}(t_0, \rho_e, \rho_i)}} (\rho_e \cup \bigcup_{j \in [1;n]} \widehat{E}(t_j, \rho_e, \rho_i), \rho_i)$$

$$\sqcup \bigsqcup_{(\lambda x_1 \ldots x_n . \ s)^{\ell} \in \rho_e \cup Toplevel} (\rho_e, \rho_i \ \dot{\cup} \ [\overline{x} \mapsto (\rho_e \cup \{\mathbf{xproc}\} \cup Toplevel)])$$

$$\sqcup \bigsqcup_{\substack{\{(t_0 \ t_1 \ldots t_n)^\ell\} \subseteq P_i \\ (\lambda x_1 \ldots x_n . \ s)^{\ell'} \in \widehat{E}(t_0, \rho_e, \rho_i)}} (\rho_e, \rho_i \ \dot{\cup} \ [\overline{x} \mapsto \widehat{E}(\overline{t}, \rho_e, \rho_i)])$$

Modular Heap Analysis for Higher-Order Programs

Ravichandhran Madhavan, G. Ramalingam, and Kapil Vaswani

Microsoft Research, India
{t-rakand,grama,kapilv}@microsoft.com

Abstract. We consider the problem of computing summaries for procedures that soundly capture the effect of calling a procedure on program state that includes a mutable heap. Such summaries are the basis for a compositional program analysis and key to scalability. Higher order procedures contain callbacks (indirect calls to procedures specified by callers). The use of such callbacks and higher-order features are becoming increasingly widespread and commonplace even in mainstream imperative languages such as $C^\sharp$ and Java. Such callbacks complicate compositional analysis and the construction of procedure summaries. We present an abstract-interpretation based approach to computing summaries (of a procedure's effect on a mutable heap) in the presence of callbacks in a simple imperative language. We present an empirical evaluation of our approach.

1 Introduction

In this paper, we present a compositional approach to heap analysis for an imperative language with dynamic memory allocation and higher order functions (or callbacks). Modular/compositional program analysis [1] is a key technique for scaling static analysis to large programs. Our interest is in techniques to compute a *summary* for each procedure that approximates its relational semantics (relating input states to output states). A significant benefit of this approach is that libraries can be analyzed once and the computed library summaries reused for any program that uses the library. This is particularly significant since modern applications rely on large libraries and frameworks.

A typical approach to computing procedure summaries is to first construct a call-graph and then analyze procedures in the call-graph in a bottom-up fashion. Any collection of mutually recursive procedures is iteratively analysed until their summaries reach a fixed point. This approach is feasible when the call-graph can be constructed easily and precisely, e.g., for languages with only direct calls. However, most modern languages permit *indirect* calls (virtual methods, delegates, etc.), which pose several challenges. Determining the targets of indirect calls (which depend on runtime values) is itself a complex analysis, and depends upon the results of heap analysis. One possibility is to integrate heap analysis and the call-graph construction into a single analysis. However, the direct way of doing this gives up on modularity and resorts to a top-down whole-program analysis. An alternative is to use a less precise call-graph construction technique that does not require heap analysis: e.g., type-based techniques such as Class Hierarchy Analysis (CHA). This approach too suffers from several drawbacks.

(a) A library procedure may *call back* a procedure defined by a client of the library. This means that a conservative call-graph cannot be constructed for a library *independent*

A. Miné and D. Schmidt (Eds.): SAS 2012, LNCS 7460, pp. 370–387, 2012.

of its client. Hence, the library cannot be analyzed independent of its client. Thus, we are again forced to resort to a whole-program analysis of each application separately.

(b) A conventional call-graph is necessarily context-insensitive. it identifies the possible targets of an indirect call in a procedure, but the targets actually called may vary with calling contexts. A modular analysis, based on such a call-graph, will compute a procedure summary that is context-insensitive (in terms of precision).

(c) A type-based call-graph can be very imprecise. Assuming that a delegate call, in $C^\sharp$, can invoke any delegate (essentially a lambda expression) defined in the program can be disastrous. The imprecision of type-based resolution also leads to significant scalability problems, especially with common methods such as equals or hashcode and common interfaces such as iterators.

Our Approach. Computing summaries describing heap effects is challenging even in the absence of indirect calls, as the summary must capture the effects of a procedure on the heap, without making assumptions about the aliasing in the input heap. Previously, we had presented an abstract-interpretation approach to computing such *first-order heap-effect summaries* (based on prior work by Whaley, Salcianu, and Rinard) [11,8,4]. In this paper, we extend this approach to deal with callbacks and higher-order procedures modularly, by constructing *higher-order heap-effect summaries*. The intuition behind our approach is informally described in Section 2.

The key and first step is to formulate a compositional concrete semantics for a language with higher order procedures in a form suitable for abstraction, as shown in Section 3. We then mimic the same structure to define an abstract semantics for procedures and libraries (Sections 4 and 5), which serves as the basis for our analysis, which can be applied to a library independent of its client(s).

We have implemented our analysis for $C^\sharp$ and evaluated it on a collection of large applications (Section 6). We find that indirect method calls are a widely used feature of modern languages. We also find that call graphs based on our approach are significantly more precise and compact compared to conventional class hierarchy analysis. As a result, our heap analysis is able to scale to larger applications.

The ideas behind our approach are similar to those used in analyses presented by Vivien *et al.* [10] and Lattner *et al.* [3]. However, neither of these analyses has a theoretical formulation or a correctness proof. We believe that these two seemingly different analyses can be seen as instances of our abstract interpretation formulation. A comparison of our work with these analyses and other related work appears in Section 7.

2   An Informal Overview

We now present an informal overview of how we extend our previous approach [4] to handle higher-order procedures. The previous approach computes a shape-graph like summary for first-order procedures that can be concretized as a transformer of concrete heap graphs. We refer to these representations as transformer graphs. Let τ range over such transformer graphs. We present a formal definition of transformer graphs later, as the intuition behind the extension to higher-order procedures does not depend on this.

Representing Higher-Order Summaries. The basic idea is to extend the summary representation to capture information about callbacks that can occur, delaying instantiating

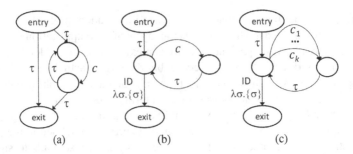

Fig. 1. Informal interpretation of summary

the effects of the callback until sufficient context information is available to determine the actual procedure(s) that are called, using first-order summaries (i.e., transformer graphs) to represent code-fragments that are free of unresolved (indirect) calls.

Consider a procedure whose body is of the form $S_1; S_2; S_3$, where S_1 and S_3 are free of unresolved calls, and S_2 consists of a single unresolved call. In this case, we can compute graph transformers τ_1 and τ_3 that are abstractions of S_1 and S_3 respectively, and utilize a symbolic summary of the form $\tau_1; S_2; \tau_3$ for the procedure. While this is basic idea behind our approach, we refine this idea in several ways.

Exploiting Local Context. Though we don't know the exact side-effects of the indirect call in S_2, we can restrict the scope of these side-effects: the call can affect only the part of the heap reachable via the call parameters and global variables. This observation lets us decompose τ_3 into two parts: τ_3^ℓ, concerning locations that cannot be modified by the call in S_2, and τ_3^g, concerning locations that could be modified by the call. We can then write the summary as $\tau_1; S_2; \tau_3^\ell; \tau_3^g$, which simplifies to $\tau_1 \circ \tau_3^\ell; S_2; \tau_3^g$. Note that the composition "$\tau_1 \circ \tau_3^\ell$" can be computed once, even before the target of the indirect call is determined, simplifying the summary.

A Flow-Insensitive Abstraction. In general, when the procedure contains many unresolved calls, this approach will lead to a summary representation that looks like a control-flow-graph where every vertex (other than entry/exit vertices) represents a call-statement, and every edge is annotated with a transformer graph. For efficiency reasons, we utilize a more aggressive, but less precise, flow-insensitive abstraction that uses a single graph transformer τ (instead of one per edge) and a set of call-statements w (thus forgetting the control-flow between call-statements). For our previous example, this produces a summary $(\tau, \{S_2\})$, where τ conservatively approximates both $\tau_1 \circ \tau_3^\ell$ and τ_3^g. Informally, a summary $(\tau, \{c\})$ can be interpreted as the control-flow-graph shown in Fig. 1(a). Since the transformers τ we use are isotonic (i.e., τ is a sound approximation of the identity relation), this interpretation can be simplified to the one shown in Fig. 1(b), which is the basis for our subsequent formalization. A summary $(\tau, \{c_1, \cdots, c_k\})$ is interpreted as shown in Fig. 1(c).

Computing Higher Order Summaries. We present an algorithm that constructs the desired transformer τ using a Sharir-Pnueli style interprocedural analysis. We present details of this analysis later, but list some of the key components of the analysis here.

Intraprocedural Analysis. We present an abstract semantics for primitive statements that maps an input summary (τ, ω) to an output summary (τ', ω').

Direct and Indirect Calls. The abstract semantics of a direct call statement is defined using a *composition* operator that combines an input summary (τ_r, ω_r) and the called procedure's summary (τ_e, ω_e) into an output summary, after accounting for parameter passing. Initially, an indirect call c is handled in a straightforward fashion, by updating the input summary to include c as an unresolved call. However, as the analysis proceeds, sufficient context information may become available to resolve indirect calls: e.g., when a procedure summary containing unresolved call is instantiated at a particular call-site. Our analysis identifies indirect calls whose targets can be resolved. If a resolved target's summary is available, then it is instantiated. This is an iterative process, as instantiating a resolved target's summary may create further opportunities for resolving more indirect calls.

Eliminating Indirect Calls. Completely resolving an indirect call can be a multi-stage process. At intermediate stages, we might be able to identify some of the potential targets of an indirect call, but cannot be sure whether all possible targets of the indirect call have been identified. Eventually, sufficient context information may become available to let us determine that all possible targets of the indirect call have been identified. At this point, the indirect call can be dropped from the summary.

3   The Language and Its Concrete Semantics

Syntax. A library (LP,LL) consists of a set of procedures LP and a set of nested libraries LL (denoting libraries it is linked with). A procedure P consists of a name (belonging to the set *Procs*) and a control-flow graph, with an entry vertex $entry(\textsf{P})$ and an exit vertex $exit(\textsf{P})$. The entry vertex has no predecessor and the exit vertex has no successor. Every edge of the control-flow graph is labelled by a primitive statement. The set of primitive statements are shown in Fig. 2. We use $u \xrightarrow{S} v$ to indicate an edge in the control-flow graph from vertex u to vertex v labelled by statement S. In the sequel, we abuse notation and do not distinguish between a procedure and its name, e.g. if P is a procedure then P also denotes its name.

We use "function pointers" as the primitive for indirect calls. The statement "$x = \&\textsf{P}$" assigns the address of procedure P to variable x, and the indirect call "$(*x)(a_1, \cdots, a_k)$" calls the procedure pointed to by x. This is sufficient to model common indirect call mechanisms such as virtual functions and delegates. A closure c can be realized as a pair consisting of a function pointer $c.f$ and a data pointer $c.d$, and the call to c modelled as "$(*(c.f))(c.d)$".

Concrete Semantics Domain. Let *Vars* denote a set of identifiers used as variable names, partitioned into the following disjoint sets: the set of global variables *Globals*, the set of local variables *Locals* (assumed to be the same for every procedure), and the set of formal parameter variables *Params* (assumed to be the same for every procedure). Let *Fields* denote a set of identifiers used as field names. We use a simple language with only two primitive types: pointers to heap objects and function-pointers.

We use a graph-based representation for the concrete state. We use a level of indirection in representing function-pointer variables: the variable stores a procedure-id (identifying a procedure), and a separate table maps the procedure-id to its semantic value (as formalized below). We use procedure-ids, instead of procedure names, to ensure uniqueness of ids, for reasons explained soon.

Let N_c be an unbounded set of heap locations. Let PV_c be an unbounded set of values, disjoint from N_c, used as procedure-ids. A concrete (points-to) graph $g \in \mathbb{G}_c$ is a triple (V, E, σ), where $V \subseteq N_c \cup PV_c$ represents the set of objects in the heap, $E \subseteq (V \cap N_c) \times \textit{Fields} \times V$ represents values of pointer fields in heap objects, and $\sigma \in \Sigma_c = \textit{Vars} \mapsto V$ represents the values of program variables. N_c includes a special element $\textit{null}$. Variables and fields of new objects are initialized to $\textit{null}$.

Let $\mathcal{F}_c = \mathbb{G}_c \mapsto 2^{\mathbb{G}_c}$ be the set of functions that map a concrete graph to a set of concrete graphs. An element of $\mathcal{F}_c$ may also be thought of as a (binary) relation on concrete graphs. The semantics of statements (and procedures), in the absence of indirect calls, can be described using elements of $\mathcal{F}_c$.

We now enrich the domain to support indirect procedure calls. We define two domains $\mathcal{P}_c$ and $\mathcal{T}_c$ recursively as follows: $\mathcal{T}_c = PV_c \hookrightarrow \mathcal{P}_c$ and $\mathcal{P}_c = \mathbb{G}_c \times \mathcal{T}_c \to_i 2^{\mathbb{G}_c \times \mathcal{T}_c}$. An element of $\mathcal{T}_c$ is a partial function, binding procedure-ids to their semantics. (We may think of this as a simple "virtual-function table".) The concrete state is enriched by such a table. A procedure uses such a table to dispatch indirect calls (including callbacks). But the procedure may also update the table (e.g., if it returns a procedure-value). However, the procedure can only *add* new entries to the table, but not modify pre-existing entries. The construct $\to_i$ includes only such functions. A function f in $\mathbb{G}_c \times \mathcal{T}_c \to 2^{\mathbb{G}_c \times \mathcal{T}_c}$ is defined to be in $\mathbb{G}_c \times \mathcal{T}_c \to_i 2^{\mathbb{G}_c \times \mathcal{T}_c}$ iff: $(g', t') \in f(g, t)$ implies $\forall n \in \text{dom}(t).t'(n) = t(n)$. The domain $\mathcal{P}_c$ generalizes $\mathcal{F}_c$ and is used to give semantics to higher-order statements and procedures. We define $\mathcal{L}_c$ to be $\textit{Procs} \hookrightarrow \mathcal{P}_c$.

We define a partial order $\sqsubseteq_c$ on $\mathcal{F}_c$ as: $f_a \sqsubseteq_c f_b$ iff $\forall g \in \mathbb{G}_c.f_a(g) \subseteq f_b(g)$. Let $\sqcup_c$ denote the corresponding least upper bound (join) operation defined by: $f_a \sqcup_c f_b = \lambda g.f_a(g) \cup f_b(g)$. For any $f \in \mathcal{F}_c$, we define $\hat{f} : 2^{\mathbb{G}_c} \mapsto 2^{\mathbb{G}_c}$ by: $\hat{f}(G) = \cup_{g \in G} f(g)$. We define the relational composition of two elements in $\mathcal{F}_c$ as: $f_a \circ f_b = \lambda g.\hat{f}_b(f_a(g))$. We extend these operators to the domain $\mathcal{P}_c$, $\mathcal{T}_c$ and $\mathcal{L}_c$ following the structure of their recursive definitions. E.g, $\sqsubseteq_c$ is extended as follows: for any $p_1, p_2 \in \mathcal{P}_c, p_1 \sqsubseteq_c p_2$ iff $(g', t') \in p_1(g, t) \Rightarrow \exists (g'', t'') \in p_2(g, t)$ s.t. $g' = g'', t' \sqsubseteq_c t''$ where $t_1 \sqsubseteq_c t_2$ iff $\forall n \in \text{dom}(t_1), t_1(n) \sqsubseteq_c t_2(n)$. For any $l_1, l_2 \in \mathcal{L}_c, l_1 \sqsubseteq_c l_2$ iff $\forall P \in \text{dom}(l_1), l_1(P) \sqsubseteq_c l_2(P)$.

Concrete Semantics. A primitive statement S has a semantics $[\![S]\!]_c \in \mathcal{P}_c$, as shown in Fig. 2. The semantics of call statements and the semantics of the procedures and libraries that contain them are mutually interdependent. Hence, we parameterize the semantics of call statements with a parameter AP, defined as follows. Let (LP, LL) be a library consisting of a set of procedures LP and a set of nested libraries LL. Let LLP denote the set of all procedures in LL. A direct call in the library can only reference procedures defined in LP or in LL. The semantics of (LP, LL) is defined as the least fixed point of a collection of equations (defined below) which contains a variable φ_P for every procedure P in LP. Define the partial function AP as follows: AP maps every $P \in LP$ to variable φ_P, and it maps every $P \in LLP$ to its semantics $[\![P]\!]_c$. For simplicity, we assume

Statement S	Concrete semantics $[\![S]\!]_c\,((\mathsf{V},\mathsf{E},\sigma),t)$
$v_1 = v_2$	$\{\,((\mathsf{V},\mathsf{E},\sigma[v_1 \mapsto \sigma(v_2)]),t)\,\}$
$v = new\ C$	$\{\,((\mathsf{V}\cup\{n\},\mathsf{E}\cup\{n\}\times Fields\times\{null\},\sigma[v\mapsto n]),t) \mid n\in N_c\setminus\mathsf{V}\,\}$
$v_1.f = v_2$	$\{\,((\mathsf{V},\{\langle u,l,v\rangle\in\mathsf{E}\mid u\neq\sigma(v_1)\vee l\neq f\}\cup\{\langle\sigma(v_1),f,\sigma(v_2)\rangle\},\sigma),t)\,\}$
$v_1 = v_2.f$	$\{\,((\mathsf{V},\mathsf{E},\sigma[v_1\mapsto n]),t) \mid \langle\sigma(v_2),f,n\rangle\in\mathsf{E}\,\}$
$v = \&\mathsf{P}$	**if** $\mathsf{P}\in dom(\mathsf{AP})$ **then** $\{\,((\mathsf{V},\mathsf{E},\sigma[v\mapsto n]),t[n\mapsto\mathsf{AP}(\mathsf{P})]) \mid n\notin dom(t)\,\}$ **else** $\{\}$
$\mathsf{P}(v_1,\cdots,v_k)$	**if** $\mathsf{P}\in dom(\mathsf{AP})$ **then** $Call_S(\mathsf{AP}(\mathsf{P}))$ **else** $\{\}$
$(*v)(v_1,\cdots,v_k)$	**if** $\sigma(v)\in dom(t)$ **then** $Call_S(t(\sigma(v))))$ **else** $\{\}$

Fig. 2. Statements in our language and their concrete semantics

that procedure names are unique across LP and LL. We can eliminate this assumption by using unique qualified names for procedures. However, the semantics presented is valid for all clients, including those that may reuse procedure names used in LP or LL. To avoid name-capture when control flows back and forth between a client and the library via callbacks, we identify procedures using unique ids generated at runtime, as illustrated by the semantics of the statement "$v = \&\mathsf{P}$". These unique ids are used as indices into the "virtual function table" t.

A direct call to procedure P or taking the address of procedure P is valid only if $\mathsf{P}\in dom(\mathsf{AP})$. In this case, the semantics of the statement is defined in terms of $\mathsf{AP}(\mathsf{P})$. An indirect call, however, may reference other procedures, e.g., such as those defined by clients of the libraries. The run-time parameter t is used to resolve indirect calls. Given $f\in\mathcal{P}_c$, $Call_S(f)$ is essentially the same as f, but accounts for parameter passing and pushing/popping activation records and is defined in the Appendix.

Semantics of Procedures. We now define the concrete summary semantics $[\![\mathsf{P}]\!]_c\in\mathcal{P}_c$ for every procedure P in LP using the following equations, in the style of Sharir-Pnueli. For every procedure P in LP, we introduce a new variable φ_u for every vertex in the control-flow graph (of P) and a new variable $\varphi_{u,v}$ for every edge $u\to v$ in the control-flow graph. We also introduce a variable φ_P. The semantics is defined as the least fixed point of the following set of equations. The value of φ_u in the least fixed point is a function that maps any concrete state (g,t) to the set of concrete states that arise at program point u when the procedure containing u is executed with an initial state (g,t). Similarly, $\varphi_{u,v}$ captures the states after the execution of the statement labelling edge $u\to v$.

$$\varphi_v = \lambda(g,t).\,\{(g,t)\} \qquad\qquad v \text{ is an entry vertex} \qquad (1)$$

$$\varphi_v = \bigsqcup_c\{\varphi_{u,v}\mid u\to v\} \qquad\quad v \text{ is not an entry vertex} \qquad (2)$$

$$\varphi_{u,v} = \varphi_u\circ[\![S]\!]_c \qquad\qquad\quad \text{where } u\xrightarrow{S} v \qquad\qquad (3)$$

$$\varphi_\mathsf{P} = \varphi_{exit(\mathsf{P})} \qquad\qquad\qquad\qquad\qquad\qquad\qquad (4)$$

We define $[\![\mathsf{P}]\!]_c$ to be the value of φ_P in the least fixed point of equations (1)-(4).

Semantics of Libraries. (Note that an application or program is just a special case of a library.) The semantics of a library is captured by an element of $\mathcal{L}_c$, that maps (the name of) every procedure in the library to its semantics: $[\![(LP, LL)]\!]_c = \{ (P, [\![P]\!]_c) \mid P \in LP \}$.

4   Abstract Domains and Concretization

We now formally present an abstract interpretation that analyzes a library (LP, LL) and computes a sound approximation of its concrete semantics presented earlier. Our algorithm first analyzes all the libraries in LL, uses these results to analyze and compute a summary for every procedure in LP. The algorithm can also be used to analyze an application (whole program) or a single method in isolation, which are just special cases of a library.

The Abstract Graph Domain. We utilize an abstract (points-to) graph to represent a set of concrete graphs. Our formulation is parameterized by a set N_a, the universal set of all abstract graph nodes, and a set PV_a, the set of abstract procedure-ids. An abstract graph $g \in \mathbb{G}_a$ is a triple (V, E, σ), where $V \subseteq N_a \cup PV_a$ represents the set of abstract heap objects, $E \subseteq (V \cap N_a) \times \textit{Fields} \times V$ represents possible values of pointer fields in the abstract heap objects, and $\sigma \in \textit{Vars} \mapsto 2^V$ is a map representing the possible values of program variables. Given a concrete graph $g_1 = \langle V_1, E_1, \sigma_1 \rangle$ and an abstract graph $g_2 = \langle V_2, E_2, \sigma_2 \rangle$ we say that a function $h : V_1 \mapsto V_2$ is an embedding of g_1 into g_2, denoted $g_1 \preceq_h g_2$, iff:

$$\langle x, f, y \rangle \in E_1 \Rightarrow \langle h(x), f, h(y) \rangle \in E_2, \qquad \forall v \in \textit{Vars}. \ \{ h(\sigma_1(v)) \} \subseteq \sigma_2(v)$$

The concretization $\gamma_G(g_a)$ of an abstract graph g_a is defined to be the set of all concrete graphs that can be embedded into g_a: $\gamma_G(g_a) = \{ g_c \in \mathbb{G}_c \mid \exists h. g_c \preceq_h g_a \}$

The Transformer Graph Domain. A transformer graph τ [4] is a graph-based representation that can be used to abstract the relational semantics of a first-order procedure or code fragment. It is based on weak-updates to the heap. Hence, given any input graph, a transformer graph identifies a set of heap objects that may be added to the input graph, and a set of points-to edges that may be added to the input graph.

The set $\mathcal{F}_a$ of transformer graphs is defined as follows. An element $\tau \in \mathcal{F}_a$ is a tuple $(EV, EE, \pi, IV, IE, \sigma)$ where, $EV \subseteq N_a$ is the set of external vertices, $IV \subseteq N_a \cup PV_a$ is the set of internal vertices, $EE \subseteq V \times \textit{Fields} \times EV$ is the set of external edges, where $V = EV \cup IV$, $IE \subseteq V \times \textit{Fields} \times V$ is the set of internal edges, $\pi \in \textit{Vars} \mapsto 2^V$ is a map representing the possible values of program variables in the initial state and $\sigma \in \textit{Vars} \mapsto 2^V$ is a map representing the possible values of program variables in the final state. Internal nodes and edges are used to represent new nodes and points-to edges to be added to the input graph. External nodes and external edges are used to create symbolic access-paths evaluated against an input graph to determine the sources and targets of edges to be added. More generally, an external node in the transformer graph acts as a proxy for a set of *vertices in the final output graph*, which may include nodes that exist in the input graph as well as new nodes added to the input graph.

Formally, let τ be $(\mathsf{EV}, \mathsf{EE}, \pi, \mathsf{IV}, \mathsf{IE}, \sigma)$ and $g_c \in \mathbb{G}_c$ be $(\mathsf{V}_c, \mathsf{E}_c, \sigma_c)$. To apply τ to g_c, we first compute a mapping $\eta : \mathsf{EV} \cup \mathsf{IV} \mapsto (\mathsf{IV} \cup \mathsf{V}_c)$, as illustrated in the Appendix. (See [4] for more details.) We define the resulting output graph $\tau\langle g_c \rangle$ to be $(\mathsf{V}', \mathsf{E}', \sigma')$ where $\mathsf{V}' = \mathsf{V}_c \cup \mathsf{IV}$, $\mathsf{E}' = \mathsf{E}_c \cup \{\langle v_1, f, v_2 \rangle \mid \langle u, f, v \rangle \in \mathsf{IE}, v_1 \in \eta(u), v_2 \in \eta(v)\}$, and $\sigma' = \lambda x.\hat{\eta}(\sigma(x))$. (Note that the output graph contains concrete and abstract vertices, but can be considered an abstract graph for suitably defined N_a and PV_a.) We define the concretization function $\gamma_T : \mathcal{F}_a \to \mathcal{F}_c$ as follows: $\gamma_T(\tau) = \lambda g_c . \gamma_G(\tau\langle g_c \rangle)$.

Define a partial order $\sqsubseteq_{co}$ on $\mathcal{F}_a$ as follows: $\tau_1 \sqsubseteq_{co} \tau_2$ iff $\mathsf{EV}_1 \subseteq \mathsf{EV}_2$, $\mathsf{EE}_1 \subseteq \mathsf{EE}_2$, $\mathsf{IV}_1 \subseteq \mathsf{IV}_2$, $\pi_1 \sqsubseteq \pi_2$, $\mathsf{IE}_1 \subseteq \mathsf{IE}_2$ and $\sigma_1 \sqsubseteq \sigma_2$, where $\sqsubseteq$ for π and σ is defined as pointwise inclusion: $\sigma_1 \sqsubseteq \sigma_2$ iff $\forall x.\sigma_1(x) \subseteq \sigma_2(x)$.

Higher Order Summaries. As explained earlier, we represent abstract higher order summaries as pairs (τ, ω) consisting of a transformer graph τ and a set of (indirect) call-statements ω. Formally, let $CallStmt = Vars \times Vars^*$ denote the set of all indirect call-statements. We define the abstract summary domain $\mathcal{P}_a = \mathcal{F}_a \times 2^{CallStmt}$. We extend $\sqsubseteq_{co}$ to $\mathcal{P}_a$ as follows: $(\tau_1, \omega_1) \sqsubseteq_{co} (\tau_2, \omega_2)$ iff $\tau_1 \sqsubseteq_{co} \tau_2$ and $\omega_1 \subseteq \omega_2$. We define $\mathcal{L}_a$ to be the set $Procs \hookrightarrow \mathcal{P}_a$ (of partial functions from $Procs$ to $\mathcal{P}_a$).

As explained above, a first-order procedure can be summarized using a transformer graph. Now consider a procedure that has no indirect calls, but has statements of the form "$x = \&\mathsf{P}$". A transformer graph τ is sufficient, in this case, to capture the procedure's effect on the graph component of state. However, the procedure's effect also includes updates to the function-table component of the state. In our approach, this effect is captured by the entire library summary (an element of $\mathcal{L}_a$), which also summarizes the effects of procedures (such as "P" above). Thus, the complete meaning of τ (in this case) can be captured only in the context of a library summary $\mathsf{L}_a \in \mathcal{L}_a$. The function $\gamma_\mathsf{M} : \mathcal{F}_a \times \mathcal{L}_a \to \mathcal{P}_c$ formalizes this below. The semantics of a higher-order summary $(\tau, \omega) \in \mathcal{P}_a$ is, in turn, formalized by $\gamma_\mathsf{H} : \mathcal{P}_a \times \mathcal{L}_a \mapsto \mathcal{P}_c$, as this too is dependent on the entire library summary. Finally, the semantics of a library summary $\mathsf{L}_a \in \mathcal{L}_a$ is formalized by a function $\gamma : \mathcal{L}_a \mapsto \mathcal{L}_c$. These functions are mutually recursive.

Given $f \in \mathcal{P}_c$, we define f^i inductively as $f^0 = \lambda t.\lambda g.\{g\}$ and $f^{i+1} = f^i \circ f$. We define f^* to be $\bigsqcup_c \{f^i \mid i \geq 0\}$. We define $\gamma_\mathsf{M}, \gamma_\mathsf{H}, \gamma$ as below.

$$\gamma_\mathsf{M}(\tau, \mathsf{L}_a) = \lambda(g_c, t_c).\{ (g_c', t_c') \mid \exists h.g_c \preceq_h \tau\langle g_c\rangle \wedge$$
$$t_c' = t_c \uplus \{ (n, \gamma(\mathsf{L}_a)(h(n))) \mid h(n) \in \mathrm{dom}(\mathsf{L}_a) \} \}$$

$$\gamma_\mathsf{H}((\tau, \omega), \mathsf{L}_a) = \gamma_\mathsf{M}(\tau, \mathsf{L}_a) \circ (\bigsqcup_c (\{[\![S]\!]_c \circ \gamma_\mathsf{M}(\tau, \mathsf{L}_a) \mid S \in \omega\}))^*$$

$$\gamma(\mathsf{L}_a) = \{ (\mathsf{P}, \gamma_\mathsf{H}(\mathsf{L}_a(\mathsf{P}), \mathsf{L}_a)) \mid \mathsf{P} \in \mathrm{dom}(\mathsf{L}_a) \}$$

The definition of $\gamma(\mathsf{L}_a)$ is straight forward: it maps every procedure P in the library L_a to the concretization of its abstract summary given by $\mathsf{L}_a(\mathsf{P})$. The function $\gamma_\mathsf{H}((\tau, \omega), \mathsf{L}_a)$ interprets (τ, ω) as a control flow graph, as shown in Figure 1, and computes the concrete state transformer in $\mathcal{P}_c$ at the exit point of the control flow graph (via a fix-point computation) where the transfer functions for the edges labelled by τ are given by $\gamma_\mathsf{M}(\tau, \mathsf{L}_a)$ and the transfer functions for the edges labelled by the call statements are given by their concrete semantics defined in Figure 2. $\gamma_\mathsf{M}(\tau, \mathsf{L}_a)$ is defined as the function in $\mathcal{P}_c$ that maps a concrete state (g_c, t_c) to the set of all concrete states that are compatible with the abstract graph $\tau\langle g_c \rangle$ and the abstract library L_a. A concrete state (g'_c, t'_c) is compatible with an abstract graph, abstract library pair (g_a, L_a) iff $g'_c \preceq_h g_a$ and every entry (n, f) in the virtual function table t'_c either belongs to the input table t_c or f is the concrete image of the abstract summary of the procedure $h(n)$. ($\gamma_\mathsf{M}(\tau, \mathsf{L}_a)$ assumes that the abstract procedure ids PV_a are procedure names *Procs*.)

5   Abstract Semantics

Let $(\mathsf{LP}, \mathsf{LL})$ be a library, consisting of a set of procedures LP and a set of other libraries LL it links to. Let LLP denote the set of all procedures in LL. Assume that we have analyzed LL and computed summaries for every procedure in LLP. The abstract semantics of $(\mathsf{LP}, \mathsf{LL})$ is captured by an element of $\mathcal{L}_a$ as follows: $[\![(\mathsf{LP}, \mathsf{LL})]\!]_a = \{ (\mathsf{P}, [\![\mathsf{P}]\!]_a) \mid \mathsf{P} \in \mathsf{LP} \}$, where, $[\![\mathsf{P}]\!]_a$ is the value of the variable ϑ_P in the least fix point of the collection of abstract semantic equations defined shortly. Define function $\mathsf{L}_s \in \mathcal{L}_a$ with domain $\mathsf{LP} \cup \mathsf{LLP}$ as follows: L_s maps every $\mathsf{P} \in \mathsf{LP}$ to variable ϑ_P, and it maps every $\mathsf{P} \in \mathsf{LLP}$ to its pre-computed summary.

Node Abstraction. First, we fix the set N_a and PV_a. Recall that the domain $\mathcal{F}_a$ defined earlier is parameterized by these sets. We utilize an allocation-site based merging strategy for bounding the size of the transformer graphs. We utilize the labels attached to statements as allocation-site identifiers. Let *Labels* denote the set of statement labels in the given program. We define N_a to be $\{n_x \mid x \in \textit{Labels} \cup \textit{Params} \cup \textit{Globals}\}$. We define PV_a to be the set *Procs* of procedure names.

The Sharir-Pnueli Equations. For every procedure $\mathsf{P} \in \mathsf{LP}$, we define the following set of equations, approximating the concrete semantics equations 1-3. We introduce a variable ϑ_u for every vertex u in the control-flow graph of P, and a variable $\vartheta_{u,v}$ for every edge $u \to v$ in the control-flow graph.

$$\vartheta_v = (\mathsf{ID}, \emptyset) \qquad\qquad v \text{ is an entry vertex} \qquad (5)$$

$$\vartheta_v = \sqcup_{co}\{\vartheta_{u,v} \mid u \xrightarrow{S} v\} \qquad v \text{ is not an entry vertex} \qquad (6)$$

$$\vartheta_{u,v} = [\![S]\!]_a(\vartheta_u) \qquad\qquad \text{where } u \xrightarrow{S} v \qquad (7)$$

$$\vartheta_\mathsf{P} = \textit{simplify } \mathsf{L}_s\ \vartheta_{exit(\mathsf{P})} \qquad\qquad (8)$$

Here, ID is a transformer graph consisting of a external vertex for each global variable and each parameter (representing the identity function). Formally, $\mathsf{ID} = (\mathsf{EV}, \emptyset, \pi, \emptyset, \emptyset, \pi)$, where $\mathsf{EV} = \{n_x \mid x \in \textit{Params} \cup \textit{Globals}\}$ and $\pi = \lambda v.\ v \in \textit{Params} \cup \textit{Globals} \to \{n_v\} \mid v \in \textit{Locals} \to \{null\}$.

These equations are straightforward, as they leave the abstraction work to the abstract semantics of statements, explained below. The summary for the procedure, ϑ_P, is obtained by simplifying the abstract value $\vartheta_{exit(\mathsf{P})}$ associated with the exit vertex of the procedure as explained later.

Primitive Statements. The abstract semantics $[\![S]\!]_a$ of primitive statements other than call-statements is shown in Fig. 3. Given a set-valued function $f : A \mapsto B$ and $a \in A, b \in B$, we use $f[a \hookrightarrow b]$ to denote a weak update of a i.e, $f[a \hookrightarrow b] = f[a \mapsto$

$$
\begin{aligned}
&[\![v_1 = v_2]\!]_a(\tau, \omega) &&= (\tau[\sigma \mapsto \sigma[v_1 \hookrightarrow \sigma(v_2)]]), \omega) \\
&[\![l : v = new\ C]\!]_a(\tau, \omega) &&= ((\mathsf{EV}, \mathsf{EE}, \pi, \mathsf{IV} \cup \{n_l\}, \mathsf{IE} \cup \{n_l \times Fields \times \{null\}\}, \sigma[v \hookrightarrow n_l]), \omega) \\
&[\![v_1.f = v_2]\!]_a(\tau, \omega) &&= (\tau[\mathsf{IE} \mapsto \mathsf{IE} \cup \{(\sigma(v_1) \setminus \mathsf{PV}_a) \times \{f\} \times \sigma(v_2)\}], \omega) \\
&[\![l : v_1 = v_2.f]\!]_a(\tau, \omega) &&= \textbf{let } A = \{n \mid \exists n_l \in \sigma(v_2), \langle n_l, f, n \rangle \in \mathsf{IE}\} \textbf{ in} \\
& && \quad \textbf{let } X = (\sigma(v_2) \setminus \mathsf{PV}_a) \textbf{ in} \\
& && \quad \textbf{let } B = X \cap Escaping(\tau) \textbf{ in} \\
& && \quad \textbf{if } (B = \emptyset) \textbf{ then } (\tau[\sigma \mapsto \sigma[v_1 \hookrightarrow A]], \omega) \\
& && \quad \textbf{else} \\
& && \quad ((\mathsf{EV} \cup \{n_l\}, \mathsf{EE} \cup B \times \{f\} \times \{n_l\}, \pi, \mathsf{IV}, \mathsf{IE}, \sigma[v_1 \hookrightarrow A \cup \{n_l\}]), \omega) \\
&[\![v = \&\mathsf{P}]\!]_a(\tau, \omega) &&= (\tau[\sigma \mapsto \sigma[v_1 \hookrightarrow \{\mathsf{P}\}]], \omega)
\end{aligned}
$$

Fig. 3. Abstract semantics of primitive statements, where $\tau = (\mathsf{EV}, \mathsf{EE}, \pi, \mathsf{IV}, \mathsf{IE}, \sigma)$

$$
\begin{aligned}
&Call_S^\sharp((\tau_r, \omega_r), (\tau_e, \omega_e)) &&= (pop_S^\sharp(\tau_e \langle\!\langle push_S^\sharp(\tau_r) \rangle\!\rangle_a, \tau_r), \omega_r \cup \omega_e) \\
&[\![\mathsf{P}(v_1, \cdots, v_k)]\!]_a(\tau, \omega) &&= Call_S^\sharp((\tau, \omega), \mathsf{L}_s(\mathsf{P})) \\
&MarkParam(\tau, X) &&= \tau[\pi \mapsto \lambda x.\textbf{if } x \in X \textbf{ then } \pi(x) \cup \sigma(x) \textbf{ else } \pi(x)] \\
&[\![(*v)(v_1, .., v_k)]\!]_a(\tau, \omega) &&= (MarkParam(\tau, \{v_1, .., v_k\} \cup Globals), \omega \cup \{(*v)(v_1, .., v_k)\})
\end{aligned}
$$

Fig. 4. Abstract semantics of calls

$f(a) \cup b]$. Given $\tau = (\mathsf{EV}, \mathsf{EE}, \pi, \mathsf{IV}, \mathsf{IE}, \sigma_1)$, let $\tau[\sigma \mapsto \sigma_2]$ denote $(\mathsf{EV}, \mathsf{EE}, \pi, \mathsf{IV}, \mathsf{IE}, \sigma_2)$ and we use a similar notation for updating other components of τ. The set $Escaping(\tau)$ used in the semantics of $l : v_1 = v_2.f$ is defined as $\{x \mid \exists w \in range(\pi).\ x$ is reachable from w via $\mathsf{EE} \cup \mathsf{IE}$ edges $\}$. Our abstract semantics closely resembles the one used in [4], with one difference. Unlike in the earlier analysis, we perform weak updates on all the variables (to conservatively over-approximate the transformers of all the code segments between the indirect calls). In our implementation, we minimize the precision loss due to weak updates via variable renaming.

Call Statements. Fig. 4 presents the abstract semantics of call statements. The abstract semantics of a direct call statement utilizes the function L_s defined earlier, which maps every $\mathsf{P} \in \mathsf{LP}$ to variable ϑ_P, and every $\mathsf{P} \in \mathsf{LLP}$ to its pre-computed summary. The operation $Call^\sharp(,)$ composes the graph transformer τ_r before the call-site with the graph transformer τ_e of the callee's summary, to find the resultant graph transformer. The ω component is obtained simply by taking the union of the set of indirect calls in the caller and callee. We use operations $push_S^\sharp$ and $pop_S^\sharp$ as abstractions of the parameter passing mechanism and pushing/popping an activation record. These operations, defined in the Appendix, are straightforward, except for one point: $pop_S^\sharp$ updates local variables of the caller *weakly*, defining their value as the join of their original value (in the caller) and their final value (in the callee). This is done so that variables referred to in indirect call-sites from the callee's summary that are added to the caller can be interpreted soundly.

The definition of $\langle\!\langle\rangle\!\rangle$ is analogous to the definition of the $\langle\rangle$ operator used to define the concretization function. While $\tau\langle g \rangle$ models *relation application* (it returns a representation of all graphs related to g by τ), $\tau_1 \langle\!\langle \tau_2 \rangle\!\rangle_a$ models *relation composition*. A formal definition of this operation appears in the appendix. When a callee's summary is instantiated at a call-site as above, we may be able to *resolve* some of the indirect calls in the callee (i.e., determine the actual targets of these calls). The procedure *simplify* is used to perform such resolution and simplify the result, as explained later.

The semantics of indirect call statements is mostly straightforward: the statement is simply added to the list of unresolved calls. However, the transformer graph is updated as indicated by function *MarkParam*. Recall that we wish to construct a transformer graph that simultaneously approximates multiple code fragments, each starting/ending at an indirect-call, entry vertex, or exit vertex. The code fragment starting after the given indirect call may be thought of as having parameters $\{ v_1, \cdots, v_k \} \cup Globals$: these are the roots of part of the caller's heap that is accessible to and may be modified by the callee. Hence, nodes pointed to by these variables are marked as parameter nodes.

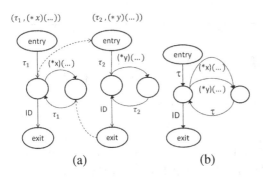

(a)   (b)

Fig. 5. Resolving an indirect call

Resolving Indirect Calls. We now describe how a summary is simplified when an indirect call is resolved. Consider the scenario shown in Fig. 5(a). Let $(\tau_1, \{(*x)(\cdots)\})$ be a summary computed during the analysis. Suppose the possible values of x includes a procedure P (i.e., P $\in \sigma_{\tau_1}(x)$). Then, the indirect call in the summary may invoke P. Let $(\tau_2, \{(*y)(\cdots)\})$ be the summary of P (either a precomputed summary or a partially-computed summary if P is part of the analysis scope). Fig. 5(a) shows the combined control-flow graph we get from the two summaries. The goal of the resolution process is to simplify, via abstraction, this control-flow graph to one in normal form, as shown in Fig. 5(b). A couple of points are worth noting about the summary shown in Fig. 5(b). Firstly, the original indirect call instruction $(*x)(\cdots)$ is still present in the summary. This cannot be dropped until all possible targets of x have been determined and instantiated (as detailed later). Secondly, the indirect calls $(*x)(\cdots)$ and $(*y)(\cdots)$ are treated as if they are indirect calls of the summarized method. In reality, the second is an indirect call in a target of the first.

The above procedure can be generalized to the case of summaries with multiple indirect calls. In general, instantiating a summary can trigger further summary instantiations: e.g., sufficient context information may become available to resolve other indirect calls. Hence, the resolution process is an iterative one of identifying indirect calls that can be resolved and then instantiating summaries of identified targets. The operation *inline* : $\mathcal{L}_a \mapsto (\mathcal{P}_a \mapsto \mathcal{P}_a)$ that realizes this iterative procedure is defined in Fig. 6.

The function *inlineCall* (in Fig. 6) performs the inlining operation for a single indirect call as illustrated in Fig. 5, which involves a fix-point computation. Notice the cycle in the control flow graph in Fig. 5(a) passing though the edges labelled τ_1 and τ_2, the transformer graph τ shown in Fig. 5(b) is the fixed point of this cycle; *inlineCall* computes this fixed point. The functions *inlineOnce* (and *inlineCalls*) extend the *inlineCall* operation to a set of indirect calls by applying it sequentially on every resolvable call in the input summary. (An indirect call is resolvable if its

$$lfp \ f \ v = \text{if } (f \ v) = v \text{ then } v \text{ else } lfp \ f \ (f \ v)$$

$$inlineCall \ ((\tau_e, \omega_e), S) \ (\tau_r, \omega_r) =$$

$$\text{let } \tau_1 = Call^{\sharp}_S((\tau_r, \omega_r), (\tau_e, \omega_e)) \text{ in}$$

$$\text{let } \tau_2 = \tau_r \langle\!\langle \tau_1 \rangle\!\rangle_a \text{ in}$$

$$\text{let } \tau_3 = lfp \ (\lambda f. f \langle\!\langle f \rangle\!\rangle_a) \ \tau_2 \text{ in}$$

$$(\tau_3 \langle\!\langle \tau_r \rangle\!\rangle_a, \omega_r \cup \omega_e)$$

$$inlineCalls \ \Sigma \ \psi = \begin{cases} \psi & \text{if } \Sigma = \{\} \\ inlineCalls \ \Sigma' \ (inlineCall \ x \ \psi) & \text{if } \Sigma = \{x\} \uplus \Sigma' \end{cases}$$

$$inlineOnce \ L_a \ (\tau, \omega) =$$

$$\text{let } \Sigma = \{(L_a(\text{P}), c) \mid c \in \omega \wedge c = (*v)(v_1, \cdots, v_k) \wedge \text{P} \in \sigma(v) \cap \text{dom}(L_a)\} \text{ in}$$

$$inlineCalls \ \Sigma \ (\tau, \omega)$$

$$inline \ L_a \ \psi = lfp \ (\lambda \psi'. \ inlineOnce \ L_a \ \psi') \ \psi$$

Fig. 6. Definition of *inline*

target variable points to (abstract) procedure ids.) However, applying *inlineOnce* function may result in more resolvable indirect calls. Moreover, the summaries inlined by *inlineOnce* could be mutually inter-dependent (if the procedures they correspond to are mutually recursive in the context of the input summary). Both these cases are uniformly handled by the *inline* function which repeatedly applies the *inlineOnce* operation until a fixed point.

Eliminating Calls. Once all targets of an indirect call $(*x)(\cdots)$ have been identified and their summaries instantiated, the call can be omitted from the summary. Transformer graphs use external nodes to represent *unresolved values*: e.g., input parameters. If x does not point to any external node, then all possible values of x are known. However, the converse is not true: even if x points to an external node, all possible values of x may already have been determined, as illustrated by the example in Fig. 7.

```
R () {
  r = new T(); r.f = &P;
  x = new T(); x.f = &Q;
  while(*) {
    t1 = r.f; (*t1)(x);
    t2 = x.f; (*t2)(r);
  } }
```

Fig. 7. Example program

The indirect calls in lines 4 and 5 can potentially call procedures P and Q. However, these indirect calls could also potentially update the values of $x.f$ or $r.f$, thus changing the procedures that are called in subsequent executions of these statements. The transformer graphs correctly account for this possibility by creating external nodes (that represent the *updated* values of $x.f$ and $r.f$ after these indirect calls). However, assume that procedures P and Q do *not* update the values of $x.f$ and $r.f$. Once the summaries of P and Q are instantiated in the summary of R, we can determine that no new values are possible for $t1$ and $t2$, even though they point to external nodes, and that all possible targets of these indirect calls have been instantiated. We can, hence, eliminate these indirect calls from the summary. The algorithm in Fig. 8 iteratively identifies potentially unresolved calls and eliminates the other calls. This elimination creates opportunities to identify and eliminate useless external nodes. Due to space constraints, we do not describe how this is done.

$dropResolvedCalls\ ((\mathsf{EV}, \mathsf{EE}, \pi, \mathsf{IV}, \mathsf{IE}, \sigma), \omega) \ =$

let $reach(X) = \{y \mid \exists x \in X.\ y$ is reachable from x via. $\mathsf{IE} \cup \mathsf{EE}$ edges $\}$

let $e_{init} = reach(\cup\{\ \pi(x) \mid x \in Params \cup Globals\ \})$

let $e_m((*x)(a_1, \ldots, a_k)) = reach(\pi(a_1)) \cup \ldots \cup reach(\pi(a_k))$

let $unresolved = lfp\ (\lambda X.\{(*x)(a_1, \ldots, a_k) \in \omega \mid (\sigma(x) \cap \mathsf{EV}) \in \widehat{e_m}(X) \cup e_{init}\})\ \emptyset$

$((\mathsf{EV}, \mathsf{EE}, \pi, \mathsf{IV}, \mathsf{IE}, \sigma), unresolved)$

$simplify\ L_a\ \psi\ =\ dropResolvedCalls(inline\ L_a\ \psi)$

Fig. 8. The Simplification Procedure

Other Optimizations and Details. Our analysis computes the fixed point of a (large) collection of equations generated from a given library. Similar to a conventional modular analysis, we analyze each procedure one at a time. Typically, in a modular analysis, the *dependences* between the equations can be identified statically and guide the order in which equations are processed for fixed point computation (which generally is a bottom-up or reverse topological order of the call-graph). Indirect calls, however, mean that some of the dependences can only be identified during the course of the analysis making it impossible to devise an optimal order of processing. We use a combination of an initial approximate call-graph constructed using class hierarchy analysis and call-graph edges identified dynamically during our analysis to guide the order in which procedures are iteratively analyzed. We also exploit an optimization to identify and merge *equivalent* call statements: $(*a_0)(a_1, \cdots, a_k)$ and $(*b_0)(b_1, \cdots, b_k)$ are equivalent if the abstract values of a_i and b_i are the same for every i. Finally, at the exit point of each method (after the *simplify* operation) we remove the internal/external vertices not reachable from $Params, Globals$ and the arguments of unresolved indirect calls from the method summary (analogous to *garbage collection*). We omit details of several other optimizations due to space constraints.

Correctness. We say that a concrete value $\mathsf{L}_c \in \mathcal{L}_c$ is *correctly represented* by an abstract value $\mathsf{L}_a \in \mathcal{L}_a$, denoted $\mathsf{L}_c \sim \mathsf{L}_a$, iff $\mathsf{L}_c \sqsubseteq_c \gamma(\mathsf{L}_a)$, and similarly for the other domains as well.

Theorem 1. $[\![(\mathsf{LP}, \mathsf{LL})]\!]_c \sim [\![(\mathsf{LP}, \mathsf{LL})]\!]_a.$

6   Experimental Evaluation

We have implemented a flow-insensitive version of our analysis for $C^\sharp$ using the *Microsoft Phoenix framework*. Our implementation, referred to as *SEAL* (for Side-Effects Analysis), is available at *http://www.rise4fun.com/seal*. SEAL is reasonably well tested, with over 50 testcases, many using higher-order features of $C^\sharp$ such as delegates and LINQ. However, SEAL does not currently handle reflection and concurrency.

Fig. 9 shows the benchmarks used in our empirical evaluation along with their source code sizes. All benchmarks except *System. Core* which is a part of the .NET framework, are popular open source libraries from *http://www.codeplex.com*. We analysed each benchmark using the pre-computed summaries for parts of the .NET framework, namely,

Benchmark	LOC	Methods	Pure	Cond. Pure	Impure	Impure & incomp	Time
DocX *(dx)*	10K	612	285	89	61	177	1m17s
Facebook APIs *(fb)*	21K	4112	1886	91	1336	799	1m59s
Dynamic Data Display *(ddd)*	25K	2266	1285	334	258	389	3m58s
TestApis *(test)*	25K	1080	503	205	189	183	2m50s
Newtonsoft Json *(json)*	27K	1867	675	532	234	426	27m34s
Quickgraph *(qg)*	34K	3380	1703	653	628	396	1m50s
NRefactory *(nr)*	43K	3004	998	1036	262	708	21m49s
CUL *(cul)*	56K	3963	1519	1275	855	314	5m13s
PdfSharp *(pdf)*	96K	3883	1405	344	1031	1103	9m53s
DotSpatial *(ds)*	250K	11579	4656	2718	1737	2468	1h51m2s
System.core *(sys)*	unknown	3092	1190	752	445	705	11m28s

Fig. 9. Results of running SEAL on 11 benchmark programs. On all the benchmarks, SEAL used at most 4GB of memory.

mscorlib, system and *system.core* DLLs. Unlike a typical whole-program analysis that would (re) analyse the .NET DLLs while analysing every benchmark, SEAL analyses the .NET DLLs once and reuses their summaries during the subsequent analyses. Furthermore, *DotSpatial* consists of 7 inter-dependent DLLs which were analysed one at a time in a modular fashion (the numbers presented are the aggregate of all the DLLs).

Except in the case of a few commonly used methods (like System.Array members) for which we used manually written stubs, we treated calls to methods for which code was unavailable (such as native, GUI and database libraries) heuristically . Hence, our analysis could be unsound in the presence of such calls.

Performance and Purity Classification. SEAL classifies every method into 4 categories. A *pure* method does not have any externally visible side-effects and does not have any unresolved calls. A *conditionally pure* method has no side-effects but has one or more unresolved calls and hence its purity depends on the calling-context. An *impure* method has side-effects but has no unresolved calls. An *impure & incomplete* method has side-effects and unresolved calls.

Fig. 9 shows the results of running SEAL on our benchmarks on a 2.83 GHz, 4 core, Intel Xeon server running Windows Server 2008. We observe that SEAL scales to large, real world C# libraries with thousands of methods within reasonable time and memory overhead. Also observe that there exists a significant number of procedures whose purity and side-effects depends on unresolved calls, highlighting the need for a sound and precise treatment of call-backs.

Fig. 10 presents statistics that provide interesting insights into the analysis. The first column in Fig. 10 shows the average number of unresolved calls in the summary of a method, i.e., the size of the ω component of the summaries (the absolute deviation, i.e., the average of differences of the each of the values from mean is shown within parenthesis). It can be seen that, across all benchmarks, SEAL finds at least 2 unresolved calls per method on an average. In fact, many methods have many more unresolved calls, as indicated by the large absolute deviation. (up to 7 unresolved calls per method on average in *json* and *sys*).

Bench-mark	Unresolved calls	Completely resolved calls	Non-escaping internal nodes
dx	4.05 (5.42)	7% (10%)	33% (36%)
fb	2.55 (4.07)	6% (10%)	9% (15%)
ddd	2.10 (3.22)	1% (2%)	30% (37%)
test	2.52 (3.61)	5% (9%)	27% (34%)
json	7.32 (10.61)	6% (9%)	31% (35%)
qg	2.06 (3.13)	1% (3%)	10% (17%)
nr	4.04 (5.04)	1% (2%)	24% (32%)
cul	2.14 (2.84)	6% (11%)	19% (28%)
pdf	3.50 (5.13)	2% (3%)	37% (34%)
sys	6.87 (10.42)	4% (7%)	41% (35%)
ds	5.93 (8.77)	3% (5%)	10% (11%)

Fig. 10. Prevalence of unresolved calls and utility of *dropResolvedCalls*/ garbage collection

The second column of Fig. 10 shows the average percentage of indirect calls in *unsimplified* method summaries that are classified as completely resolved (and removed) by *simplify*. The third column shows the average percentage of internal nodes allocated by a method (and its callees) that are non-escaping. This shows that in spite of unresolved calls, the analysis is able to identify a significant percentage (25% on average) of locally allocated objects as non-escaping and eliminate them from the summaries.

A Comparison with CHA Callgraph Based Modular Analysis. We now compare SEAL with an alternative call-graph-based compositional heap analysis, which we refer to as CCC. CCC works by first constructing a call-graph using *Class Hierarchy Analysis (CHA)*. It then processes procedures in bottom-up order over this call-graph, using our first-order compositional heap analysis technique [4].

Our implementation of CCC is unsound for reasons explained below. However, our intention is solely to use the reported numbers as an upper bound for precision and lower bound for analysis time for a sound version of CCC. Our CCC implementation constructs the call-graph of libraries independent of the application (or client), which is potentially unsound due to callbacks. We exclude *DotSpatial* from this experiment due to the complications in constructing a reasonably sound call-graph spanning multiple DLLs. We found that conservatively modelling calls to virtual methods like *equals* and *hashCode* (defined in the root class *Object*) as dispatching to any of their overridden implementations doesn't scale to even a 10 line program within reasonable time limits when the referenced libraries are also included. For this reason, CCC heuristically (and unsoundly) treats calls to such top-level interface methods (as having no side-effect). (In contrast, SEAL does not resort to any such heuristics.)

The results in Fig. 11 show that CCC is dramatically slower than SEAL. The table includes statistics about the call-graphs in the two cases which suggest that the performance difference is likely due to the imprecision of the CCC call-graph. The SEAL call-graph is a bit different from a conventional static call-graph, as it includes some (but not all) transitive caller-callee relationships because of the way it inlines summaries. However, these numbers capture (in both cases) the dependences that exist between the summaries of different procedures. These numbers indicates that decoupling call-graph construction from the heap analysis leads to over-estimating these dependences and larger SCCs, which make the analysis slower and make a case for integrating the call-graph construction with the heap analysis, as we do in a compositional fashion.

	SEAL	CCC	CCC call-graph				SEAL call-graph			
	Time	Time	#Edges	#SCCs	Avg SCC Size	Max SCC Size	#Edges	#SCCs	Avg SCC Size	Max SCC Size
dx	1m17s	12m52s	684	0	NA	NA	1273	0	NA	NA
fb	1m59s	23m13s	4052	3	3.33	4	4090	1	2	2
ddd	3m58s	∞	9105	6	18.17	99	3666	1	2	2
test	2m50s	16m7s	2532	13	5	25	1891	7	4	7
json	27m34s	∞	10701	18	28.06	450	13033	8	4.63	12
qg	1m50s	∞	296982	11	66.73	658	3416	1	2	2
nr	21m49s	∞	20763	14	79.43	911	10976	10	14.4	55
cul	5m13s	2h34m12s	34231	11	35.82	354	4740	3	2.67	3
pdf	9m53s	23m31s	7339	21	3.62	19	14434	6	2.33	3
sys	11m28s	3h44m55s	56712	10	58.30	508	7292	11	8.45	45

Fig. 11. Comparison of SEAL and CCC. ∞ indicates timeout after 4 hours.

7 Related Work

This paper extends our previous work [4,5] on compositional heap analysis for first-order procedures. The problem of resolving indirect calls has attracted a lot of attention, ranging from various call-graph construction algorithms for object-oriented languages to control-flow analysis algorithms for functional languages, e.g., see [9,2,6]. Many of these algorithms, however, take a top-down, whole-program, analysis approach. In contrast, we have focused on a compositional, bottom-up, approach that can be used to compute summaries for libraries that can be reused for any client of the library.

Rountev et al. [7] present a framework for modular analysis of libraries in the presence of call-backs by extending Sharir and Pnueli's functional approach. For procedures containing indirect calls (directly or transitively), their approach constructs a simplified control flow graph as a (higher-order) summary, by simplifying paths that contain only direct calls to procedures that have a first-order summary to an edge labelled by its transformer. This is similar to the starting point of our approach, but we push this approach further. We show how to inline a higher-order summary at a call-site, simplify the resulting summary, resolve indirect calls when possible, and integrate a heap analysis within this approach. (E.g., they rely on other, separate, analyses to identify targets of indirect calls when a library's summary is instantiated in the context of a client.)

Vivien et al. [10] present an approach for analyzing an arbitrary set of procedures in a complete program. Their approach permits the summary computed for a procedure to be incrementally refined using the summaries of callees when they become available. However, this approach does not handle indirect calls, and assumes that a call-graph is available. In contrast, we deal with indirect calls and callbacks, and construct a call-graph during the analysis in a compositional fashion. Furthermore, the approach doesn't have a theoretical formalization or proof of correctness. We believe that our abstract interpretation formalization can be easily adapted to express Vivien et al.'s approach.

Lattner et al. [3] present a modular unification-based pointer analysis for C programs in the presence of function pointers. Our approach shares several elements with the Lattner et al. approach, most notably combining a (first-order) transformer with a set of unresolved calls into a summary, but we use a more precise (non-unification) pointer analysis. [3] does not simplify summaries as aggressively as we do, does not explain identification/elimination of completely resolved calls, does not have an abstract interpretation formulation and is quite complex. We believe that our formalization can be adapted with minor modifications to formalize Lattner *et al.* analysis. An interesting aspect of [3] is the use of a context-sensitive heap abstraction (or heap cloning). Conceptually, it is straight forward to incorporate heap cloning into our analysis by altering the definition of N_a and the abstract semantics of call statements, in fact, our implementation (SEAL) supports heap cloning. However, it has far reaching implications on the precision and scalability of the analysis; initial evaluations indicate a dramatic increase in the sizes of the transformer graphs and the number of unresolved indirect calls. In the future, we plan to investigate ways of efficiently incorporating heap cloning into our analysis.

References

1. Cousot, P., Cousot, R.: Modular Static Program Analysis. In: CC 2002. LNCS, vol. 2304, pp. 159–179. Springer, Heidelberg (2002)
2. Grove, D., DeFouw, G., Dean, J., Chambers, C.: Call graph construction in object-oriented languages. In: OOPSLA, pp. 108–124 (1997)
3. Lattner, C., Lenharth, A., Adve, V.S.: Making context-sensitive points-to analysis with heap cloning practical for the real world. In: PLDI, pp. 278–289 (2007)
4. Madhavan, R., Ramalingam, G., Vaswani, K.: Purity Analysis: An Abstract Interpretation Formulation. In: Yahav, E. (ed.) SAS 2011. LNCS, vol. 6887, pp. 7–24. Springer, Heidelberg (2011)
5. Madhavan, R., Ramalingam, G., Vaswani, K.: Purity analysis: An abstract interpretation formulation. Tech. rep., Microsoft Research (2011)
6. Might, M., Smaragdakis, Y., Horn, D.V.: Resolving and exploiting the k-cfa paradox: Illuminating functional vs. object-oriented program analysis. In: PLDI, Toronto, Canada, pp. 305–315 (June 2010)
7. Rountev, A., Kagan, S., Marlowe, T.: Interprocedural Dataflow Analysis in the Presence of Large Libraries. In: Mycroft, A., Zeller, A. (eds.) CC 2006. LNCS, vol. 3923, pp. 2–16. Springer, Heidelberg (2006)
8. Sălcianu, A., Rinard, M.: Purity and Side Effect Analysis for Java Programs. In: Cousot, R. (ed.) VMCAI 2005. LNCS, vol. 3385, pp. 199–215. Springer, Heidelberg (2005)
9. Shivers, O.G.: Control-Flow Analysis of Higher-Order Languages or Taming Lambda. Ph.D. thesis, Carnegie-Mellon Univeristy (May 1991)
10. Vivien, F., Rinard, M.: Incrementalized pointer and escape analysis. In: PLDI, pp. 35–46 (2001)
11. Whaley, J., Rinard, M.C.: Compositional pointer and escape analysis for java programs. In: OOPSLA, pp. 187–206 (1999)

A   Appendix

Definition of $Call_S$. Let S be a procedure call statement with arguments $a_1,...,a_k$. Let $Param(i)$ denote the i-the formal parameter. Define the functions $push_S \in \Sigma_c \mapsto \Sigma_c$,

$pop_S \in \Sigma_c \times \Sigma_c \mapsto \Sigma_c$, and $Call_S$ as follows:

$$push_S(\sigma) = \lambda v.\ v \in Globals \to \sigma(v)\ |\ v \in Locals \to null\ |\ v = Param(i) \to \sigma(a_i)$$
$$pop_S(\sigma, \sigma') = \lambda v.\ v \in Globals \to \sigma'(v)\ |\ v \in Locals \cup Params \to \sigma(v)$$
$$Call_S(f) = \lambda((\mathsf{V}, \mathsf{E}, \sigma), t).\{\ ((\mathsf{V}', \mathsf{E}', pop_S(\sigma, \sigma')), t')\ |$$
$$((\mathsf{V}', \mathsf{E}', \sigma'), t') \in f\ ((\mathsf{V}, \mathsf{E}, push_S(\sigma)), t)\ \}$$

Definition of η. Let $\tau \in \mathcal{F}_a$ be $(\mathsf{EV}, \mathsf{EE}, \pi, \mathsf{IV}, \mathsf{IE}, \sigma)$ and $g_c \in \mathbb{G}_c$ be $(\mathsf{V}_c, \mathsf{E}_c, \sigma_c)$. The function η used in the definition of $\tau\langle g_c \rangle$ is defined as follows. Define a mapping η : $(\mathsf{EV} \cup \mathsf{IV} \cup \mathsf{PV}_a) \mapsto (\mathsf{IV} \cup \mathsf{V}_c)$ that maps every vertex (and procedure ids) in τ to a set of values, as follows: Let $Escaping(\tau) = \{x\ |\ \exists w \in range(\pi).\ x$ is reachable from w via $\mathsf{EE} \cup \mathsf{IE}$ edges $\}$.

$$v \in \pi(x) \Rightarrow \sigma_c(x) \subseteq \mu(v)$$
$$v \in \mathsf{IV} \cup \mathsf{PV}_a \Rightarrow v \in \mu(v)$$
$$\langle u, f, v \rangle \in \mathsf{EE}, u' \in \mu(u), \langle u', f, v' \rangle \in \mathsf{E}_c \Rightarrow v' \in \mu(v)$$
$$\langle u, f, v \rangle \in \mathsf{EE}, (\mu(u) \cap \mu(u') \setminus \mathsf{PV}_c \setminus \mathsf{PV}_a) \neq \emptyset, \langle u', f, v' \rangle \in \mathsf{IE},$$
$$u \in Escaping(\tau) \Rightarrow \mu(v') \subseteq \mu(v)$$

Definition of $push_S^\sharp$ and $pop_S^\sharp$. Let S be a direct/indirect call statement with arguments $a_1, \ldots, a_n$ and $\tau_1 = (\mathsf{EV}_1, \mathsf{EE}_1, \pi_1, \mathsf{IV}_1, \mathsf{IE}_1, \sigma_1)$, $\tau_2 = (\mathsf{EV}_2, \mathsf{EE}_2, \pi_2, \mathsf{IV}_2, \mathsf{IE}_2, \sigma_2)$ $push_S^\sharp(\tau_1) = (\mathsf{EV}_1, \mathsf{EE}_1, \pi_1, \mathsf{IV}_1, \mathsf{IE}_1, \sigma_1')$ and $pop_S^\sharp(\tau_2, \tau_1) = (\mathsf{EV}_2, \mathsf{EE}_2, \pi_2, \mathsf{IV}_2, \mathsf{IE}_2, \sigma_2')$ where, $\sigma_1' = \lambda v.\ (v = Param(i) \to \sigma_1(a_i)\ |\ v \in Globals \to \sigma_1(v)\ |\ v \in Locals \to null)$ and $\sigma_2' = \lambda v.\ (v \in Params \cup Locals \to \sigma_1(v) \cup \sigma_2(v)\ |\ v \in Globals \to \sigma_2(v))$

Definition of Relational Composition Operator $\langle\!\langle\rangle\!\rangle$. Let $\tau_1 = (\mathsf{EV}_1, \mathsf{EE}_1, \pi_1, \mathsf{IV}_1, \mathsf{IE}_1, \sigma_1)$, $\tau_2 = (\mathsf{EV}_2, \mathsf{EE}_2, \pi_2, \mathsf{IV}_2, \mathsf{IE}_2, \sigma_2)$. We define $\tau_2\langle\!\langle\tau_1\rangle\!\rangle_a$ to be $\tau_2\langle\!\langle\tau_1, \eta_a\rangle\!\rangle$, where η_a is the least solution of the following set of constraints over the variable μ_a.

$$u \in \pi_2(p) \Rightarrow \sigma_1(p) \subseteq \mu_a(u)$$
$$u \in (\mathsf{IV}_2 \cup \mathsf{PV}_a) \Rightarrow u \in \mu_a(u)$$
$$\langle u, f, v \rangle \in \mathsf{EE}_2, u' \in \mu_a(u), \langle u', f, v' \rangle \in \mathsf{IE}_1 \Rightarrow v' \in \mu_a(v)$$
$$\langle u, f, v \rangle \in \mathsf{EE}_2, (\mu_a(u) \cap \mu_a(u') \setminus \mathsf{PV}_a) \neq \{\}, \langle u', f, v' \rangle \in \mathsf{IE}_2 \Rightarrow \mu_a(v') \subseteq \mu_a(v)$$
$$\langle u, f, v \rangle \in \mathsf{EE}_2, \mu_a(u) \cap Escaping(\tau_2\langle\!\langle\tau_1, \mu_a\rangle\!\rangle) \neq \{\} \Rightarrow v \in \mu_a(v)$$

Define $\tau_2\langle\!\langle\tau_1, \nu\rangle\!\rangle$ to be $\tau' = (\mathsf{V}' \cap (\mathsf{IV}_1 \cup \mathsf{IV}_2), \mathsf{EE}', \pi', \mathsf{V}' \cap (\mathsf{EV}_1 \cup \mathsf{EV}_2), \mathsf{IE}', \sigma')$ where,

$$\mathsf{V}' = (\mathsf{IV}_1 \cup \mathsf{EV}_1) \cup \hat{\nu}(\mathsf{IV}_2 \cup \mathsf{EV}_2)$$
$$\mathsf{IE}' = \mathsf{IE}_1 \cup \{\langle v_1, f, v_2 \rangle\ |\ \langle u, f, v \rangle \in \mathsf{IE}_2, v_1 \in \nu(u) \setminus \mathsf{PV}_a, v_2 \in \nu(v)\}$$
$$\mathsf{EE}' = \mathsf{EE}_1 \cup \{\langle u', f, v \rangle\ |\ \langle u, f, v \rangle \in \mathsf{EE}_2, u' \in \nu(u), u' \in Escaping(\tau')\}$$
$$\pi' = \lambda var.\ \pi_1(var) \cup \hat{\nu}(\pi_2(var))$$
$$\sigma' = \lambda var.\ \sigma_1(var) \cup \hat{\nu}(\sigma_2(var))$$

Binary Reachability Analysis
of Higher Order Functional Programs

Ruslán Ledesma-Garza and Andrey Rybalchenko

Technische Universität München

Abstract. A number of recent approaches for proving program termination rely on transition invariants – a termination argument that can be constructed incrementally using abstract interpretation. These approaches use binary reachability analysis to check if a candidate transition invariant holds for a given program. For imperative programs, its efficient implementation can be obtained by a reduction to reachability analysis, for which practical tools are available. In this paper, we show how a binary reachability analysis can be put to work for proving termination of higher order functional programs.

1   Introduction

Tools and techniques for proving program termination are important for increasing software quality [5]. System routines written in imperative programming languages received a significant amount of attention recently, e.g., [2,3,4,19,24,32]. A number of the proposed approaches rely on transition invariants – a termination argument that can be constructed incrementally using abstract interpretation [25]. Transition invariants are binary relations over program states. Checking if an incrementally constructed candidate is in fact a transition invariant of the program is called binary reachability analysis. For imperative programs, its efficient implementation can be obtained by a reduction to the reachability analysis, for which practical tools are available, e.g., [1,11,12,22]. The reduction is based on a program transformation that stores one component of the pair of states under consideration in auxiliary program variables, and then checks if the pair is in the transition invariant [4]. The transformed program is verified using an existing safety checker. If the safety checker succeeds then the original program terminates on all inputs.

For functional programs, recent approaches for proving termination apply the size change termination (SCT) argument [20]. This argument requires checking the presence of an infinite descent within data values passed to application sites of the program on any infinite traversal of the call graph. This check can be realized in two steps. First, every program function is translated into a set of so-called size-change graphs that keep track of decrease in values between the actual arguments and values at the application sites in the function. Second, the presence of a descent is checked by computing a transitive closure of the size-change graphs. Originally, the SCT analysis was formulated for first order

A. Miné and D. Schmidt (Eds.): SAS 2012, LNCS 7460, pp. 388–404, 2012.

functional programs manipulating well-founded data, yet using an appropriate control-flow analysis, it can be extended to higher order programs, see e.g., [28, 29, 30]. Alternatively, an encoding into term rewriting can be used to make sophisticated decidable well-founded orderings on terms applicable to proving termination of higher order programs [9].

The SCT analysis is a decision problem (that checks if there is an infinite descent in the abstract program defined by size change graphs), however it is an incomplete method for proving termination. SCT can return "don't know" for terminating programs that manipulate non-well-founded data, e.g., integers, or when an interplay of several variables witnesses program termination. In such cases, a termination prover needs to apply a more general termination argument. Usually, such termination arguments require proving that certain expressions over program variables decrease as the computation progresses and yet the decrease cannot happen beyond a certain bound.

In this paper, we present a general approach for proving termination of higher order functional programs that goes beyond the SCT analysis. Our approach explores the applicability of transition invariants to this task by proposing an extension (wrt. imperative case) that deals with partial applications, a programming construct that is particular for functional programs. Partial applications of curried functions, i.e., functions that return other functions, represent a major obstacle for the binary reachability analysis. For a curried function, the set of variables whose values need to be stored in auxiliary variables keeps increasing as the function is subsequently applied to its arguments. However these arguments are not necessarily supplied simultaneously, which requires intermediate storage of the argument values given so far. In this paper, we address such complications.

We develop the binary reachability analysis for higher order programs in two steps. First, we show how intermediate nodes of program evaluation trees, so-called judgements, can be augmented with auxiliary values needed for tracking binary reachability. The auxiliary values store arguments provided at application sites. Then, we show how this augmentation can be performed on the program source code such that the evaluation trees of the augmented program correspond to the result of augmenting the evaluation trees of the original program. The source code transformation introduces additional parameters to functions occurring in the program. For curried functions, these additional parameters are interleaved with the original parameters, which allows us to deal with partial applications.

Our binary reachability analysis for higher order programs opens up an approach for termination proving in the presence of higher order functions that exploits a highly optimized safety checker, e.g., [13, 14, 16, 18, 33], for checking the validity of a candidate termination argument. Hence, we can directly benefit from sophisticated abstraction techniques and algorithmic improvements offered by these tools, as inspired by [4].

In summary, this paper makes the following contributions.

- A notion of binary reachability analysis for higher order functional programs.

- A program transformation that reduces the binary reachability analysis to the reachability analysis.
- An implementation of our approach and its evaluation on micro benchmarks from the literature.

2   Illustration

In this section we illustrate what our transformation adds to the program in order to keep track of pairs of argument valuations for checking a transition invariant candidate.

We consider the following curried function f that has a type x:int -> y:int -> ret:int. Here, we annotated the parameter and return value types with identifiers to improve readability.

```
let rec f x = if x > 0 then f (x-1) else fun y -> f x y
```

This function shows that – in contrast to proving termination of recursive procedures in imperative programs – it is important to differentiate between partial and complete applications when dealing with curried functions. First, we observe that any partial application of f terminates. For example, f 10 stops after ten recursive calls and returns a function fun y -> f 0 y where f is bound to a closure. That is, there is no infinite sequence of f applications that are passed only one argument. In contrast, any complete application of f does not terminate. For example, f 1 1 will lead to an infinite sequence of f applications such that each of them is given two arguments.

Our binary reachability analysis takes as input a specification that determines which kind of applications we want to keep track of. The specification consists of a function identifier, e.g., f, a number of parameters, e.g., one, and a transition invariant candidate. Then, such a specification requires that applications of f to one argument satisfy the transition invariant candidate. Alternatively, we may focus on applications of f to two arguments.

Once the specification is given, we transform f into a function f_m that keeps track of arguments on which f was applied using additional parameters old_x and old_y. As a result, f_m fulfills two requirements. First, it computes a result value res such that res = f x y. Second, it computes new values of additional parameters. If f_m were an imperative program, we would obtain the type

```
x:int * y:int * copied:bool * old_x:int * old_y:int ->
    ret:int * new_copied:bool * new_x:int * new_y:int
```

where new_x and new_y are computed as follows. If old_x already stores a value that was given to x in the past, i.e., if copied = true, then new_x = old_x. Otherwise, f_m can nondeterministically either store x in new_x and set new_copied = true, or leave new_x = old_x and new_copied = false. The computation of new_y is similar. Given a transformed program, checking binary reachability amounts to checking that at each application site the pair of tuples (old_x, old_y) and (x, y) satisfies the transition invariant whenever copied is true.

Due to partial applications we cannot expect that values of x and y are provided simultaneously, which complicates both computation of new_x and new_y and checking if (old_x, old_y) together with (x, y) satisfy the transition invariant. Hence, we need to keep track of arguments as they are provided, which requires "waiting" for missing arguments. We implement this waiting process by introducing additional parameters old_state_x and old_state_y for each partial application, together with their updated versions new_state_x and new_state_y. Each additional parameter accumulates arguments in its first component, and it keeps a tuple of previously provided arguments in its second component. We obtain the following type for f_m.

```
x:int
-> old_state_x:((int * int) *           (* accumulate x and y      *)
                (bool * int * int))     (* store copied, x, and y *)
-> (y:int
    -> old_state_y:((int * int) *       (* accumulate x and y      *)
                    (bool * int * int)) (* store copied, x, and y *)
    -> ret:int * new_state_y:((int * int) *
                              (bool * int * int))) *
   new_state_x:((int * int) *
                (bool * int * int))
```

We refer to (int * int) * (bool * int * int) as state. Then f_m has the type:

```
x:int -> old_state_x:state ->
(y:int -> old_state_y:state -> ret:int * new_state_y:state) *
new_state_x:state
```

We formalize the above transformation in Section 5. Figure 8 presents a detailed execution protocol of applying our transformation on the above program.

Note that if complete applications of a function terminate, then every partial application of the function terminates. For example, consider the following function g.

```
let rec g x = if x > 0 then g (x-1) else fun y -> x+y
```

This function does not have any infinite application sequences neither for complete nor for partial applications.

3   Preliminaries

In this section we describe Mini-OCaml, the programming language that we use to represent programs. We also present the logger monad [34] extended with an update operation.

Mini-OCaml Syntax. Let X be a set of *variables*, e.g., x, List.map, and myVar. Let C be a set of *constants*, e.g., +, 1, 2.5, and "h". Let C be a set of *constructors*, e.g., ::, Some, [], and true. We assume $s, x \in X$, $c \in C$,

$$E \ni e ::= \quad c$$
$$|\ x$$
$$|\ c(e, \ldots, e)$$
$$|\ e\ e$$
$$|\ \texttt{fun}\ x\ \texttt{->}\ e$$
$$|\ \texttt{let}\ p\ \texttt{=}\ e\ \texttt{in}\ e$$
$$|\ \texttt{let rec}\ x\ \texttt{=fun}\ x\ \texttt{->}e\ \texttt{in}\ e$$
$$|\ \texttt{match}\ e\ \texttt{with}$$
$$\quad |\ c(x, \ldots, x)\ \texttt{->}\ e$$
$$\quad \ldots$$
$$\quad |\ c(x, \ldots, x)\ \texttt{->}\ e$$
(a)

$$\tau ::= \iota$$
$$|\ \alpha$$
$$|\ \tau\ \texttt{->}\ \tau$$
$$|\ (\tau, \ldots, \tau)\ \iota$$
(b)

$$V \ni v ::= c$$
$$|\ c(v, \ldots, v)$$
$$|\ (\texttt{fun}\ x\ \texttt{->}\ e,\ \mathcal{E})$$
$$|\ (x, \texttt{fun}\ x\ \texttt{->}\ e, \mathcal{E})$$
(c)

$$\overline{\mathcal{E} \vdash c \Rightarrow c} \qquad \frac{x \in Dom\ \mathcal{E}}{\mathcal{E} \vdash x \Rightarrow \mathcal{E}\,x}$$

$$\frac{\mathcal{E} \vdash e_n \Rightarrow v_n \quad \ldots \quad \mathcal{E} \vdash e_1 \Rightarrow v_1}{\mathcal{E} \vdash c(e_1, \ldots, e_n) \Rightarrow c(v_1, \ldots, v_n)}$$

$$\frac{\mathcal{E} \vdash e_p \Rightarrow v_p \quad \mathcal{E} \vdash e_f \Rightarrow c}{\mathcal{E} \vdash e_f\ e_p \Rightarrow c\,v_p}$$

$$\frac{\mathcal{E} \vdash e_p \Rightarrow v_p \quad \mathcal{E} \vdash e_f \Rightarrow (\texttt{fun}\ x\ \texttt{->}\ e_b, \mathcal{E}_b)}{\mathcal{E}_b + x \mapsto v_p \vdash e_b \Rightarrow v}{\mathcal{E} \vdash e_f\ e_p \Rightarrow v}$$

$$\frac{\mathcal{E} \vdash e_p \Rightarrow v_p \quad \mathcal{E} \vdash e_f \Rightarrow (x_f, \texttt{fun}\ x\ \texttt{->}\ e_b, \mathcal{E}_b)}{\mathcal{E}_b + x_f \mapsto (x_f, \texttt{fun}\ x\ \texttt{->}\ e_b, \mathcal{E}_b) + x \mapsto v_p \vdash e_b \Rightarrow v}{\mathcal{E} \vdash e_f\ e_p \Rightarrow v}$$

$$\frac{\mathcal{E} \vdash e_1 \Rightarrow v_1 \quad \mathcal{E} + \text{Bindings}\ p\ v_1 \vdash e_2 \Rightarrow v}{\mathcal{E} \vdash \texttt{let}\ p\ \texttt{=}\ e_1\ \texttt{in}\ e_2 \Rightarrow v}$$

$$\overline{\mathcal{E} \vdash \texttt{fun}\ x\ \texttt{->}\ e_b \Rightarrow (\texttt{fun}\ x\ \texttt{->}\ e_b, \mathcal{E})}$$

$$\frac{\mathcal{E} + x_f \mapsto (x_f, \texttt{fun}\ x\ \texttt{->}\ e_b, \mathcal{E}) \vdash e_2 \Rightarrow v}{\mathcal{E} \vdash \texttt{let rec}\ x_f\ \texttt{=}\ \texttt{fun}\ x\ \texttt{->}\ e_b\ \texttt{in}\ e_2 \Rightarrow v}$$

$$\frac{\mathcal{E} \vdash e_m \Rightarrow v_m}{c_k(\ldots_k)\ \text{is the first pattern to match}\ v_m}{\mathcal{E} + \text{Bindings}\ (c_k(\ldots_k))\ v_m \vdash e_k \Rightarrow v}{\mathcal{E} \vdash (\texttt{match}\ e_m\ \texttt{with}\ |\ \ldots) \Rightarrow v}$$

(d)

Fig. 1. Mini-OCaml syntax (a), types (b), and evaluation rules (c). Rule premises are ordered from left to right and from top to bottom. Patterns in (Match) are ordered from top to bottom.

and $c \in C$. Figure 1(a) presents the syntax of Mini-OCaml expressions. We encode `if-then-else` expressions using match expressions. Function applications are left associative. We assume that tuples of values are encoded using tuple constructors. We assume that text in `type writer font` is Mini-OCaml code.

Mini-OCaml Types. We use the OCaml type system [21] to type Mini-OCaml expressions. Let B be a set of base types, e.g., `int`, `string`, and `in_channel`. Let A be a set of type variables, e.g., `'a` and `'b`. Let $\boldsymbol{B}$ be a set of type constructors, e.g., `list`, `option`, and `bool`. We assume $\iota \in B$, $\alpha \in A$, and $\iota \in \boldsymbol{B}$. Figure 1(b) presents the set of Mini-OCaml types. We write the typing proposition $e\ :\ \tau$ if expression e is of type τ under some typing context. We say that expression e is well-typed if there exists a type τ such that $e\ :\ \tau$. Examples of valid propositions are `1 : int` and `+ : int -> int -> int`.

Mini-OCaml Semantics. Figure 1(c) presents *values* computed by Mini-OCaml programs using judgements j of the form

$$J \ni j ::= \mathcal{E} \vdash e \Rightarrow v$$

Every judgement is derived by applying rules shown in Figure 1(d). A judgement j is *valid* if there exists an evaluation tree with j as the root. Each evaluation tree is given by the set of its edges. Each edge is a sequence of judgements $j_1, \ldots, j_n, j$, where $j_1, \ldots, j_n$ are the predecessor nodes and j is the successor node. If $n = 0$ then the edge represents a leaf node.

For example, we consider the evaluation tree t for 1 + 2 as shown below.

$$
\frac{
  \quad\quad\quad\quad
  \dfrac{
    \dfrac{}{\emptyset \vdash 1 \Rightarrow 1} \quad \dfrac{}{\emptyset \vdash + \Rightarrow +}
  }{\emptyset \vdash (+) \; 1 \Rightarrow +_1}
}{\dfrac{}{\emptyset \vdash 2 \Rightarrow 2} \quad\quad\quad \emptyset \vdash 1 + 2 \Rightarrow 3}
$$

Let $j_1 = (\emptyset \vdash 1+2 \Rightarrow 3)$, $j_2 = (\emptyset \vdash 2 \Rightarrow 2)$, $j_3 = (\emptyset \vdash (+) \; 1 \Rightarrow +_1)$, $j_4 = (\emptyset \vdash 1 \Rightarrow 1)$, $j_5 = (\emptyset \vdash + \Rightarrow +)$. The evaluation tree t is given by the set of five edges below.

$$ t = \{j_2, j_4, j_5, (j_4, j_5, j_3), (j_2, j_3, j_1)\} $$

Let eval $\mathcal{E}$ e be the value of expression e in the environment $\mathcal{E}$, i.e., $v =$ eval $\mathcal{E}$ e if there is an evaluation tree for $\mathcal{E} \vdash e \Rightarrow v$.

Recursion Relations and Binary Reachability. We are interested in keeping track of (possibly partial) applications of a function defined in a program. Let f be a function identifier of type $\tau_1 \to \ldots \to \tau_m \to \tau$ that is bound using a let-rec binding, and N be a number between 1 and m. An f/N-*application judgement* describes evaluation of an application of f to N-many actual parameters, i.e., it is a judgement of the form $\mathcal{E} \vdash f \; e_1 \; \ldots \; e_n \Rightarrow v$. A f/N-*recursion relation* consists of pairs of value tuples $(v_1, \ldots, v_N)$ and $(u_1, \ldots, u_N)$ that satisfy the following condition. For each $(v_1, \ldots, v_N)$ and $(u_1, \ldots, u_N)$ in the relation we require existence of a pair of valid f/N-application judgements $j_1 = \mathcal{E}_1 \vdash f \; e_1 \; \ldots \; e_N \Rightarrow v$ and $j_2 = \mathcal{E}_2 \vdash f \; e_1 \; \ldots \; e_N \Rightarrow u$ such that j_2 appears in the evaluation tree of j_1 and for each $i \in 1..N$ we have eval $\mathcal{E}_1$ $e_i = v_i$ and eval $\mathcal{E}_2$ $e_i = u_i$.

The goal of *binary reachability analysis* is to check if the f/N-recursion relation of the program is contained in a given binary relation.

We fix f, N, and a binary relation TI for the rest of this paper. Furthermore, we assume that TI is represented as an assertion over tuples of variables $(a_1, \ldots, a_N)$ and $(m_1, \ldots, m_N)$. This assumption will be used in Figure 6.

4   Binary Reachability on Evaluation Trees

In this section we make the first step towards our program transformation. We present an augmentation of evaluation trees that allows us to reduce the binary reachability analysis to the validity analysis of annotated judgements. Each judgement is augmented with a boolean and an N-ary tuple of values, which we will refer to as a *state*.

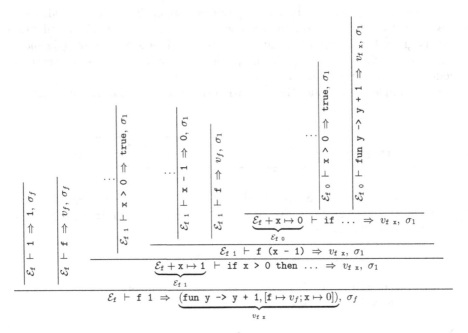

Fig. 2. Annotation of the evaluation tree for `f 1` in the environment $\mathcal{E}_f = $ (f,fun x -> if x > 0 then f (x - 1) else fun y -> y + 1, $\emptyset$). The initial judgement is annotated with $\sigma_f = (false, 0)$. The annotation changes from σ_f to $\sigma_1 = (true, 1)$ after the first call to `f`. Due to the lack of width, we had to rotate several judgements.

Before presenting the augmentation procedure, we consider examples of tree augmentation shown in Figure 2. The root of the tree is augmented with a state $\sigma_f = (false, 0)$, where *false* indicates that no argument has been used for the augmentation yet. We use s to augment judgements in the subtree for the branches that do not correspond to the evaluation of the body of `f`. When augmenting the subtree that deals with the body, we can nondeterministically decide to start augmenting with a state that records the argument of the current application. That is, in the body subtree we augment with the state $\sigma_1 = (true, 1)$. Here, *true* indicates that we took a snapshot of the current application argument, and 1 is the argument value. The remaining judgements are augmented with σ_1, since we will not change the snapshot if it was taken, i.e., if the first component of the augmenting state is *true*.

We proceed with an algorithm **Augment** that takes as input an initial state and an evaluation tree and produces an augmented tree. Each augmented judgement is of the form $\mathcal{E} \vdash e \Rightarrow v, \sigma$, where σ is a state. As an *initial* state we take a pair $(false, (v_1 \ldots, v_N))$ where $v_1 \ldots, v_N$ are some values.

See Figure 3. **Augment** traverses the input tree recursively, by starting from the root. Whenever the current judgement is a f/N-application judgement, then we choose whether to create a snapshot of the arguments and store them in the

```
1   let Augment ((c, _) as σ) t =
2     let j = root t in
3     match j with
4     | ℰ ⊢ f e₁ ... eₙ ⇒ v →
5         let v₁, ..., vₙ = eval ℰ e₁, ..., eval ℰ eₙ in
6         let σ' = if ¬c ∧ nondet() then (true, v₁, ..., vₙ) else σ in
7         let tₚ, tf, t_b = immediate subtrees of t in
8         let t'ₚ, t'f, t'_b = Augment σ tₚ, Augment σ tₚ, Augment σ' t_b in
9         ({root t'ₚ, root t'f, root t'_b, (j, σ))} ∪ t'ₚ ∪ t'f ∪ t'_b
10    | _ →
11        let t₁, ..., tₙ = immediate subtrees of t in
12        let t'₁, ..., t'ₙ = Augment σ t₁, ..., Augment σ tₙ in
13        ({root t'₁, ..., root t'ₙ, (j, σ))} ∪ t'₁ ∪ ··· ∪ t'ₙ
```

Fig. 3. Evaluation tree monitoring. The input consists of a monitor state σ and an evaluation tree t. **nondet()** non-deterministically returns either *true* or *false*.

state that is used to augment the subtree that evaluates the body. We only create a snapshot if the Boolean component of the current state is *false*. In case we currently do not deal with a f/N-application judgement, no state change happens and we proceed with the subtrees. Once we obtain the augmented versions of the subtrees, we put them together by creating a node that connects the roots of the subtrees.

We establish a formal relationship between the f/N-recursion relation with the augmented judgements obtained by applying Augment using the following theorem.

Theorem 1 (Augment keeps track of f/N-recursion relation). *A pair* $(v_1, \ldots, v_N)$ *and* $(u_1, \ldots, u_N)$ *is in the f/N-recursion relation if and only if the result of applying Augment wrt. some sequence of nondeterministic choices on* j *and an initial state contains an augmented judgement of the form*

$$\mathcal{E} \vdash f\ e_1 \ldots e_N \Rightarrow v, (true, (v_1, \ldots, v_N))$$

such that for each $i \in 1..N$ *we have eval* $\mathcal{E}\ e_i = u_i$

5   Program Transformation

In this section we present a program transformation that realizes the function Augment presented in Section 4. To implement the state passing between judgments we apply a so-called logger monad.

```
1  (* logger monad type *)
2  type 'a m = state -> 'a * state
3  (* unit operator *)
4  let unit a = fun s -> (a, s)
5  (* bind operator *)
6  let ( >>= ) m k = fun s0 ->
7                      let v1, s1 = m s0 in
8                      k v1 s1
9  (* state transform operator *)
10 let update f = fun s -> ( (), f s )
```

Fig. 4. Logger monad with state transform operator **update**. The unit operator takes a value and constructs a monadic value. The bind operator takes a monadic value and a function returning a monadic value, and constructs a new monadic value. The state transform operator creates a new monadic value by applying the state transformer **f**.

Logger Monad. A *monad* consists of a type constructor m of arity 1 and two operations

```
unit : 'a -> 'a m
( >>= ) : 'a m -> ('a -> 'b m) -> 'b m
```

These operations need to satisfy three conditions called *left unit*, *right unit*, and *associative* [35]. We assume that state is a given type. Figure 4 presents a variant of the *logger monad* [34]. The state update operator update is of type (state -> state) -> unit m. A monadic expression (resp. value) is an expression (resp. value) of the logger monad type.

For example, the monadic expression unit 1 evaluates to a function that takes a state σ and returns a pair $(1, \sigma)$. As another example, the following monadic expression evaluates to a function that takes a state σ and returns a pair $(1, \sigma + 1)$.

```
update (fun s -> s + 1) >>= fun () -> unit 1
```

Transformation of Types. We transform each program expression into a monadic expression that keeps track of the state that results in the judgement augmentation. Figure 5 presents the function monadic that maps types of expressions in the original program to types of the transformed program. Function monadic indicates that a transformed program is a Mini-OCaml function that takes an initial state and returns a pre-monadic program value together with a final state.

For example, consider the following applications of monadic.

```
monadic (int -> (int -> int)) = (int -> ((pre_m int -> int)) m)) m
                                (int -> ((int -> int m) m)) m
```

```
1 let rec monadic τ = (pre_m τ) m

2 and pre_m = function
3   | τ₁ -> τ₂ → (pre_m τ₁) -> (pre_m τ₂) m
4   | (τ₁, ..., τₙ) ι → ((pre_m τ₁), ..., (pre_m τₙ)) ι
5   | τ → τ
```

Fig. 5. Type transformation function monadic

```
1   let enter = function
2     | f e₁ →
3        " fun v -> fun ((_, a₂, ..., a_N), m) -> (v, a₂, ..., a_N), m "
         ⋮
4     | ( ... (f e₁) ... e_{N−1}) →
5        " fun v -> fun ((a₁, ..., a_{N−2}, _, a_N), m) ->
6                        (a₁, ..., a_{N−2}, v, a_N), m "
7     | ( ... (f e₁) ... e_N) →
8        " fun v -> fun ((a₁, ..., a_{N−1}, _), m) ->
9                     let a = a₁, ..., a_{N−1}, v in
10                    let m_c, m_1, ..., m_N = m in
11                    if m_c then assert TI;
12                    a, if not m_c && nondet () then true, a else m "
13    | _ → " fun _ -> id "

14 let exit = function
15   | f e₁ | ... | ( ... (f e₁) ... e_{N−1}) → " fun _ s -> (fun _ -> s)  "
16   | ( ... (f e₁) ... e_N) → " fun s _ -> (fun _ -> s)  "
17   | _ → " fun _ _ -> id "
```

Fig. 6. The transformer selector functions enter and exit. The operator " · " emits a Mini-OCaml expression after evaluating expressions that are embedded using ' · '.

Transformation of Expressions. We present the transformation function Transform in Figure 7. Transform uses two auxiliary functions enter and exit shown in Figure 6.

For an expression e, Transform traverses the abstract syntax tree of e and gives a core monadic expression that evaluates the user program together with two state transform operations. Transform generates Mini-OCaml expressions using the "·" function. For example, "let x = 1 in 1" emits the expression let x = 1 in 1. Within "·" we can perform an evaluation by applying ' · '. For example, "let x = '1+2' in 1" emits let x = 3 in 1.

The important case is the transformation of f/N-applications. Such applications are recognized in enter and exit. The emitted code either saves the argument

```
1  let Transform e =
2    match e with
3    | c →
4      let x₁, ..., x_Arity c = FreshVar (), ..., FreshVar () in
5        " unit (fun x₁->
6              ...
7                  unit (fun x_Arity c->
8                      unit (c x₁ ... x_Arity c)) ... ) "
9    | x → " unit x "
10   | c(e₁, ..., eₙ) →
11     let x₁, ..., xₙ = FreshVar (), ..., FreshVar () in
12       "  'Transform eₙ' >>= fun xₙ ->
13             ...
14           'Transform e₁' >>= fun x₁ ->
15             unit (c(x₁, ..., xₙ))  "
16   | e_f e_p →
17     let x_app, x_p, s_full s_partial = FreshVar (), FreshVar (), FreshVar (), FreshVar () in
18       "  fun s_full ->
19              ('Transform e_p' >>= fun x_p ->
20              'Transform e_f' >>= fun x_f ->
21              update ('enter e' x_p) >>= fun () s_partial ->
22              (x_f x_p >>= fun x_app ->
23              update ('exit e' s_full s_partial) >>= fun () ->
24              unit x_app) s_partial) s_full   "
25   | fun x -> e_b → " unit (fun x -> 'Transform e_b') "
26   | let p = e₁ in e₂ → " ( 'Transform e₁' >>= fun p -> 'Transform e₂' ) "
27   | let rec x_f = fun x -> e_b in e₂ →
28       " ( let rec x_f = fun x -> 'Transform e_b' in 'Transform e₂') "
29   | match e_m with | e₁ᵖ -> e₁  ... | eᵢᵖ -> eᵢ →
30       let x_m  = FreshVar () in
31         "  'Transform e_m' >>= fun x_m ->
32           ( match x_m with
33               | e₁ᵖ -> 'Transform e₁'
34               ...
35               | eᵢᵖ -> 'Transform eᵢ'
36           )  "
```

Fig. 7. The transformation function Transform. The operator " · " emits a Mini-OCaml expression after evaluating expressions that are embedded using ' · '.

values into the state, or propagates further the current state. Furthermore, enter performs a check if the snapshot stored in a state together with the arguments of a f/N-application satisfy the transition invariant candidate TI. This check is guarded by the condition that the snapshot must have been stored previously.

We show an example application of Transform in Figure 8 for analyzing f/1-applications. First, we present subexpressions of the program and then show the result of the application of Transform on them (we have partially simplified the transformed expressions to improve readability).

We establish a relationship between augmented evaluation trees and evaluation trees of the transformed program in the following theorem.

Theorem 2 (Transform Implements Augment). *A pair $(v_1, \ldots, v_N)$ and $(u_1, \ldots, u_N)$ is obtained from the augmented evaluation tree as described in Theorem 1 if and only if a judgement of the following form appears in the evaluation tree of the program obtained by applying* Transform:

$$\mathcal{E} \vdash f \; e_1 \; \_ \; \ldots \; e_N \; s \; \Rightarrow \; v,$$

such that eval $\mathcal{E} \; s \; = \; (true, (v_1, \ldots, v_N))$ *and for each $i \in 1..N$ we have* eval $\mathcal{E} \; e_i = u_i$.

The following corollary of Theorem 2 allows one to rely on the assertion validity in the transformed program to implement the binary reachability analysis of the original program.

Theorem 3 (Binary Reachability Analysis as Assertion Checking). *Each pair $(v_1, \ldots, v_N)$ and $(u_1, \ldots, u_N)$ in the f/N-recursion relation of the program satisfies TI if and only if the assertion inserted by* enter *is valid in the transformed program.*

6   Experimental Evaluation

In this section we describe our implementation and the corresponding experimental evaluation.

Implementation. We implemented Transform as an extension to the Camlp4 parser [26]. Our implementation takes as input a user program and a specification consisting of a function name, an arity, and candidate transition invariant. Our implementation produces a transformed program following the procedure depicted in Figure 8.

Experiments. Our experiments consisted of two steps. First we applied our transformation to the set of benchmarks summarized in Figure 9. Then we analyzed the transformed benchmarks using the reachability checker Dsolve [16,17]. The set of benchmarks is available at http://www7.in.tum.de/~ruslan/binreach/. Our benchmarks feature higher order functions and algebraic data types (lists). We summarize our verified benchmarks in Figure 9. Benchmarks 11-15 correspond to the higher-order programs in [28] that are strict and type-check.

```
e = let rec f x = if x > 0 then f (x - 1) else fun y -> f x y in f 1
e1 = if x > 0 then f (x - 1) else fun y -> f x y
e2 = x > 0
e3 = 0
e4 = (>) x
e5 = x
e6 = (>)
e7 = f (x - 1)
...


Transform e = let rec f = fun x -> 'Transform e1' in 'Transform e20'
Transform e1 = 'Transform e2' >>= fun x2 -> (if x2 then 'Transform e7'
                                             else 'Transform e14')
Transform e2 = fun s_full -> ('Transform e3' >>= fun x3 ->
                              'Transform e4' >>= fun x4 ->
                              update (fun s -> s) >>= fun () s_partial ->
                              (x4 x3 >>= fun xapp2 ->
                              update (fun s -> s) >>= fun () ->
                              unit xapp2) s_partial) s_full
Transform e3 = unit 0
Transform e4 = fun s_full -> ('Transform e5' >>= fun x5 ->
                              'Transform e6' >>= fun x6 ->
                              update (fun s -> s) >>= fun () s_partial ->
                              (x6 x5 >>= fun xapp4 ->
                              update (fun s -> s) >>= fun () ->
                              unit xapp4) s_partial) s_full
Transform e5 = unit x
Transform e6 = unit (fun z1 -> unit (fun z2 -> unit (z1 > z2)))
Transform e7 = fun s_full -> ('Transform e8' >>= fun x8 ->
                              'Transform e13' >>= fun x13 ->
                              update (fun ( _, m ) ->
                                let m_c, m_1 = m in
                                if m_c then assert ( x8 > 0 && m_1 > x8 );
                                x8, if not m_c && nondet () then true, x8
                                    else m
                              ) >>= fun () s_partial ->
                              (x13 x8 >>= fun xapp7 ->
                              update (fun _ -> s_full) >>= fun () ->
                              unit xapp7) s_partial) s_full
...
```

Fig. 8. Example application of Transform with $N = 1$ and $TI = (a_1 > 0 \wedge m_1 > a_1)$. Given a stored snapshot, the transformed application f (x - 1) checks that the current actual satisfies TI.

The experiments show that our transformation can be used together with a state of the art static analyzer to prove termination of higher-order programs found in the literature.

#	Name	Description	Disjuncts in TI	FunV wall time
1	ack	The Ackermann function	2	0m1.320s
2	chop	Chop the first n elements of a list	2	1m14.507s
3	dictionary	An algebraic data type recursive manipulation	1	0m37.219s
4	fold2 (H)	Fold a pair of lists	2	12m17.410s
5	mccarthy91	The McCarthy 91 function	1	0m20.142s
6	mult	Recursive definition of multiplication	2	1m14.957s
7	rev_append	Append a list reversed	1	0m11.829s
8	rev_merge	Merge two lists	2	0m2.279s
9	simple-rec	A simple recursive function	1	0m5.293s
10	sum	The sum of the first n naturals	1	0m8.268s
11	sereni29 (H)	map applied to a function constructed with compose and a list	1	0m3.843s
12	sereni56 (H)	Computation of the n-th Church numeral using compose	1	0m4.046s
13	sereni81 (H)	Fold left defined using fold right	1	0m9.859s
14	sereni85 (H)	A program with two call sites to map	1	0m5.230s
15	sereni163 (H)	A parameter function applied to a non-terminating parameter function	1	0m2.002s

Fig. 9. Verified benchmarks. Benchmarks with higher order functions are marked with (H). We show the number of disjuncts of the corresponding transition invariant in the next to last column.

7   Related Work

Termination and control-flow analysis. Traditionally, termination analysis of higher-order programs is developed on top of a control-flow analysis [28, 29, 30]. Our approach relies on the applied safety checker to keep track of control flow. In principle, our transformation could benefit from the results of control-flow analysis, as discussed in Section 8. Practically, such additional information was not necessary when proving termination of all examples presented in [28, 29, 30]. Adding a control-flow analysis pass [8, 23, 27, 31] before the transformation would be akin to the application of (function) pointer analysis for imperative programs. We leave a study of such an integration as future work.

Abstraction for termination. The size change termination argument [20] can be extended to higher-order functional programs, see e.g. [15, 30]. This argument requires checking the presence of an infinite descent in values passed to application sites of the program on any infinite traversal of the call graph. In contrast, our approach can keep track of a rank descent in arbitrary expressions over program values. In principle, SCT can be seen a specific abstract domain that yields termination arguments related to disjunctive well-foundedness [10]. We leave the question if general abstraction techniques for termination [6, 7] can be reduced by an appropriate source to source transformation as future work.

Contract checking. Contracts are pre- and post-condition specifications for functions. Xu created a verification tool [36] for Haskell that is based on contracts and partial evaluation. Their approach works well for checking safety properties, and can even detect divergence of programs. In contrast, our approach is specialized to the verification of termination, and is a step towards the auto-mated verification of termination through counterexample guided abstraction refinement.

Liquid typing. Dsolve [16] is a reachability checker based on refinement type inference. The type inference algorithm consists of two parts. First, a set of constraints over refinement predicates is generated from program code. Second, an iterative algorithm tests candidate solutions constructed from a set of predicate schemes in the theory of linear arithmetic and uninterpreted functions. As our experiments show, the composition of our transformation and Dsolve yields a binary reachability analysis tool.

8   A Limitation and Future Work

Compared to imperative programs, higher order functions impose additional complication on the binary reachability analysis. The major current limitation of our approach lies in the treatment of partial applications when arguments are provided at different program points, as illustrated by the following example.

```
let rec f x = if x > 0 then f (x - 1) else fun y -> y + 1 in
let g = f 1 in
g 2
```

Proving termination of f/2 applications is not possible, since the second argument to f is given indirectly through an application of g. Without a control-flow analysis, we cannot store 2 in the auxiliary state since it is not known syntactically that 2 is the second argument for f. Removing the above limitation is an important step for future work, which can be accomplished either by relying on results of a control-flow analysis, e.g. [27], that is performed before the transformation takes place. In simple cases, by using the following transformation that is based on β reduction.

```
let rec f x = if x > 0 then f (x - 1) else fun y -> y + 1 in
(* let g = f 1 in *)
(f 1) 2
```

In the transformed program, both arguments are given to f directly.

Acknowledgements. Ruslán Ledesma-Garza is supported by the Deutsche Forschungsgemeinschaft, through the research training group 1480 - Program and Model Analysis.

References

1. Ball, T., Rajamani, S.K.: The SLAM project: debugging system software via static analysis. In: POPL (2002)
2. Berdine, J., Cook, B., Distefano, D., O'Hearn, P.W.: Automatic Termination Proofs for Programs with Shape-Shifting Heaps. In: Ball, T., Jones, R.B. (eds.) CAV 2006. LNCS, vol. 4144, pp. 386–400. Springer, Heidelberg (2006)

3. Chawdhary, A., Cook, B., Gulwani, S., Sagiv, M., Yang, H.: Ranking Abstractions. In: Drossopoulou, S. (ed.) ESOP 2008. LNCS, vol. 4960, pp. 148–162. Springer, Heidelberg (2008)
4. Cook, B., Podelski, A., Rybalchenko, A.: Termination proofs for systems code. In: PLDI (2006)
5. Cook, B., Podelski, A., Rybalchenko, A.: Proving program termination. Commun. ACM 54(5) (2011)
6. Cousot, P., Cousot, R.: Invited talk: Higher order abstract interpretation (and application to comportment analysis generalizing strictness, termination, projection, and per analysis. In: ICCL (1994)
7. Cousot, P., Cousot, R.: An abstract interpretation framework for termination. In: POPL (2012)
8. Earl, C., Might, M., Horn, D.V.: Pushdown control-flow analysis of higher-order programs: Precise, polyvariant and polynomial-time. In: Scheme (2010)
9. Giesl, J., Raffelsieper, M., Schneider-Kamp, P., Swiderski, S., Thiemann, R.: Automated termination proofs for haskell by term rewriting. ACM Trans. Program. Lang. Syst. 33 (2011)
10. Heizmann, M., Jones, N.D., Podelski, A.: Size-Change Termination and Transition Invariants. In: Cousot, R., Martel, M. (eds.) SAS 2010. LNCS, vol. 6337, pp. 22–50. Springer, Heidelberg (2010)
11. Henzinger, T.A., Jhala, R., Majumdar, R., Sutre, G.: Lazy abstraction. In: POPL (2002)
12. Ivančić, F., Yang, Z., Ganai, M.K., Gupta, A., Shlyakhter, I., Ashar, P.: F-SOFT: Software Verification Platform. In: Etessami, K., Rajamani, S.K. (eds.) CAV 2005. LNCS, vol. 3576, pp. 301–306. Springer, Heidelberg (2005)
13. Jhala, R., Majumdar, R.: Counterexample refinement for functional programs (2009), http://www.cs.ucla.edu/~rupak/Papers/CEGARFunctional.ps
14. Jhala, R., Majumdar, R., Rybalchenko, A.: HMC: Verifying Functional Programs Using Abstract Interpreters. In: Gopalakrishnan, G., Qadeer, S. (eds.) CAV 2011. LNCS, vol. 6806, pp. 470–485. Springer, Heidelberg (2011)
15. Jones, N.D., Bohr, N.: Termination Analysis of the Untyped λ-Calculus. In: van Oostrom, V. (ed.) RTA 2004. LNCS, vol. 3091, pp. 1–23. Springer, Heidelberg (2004)
16. Kawaguchi, M., Rondon, P.M., Jhala, R.: Type-based data structure verification. In: PLDI (2009)
17. Kawaguchi, M., Rondon, P.M., Jhala, R.: Dsolve: Safety Verification via Liquid Types. In: Touili, T., Cook, B., Jackson, P. (eds.) CAV 2010. LNCS, vol. 6174, pp. 123–126. Springer, Heidelberg (2010)
18. Kobayashi, N., Sato, R., Unno, H.: Predicate abstraction and CEGAR for higher-order model checking. In: PLDI (2011)
19. Kroening, D., Sharygina, N., Tsitovich, A., Wintersteiger, C.M.: Termination Analysis with Compositional Transition Invariants. In: Touili, T., Cook, B., Jackson, P. (eds.) CAV 2010. LNCS, vol. 6174, pp. 89–103. Springer, Heidelberg (2010)
20. Lee, C.S., Jones, N.D., Ben-Amram, A.M.: The size-change principle for program termination. In: POPL (2001)
21. Leroy, X.: Polymorphic typing of an algorithmic language. Research report 1778, INRIA (1992)
22. McMillan, K.L.: Lazy Abstraction with Interpolants. In: Ball, T., Jones, R.B. (eds.) CAV 2006. LNCS, vol. 4144, pp. 123–136. Springer, Heidelberg (2006)
23. Might, M., Shivers, O.: Exploiting reachability and cardinality in higher-order flow analysis. J. Funct. Program. 18(5-6) (2008)

24. Otto, C., Brockschmidt, M., von Essen, C., Giesl, J.: Automated termination analysis of java bytecode by term rewriting. In: RTA (2010)
25. Podelski, A., Rybalchenko, A.: Transition invariants. In: LICS (2004)
26. Pouillard, N.: Camlp4 (retrieved on July 11, 2011)
27. Prabhu, T., Ramalingam, S., Might, M., Hall, M.W.: Eigencfa: accelerating flow analysis with GPUs. In: POPL (2011)
28. Sereni, D.: Termination Analysis of Higher-Order Functional Programs. PhD thesis, University of Oxford (2006)
29. Sereni, D.: Termination analysis and call graph construction for higher-order functional programs. In: ICFP (2007)
30. Sereni, D., Jones, N.D.: Termination Analysis of Higher-Order Functional Programs. In: Yi, K. (ed.) APLAS 2005. LNCS, vol. 3780, pp. 281–297. Springer, Heidelberg (2005)
31. Shivers, O.: Control-flow analysis in scheme. In: PLDI (1988)
32. Spoto, F., Mesnard, F., Payet, É.: A termination analyzer for java bytecode based on path-length. ACM Trans. Program. Lang. Syst. 32(3) (2010)
33. Terauchi, T.: Dependent types from counterexamples. In: POPL (2010)
34. Voigtländer, J.: Free theorems involving type constructor classes: functional pearl. In: ICFP (2009)
35. Wadler, P.: Monads for functional programming. In: Advanced Functional Programming, pp. 24–52 (1995)
36. Xu, D.N.: Static Contract Checking for Haskell. PhD thesis. University of Cambridge (August 2008)

On the Limits of the Classical Approach to Cost Analysis

Diego Esteban Alonso-Blas and Samir Genaim

DSIC, Complutense University of Madrid (UCM), Spain

Abstract. The classical approach to static cost analysis is based on transforming a given program into cost relations and solving them into closed-form upper-bounds. It is known that for some programs, this approach infers upper-bounds that are asymptotically less precise than the actual cost. As yet, it was assumed that this imprecision is due to the way cost relations are solved into upper-bounds. In this paper: (1) we show that this assumption is partially true, and identify the reason due to which cost relations cannot precisely model the cost of such programs; and (2) to overcome this imprecision, we develop a new approach to cost analysis, based on SMT and quantifier elimination. Interestingly, we find a strong relation between our approach and amortised cost analysis.

1 Introduction

Cost analysis (a.k.a. resource usage analysis) aims at *statically* determining the amount of resources required to safely execute a given program, i.e., without running out of resources. By *resource*, we mean any quantitative aspect of the program, such as memory consumption, execution steps, etc. Several cost analysis frameworks are available [2,10,12,14,15,17]. Although different in their underlying theory, all of them usually report the cost of a program as an upper-bound function (UBF for short) such that: when evaluated on (an abstraction of) a given input, the UBF gives an upper-bound on the amount of resources required for safely running the program on that specific input.

Many automatic cost analysis tools are based on the *classical approach* of Wegbreit [22], which we describe using its extension for JAVA bytecode [2]. This analysis is done in three steps: (1) the JAVA program is transformed into an *abstract program*, in which data-structures are abstracted to their sizes, e.g., length of lists, depth of trees, etc.; (2) the abstract program is transformed into a set of *cost relations* (CRs for short), which are a non-deterministic form of *recurrence equations* that define the cost of executing the program in terms of its *input* parameters; and (3) the CRs are solved into UBFs.

This analysis performs well in practice, however, for some classical examples, it infers UBFs that are asymptotically less precise than the actual cost. Clearly, the abstraction at step (1) may involve a loss of precision since it can introduce spurious traces, which do not occur in the original program. This imprecision is out of the scope of this paper. Instead, we focus on the imprecision at steps (2)

A. Miné and D. Schmidt (Eds.): SAS 2012, LNCS 7460, pp. 405–421, 2012.

and (3). As yet, it was *assumed* that this imprecision is due to the way CRs are solved into UBFs in step (3), and that, in principle, it could be overcome using more precise resolution techniques.

The *first contribution* of this paper shows that this assumption is not true, namely, that the cost of some programs cannot be modeled precisely with CRs. This is because CRs are defined only in terms of the input parameters, and thus they fail to capture dependencies between the output of a program and its cost. These dependencies are crucial for programs in which the output of one part is passed as input to another part, and transforming them into CRs introduces spurious scenarios. Any resolution technique that solves CRs into UBFs must cover these spurious scenarios, hence it would fail to obtain precise UBFs.

To eliminate these spurious scenarios, an UBF must be defined in terms of both input and output. Our *second contribution* is a novel cost analysis that uses the this notion of cost. It is based on quantifier elimination and template UBFs. Briefly, it takes a given set of template UBFs, with some unknown parameters, and uses satisfiability modulo theory (SMT) and quantifier elimination to instantiate those parameters, such that the resulting UBFs are safe.

The rest of the paper is organised as follows. Sec. 2 presents our running examples and formally defines the language on which we apply our analysis. Sec. 3 studies the limitations of CRs. Secs. 4 and 5 are the technical core of the paper, in which we develop our cost analysis. Sec. 6 discusses the relation of our analysis to amortised cost analysis. Sec. 7 describes a prototype implementation. Sec. 8 overviews related work, and Finally, Sec. 9 concludes.

2   Motivating Examples and Preliminaries

In this section we describe an *abstract cost rules* (ACR for short) language [2], which we use to formally present our cost analysis. In [2], a JAVA program is *automatically abstracted* to this language. The abstraction guarantees that every *concrete* trace has a corresponding *abstract* one with the same cost, but there might be spurious abstract traces, which do not correspond to concrete ones. Recall that our interest is in analysing ACR programs, the translation from JAVA is out of the scope of this paper. We first explain the language using some examples that we use along the paper. Then, we formally define its syntax, semantics and the concrete notions of cost. As a notation, we refer to line number n in a given JAVA (resp. ACR) program by Jn (resp. An).

Example 1. The JAVA code of the first example is depicted in Fig. 1 (on the left). It implements a Stack data-structure using a linked list whose first element is the top of the stack (field top points to this list). Method main has a loop (J14-19) that in each iteration invokes method randPop (J15), which in turn pops an arbitrary number of elements (J6-9), and then pushes a new element (J16). Note that coin() at J6 non-deterministically returns *true* or *false*. Each pop operation consumes m resources, as specified by the annotation @acquire(m) at J8, and each push consumes 1 resource (J17). This example is based on a classical example for amortised analysis [9], the only difference is that pop costs m units instead

```
 1 class Stack {
 2   Node top;
 3
 4   //@requires m >= 1
 5   void randPop(int m) {
 6     while( top != null && coin() ) {
 7       top=top.next; //pop
 8       //@acquire(m)
 9     }
10   }
11
12   //@requires m >= 0
13   void main(int m) {
14     while( m > 0 ) {
15       randPop(m);
16       top = new Node('a',top); //push
17       //@acquire(1)
18       m = m−1;
19     }
20   }
21 }
```

$$1 \quad rpop([s, m], [s_1]) \leftarrow$$
$$2 \quad m \geq 1,$$
$$3 \quad s \geq 0,$$
$$4 \quad s_1 = s.$$
$$5 \quad rpop([s, m], [s_1]) \leftarrow$$
$$6 \quad m \geq 1,$$
$$7 \quad s \geq 1,$$
$$8 \quad acq(m),$$
$$9 \quad s_2 = s - 1,$$
$$10 \quad rpop([s_2, m], [s_1]).$$
$$11$$
$$12 \quad main([s, m], [s_1]) \leftarrow$$
$$13 \quad m = 0,$$
$$14 \quad s_1 = s,$$
$$15 \quad main([s, m], [s_1]) \leftarrow$$
$$16 \quad m \geq 1,$$
$$17 \quad rpop([s, m], [s_2]),$$
$$18 \quad s_3 = s_2 + 1,$$
$$19 \quad acq(1),$$
$$20 \quad m_1 = m - 1,$$
$$21 \quad main([s_3, m_1], [s_1]).$$

Fig. 1. Java code for Stack and its ACR program

of 1, to showcase some unique features of our analysis. These m units can be seen as the cost of executing m iterations of a loop (which we omit).

Fig. 1 (on the right) includes the ACR version of Stack. It has been automatically generated, and simplified for clarity, using the tools of [2]. A1-10 define a procedure $rpop$ that corresponds to randPop. It has two input parameters: s is the size of the stack (i.e., the length of list top); and m is the value of variable m. Note that s is an abstraction of top. It also has one output parameter s_1 which corresponds to the size of the stack upon exit from randPop. Procedure $rpop$ is defined by means of two rules: the first one (A1-4) corresponds to the case in which we do not enter the loop; and the second one (A5-10) corresponds to executing one iteration and calling $rpop$ recursively (A10) for more iterations. The instruction $s_2 = s - 1$ at A9 corresponds to removing an element from the stack (J7). The translation of method main into procedure $main$ (A12-20) is done in a similar way. Just note that calling $rpop$ (A17) with a stack of size s results in a stack of size s_2, and that $s_3 = s_2 + 1$ at A18 corresponds to J16.

A call $main([s, m], [s_1])$ executes exactly m push operations, and thus, it can execute at most $s + m$ pop operations. Each push costs exactly 1, and each pop at most m. Since m varies from one call to $rpop$ to another, then $s \cdot m + \frac{1}{2}(m^2 + m)$ is an UBF on the resource consumption of $main([s, m], [s_1])$. The analysis of [2] infers the cubic UBF $m^3 + s \cdot m^2 + m$, which is asymptotically less precise.

```
1 //@requires n>=0          10 //@requires n>=1
2 void p(int n) {           11 int q(int n) {
3   if (n > 0) {            12   int i = n/2;
4     m = q(n);             13   do {
5     //@release(m)         14     A x = new A();
6     p(n−m);               15     B y = new B();
7     //@release(m)         16     //@acquire(2)
8   }                       17     i−−;
9 }                         18     // [...]
                            19   } while(i>0 && coin());
                            20   return n/2 − i;
                            21 }
```

1 $p([n],[\ ]) \leftarrow$	14 $l([i],[i_1]) \leftarrow$
2 $n = 0.$	15 $i \geq 1,$
3 $p([n],[\ ]) \leftarrow$	16 $\mathtt{acq}(2),$
4 $n \geq 1,$	17 $i_2 = i - 1,$
5 $q([n],[m]),$	18 $l([i_2],[i_1]).$
6 $\mathtt{rel}(m),$	19 $q([n],[m]) \leftarrow$
7 $n_1 = n - m,$	20 $n \geq 1$
8 $p([n_1],[\ ]),$	21 $i = n/2,$
9 $\mathtt{rel}(m).$	22 $l([i],[i_1]),$
10 $l([i],[i_1]) \leftarrow$	23 $m = i - i_1.$
11 $i \geq 0,$	
12 $\mathtt{acq}(2),$	
13 $i_1 = i - 1.$	

Fig. 2. Java code for the peak, and its ACR program

Example 2. The second example is depicted in Fig. 2. We use it to explain the notion of *peak* resource consumption. Method q (J10-21) receives an integer n, executes at least 1 and at most n/2 iterations of a loop (J13-19), and returns the number of iterations that have been performed. This loop creates 2 objects in each iteration (J14-15). Method p executes a loop (using recursion) where in each iteration it calls q with the current value of the loop counter n, and then performs a recursive call where the loop counter is decremented by m (the number of iterations that q has performed). The ACR version, depicted in Fig. 2 on the right, its relation to the JAVA code is as in Ex. 1. We skip details and only comment that procedure l (A10-23) corresponds to the while loop (J13-19). Note that the ACR includes explicit resource release instructions (A6 and A9).

A call $p([n],[\ ])$ creates exactly $2 \cdot n$ objects. However, assuming that objects of type A (resp. B) become unreachable at J5 (resp. J7), then m objects can be garbage collected when reaching J5 (resp. J7). Thus, at any given moment there cannot be more than n reachable objects, which means that a memory for n objects (the peak consumption) is enough for safely executing this program. The analysis of [2,3] infers the UBF $\frac{n \cdot (n+1)}{2}$ which is asymptotically less precise.

In both programs of Exs. 1 and 2, the resource consumption is specified with the annotations $\mathtt{acq}(e)$ and $\mathtt{rel}(e)$, for acquiring and releasing e resources respectively. It should be clear that we are interested in inferring safe UBFs assuming the given annotations, and not in inferring the annotations.

Syntax. Formally, an ACR program is a set of procedures. A procedure p is defined by a set of rules of the form $p(\bar{x}, \bar{y}) \leftarrow b_1, b_2, \ldots, b_n$ where $\bar{x}$ (resp. $\bar{y}$) is a sequence of input (resp. output) parameters, and each b_i is one of the following instructions: a (linear) constraint φ; a procedure call $q(\bar{w}, \bar{z})$; or a resource consumption instruction $\mathtt{acq}(e)$ or $\mathtt{rel}(e)$ where e is an arithmetic expression that evaluates to a non-negative value. In the rest of the paper we assume a given program P (to avoid repeating "for a given program P").

$$\text{①} \quad \frac{q(\bar{x}, \bar{y}) \leftarrow \bar{b}' \in P}{\langle \psi, q(\bar{x}, \bar{y}) \cdot \bar{b} \rangle \xrightarrow{0} \langle \psi, \bar{b}' \cdot \bar{b} \rangle} \qquad \text{②} \quad \frac{\psi \wedge \varphi \not\models \text{false}}{\langle \psi, \varphi \cdot \bar{b} \rangle \xrightarrow{0} \langle \psi \wedge \varphi, \bar{b} \rangle}$$

$$\text{③} \quad \frac{eval(e, \psi) = v \geq 0}{\langle \psi, \text{acq}(e) \cdot \bar{b} \rangle \xrightarrow{v} \langle \psi, \bar{b} \rangle} \qquad \text{④} \quad \frac{eval(e, \psi) = v \geq 0}{\langle \psi, \text{rel}(e) \cdot \bar{b} \rangle \xrightarrow{-v} \langle \psi, \bar{b} \rangle}$$

Fig. 3. Semantics of ACR programs

Semantics. A state s takes the form $\langle \psi, \bar{b} \rangle$, where $\bar{b}$ is a sequence of instructions pending for execution, and ψ is a constraint over $vars(\bar{b})$ and possibly other existentially quantified variables. The *store* ψ imposes relations between variables (e.g., $x = 1$, $x > y$). An execution starts from an initial state $\langle \bar{x} = \bar{v}, p(\bar{x}, \bar{y}) \rangle$, where $\bar{v}$ is a sequence of integers, which is then rewritten according to the rules in Fig. 3. These rules define a transition relation $s_1 \xrightarrow{v} s_2$, meaning that there is a transition from s_1 to s_2 that consumes v resources. Rule ① handles procedure calls, it (non-deterministically) selects a rule from P that matches the call, and adds its instructions $\bar{b}'$ to the sequence of pending instructions. Variables in $\bar{b}'$ (except $\bar{x} \cup \bar{y}$) are renamed such that they are different from $vars(\bar{b}) \cup vars(\psi)$. Rule ② handles constraints by adding them to the store, if the resulting state is satisfiable. Rules ③-④ handle resource consumption. They evaluate e to a non-negative value v, and label the corresponding transition with v or $-v$.

The execution stops when no rule is applicable, which happens when the execution reaches (1) a *final state* $\langle \psi', \epsilon \rangle$ where ϵ is the empty sequence; or (2) a *blocking state* $\langle \psi', \varphi \cdot \bar{b} \rangle$ where $\varphi \wedge \psi' \models false$. A trace t is a finite or infinite sequence of states in which there is a valid transition between each pair of consecutive states. Traces that end in a final state and infinite traces are called *complete*. Namely, we exclude traces that end in a blocking state. We write $s_1 \xrightarrow{*} s_2$ for a finite trace starting from s_1 and ending at s_2.

Definition 1 (trace cost). *Given a finite trace t, its net-cost $\tilde{\tau}(t)$ is the sum of the cost labels on its transitions. Given a complete trace t, its peak-cost $\hat{\tau}(t)$ is defined as* $\max\{\tilde{\tau}(t') \mid t' \text{ is a prefix of } t\}$.

Note that the peak-cost is always non-negative since the empty trace is a prefix of any trace t. However, the net-cost can be also negative. This is because we do not require that resources are acquired before they are released. This is useful for modeling consumer/producer programs, where the produced data can be viewed as resources. Though, we do not address such scenarios in this paper.

Definition 2 (procedure cost). *Given a procedure p with m input and n output parameters, its net-cost $\tilde{\pi}(p)$ and peak-cost $\hat{\pi}(p)$ are defined as*

$$\tilde{\pi}(p) = \{\langle \bar{v}_1, \bar{v}_2, \tilde{\tau}(t) \rangle \mid \bar{v}_1 \in \mathbb{Z}^m, \bar{v}_2 \in \mathbb{Z}^n, t \equiv \langle \bar{x} = \bar{v}_1, p(\bar{x}, \bar{y}) \rangle \xrightarrow{*} \langle \psi, \epsilon \rangle, \bar{y} = \bar{v}_2 \models \psi\}$$
$$\hat{\pi}(p) = \{\langle \bar{v}_1, \hat{\tau}(t) \rangle \quad \mid \bar{v}_1 \in \mathbb{Z}^m, t \text{ is a complete trace and starts in } \langle \bar{x} = \bar{v}_1, p(\bar{x}, \bar{y}) \rangle\}$$

Intuitively, the net-cost tells what is the balance between the resources that have been acquired and released during the execution of p. Note that it only considers traces that terminate in a final state. The peak-cost tells what is the maximum amount of resources that a program can hold (i.e., acquired but not released yet) at any given state during the execution. Note that Def. 2 does not consider traces that terminate in a blocking state. This is because they do not correspond to valid traces in the JAVA program, and obtained due to the abstraction.

We say that $C \geq 0$ resources are enough for safely executing $p(\bar{v}, \bar{y})$ without running out of resources if $C \geq \max\{c \mid \langle \bar{v}, c \rangle \in \hat{\pi}(p)\}$. Note that for terminating programs that only acquires resources, one could also use $C \geq \max\{c \mid \langle \bar{v}, \bar{v}', c \rangle \in \hat{\pi}(p)\}$. This is the case for example of the Stack program. Our main interest is in inferring UBFs on the peak-cost of each procedure, however, this will require inferring first UBFs on the net-cost of each procedure p as we will see later.

3   Shortcomings of the Classical Approach to Cost Analysis

As explained in Sec. 1, the classical approach to cost analysis first transforms a given program into a set of CRs, and then solves these CRs into UBFs. The following CRs are automatically generated by [2] for the Stack program of Fig. 1

(1) $rpop(s, m) = 0$ $\{m \geq 1 \land s \geq 0\}$
(2) $rpop(s, m) = m + rpop(s_2, m)$ $\{m \geq 1 \land s \geq 1 \land s_2 = s - 1\}$
(3) $main(s, m) = 0$ $\{m = 0 \land s \geq 0\}$
(4) $main(s, m) = 1 + rpop(s, m) + main(s_3, m_1)$ $\{m \geq 1 \land s_3 = s_2 + 1 \land m_1 = m - 1 \land \underline{s \geq s_2 \geq 0}\}$

Eqs. (1)-(2) capture the cost of executing procedure $rpop$ on the input s and m, and Eqs. (3)-(4) capture the cost of executing procedure $main$ on the input s and m. Eq. (4) states that when $m \geq 1$, the cost of executing $main(s, m)$ is 1 (for the push operation); plus the cost of executing $rpop(s, m)$; plus the cost of executing $main(s_3, m_1)$. The constraints on the right side of each equation define the applicability conditions for that equation (e.g., $m \geq 1$) and relations between its variables (e.g., $s_3 = s_2 + 1$). Note that the above CRs have a similar structure to the corresponding ACR program of Fig. 1.

A fundamental difference between ACRs and CRs is that the latter do not include the output parameters. For example, in Eq. (4), the output parameter s_2 in the call to $rpop$ has been removed, and the constraint $s \geq s_2 \geq 0$ (underlined in Eq. (4)) has been added to indicate that, upon exit from $rpop$, the value of s_2 is non-negative and smaller than or equal to s. Note that this is the most precise relation between the input and the output parameters of $rpop$. This information is obtained by value analysis (at the level of the ACR program) that infers relations between the input and the output parameters [6].

CRs can be evaluated (they are similar to a functional program with constraints) to obtain the cost of a corresponding procedure. E.g., $main(v_1, v_2)$ can be evaluated to obtain the cost of executing $main([v_1, v_2], [y])$. Clearly, due to the non-determinism (e.g., in the constraints), the evaluation of $main(v_1, v_2)$ might result in several possible values. Soundness requires that the cost of any trace for $main([v_1, v_2], [y])$ is a possible result for $main(v_1, v_2)$. Nevertheless, the interest is not in evaluating CRs, since it is like executing the ACR program, but rather in statically computing UBFs that bound their results. For example, the solver of [1] infers the UBF $m^3 + m^2 \cdot s + m$ for $main(s, m)$. Intuitively, it does this as follows: (a) it infers the maximum number of iterations that $main$ can perform, which is m; (b) it infers a worst-case behaviour for all iterations, which is $1 + (s + m) \cdot m$ since the stack can have at most $s + m$ elements; and (c) it multiplies (a) and (b) to get the above UBF.

It is known that, in practice, cost analysers that are based on CRs fail to obtain the desired UBFs for programs like those in Fig. 1 and 2. Moreover, as yet, it was assumed that this failure is due to (i) the way CRs are solved into UBFs; and (ii) the imprecision in the value analysis which is used to infer input-output relations (as $s \geq s_2 \geq 0$ above). It was also assumed that, in principle, one could develop more sophisticated techniques for solving CRs [4] or use more precise value analysis (e.g., non-linear) that would obtain precise UBFs for such programs. In what follows we show that these assumptions are not true. In particular, that Eqs. (3)-(4) in the above CRs do not model *precisely* the cost of procedure $main$, and thus any sound UBF for $main$ would be imprecise.

Let us consider an evaluation of $main(s, m)$ in the above CRs. It is easy to see that, using Eq. (4), we can choose $s_2 = s$ and thus get $main(s, m) = 1 + rpop(s, m) + main(s + 1, m - 1)$. Then, in the same way, we can get $main(s + 1, m - 1) = 1 + rpop(s + 1, m - 1) + main(s + 2, m - 2)$, and so on for each $main(s+i, m-i)$. Thus, an evaluation of $main(s, m)$ admits $\sum_{i=0}^{m-1}(1 + rpop(s + i, m - i))$ as a possible result. Since $rpop(s, m)$ can always evaluate to $s \cdot m$, the above sum can be reduced to $u(s, m) = \frac{(m-1)}{6} \cdot (m^2 + 3 \cdot s \cdot m + m + 6)$. This means that any UBF $f(s, m)$ for Eqs. (3)-(4) must satisfy $\forall s, m : f(s, m) \geq u(s, m)$, which is asymptotically less precise than the UBF from Ex. 1. Thus, we conclude that the imprecision is not related to how CRs are solved, and not to imprecision in the value analysis since the input-output relation $s \geq s_2 \geq 0$ that we used above is the most precise one.

The actual reason for this imprecision is that, in Eq (4), the value for s_2, i.e., the output of $rpop$, and the cost of $rpop(m, s)$ can be chosen independently. For example, in the original program it is not possible that $s_2 = s$ and that the cost of $rpop(s, m)$ is $s \cdot m$, in which case s_2 must be 0. However, in the above CRs this scenario is possible. This relation cannot be captured if the UBFs are defined only in terms of the input parameters, an observation that lead us to the idea of defining UBFs in terms of both input and output parameters.

Example 3. Consider again procedure $rpop([s, m], [s'])$ of Fig. 1. The CRs-based approach infers the UBF $s \cdot m$ for $rpop$, which depends only on the input parameters s and m. This indeed is the most precise UBF if only input parameters are allowed, since there exists an execution in which we remove all stack elements. However, if we allow the use of output parameters also, then $(s - s') \cdot m$ describes the exact cost of $rpop$: $s - s'$ is the number of elements that have been removed from the stack, and removing each one costs m.

At this point, the use of output parameters to define UBFs might look inappropriate. This is because UBFs are usually used to *statically* estimate the amount of resource required for safely executing the program. However, requiring information on the output parameters in order to evaluate a given UBF is like actually requiring to execute the program. This is not really the case because of the following two reasons. First, when inferring UBFs on the net-cost, we distinguish between the entry procedure (e.g., *main*), and intermediate procedures (e.g., *rpop*). The UBF for the entry procedure will (almost always) be definable in terms of its input parameters only, however, in order to infer a precise UBF for the entry procedure, we need UBFs for the intermediate procedures in terms of input and output parameters. Second, UBFs on the peak-cost, which are the important ones for safety, will use only input parameters, however, inferring them will make use of net-cost UBFs that depend on input and output parameters.

4   Inference of Net-Cost

In this section we describe our approach for inferring UBFs on the net-cost of the program's procedures, which is based on defining the cost in terms of the input and output parameters. We show that it can infer the precise cost of the Stack example of Fig. 1. In Sec. 5, we extend it to infer UBFs on the peak-cost.

Definition 3 (safe net-cost UBFs). *Let p be a procedure with n input and m output parameters. A function $\tilde{f}_p : \mathbb{Z}^{n+m} \mapsto \mathbb{Q}$ is a safe UBF on the net-cost of p iff for any $\langle \bar{v}_1, \bar{v}_2, c \rangle \in \tilde{\pi}(p)$ it holds $\tilde{f}_p(\bar{v}_1, \bar{v}_2) \geq c$.*

Intuitively, a function $\tilde{f}_p$ is an UBF on the net-cost of p if for any possible execution that starts with input $\bar{v}_1$, terminates in a final state with an output $\bar{v}_2$, and have net-cost c, it holds that $\tilde{f}_p(\bar{v}_1, \bar{v}_2) \geq c$. Clearly, CRs cannot be used to infer such UBFs, since they do not use the output parameters.

In what follows we develop a novel approach for inferring such UBFs that is based on the use of quantifier elimination. We present our approach in two steps: (1) *verification*: in which we are given a set of *candidate* UBFs on the net-cost of each procedure, and our interest is to verify that these functions are safe, i.e., satisfy Def. 3; and (2) *inference*: in which we are given a set of *template* UBFs, and our interest is to instantiate the templates parameters into safe UBFs.

Verification of UBFs on the Net-Cost. Let us start by explaining the basics of the verification step. Assume that we have a procedure p defined by the following single rule

$$p(\bar{x}, \bar{y}) \leftarrow \mathsf{acq}(e), q_1(\bar{x}_1, \bar{y}_1), \ldots, q_n(\bar{x}_n, \bar{y}_n)$$

and that we have a set of *safe* UBFs $\tilde{f}_{q_1}, \ldots, \tilde{f}_{q_n}$ on the net-cost of $q_1, \ldots, q_n$. To verify that a given $\tilde{f}_p$ is a safe UBF on the net-cost of p, it is *sufficient* to check that the condition $\tilde{f}_p(\bar{x}, \bar{y}) \geq e + \tilde{f}_{q_1}(\bar{x}_1, \bar{y}_1) + \cdots + \tilde{f}_{q_n}(\bar{x}_n, \bar{y}_n)$ holds for any values of the program variables. Applying this principle to all rules of the program, it is possible to verify the safety of several candidate UBFs simultaneously.

Given a set $\tilde{F}$ of candidate UBFs on the net-cost that includes a function $\tilde{f}_p : \mathbb{Z}^{n+m} \mapsto \mathbb{Q}$ for each procedure $p \in P$, we build a *verification condition* (VC for short) whose validity implies the safety of each $\tilde{f}_p \in \tilde{F}$. The net-cost VC is generated from the program rules as follows.

Definition 4 (Net-cost VC). *Given a set $\tilde{F}$ of candidate UBFs, for each rule $r \equiv p(\bar{x}, \bar{y}) \leftarrow b_1, b_2, \ldots, b_n$, we generate a condition ψ_r as follows:*

1. *let φ be the conjunction of all constraints in r;*
2. *let the net-cost $\tilde{b}$ of an instruction b be defined as follows: if $b \equiv q_i(\bar{x}_i, \bar{y}_i)$ then $\tilde{b} \equiv \tilde{f}_q(\bar{x}_i, \bar{y}_i)$, if $b \equiv acq(e)$ then $\tilde{b} \equiv e$, if $b \equiv rel(e)$ then $\tilde{b} \equiv -e$, and if b is a constraint then $\tilde{b} \equiv 0$;*
3. *let $\psi_r \equiv \forall \bar{w} : \varphi \Rightarrow \tilde{f}_p(\bar{x}, \bar{y}) \geq \tilde{b}_1 + \cdots + \tilde{b}_n$ where $\bar{w} = vars(r)$.*

Then, the net-cost VC is defined as $\Psi(\tilde{F}) = \wedge_{r \in P} \psi_r$.

Note that ψ_r is the condition we explained before, but taking into account the constraints φ of the rule r which define the context in which this condition holds.

Example 4. Consider the program in Fig. 1, and let $\tilde{f}_r(s, m, s_1)$ and $\tilde{f}_m(s, m, s_1)$ be candidate UBFs on the net-cost of $rpop([s, m], [s_1])$ and $main([s, m], [s_1])$, respectively. The verification condition for this program w.r.t. $\tilde{F} = \{\tilde{f}_r(s, m, s_1), \tilde{f}_m(s, m, s_1)\}$ is $\Psi(\tilde{F}) = \psi_{r_1} \wedge \psi_{r_2} \wedge \psi_{r_3} \wedge \psi_{r_4}$ where:

$$\psi_{r_1} \equiv \forall \bar{w}_1 : m \geq 1 \wedge s \geq 0 \wedge s_1 = s \Rightarrow \tilde{f}_r(s, m, s_1) \geq 0$$
$$\psi_{r_2} \equiv \forall \bar{w}_2 : m \geq 1 \wedge s \geq 1 \wedge s_2 = s - 1 \Rightarrow \tilde{f}_r(s, m, s_1) \geq m + \tilde{f}_r(s_2, m, s_1)$$
$$\psi_{r_3} \equiv \forall \bar{w}_3 : m = 0 \wedge s_1 = s \wedge s \geq 0 \Rightarrow \tilde{f}_m(s, m, s_1) \geq 0$$
$$\psi_{r_4} \equiv \forall \bar{w}_4 : \begin{matrix} m \geq 1 \wedge s_3 = s_2 + 1 \wedge \\ m_1 = m - 1 \wedge s \geq 0 \end{matrix} \Rightarrow \tilde{f}_m(s, m, s_1) \geq \tilde{f}_r(s, m, s_2) + 1 + \tilde{f}_m(s_3, m_1, s_1)$$

The condition ψ_{r_4}, for example, corresponds to the second rule of procedure *main*. It states that $\tilde{f}_m(s, m, s_1)$ is a safe UBF if it is greater than the cost of the call to *rpop*, i.e., $\tilde{f}_r(s, m, s_2)$, plus 1 for the push operation, plus the cost of the recursive call to *main*, i.e, $\tilde{f}_m(s_3, m_1, s_1)$. This condition should hold for any values that satisfy the constraint $m \geq 1 \wedge s_3 = s_2 + 1 \wedge m_1 = m - 1 \wedge s \geq 0$, i.e., in the context of the second rule. Let us consider now the validity of $\Psi(\tilde{F})$ for the following possible concrete definitions of $\tilde{f}_r(s, m, s_1)$ and $\tilde{f}_m(s, m, s_1)$

(a) $\tilde{f}_m(s, m, s_1) = s{\cdot}m + \frac{1}{2}(m^2 + m)$, and $\tilde{f}_r(s, m, s_1) = (s - s_1){\cdot}m$.
(b) $\tilde{f}_m(s, m, s_1) = s{\cdot}m + \frac{1}{2}(m^2 + m)$, and $\tilde{f}_r(s, m, s_1) = s{\cdot}m$.

Using (a), we get that $\Psi(\tilde{F})$ is a valid formula. Note that here we use the optimal UBFs for *main* and *rpop*. Using (b), we get that $\Psi(\tilde{F})$ is invalid, though both UBF are safe. This is because, in this case, using $s{\cdot}m$ as an UBF for *rpop* is not enough for proving that $s{\cdot}m + \frac{1}{2}(m^2 + m)$ is an UBF for *main*.

Theorem 1. *Given a set $\tilde{F}$ of candidate UBFs, if $\models \Psi(\tilde{F})$ then $\tilde{F}$ is safe.*

Note that checking the validity of $\Psi(\tilde{F})$ is a first order problem that can be solved using SMT solvers (see Sec. 7).

Inference of UBFs on the net-cost. For many applications it is useful to infer the set $\tilde{F}$, instead of verifying the correctness of a given one. This can be formulated as seeking a set $\tilde{F}$ of UBFs for which $\Psi(\tilde{F})$ is valid, which means solving the formula $\exists \tilde{f}_1 \tilde{f}_2 \ldots \tilde{f}_k : \Psi(\tilde{F})$. However, this is a second order problem and solving it in general is impractical. A common approach to avoid solving a second order formula is the use of template functions that restrict the form of functions that we are looking for. A template for $\tilde{f}_p(\bar{x}, \bar{y})$ is a function with a fixed structure, defined over the variables $\bar{x} \cup \bar{y}$, and some unknown template parameters.

Example 5. The following are UBF templates for procedure *main* and *rpop*:

1. $\tilde{f}_r(s, m, s_1) = \lambda_1 \cdot s \cdot m + \lambda_2 \cdot s_1 \cdot m + \lambda_3 \cdot s + \lambda_4 \cdot m + \lambda_5 \cdot s_1 + \lambda_0$
2. $\tilde{f}_m(s, m, s_1) = \mu_1 \cdot s \cdot m + \mu_2 \cdot m^2 + \mu_3 \cdot s_1 \cdot m + \mu_4 \cdot s + \mu_5 \cdot m + \mu_6 \cdot s_1 + \mu_0$

The variables $\bar{\lambda}$ and $\bar{\mu}$ are the template parameters.

Assuming that $\tilde{F}$ is a set of candidate UBF templates, and that $\mathcal{P}$ is the set of template parameters, the inference problem is reduced to solving the first order problem $\exists \mathcal{P} : \Psi(\tilde{F})$. This can be solved by combining quantifier elimination and SMT solvers (see Sec. 7). The idea behind UBF templates is that later we will assign values to the template parameters such that the resulting UBFs are safe.

Note that in Ex. 5 we have chosen simple templates just to keep the technical details in the next examples simple. We could also choose a cubic polynomial template, and later try to find an instantiation such that the parameters of the cubic parts are assigned 0 (in order to get the quadratic UBF). In principle, any template UBF can be used as far as it uses arithmetic expressions that are supported by the quantifier elimination procedure (see Sec. 7).

Example 6. Using the templates of Ex. 5 in the VC of Ex. 4, we get a VC $\Psi(\tilde{F})$ in which the template variables $\bar{\lambda} \cup \bar{\mu}$ are free variables. Eliminating the universally quantified variables, we get a formula ξ over $\bar{\lambda} \cup \bar{\mu}$ that is a conjunction of the following equalities and inequalities:

$\lambda_1 \geq 1$	$\lambda_2 = -\lambda_1$	$\lambda_1 + \lambda_3 \geq 1$	$\mu_6 \geq \lambda_5 - \lambda_1$	$2 \cdot \mu_2 \geq \lambda_1 + \lambda_4$
$\lambda_4 \geq 0$	$\mu_1 = \lambda_1$	$\lambda_3 + \lambda_5 \geq 0$	$\mu_4 = \lambda_1 - \lambda_5$	$\mu_5 + \mu_2 \geq \mu_4 + \lambda_0 + \lambda_4 + 1$
$\mu_0 \geq 0$	$\mu_3 = 0$	$\lambda_0 + \lambda_4 \geq 0$	$\lambda_1 \geq \lambda_3 + \lambda_5$	

Each model of ξ assigns values to the template parameters $\bar{\lambda}$ and $\bar{\mu}$ such that $\tilde{f}_r(s, m, s_1)$ and $\tilde{f}_m(s, m, s_1)$ of Ex. 5 are safe UBFs for *rpop* and *main* respectively. For example, it is easy to check that

$$\mu_1 = 1, \mu_2 = \mu_5 = \frac{1}{2}, \mu_4 = \mu_6 = \mu_0 = 0, \lambda_1 = 1, \lambda_2 = -1, \lambda_3 = \lambda_4 = \lambda_5 = 0$$

is a model of ξ, which corresponds to the desired UBFs $s \cdot m + \frac{1}{2}(m^2 + m)$ and $(s - s_1) \cdot m$ for procedures *main* and *rpop* respectively. It is worth noting that the inequalities $\lambda_1 \geq 1$ and $\lambda_2 = -\lambda_1$, meaning that any UBF for *rpop* *must* involve both $s \cdot m$ and $s_1 \cdot m$ (recall that s_1 is its output parameter). If we analyse *rpop* alone this would not be the case, and UBFs like $s \cdot m$ would be possible, however, this is essential in order to obtain the quadratic UBF for *main*.

It is important to note that once the constraints over the template parameters (i.e., ξ in the above example) are generated, then one should try to find a model of ξ that results in a tight UBF. This process usually depends on the kind of expression used in the templates. For example, in the case of polynomial templates one could try to first set the parameters of the higher degree components to 0, etc. Another possibility is to start from a polynomial with low degree, and increment it gradually until an UBF is found.

5   Inference of Peak-Cost

When a given program only acquires resources, the net-cost analysis can be used to estimate the amount of resources required for safely executing the program. This, however, is not the case when the program can also release resources. For example, the net-cost of the program in Fig 2 is 0, since all resources are released either at J5 or J7, however, it requires at least $n + 1$ resources in order to execute correctly. In order to estimate the amount of resources required for safely executing such programs, what we need is the peak-cost, which is the maximum amount of resources that a program can hold simultaneously.

Definition 5 (safe peak-cost UBFs). *Let p be a procedure with n input parameters. A function $\hat{f}_p : \mathbb{Z}^n \mapsto \mathbb{Q}$ is a safe UBF on the peak-cost of p, iff for any $\langle \bar{v}_1, c \rangle \in \hat{\pi}(p)$ it holds $\hat{f}_p(\bar{v}_1) \geq c$.*

Our approach for inferring UBFs on the peak-cost is done in two steps, verification and inference, similar to the case of net-cost.

Verification of UBFs on the Peak-Cost. Let us start by explaining the basics of the verification step. Assume that we have a procedure p defined by the following single rule

$$p(\bar{x}, \bar{y}) \leftarrow q_1(\bar{x}_1, \bar{y}_1), q_2(\bar{x}_2, \bar{y}_2)$$

and assume that we have UBFs $\hat{f}_{q_1}$ and $\hat{f}_{q_2}$ on the peak-cost of q_1 and q_2 respectively. We are interested in verifying that a given function $\hat{f}_p(\bar{x})$ is indeed a safe UBF on the peak-cost of p. When executing p, the peak-cost might be reached while executing q_1 or q_2. If it is reached during q_1, then the peak-cost of p is like that of q_1, and if it is reached during q_2, then the peak-cost of p is like that of q_2 plus the amount of resources that p holds before calling q_2. Now note that this last amount is exactly the net-cost of q_1. Thus, in order to verify the correctness of $\hat{f}_p$ it is sufficient to check that the condition $\hat{f}_p(\bar{x}) \geq \hat{f}_{q_1}(\bar{x}_1) \wedge \hat{f}_p(\bar{x}) \geq \tilde{f}_{q_1}(\bar{x}_1, \bar{y}_1) + \hat{f}_{q_2}(\bar{x}_1)$ holds for any values of the program variables, where $\tilde{f}_{q_1}(\bar{x}_1, \bar{y}_1)$ is a safe UBF on the *net-cost* of q_1. Applying this principle to all rules of the program, it is possible to verify the correctness of several UBFs simultaneously.

Given a set $\hat{F}$ of candidate UBFs on the peak-cost, which includes a function $\hat{f}_p : \mathbb{Z}^n \mapsto \mathbb{Q}$ for each procedure $p \in P$, we want to build a VC whose validity implies that each $\hat{f}_p$ is indeed a safe UBF. For this, we assume a given set $\tilde{F}$ of safe UBFs on the net-cost of each procedure (later we will see that $\hat{F}$ and $\tilde{F}$ can be verified or inferred simultaneously). The peak-cost VC, denoted by $\Phi(\tilde{F}, \hat{F})$, is generated from the program rules as we explain next.

Definition 6 (Peak-cost VC). *Let $\hat{F}$ be a set of candidate UBFs on the peak-cost, and $\tilde{F}$ be a set of safe UBFs on the net-cost. For each rule $r \equiv p(\bar{x}, \bar{y}) \leftarrow b_1, b_2, \ldots, b_n$, we generate a condition ϕ_r according to the following steps*

1. *let $b_{\ell_1}, \ldots, b_{\ell_k}$, with $1 \leq \ell_1 < \cdots < \ell_k \leq n$, be all elements of the body that are of the form $q_{\ell_i}(\bar{x}_{\ell_i}, \bar{y}_{\ell_i})$ or $\mathsf{acq}(e)$. We assume there is at least one such element, otherwise we add $\mathsf{acq}(0)$ at the end of r;*
2. *let φ_i be the conjunction of all constraints in r up to b_{ℓ_i};*
3. *the peak-cost $\hat{b}_{\ell_i}$ of an instruction b_{ℓ_i} is defined as follows: if $b_{\ell_i} \equiv q_{\ell_i}(\bar{x}_{\ell_i}, \bar{y}_{\ell_i})$ then $\hat{b}_{\ell_i} \equiv \hat{f}_q(\bar{x}_{\ell_i})$, and if $b_{\ell_i} \equiv \mathsf{acq}(e)$ then $\hat{b}_{\ell_i} \equiv e$;*
4. *let ϕ_r be the formula below where $\bar{w} = vars(r)$ and $\tilde{b}_j$ are as in Def. 4.*

$$\phi_r \equiv \underbrace{(\wedge_{i=1}^k \forall \bar{w} : \varphi_i \Rightarrow \hat{f}_p(\bar{x}) \geq (\Sigma_{j=1}^{\ell_i - 1} \tilde{b}_j) + \hat{b}_j))}_{\mathcal{A}} \wedge \underbrace{(\forall \bar{w} : \varphi_1 \Rightarrow \hat{f}_p(\bar{x}) \geq 0))}_{\mathcal{B}}$$

Then, the peak-cost VC is $\Phi(\tilde{F}, \hat{F}) = \wedge_{r \in P} \phi_r$.

Let us explain the parts of ϕ_r: ($\mathcal{A}$) this part generalises the intuition that we have explained before. Intuitively, the instructions $b_{\ell_1}, \ldots, b_{\ell_k}$ are those that might *increase* the resource consumption, thus, the peak-cost of p should be greater than or equal to the peak-cost $\hat{b}_{\ell_i}$ of each b_{ℓ_i} plus the resources $\Sigma_{j=1}^{\ell_i - 1} \tilde{b}_j$ that p holds before executing $\hat{b}_{\ell_i}$ (note the use of the net-cost $\tilde{b}_j$); and ($\mathcal{B}$) this part requires that the peak function is non-negative. Note that in principle we should require $\forall \bar{w} : \varphi_i \Rightarrow \hat{f}_p(\bar{x}) \geq 0$ for all $i \in [1 \ldots k]$, however, requiring $\mathcal{B}$ is enough since $\varphi_i \Rightarrow \varphi_1$ for all $i \in [2 \ldots k]$. In the examples below we sometimes omit the second part $\mathcal{B}$ when it is redundant.

Example 7. The peak-cost VC for the program of Fig. 2, w.r.t. (some generic) $\tilde{F}$ and $\hat{F}$, is $\Phi(\tilde{F}, \hat{F}) = \phi_{r_1} \wedge \cdots \wedge \phi_{r_5}$ where

$$\phi_{r_1} \equiv \forall \bar{w}_1 : n = 0 \Rightarrow \hat{f}_p(n) \geq 0$$
$$\phi_{r_2} \equiv (\forall \bar{w}_2 : n \geq 1 \Rightarrow \hat{f}_p(n) \geq \hat{f}_q(n)) \wedge$$
$$(\forall \bar{w}_2 : n \geq 1 \wedge n_1 = n - 1 \Rightarrow \hat{f}_p(n) \geq \tilde{f}_q(n, m) - m + \hat{f}_p(n_1)) \wedge$$
$$(\forall \bar{w}_2 : n \geq 1 \Rightarrow \hat{f}_p(n) \geq 0)$$
$$\phi_{r_3} \equiv \forall \bar{w}_3 : i \geq 0 \Rightarrow \hat{f}_1(i) \geq 2$$
$$\phi_{r_4} \equiv (\forall \bar{w}_4 : i \geq 1 \Rightarrow \hat{f}_1(i) \geq 2) \wedge (\forall \bar{w}_4 : i \geq 1 \wedge i_2 = i - 1 \Rightarrow \hat{f}_1(i) \geq 2 + \hat{f}_1(i_2))$$
$$\phi_{r_5} \equiv (\forall \bar{w}_5 : n \geq 1 \wedge i = \tfrac{n}{2} \Rightarrow \hat{f}_q(n) \geq \hat{f}_1(i)) \wedge (\forall \bar{w}_5 : n \geq 1 \wedge i = \tfrac{n}{2} \Rightarrow \hat{f}_q(n) \geq 0)$$

Formula ϕ_{r_2}, for example, corresponds to the second rule of procedure p. It consists of 3 subformulas, the first two are the $\mathcal{A}$-part and the last is the $\mathcal{B}$-part. In the second, note the expression $\tilde{f}_q(n, m) - m$ which is the amount of resource that p holds before the recursive call to p. Using $\tilde{f}_q(n, m) = 2 \cdot m$, $\hat{f}_p(n) = n + 2$,

$\hat{f}_q(n) = n+2$, and $\hat{f}_i(i, i_1) = 2 \cdot i_1 + 2$, it is possible to verify that $\Phi(\tilde{F}, \hat{F})$ is valid. However, using another safe UBF on the net-cost of q, e.g., $\tilde{f}_q(n, m) = n + 2$, then $\Phi(\tilde{F}, \hat{F})$ is not valid. Indeed, $2 \cdot m$ is the most precise UBF on the net-cost of q, and is the one needed to verify the above UBF on the peak-cost of p.

Theorem 2. *Given a set $\tilde{F}$ of safe UBFs on the net-cost (Th. 1), and a set $\hat{F}$ of candidate UBFs on the peak-cost, if $\models \Phi(\tilde{F}, \hat{F})$, then $\hat{F}$ is safe.*

As in the case of $\Psi(\tilde{F})$ cost, checking the validity of $\Phi(\tilde{F}, \hat{F})$ reduces to a satisfiability problem of first order logic.

Inferring UBFs on the Peak-Cost. Our main interest is in inferring $\hat{F}$ rather than verifying the correctness of a given one. This can be done using template UBFs as the case of net-cost. However, an important point is that instead of assuming a given set $\tilde{F}$ of UBFs on the net-cost, we can infer it at the same time as $\hat{F}$, simply by considering the VC $\Phi(\tilde{F}, \hat{F}) \wedge \Psi(\tilde{F})$. This is actually essential in practice, since as we have seen in Ex. 7 not any safe UBF on the net-cost can be used to infer the peak-cost. Inferring them simultaneously will force choosing the required one.

Example 8. Let $\tilde{F}$ and $\hat{F}$ be defined by the following linear UBF templates:

$$\tilde{f}_p(n) = \lambda_1 \cdot n + \lambda_2 \quad \tilde{f}_q(n, m) = \lambda_3 \cdot n + \lambda_4 \cdot m + \lambda_5 \quad \tilde{f}_i(i, i_1) = \lambda_6 \cdot i + \lambda_7 \cdot i_1 + \lambda_8$$
$$\hat{f}_p(n) = \mu_1 \cdot n + \mu_2 \qquad \hat{f}_q(n) = \mu_3 \cdot n + \mu_4 \qquad \hat{f}_i(i) = \mu_5 \cdot i + \mu_6$$

and let $\Phi(\tilde{F}, \hat{F})$ be the VC of Ex. 7 using these $\tilde{F}$ and $\hat{F}$. Moreover, let $\Psi(\tilde{F}) = \psi_{r_1} \wedge \cdots \wedge \psi_{r_5}$ be the corresponding net-cost VC using the above $\tilde{F}$, where

$$\psi_{r_1} \equiv \forall \bar{w}_1 : n = 0 \Rightarrow \tilde{f}_p(n) \geq 0$$
$$\psi_{r_2} \equiv \forall \bar{w}_2 : n \geq 1 \wedge n_1 = n - 1 \Rightarrow \tilde{f}_p(n) \geq \tilde{f}_q(n, m) - m + \tilde{f}_p(n_1) + m$$
$$\psi_{r_3} \equiv \forall \bar{w}_3 : i \geq 0 \wedge i_1 = i - 1 \Rightarrow \tilde{f}_i(i, i_1) \geq 2$$
$$\psi_{r_4} \equiv \forall \bar{w}_4 : i \geq 1 \wedge i_2 = i - 1 \Rightarrow \tilde{f}_i(i, i_1) \geq 2 + \tilde{f}_i(i_2, i_1)$$
$$\psi_{r_5} \equiv \forall \bar{w}_5 : n \geq 1 \wedge i = \tfrac{n}{2}, m = i - i_1 \Rightarrow \tilde{f}_q(n, m) \geq \tilde{f}_i(i, i_1)$$

Then, applying quantifier elimination on $\Phi(\tilde{F}, \hat{F}) \wedge \Psi(\tilde{F})$ to eliminate the universally quantified variables, we get a formula ξ over the template parameters that is a conjunction of the following equalities and inequalities

$\lambda_2 \geq 0$	$\lambda_3 = 0$	$\lambda_8 \leq \lambda_5 \leq 0$	$\lambda_1 = \lambda_4 - 2$	$\lambda_6 + \lambda_8 \geq 2$
$\lambda_6 \geq 2$	$\mu_6 \geq 2$	$\mu_1 = \lambda_1 + 1$	$\lambda_4 = \lambda_6 = -\lambda_7$	$2 \cdot \mu_6 + \mu_5 \leq 2 \cdot \mu_4 + 2 \cdot \mu_3$
$\mu_5 \geq 2$	$\mu_2 \geq 0$	$2 \cdot \mu_3 \geq \mu_5$	$\lambda_6 \geq \mu_3 + 1$	$\mu_1 + \mu_2 \geq \mu_3 + \mu_4$

The models of ξ define possible instantiations $\tilde{F}$ and $\hat{F}$ such that they are safe UBFs. E.g., there is a model of ξ with $\mu_1 = 1$ and $\mu_2 = 2$ which defines the UBF $n + 2$ on the peak-cost of p. Note the constraint $\lambda_3 = 0$, which means that the UBF on the net-cost of q must not depend on the input n (in Ex. 7 we failed with $\tilde{f}_q(n, m) = n + 2$). This demonstrates how the peak-cost VC affects the net-cost one. Note that, for p, we have inferred the UBF $n + 2$ and not the optimal one $n + 1$ because the quantifier elimination is done over $\mathbb{R}$ and not over $\mathbb{Z}$.

Example 9. Let us finish with an example of a non-terminating program. Consider the following (contrived) program, which is defined by a single rule

$$p([n], [y_1]) \leftarrow n \geq m \geq 0, \mathsf{acq}(m), n_1 = n - m, p([n_1], [y_1]).$$

Procedure p receives a non-negative integer n, non-deterministically chooses a non-negative value $m \leq n$, acquires m resources, and then calls p recursively with $n - m$. The peak-cost of this program is exactly n, since any infinite trace cannot acquire more than n resources and there are infinite traces that acquire exactly n. The peak-cost VC for this program is

$$(\forall n, m : n \geq m \geq 0 \Rightarrow \hat{f}_p(n) \geq m) \wedge (\forall n, m : n \geq m \geq 0 \Rightarrow \hat{f}_p(n) \geq m + \hat{f}_p(n_1)$$

Assuming the template UBF $\hat{f}_p(n) = \lambda_1 \cdot n + \lambda_2$, the elimination of the universally quantified variables result in the formula $\xi = \lambda_1 \geq 1 \wedge \lambda_2 \geq 0$. Since $\lambda_1 = 1$ and $\lambda_2 = 0$ is a model of ξ, then $\hat{f}_p(n) = n$ is a safe UBF.

6   Relation to Amortised Cost Analysis

In this section we discuss an interesting relation that we have observed between UBFs that are defined in terms of both input and output parameters, and the notion of potential functions used in the context of amortised cost analysis. This may provide a semantics-based explanation to why amortised analysis can obtain more precise UBFs.

A potential function, in the context of an ACR, is a function that maps a given state to a non-negative rational number, which is called the potential of the state. This potential can be interpreted as the amount of resources available in the given state. An automatic amortised cost analysis [15] assigns to each procedure $p(\bar{x}, \bar{y})$ two potential functions: *input* $P_p(\bar{x})$, and *output* $Q_p(\bar{y})$. Intuitively, the input potential $P_p(\bar{x})$ must be large enough to pay for the cost of executing $p(\bar{x}, \bar{y})$, and, upon exit, leaving at least $Q_p(\bar{y})$ resources to be consumed later. Thus, if c is the net-cost of p, then $P_p(\bar{x}) \geq c + Q_p(\bar{y})$ must hold. This later expression can be rewritten as $P_p(\bar{x}) - Q_p(\bar{y}) \geq c$, which means that $P_p(\bar{x}) - Q_p(\bar{y})$ is an UBF on the net-cost of p, but also is an UBF that uses input and the output parameters. Thus, the above potential functions are in principle UBFs as defined in Def. 3, however, they are just a special case since $P_p(\bar{x}) - Q_p(\bar{y})$ does not allow using, for example, expressions like $s_1 \cdot m$.

We have tried to analyse (a functional version of) the Stack example using the amortised analysis of [15], which uses the above notion of potential functions. The analysis failed to obtain the expected quadratic UBF, and instead, it reported a cubic UBF. This failure confirms that it is essential to define the output potential for *rpop* as $s_1 \cdot m$, which cannot be defined using the above kind of potential functions. Note that this should not be interpreted as a fundamental limitation of [15], since their underlying machinery can be easily adapted to support potential functions of this form. In addition, the above discussion should be considered only in the context of the ACR language, since amortised analysis has many other features that goes beyond the ACR language.

7   Implementation and Experiments

A prototype implementation of our analysis is available at http://costa.ls.fi.upm.es/acrp. It receives as input an ACR program and a set of template UBFs. Then, it generates the VCs described in Secs. 4 and 5 as a REDUCE script [20], executes the script to eliminate the universally quantified variables, and finally outputs the template parameters constraints in SMT2-LIB format, which can be then solved using off-the-shelf SMT solvers.

For the quantifier elimination, the REDUCE script uses the REDLOG package [11] with the theory of *real closed fields*. This theory allows using a wide range of template UBFs, such as multivariate polynomial, max and min operations, etc. As done in [19], REDLOG can be switched to use SLFQ [7], which is a formula simplifier for the theory of real closed fields. Using SLFQ significantly reduces the size of the template parameters constraints, and thus improves the overall performance. For solving the template parameters constraints we have used Z3 [21], employing the logic of *non linear real arithmetic* (QF_NRA). Currently, we only ask the SMT solver for a satisfying assignment, which in turn instantiate the templates to safe UBFs. Looking for an assignment that gives the tightest UBFs is left for future work.

We have applied the analyser on small examples collected from cost analysis literature. All are available in the above address. For these examples we obtained the expected precise UBFs. Unfortunately, being based on real quantifier elimination, our procedure does not yet scale for large programs. In a future work we plan to explore patterns of ACR programs for which (a variation of) the analysis scales, e.g., for the case of the multivariate polynomials of [15].

8   Related Work

Static cost analysis dates back to the seminal work of Wegbreit [22]. Recently it has received a considerable attention which resulted in several cost analysers for different programming languages [2,10,12,15]. The research in this paper is mostly related to [2] and [15], in the sense that our research was motivated by the limitations of [2], and our solution turned to have common ideas with of [15] as we have explained in Sec. 6. When comparing [15], the advantage of our analysis is in that it has a more general notion of potential functions, it is not limited to polynomial templates, and can handle variables with negative values. However, unlike ours, their techniques can handle data-structures by assigning potentials to its parts, and their tool is reasonably scalable and performs very well in practice.

Our peak-cost constraints are similar to those of [3], they were used for inferring memory consumption in the presence of garbage collection. The limitations of CRs have been considered also in [4], but from a different perspective. Solving CRs using template function and real quantifier elimination has been considered before in [5]. However, it cannot handle the limitations we pointed out in this paper, and cannot handle non-terminating programs. Also [13,23] deal with similar problems, however, they cannot handle the limitation described in this paper, and cannot handle non-terminating programs. Real quantifier elimination has been used for program verification in [8,16,18].

9   Conclusions

In this paper we have studied well known limitations of cost analysis approaches that are based on the use of CRs. We have shown that, unlike it was assumed so far, the reason for these limitations is that CRs ignore the output values of procedures. In particular, we have shown that there are programs whose cost cannot be modeled precisely using CRs. In order to overcome these limitations, we have defined the notion of UBFs that use both input and output parameters, and developed a novel approach for cost analysis that is based on this kind of UBFs. Interestingly, we have found a relation between this kind of UBFs and potential functions that are used in automatic amortised cost analysis [15], which might give an alternative explanation to why amortised analysis (of ACR programs) can be more precise than the classical approach.

Starting from template UBFs, our analysis generates a verification condition over these templates in which the program variables are universally quantified. Eliminating these variables using quantifier elimination tools results in a (possibly non-linear constraint) whose models define possible instantiations for the templates such that they are safe UBFs. An important feature of approach is that it can be used for inferring lower-bounds (for terminating programs) with minimal changes: just replacing $\geq$ by $\leq$ in the VC, and, in addition, $\wedge$ by $\vee$ in each peak-cost condition ϕ_r. Due to lack of space we skipped the details. We have also reported on a preliminary implementation and its evaluation on small examples. For future work, we would like to find some special cases of ACR program for which the analysis can scale to large programs.

Acknowledgements. This work was funded in part by the Information & Communication Technologies program of the European Commission, Future and Emerging Technologies (FET), under the ICT-231620 *HATS* project, by the Spanish Ministry of Science and Innovation (MICINN) under the TIN-2008-05624 and PRI-AIBDE-2011-0900 projects, by UCM-BSCH-GR35/10-A-910502 grant and by the Madrid Regional Government under the S2009TIC-1465 *PROMETIDOS-CM* project. Diego Alonso is supported by the UCM PhD scholarship program.

References

1. Albert, E., Arenas, P., Genaim, S., Puebla, G.: Closed-Form Upper Bounds in Static Cost Analysis. Journal of Automated Reasoning 46(2), 161–203 (2011)
2. Albert, E., Arenas, P., Genaim, S., Puebla, G., Zanardini, D.: Cost Analysis of Object-Oriented Bytecode Programs. Theoretical Computer Science 413(1), 142–159 (2012)

3. Albert, E., Genaim, S., Gómez-Zamalloa, M.: Parametric Inference of Memory Requirements for Garbage Collected Languages. In: ISMM, pp. 121–130. ACM, New York (2010)
4. Albert, E., Genaim, S., Masud, A.N.: More Precise Yet Widely Applicable Cost Analysis. In: Jhala, R., Schmidt, D. (eds.) VMCAI 2011. LNCS, vol. 6538, pp. 38–53. Springer, Heidelberg (2011)
5. Anderson, H., Khoo, S.-C., Andrei, Ș., Luca, B.: Calculating Polynomial Runtime Properties. In: Yi, K. (ed.) APLAS 2005. LNCS, vol. 3780, pp. 230–246. Springer, Heidelberg (2005)
6. Benoy, F., King, A.: Inferring Argument Size Relationships with CLP(R). In: Gallagher, J.P. (ed.) LOPSTR 1996. LNCS, vol. 1207, pp. 204–223. Springer, Heidelberg (1997)
7. Brown, C.W., Gross, C.: Efficient Preprocessing Methods for Quantifier Elimination. In: Ganzha, V.G., Mayr, E.W., Vorozhtsov, E.V. (eds.) CASC 2006. LNCS, vol. 4194, pp. 89–100. Springer, Heidelberg (2006)
8. Chen, Y., Xia, B., Yang, L., Zhan, N., Zhou, C.: Discovering Non-linear Ranking Functions by Solving Semi-algebraic Systems. In: Jones, C.B., Liu, Z., Woodcock, J. (eds.) ICTAC 2007. LNCS, vol. 4711, pp. 34–49. Springer, Heidelberg (2007)
9. Cormen, T.H., Leiserson, C.E., Rivest, R., Stein, C.: Introduction to Algorithms, 3rd edn. MIT Press (2009)
10. Debray, S.K., Lin, N.-W.: Cost Analysis of Logic Programs. ACM Transactions on Programming Languages and Systems 15(5), 826–875 (1993)
11. Dolzmann, A., Sturm, T.: REDLOG: Computer Algebra meets Computer Logic. ACM SIGSAM Bulletin 31(2), 2–9 (1997)
12. Gulwani, S., Mehra, K.K., Chilimbi, T.M.: SPEED: Precise and Efficient Static Estimation of Program Computational Complexity. In: Proc. of POPL 2009, pp. 127–139. ACM (2009)
13. Gulwani, S., Zuleger, F.: The Reachability-Bound Problem. In: PLDI, pp. 292–304. ACM (2010)
14. Hickey, T.J., Cohen, J.: Automating Program Analysis. J. ACM 35(1), 185–220 (1988)
15. Hofmann, M., Hoffmann, J., Aehlig, K.: Multivariate Amortized Resource Analysis. In: POPL 2011, pp. 357–370. ACM (2011)
16. Kapur, D.: Automatically generating loop invariants using quantifier elimination. In: Deduction and Applications, vol. 05431 (2006)
17. Le Métayer, D.: ACE: An Automatic Complexity Evaluator. ACM Trans. Program. Lang. Syst. 10(2), 248–266 (1988)
18. Monniaux, D.: Automatic modular abstractions for template numerical constraints. Logical Methods in Computer Science 6(3) (2010)
19. Sturm, T., Tiwari, A.: Verification and Synthesis using Real Quantifier Elimination. In: ISSAC 2011, pp. 329–336. ACM (2011)
20. REDUCE Computer Algebra System. REDUCE home page
21. Z3 Theorem Prover. Z3 home page
22. Wegbreit, B.: Mechanical Program Analysis. Communications of the ACM 18(9) (1975)
23. Zuleger, F., Gulwani, S., Sinn, M., Veith, H.: Bound Analysis of Imperative Programs with the Size-Change Abstraction. In: Yahav, E. (ed.) SAS 2011. LNCS, vol. 6887, pp. 280–297. Springer, Heidelberg (2011)

Termination Proofs for Linear Simple Loops[*]

Hong Yi Chen[1], Shaked Flur[2], and Supratik Mukhopadhyay[1]

[1] Department of Computer Science
Louisiana State University
Baton Rouge, LA 70803
hchen11@lsu.edu, supratik@csc.lsu.edu
[2] Department of Computer Science
The Technion
Haifa 32000, Israel
fshaked@cs.technion.ac.il

Abstract. Analysis of termination and other liveness properties of an imperative program can be reduced to termination proof synthesis for simple loops, *i.e.*, loops with only variable updates in the loop body. Among simple loops, the subset of *Linear Simple Loops* (LSLs) is particular interesting because it is common in practice and expressive in theory. Existing techniques can successfully synthesize a linear ranking function for an LSL if there exists one. However, when a terminating LSL does not have a linear ranking function, these techniques fail. In this paper we describe an automatic method that generates proofs of universal termination for LSLs based on the synthesis of disjunctive ranking relations. The method repeatedly finds linear ranking functions on parts of the state space and checks whether the transitive closure of the transition relation is included in the union of the ranking relations. Our method extends the work of Podelski and Rybalchenko [27]. We have implemented a prototype of the method and have shown experimental evidence of the effectiveness of our method.

1   Introduction

Termination proof synthesis for simple loops, *i.e.*, loops with only variable updates in the loop body, are the building blocks of the liveness analysis of large complex systems [16, 29, 17, 10, 23, 26, 25, 28, 22, 24]. In particular, we consider a subclass of simple loops which contain only linear updates with the flexibility of handling nondeterminism. We call them *Linear Simple Loops* (LSLs). LSLs are interesting because most loops in practice are indeed linear; more importantly, with its capability to handle nondeterminism LSLs are expressive enough to serve as a foundational model for other simple loops.

---

[*] This research is partially supported by NSF under the grant 0965024. Any opinions, findings, and conclusions or recommendations expressed in this material are those of the author(s) and do not necessarily reflect the views of the National Science Foundation.

A. Miné and D. Schmidt (Eds.): SAS 2012, LNCS 7460, pp. 422–438, 2012.

It is well known that termination of simple loops with linear guards and linear assignments (they form the deterministic subclass of LSL) over rationals or reals is decidable [34]. The termination problem for "homogeneous cases" over integers, of the deterministic LSL subclass is also decidable [9]. Ben-Amram *et al.* recently proved termination of LSLs is undecidable when the the coefficients are from $\mathbb{Z} \cup \{r\}$ with r being an arbitrary irrational number [2]. However, when we reduce the analysis of a complex system to that of an LSL, knowing whether or not the LSL terminates is not enough, we often need to obtain a termination proof, such as a ranking function or a ranking relation, that the overall analysis can build upon [16, 29, 17, 10, 23, 26, 25, 28]. When it comes to finding termination proofs for LSLs, Podelski and Rybalchenko's technique [27] can generate a linear ranking function if there exists one. This method is based on Farkas's lemma [33] that provides a technique to derive hidden constraints from a system of linear inequalities. The method is complete when LSLs range over rationals or reals. However, if a terminating LSL has only non-linear ranking functions, this method will return failure. In this paper, we extend the method of Podelski and Rybalchenko, and solve cases for which only non-linear ranking functions exist.

Our approach is closely related to the previous work on termination proof synthesis based on disjunctive ranking relations. The traditional method for proving program termination, proposed by Turing [35], relies on proving $R \subseteq \tau(f)$, where R is the program's transition relation, $\tau(f)$ is a ranking relation given by a ranking function f. The difficulty with Turing's method is that a single ranking function is usually hard to find. With LSLs in particular, non-linear ranking functions are often difficult to synthesize. To address this problem Podelski and Rybalchenko proposed [28] proving $R^+ \subseteq \tau(f_1) \cup \cdots \cup \tau(f_n)$, where R^+ is the transitive closure of R, and $\tau(f_1) \cup \cdots \cup \tau(f_n)$ is a finite union of ranking relations. Many recent approaches for proving termination for general programs are based on disjunctive ranking relations [3, 4, 1, 18, 17, 29, 26, 25]. In this paper, instead of trying to synthesize a single non-linear ranking function, we generate disjunctive linear ranking functions and check the validity of $R^+ \subseteq \tau(f_1) \cup \cdots \cup \tau(f_n)$.

To be able to apply the disjunctive ranking relation proof rule [28], we need the technique of binary reachability check (BRC). That is, given a disjunctive ranking relation T, we need to prove or disprove the inclusion $R^+ \subseteq T$. We use the technique developed by the TERMINATOR team [17] to check this inclusion. Their approach is to syntactically transform the program so that binary reachability check is reduced to unary reachability check, which is a well studied task and can be carried out on any temporal safety checker. Moreover, if the validity of $R^+ \subseteq T$ is not satisfied, the construction of the transformed program will enable the safety checker to generate an error path that violates the inclusion. In our problem setting, if the input to BRC is an LSL, the error path will induce a new LSL which is an unrolling of the original LSL. Thus we can repeatedly check for binary reachability and expand the current disjunctive ranking relation.

In this paper we provide a method for automatically generating disjunctive ranking relations as proofs of universal termination for LSLs. Roughly speaking, the idea is to repeatedly partition the state space based on trace segments [19, 31, 21] such that one of the subspace is guaranteed to have a linear ranking function. The partitioning will generate a series of linear ranking functions f_i's such that $R \subseteq \bigcup \tau(f_i)$. However this does not suffice as a termination proof since the inclusion should refer to R^+ and not to R. For a termination proof we leverage BRC; if $R^+ \subseteq \bigcup \tau(f_i)$ is satisfied, it returns success; if not, BRC provides a new LSL, and we look for the next series of ranking functions f_j's. We then again check for the inclusion $R^+ \subseteq \bigcup \tau(f_i) \cup \bigcup \tau(f_j)$. This process continues until we successfully find an over-approximation of R^+. The question that remains is how to effectively find the sub-space for which a linear ranking function exists. To answer this question, we resort to the simple fact that when variables range over $\mathbb{Z}$ and updates are deterministic, two constraints $x \geq b$ and $x > x'$, where b is a number, x' represents the value of x after one transition, guarantees x to be a ranking function. Similarly, whenever we have a constraint of the form $\varphi \geq b$, we partition the state space by constraint $\varphi > \text{SHIFT}(\varphi)$ (function Shift is formally defined in Section 4.2) and its negation $\varphi \leq \text{SHIFT}(\varphi)$. When the variables range over $\mathbb{Q}$ or $\mathbb{R}$, or updates are nondeterministic, more complicated partition needs to be performed, as is described in Section 3.2 and 4.2.

Lastly, we provide experimental results showing that our method outperforms both linear ranking function synthesis [27] and polyranking method [7] on a suite of LSL examples provided in [11].

Related Work. Rather than looking for disjunctive ranking relations as the termination proof, Cousot [20] shows how non-linear ranking functions can be synthesized over nonlinear loops based on the S-procedure for semi-definite programming. Colón and Sipma's work on linear loops with multiple paths and assertional transition relations achieve to synthesize linear ranking functions via polyhedral manipulation in [13, 14]. Bradley et al. show how to synthesize lexicographic linear ranking functions with supporting linear invariants over loops with linear assertional transition relations in [6]. Another type of termination proof is polyranking functions raised by Bradley et al. A polyranking function needs not always decrease but decreases eventually. It is a generalization of the regular polynomial ranking function. In [8], the authors show a method for finding bounded expressions that are eventually negative over loops with parallel transitions. In [7], the authors demonstrate a method for synthesize lexicographic linear polyranking functions with supporting linear invariants over linear loops.

Other related works include proving conditional termination, which aims to find a set of initial states, usually an underapproximation of it, that guarantees termination. Cook et al. in [15] proposed an approach that first finds potential ranking functions then solves for the sub-space that guarantees the potential ranking function to be a true ranking function. Bozga et al. represent the set of non terminating states in terms of greatest fixpoint and then utilize quantifier elimination to deduce the exact set and consequently the dual set (i.e. the terminating states).

2 Preliminaries

2.1 Loop Model and Semantics

Through out this paper, all variables range over domain $\mathbb{Z}$, $\mathbb{Q}$, or $\mathbb{R}$. The following definition provides the syntax of LSLs.

Definition 1 (Linear Simple Loops). *A Linear Simple Loop over program variables $X^0 = (x_1, x_2, \ldots, x_m)$ and its n copies $X^1, X^2, \ldots, X^n$ ($m, n \geq 1$) is a tuple $L = \langle \text{COND}, \text{UPDATE}, i, j \rangle$ where*

- COND *is a set of linear constraints of the form $a_i X^i \bowtie b$*
  ($\bowtie \in \{<, \leq, =, \geq, >\}$).
- UPDATE *is a set of linear constraints of the form $a_0 X^0 + \cdots + a_n X^n \bowtie b$*
  ($\bowtie \in \{<, \leq, =, \geq, >\}$).
- *i and j are integers and $0 \leq i < j \leq n$.*
- *a_k and b are coefficients that range over $\mathbb{Z}$ or $\mathbb{Q}$.*

We sometime refer to COND and UPDATE as loop conditions and loop updates respectively. Intuitively, L describes unrolling of a loop (and maybe some extra constraints) with a back edge from j to i.

The formal semantics of LSL is defined as follows. Let $L = \langle \text{COND}, \text{UPDATE}, i, j \rangle$ be an LSL over variables X^0 and its n copies $X^1, X^2, \ldots, X^n$. An $(n+1)$-trace of L is a tuple $(s_0, s_1, \ldots, s_n)$ such that all the constraints in COND and UPDATE are satisfied simultaneously when assigning s_0 to X^0, s_1 to X^1, ..., s_n to X^n. We denote by $R_{n+1}(L)$ the set of all $(n+1)$-traces of L and $R(L)$ the relation L describes.

$$R(L) = \{(s_i, s_j) \mid (s_0, s_1, \ldots, s_n) \in R_{n+1}(L)\}$$

The most simple LSL $L = \langle \text{COND}, \text{UPDATE}, 0, 1 \rangle$ involves only X^0 and X^1. Without explicitly stating i and j, by default we assume $i = 0$, $j = 1$. An $L = \langle \text{COND}, \text{UPDATE}, 0, 1 \rangle$ describes a transition relation from a state that is before a transition (given by X^0) to the corresponding state that is after the transition (given by X^1). For example, the following while loop

$$while \ (x > 0)$$
$$x := x - 1;$$

can be rewritten as the following LSL

$$L_1 \triangleq \langle \{x^0 > 0\}, \{x^1 = x^0 - 1\}, 0, 1 \rangle$$

An $L = \langle \text{COND}, \text{UPDATE}, 0, 1 \rangle$ can also have more than two copies of variables. For example,

$$L_2 \triangleq \langle \{x^0 > 0\}, \{x^1 = x^0 - 1, \ x^1 > 0, \ x^2 = x^1 - 1, \ x^2 \leq 0\}, 0, 2 \rangle$$

X^1 and X^0 represent the values of the variable X after and before a transition, respectively. The constraint $x^2 \leq 0$ restrains the input space of L_2 to $x^0 \in \{2\}$.

Note that $x^0 = 1$ is not in our input space, since there does not exist x^1 and x^2 satisfying L_2. In our approach, we add such constraints over future transition states such that the restrained LSL is guaranteed to have a linear ranking function.

An LSL $L = \langle \text{COND}, \text{UPDATE}, 0, k \rangle$ describes a transition relation between X^0 and X^k. For example, in

$$L_3 \triangleq \langle \{x^0 > 0, \}, \{x^1 = x^0 - 1, \ x^1 > 0, \ x^2 = x^1 - 1\}, 0, 2 \rangle$$

the transition pairs described by L_3 include: $(5,3), (4,2), (3,1), \ldots$. We often use $L = \langle \text{COND}, \text{UPDATE}, 0, k \rangle$ when we are looking at the k-th unrolling of some $L' = \langle \text{COND}', \text{UPDATE}', 0, 1 \rangle$.

To further generalize our loop model, we provide the ability not only to look ahead, but also to look back.

$$L_4 \triangleq \langle \{x^1 > 0\}, \{x^0 > 0, \ x^1 = x^0 - 1, \ x^2 = x^1 - 1, \ x^2 \leq 0\}, 1, 2 \rangle$$

Despite having the same constraints as in L_2, the input space of $L_4(1,2)$ is $x^1 \in \{1\}$.

Note that LSLs allow nondeterminism. To be specific, we can have linear expressions on both sides of an update statement, and inequalities instead of equal relation. This gives us more flexibility to model nondeterministic inputs or non-linear operations. For example, we can have an LSL such as

$$L_5 \triangleq \langle \{x^0 > 0\}, \{x^0 + x^1 \leq 1\}, 0, 1 \rangle$$

that cannot be expressed in any conventional programming language.

2.2   Disjunctive Ranking Relations

Definition 2 (Well-Ordered Sets). *A set D is well-ordered with respect to a relation $<$ if,*

1. *$<$ is a strict total ordered and,*
2. *There is no infinite sequence $d_0, d_1, d_2, \ldots$ of elements in D such that $d_{i+1} < d_i$ for every $i \in \mathbb{N}$.*

Definition 3 (Ranking Functions). *Given a transition relation $R \subseteq S \times S$, a function $r : S \to D$ is a ranking function, if D is a well-ordered set and for every $(s_1, s_2) \in R$ we have $r(s_2) < r(s_1)$, where $<$ is the well order associated with D.*

A Ranking Function is called linear (Linear Ranking Function) if r is linear.

Definition 4 (Ranking Relations). *Given a ranking function $r : S \to D$ we define the corresponding ranking relation by*

$$\tau(r) = \{(s_1, s_2) \mid r(s_2) < r(s_1)\}$$

where $<$ is the well order associated with D.

Definition 5 (Disjunctive Ranking Relations). *A disjunctive ranking relation T is a finite union of ranking relations. That is,*

$$T = T_1 \cup \cdots \cup T_n$$

where T_i is a ranking relation for $1 \leq i \leq n$, $n \in \mathbb{N}$

The relation between disjunctive ranking relations and termination has been established in [28] using Ramsey's theorem [30]. Let P be a program, R be the corresponding transition relation induced by P, R^+ be the non-reflexive transitive closure of R, then P is terminating if and only if

$$R^+ \subseteq T$$

for some disjunctive ranking relation T.

2.3   Binary Reachability Check

Given an LSL L and a disjunctive ranking relation T, the goal of binary reachability check is to verify whether $R^+(L) \subseteq T$. If yes, the procedure returns "true". Otherwise, the procedure returns an error path which induces a new LSL L' such that L' is an unrolling of L and $R(L') \not\subseteq T$. The input and output of procedure BRC is described as follows (see [17] for more details):

input
LSL L, disjunctive ranking relation T
output
if $(R^+(L) \subseteq T)$ return "true"
else return LSL L' such that L' is an unrolling of L and $R(L') \not\subseteq T$

2.4   Simple Linear Ranking Function Synthesis

The following theorem is proved in [27].

Theorem. *An LSL given by the system $(A^0 A^1)\binom{x^0}{x^1} \leq b$ (i.e. $i = 0, j = 1$) is terminating if there exist nonnegative vectors λ_1, λ_2 over rationals such that the following system is satisfiable:*

$$\lambda_1 A^1 = 0 \tag{1}$$

$$(\lambda_1 - \lambda_2)(A^0) = 0 \tag{2}$$

$$\lambda_2(A^0 + A^1) = 0 \tag{3}$$

$$\lambda_2 b < 0 \tag{4}$$

More over, the LSL has a linear ranking function of the form

$$\rho(X^0) = \begin{cases} rX^0 & \text{if exists } X^1 \text{ such that } (A^0 A^1)\binom{x^0}{x^1} \leq b \\ \delta_0 - \delta & \text{otherwise} \end{cases}$$

where $r \triangleq \lambda_2 A^1$, $\delta_0 \triangleq -\lambda_1 b$, and $\delta \triangleq -\lambda_2 b$.

We will extend this method in Section 4 so that it works for the general form of LSLs.

3   Example

We first demonstrate our technique with a simple deterministic LSL over the integers. Then we will extend our technique for nondeterministic updates and rational / real variables.

3.1   Deterministic Updates over Integer Domain

Consider the while loop in Figure 1. It has only 3 simple assignments, but it is not obvious whether it is terminating. It is easy to see that the traces of z are composed of two alternating numbers, one negative the other non-negative, and that the negative number has a higher value. The variable y always gets assigned to value of z from the previous state. Hence it behaves like z, except being one step behind. The variable x increments itself with y. Therefore x will alternatively increase (or stay unchanged) and decrease. Moreover the decrease is larger than the increase, hence x will eventually become negative and the loop will terminate.

```
int x, y, z;
while (x ≥ 0)
    x := x + y;
    y := z;
    z := -z - 1;
```

Fig. 1. Example

Let us first convert the while loop above to an LSL.

$$L = \langle \{x^0 \geq 0\}, \{x^1 = x^0 + y^0,\ y^1 = z^0,\ z^1 = -z^0 - 1\}, 0, 1 \rangle$$

If we apply the method of Section 2.4 to L, it will return failure since L does not have a linear ranking function. As mentioned earlier, we want to construct multiple linear ranking functions, each of them over a restrained input space. We do this by adding constraints to L such that the new LSL is guaranteed to have a linear ranking function. From COND_L we see that we already have the linear expression x^0 that is bounded, $i.e.$, $x^0 \geq 0$. If we add to L a constraint $x^0 > x^1$, then we know x^0 can serve as a ranking function for the restrained LSL because x^0 has a lower bound and is strictly decreasing, which is a sufficient condition for x^0 to become a ranking function over the integer domain.

We break L into two LSLs $L_{1.1}$ and $L_{1.2}$ such that $L_{1.1}$ is obtained by combining L with constraint $x^0 > x^1$, and $L_{1.2}$ is obtained by combining L with the negation of the constraint, namely $x^0 \leq x^1$.

$$L_{1.1} = \langle \text{COND}_L, \text{UPDATE}_L \cup \{x^0 > x^1\}, 0, 1 \rangle \qquad \text{(trivial case)}$$
$$L_{1.2} = \langle \text{COND}_L, \text{UPDATE}_L \cup \{x^0 \leq x^1\}, 0, 1 \rangle \qquad \text{(synthesis case)}$$

We call $L_{1.1}$ the *trivial case* since we immediately obtain a linear ranking function from it.

$$\rho_1(X^0) = \begin{cases} x^0 & \text{if } \exists X^1 \text{ such that } X^0, X^1 \text{ satisfies } L_{1.1} \\ -1 & \text{otherwise} \end{cases}$$

We call $L_{1.2}$ the *synthesis case* since it needs further examination. We call COND_L the *Seed* for partitioning L.

From this point onwards, we only need to take care of $L_{1.2}$. First we check whether $L_{1.2}$ has a linear ranking function already. In this particular case we find out that this is not true. Next, we would like to repeat the earlier process on $L_{1.2}$, *i.e.*, adding constraints to $L_{1.2}$ such that a linear ranking function must exist. Since $L_{1.2}$ already includes $x^0 \leq x^1$, using $x^0 \geq 0 \wedge x^0 > x^1$ again will no longer make sense. However observe that the new constraint in $L_{1.2}$ gives a new linear expression that is bounded below, *i.e.*, $x^1 \geq x^0$. This constraint will become our new *Seed*, and we can use it to partition $L_{1.2}$. This time we partition with the constraint $(x^1 - x^0) > (x^2 - x^1)$ and its negation.

At this point a new issue arises, x^2 is introduced to denote the value of x after one transition from x^1. However from $L_{1.2}$ alone, there is no such information about x^2. To remedy this situation, we first need to unroll L so that the unrolled transition involves x^2. We do this by making a copy of all the loop constraints in L, then changing X^1 to X^2, X^0 to X^1 (the process is formally described by $\mathrm{UNROLL}(L)$ in Section 4). We get L_2 as follows.

$$L' = \mathrm{UNROLL}_2(L)$$
$$= \langle \{x^0 \geq 0\}, \{x^1 = x^0 + y^0, \ y^1 = z^0, \ z^1 = -z^0 - 1,$$
$$x^1 \geq 0, \ x^2 = x^1 + y^1, \ y^2 = z^1, \ z^2 = -z^1 - 1\}, 0, 1 \rangle$$
$$L_2 = \langle \mathrm{COND}_{L'}, \mathrm{UPDATE}_{L'} \cup Seed, 0, 1 \rangle$$
$$= \langle \{x^0 \geq 0\}, \{x^1 = x^0 + y^0, \ y^1 = z^0, \ z^1 = -z^0 - 1,$$
$$x^1 \geq 0, \ x^2 = x^1 + y^1, \ y^2 = z^1, \ z^2 = -z^1 - 1\} \cup \{x^1 \geq x^0\}, 0, 1 \rangle$$

Now we can partition L_2 using the constraint mentioned above.

$$L_{2.1} = \langle \mathrm{COND}_{L_2}, \mathrm{UPDATE}_{L_2} \cup \{(x^1 - x^0) > (x^2 - x^1)\}, 0, 1 \rangle \qquad \text{(trivial case)}$$
$$L_{2.2} = \langle \mathrm{COND}_{L_2}, \mathrm{UPDATE}_{L_2} \cup \{(x^1 - x^0) \leq (x^2 - x^1)\}, 0, 1 \rangle \quad \text{(synthesis case)}$$

$L_{2.1}$ is again the trivial case, where a linear ranking function is guaranteed

$$\rho_2(X^0) = \begin{cases} x^1 - x^0 = y^0 & \text{if } \exists X^1, X^2 \text{ such that } X^0, X^1, X^2 \text{ satisfies } L_{2.1} \\ 0 & \text{otherwise} \end{cases}$$

Now we check whether the synthesis case has a linear ranking function. Notice that this time we can not use the method described in Section 2.4 any more, since now the synthesis case LSL involves X^2. In Section 4, we describe a general ranking function synthesis method which can handle this general form of LSLs.

If we feed $L_{2.2}$ to the method in Section 4, we get the following linear ranking function.

$$\rho_3(X^0) = \begin{cases} 2x^0 + z^0 & \text{if } \exists X^1, X^2 \text{ such that } X^0, X^1, X^2 \text{ satisfies } L_{2.2} \\ -1 & \text{otherwise} \end{cases}$$

As shown in Figure 2, up to this point we have divided L to three LSLs, $L_{1.1}$, $L_{2.1}$, and $L_{2.2}$. Each of these three has a linear ranking function. Let $T = \tau(\rho_1) \cup \tau(\rho_2) \cup \tau(\rho_3)$. Theorem 2 in Section 4 shows us that $R(L) \subseteq T$. That is, any two consecutive states form a pair that belongs to T.

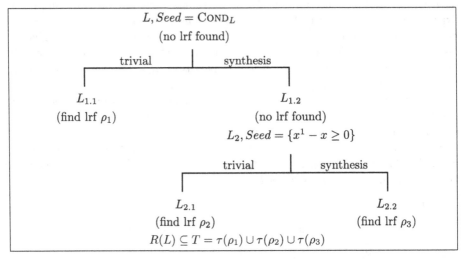

Fig. 2. Execution of $L \triangleq \langle \{x^0 \geq 0\}, \{x^1 = x^0 + y^0, y^1 = z^0, z^1 = -z^0 - 1\}, 0, 1\rangle$

Recall that our goal is to find a T such that $R^+(L) \subseteq T$. We first check whether the T we found already satisfies $R^+(L) \subseteq T$. As it turns out for this particular case, it is not. BRC gives an error path that executes L twice. Therefore we get a new LSL L'' that unrolls L twice and L'' describes a relation from X^0 to X^2.

$$L'' = \text{UNROLL}_2(L) \text{ with } i_{L''} = 0, j_{L''} = 2$$

Note L'' has the same set of constraints as L', but has different backedge. We feed L'' to the method described in Section 4.1. It shows that L'' has a linear ranking function already.

$$\rho_4(X^0) = \begin{cases} x^0 + y^0 & \text{if } \exists X^1, X^2 \text{ such that } X^0, X^1, X^2 \text{ satisfies } L' \\ -1 & \text{otherwise} \end{cases}$$

Again we update T by $T = T \cup \tau(\rho_4)$ and this time the test $R^+(L) \subseteq T$ succeeds, i.e., we have successfully found a disjunctive ranking relation T for the original LSL L.

3.2 Variables over $\mathbb{Q}$ or $\mathbb{R}$ and Nondeterministic Updates

Notice that when variables range over $\mathbb{Q}$ or $\mathbb{R}$, the two constraints $\varphi \geq b$ and $\varphi > \text{SHIFT}(\varphi)$ can no longer guarantee φ to be a linear ranking function. One way to remedy that is to pick a small positive value c and partition the state space by $\varphi - \text{SHIFT}(\varphi) > c$ and its negation $\varphi - \text{SHIFT}(\varphi) \leq c$. Similar to the integer example, the former constraint will generate the trivial case, and the latter constraint will generate the synthesis case.

Another way is to still partition with $\varphi > \text{SHIFT}(\varphi)$ and its negation $\varphi \leq \text{SHIFT}(\varphi)$. However since the former can no longer generate a trivial case, we need to continue the partition process on the trivial case as well.

Nondeterministic updates are also an issue. If we look at ranking function ρ_2 above, the expression y^0 originates from the expression $x^1 - x^0$. We cannot use $x^1 - x^0$ directly because the ranking functions need to be expressed in terms of X^0. With deterministic updates, we can get rid of x^1 by substituting it with $x^0 + y^0$. With nondeterministic updates, we may not be able to simplify the expression in this manner. Therefore we need to apply Theorem 1 in Section 4.1 to generate ranking functions on X^0 only, and when we fail to find one, we need to partition the trivial case further. In our algorithm shown in Figure 4, this is the approach we take in all situations.

4 Algorithm for Synthesizing Disjunctive Ranking Relations

4.1 Extended Linear Ranking Function Synthesis

Let $\boldsymbol{A}$ denote the row vector $(A^0 \ldots A^i \ldots A^j \ldots A^n)$, $\boldsymbol{A}_i$ denote the i-th element A^i, $\boldsymbol{A}_{-i}$ denote the row vector with all but the i-th element $(A^0 \ldots A^{i-1} A^{i+1} \ldots A^j \ldots A^n)$. Similarly we define column vectors $\boldsymbol{X}$, $\boldsymbol{X}_i$, and $\boldsymbol{X}_{-i}$. Then we prove the following theorem.

Theorem 1. *An LSL $L = \langle \text{COND}, \text{UPDATE}, i, j \rangle$ given by the system $\boldsymbol{A}\boldsymbol{X} \leq b$ is terminating if there exist non-negative vectors λ_1, λ_2 over rationals such that the following system is satisfied:*

$$\lambda_1 \boldsymbol{A}_{-i} = 0 \tag{1}$$
$$\lambda_2 \boldsymbol{A}_{-i,-j} = 0 \tag{2}$$
$$(\lambda_1 - \lambda_2)\boldsymbol{A}_i = 0 \tag{3}$$
$$\lambda_2(\boldsymbol{A}_i + \boldsymbol{A}_j) = 0 \tag{4}$$
$$\lambda_2 b < 0 \tag{5}$$

More over, the LSL has a linear ranking function of the form

$$\rho(X^i) = \begin{cases} rX^i & \text{if exists } X^j \text{ such that } (X^i, X^j) \in R(L) \\ \delta_0 - \delta & \text{otherwise} \end{cases}$$

where $r \triangleq \lambda_2 \boldsymbol{A}_j$, $\delta_0 \triangleq -\lambda_1 b$, and $\delta \triangleq -\lambda_2 b$.

Note that Theorem 1 cannot be replaced by using the Theorem in Section 2.4 because Theorem 1 guarantees to generate ranking functions expressed in X^i only, while the original theorem does not. Just as in [27], the converse of the above theorem is true for rationals and reals. Since this paper does not focus on the application of the converse theorem, we do not elaborate it here.

4.2 Formal Description

To help describing the algorithm, we need to define a few notations here. We start by defining SHIFT which is the process of transforming constraint from a certain copy of X to a higher copy. It does so by incrementing the superscript of each X^i. For example, SHIFT$(x^0 - x^1 < 1) = x^1 - x^2 < 1$.

Definition 6 (Shift). *Given a linear combination* $\psi : a_0 X^0 + a_1 X^1 + \cdots + a_n X^n$, *a linear constraint* $\varphi : \psi \leq b$, *a set of linear constraints* C, *where* $b \in \mathbb{Z}$, *we define*

$$\text{SHIFT}(\psi) \triangleq a_0 X^1 + a_1 X^2 + \cdots + a_n X^{n+1}$$

$$\text{SHIFT}_1(\varphi) \triangleq \text{SHIFT}(\psi) \leq b$$

$$\text{SHIFT}_{k+1}(\varphi) \triangleq \text{SHIFT}_k(\text{SHIFT}(\psi) \leq b)$$

$$\text{SHIFT}_k(C) \triangleq \{\text{SHIFT}_k(\varphi) \mid \varphi \in C\}$$

Next we define function UNROLL. This function produces an LSL with the same traces as the original but with more copies of X. It does so by adding SHIFT of the constraints to itself. Note that function UNROLL is used in the partitioning process (see L' in Section 3.1). The BRC procedure also unrolls an LSL (see L'' in Section 3.1). The only difference between the two unrolling is that BRC changes the value of j to the number of iterations in the error path.

Definition 7 (Unroll). *Given a set of linear constraints* C, *an LSL* $L = \langle \text{COND}, \text{UPDATE}, i, j \rangle$, *we define*

$$\text{UNROLL}_{1,d}(C) \triangleq C$$

$$\text{UNROLL}_{k+1,d}(C) \triangleq C \cup \text{SHIFT}_d(\text{UNROLL}_{k,d}(C))$$

$$\text{UNROLL}_k(L) \triangleq \langle \text{COND}, \text{UNROLL}_{k,j-i}(\text{COND} \cup \text{UPDATE}), i, j \rangle$$

Lastly we define function DIFF. This function creates new constraints that we use to partition the original LSL. It does so by taking constraint, shifting it and then binding the constraint and its shift with $>$ or $\leq$. For instance, for constraint $\varphi : x^0 \leq 0$ we have DIFF$_{1,>}(\varphi) = x^1 > x^0$ and DIFF$_{1,\leq}(\varphi) = x^1 \leq x^0$.

Definition 8 (Diff). *Given a linear constraint* $\varphi : \psi \leq b$ *and set of constraints* Seed, *where* $b \in \mathbb{Z}$. *We define*

$$\text{DIFF}_{i,\sim}(\varphi) \triangleq \text{SHIFT}_i(\psi) \sim \psi$$

$$\text{DIFF}_{i,\sim}(Seed) \triangleq \{\text{DIFF}_{i,\sim}(\varphi) \mid \varphi \in Seed\}$$

where $\sim$ *is one of* $\{>, \leq\}$.

Now we give two procedures Main and DRR (for "Disjunctive Ranking Relation"). DRR, described in Figure 4, is a recursive procedure, that given an LSL L returns a disjunctive ranking relation T such that $R(L) \subseteq T$. Procedure Main, described in Figure 3, repeatedly calls DRR while $R^+(L) \not\subseteq T$, each time feeding DRR with an unrolling of the original L.

---

procedure Main
input: LSL $L_{original} = \langle \text{COND}, \text{UPDATE}, 0, 1 \rangle$
output: disjunction ranking relation T or "fail"
begin
    $L \leftarrow L_{original}$
    $T \leftarrow \emptyset$
    do
        if DRR(L,COND$_L$) succeeds with disjunctive ranking relation T'
            $T \leftarrow T \cup T'$
        else
            return "fail"
    while (binary reachability check on $(L_{original}, T)$ fails with updated L)
    return T
end.

Fig. 3. Procedure Main

Suppose that DRR is called recursively k times with inputs $(L_1, Seed_1)$, $(L_2, Seed_2)$, ..., $(L_k, Seed_k)$. If the linear ranking function synthesis for L_k succeeds and return the parameters r, δ_0, δ the following is the ranking function we use,

$$\rho_k(X) = \begin{cases} r(X) & \text{if exists } X^1 \text{ such that} \\ & (X, X^1) \in R(L_k) \text{ [case-0]} \\ \delta_0 - \delta & \text{else if exists } X^1 \text{ such that} \\ & (X, X^1) \in R(L_{k-1}) \text{ [case-1]} \\ \delta_0 - 2\delta & \text{else if exists } X^1 \text{ such that} \\ & (X, X^1) \in R(L_{k-2}) \text{ [case-2]} \\ \vdots & \vdots \\ \delta_0 - (k-1)\delta & \text{else if exists } X^1 \text{ such that} \\ & (X, X^1) \in R(L_1) \text{ [case-(k-1)]} \\ \delta_0 - k\delta & \text{otherwise [case-k]} \end{cases} \quad (\sharp)$$

4.3 Correctness Proof

Theorem 2 insures the disjunctive ranking relation returned by DRR is large enough to contain the transition relation of the input LSL. This, in turn, insures that BRC will give a new counterexample for each iteration (until $R^+(L) \subseteq T$)

```
procedure DRR
input: LSL L = ⟨COND, UPDATE, 0, j⟩, and Seed a subset of COND ∪ UPDATE.
output: disjunction ranking relation T
begin
    if linear ranking function synthesis on L succeeds with function r
        return τ(r)
    L_unroll ← UNROLL2(L)
    for each φ ∈ Seed
        Seed_triv ← {DIFF_{j,>}(φ)}
        L_triv ← ⟨COND_{L_unroll}, UPDATE_{L_unroll} ∪ Seed_triv, 0, j⟩
        T ← T∪ DRR(L_triv, Seed_triv)
        Seed ← DIFF_{j,≤}(Seed)
        L ← ⟨COND_{L_unroll}, UPDATE_{L_unroll} ∪ Seed, 0, j⟩
    return T∪ DRR(L, Seed)
end.
```

Fig. 4. Procedure DRR

and the termination condition converges towards a solution. The proof of theorem 2 relies on lemma 1. Lastly theorem 3 asserts the correctness of the algorithm.

Lemma 1. *Let $s_0, \ldots, s_j, \ldots, s_{m \cdot j}$ be an $(m \cdot j + 1)$-trace of some $L = \langle \text{COND}, \text{UPDATE}, 0, j \rangle$ and let Seed be over $X^0, \ldots, X^{m \cdot (j-1)}$. If DRR is called with L and Seed as input and it succeeds then (s_0, s_j) is contained in the return set of DRR.*

Theorem 2. *Suppose that DRR is called with input $(L = \langle \text{COND}, \text{UPDATE}, 0, j \rangle$, Seed) where L is over $X^0, \ldots, X^j$ and Seed = COND_L. If DRR terminates successfully with return value T then $R(L) \subseteq T$.*

Theorem 3. *If procedure Main terminates successfully on a program P, then P terminates and has a disjunctive linear ranking relation T.*

4.4   Termination and Complexity of the Algorithm

The procedures Main and DRR as given in this section may not always terminate, in particular when the input LSL is not terminating. When implemented we need to bound the recursion depth of DRR and the number of iterations of the main loop. When the input LSL is deterministic and the variables range over $\mathbb{Z}$, the recursive calls to DRR for each $\varphi \in Seed$ will succeed with no further calls and therefore the number of calls to DRR will be linear in the depth bound. When the LSL is non-deterministic or the variables range over $\mathbb{Q}$ or $\mathbb{R}$, the number of calls to DRR in the worst case is exponential in the depth bound. Finally we note that the LSL $\text{UNROLL}_k(L)$ has k times as many constraints and variables as in L.

Table 1. Experiment results

#	Vars	Terminating	Linear	Polyrank	Ours	BRC	DRR	Failed Proc
1	1	yes	no	no	no	-	-	DRR
2	1	yes	yes	yes	yes	0	1	-
3	1	yes	yes	yes	yes	0	1	-
4	1	yes	yes	yes	yes	0	1	-
5	1	yes	yes	no	yes	0	1	-
6	2	yes	no	no	yes	0	2	-
7	2	no	-	-	-	-	-	DRR
8	2	no	-	-	-	-	-	DRR
9	2	no	-	-	-	-	-	DRR
10	2	no	-	-	-	-	-	DRR
11	2	yes	no	no	no	-	-	DRR
12	2	yes	no	no	yes	0	2	-
13	2	yes	no	no	yes	0	2	-
14	2	yes	no	no	yes	0	2	-
15	2	yes	yes	no	yes	0	1	-
16	2	no	-	-	-	-	-	DRR
17	2	no	-	-	-	-	-	DRR
18	2	yes	no	no	yes	0	2	-
19	2	no	-	-	-	-	-	DRR
20	2	no	-	-	-	-	-	DRR
21	2	yes	no	no	yes	0	2	-
22	2	no	-	-	-	-	-	DRR
23	2	yes	no	no	yes	0	2	-
24	2	yes	no	no	yes	0	2	-
25	2	yes	yes	yes	yes	0	1	-
26	2	yes	no	no	yes	0	2	-
27	2	yes	no	no	yes	0	2	-
28	3	yes	no	no	yes	0	2	-
29	3	no	-	-	-	-	-	DRR
30	3	yes	no	no	no	∞	3	BRC
31	3	yes	no	no	yes	0	2	-
32	3	yes	no	no	yes	0	2	-
33	3	no	-	-	-	-	-	DRR
34	3	yes	no	no	yes	1	3	-
35	3	yes	no	no	yes	0	2	-
36	3	yes	no	no	yes	0	2	-
37	3	yes	yes	yes	yes	0	1	-
38	4	yes	no	no	yes	0	2	-

5   Experiments

We created a test suite of LSL loops. To our knowledge it is the first LSL test
suite. The loops are collected from other research work [27, 15, 34, 28, 9, 12, 6, 8,

13, 5] and real code. The test suite is still growing. At the time of our submission, it contains 38 LSL loops. Among them 11 are non-terminating loops, 7 are terminating with linear ranking functions, 20 are terminating with non-linear ranking functions. Moreover, 6 are non-deterministic, 32 are deterministic, 5 have 1 variable, 22 have 2 variables, 10 have 3 variables, and one has 4 variables. All loops are executed over domain $\mathbb{Z}$. The test suite as well as the implementation are available at [11].

We compared our method to linear ranking function synthesis method [27] using the implementation found in [32], and the polyranking method [7] using the implementation found in [5]. Detailed experimental results are provided in Table 1. The "Vars" column indicates the number of variables used in the LSL. The "Terminating" column indicate whether the LSL terminates. The columns of "Linear", "Polyrank", and "Ours" indicate whether the methods of Podelski *et al.*'s linear ranking function synthesis method [27], Bradley *et al.*'s polyranking method [7], and our method, respectively, have successfully found a termination proof. The "BRC" column states the number of times procedure BRC was called and the "DRR" column states the accumulative depth of DRR recursion. The "Failed Proc" column indicates which procedure, Main or DRR, failed terminating if the whole process failed to terminate. Since the runtime for all three methods was in the magnitude of a few milliseconds we omitted them from the table.

As shown in the table, our method considerably outperformed the other two methods. We succeed for all 7 loops with a linear ranking function. Out of the 20 terminating loops that have no linear ranking function we are successful for 17. For all non-terminating loops, the execution needs to be manually terminated. Except for one loop, all the proof searches fail in procedure DRR. In comparison, the linear ranking function synthesis method [27] succeeds for all the 7 loops with a linear ranking function; it fails to find a termination proof for all the 20 examples among the rest that were terminating. The polyranking method [7] succeeds in proving termination for 5 out of the 7 examples with a linear ranking function; it fails to find a termination proof for all the 20 examples among the rest that were terminating. We set the tree depth to be 100 for the polyranking method.

6   Conclusions

This paper describes an automatic method for generating disjunctive ranking relations for Linear Simple Loops. The method repeatedly finds linear ranking functions on restricted state space until it reaches an over-approximation of the transitive closure of the transition relation. As demonstrated experimentally we largely expanded the scope of LSLs that can be solved. We also extended an existing technique for linear ranking function synthesis. The extended method can handle more general form of LSLs. Another contribution is that we created the first LSL test suite.

Acknowledgments. We thank Byron Cook for providing inspiring examples. We thank the anonymous reviewers for their valuable insights.

References

[1] Balaban, I., Cohen, A., Pnueli, A.: Ranking Abstraction of Recursive Programs. In: Emerson, E.A., Namjoshi, K.S. (eds.) VMCAI 2006. LNCS, vol. 3855, pp. 267–281. Springer, Heidelberg (2005)

[2] Ben-Amram, A.M., Genaim, S., Masud, A.N.: On the Termination of Integer Loops. In: Kuncak, V., Rybalchenko, A. (eds.) VMCAI 2012. LNCS, vol. 7148, pp. 72–87. Springer, Heidelberg (2012)

[3] Berdine, J., Chawdhary, A., Cook, B., Distefano, D., O'Hearn, P.: Variance analyses from invariance analyses. In: Proceedings of the 34th Annual ACM SIGPLAN-SIGACT Symposium on Principles of Programming Languages, POPL 2007, pp. 211–224. ACM, New York (2007)

[4] Berdine, J., Cook, B., Distefano, D., O'Hearn, P.W.: Automatic Termination Proofs for Programs with Shape-Shifting Heaps. In: Ball, T., Jones, R.B. (eds.) CAV 2006. LNCS, vol. 4144, pp. 386–400. Springer, Heidelberg (2006)

[5] Bradley, A.R.: polyrank: Tools for termination analysis (2005), http://theory.stanford.edu/~arbrad/software/polyrank.html

[6] Bradley, A.R., Manna, Z., Sipma, H.B.: Linear Ranking with Reachability. In: Etessami, K., Rajamani, S.K. (eds.) CAV 2005. LNCS, vol. 3576, pp. 491–504. Springer, Heidelberg (2005)

[7] Bradley, A.R., Manna, Z., Sipma, H.B.: The Polyranking Principle. In: Caires, L., Italiano, G.F., Monteiro, L., Palamidessi, C., Yung, M. (eds.) ICALP 2005. LNCS, vol. 3580, pp. 1349–1361. Springer, Heidelberg (2005)

[8] Bradley, A.R., Manna, Z., Sipma, H.B.: Termination of Polynomial Programs. In: Cousot, R. (ed.) VMCAI 2005. LNCS, vol. 3385, pp. 113–129. Springer, Heidelberg (2005)

[9] Braverman, M.: Termination of Integer Linear Programs. In: Ball, T., Jones, R.B. (eds.) CAV 2006. LNCS, vol. 4144, pp. 372–385. Springer, Heidelberg (2006)

[10] Chawdhary, A., Cook, B., Gulwani, S., Sagiv, M., Yang, H.: Ranking abstractions. Technical report (2008)

[11] Chen, H.Y., Flur, S., Mukhopadhyay, S.: Lsl test suite, https://tigerbytes2.lsu.edu/users/hchen11/lsl/

[12] Colon, M.A., Uribe, T.E.: Generating Finite-State Abstractions of Reactive Systems Using Decision Procedures. In: Hu, A.J., Vardi, M.Y. (eds.) CAV 1998. LNCS, vol. 1427, pp. 293–304. Springer, Heidelberg (1998)

[13] Colón, M.A., Sipma, H.B.: Synthesis of Linear Ranking Functions. In: Margaria, T., Yi, W. (eds.) TACAS 2001. LNCS, vol. 2031, pp. 67–81. Springer, Heidelberg (2001)

[14] Colón, M.A., Sipma, H.B.: Practical Methods for Proving Program Termination. In: Brinksma, E., Larsen, K.G. (eds.) CAV 2002. LNCS, vol. 2404, pp. 442–454. Springer, Heidelberg (2002)

[15] Cook, B., Gulwani, S., Lev-Ami, T., Rybalchenko, A., Sagiv, M.: Proving Conditional Termination. In: Gupta, A., Malik, S. (eds.) CAV 2008. LNCS, vol. 5123, pp. 328–340. Springer, Heidelberg (2008)

[16] Cook, B., Podelski, A., Rybalchenko, A.: Abstraction Refinement for Termination. In: Hankin, C., Siveroni, I. (eds.) SAS 2005. LNCS, vol. 3672, pp. 87–101. Springer, Heidelberg (2005)

[17] Cook, B., Podelski, A., Rybalchenko, A.: Termination proofs for systems code. In: Proceedings of the 2006 ACM SIGPLAN Conference on Programming Language Design and Implementation, PLDI 2006, pp. 415–426. ACM, New York (2006)

[18] Cook, B., Rybalchenko, A.: Proving that programs eventually do something good. In: POPL 2006: Principles of Programming Languages, pp. 265–276. Springer (2007)

[19] Cousot, P.: Semantic foundations of program analysis. In: Muchnick, S.S., Jones, N.D. (eds.) Program Flow Analysis: Theory and Applications, ch. 10, pp. 303–342. Prentice-Hall, Inc., Englewood Cliffs (1981)

[20] Cousot, P.: Proving Program Invariance and Termination by Parametric Abstraction, Lagrangian Relaxation and Semidefinite Programming. In: Cousot, R. (ed.) VMCAI 2005. LNCS, vol. 3385, pp. 1–24. Springer, Heidelberg (2005)

[21] Cousot, P., Cousot, R.: An abstract interpretation framework for termination. In: POPL, pp. 245–258 (2012)

[22] Gulwani, S., Jain, S., Koskinen, E.: Control-flow refinement and progress invariants for bound analysis. SIGPLAN Not. 44, 375–385 (2009)

[23] Gulwani, S., Mehra, K.K., Chilimbi, T.: Speed: precise and efficient static estimation of program computational complexity. In: Proceedings of the 36th Annual ACM SIGPLAN-SIGACT Symposium on Principles of Programming Languages, POPL 2009, pp. 127–139. ACM, New York (2009)

[24] Gulwani, S., Zuleger, F.: The reachability-bound problem. In: Proceedings of the 2010 ACM SIGPLAN Conference on Programming Language Design and Implementation, PLDI 2010, pp. 292–304. ACM, New York (2010)

[25] Kroening, D., Sharygina, N., Tsitovich, A., Wintersteiger, C.M.: Termination Analysis with Compositional Transition Invariants. In: Touili, T., Cook, B., Jackson, P. (eds.) CAV 2010. LNCS, vol. 6174, pp. 89–103. Springer, Heidelberg (2010)

[26] Podelski, A., Rybalchenko, A.: Software model checking of liveness properties via transition invariants. Technical report (2003)

[27] Podelski, A., Rybalchenko, A.: A Complete Method for the Synthesis of Linear Ranking Functions. In: Steffen, B., Levi, G. (eds.) VMCAI 2004. LNCS, vol. 2937, pp. 239–251. Springer, Heidelberg (2004)

[28] Podelski, A., Rybalchenko, A.: Transition invariants. In: LICS, pp. 32–41 (2004)

[29] Podelski, A., Rybalchenko, A.: Transition predicate abstraction and fair termination. In: Proceedings of the 32nd ACM SIGPLAN-SIGACT Symposium on Principles of Programming Languages, POPL 2005. ACM (2005)

[30] Ramsey, F.P.: On a problem of formal logic. Proc. London Math. Soc. 30, 491–504 (1930)

[31] Rival, X., Mauborgne, L.: The trace partitioning abstract domain. ACM Trans. Program. Lang. Syst. 29(5) (August 2007)

[32] Rybalchenko, A.: Rankfinder, http://www.mpi-sws.org/~rybal/rankfinder/

[33] Schrijver, A.: Theory of linear and integer programming. John Wiley & Sons, Inc., New York (1986)

[34] Tiwari, A.: Termination of Linear Programs. In: Alur, R., Peled, D.A. (eds.) CAV 2004. LNCS, vol. 3114, pp. 70–82. Springer, Heidelberg (2004)

[35] Turing, A.M.: Checking a large routine. Report of a Conference on High Speed Automatic Calculating Machines, pp. 67–69 (1948)

Finding Non-terminating Executions in Distributed Asynchronous Programs

Michael Emmi[1],[*] and Akash Lal[2]

[1] LIAFA, Université Paris Diderot
mje@liafa.univ-paris-diderot.fr
[2] Microsoft Research India
akashl@microsoft.com

Abstract. Programming distributed and reactive asynchronous systems is complex due to the lack of synchronization between concurrently executing tasks, and arbitrary delay of message-based communication. As even simple programming mistakes have the capability to introduce divergent behavior, a key liveness property is *eventual quiescence*: for any finite number of external stimuli (e.g., client-generated events), only a finite number of internal messages are ever created.

In this work we propose a practical three-step reduction-based approach for detecting divergent executions in asynchronous programs. As a first step, we give a code-to-code translation reducing divergence of an asynchronous program P to completed state-reachability—i.e., reachability to a given state with no pending asynchronous tasks—of a polynomially-sized asynchronous program P'. In the second step, we give a code-to-code translation under-approximating completed state-reachability of P' by state-reachability of a polynomially-sized recursive sequential program $P''(K)$, for the given analysis parameter $K \in \mathbb{N}$. Following Emmi et al. [8]'s delay-bounding approach, $P''(K)$ encodes a subset of P''s, and thus of P's, behaviors by limiting scheduling nondeterminism. As K is increased, more possibly divergent behaviors of P are considered, and in the limit as K approaches infinity, our reduction is complete for programs with finite data domains. As the final step we give the resulting state-reachability query to an off-the-shelf SMT-based sequential program verification tool.

We demonstrate the feasibility of our approach by implementing a prototype analysis tool called ALIVE, which detects divergent executions in several hand-coded variations of textbook distributed algorithms. As far as we are aware, our easy-to-implement prototype is the first tool which automatically detects divergence for distributed and reactive asynchronous programs.

1 Introduction

The ever-increasing popularity of online commercial and social networks, along with proliferating mobile computing devices, promises to make distributed software an even more pervasive component of technological infrastructure. In a

---

[*] Supported by a Fondation Sciences Mathématiques de Paris post-doctoral fellowship.

A. Miné and D. Schmidt (Eds.): SAS 2012, LNCS 7460, pp. 439–455, 2012.

distributed program a network of physically separated asynchronous processors coordinate by sending and asynchronously receiving messages. Such systems are challenging to implement because of several uncertainties, including processor timings, message delays, and processor failures. Although simplifying mechanisms such as *synchronizers* and shared-memory simulation do exist [16], they add significant runtime overhead which can be unacceptable in many situations.

Because of the inherit complexity in distributed asynchronous programming, even subtle design and programming mistakes have the capability to introduce erroneous or divergent behaviors, against which the usual reliability measures are much less effective. The great amount of nondeterminism in processor timings and message delays tends to make errors elusive and hard to reproduce in simulation and testing. The combinatorial explosion incurred by the vast number of processor interleavings and message-buffer contents tends to make formal verification techniques intractable. Though many distributed algorithms are proposed along with manual correctness proofs, key properties such as *eventual quiescence*—i.e., for any number of external stimuli such as client-generated events, only a finite number of internal network messages are ever created—remain difficult to ensure with automatic techniques. Practically speaking, such properties ensure the eventual construction of network spanning trees [16], the eventual election of network leaders [20], and the eventual acceptance of network peer proposals, e.g., according to the Paxos protocol [15].

In this work we develop an automatic technique to detect violations to eventual quiescence, i.e., executions of distributed systems for which a finite number of external stimuli result in an infinite number of internal messages. Our reduction-based approach works in three steps. First, we reduce the problem of finding nonterminating executions of a given (distributed) asynchronous program P to the problem of computing reachability in a polynomially-sized (distributed) asynchronous program P'. This reduction is complete for programs with finite data domains, in the sense that an answer to the reachability query on P' is a precise answer to the nontermination query on P. In the second step, we reduce reachability in P' to reachability in a polynomially-sized recursive sequential program P''—without explicitly encoding the concurrent behavior of P' as data in P''. This step is parameterized by an integer $K \in \mathbb{N}$; for small K, P'' encodes few concurrent schedules of P'; as K is increased, P'' encodes and increasing number of concurrent reorderings, and in the limit as K approaches infinity, P'' codes all possible behaviors of P'—and thus P. Finally, using existing sequential program verification tools, we check reachability in P'': a positive result indicates a nonterminating execution in P, though the lack of nonterminating executions in P can only be concluded in the limit as K approaches infinity. Our technique supports *fairness*, in that we may consider only infinite executions in which no message is ignored forever.

We demonstrate the feasibility of our reduction-based approach by implementing a prototype analysis tool called ALIVE, which detects violations to eventual quiescence in several hand-coded variations to textbook distributed algorithms [16]. Our relatively easy-to-implement prototype leverages existing

SMT-based program verification tools [14], and as far as we are aware, is the first tool which can automatically detect divergence in distributed asynchronous programs.

To begin in Section 2, we introduce a program model of distributed computation. In Section 3 we describe our reduction to sequential program analysis, and provide code-to-code translations which succinctly encode the reduction. Following in Section 4 we describe our experimental results in analyzing textbook distributed algorithms, and we conclude by discussing related work in Section 5.

2 Distributed Asynchronous Programs

We consider a distributed message-passing program model in which each processor is equipped with a procedure stack and an unordered buffer of pending messages. Initially all processors are idle. When an idle processor's message buffer is non-empty, some message is removed, and a message-dependent *task* is executed to completion. Each task executes essentially as a recursive sequential program, which besides accessing its own processor's global storage, can *post* messages to the buffers of any processor, including its own. When a task does complete, its processor again becomes idle, chooses a next pending message to remove, and so on. The distinction between messages and handling tasks is purely aesthetic, and we unify the two by supposing each message is a procedure-and-argument pair. Though in principle many message-passing systems, e.g., in Erlang and Scala, allow reading additional messages at any program point, we have observed that common practice is to read messages only upon completing a prior task [21].

Our choice to model message-passing programs with *unordered* buffers has two important consequences. First, although some programming models do not ensure messages are received in the order they are sent, others do; our unordered buffer model should be seen as an abstraction of a model with faithful message queues, since ignoring message order allows behaviors infeasible in the queue-ordered model. Second, when message order is ignored, distributed executions are *task-serializable*—i.e., equivalent to executions where the tasks across all processors execute serially, one after the other. Intuitively this is true because (a) tasks of different processors access disjoint memory, and (b) message posting operations commute with each other. (Message posting operations do not commute when buffers are ordered.) To simulate a distributed system with a single processor we combine each processor's global storage, and ensure each processor's tasks access only their processor-indexed storage. Since serializability implies that single processor systems precisely simulate the behavior of distributed systems, we limit our discussion, without loss of generality, to single-processor asynchronous programs [19].

2.1 Program Syntax

Let Procs be a set of procedure names, Vals a set of values, Exprs a set of expressions, Pids a set of processor identifiers, and let T be a type. Figure 1 gives

$$P ::= \mathbf{var}\ g{:}T\ (\mathbf{proc}\ p\ (\mathbf{var}\ 1{:}T)\ s)^*$$
$$s ::= s;\ s\ \mid\ \mathbf{skip}\ \mid\ x := e$$
$$\mid\ \mathbf{assume}\ e$$
$$\mid\ \mathbf{if}\ e\ \mathbf{then}\ s\ \mathbf{else}\ s$$
$$\mid\ \mathbf{while}\ e\ \mathbf{do}\ s$$
$$\mid\ \mathbf{call}\ x := p\ e$$
$$\mid\ \mathbf{return}\ e$$
$$\mid\ \mathbf{post}\ p\ e$$
$$x ::= g\ \mid\ 1$$

Fig. 1. The grammar of asynchronous message-passing programs P. Here T is an unspecified type, and e and p range over expressions and procedure names.

DISPATCH
$$\frac{}{\langle g, \varepsilon, m \cup \{f\}\rangle \to \langle g, f, m\rangle}$$

COMPLETE
$$\frac{f = \langle \ell, \mathbf{return}\ e;\ s\rangle}{\langle g, f, m\rangle \to \langle g, \varepsilon, m\rangle}$$

POST
$$\frac{s_1 = \mathbf{post}\ p\ e;\ s_2 \qquad \ell_2 \in e(g, \ell_1) \qquad f = \langle \ell_2, s_p\rangle}{\langle g, \langle \ell_1, s_1\rangle\, w, m\rangle \to \langle g, \langle \ell_1, s_2\rangle\, w, m \cup \{f\}\rangle}$$

Fig. 2. The transition relation $\to$ of asynchronous message-passing programs

the grammar of *asynchronous message-passing programs*. We intentionally leave the syntax of expressions e unspecified, though we do insist Vals contains **true** and **false**, and Exprs contains Vals and the *(nullary) choice operator* $\star$. We say a program is *finite-data* when Vals is finite.

Each program P declares a single global variable g and a procedure sequence, each $p \in$ Procs having a single parameter 1 and top-level statement denoted s_p; as statements are built inductively by composition with control-flow statements, s_p describes the entire body of p. The set of program statements s is denoted Stmts. Intuitively, a **post** $p\ e$ statement is an asynchronous call to a procedure p with argument e. The **assume** e statement proceeds only when e evaluates to **true**, and this statement plays a role in disqualifying executions in our subsequent reductions of Section 3. The programming language we consider is simple, yet very expressive, since the syntax of types and expressions is left free, and we lose no generality by considering only single global and local variables.

2.2 Program Semantics

A *(procedure) frame* $f = \langle \ell, s\rangle$ is a current valuation $\ell \in$ Vals to the procedure-local variable 1, along with a statement $s \in$ Stmts to be executed. (Here s describes the entire body of a procedure p that remains to be executed, and is initially set to p's top-level statement s_p; we refer to initial procedure frames $t = \langle \ell, s_p\rangle$ as *tasks*, to distinguish the frames that populate task buffers.) The set of all frames is denoted Frames. A *configuration* $c = \langle g, w, m\rangle$ is a current valuation $g \in$ Vals to the processor-global variable g, along with a procedure-frame stack $w \in$ Frames* and a multiset $m \in \mathbb{M}[\text{Frames}]$ representing the pending-tasks buffer. The configuration c is called *idle* when $w = \varepsilon$, and *completed* when $w = \varepsilon$ and $m = \emptyset$. The set of configurations is denoted Configs.

Figure 2 defines the transition relation $\to$ for the asynchronous behavior. (The transitions for the sequential statements are standard.) The POST rule creates a new frame to execute the given procedure, and places the new frame in the pending-tasks buffer. The COMPLETE rule returns from the final frame of a task, rendering the processor idle, and the DISPATCH rule schedules a pending task on the idle processor.

An *execution* of a program P (from c_0) is a configuration sequence $\xi = c_0 c_1 \ldots$ such that $c_i \to c_{i+1}$ for $i \geq 0$; we say each configuration c_i is *reachable* from c_0. An *initial condition* $\iota = \langle g_0, \ell_0, p_0 \rangle$ is a global-variable valuation $g_0 \in \mathsf{Vals}$, along with a local-variable valuation $\ell_0 \in \mathsf{Vals}$, and a procedure $p_0 \in \mathsf{Procs}$. A configuration $c = \langle g_0, \langle \ell_0, s_{p_0} \rangle, \emptyset \rangle$ of a program P is called $\langle g_0, \ell_0, p_0 \rangle$-*initial*. An execution $\xi = c_0 c_1 \ldots$ is called *infinitely-often idle* when there exists an infinite set $I \subseteq \mathbb{N}$ such that for each $i \in I$, c_i is idle.

Definition 1 (state-reachability). *The* (completed) state-reachability problem *is to determine for an initial condition ι, global valuation g, and program P, whether there exists a (completed) g-valued configuration reachable in P from ι.*

In this work we are interested in detecting non-terminating executions due to asynchrony, rather than the orthogonal problem of detecting whether each individual task may alone terminate. Our notion of non-termination thus considers only executions which return to idle configurations infinitely-often.

Definition 2 (non-termination). *The* non-termination problem *is to determine for an initial condition ι and a program P, whether there exists an infinitely-often idle execution of P from some ι-initial configuration.*

3   Detecting Non-termination

Though precise algorithms for detecting (fair) non-termination in finite-data asynchronous programs are known (see Ganty and Majumdar [10]), the fair non-termination problem is polynomial-time equivalent to reachability in Petri nets, which is an EXPSPACE-hard problem for which only non-primitive recursive algorithms are known. Though worst-case complexity is not necessarily an indication of feasibility on practically-occurring instances, here we are interested in leveraging existing tools designed for more tractable problems whose solutions can be used to incrementally under-approximate non-termination detection; i.e., where for a given analysis parameter $k \in \mathbb{N}$ we can efficiently detect non-termination from an interesting subset B_k of program behaviors.

Our strategy is to reduce the problem of detecting non-terminating executions in asynchronous programs to that of completed state-reachability in asynchronous programs. We perform this step using the code-to-code translation of Section 3.1, and in Section 3.2 we consider extensions to handle fairness. Then, in the second step of Section 3.3, we apply an incrementally underapproximating reduction from state-reachability in asynchronous programs to state-reachability in sequential program [8, 4], and discharge the resulting program analysis problem using existing sequential analysis tools.

3.1   Reduction from Non-termination to Reachability

In the first step of our reduction, we use the fact that every infinite execution eventually passes through two configurations c_1, and then c_2, such that every possible execution from c_1 is also possible from c_2; e.g., when c_1 and c_2 are idle configurations with the same global valuation in which all tasks pending at c_1 are also pending at c_2. Formally, given two configurations $c_1 = \langle g_1, w_1, m_1 \rangle$ and $c_2 = \langle g_2, w_2, m_2 \rangle$ we define the order $c_1 \preceq c_2$ to hold when $g_1 = g_2$, $w_1 = w_2$, and $m_1 \subseteq m_2$.[1] An execution $c_0 c_1 \ldots$ is called *periodic* when $c_i \preceq c_j$ for two idle configurations c_i and c_j such that $i < j$.[2] The following lemma essentially exploits the fact that $\preceq$ is a well-quasi-ordering on idle configurations.

Lemma 1. *A finite-data program P has an infinitely-often idle execution from ι if and only if P has a periodic execution from ι.*

Proof. Suppose $c_0 c_1 \ldots$ is the sequence of idle configurations in an infinitely-often idle execution ξ. As the subset order $\subseteq$ on multisets is a well-quasi order, and the domain Vals of global variables is finite, $\preceq$ is a well-quasi order on idle configurations. Thus there exists $i < j$ such that $c_i \preceq c_j$, so ξ is also periodic.

Supposing $\xi = c_0 c_1 \ldots$ is a periodic execution from ι, there exists idle configurations c_i and c_j of ξ such that $i < j$ and $c_i \preceq c_j$; let $c_i = \langle g_i, \varepsilon, m_i \rangle$ and $c_j = \langle g_j, \varepsilon, m_j \rangle$. Since $g_i = g_j$ and $m_i \subseteq m_j$, by definition of $\preceq$, the sequence of execution steps between c_i and c_j is also enabled from configuration c_j—we may simply ignore the extra tasks $m_j \setminus m_i$ pending in c_j. For any $k, l \in \mathbb{N}$ and task buffer $m \in \mathbb{M}[\mathsf{Frames}]$ such that $k < l < |\xi|$, let $\xi_{k,l}^m$ be the sequence of configurations $c_k c_{k+1} \ldots c_{l-1}$ of ξ, each with additional pending tasks m. Furthermore, let $k \cdot m$ be the multiset union of k copies of m. Letting $m = m_j \setminus m_i$, then $\xi_{0,i} \xi_{i,j} \xi_{i,j}^m \xi_{i,j}^{2m} \xi_{i,j}^{3m} \ldots$ is an infinitely-often idle execution from ι which periodically repeats the same transitions used to construct ξ between c_i and c_j.

We reduce the detection of periodic executions to completed state reachability in asynchronous programs. Essentially, such a reduction must determine multiset inclusion between the unbounded task buffers at two idle configurations; i.e., for some idle configuration $c_i = \langle g_i, \varepsilon, m_i \rangle$ reachable in an execution $c_0 c_1 \ldots$, there exists $j > i$ such that $c_j = \langle g_j, \varepsilon, m_j \rangle$ with $g_i = g_j$ and $m_i \subseteq m_j$. As the set m_i of pending tasks at c_i is unbounded, any reduction cannot hope to store arbitrary m_i for later comparison with m_j using finite-domain program variables.

Our reduction determines the correspondence between unbounded task buffers in the source program using only finite-domain program variables by leveraging the task buffers of the target program. For each instance of a task t which is pending in c_i, we post an additional task $\mathrm{pro}(t)$ when t is posted; for each task t pending in c_j, we either post an additional task $\mathrm{anti}(t)$ instead of t, or we post nothing, to handle the case where t is never dispatched. We then check that for each executed $\mathrm{pro}(t)$ a matching $\mathrm{anti}(t)$ is also executed, and that

---

[1] Here $\subseteq$ is the multiset subset relation.
[2] As our definition of $\preceq$ only relates configurations with equal global valuations, our notion of periodic is only complete for finite-data programs.

```
 1 // translation of var g: T          13 // translation of g               26 // translation of post p e
 2 var repeated: B                      14 G[period]                         27 if * then
 3 var turn: B                          15                                   28     assume !period;
 4 var last: Procs × Vals               16 // additional procedures          29     post pro (p,e);
 5 var G[B]: T                          17 proc pro(var t: Procs × Vals)      30     post p (e,true);
 6                                       18     assume turn;                  31     repeated := true
 7 // translation of                    19     last := t;                    32 else if * then
 8 // proc p (var l: T) s               20     turn := false;                33     assume period;
 9 proc p (var l:T, period:B) s         21     return                        34     post anti (p,e)
10                                       22 proc anti(var t: Procs × Vals)    35 else if * then
11 // translation of call x := p e      23     assume !turn ∧ last = t;       36     skip
12 call x := p (e,period)               24     turn := true;                 37 else
                                         25     return                        38     post p (e,period)
```

Fig. 3. The translation $((P))_{nt}$ of an asynchronous program P

at some point no $\mathtt{pro}(t)$ nor $\mathtt{anti}(t)$ tasks are pending. By considering executions which alternate between tasks of $\{\mathtt{pro}(t) : t \in m_i\}$ and $\{\mathtt{anti}(t) : t \in m'_j\}$—where $m'_j \subseteq m_j$ such that $m_j \setminus m'_j$ correspond to the dropped tasks—we can ensure each instance of an m_i task has a corresponding instance in m_j, storing only the last encountered $\mathtt{pro}(t)$ task, for $t \in m_i$.

Figure 3 lists our code-to-code translation $((P))_{nt}$ reducing non-termination in an asynchronous program P to completed state reachability in the asynchronous program $((P))_{nt}$. Besides the auxiliary variable $\mathtt{last}$ used to store the last encountered $\mathtt{pro}(t)$ task, for $t \in m_i$, we introduce Boolean variables $\mathtt{repeated}$, to signal whether m_i is non-empty, and $\mathtt{turn}$, to signal whether an $\mathtt{anti}(t)$ task has been executed since the last executed $\mathtt{pro}(t)$ task. We also divide the execution of tasks into two phases by introducing a task-local Boolean variable $\mathtt{period}$. The first phase ($\mathtt{!period}$) corresponds to the execution $c_0 c_1 \ldots c_i$, while the second phase ($\mathtt{period}$) corresponds to $c_{i+1} c_{i+2} \ldots c_j$. Initially pending tasks occur in the first non-$\mathtt{period}$ phase. Then each time a new task t is posted, a non-deterministic choice is made for whether t will execute in the non-$\mathtt{period}$ phase, in the $\mathtt{period}$ phase, or never.

Finally, to determine which finite asynchronous executions prove the existence of infinite asynchronous executions, we define the predicate φ_{nt} over initial conditions ι and configuration c as

$$\varphi_{nt}(\iota, c) \overset{\text{def}}{=} \begin{cases} \mathtt{true} & \text{when } \neg\mathtt{repeated}(\iota) \text{ and } \mathtt{turn}(\iota) \\ & \text{and } \mathtt{repeated}(c) \text{ and } \mathtt{turn}(c) \\ & \text{and } \mathtt{G[0]}(c) = \mathtt{G[1]}(\iota) = \mathtt{G[1]}(c) \\ \mathtt{false} & \text{otherwise,} \end{cases}$$

along with the mapping ϑ_{nt} which projects the initial conditions of $((P))_{nt}$ to those of P, as $\vartheta_{nt}(\langle g, \ell, p \rangle) \overset{\text{def}}{=} \langle g', \ell', p' \rangle$ when $\mathtt{g}(g') = \mathtt{G[0]}(g)$, $\mathtt{l}(\ell') = \mathtt{l}(\ell)$, and $p' = p$. Essentially, in any completed configuration c reachable from ι satisfying $\varphi_{nt}(\iota, c)$, we know that some task has executed during the period (since $\mathtt{repeated}$ evaluates to $\mathtt{true}$), and that for each task pending at the beginning of the period, an identical task is pending at the end of the period (since $\mathtt{turn}$ evaluates to true, and there are no pending tasks in c). Finally, the conditions on the global variable G ensure that the beginning and end of each period reach the same global valuation.

Lemma 2. *A finite-data program P has an infinitely-often idle execution from ι_0 if and only if a completed configuration c is reachable in $((P))_{nt}$ from some ι such that $\varphi_{nt}(\iota, c) = \textbf{true}$ and $\vartheta_{nt}(\iota) = \iota_0$.*

Proof. For the forward direction, by Lemma 1, P also has a periodic execution $\xi = \xi_{0,i}\xi_{i,j}\xi_{j,\omega}$ from ι_0—where $\xi_{k,l} \stackrel{\text{def}}{=} c_k c_{k+1} \ldots c_{l-1}$ for $k < l < |\xi|$—and $c_i \preceq c_j$ for idle configurations $c_i = \langle g, \varepsilon, m_1 \rangle$ and $c_j = \langle g, \varepsilon, m_2 \rangle$. We build an execution $\xi' = \xi'_{0,i}\xi'_{i,j}\xi_{\text{match}}$ of $((P))_{nt}$ such that

- the configurations c'_k of $\xi'_{0,i}$ correspond to configurations c_k of $\xi_{0,i}$, with $g(c_k) = $ G[0](c'_k), G[1]$(c'_k) = g$,
- the configurations c'_k of $\xi'_{i,j}$ correspond to configurations c_k of $\xi_{i,j}$, with $g(c_k) = $ G[1](c'_k) and G[0]$(c'_k) = g$,
- the pending tasks of each configuration c'_k of $\xi'_{0,j}$, excluding **pro** and **anti** tasks, are contained within those of c_k,
- the local valuations of each configuration c'_k of $\xi'_{0,i}$ (resp., of $\xi'_{i,j}$) match those of c_k, except **period** evaluates to 0 (resp., to 1) in every frame of c'_k, and
- the sequence ξ_{match} alternately executes **pro** and **anti** tasks such that each **pro**(t) task is followed by a matching **anti**(t) task.

It follows that we can construct such a ξ' which reaches a completed configuration c from some ι such that $\varphi_{nt}(\iota, c)$, $\vartheta_{nt}(\iota) = \iota_0$, and G[0]$(c) = $ G[1]$(c) = g$.

For the backward direction, the reachability of a completed configuration c of $((P))_{nt}$ from ι such that $\varphi_{nt}(\iota, c)$ implies that there exists a periodic execution $\xi = c_0 c_1 \ldots$ of P; in particular, there exist configurations $c_i \preceq c_j$ of ξ with $i < j$, and which have the global valuations $g(c_i) = g(c_j) = $ G[0]$(c) = $ G[1](c) reached at the end of each period of $((P))_{nt}$'s execution, and the set of pending tasks m in c_i are those second-period tasks posted by $((P))_{nt}$ from first-period tasks. Since the set of tasks posted and pending by the end of the second period must contain m—otherwise unexecutable **pro** tasks would remain pending—we can construct a run where the pending tasks of c_j contain the pending tasks of c_i, and so P has a periodic execution. By Lemma 1 we conclude that P also has an infinitely-often idle execution.

3.2 Ensuring Scheduling Fairness

In many classes of asynchronous systems there are (at least) two sensible notions of scheduling fairness against which to determine liveness properties: an infinite execution is called *strongly-fair* if every infinitely-often enabled transition is fired infinitely often, and *weakly-fair* if every infinitely-often *continuously* enabled transition is fired infinitely often. In our setting where asynchronous tasks execute serially from a task buffer, weak fairness becomes irrelevant; while one task executes no other transitions are enabled, and when idle (i.e., while no tasks are executing), all pending tasks become enabled. Furthermore once a task is posted, it becomes pending, and it is thus enabled in all subsequent idle configurations until dispatched. We thus define fairness according to what is normally referred to as strong fairness: an execution is *fair* when each infinitely-often posted task is infinitely-often dispatched.

To extend our reduction so that only fair infinite executions are considered we make two alterations to the translation of Figure 3. First, on Line 36 we replace **skip** with **assume period**; this ensures participation of all tasks pending at the beginning of each period. Second, we add auxiliary state to ensure at least one instance of each task posted during the period is dispatched. This can be encoded in various ways; for instance, we can add two arrays dropped and dispatched of index type Procs × Vals and element type $\mathbb{B}$ that indicate whether each task has been dropped/dispatched during the period phase (i.e., where the local variable period evaluates to **true**). Initially dropped$[t]$ = dispatched$[t]$ = **false** for all $t \in$ Procs × Vals. Each time a post to task t is dropped during the period phase (i.e., Line 36) we set dropped$[t]$ to **true**, and each time task t is executed during the period phase (i.e., Line 38 when period is **true**) we set dispatched$[t]$ to **true**. (Note that we need not consider the non-post of t on Line 34 as dropped, since t is necessarily dispatched during the period phase; otherwise there would remain a pending anti(t) task.) Finally, we add to our reachability query the predicate $\forall t.$ dropped$[t]$ $\Rightarrow$ dispatched$[t]$, thus ensuring that when all asynchronous tasks have completed the only dropped tasks have been dispatched during the period.

Alternatively, we may also encode this fairness check by posting auxiliary dropped and dispatched tasks to the task buffer, in place of using the dropped and dispatched arrays. Essentially for each task t dropped during the period phase on Line 36 we add **post** dropped(t), and for each task t posted into the period phase we add **post** dispatched(t). Then, using a single additional variable of type Procs × Vals we ensure that for every executed dropped(t) task some dispatched(t) task also executes; a single variable suffices for this check because we may consider only schedules where all dropped(t) and dispatch(t) tasks execute contiguously for each t.

3.3   Delay-Bounded Reachability

Following the reduction from (fair) nontermination, we are faced with a highly-complex problem: determining completed state-reachability in finite-data programs is polynomial-time equivalent to computing exact reachability in Petri nets (i.e., such that all places representing pending tasks are empty), or alternatively in vector addition systems (i.e., such that all vector components counting pending tasks are zero). Though these problems are known to be decidable, there is no known primitive-recursive upper complexity bound.

Rather than dealing with such difficult problems, our strategy is to consider only a restricted yet interesting set of actual program behaviors. Following Emmi et al. [8]'s delay-bounding scheme, we equip some deterministic task scheduler with the ability to deviate from its deterministic schedule only a bounded number of times (per task). As this development is very similar to Emmi et al. [8]'s,

```
 1 // translation of var g: T
 2 var g: T
 3 var G[K]: T
 4
 5 // translation of
 6 // proc p (var l: T) s
 7 proc p (var l: T, k: K) s
 8
 9 // translation of call x := p e
10 call x := p (e,k)
```
```
11 // translation of post p e
12 let temp: T = g
13 and guess: T
14 and k': K in
15     assume k ≤ k' < K;
16     g := G[k'];
17     G[k'] := guess;
18     call p (e,k');
19     assume g = guess;
20     g := temp;
```

Fig. 4. The K delay sequential translation $((P))_{db}^K$ of an asynchronous program P

we refer the interested reader there. We recall in Figure 4 the essential delay-bounded asynchronous to sequential translation.

To determine which executions of the sequential program $((P))_{db}^K$ prove the existence of a valid asynchronous execution, we define the predicate φ_{db} over initial conditions ι and configuration c as

$$\varphi_{db}(\iota, c) = \begin{cases} \textbf{true} & \text{when } \texttt{G[0]}(\iota) = \texttt{g}(c) \\ & \text{and } \forall i \in \mathbb{N}. 0 < i < K \Rightarrow \texttt{G}[i](\iota) = \texttt{G}[i-1](c) \\ \textbf{false} & \text{otherwise,} \end{cases}$$

along with the mapping ϑ_{db} from initial conditions of $((P))_{db}^K$ to those of P as $\vartheta_{db}(\langle g, \ell, p \rangle) \stackrel{\text{def}}{=} \langle g', \ell', p' \rangle$ when $\texttt{g}(g') = \texttt{g}(g)$, $\texttt{l}(\ell') = \texttt{l}(\ell)$, and $p' = p$. Essentially, in any completed configuration c reachable from ι satisfying $\varphi_{db}(\iota, c)$, we know that the initially pending task returned with the shared global valuation $\texttt{G[0]}(\iota)$ resumed by the first-round tasks, and that the last $(i-1)$ round task, for $0 < i < K$, returned with the shared global valuation $\texttt{G}[i](c)$ resumed by the first i round task. The following lemma follows from Emmi et al. [8].

Lemma 3. *A valuation g is reachable in some completed configuration of a program P from ι_0 if some g-valued completed configuration c is reachable in $((P))_{db}^K$ from some ι, such that $\varphi_{db}(\iota, c) = \textbf{true}$ and $\vartheta_{db}(\iota) = \iota_0$, for some $K \in \mathbb{N}$.*

4   Experience

We have implemented a prototype analysis tool called ALIVE. Our tool takes as input distributed asynchronous programs written in a variation of the Boogie language [2] in which message posting is encoded with specially-annotated procedure calls. Given a possibly non-terminating input program P, ALIVE translates P into another asynchronous program P' (according to the translation of Sections 3.1 and 3.2) that may violate a particular assertion if and only if P has a (fair) non-terminating execution. Then ALIVE passes P' and a bounding parameter $K \in \mathbb{N}$ to our ASYNCCHECKER delay-bounded asynchronous program analysis tool [9] which attempts to determine whether the assertion can be

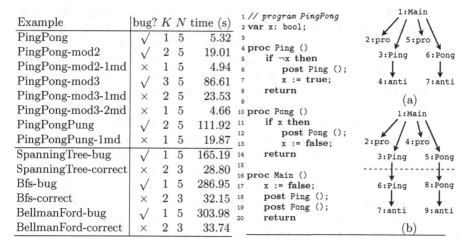

Example	bug?	K	N	time (s)
PingPong	√	1	5	5.32
PingPong-mod2	√	2	5	19.01
PingPong-mod2-1md	×	1	5	4.94
PingPong-mod3	√	3	5	86.61
PingPong-mod3-1md	×	2	5	23.53
PingPong-mod3-2md	×	1	5	4.66
PingPongPung	√	2	5	111.92
PingPongPung-1md	×	1	5	19.87
SpanningTree-bug	√	1	5	165.19
SpanningTree-correct	×	2	3	28.80
Bfs-bug	√	1	5	286.95
Bfs-correct	×	2	3	32.15
BellmanFord-bug	√	1	5	303.98
BellmanFord-correct	×	2	3	33.74

```
1 // program PingPong
2 var x: bool;
3
4 proc Ping ()
5     if ¬x then
6         post Ping ();
7         x := true;
8     return
9
10 proc Pong ()
11     if x then
12         post Pong ();
13         x := false;
14     return
15
16 proc Main ()
17     x := false;
18     post Ping ();
19     post Pong ();
20     return
```

Fig. 5. Experimental results with ALIVE. Here K indicates the delay-bound, and N the recursion-depth bound.

Fig. 6. The PingPong program, along with asynchronous executions of the translations $((\text{PingPong}))_{nt}$ (a) and $((\text{PingPong-mod2}))_{nt}$ (b). Task order is indicated by numeric prefixes; the dotted line indicates delaying.

violated (in an execution using at most K delay operations, per task). ASYNC-CHECKER essentially performs a variation of our delay-bounded translation of Section 3.3—which results in a sequential Boogie program—and hands the resulting program P'' to the CORRAL SMT-based bounded model checker [14] to detect assertion violations.

Our implementation is able to find (fair) non-terminating executions in several toy examples, and handed-coded implementations of textbook distributed algorithms [16]; the source code of our examples can be found online [7]. Figure 5 summarizes our experiments on two families of examples which we discuss below: the PingPong family of toy examples, and the SpanningTree family of textbook examples. For each family, Figure 5 lists both "buggy" variations (i.e., those with infinite executions) and "correct" variations (those without infinite executions—at least up to the given delay bound). In each case the delay bound is given by K, and a recursion bound is given by N; our back-end bounded model checker CORRAL only explores executions in which the procedure stack never contains more than N frames of any procedure, for a given recursion bound $N \in \mathbb{N}$. Note that our implementation is a simple unoptimized prototype; the running times are simply listed as a validation that our reduction is feasible.

4.1 PingPong

As a simple example of a non-terminating asynchronous program, consider the PingPong program of Figure 6. Initially the Main procedure initializes the Boolean variable x to **false** and posts asynchronous calls to Ping and Pong. When Ping executes and x is **false**, then Ping posts a subsequent call to Ping, and sets x to **true**; otherwise Ping simply returns. Similarly, when Pong executes and x is **true**, then Pong posts a subsequent call to Pong, and sets x to **false**; otherwise Pong simply returns. This program has exactly one non-terminating execution: that where the pending instances to Ping and Pong execute in alternation. This execution is periodic, as the configuration where x=**false**, and both Ping and Pong have a single pending instance, is encountered infinitely often.

Figure 6a depicts an execution of the program resulting from our translation (Section 3.1) of the PingPong program. Following our translation, the Main procedure takes the branch of Line 28 in Figure 3, posting both pro(Ping) and Ping, then both pro(Pong) and Pong. Without using any delay operations, the scheduler encoded by AsyncChecker executes the posted tasks in depth-first order over the task-creation tree [8, 9]. Thus following Main, pro(Ping) executes, then Ping, followed by anti(Ping). Subsequently, pro(Pong), Pong, and anti(Pong) execute, in that order. Luckily this execution provides a witness to nontermination without spending a single delay.

Our experiments include several variations of this example. The -mod2 and -mod3 variations add an integer variable i which is incremented (modulo 2, resp., 3) by each call of Ping. The addition of this counter complicates the search for a repeated configuration, since besides the global variable x and pending tasks Ping and Pong, the value of i must also match in the repeating configuration. This addition also increases the number of delay operations required to discover an infinite execution, as the depth-first task scheduler without delaying considers only executions where all Ping tasks execute before all Pong tasks—see Figure 6b; since, for instance, modulo 2 incrementation requires two of each Ping and Pong tasks to return to a repeating configuration (i.e., with i=0), the second Ping task must delay in order to occur after the first Pong task. In the -1md and -2md variations, we reduce the budget of task delaying, and observe that indeed the additional delay budgets are required to witness nonterminating executions. The PingPongPung variation is an even more intricate variation in which each task (i.e., Ping, Pong, or Pung) posts a different task.

4.2 SpanningTree

In Figure 7 we consider two examples of distributed algorithms taken from the textbook of Lynch [16], and modified to introduce nonterminating executions. Essentially, SpanningTree attempts to compute a spanning tree for an arbitrary network by building a **parent** relation from message broadcasts. When the **parent** link is established asynchronously there exist (unfair) executions in which nodes cyclically propagate their search messages without ever establishing the parent relation. The BellmanFord algorithm is a generalization of SpanningTree in which links between nodes have weights; the algorithm attempts to establish a spanning tree in which each node is connected by a minimal-weight path. Our injection of a bug demonstrates that even the most trivial of

```
 1 // program SpanningTree
 2 type Pid;
 3 var parent[Pid]: Pid;
 4 var reported[Pid]: bool;
 5
 6 proc Main ()
 7     var root: Pid;
 8     assume ∀p: Pid. reported[p] = false;
 9     post search (root, root);
10     return
11
12 proc search (var this: Pid, sender: Pid)
13     var neighbor: Pid;
14
15     if ¬reported[this] then
16
17         // BUG: should be done synchronously!
18         post parent (this, sender);
19
20         while ⋆ do
21             let neighbor: Pid in
22             assume neighbor ≠ this;
23             assume neighbor ≠ sender;
24             post search (neighbor, this);
25
26     return
27
28 proc parent (var this: Pid, p: Pid)
29     parent[this] := p;
30     reported[this] := true;
31     return
```

```
 1 // program BellmanFord
 2 type Pid;
 3 type Val;
 4 var dist [Pid]: int;
 5 var parent [Pid]: Pid;
 6 const weight [Pid, Pid]: int;
 7
 8 proc Main ()
 9     var root: Pid;
10     assume ∀p: Pid. dist[p] = INF;
11     post bellmanFord (root, 0, root);
12     return
13
14 proc bellmanFord (var this: Pid, w: int,
15                               sender: Pid)
16     var neighbor: Pid;
17
18     // BUG: should check <, not ≤
19     if w + weight[this,sender] ≤ dist[this]
20     then
21         dist[this] := w + weight[this,sender];
22         parent[this] := sender;
23
24         while ⋆ do
25             let neighbor: Pid in
26             assume neighbor ≠ this;
27             assume neighbor ≠ sender;
28             post bellmanFord
29                 (neighbor, dist[this], this);
30     return
```

Fig. 7. Two distributed asynchronous programs with divergent infinite executions

programming errors (e.g., typing $\leq$ rather than $<$) can introduce fair nonterminating executions. ALIVE automatically discovers these nonterminating executions for an arbitrary, unspecified network.

4.3 Paxos

Lamport's Paxos algorithm [15] provides a two-phase protocol for collaboratively choosing a (numeric) value from a set of values proposed by various nodes in a network; Figure 8 lists a basic variation of the algorithm. Initially a set of *proposers* choose a unique value to propose, and broadcast their intention to the set of *acceptors* via the **prepare** message. Each acceptor then decides whether to support the proposed value, depending on whether or not a higher proposal has already been seen. When a **proposal_OK** message is received, the proposer checks whether a majority has been achieved, and if so broadcasts an **accept** message. If in the meantime the acceptors have not encountered a higher proposal, they agree on the given proposal by setting **accepted** on Line 46.

Even in fair executions, divergent behavior can arise from several places. As in the program of Figure 8, the proposers may periodically post higher proposals in case their initial proposal is not answered within a timeout (Line 12), when NOTIFY_DECLINED is false. Then even an individual proposer may repeatedly **propose** new values just before receiving the acceptors' **proposal_OK** messages.

The acceptors, in turn, may continue to increment their **prepared** values, such that previously agreed proposals will no longer be accepted (see the condition on Line 40). Even preventing such behavior by assuming the proposers only submit new proposals upon the reception of **declined** messages (i.e., suppose **NOTIFY_DECLINED** is true), fair nonterminating executions may still arise by competition between two or more proposers; for instance where two proposers continuously outbid the other before either's proposal has been accepted.

Since each subsequent proposal in the Paxos algorithm proposed an increasingly large number, strictly speaking our detection algorithm will not discover such nonterminating executions, since the same values of **proposal** and **prepared** will not be encountered twice. Essentially we must extend our well-quasi-ordering of Section 3.1 by relaxing the equality on global state valuations to a well-quasi-ordering which is compatible with the program's transition relation. For the purpose of our experiments, we have encoded manually such an order $\preceq'$ for our variations on the Paxos algorithm; the order relates global valuations $g_1 \preceq' g_2$ when there exists some $\delta \in \mathbb{N}$ such that the values of **proposal** for proposing processes, and **prepared** for accepting processes, in g_1 and g_2 uniformly increase by δ, and all other variables in g_1 and g_2 are equal. With this small manual effort, ALIVE is able to discover the "individual" nonterminating execution described above, and while ALIVE can also detect the "competing" nonterminating execution in theory, ASYNCCHECKER times out on the reachability check after 30 minutes.

5   Related Work

Contrary to much work on sequential program (non)termination detection [5, 11], less attention has been paid to concurrent programs, where nontermination can arise from asynchronous interaction rather than diverging data values. Though both Cook et al. [6] and Popeea and Rybalchenko [17] have proposed techniques to prove termination in multithreaded programs, failure to prove termination does not generally indicate the existence of nonterminating executions. In very recent work, Atig et al. [1] suggest compositional nontermination detection for multithreaded programs based on bounded context-switch; their technique detects infinite executions between a group of interfering, and each non-terminating, threads. Our approach is orthogonal, as we detect infinite executions in which every task terminates; nontermination arises from the never-ending creation of new tasks. Technically, while Atig et al. [1] explore the behaviors between statically-known threads, our problem is to detect the repetition of an unbounded set of dynamically-created tasks.

Our reduction-based technique follows a recent trend of compositional translations to sequential program analysis by considering bounded program behaviors. Based on the notion of bounded context-switch [18], Lal and Reps [13] proposed a reduction from detecting safety violations in multithreaded programs (with a finite number of statically-known threads) to detecting safety violations in sequential programs; shortly after La Torre et al. [12] extended this result to handle an arbitrary number of parametric threads, which was further extended by Emmi et al. [8]

```
 1 // The Proposers
 2 var proposal[Pid]: int;              26 // The Accepters
 3 var agreed[Pid]: int;                27 var prepared[Pid]: int;
 4                                       28 var accepted[Pid]: int;
 5 proc propose (var p: Pid)            29
 6     let n: int = gen_proposal_number () in  30 proc prepare (var p: Pid, sender: Pid, n: int
 7     proposal[p] := n;                            )
 8     agreed[p] := 0;                   31     if prepared[p] ≥ n then
 9     post prepare (ACCEPTOR, p, n);    32         if NOTIFY_DECLINED then
10                                       33             post declined(sender, n)
11     if ¬NOTIFY_DECLINED then          34     else
12         post propose(p);              35         prepared[p] := n;
13     return                            36         post proposal_OK(sender, accepted[p])
14                                       37     return
15 proc proposal_OK (var p: Pid, n: int) 38
16     agreed[p] := agreed[p] + 1;       39 proc accept (var p: Pid, sender: Pid, n: int)
17     if agreed[p] ≥ MAJORITY then      40     if prepared[p] > n then
18         post accept (ACCEPTOR, p,     41         if NOTIFY_DECLINED then
19                    proposal[p]);      42             post declined(sender, n)
20     return                            43     else
21                                       44         // do there exists infinite runs
22 proc declined (var p: Pid, n: int)    45         // which never accept any proposal?
23     call propose (p);                 46         accepted[p] := n
24     return                            47     return
```

Fig. 8. A basic variation of the Paxos distributed algorithm; for simplicity we suppose there is only a single accepting process named ACCEPTOR

to handle dynamic thread creation—including the case of task-buffer based "asynchronous programs" [19]. More recently Bouajjani and Emmi [3] proposed a reduction from safety violations in distributed asynchronous programs with ordered message queues. Thus far, only the recent (yet orthogonal—see above) work of Atig et al. [1] considers liveness properties such as nontermination.

Finally, although reductions from fair nontermination of task-buffer based finite-data asynchronous programs (alternatively, Petri nets) are known—e.g., by encoding into Petri net path logic formalæ [10]—our encoding *into* asynchronous programs is original, and takes advantage of existing program analysis tools with efficient under-approximating exploration strategies. Technically, Ganty and Majumdar [10]'s encoding uses constraints on marking-valued variables to ensure that each task pending at the beginning of a repeating period is re-posted and pending at the period's end; a path-logic solver must then determine satisfiability under those constraints. Our encoding handles the matching of pre- and post-period pending tasks directly; we pose an asynchronous program reachability query on a program whose additional tasks block executions in which pre- and post-period tasks cannot be matched.

6 Conclusion

We have proposed a practical reduction-based algorithm for detecting divergent executions in distributed asynchronous programs. By incrementally increasing possible task reordering, our approach explores an increasing number of possibly-divergent behaviors with increasing analysis cost, and any possibly-divergent behavior is considered at some cost. By reducing divergence of distributed asynchronous programs to assertion violation in sequential programs, our approach leverages efficient off-the-shelf sequential program analysis tools. Using our prototype tool, ALIVE, we demonstrate that the approach is able to find divergent executions in modified versions of typical textbook distributed algorithms.

References

[1] Atig, M.F., Bouajjani, A., Emmi, M., Lal, A.: Detecting Fair Non-termination in Multithreaded Programs. In: Madhusudan, P., Seshia, S.A. (eds.) CAV 2012. LNCS, vol. 7358, pp. 210–226. Springer, Heidelberg (2012)

[2] Barnett, M., Leino, K.R.M., Moskal, M., Schulte, W.: Boogie: An intermediate verification language, http://research.microsoft.com/en-us/projects/boogie/

[3] Bouajjani, A., Emmi, M.: Bounded Phase Analysis of Message-Passing Programs. In: Flanagan, C., König, B. (eds.) TACAS 2012. LNCS, vol. 7214, pp. 451–465. Springer, Heidelberg (2012)

[4] Bouajjani, A., Emmi, M., Parlato, G.: On Sequentializing Concurrent Programs. In: Yahav, E. (ed.) SAS 2011. LNCS, vol. 6887, pp. 129–145. Springer, Heidelberg (2011)

[5] Cook, B., Podelski, A., Rybalchenko, A.: Termination proofs for systems code. In: PLDI 2006: Proc. ACM SIGPLAN 2006 Conference on Programming Language Design and Implementation, pp. 415–426. ACM (2006)

[6] Cook, B., Podelski, A., Rybalchenko, A.: Proving thread termination. In: PLDI 2007: Proc. ACM SIGPLAN 2007 Conference on Programming Language Design and Implementation, pp. 320–330. ACM (2007)

[7] Emmi, M., Lal, A.: Finding non-terminating executions in distributed asynchronous programs (May 2012), http://hal.archives-ouvertes.fr/hal-00702306/

[8] Emmi, M., Qadeer, S., Rakamarić, Z.: Delay-bounded scheduling. In: POPL 2011: Proc. 38th ACM SIGPLAN-SIGACT Symposium on Principles of Programming Languages, pp. 411–422. ACM (2011)

[9] Emmi, M., Lal, A., Qadeer, S.: Asynchronous programs with prioritized task-buffers. Technical Report MSR-TR-2012-1, Microsoft Research (2012)

[10] Ganty, P., Majumdar, R.: Algorithmic verification of asynchronous programs. CoRR, abs/1011.0551 (2010), http://arxiv.org/abs/1011.0551

[11] Gupta, A., Henzinger, T.A., Majumdar, R., Rybalchenko, A., Xu, R.-G.: Proving non-termination. In: POPL 2008: Proc. 35th ACM SIGPLAN-SIGACT Symposium on Principles of Programming Languages, pp. 147–158. ACM (2008)

[12] La Torre, S., Madhusudan, P., Parlato, G.: Model-Checking Parameterized Concurrent Programs Using Linear Interfaces. In: Touili, T., Cook, B., Jackson, P. (eds.) CAV 2010. LNCS, vol. 6174, pp. 629–644. Springer, Heidelberg (2010)

[13] Lal, A., Reps, T.W.: Reducing concurrent analysis under a context bound to sequential analysis. Formal Methods in System Design 35(1), 73–97 (2009)

[14] Lal, A., Qadeer, S., Lahiri, S.K.: Corral: A Solver for Reachability Modulo Theories. In: Madhusudan, P., Seshia, S.A. (eds.) CAV 2012. LNCS, vol. 7358, pp. 427–443. Springer, Heidelberg (2012)

[15] Lamport, L.: The part-time parliament. ACM Trans. Comput. Syst. 16(2), 133–169 (1998)

[16] Lynch, N.A.: Distributed Algorithms. Morgan Kaufmann (1996) ISBN 1-55860-348-4

[17] Popeea, C., Rybalchenko, A.: Compositional Termination Proofs for Multi-threaded Programs. In: Flanagan, C., König, B. (eds.) TACAS 2012. LNCS, vol. 7214, pp. 237–251. Springer, Heidelberg (2012)

[18] Qadeer, S., Rehof, J.: Context-Bounded Model Checking of Concurrent Software. In: Halbwachs, N., Zuck, L.D. (eds.) TACAS 2005. LNCS, vol. 3440, pp. 93–107. Springer, Heidelberg (2005)

[19] Sen, K., Viswanathan, M.: Model Checking Multithreaded Programs with Asynchronous Atomic Methods. In: Ball, T., Jones, R.B. (eds.) CAV 2006. LNCS, vol. 4144, pp. 300–314. Springer, Heidelberg (2006)

[20] Svensson, H., Arts, T.: A new leader election implementation. In: Erlang 2005: Proc. 2005 ACM SIGPLAN Workshop on Erlang, pp. 35–39. ACM (2005)

[21] Trottier-Hebert, F.: Learn you some Erlang for great good!, http://learnyousomeerlang.com/

Author Index